Wilfried Engemann
**Homiletics**

# Wilfried Engemann
# **Homiletics**

———

Principles and Patterns of Reasoning

Translated by
Helen Heron und Anna Walchshofer

**DE GRUYTER**

ISBN 978-3-11-041962-7
e-ISBN (PDF) 978-3-11-044025-6
e-ISBN (EPUB) 978-3-11-044026-3

**Library of Congress Control Number: 2018947016**

**Bibliografische Information der Deutschen Nationalbibliothek**
Die Deutsche Nationalbibliothek verzeichnet diese Publikation in der Deutschen Nationalbibliografie; detaillierte bibliografische Daten sind im Internet über http://dnb.dnb.de abrufbar.

# Table of Contents

## Part III  Theology of Preaching

# Part IV  Guidelines for Sermon Preparation Process

# Part V  **Appendix**

# List of Figures

https://doi.org/10.1515/9783110440256-201

# Preface

Are sermons still a thing? In the past decades, this question has not only been posed rhetorically, but has also skeptically been brought up out of empirical perceptions, obvious assumptions and serious convictions.[1] The springboard to this question included changing communication habits associated with the use of new media, profound reforms in the field of religious education and theological reservations about a homiletic practice in which preaching was primarily used to spread information about salvation, without much consideration for the listeners in their personal responsibility as Christians and contemporaries.[2]

The fact that today still millions of people worldwide attend church services Sunday after Sunday and hear a sermon is – also in comparison to other public events – an expression of a considerable participatory behavior as well as a whole range of expectations that are not to be underestimated. Time and again, the sermon is faced with the challenge of not disappointing those present in the service but to encourage them to live by faith[3]. This includes, among other things, taking a step towards freedom, the giving and receiving of love and appreciation, going through the day with a good attitude of life, knowing what you want and the reasons for it, showing solidarity and not neglecting one's friendship with oneself, to name just a few examples. The need for such sermons will never run dry. The simple fact that they still exist is probably also an indication for their success in meeting these needs every now and then.

This highlighting of the expectations put on a sermon already suggests to what a great extent the homiletic premises of preachers, their understanding of faith, their ideal of life, their image of humanity and God etc. influence their idea of a "good sermon". Therefore, it is essential to take a closer look at the associated patterns of argumentation. Accordingly, this work offers a differentiated overall portrait of the homiletic issues that were formative in the debates surrounding the premises, challenges, methods, and goals of the sermon. Most significant – in addition to individual impulses from the first half of the 20th century – are those

---

1 Cf. the title of the book edited by H. Zeddies, 1975: "Immer noch Predigt?"
2 Cf. i.e. the critical remarks in H.-E. Bahr, 1968.
3 The phrase "living by faith" (German: "Leben aus Glauben") focuses on the serviceableness of faith for life. To believe is not an end in itself but supports, for example, a person's the access to experiencing freedom. Faith exists only as someone's way of believing, as lived faith. Faith is a resource of life. I generally refrain from using phrases such as life of faith, life in faith, and life through faith to counter the misconception that faith is, above all, an "obedient life of faith". By contrast, to live by faith embraces the strengthening of a conscience-based autonomy as a facet of the Christian art of living.

https://doi.org/10.1515/9783110440256-202

homiletic approaches and perspectives of reflection developed after the Second World War.[4] The contents of these discourses are discussed theologically as well as in dialog with human sciences and put into a methodically convergent context within the framework of my own homiletic concept.

The resulting homiletic principles follow the systematics of a concept that I have continuously developed by integrating aspects of communication studies since the late 1980s. Abridged versions have already been published in various individual contributions on the person of the preacher, the role of the listener, on how to refer to a text in the sermon, on the language of the sermon as well as the requirements for its reception. In 2002, these contributions were released conjointly for the first time.[5] The present volume is a complete revision of the second (German) edition of 2011.[6]

The didactic concern of this textbook is, inter alia, a *coherent view of all elements of the homiletic process:* The preaching event as a process of communication with its own conditions and requirements is taken into account – rather than following the individual questions that have arisen in the course of the history of Homiletics in a chronological order or treating the classical themes of Homiletics without reference to their context in the preaching event in its entirety. First, however, all criteria for the design of a sermon must be measured by whether they adequately consider the elementary conditions of a sermon as a speech from person to person – that is, the indissoluble conditions of communication and comprehension.

If a sermon is, at the same time, a *religious speech in the tradition of Christianity* as well as in the context of church and congregation, then one must ask how those requirements of communication should be considered and accentuated from a theological standpoint, how they can be incorporated hermeneutically and what consequences they have for preaching as a form of the Christian practice.

This program is implemented in the four main parts of this book as follows:

*Part I:* The starting point and focus of this Homiletics is the systematic development of the preaching event as a complex process of communication and comprehension with specific elements, phases and situations. The plausibility of the resulting interrelationship hinges on the coherence and convergence of the arguments referred to in the course of the homiletic discussion of the individual

---

4 For the main points and structure of this discourse between 2000 and 2015 in an exemplary manner cf. W. Engemann, 2010a, 2010b, 2016b, 2016c.

5 W. Engemann, 2002.

6 W. Engemann, 2011.

aspects. These aspects include, above all, the biblical tradition, the preacher as the subject[7], the language of the sermon, its concept and structure, the reality of life of those potentially listening to the sermon as well as the liturgical context of the worship service in its entirety.

Structuring the complex preaching event into four phases (the tradition, the preparation, the verbalization and the realization or reception)[8] is connected to the specification of key situations in which certain processes of human understanding and communication are repeated: What is usually dealt with in the form of different "approaches to Homiletics" (text-oriented, subject-oriented, listener-oriented approach, etc.) will in this book appear like a wandering focus. The sermon is a communication event and the homiletic perspectives may change from case to case.

Conditio sine qua non for a professional approach to Homiletics is an adequate understanding of the challenges and problems that the sermon actually faces. Therefore, in this book, the problem orientation, combined with a subsequent deepening as well as the presentation of corresponding consequences, plays a prominent role:

1. First, all the main chapters of the part I, which deal with the methodological and theological foundations of the sermon, will start with *empirical observations and corresponding analyses of concrete problems of contemporary sermons*.

2. Further, the discussion of each individual focus of the sermon process is combined with a *brief summary of the respective homiletic problems in the course of history*.

3. Each chapter offers a *deepening of the issues raised in the context of contemporary Homiletics*.

4. All chapters of part I end with the endeavor to develop – out of the respective observations and deliberations – *criteria for a particular area in the process of sermon preparation*.

---

**7** To refer to *the preacher as the subject* of the sermon is so important for the homiletic-interdisciplinary discourse that this phrase could not be dispensed with, even though in English the term "subject of" widely announces an object. When this book speaks of the preacher as the subject of the sermon, it is always referring to aspects that must be considered on the basis of his personality, individuality, and his being as a subject. However, to speak of the preacher as the subject by no means implies a dimension of arbitrariness, of lacking emotional distance – in short, a subjectivistic behavior in preaching; it is about *reflected subjectivity*. Otto Haendler has captured the essence of this aspiration in a nutshell, when he writes: "If someone proclaims the gospel with his own mouth with words in his own language, with the help of his own experience and knowledge, Sunday after Sunday, his own person is consequently so important for the sake of the matter that we must grant him the greatest attention" (O. Haendler, [1941] 2017b, 298.)
**8** Cf. Fig. 2, p. 50.

*Part II:* The priorities mentioned above likewise provide the structure for the presentation of approaches and methods for the sermon analysis in Part II. Forms of sermon analysis that have their focus on the text form (e.g. speech act-theoretical, semantic or ideological-critical approaches) are contrasted with forms of analysis that focus on the interaction between preacher and listener (e.g. models of depth psychology and the transactional analysis) as well as on the reception by the congregation. Further, the latest results of the so-called preaching reception research and the associated possibilities of analysis are considered in this part of the book.

*Part III:* Part of the in-depth study of the preaching process is the theological contextualization of the perspectives of reflection unfolded in Part I. This corresponds to the discussion of basic theological questions concerning the theory and practice of preaching. The theology of preaching developed herein draws on a theological discussion of empirical problems of preaching. Further, since it is matter of *reflecting the sermon theologically as a communicative event*, it also refers to the heretofore unfolded arguments of communication studies, psychology, text hermeneutics and linguistics. In doing so, fundamental questions particularly concerning the task of the sermon, the anthropology that defines it and its concept of faith, are taken into account. Of course, a theological annotation on preaching cannot be limited to statements regarding the premises and *Credenda* of Homiletics – that is, what one would like to believe regarding the effect of the sermon. Therefore, theological positions, attitudes and decisions must also be related to the *Facienda* influencing the preaching process – that is, questions of how *to compose* a sermon.

*Parts IV and V:* Guidelines for Sermon Preparation (Part IV) and Indices (Part V) take into account the practical requirements of a homiletic textbook and study book. By way of a model for preparing a sermon (p. 519–533), a detailed guide to the implementation of the individual methodological steps is given. The instruction sheet (p. 534–536) contains an annotated checklist for sermon drafts and the necessary preliminary work according to what is generally expected in seminars and theological exams at German-speaking universities. The numerous integrated overviews, tables and schematics are the collective result of decades work of lectures and courses held and are summarized in a directory at the beginning of the book (p. XVII–XVIII). They conform to the expectation of systematizing and visualizing the treated material.

Lastly, the herewith presented teaching- and study book on Homiletics is also intended to promote the international dialog on preaching. Cross-border and cross-continental exchanges are all too often hampered by linguistic barriers. By outlining important impulses – especially those of Homiletics within the German speaking world – in English, this work not only creates possibilities of comparison and connection between established argumentation patterns of German and North American or English-speaking preaching theory, but also highlights the theological and societal problems surrounding a contemporary sermon culture as a *common* challenge. This is supported by illustrating analogies as well as points of dispute and points of contact between discourses in English-speaking and German-speaking countries.

A book that deals with the theory of preaching practice would do well to take empirical details of this practice into account. What topics a homiletic textbook should address does not only result of the potential theories arising out of scientific studies held in this discipline. It is also a result of certain *habits* in the crafting of sermons, of prevailing *views* on the task of preaching, of different premises regarding the meaning of the biblical tradition for the worship service etc. Some of the problems that have come to light are of a fundamental nature and have made the communication of the gospel difficult at all times. Other difficulties are due to unresolved misunderstandings or concrete preconceptions about the nature of the sermon and the resulting routines. From this emerges the recurring structural element of the "snapshots"[9], which are to act as indicators of problematic areas within Homiletics, without actually depicting the entity of the current preaching practice. The individual potential problems are combined with some initial suggestions and hints for the application of suitable homiletic criteria, which are then specified and further elaborated on in the course of the individual chapters. The almost 35-year-long collaboration with students has shown that becoming aware of certain problematic areas of sermons is a crucial step towards giving up unnecessary homiletic habits.

However, the concomitant acquisition of the respective knowledge and skills not only serves the critical distance to the demands of ministry, that is, the possibility to cut oneself short (in the sense of an objection) in the preparation of the sermon. Despite or because of its particular challenges, homiletic work is first and foremost an enriching enterprise that has a privileged character: in which profession is one asked to regularly once a week deal with existential issues – including the consideration of one's own life – as well as with the experiences of life and faith of others and to explore the coordinates of living by faith in the here and now?

In this context, a note on the language relating to gender in this book: Preachers are spoken of in the plural, when it comes to the corresponding professional groups of women and men in concrete social or ecclesiastical contexts, who have to cope with certain tasks in the context of ecclesiastical orders and societal challenges.

---

9 Cf. I.2.1, I.3.1, I.4.1, I.5.1 etc. For further explanations on the principle of problem orientation cf. below at I.2.1, p. 15f.

However, when it comes to categorical statements (the preacher as a subject) or basal relations (the relationship between text and preacher), that is, when the preacher comes into view as a structural element of the homiletic process, "preacher" is used as a collective noun in the singular and the explicit marking of the two genders (the preacher and his or her text) is omitted. This is done to avoid semantic confusions.

A particular challenge in the translation of this book came through its interdisciplinary reasoning and the abundance of conceptual worlds and terms connected to it. In addition, the various questions to be dealt with when talking about "sermons" not only touch upon several different areas of science but also – in this work – some discourses specific to the German-speaking world that come with their own terminology, for which there are no suitable equivalent terms in English. Established terminologies from linguistics and literary criticism as well as psychological, sociological, hermeneutic, exegetical, semiotic, rhetorical, philosophical and dogmatic expressions of the German "technical jargon" had to be translated into another linguistic world. If this German-American walk through the conceptual worlds of Homiletics leads to reviving the homiletic dialog between the continents, it would be a great gain for dialog about the premises, goals and avenues of a contemporary preaching culture.

Since not only technical terms, but also humorous allusions, ironically accentuated nuances, puns, etc., can often only be transported "with losses" from one language to another, I would like to point out that a 3rd, completely revised edition of the German original edition of my "Introduction to Homiletics" (2nd edition 2011) will be published by Narr Francke Attempto GmbH (Tübingen) in 2019. This work may be used as an "interpretation aid" as needed. Furthermore, I am glad to receive tips on improving the English text and would like to thank the readers for their cooperation in advance.

Many people whom I have to thank for their suggestions, criticism and encouragement over the years are listed in the bibliography. I'd also like to thank Helen Heron, who made the rough draft of this translation, as well as Anna Walchshofer and her colleague Carina Ratzka for their patience and diligence in the elaborate proofreading. Birte Bernhardt and Bernhard Lauxmann, assistants at the Department of Practical Theology and Psychology of Religion, were a great help in coordinating and directing the many steps in the translation and publication process and in researching international homiletic literature. Jeanine Lefèvre, administrator of our Department, meticulously monitored the compliance with numerous formalities and contributed to standardizing the text. Sincere thanks to you all here.

Vienna, July 2018

Part I: **The Preaching Event. Its Components
and Perspectives, Phases and Situations**

# 1 Preaching as a Process of Comprehension and Communication. A Synopsis

## Preliminary Remarks

There is a wide range of different approaches to Homiletics, and not all of them place the focus of interest on the sermon as a "product", i.e. as a manuscript or lecture. It is certainly true that some older homiletic concepts seem to suggest that the listing of theological postulates and criteria concerning the "act of proclamation" make up the core of homiletic reflection. However, Homiletics must be viewed as more than mere instructions on how to impart knowledge gained from another source but instead as a theory-grounding discipline and must focus on the entire homiletic process. This includes detailed analyses of each component, the defining phases and the overall context.

The core questions of Homiletics must concern the specific *prerequisites and requirements of a sermon's synthesis, presentation and reception*. Personal, communicative, contextual and other impacting factors, each influencing the process of preaching, must be taken into account. This allows the drawing of conclusions for the homiletic work which are appropriate and homiletically justifiable rather than merely pleasant to the dogmatic ear.

A homiletic textbook, therefore, must go beyond theological comments or justifications of certain sermon definitions. First and foremost, the circumstances which co-determine the development and the effect of a sermon *independently* of subordinate definitions are to be examined. Different perspectives of reflection, or approaches to Homiletics respectively, are therefore presented in the context of *sermons as processes of comprehension and communication*. Thus, the focus is on a sermon's structural conditions and prerequisites, which are in fact building blocks in the basis of any kind of homiletic approach – despite the fact that they may not receive any kind of consideration in some.

The Event of Preaching can be subdivided into several phases of *text interpretations and text productions*. In each of them, there is a struggle for comprehension and communication. The first part of this textbook will demonstrate the existence, and the nature, of the links between different homiletic approaches which are commonly – and wrongly – considered mutually exclusive. Their core relations are clearly determinable, and they are to be understood as elaborations and amplifications of the structural components making up the processes outlined below. This process can be depicted in a graph (see Fig. 1, p. 4) as follows:

https://doi.org/10.1515/9783110440256-001

## The Components, Phases and Situations of the Sermon Process

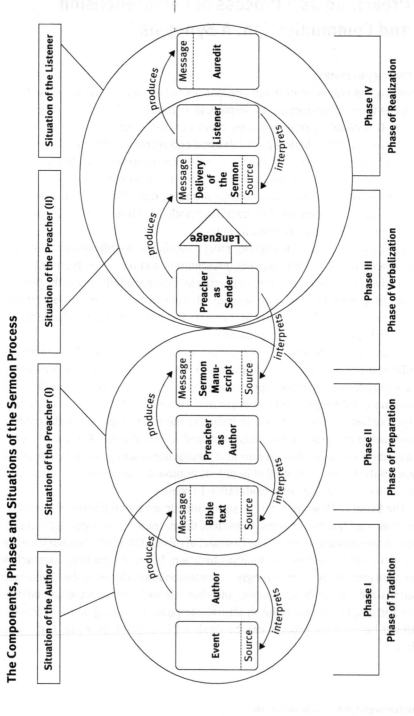

**Fig. 1:** The components, phases and situations of the sermon process

## 1.1 The Phase of Tradition: From the Event to the Biblical Text

At the beginning of every text-based tradition there are particular →*events*[1] (processes, acts, situations, stories, perceptions) which stimulate an →*author*[2] to translate them into speech, to put them into narrative form or to put down in writing their meaning in reference to his own understanding of a →*(Bible)text*. The narrator or author is presented with a →*source* (which may be already circulating narratives or texts) from which he draws, from which he selects particular aspects as relevant, and which he finally structures by supplying *his own* words as an explanatory accompanying text to the source. On the one hand, this process is based on the →*interpretation* of a source; on the other hand, it implies the →*production* of a text.[3]

Writers usually wish to enter into communication with their readers. They have a →*message* that they wish to convey to others, or else they would not write. The text that emerges is embedded in a particular situation (*situation 1*). Authors are not only writing under specific personal conditions, e.g. from prison (→*situation of the author*). It is also in their interest to be understood against *the given background situation of the addressees* and to contribute to finding answers to pending questions. The text is therefore – although in itself a "message" – the product of a *situation-related analysis* of the (e.g. verbally transmitted) gospel, which in turn is preceded by experiences of God, encounters with Jesus or other forms of "revelation" in certain situations. The texts themselves are so heavily loaded with situational context that one cannot understand their testimony if they are abstracted from the conditions under which they were formulated.

Whether the author has understood or perceived everything "correctly", or whether his text offers an adequate view of the source of the event (e.g. the life, work and intention of Jesus) is not relevant to the *comprehensibility* of the text. Anyone who works with biblical reports, or with literature in general, must be open to finding in the text itself the decisive knowledge necessary for its comprehension. The interpreters can never be "aequi" (contemporaneous) with the authors – as the hermeneutics of the Enlightenment strove to do.

---

[1] The arrow (→) before a word refers to the corresponding term in the graph. A detailed introduction to the complexity of this process and to the textual term behind it can be found in W. Engemann, 2000a. The most important hermeneutic steps are summarized in W. Engemann, 2003e, 133–140.

[2] In this context it is enough to reduce to the term "author" the complex process of the tradition from an initial narrative to a possible final editing and the thus possible co-authorship of a text. For more detailed information on this matter see W. Engemann, 2000a.

[3] Cf. the relevant actions in Fig. 1.

For that reason alone it is important to pay sufficient attention to the text, and to study its own independent existence. One cannot reduce texts to universal key statements. Readers need the *whole text* to allow themselves to open up to new frameworks of interpretation, which cannot be achieved by means of simply recalling historical-critical information. The author may not (any longer) be considered as an aid to interpretation, but in the text itself measures have been taken which encourage certain interpretations, while others are hindered.

→*Phase 1 (phase of the tradition)* in Fig. 1 depicts a process that precedes the preacher's work on the sermon. It is part of a process of transmission, which is – at a later point in time – essential for the accomplishment of a sermon based on the relevant biblical text. Yet even in this phase, a hermeneutic principle is at work: the written testimonies found in Scripture are themselves formed within the framework of a process of reception and production. In the course of this, some of the many pieces of information, which a source potentially has in store, are selected, supplemented with an interpretation, or converted into a message.

When they put down in writing their interpretation of what they "have seen and heard"[4], the authors of the biblical texts do *not* simply limit themselves to documenting their visual and auditory perceptions: one cannot actually see and hear that in Jesus of Nazareth, God himself became human and died for us, and that the death and resurrection of Jesus has saved our lives. Only someone who has understood their own part and has not shied away from an existential interpretation can come to such a judgment.

The hermeneutic act mentioned above recurs in the course of the construction of the sermon, when the →*preacher* approaches the text (→*Phase II; phase of preparation*), when he performs the sermon from the pulpit (→*Phase III: phase of verbalization*) and when, later, the →*listener* deals with the sermon in order to understand what significance it might have for him (→*Phase IV: phase of realization*). Homiletics must be able to argue how this process is to be "influenced" and structured and to explain what it is that can impede, disrupt or obstruct the process. Moreover, it naturally deals with the specific homiletic arguments which challenge the legitimacy of the *successio hermeneutica* (in German: "hermeneutischer Sukzessiv"[5]) suggested here.

---

4 Cf. Acts 4:20.

5 When I speak of the *successio hermeneutica* or a "hermeneutic succession" within the meaning of a successive hermeneutic process in relation to the communication of the gospel, I wish to stress the fact that Christian witness to faith in the form of sermons has always been connected with an irrevocable "It's your turn now!" Understanding the gospel always means comprehending it in relation to one's own life, i.e. to allow oneself to become a transmitter of the gospel in the course of the understanding. Cf. on this below, III.4.4.

Where does the *actual* process of the sermon begin? The most tangible starting point is naturally the phase of the direct preaching and listening, when the preacher takes the floor and the listeners begin to take in what they have heard, to interpret it in their own way – i.e. to make it their own – and to integrate it into their own personal lives in a productive way. However, this approximately 20-minute long communication process is already the result of preceding homiletic endeavor; it results from other, analogous forms of the communication of the gospel. This takes us to the components of the second phase.

## 1.2 The Phase of Preparation: From the Biblical Text to the Sermon Manuscript

We must therefore speak about the biblical text a second time. Looking at our graph[6], one might initially find that the →*Bible text* represents the first concrete component in the process of the sermon. However, it would be wrong to conclude from the presented order of sequence (the text preceding the →*preacher*) that the sermon process begins with the text. The preparation process of a specific sermon is ideally initiated when a preacher begins to work with a certain text. Therefore, it will be necessary to discuss in detail how Homiletics can ensure that the text, in its confronting, criticizing and confirming functions,[7] is also taken into consideration in the →*phase of preparation* of the sermon.

Yet to say that the sermon process begins with the encounter of text and preacher is not a convincing argument either, for the reading of the text is in no way point zero. The reception of the text, after all, happens against the background of all the experiences which determine the current →*situation* of the preachers. They read the text from the perspective of much-discussed questions and problems that concern either the preachers themselves, or members of their congregation. Consequently, there is an actual, irrevocable simultaneity between the situation of the preachers and their text from the very beginning, and it is fruitless to ask whether the work on the sermon should begin with the examination of the situation *or* the analysis of the text. The definitive point is that both sides influence the work on the sermon. Otherwise there is the danger of far-reaching mistakes as described in detail in I.3.1 and I.4.1.

Hence the Bible text which has been read naturally belongs to two situations. It belongs – cf. the overlapping of the relevant areas in Fig. 1 – entirely to the situation

---

6 Cf. the Phase of Preparation (Phase II) in Fig. 1.
7 The details of this fundamental function are explained in detail in 3.3.3.

of the author and entirely to the situation of the preacher. This distinguishes it from a speech or a conversation[8] and has consequences for the understanding of its "historicity".[9] Preachers, paradoxically, are not tasked with making a historical text topical. They are tasked with *allowing* the ever-current Bible text to become historical: it is important for the preachers that, in dealing with the text, they provide a *new* text, a sermon that conveys what this text means for themselves and their contemporaries' situation today. Just like once an author, in his time, established his faith and put it into words, it is now the turn of the preacher.

A sermon which takes the listeners back into *that moment in time*, embellishes the text with some modern-day veneer and finally attempts to make clear what the *writer at that time* wanted, obstructs rather than carries forward the process of the tradition of the gospel. A sermon which reflects the message gained from the text in the present context and transforms it into a new text, on the other hand, will pass the gospel down in its real sense without having to exhaust it.[10]

On the one hand, the desire to understand the text has to do with studying its open, yet not arbitrary structure, to follow its sometimes sense-generating, sometimes sense-denying fabric. On the other hand, texts, and biblical texts in particular, assume the personal initiative of their readers in order to become alive again. Therefore, we must devote due attention to the co-operation between text and preacher.[11]

Naturally it is not only their relationship to the text that animates preachers to work on the sermon. It is determined by various factors, including the person and subjectivity of the preachers themselves. A preacher's personality structure influences the way he deals with the text, as well as his attempt to put it in relation to the listeners' questions about life and faith. The question is, therefore, whether personal competence can be regarded as a homiletic category, and to what extent such a competence is a fundamental precondition for the comprehensibility, credibility and witness-bearing function of the sermon. In this context, it is important to discuss the significance of the preachers' personality for their competence in communication and confession.[12]

---

**8** On the literary-theoretical explosive nature of this differentiation cf. K. Weimar, 1993, esp. 38–41.

**9** If one only allows the text to be "historical" because it is "old" one overlooks e.g. that in contrast to other ancient artifacts it is preserved unchanged, that it is equally present as the same text to every reader. The text *becomes* historical when someone interprets it, uses it as a source and makes use of it for the draft of a new text.

**10** Cf. III.4.5.2d.

**11** Cf. I.3.3.1.

**12** Cf. I.2.3.3 – I.2.3.5.

This competence – or the lack thereof – is initially expressed in the →*sermon manuscript*[13] as the result of the preachers' critical analysis of the text. Preachers derive a →*message* from the Bible text, which is originally *their* message, before it is conveyed to the congregation. Their personality structure, their basic attitude to the "world", their conception of God, their understanding of faith, their hopes and fears etc. are expressed in the topics they discuss, in their appeals and in the confessions they dare to make. This can be illustrated with the help of various forms of sermon analysis. For homiletic reasons, it is therefore imperative to define personal competence in relation to the necessity of the preachers' self-perception.

## 1.3 The Phase of Verbalization: From the Sermon Manuscript to the Sermon from the Pulpit

In the →*delivery of the sermon* preachers become the interpreters of their own sermon. Their manner, their voice, language and posture contribute to the clarification, or indeed the obscuring, of what they desire to say. For this reason, it is important to look at the verbal and non-verbal signs they use to transmit their *manuscript*. This phase is significant enough to warrant a look at →*language* as separate element, or the particular medium of the preaching process. It is quite obvious that one and the same sentence – and one and the same text even more so – can take on quite different meanings when spoken by different people, or in different situations. Even without any changes to the textual or the semantic content, a written speech may achieve an entirely different effect when it is "performed": a sermon whose contents are intended to encourage, for example, can have a depressing effect; a sermon which is intended to motivate a particular action can turn into a reprimand. It is therefore important to look at the specific characteristics of verbal communication in a sermon.

There is a big difference between the →*situation* (II) of the preachers as speakers, and their situation as readers and authors: now, preachers are no longer alone with the text and the manuscript. Instead, they have entered into a situation of speaking and →*listening*, which forms the core of the preaching event.[14]

---

13 In this context it does not matter whether the text has been put into writing in its entirety, or partially, or at all. What is important in this phase of the process of a sermon, is the fact that the content and intention of the sermon are established for the preacher before they ascend to the pulpit.

14 On this cf. the overlapping of the situations of the preacher (II) and the listener in the figure introduced (Fig. 1, p. 4).

They now have an audience, a living counterpart. We know from communication studies that human processes of understanding – in contrast to data exchange between machines – are not restricted to the mere forwarding of information but also define relationships. Consequently, we shall ask about the relevance of appropriate communication strategies for the sermon.

While the preacher and the author of the text belong to different situations, in this phase simultaneity between preacher and listener is established due to the oral presentation of the sermon. This poses the following problem: preacher and listener come to the church service from their respective situations, yet the sermon delivered should be equally relevant for both. How can this expectation be met? The competencies required for the preparation phase are no longer sufficient: the process of making oneself understood is different from that of understanding. If the sermon (already) fails *as a process of communication*, the "dissemination of the gospel" will naturally be affected; as a result, the sermon cannot be taken in by those for whom it was intended. Hence the preacher must consider specific rules, which foster the acceptability and the usability of the sermon, i.e. its inherent potential to be understood and made use of by the listener.

## 1.4 The Phase of Realization: From the Sermon to the Listener's Comprehension

This phase is called *realization* because the preaching event only achieves its goal if it reaches the →*listener,* and is adopted by them in such a way that they themselves recognize its significance. It is not enough for addresses to "be correct" and to contain no "mistakes" in the interpretation of the Bible; such a sermon will remain incomplete if it does not inspire or encourage the listeners to implement and continue with what has been said in some way. In this context, "continuation" means the repetition of the listeners' processes of interpretation and productive comprehension to the point of the creation of their own witness – cf. Phases I and II.[15] The coupling of the two sequences →*presentation of the sermon and the receiving person* is essential in this chain of passed-down interpretations of passed-down texts, for it is only through this linking that the recipients can obtain a →*message* which is *entirely theirs* – a message for *them in particular*. If this is not the case, the sermon is missing a vital element.

What has been said about the comprehension of biblical texts, in some way also applies to the actual insight listeners take away from the sermon: The one

---

15 Here and for what follows again cf. Fig. 1, p. 4.

who has understood the sermon best is not the one who can repeat it by heart, but the one who has internalized the meaning of what has been read or heard and is thus able to pass on the message, should the need arise. The term →*Auredit* can be used to explicitly mark the factual textual character of this personal comprehension as a (communicative) goal of the sermon. Analogous to the word "manuscript" (= "written by hand"), "Auredit" is constructed from the ablative of *auris* and the passive participle of *audire* (= "heard with the ear").[16] It is less a matter of a linguistic analogy but rather a basic, structural analogy in the process of the sermon: as the manuscript is created from the preacher's study of the text, the *Auredit* comes into being as a result of the listeners' analysis of the sermon they have heard.

The →*situation of the listener* during the sermon is determined by various factors:

a) First of all there is the situation which we have previously defined more precisely as "day-to-day reality". It is true that listeners come to the church service from their everyday life; but they do not leave this everyday life behind at the door. They are accompanied by their everyday lives, and they may even be particularly aware of this – the problems of their workaday lives may be part of the reason why they are coming to church in order to hear a sermon, to sing, and to pray. We must consider this situation adequately. Consequently, we shall have to ask how the listeners' day-to-day reality can be included homiletically into the work on the sermon, which questions and criteria play a part here, and how the preachers' perception of their *own* reality of life may have an effect on the situational suitability of a sermon.

The homiletic efforts carried out by a preacher in working out and "performing" a sermon should therefore extend beyond the situation of "we are a congregation listening to a sermon". Basically, the above model should be expanded by a "Situation of the Listener II"; for after hearing the sermon the listener is faced with the task of mediating afresh between tradition and (the day-to-day) situation. From the point of view of the homiletic process, the listener is the final instance in the sermon-related process of transmission. Whether and how they become "doers of the Word"[17] (cf. Jas 1:22), reveals which processes can be triggered by the communication of the gospel in our times. This does not mean "deeds" as attempts of

---

16 To understand the Auredit, cf. in more detail W. Engemann, 2003c, 24–28, and the productive adoption of this concept by several authors including K.-H. Bieritz, 1998; A. Freund, 2000; J. Cornelius-Bundschuh, 2001; U. Pohl-Patalong, 2003; T. Klie, 2003; S. Wolf-Withöft, 2004; S. Rolf, 2008.

17 Here I am by no means thinking only of the pragmatic appropriation or active dimension of a sermon. The question is rather whether something takes place in, with or through the listener,

self-justification so much as changes in, with and among people, especially such processes that affect the experience of freedom, and the giving and receiving of love[18].

b) The preacher also plays a part in the situation of the listener, at least for the duration of the sermon, as the listeners cannot disassociate the words they hear from the person who speaks them.[19] At the same time, they are in a dialog with themselves, and attempt to connect what they have heard with their own experiences, as well as with other perceptions while listening (e.g. the posture or appearance of the preacher). As partners in this communicative event of preaching, they will follow the sermon not only on the level of content. The relationship level, which develops between preacher and listener in the course of the sermon, is influenced by sympathies or antipathies. The associated experiences of confirmation or rejection, or of a reprimand, positively or negatively affect the reception of the sermon. This is why we must talk about the listen*er* as well as about the listen*ing*. The preacher, therefore, has to consider not only the prerequisites of a linguistically and theologically successful address, but also strategies of (e.g. selective) auditory attention.

This brief introduction to the reflection perspectives of analysis and presentation of the event of preaching shows that the individual aspects cannot always be sharply distinguished from one another. On the contrary, the breaking down of the sermon process into its components, phases and situations has highlighted connections, which, for example, do not permit us to isolate the *biblical text* from its different ways of reception, to speak of *preachers* without recognizing their relationship with the listeners, to judge the *sermon* only on the level of its theological content, or to consider the *listeners* simply as recipients of communication.

There is a frequently occurring *simultaneity of factors*, due to different situations and practices of reception, which determines both the interpretation and the production of text and speech in the individual phases of the preaching event. This simultaneity requires a specific reconstruction and discussion of homiletic problems: It is imperative not to discuss each individual component of the preaching event in itself, but instead with a view to the acts of "interpretation" and "production" that have to be performed by the preacher as well as the

---

whether the sermon process is able to set something into motion, to introduce change, or lead to stabilization – occurrences which would not have happened without this process.

**18** "Love" in this context means all the conceivable forms of social solicitude and the experiences of attention, care and consideration connected to them.

**19** Cf. the corresponding situation sector in Fig. 1, p. 4.

listener. This includes an analysis of agencies conducive or obstructive to these acts. Perhaps formally this insight would be best accommodated by declaring the individual positions of interpretation, as well as the redrafting of texts, the structuring devices of Homiletics: the biblical text as a source for the preacher, the preacher as an interpreter of the text, the work on the sermon etc.

For didactic reasons, I have chosen a different way. In order to make it easier for the readers to localize the previously mentioned basic homiletic problems, the structure of this introduction is based on those components of the sermon process that simultaneously form the material basis for particular homiletic concepts: on the preacher (I.2 Preaching as One's Own Person), on the biblical tradition (I.3 Preaching with a Text), on the form of the sermon itself (I.4 Preaching with a Structure), on the sermon as speech (I.5 Preaching under the Conditions of Language), on the listener or the situation (I.6 Preaching for the Individual) and on the liturgical context (I.7 Preaching in the Worship Service).

The individual components will be introduced, presented and discussed in such a way that they may simultaneously become visible as components of the process outlined above. This requires individual homiletic foci to be addressed outside of their respective primary thematic classification: thus, a discussion of the situation, will not be reduced to the listener's later "Sitz im Leben", for example; likewise, the question of the preacher cannot be answered conclusively under aspects relating specifically to his personality but must be looked at again from the perspective of the listener.

The simplifying model (Fig. 1) shows that the actual sermon process begins when the preacher approaches a text to rework its significance within the realms of his own present time and age.[20] Preachers are not simply persons who have been appointed, and usually ordained; they are first and foremost individuals. They are subjects, persons with very specific experiences and expectations, with preferences and aversions, with particular, pre-formed images of God and concepts of faith. What does it mean that the communication of the gospel is initiated by the preacher *as a person*? A sermon is an initiation of the communication of the gospel, and therefore it is sensible, at least from a structural point of view, to start the discussion of the segments of the preaching event with the question of the function and role of the preacher.

---

**20** In a purely empirical approach, one could naturally never state definitively where the process of the emergence of a sermon had its beginning, as this process always contains what preachers already knew before they read a text, what they have experienced in the last weeks, what happened to them years ago, what theological literature they have read in the last month and what has possibly gripped their attention, what visits they have paid and what conversations they have had, what ideas have inspired them etc.

# 2 Preaching as One's Own Person. On the Preacher as the Subject of the Sermon

The process of the communication of the gospel inevitably involves people with different experiences, qualifications, approaches to life, and attitudes to faith. What does this mean, both theologically and methodically? Reflections on the role of the preacher as "subject", "individual", "personality", "sinner", "impediment," "mouthpiece of the Spirit" etc. have been part of theoretical homiletic approaches since the very beginning of preaching, even in its initial stages. Yet it would be misleading to say it has always been a line of homiletic tradition, since the reasons and assumptions for addressing the role of the preacher differ too greatly from one another.

Before we discuss the most important aspects of this issue's theoretical and problem-specific history, a few "snapshots" are presented in this chapter.[21] The empirical indicators of problems connected to this matter should clarify the need for a homiletic discussion of the well-known fact that preachers must always turn to their congregation "in person".

## 2.1 Snapshots. Empirical Indicators of Problems

The following problem-related sketches are not an expression of a preference for "bad examples" nor the nagging of someone more knowledgeable in pastoral practice, but the result of decades of positive experiences with problem-based learning: "Problems are not just 'cold' cognitive structures, but they belong to the 'hot cognitions' by dynamizing our spiritual life and giving motivation and direction to our searching and learning. The ability for problem-oriented learning and thus for dealing with problems productively is an essential resource of lifelong learning to be cultivated, and working on problems, be it as a means or as an end, is a central task of didactics."[22] When a problem arises, one can learn to articulate and demonstrate clearly what is wrong. Irritations caused by sermons provoke the search for alternatives in language, theology, one's image of the listener, ideals of life, comprehension of texts, etc. Above all, problem analysis pushes to the question of why a sermon has triggered certain irritations, misunderstandings,

---

21 The category "Snapshots. Empirical Indicators of Problems" is repeated in the main chapters of Part I, which is devoted to the deduction of the individual components and phases of the sermon process.
22 K. Reusser, 2005, 163f.

https://doi.org/10.1515/9783110440256-002

defiant reactions, etc. Preaching (just like other competencies that are required for studying) is learned by the imitation of "positive examples" to a much lesser degree – i.e. not without the knowledge of the shoals and abysses one has to pass when crafting and presenting a sermon. It goes without saying that students are also provided with other sermons as reference material which – in terms of their language or their wording – formally and content-wise conform to the standards of a "good sermon".

As in the first and second German edition, I partly resort to seminar and exam sermons; additionally I select examples from other sermon manuscripts, all of which have been anonymized. The inclusion of work of students in a homiletic textbook occurs for three reasons: (1) The respective sermons reflect representative listening-experiences with sermons. To a certain extent, the preaching of future pastors is an – though often unconscious – individual reconstruction or "imitation" of what they have perceived and internalized as preaching in, for example, their home churches. If viewed from this perspective, the respective quotations from sermons by students certainly partly document a common preaching practice. Some of the questions, which are further elaborated on with the help of these texts, may therefore also be present in a modified form in the sermons of more experienced preachers. (2) A notable advantage of also including sermons of students is that the submitted drafts are coupled with exegetical, systematic-theological and hermeneutical preliminary work. Thereby, one can see the reasoning of a particular sermon step-by-step and understand on the basis of which reflections the sermon took the shape it did as well as why the theological reasoning took a certain direction. (3) Moreover, these designs are the result of theological study. They show what young theologians and theologians today consider to be a sermon and what it means for them to practice theology.

### 2.1.1 Unreflected Subjectivity

The subjectivity of the preacher belongs to the constitutive requirements of the sermon, not although but specifically *because* the sermon is a form of the communication of the gospel. To proclaim the gospel as the "power of God for salvation to everyone who believes" (Rom 1:16) does not exclude but includes the human being *in person* as a witness to the gospel who expresses in his own words what living by faith actually means.

The preacher's existence as subject is of elementary significance, not only for the credibility and plausibility of a sermon's "testimony". In its context of active processes of communication, the subjectivity also plays a role with regard to the contextual and argumentative *position-taking* of the preacher: as a rule, a sermon is delivered by only one person. Even when several people are involved in the preaching event – e.g. in a dialog sermon – the sermon is not the result of a democratic decision-making process but gains its very credibility from its *intersubjectivity*, i.e. that the different individuals work towards the visualization of the capabilities of living by faith. This means that disparate experiences, contrasting images of God, or personal ways of believing are not leveled out or played off against one another; instead, they achieve a specific profile through the position-taking which inevitably occurs in this process. They mark a location in space and time, which others refer to, or from which they can distance themselves, as the case may be. In this sense, a preacher's subjectivity has little to do with the exposure of personal information – in contrast to the following quotation.

"The goal of the sermon is to involve the congregation in the preacher's encounter with the text that forms the basis of the sermon. A reference to real life is achieved through the inclusion of biographical tales."[23] – No, that is exactly not the point here. In such an approach, the listeners are all too often confronted with issues of the preacher *as an expert*. Questions do not become any more personal, or more interesting, because they reflect the preacher's theological thinking. Likewise, the "biographical tales" mentioned in the quotation are not of interest, let alone relevant, for the listeners simply because they refer somehow to snippets from the personal life of the preacher, particularly if they are put under the catchphrase: "How I personally, as pastor, encountered the biblical text."

The reason why subjectivity is often not acknowledged as a requirement of a credible sermon is that it is confused with arbitrariness and randomness, and consequently suspected of contributing to the departure from the Reformation Scriptural principle. Hence, a "subjective personal sermon" is often misinterpreted as the opposite to an "objective textual sermon". Several misunderstandings form the basis of this approach: the homiletic maxim (that one should strive for a sermon for which a subject takes responsibility, or, more precisely, to pursue a manner of preaching supported by one's own subjectivity) has a *reflected subjectivity* in mind. The programmatic abstention from reflecting one's own subjectivity does not by any means lead to more objectivity; rather, the denial or suppression of the preacher's subjective self is accompanied by the effects of an unreflected subjectivity which is presented to the listeners – perhaps with the deceptive claim of objectively staying true to the "source text". Consequently, preachers may fall for a problematic self-image instead of presenting each individual sermon's intention with an awareness of their own existence as subject, their personal experiences and expectations, including their personal inclinations and anxieties, preferences and disassociations.

"I must not believe that God is by my side when I am on the wrong path! If I do things against his will, I must of course reckon with difficulties, which God will not remove from my path. I

---

**23** From the preparatory work on a sermon draft on 1 Cor 12:4–11.

should turn back, after all. So I shall have to struggle with those problems on my own, problems which I would not have if only I had gone the way God had planned for me. This is also true for my prayers. If I am moving in a false direction, God will naturally not hear them, for my own sake, until I have come to my senses and have focused my intention on the good he has planned for me."[24]

There is more than one problem with this text. There is the theologically dubious argumentation that we cannot expect a positive intervention by God as long as we do not fulfill our religious duty to obey[25] (as if we could find the will of God as daily instructions on the kitchen table in the morning). More importantly, in this context, there is also a presumptuous claim of authority in the *exemplary "I"* of the preacher, through which this "I" loses its credibility as an "example": preachers who appear to know so much about God's principles of intervention, as if they habitually had breakfast together, indicate through this preaching style that they themselves would never possibly follow such wrong paths. "Naturally" they know the rules, and are simply passing them on – and they would never be so ignorant as to violate God's rules of the game. An examination of the way these preachers appear to see themselves could help them lend this exemplary "I" a searching component, or a component of solidarity, which would show that they are in no way ahead of their listeners in questions of the praxis pietatis or in ethics, and thus highlight that they are not speaking to the congregation as pastors because they are advanced in regard to issues of faith and life.

In the following example, the preacher appears to view himself as a kind of larger-than-life father figure for the congregation. This entails a claim to a high level of authority, which is enforced in assuming the position of the apostle Paul – as he is perceived by the preacher – rebuking the congregation: "'You are behaving like small, immature children! If you do not look out, you will ruin everything like squabbling children!' And as a father reprimands his children in dangerous situations so that no harm will come to them, Paul admonishes the Corinthians and says: 'Do not be vain about your gifts which the Spirit has apportioned to you at his discretion; Be amazed at them rather and rejoice in them!'"[26] Moreover, at the beginning and at the end of the sermon, the situations presented resemble a classroom setting, with the listeners being expected to recognize themselves as the pupils of an inspired teacher: they should be happy to have someone like the preacher, who "knows what it's all about".

Preachers who are unaware of, or even denying, the "I in the pulpit"[27] not only harm the sermon's function as testimony but also practice a specific type of

---

24 Sermon on Heb 5:7–9.
25 Here Paul has a different view: "Do you not know that God's kindness is meant to lead you to repentance?" (Rom 2:4)
26 Sermon draft on 1 Cor 12:1–11.
27 M. Josuttis, 2003, esp. 91–96.

subjectivism, with God, the Prophets, Jesus, Paul, and the great men in church history being subordinated to a dubious self-presentation: the preachers put words into their mouths which they consider to be right, with no awareness of their own subjective selection (or suppression) strategies in terms of themes, information, or perspectives.

The present but permanently hidden effect of the "I" makes it difficult for the listener to take up a position to a sermon. Deliberations which are relevant and appropriate to the gospel appear as pearls of wisdom in a world existing for itself; lacking a recognizable relationship to the person of the preacher, they will be perceived as having scarcely any significance for the people present as listeners either.

It is certainly true that the unconscious or conscious attempt of the preachers to hide behind their testimony cannot prevent their revealing something about themselves *by speaking*, thus displaying their own *intention*. If their intention contradicts the words of the sermon, as is often the case, the sermon appears rather less credible. This is especially true when preachers find themselves in a position of disassociating themselves from the very matter they ought to represent – the message and raison d'être of their sermon. Such disassociating tendencies could reinforce the listeners' impression that preachers are arrogant and understand themselves as representatives of a religious elite. The following excerpt from a sermon is an example of this:

"The Holy People should be aware of their chosenness. We Christians today, like the Israelites in Canaan at the time of the acquisition of the land, live as a minority among the worshipers of alien gods, as the people of God among alien peoples. [...] Many of us have Turkish neighbors or colleagues who are Muslims. [...] There is the building contractor [...] with a wife from East Asia, who was brought up as a Buddhist, and with a daughter who has a Turkish boyfriend. As a Christian under these circumstances, one very quickly feels the need to give reasons for one's own Christianity. How is one to react to this situation? I do not have to sit in a corner as a moral coward or a sanctimonious hypocrite. [...] I do not have to travel to foreign lands and destroy Buddhist temples there, or burn down Turkish places of prayer here. Neither do I have to be a religious fanatic, committing attacks on the temples of the gods of our everyday life, e.g. on the consumer temples in our cities in which other gods are worshiped than the God who has revealed himself to us in Jesus Christ. Neither I nor you have to do any of this. But what should the people of God, the Christians, what should I myself do, what should I not do? We have been told what to do! To keep God's commandments. But what does it mean today – to keep God's commandments? It is a widespread misunderstanding among Protestant Christians that the commandments are not important for us."[28]

---

28 Sermon draft on Deut 7:6–12.

In this sermon, two demarcations are made: first, against those "heathens", who belong to many different groups and religions and who are not part of "God's Chosen People" and second, against an indistinct but widespread group of Christians who do not take the Ten Commandments seriously. Though the preacher assures not to belong to the chosen due to his own achievements, but thanks to the electing love of God, he still draws elaborate pictures of what one could do to the heathens if one "had to" and presents a specific view of today's Protestant Christianity, along with a specific way of quoting biblical motifs and popular expressions. All of this suggests that the preacher must be one of the very few who can truly match up to the Ten Commandments: "We have been told that we should not sit in the seat of scoffers (Ps 1:1) [...]", "So let your light so shine before men, that they may see your good works and give glory to your Father who is in heaven" (Matt 5:16)".[29]

The ambivalence of Christian existence – summed up in the known phrase *simul iustus et peccator* –, the experience of desiring to make the ethics of the Christian tradition one's own and yet suffering set-backs, the experience of not believing in the "God of commerce" but yet making sacrifices to him etc. – all of this is not taken into account in this bold template of Christian faith, which is based on the preacher's self-image.


### 2.1.2 The We-All-Syntax

An inappropriate use of the "we" form in the sermon can convey two things: on the one hand, the attempt of the preacher to hide behind or among "us all" in order not to have to openly take position or not to provoke opposite standpoints; on the other hand, this manner of speaking may imply a concealed reprimand for the listeners. In the latter case preachers may say "we", yet from the context of the address it becomes clear that they are not actually talking about themselves but *only* about their listeners – or rather their image of the listeners: "Today we have virtually forgotten how to live with the certainty of the support of the Holy Spirit."[30] "Since we do not pay sufficient respect to this issue [of our sanctification] there is theft and deceit among us: at the workplace, in the restaurant and at the car dealer's."[31]

This use of the we-form appears particularly often in ironical and cynical formulations, which have an accusatory tenor and convey a certain sense of a

---

29 Ibid.
30 Sermon draft on Rom 8:26–30.
31 Sermon draft on 1 Thess 4:1–8.

decree; for instance, in the question: "What have we done wrong now?" There is an unmistakably aggressive undertone, which can be understood as a verbally derived auto-aggression: preachers spare themselves the examination of their self-perception by projecting it onto the listeners.

"Do you know Wilhelm Busch? Yes? Then you certainly know Max and Moritz. One day, these two stole Widow Tibbets' freshly prepared hens in a smart way and feasted on them. After the meal, the two lay in the grass – replete and self-satisfied. [...] These two – that is all of us, you and I; we, whose guilt can be seen upon our faces, we, you and I, who can never have enough attention, money, love for ourselves, success, or being left in peace by our neighbors. – Now, after all this gorging, we are so full that we cannot utter another word. We choke on all the things that we cannot get enough of and in the meantime, have forgotten the simplest thing: to turn to God and pray. We cannot pursue our day-to-day tasks from Monday to Friday – and often also at the weekend – and only on Sunday, when the church bells are ringing, pause for a couple of hours and follow God's call."[32]

The "we" is also frequently used to suggest a "state of harmony"[33] where there is none – as the preacher clearly suspects, or is aware of unconsciously. In such cases the use of "we" serves to avoid argumentation and thus comes close to manipulation. If the "we" is not applied in the interests of those present, and its use is not guided by an attempt to represent them too, the individuals in question are misused as "window-dressing"[34] for the preacher's theories.

Pointing out such lapses of judgment does not mean branding the "we" in the sermon as a homiletic mistake in general. The "we" has its place in communication wherever it makes obvious how preachers are connected to their listeners, that they are facing the gospel together, that preachers and listeners are confronted with the same challenges, etc. The "we" in the sermon should be endorsed when it is used as a deliberate sign that preacher and listeners are of equal status regarding spirituality, or as a declaration of a brotherly and sisterly solidarity in questions of faith and life.

The "we" (e.g. in exhortatory formulations) is especially appropriate, indeed vital with a view to successful and credible communication, in the phrasing of liturgical elements. "'Let us pray' is a phrase which is certainly permitted in a service, since one can expect that people who attend the service have also come to pray."[35] It is a problem, however, when it is used, for example, in a rewording of the "General Confessions of Sin" – a denomination chosen with liturgical deliberation – which results in labeling the listeners as "morally completely unsatisfactory". "We think only of ourselves, it is immaterial to us that people are starving etc." Stereotypical moral carping

---

**32** Sermon draft on Rom 28:26–30.
**33** Cf. P.-L. Völzing, 1979, 230.
**34** Loc. cit., 233.
**35** Loc. cit., 228.

fails to recognize not only the basic pastoral attitude and the selflessness of a number of individuals; they are also anthropologically problematic when they equate "sins" with the failure to carry out particular obligations and justify the need for the communication of the gospel with a lack of good conduct in human beings.

### 2.1.3 Jargon, Irony and Sarcasm

Jargon, irony and sarcasm each represent verbal forms of an approach to, or a disassociation from, the subject and the communication partner: what is presented in *jargon* or slang is frequently meant to indicate *solidarity* with the listeners and signify common ground between them and the speaker. A sermon delivered in jargon indicates: "We belong together! After all, we speak the same language." At the same time this level of speech serves to create *distance* from others, who are usually not present. The use of jargon can therefore be largely determined by social motivations,[36] and it is frequently encountered where speakers feel they depend upon the goodwill of the listeners and wish to ingratiate themselves with them, as it were. From a socio-psychological perspective this means: jargon may be a symptom of a fear of *rejection,* or the *expression of ingratiation and subordination.* In this case, preaching represents a way for preachers to assure themselves of the sympathetic ear of their listeners. For the congregation, the message is one of social tenability and stability of the group-specific interaction network.

One of the problems with this strategy – aside from the psychological and theological difficulties of the expectations connected to it – lies in the fact that jargon does not achieve the desired success simply through the *use* of slang expressions. The "positive" effect of jargon is based on the real existence of common realms of action and experience between speaker and group. It is perceived as inappropriate and as an act of ingratiation if the language chosen does not correspond to the behavior anticipated by the listeners on the basis of their mutual social experience.

Regarding contents, this style is often attended by the belittlement or trivialization of particular standards of Christianity or faith, regardless of how one defines its *conditio sine qua non.* This means that such a sermon attempts to preempt potential disapproval through a diminution of possible "requirements". If, however, it is not apparent to the listeners that the preacher is indeed "one of them", faced with the same conditions of life and faith to some extent – rather than only rhetorically sharing their lives, problems and questions – the jargon,

---

36 G. Kalivoda, 1998, 713.

meant to accommodate the "man on the street", does, in fact, achieve the opposite effect.

"When somebody asks me about my existence as a Christian, I don't know what to say. I mean I don't know what that means for my life. Saying 'I am a Christian' sounds a little like a romantic escape from the world, don't you think? And on top of that, the biblical texts. To be honest, I don't even really understand their language, never mind their content. Let's just open on a random page: Phil 4:4f. [Text is read] I had better join a monastery straight away. Oh, but even there such a position is not viable. That reminds me of my aunt, who was so pious. I find it almost naïve that Paul gives such advice to the grown-up Philippians. [...] Didn't Jesus say that too, already in the Sermon on the Mount? Something like: Take no thought for your life. [...] Funny what such a word can suddenly set in motion. It's incredible how a text like this throws me right off my train of thought."[37]

Studies on jargon can be connected with observations from research in depth and communication psychology. Preachers possibly want to be "fed"; they are afraid that they may not be able to endure a situation of conflict within the congregation.[38] Whatever reasons one might find for the occurrence of such ways of speaking, they are only partially suitable for making the Christian life appear attractive or for conveying the impression of a stable bond of solidarity between a preacher and their congregation. On the contrary: it causes listeners to switch off, ignore or reinterpret what they hear, particularly when preachers transmit to the congregation their own personal problems, which may have flared up anew whilst dealing with the text or topic of the sermon.

Adopting *ironic and sarcastic tones,* or taking on corresponding attitudes has a distinct distancing effect – more than the use of jargon. It signifies a distance to people, objects or circumstances, which tends to imply a notion of invalidity or belittlement. In other words: individual sermons frequently call attention to the various dead-ends of the paradox human bustle and highlight certain flaws of the western European lifestyle, yet with – and this is the crucial point – "audibly raised eyebrows" and with the sometimes indignant, sometimes resigned comment that nothing in this will change for the time being.

On closer inspection, before long Hegel's "general irony of the world"[39] and A. Schopenhauer's thesis of the common meaninglessness of life are maltreated; soon H. Heine's understanding of the "irony of the great Dramaturge of the world

---

**37** Sermon draft on Phil 4:4–7.
**38** Cf. H.-J. Thilo, 1974, 114f.
**39** G. W. F. Hegel repeatedly speaks of the "tragic irony" of the world: "One Right stands up against the other – not as if only the one were Right, and the other Wrong, rather both are Right, conflicting, and one breaks up on the other" (Hegel, 1986, vol. 12, 393f.).

stage up there"[40] and F. Nietzsche's characterization of the world as chaos are perpetuated, and it is above all a declaration of invalidity which determines the content and tone of an ironic and sarcastic sermon. Frequently, this is connected with an attempt to distance oneself both from theologizing and from those who continue to do so – from the pulpit amongst other places. In his works on the Philosophy of Speech,[41] Paul de Man repeatedly reveals the latent propensity of irony as a deconstructive tool. He found self-destructive tendencies in relevant texts. According to him, irony stands, among other things, for *a lack of authenticity* that the writer or speaker is actually aware of; yet he also knows that this cannot be overcome. On the contrary: "You can't be 'a little ironical'."[42] Hence irony in preaching means risking a breach which does not only make it more difficult for the preacher to communicate a consistent, constructive message, but also denies the listener a clear understanding of the sermon.[43]

Jargon and irony, perhaps even sarcasm, may have their place in some communication strategies – e.g. as ultima ratio against a lack of due distance, as a defense reaction to some sorts of tactlessness, as a precautionary measure against privacy violations. Irony may certainly be used in the interest of a desired and controlled provocation or – well-measured – to ease a tense situation in conversation or to be a form of subversive humor.[44]

In case of a positive use of irony, the preacher would most likely assume the rhetorical or Socratic role of the "electric ray" who engages the listeners in a dialog (also with themselves!) and refutes their hardened opinions of themselves, of life, God and other people. In the relevant dialog Meno says to Socrates: "I consider that both in your appearance and in other respects you are extremely like the flat torpedo sea-fish; for it benumbs anyone who approaches and touches it [...]. For in truth I feel my soul and my tongue quite benumbed, and I am at loss what answer to give you."[45]

---

**40** H. Heine, 1986, vol 7.1, 111, 199 and 1979; vol. 8.1, 182.
**41** Cf. esp. P. de Man, 1989.
**42** E. Behler, 1998, 624.
**43** Cf. E. Behler: "Irony, here, is [...] not a rhetorical figure of speech among others but [...] a fissure in language, making it impossible for the author to master their text and to express something unambiguously, but just as little does it allow the reader to record an unequivocal reading report." (Ibid.) This "ambiguity" is a constructed equivocalness leading the reader, or the listener respectively, which is subordinated in the model of the "open work of art" (cf. I.4.3.4).
**44** Irony has a different significance in pastoral counseling – as in philosophical practice in general – and is common standard in professional counseling. It is a feature of purposeful interaction and does not just occur as a monological part in a conversation between two or three people. Simple repetition, exaggeration or "ironic" claiming of the opposite can open up a new path for the counselee. Whatever he has regarded as a final truth, with a great degree of determination and desperation, can be seen in a different light afterwards. Cf. W. Engemann, 2002, esp. 119–121.
**45** Plato, 1952, 297.

Jargon, irony and sarcasm are styles with a strong, habitual social functionalization and significance; therefore, they demand exceptionally fine tact and sensitivity if they are to become a constructive element of the sermon as a public address.

## 2.1.4 Drifting off into the Theological System

A drifting-off into the theological system is the result of the preachers' need for security as the reverse side of their religious and theological uncertainties in view of finding a specific, assailable statement for their sermons. They *ventilate* the text, and the theology at their disposal, so brilliantly that certain problems and aspects of their message are certainly discussed while the preachers themselves – people with a concrete view and a particular intention, based on articulated arguments – remain unmentioned. "Why do they do this? One reason is certainly that they encounter the temptation to safeguard not only their concern but also themselves. With the supply of an entire system nothing more can happen to them – and indeed nothing at all happens anymore. No one believes that someone who seeks to secure themselves and thus preaches in theological anxiety is still in any way an interpreter of the gospel. If the caution lights of the theological system light up on every word, they inevitably become 'committed to the system'."[46]

In the following sermon the listeners are constantly pushed back and forth between the promising message of justification and the associated rediscovery of paradise on the one hand, and strong reproaches for their alleged lack of interest in paradise on the other. One passage reads as follows: "Luther once said when he realized that the true faith of justification came from faith alone, that this was 'truly the gate to paradise'. This 'gate to paradise' has to a large extent been closed again for us. This is exactly why we are so embarrassed when someone asks us about our being Protestants. For Luther, 'God' was still self-evident, but he isn't for us any longer in any way. [...] In the end we are not looking for a 'merciful God' but for a reasonably happy, fulfilled life. [...] At such a sober and yet sobering stock-taking, the question naturally arises as to whether we expect anything at all from God or from the church. Certainly – a little security, some consolation in difficult situations, a sense of community with like-minded people [...]. Of the 'gate to paradise' there are only very few traces."[47] One finds no detail on either the true relevance of the experience of justification today or on the understanding of paradise which directs the preacher. A large variety of themes and questions are touched upon "somehow"; they jostle with one another and reveal the preacher to be, on the whole, a disgruntled notorious objector.

Against this background, Hans-Otto Wölber's observations and conclusions become understandable: "A diligent churchgoer once said that she always felt

---

**46** H.-O. Wölber, 1971, 369.
**47** Sermon on Rom 3:21–28, quoted by F. Lütze, 2006, 165.

that at the beginning of the sermon a hand was held out to her, but at the end this hand was drawn back again." Wölber summarizes the preachers' self-protective strategy on which such incidents are based as follows: "They may once get as far as to use a bold imperative, yet in the end they swing back to the theologically appropriate indicative. They praise the glory of God in creation, but then they add many thoughts about the decayed condition of the world. Thus, they pursue the completeness of the theological system."[48] This system itself is naturally not the gospel but at best an apparatus for theologians to make the gospel easier to explain. "The *viva vox evangelii* must be a *viva vox* not least in establishing, by virtue of a decision of faith, what is required today, instead of trying to find an ultima ratio to general theological problems."[49]

### 2.1.5 Misapprehensions Regarding the Goal of the Sermon

A sermon which the congregation perceives as out of place rather than ill-advised, trivial rather than unsubstantial, is also the result of the preachers' *internalized standards* relating to the purpose and prospects of their sermon. These standards in turn are influenced by the self-conception of the preachers and their related view of their role in the pulpit. For example, a preacher may be convinced that, every Sunday, he is purveying "salvation" to the congregation, who would have no concept of salvation without his work. (This preacher may even presume that listening to his sermon is the preferable manner of participating in salvation.) Relevant sermon analyses find that such preachers have a strong tendency towards lectures on the rediscovery of the doctrine of justification in the Reformation; what they are likely to neglect in turn are detailed examinations of their contemporaries' reality of life, and the recognition of the people's questions and experiences as adequate ground for the sermon.

Content and structure of an address depend substantially upon the respective purposes and aims that are ascribed to or expected from it. The concrete occasion for the speech or the respective situation play a special part. We are able to tell after few sentences whether we are currently listening to e.g. a birthday speech, a graduation address, or a sermon because we have internalized a kind of "standard repertoire" for the respective occasions. True, the more this repertoire is used the greater is the danger that a speech will be clichéd. To avoid this – and this holds true not only for sermons but for every other type of address, too – it is essential to continually re-examine the purpose of the speech at hand, as well as the legitimate (or unwarranted) expectations of the listeners.

---

48 H.-O. Wölber, 1971, 368.
49 Loc. cit., 369.

For many sermons, it is commonly considered enough (a) to discuss theological themes, (b) to conduct a historicizing interpretation of the text, (c) to give a general lecture on how to interact with others, or (d) to elaborate on individual aspects of Christian piety. While it is undisputed that an interpretation of the Bible, theological information, or a critical examination of everyday communication also have their place in a sermon, they remain secondary motifs. They are ends in themselves and thus put a strain on the primary function of the sermon, which is to allow people to gain a view on the different perspectives of "living by faith" in light of their experiences, their questions and resulting problems, as well as to – in the words of the parables – live under the premise of the kingdom of God today. In order for one's spoken word to correspond to the address' function, it is essential to reflect on the following questions: Why am I saying this – apart from the fact that it is part of the ceremony? What is "the case" that prompted my speech? What significance does my address have for the thoughts, feelings and actions of the listeners in their lives today? In many sermons, this manner of reflection is avoided in the ways mentioned above[50].

On a) Sermons, for example, aim at a "renewed examination of the topic of the Lord's Supper", "reiterating the history of the Trinity", and a reflection of "the theoretical question of the nature and the purpose of the congregation" as well as its "most important aspect – the unity of the church", with all the "difficulty of the idea of unity". The theological associations and considerations of the preacher are also frequently reckoned among such theological questions. Accordingly, a sermon is to be held in order to "allow the congregation to participate in the preacher's encounter with the text".[51]

A sermon, however, should never be a lecture on a topic but, at best, be *based on* a topic – e.g. "Jesus eating with his followers and with tax-collectors and sinners", to illustrate in how far I myself, 2000 years later, am invited to his table.

On b) The task of the sermon is often simply derived from the authority of Scripture or from the existence of a text. In such cases, the listeners could gain the impression that the address offered from the pulpit is primarily the consequence of the clock standing at 9.30 on that Sunday, and that a particular order of sermon texts prescribes the discussion of a particular section of the Bible. For which *further reasons* everything that is said has to be said, is therefore less than obvious.

---

**50** Cf. a) – d).
**51** From the preparatory work of student sermons with reference to 1 Cor 11:23–26, Rom 8:26–30, Eph 4:1–6 and 1 Cor 12.4:11.

In the course of such sermons, the (allegedly) central concepts of the text are put in relation to each other somehow, their scopes are defined, and their meanings are substantiated with the central concepts of other texts or theological systems. But the sermon has not fulfilled its task if it eventually puts this label on a text: "This holds true for us, too, today." A conscientious study of the text is rather a *prerequisite*, which finally enables preachers to target the task of the sermon to the best of their belief and find the appropriate words which allow the listeners to be more than the recipients of instruction on the concepts of the Christian life in Paul, or John, or the Old Testament; first and foremost, the listeners should be prepared for the arrival in their own lives, as it were, and encouraged to embrace life.

On c) General instructions on the behavior in everyday life belong to the most frequent basic motifs of preaching. These sermons, however, often lag behind everything that associations, citizens' initiatives, municipal welfare offices, or common-sense think, publish, and practice regarding matters of political correctness, environmental conservation, or neighborly help.

"Why are you hoping that things will improve at some point in time? It is your neighbor who is old and feels lonely, and you only need to cross the street and visit her. It is your beverage carton, and you can use a reusable bottle instead! [...] The Spirit drives us to change our world now because we are on the way to God's goal. And we always reach it wherever we make time for personal encounters in our everyday life, or where we open our eyes to the pollution of nature."[52] In another sermon, "it should be shown that it is false and unbiblical to divide all of mankind into winners and losers: into those who deserve immortal life and those who do not deserve it."[53] Is an analysis of Pauline theology really necessary in order to reach this insight?

The relation to everyday life as such must not be excluded from the sermon. This is, however, not achieved by instructing listeners in the basic rules of neighborliness and ecology. Day-to-day life is relevant to a sermon because of its determining experiences and because of the questions, expectations and attitudes of everyday life, which make the communication of the gospel possible and plausible in the first place.

On d) Defining the communication of the gospel exclusively as the examination of internal aspects of Christian piety is also highly problematic.

"We should think once more about how we all, every day, thoughtlessly break the commandments of Holy Scripture – and not only commandments which we consider to be specifically Jewish. God, in his benevolence and love, has established these laws for us as an expression of

---

52 Student sermon on Rom 8:26–30.
53 From the preparatory work of a student sermon on Rom 6:19–23.

his affection. We may find some laws inconvenient at first glance, but maybe they are not so dumb [...]. On the other hand, we should not follow laws and traditions blindly. We should think about them, weigh up advantages and disadvantages, and then decide to the best of our knowledge."[54]

Apart from the theological inadequacy, and the extreme legality of this accusatory argumentation, it is homiletically problematical to do nothing more than vaguely voice classical elements of Christian piety and somehow simply request them without anchoring these elements in the context of an attractive understanding of Christian spirituality or a life lived by faith. This, however, would require preachers to speak of their own joy in such a life and to be aware of their own inquisitorial attitude.

## 2.2 Indicators of Problems in the History of Homiletics

In the history of Homiletics – in so far as we establish the beginning of academic reflection on the role of the preacher in the 19th century – we can differentiate four phases or lines of argumentation: (1) At the beginning of the consideration of the role of the preacher in regard to content and form of the sermon, there was an obvious basically sympathetic opinion of his personality as a *principal possibility for the course of the preaching event.* (2) Over a long period of time, the insight that it is inevitably a subject who attends to the task of writing and delivering the sermon resulted in a catalog of *pragmatic demands* on the preacher. (3) It would be negligent not to mention the efforts to present the person of the preacher first and foremost as an *obstacle and burden* for the proclamation of the gospel. (4) The ambition to portray the preaching person as a necessary *constituent part of the preaching event, both* methodically and theologically, is, as will be seen, comparatively new.

Positions 1 to 3 will be briefly outlined in the following chapters by way of introducing the issue. The fourth position is elaborated on in due detail in I.2.3; it has characterized research in the last 70 years to an ever growing degree and appears to be the consensus in more recent Homiletics.

### 2.2.1 The Personality of the Preacher as a Principal Possibility

Even as early as at the beginning of the 19th century empirical observations suggested the perception of the personality of the preacher as basic potential for

---

**54** Student sermon on Matt 12:1–8.

convincing preaching. Commenting on the interest in the homiletic seminars which he had held, Johann F. C. Gräffe, the superintendent and leader of the homiletic institute in Göttingen, summed up in 1812: "In this institute the focus is not so much on what the preacher was attempting to say etc., but rather on what he *actually said, how* he said it and what impression he made on his listeners. That is the main thing after all!"[55]

The impression of the preachers' personality on other people is certainly not embraced for the preachers' own sake, or for some arbitrary effect. Christian Palmer, for instance, acknowledged that preachers would not have to refrain from including their own academic insight or their own mentality in their sermons, but only with the professed interest "*that the preacher states something about himself,* that, like an experience he has made, for example, will now be put to the test [...], or that can be tacitly assumed to be common experience, being individualized through expression in the first person and thus becoming *more vivid* and obtaining a curious appeal through the personal predisposition"[56]. Elsewhere Palmer states – in the sense of an advocacy of the presence of the preachers' personality in the address from the pulpit – that "a sentence which is no less than new still appears as completely new when the man who utters it is a spiritual and revitalizing personality"[57].

This more or less positive assessment of the person of the preacher mentioned above was expressed in the Homiletics of the 19th century, particularly in the fact that, at least in general, there was no rift opened between a "biblical testimony" and a "personal testimony". On the contrary, the biblical text, the person and the proclaimed gospel were considered to be in a meaningfully supplementary, convergent coherence.

"In the sermon, the eternal truth [is] delivered to the people in an abstract way, not as a dispatch [...], with the character of the messenger being entirely irrelevant since a telegraph or a carrier-pigeon could have done the same thing; but it is in fact the man with whom the biblical saying has fused so profoundly that his person draws me to the gospel."[58] Not the herald who passes on the message but the witness who is also affected personally by the message serves here as a figure of homiletic identification. It is therefore true that "the preacher must appear before the congregation in his own person with his sermon. [...] It [i.e. the sermon] is the total manifestation of the personality."[59]

---

55 J. F. C. Gräffe, 1812, 43.
56 Ch. Palmer, 1857, 547; emphasis W. E.
57 Loc. cit., 632.
58 Loc. cit., 553.
59 Loc. cit, 600. Palmer consequently regarded the forming of the personality of preachers as well as their supervision in questions of faith, as an important task of pastoral care education (e.g. within the framework of preachers' seminaries).

Palmer's approach was initially taken up in the 20th century by Helmut Schreiner. Schreiner explained that, with a change from a supposedly objective to a deliberately subjective sermon, "the witness supercedes the judge"[60]. Friedrich D. E. Schleiermacher's homiletic impulses, however, had an even greater effect in making the preacher a central theme in the homiletic process. His most significant contribution in this context was his attempt to proclaim the subjects of reflection for the sermon – the triad of text, congregation, and preacher – as equally important. On the function of the preacher he stressed: "By means of the influence of his vivacious personality he should lead the general stimulation and give it a particular direction." The preacher should never "believe that he has fulfilled his vocation if the totality of the practice of his office is not also the totality of his whole religious self-portrait"[61].

Today we may be more likely – in convergence with Schleiermacher – to highlight the necessity of an integral presence of the preacher and point out that the credibility of the preachers' words are inseparably connected to the "personality-specific creed"[62]. This does not mean condoning a preacher's personal dogmatics; rather, it means a deliberate inclusion of concretions of faith, experiences and images into which the creed of the church is translated and takes shape in different manners by each individual. The inclusion of these specifications does not harm the common creed but serves its plausibility.

It is evident that the homiletic acknowledgement of the person of the preacher was founded on reasons which even at that time had an interdisciplinary character. One of the motivations was the conviction that the comprehensibility, credibility, and effectiveness of the address from the pulpit required not only pure doctrine but also – in the today's language – an adequate level of rapport, which cannot be established without "personal authenticity" on the part of the preacher (to mention only one aspect). In other words: what should be said in the sermon is only communicable to the extent in which it affects the preachers as individuals and has become part of their conviction. "The characteristic homiletic edification is generated by the individual assimilation of the Word of God in the person. Preachers cannot truly achieve this edification if their address cannot be seen as a true possession, as their own fervent conviction.

---

60 H. Schreiner, 1936, 161.
61 F. D. E Schleiermacher, 1850, 204f. With regard to this apparently bold thesis we must certainly take into account that Schleiermacher presumes the preacher to deliberately position himself in the tradition of his church, which both trusts him with, and demands from him, a "lively protestant freedom" (loc. cit., 204).
62 Cf. K. Winkler, 1997, 267–269.

If this is missing, the listeners will distrustfully shut themselves off from the influence of the speech."[63]

Like Schleiermacher, Palmer and other Practical Theologians cited in this chapter, Alexander Schweizer argued against a naïve approval of everything personal. It is, however, also evident in his argumentation that the attempts and pleas at that time could scarcely be based on reliable methods or concrete criteria. Instead, they appear to be primarily a question of – again personal – assessment.

"From this position they say something like: 'The preacher should renounce his individuality.' This is true – if it means that it should be subordinated to the divine Word; it is false if the individuality should be considered profane and therefore expelled from the worship. The merely natural human being is profane [...]. But the new person is present in worship both in general and as he is individualized in his agitated personality; for everybody is a human being and an individual at the same time. [...] But individuality must be clearly distinguished from personality; salvation appeared personally in Christ and continues to appear only in the faithful personality, expresses itself as thought and word. [...] Only an individual that is not filled with any common basis of faith cannot appear in the worship service; on the other hand he must portray what a living expression of congregational faith is in the individual personality. [...] One must preach *the Word of God, as it fills the individual personality*, Christ, how he wins a living form in the person and reveals himself in the personal individuality."[64]

In the 19th century comparatively few reservations are expressed against the idea that the person of the preacher is in principle a possibility for the sermon.[65] The theologians who do not review, or continue, the basically positive assessment of Schleiermacher's, Palmer's, Schweizer's etc. do so less from a determinedly opposite standpoint but because they do not find a proper place for this idea in their own approaches.[66]

---

63 A. Schweizer, 1848, 172.

64 Loc. cit., 138f.; emphasis W. E.

65 Cf. e.g. C. I. Nitzsch, 1848, 46. Admittedly Nitzsch concedes – in spite of his dogmatic-deductive understanding of the sermon in which "divine Word", "interpretation of Holy Scripture" and "objective ascertainments" are to be found (loc. cit., 48f.) – that the observant "personality of the preacher" (not their "individuality" encumbered with all kinds of afflictions and passions) has a function which stimulates the effect of the sermon (loc. cit., 52). Cf. also the positive role definition of the person in the field of pastoral care (loc. cit., 2).

66 According to the assessment of the church historian Ernst Koch (1982, 223), this relates above all to the homiletic drafts which emerged from the Revivalist Movement which recognize the person of the preacher only in its potential function of witness. This aspect is discussed in more detail in III.2.2.5.

## 2.2.2 The Personality of the Preacher as a Task in Principle

The deliberate inclusion of the personality in the preaching event was at first merely regarded with favor in the Homiletics of the 19th century; it subsequently became increasingly acknowledged as a principal responsibility. Around 1890,[67] Practical Theology started to advance from simply allowing the person of the preacher. Steadily increasing expectations veered gradually into standardized demands on their personality.

"It is anyway for the most part erroneous prattle when it is requested that the preacher, as one says, 'does not add anything of his own to the Word of God'. Who does not add something of their own? Only the unthinking, unimaginative plagiarist. As soon as [...] I truly preach I make use of the Word of God in my own way. Any practical interpretation of it is made precisely through the fact, and only through it, that I allow my very self to concern the Word of Scripture."[68]

The claim of such Homiletics is clear: The presence of the "whole man", of the "expression of his very own life", in short, the "impressive personality" becomes the yardstick of a good sermon. Its impression is of the "most decisive significance for the success of the sermon"[69]. A sermon should have a stimulating effect and spread harmonious spirit, ideally, to the whole congregation through the spirit in which the preacher speaks. Original ideas are required. The sermon clearly lacks something if the preacher has not managed to relate "his very own being" to the scriptural Word.

Considerable confidence is put in the preacher, much as the demands on them are quite high: it is not enough to tackle the Word of God "personally", keep in sight "his own susceptibility to temptation", attempt to conceal "his weakness", and evoke "tones resonating with the listeners"[70]. Preachers are encouraged to make their appearance entirely deliberately and personally. The overall constitution of their appearance "with all that is known of his loyalty, veracity and kindness" has a much stronger effect upon the listeners than a rhetorically successful address, and it is more likely to be remembered by them, which in turn makes it more instrumental to them.[71]

The direct and implicit appeals for a greater inclusion of the person's own personality are no doubt the consequence of the fact that the mere proclamations of the significance of the personality for the sermon have not led to the desired result. Perhaps here they are also a reflection

---

**67** E. Koch speaks of a "new formation of Homiletics around 1890" (1982, 224).

**68** A. Krauß, 1883, 135.

**69** F. J. Winter, 1901, 985f.

**70** H. A. Köstlin, 1907, 320.

**71** F. Niebergall, 1909, 151.

of a situation which is unsatisfactory in its entirety. It appears to have been difficult to put into concrete terms the functions, ways and means of including the preacher's personality. Otherwise one would have felt the need to show the relevance of the gospel within the confines of the preacher's own existence, not continually having to differentiate it from the misunderstanding that a preacher must "speak about himself and reveal his 'own experience' from the pulpit"[72]. Then there would have been just as little reason to complain that the rhetorical skill, linguistic virtuosity or the imitation of other, famous preachers were more popular than the courage to employ one's own personal individuality and adequate forms of expression.

This spotlight on the second phase of the development of the preacher's person as a homiletic issue shows "that the significant discoveries of this generation relating to the influence of the preacher on the sermon have nevertheless left the preacher alone"[73]. "Unconditional personal veracity and total solidarity with the doubting contemporaries"[74] do not take the place of methodical reflections but demand them. Before this insight could establish itself, however, Homiletics was ruled by profound skepticism towards a role of the preacher conducive to the proclamation of the gospel.

### 2.2.3 The Personality of the Preacher as an Obstacle in Principle

Congregations who had lived through two World Wars had *the experience of the errors of people* who acted and preached in the name of God, commissioned by the institution of the church. This explains the skepticism against a positive, established role for the person of the preacher as it became established in Homiletics after 1920 more firmly than in other epochs of theoretical reflection on the sermon. This skepticism is clearly connected to the desire of theologians and preachers to free themselves from the task to lead out of the crisis. This position may also involve the interest not to be made responsible *qua* person for possible new crises.

The "radical contemplation of the message alone"[75] is the theological expression of this interest which was most clearly put into words by Eduard Thurneysen. He sees "a deep cleft [...] between the word of the preacher and the Word of God [...]. Only the deep insight that in reality one *cannot* preach allows preaching at all. Only the one who knows that God's Word can lie on *no* human

---

72 H. A. Köstlin, 1907, 321
73 E. Koch, 1982, 227.
74 Loc. cit., 224.
75 E.-R. Kiesow, 1990, 103.

lips will receive God's Word upon his lips."[76] Later, Heinrich Vogel put it in the following words: "Our word passes to this Word [of God]; it is not our property. We have no right of disposal over it, are also not the authors of the sermons."[77]

The context of the relevant formulations or supplementary comments shows that they are connected to one another by the conception that the preparation of the sermon is above all *receptive,* and the preaching is an *instrumental* act, performed by God himself. It is implied that the preacher as person and individual, as creative subject, can contribute nothing essential to promote the sermon. Hans Urner has also made a name for himself with this view. Following Thurneysen, he demands: "What he, the preacher, should say is what he hears, not what he thinks, not what he has experienced" in order so "to avoid (any) diminution of the Word of God"[78]. In fact, every sermon should be marked with the words: "The preacher as a handicap". For "everything that the preacher contributes can be restricting! He only becomes the preacher through the Word of God which is spoken to him so that he passes it on. [...] The text – as God's Word – will overcome the inevitable obstacles."[79]

This judgement – which is neither theologically convincing nor homiletically maintainable – is argued against in detail in I.1 and I.3 of this Introduction: the reception and the production of texts – including those from the Bible – not only belong together inseparably but are also to a high degree, indeed necessarily, influenced by the person who deals with these texts or drafts them.

It is difficult to tell exactly when this way of seeing the preacher first and foremost as a hindrance arose. Ernst Koch recapitulates: "After 1945 Homiletics understood the preacher as a factor of the sermon to a large degree as a burden for the sermon."[80] This certainly applies to the wide *adoption* of this approach. The decisive heralds of this homiletic position, however, had already at an earlier date expressed their reservations – it seems appropriate to state that the reversal in the view of the preacher happened even in the period after the First World War. Processes of development can only with difficulty be calculated to a precise year, particularly when it is a question of the gradual change in particular basic theological conceptions.[81] In so far as one includes the wars as one of the grounds for the change in the homiletic argumentation, we can assume that the estimation of the person was severely shaken through the

---

76  E. Thurneysen, 1921, 105–107.
77  H. Vogel, 1930, 161.
78  H. Urner, 1961, 95.
79  Loc. cit., 85.
80  E. Koch, 1982, 231.
81  As we shall see, Otto Haendler pens the most important work for the understanding of subjectivity in the sermon. This work was written and published during the Second World War (1941), even in the heyday of dialectical theology, anticipating later developments (cf. O. Haendler, 2017b).

experiences of the second decade of the 20th century. When whole conceptions of the world change fundamentally and when former ideals are experienced as being misleading (cf. analogous developments in literature, music, painting etc.) the individual person, who must somehow or other act in the world, can clearly no longer do so under the "old conditions" or under earlier assumptions.

The one-sided, stereotyped reference to the "Word of God" was conjoined with the sombre instruction that preachers should step back behind their testimony so as not to stand in the way of the Word of God.[82] There were no instructions at all as to how to do this – such directives could have suggested, after all, that the sermon was something manageable. This lack of instructions had the consequence that preachers were, again, left alone, albeit for other reasons. While in the late 19th and early 20th centuries Homiletics, in so far as it dealt with the person of the preacher, was frequently restricted to an appeal for personal charisma, the following epoch overlooked the "humiliating and helpless distress of inability"[83]. Preachers were tasked with proclaiming the kingdom of God as witnesses, but they were not given adequate orientation for how this could be achieved by "leaving their own person out of consideration."

That the "death of the preacher" was homiletically demanded, or dogmatically construed respectively, in diverse variations could scarcely be considered helpful. The tradition of argumentation can be traced from Eduard Thurneysen to Rudolf Bohren. The former stressed that "only *the one* who is willing *to die* while he is speaking of life dare be God's witness"[84]. For Thurneysen, such "dying" means in particular abstaining from rhetoric in which there is the danger of seeking something which concerns the preacher personally but is not God's concern.[85]

Fifty years after the publication of Thurneysen's essay we can read in Bohren's Homiletics: "God's Word remains God's Word, so the person who desires to proclaim it must die on the Word."[86] Likewise Bohren – in spite of minor concessions to rhetoric – reiterates Thurneysen's skepticism with regard to rhetorical efforts. To substantiate his argumentation he tells the story of a stammerer and stutterer who, of all people, was granted to appeal to him as listener – i.e. the story of a preacher who clearly did not want to disturb the true movement of God's Word with his own rhetoric and so became the suitable "dead" instrument.[87] This

---

82 On the problematic nature of this cf. III.4.2.
83 O. Haendler, 2017b, 292.
84 E. Thurneysen, 1921, 107.
85 Loc. cit., 111f.
86 R. Bohren, 1971, 218.
87 Loc. cit., 23.

argumentation is full of problems and contradictions, caused by the lack of a coherent model for the understanding of the preaching event and of a related report on the homiletic work-process.

It was obvious that matters could not be left at these assessments and appeals. In view of the crisis of the church, the progressive secularization of society, and not least of the rapidly changing conditions of the world in which the listeners live, it was not enough for preachers to simply refer to the *credenda* of Homiletics and brush aside the *facienda* with a few hints of what to do.[88] Nevertheless one must take this pre-history into account if one is to understand more recent attempts which try to look at the preacher within the frame of their own personal, communicative and confessing competence as a factor necessary for the sermon.

There is an intermediate stage on the path from a dialectical-theological problematization of the preachers' subjectivity to theory homiletically acknowledging them as persons. It can be found in the writings of Emanuel Hirsch. "If the subjectivity surges *against the cliffs of the eternal truth*, if the personal appropriation of the gospel brings about in the heart and conscience of the preacher an inner experience rich in crises and blessings, the sermon will be able to be both things at one and the same time: witness of the one Eternal One who stands *beyond every illusion and desire*, and a manifestation of a subjective heart which stands and moves *under God's authority*."[89] It is *not* the person of the preacher *as the person who he is* which becomes the starting-point of a new homiletic theory. Rather, the preacher comes to be seen merely as a subject "under God's control" and at the same time as a subject who "surges against the cliffs of the eternal truth." For the sermon process, the person of the preacher is only of significance as an unavoidable gateway for the gospel, "as a way of inner transformation of a living human heart" which the gospel takes hold of in order "to reach other human hearts"[90]. Once again the preacher appears as a potential obstacle as long as he refuses that inner alteration, and once again the true subject of the sermon is the gospel itself; again the communication of the gospel is considered in the end to be independent of the fears and desires of the preacher. This, however, means: it is not the preacher who preaches but the sermon, or God, or his Word, or the gospel respectively. Preaching is considered to be an event which – together with the preaching subject – stands entirely "under God's control". This approach underestimates both the *potential* and the *problems* of the preacher as subject.

---

**88** Incidentally, it is remarkable how poor this homiletic slogan – to say nothing other than what one hears and thereby to do without any eloquence – fits the manner of preaching of its champions. Thurneysen and Bohren failed to explain how their masterful interpretation of texts and brilliant rhetorics could be anchored within the framework of their homiletic theories. – The significance of language and the function of the address are discussed in more detail in III.4.
**89** E. Hirsch, 1964, 42. Emphasis W. E.
**90** Cf. H. M. Müller, 2002, 209.

## 2.3 Current Angles of Reflection

### 2.3.1 Personal Competence as a Homiletic Category

The decisive impulse for an integration of the person of the preacher which was conceptionally and methodically reflected upon in Homiletics came from Otto Haendler. He understands the "subject of the preacher as a starting-point and established point of contact"[91] in the doctrine of preaching: "If someone proclaims the gospel with *his own* mouth with words in *his own* language, with the help of *his own* experience and knowledge, Sunday after Sunday, his own person is consequently so important *for the sake of the matter* that we must grant him the greatest attention."[92]

Before we can focus on the contents of this approach, and how they can be stated more precisely, we must have a good look at a misunderstanding which has repeatedly found expression in the reception of Haendler's approach: Haendler never allows subjectivism to play a part.[93] On the contrary, his approach must be taken seriously *for the sake of the matter itself and the congregation or those who hear him.*[94] The attention to the preacher as subject results from the following understandings:

---

**91** Cf. O. Haendler, 2017b, 296–303. A detailed introduction to Haendler's homiletic argumentation both in the reception of his "doctrine of preaching" and his other homiletic lectures and writings can be found in Otto Haendler: Homiletik. Monographien, Aufsätze und Predigtmeditationen, edited by Wilfried Engemann (= OHPTh 2). Leipzig 2017b, 209–267. To understand the personal dimension of the sermon in Haendler cf. the extensive investigation by Christian Plate: Predigen in Person. Theorie und Praxis der Predigt im Gesamtwerk Otto Haendlers (= APrTh 53), Leipzig 2014.

**92** O. Haendler, 2017b, 298.

**93** "To be subjectivist, as a distortion of being subjective, means to disrupt the matter through one's subjectivity. To be objective means *to be carried by the matter as subject and to carry the matter as subject*" (loc. cit., 328).

**94** In this respect there is an interesting convergence between O. Haendler's intention and R. Bultmann's. Both works, Haendler's Homiletics and Bultmann's essay "New Testament and Mythology" were published at the same time (1941). Yet that is not the main reason to view the works as referring to each other; rather, it is the fact that both theologians struggle for the "elimination of false stimulations to faith": As Bultmann tackles with *rational blockades* (which result from a myth which has not been interpreted) in order to reveal the *real* outrages of the gospel, so Haendler deals with *psychological blocks*, among other things. In his view these arise partially because preachers reproduce in the sermon dogmatic doctrines without having worked out a personal expression for their content within the area of individual experience. Cf. already J. Henkys, 1990, 45 and K.-P. Jörns, 2008, 19–28.

1. The *content* of the sermon, i.e. the gospel, cannot be communicated without being expressed by a subject.
2. In addition, the *listeners*, in order to understand this gospel, are dependent upon a sermon behind which a "fellow struggler" whose address is "a true expression of the preacher's position"[95] is discernible.

On 1: Haendler's impassioned advocacy of the appropriate consideration of subjectivity is therefore connected to the demand for a new objectivity in Homiletics which can only be achieved if the preacher is "upheld by the concern as *subject*" and "upholds the concern as *subject*"[96]. "Careful research into the subject, his circumstances and possibilities" should "promote objective knowledge" and the duty of the preaching office to be "supported and secured".[97] Haendler does not demand reflection on the personality of the preacher in order to de-dogmatize the sermon for ideological reasons, but because he is convinced that precisely the insistence upon the objectivity of the message and the zealous reversion to dogmatic accuracy in the sermon will lead to the subjectivity of individual preachers having an *unchecked* effect on the process of the sermon.

The question preachers are therefore faced with is not *whether* they agree to or refuse the role and effect of their subjectivity in the course of the process of preaching, but *how* they take it into account: whether they integrate it or ignore it; knowing that the latter means that both in the preparation of the sermon and in the act of preaching, they revolve on their own axis: they follow their own individualistic ideas, preferences and fears, unchecked. "Anyone who wishes to become purely a tool in God's hand by eliminating, as far as possible, all that is subjective, will not become a tool [...], but a recording [...]. He who believes himself to be "deactivated" in this sense will find that the effect of his subjective powers are uncontrolled, non-standardized and disordered."[98]

On 2: Knowledge of one's own personality profile, and the way in which it is present in the communication of the sermon, is of crucial importance for one's relationship and interactions with the listeners. Preachers who understand their life and faith primarily as a fulfilment of their duty, and who declare obedience as the highest principle of their duty, will, according to Haendler, find it difficult to accompany the congregation into the freedom of faith.

---

95 O. Haendler, 2017b, 402.
96 Loc. cit., 328. The characterization of the preacher as subject of a concrete sermon does not exclude, but rather includes, the understanding of the church or the *congregation as a theological subject of the sermon* (cf. loc. cit., 302 and III.4.5 in this book).
97 O. Haendler, 2017b, 298. Emphasis W. E.
98 Loc. cit., 330.

"Where the preacher is still struggling against himself, he does likewise also do so against others in the sermon. Where he is still suffering without breaking through either to the freedom of the soul (i.e. to the freedom of faith) or to the freedom from compulsion, he cannot lead to freedom others who are waiting for this in his sermon."[99] In another place, Haendler explains in a similar way: Anyone who desires to stand by others by means of their sermon and "help them to their renewal" must also be able "to accept the dark side of [their] own being"[100] instead of denying it.

In other words: work on a sermon always requires an examination of one's own person and its conditions, of biographically evolved attitudes, and positions, specific ideals, preferences and fears acquired through experience. Personal competence as a homiletic category thus describes – here still provisionally defined – the preachers' ability to work out a sermon in the awareness of both the limits and possibilities of their personality structure and to therefore give the communication of the gospel a character reflecting one's own person.

This perspective in some respects undermines the position proclaimed in dialectical theology: the dilemma of having to preach but being unable to do so. Attempts to declare the diastasis between preacher and proclamation of the Word of God as the preface to all Homiletics are countered: "The best sermon does not come mostly from the gospel and least from the subject but mostly from the gospel and mostly from the subject: not from the 'ideal' but from the living subject."[101] It is thus evident: subjectivity as understood by Otto Haendler is not something which can be used as one likes. Subjectivity is something which must be developed. Accordingly, the new orientation of Homiletics with the focus on the person of the preacher deals with "a training in the use of what one [as subject] has" or a training, respectively, in how to deal with what one is, for there is "no [...] way by which one can free oneself from being a subject."[102]

It is an important aim of this homiletic endeavor to help the preacher to a real temporal synergy whereby he can serve both the matter and the listener. This objective arises from the observation that preachers – whether they have unconsciously transferred parts of their mother-fixation to the church and parts of their father-fixation to theology, or not – are in danger of losing contact with their own "self" and the world, i.e. in danger of proclaiming a theology "which has not been won and acquired but has been simply adopted from others"[103]. Then, preachers have a tendency to see central problems of life from the point of view of a "child of theology and church", as it were, but not as contemporary. *Homiletic contemporaneity*

---

99 Loc. cit., 371.
100 Loc. cit., 326.
101 Loc. cit., 332.
102 Loc. cit., 295, 331f.
103 Loc. cit., 350.

does not correlate with ingratiation-seeking topicality; it is the appropriate expression of *a preacher's ability to be aware of oneself in one's own time and to refer to its discourse*. Here, then, it is not a question of criticizing contemporary issues but of examining the present on the basis of one's own person. Particularly when one demands the sermon to include the plausibility of "truth beyond time", it is vital for the preachers to take a good look at their own temporal, limited biographical truths, in order to find an appropriate position for this "truth beyond time".

Haendler's book, "Die Predigt"[104] [The Sermon] represents a pioneering work in homiletic research which can scarcely be overestimated. It first served to express and clarify the fears of a whole generation whose conception of the *sola fide* meant that one must – in order to preclude any synergism in regard to the "effectiveness to save in the Word of God" – entertain a fundamental suspicion of everything which is connected to the creatureliness of the preacher, i.e. could come from themselves.[105] Because of this, the neglect of creativity and the suppression of destructive emotional powers were encouraged for a long time – even though these powers were by no means ineffective, but merely unappreciated.

Haendler's innovative advocacy of Homiletics which took into account both the preacher as a subject and the sermon as witness was initially not received well. His approach was misunderstood as psychologistical; his theological argumentation was largely disregarded. In the second edition of his work, Haendler gave an elaborate reply to his critics. In the preface, he wrote: "Again and again there is a concern about 'psychologizing' – i.e. about theology's mistrust of psychology and about the suspicion that the full weight of the theological position might be harmed by psychology. The problem is basically quite simple; it can be expressed in this simple sentence: "When one psychologizes, i.e. dissolves the theological truth in psychological connections, *the fault lies in himself, not in psychology.*" Without the meeting of psychology and theology, theology loses "a piece of fundamental and significant knowledge about the soul of the person, which, after all, has to be its focus of attention."[106]

From these introductory reflections on the question of the subject of the sermon, it has become clear that *personal competence* is not one skill among many others

---

**104** According to Haendler's pupil, Ernst-Rüdiger Kiesow (Rostock), the book – following Haendler's own wish – should initially bear the title "Der Prediger und seine Predigt" [The Preacher and his sermon]. It was clearly still too early at that time for such a title: The publishers did not venture to meet Haendler's wish (K. Voigt, 1992, 262, footnote 244).
**105** Cf. O. Haendler, 2017b, 302f.
**106** Loc. cit., 279, original emphasis.

which should belong to a preacher alongside exegetical, rhetorical or pedagogical competence. Instead, it is a "key competence". Before we discuss in detail different ways of perceiving this competence, we must ask about the requirements upon which the description of personal competence is based.

### 2.3.2 Personal Competence and the Preacher's Self-Perception

There can be no doubt that the epochal impulses of the human sciences in the first third of the 20th century sponsored the orientation on psychological aspects of the sermon. New empirical and academically consolidated insights furthered the shift away from mere appeals to the personal competence of the preacher as well as the turn towards overcoming the rejection of personal contributions in the proclamation out of sheer methodical helplessness. One of the key components was the overall successful attempt to analyse the personality of the person – in the sense of a working hypothesis – as a *structure* whose individual parts developed differently in each person, are functionally adapted to one another and altogether amount to a characteristic personality profile.

In this chapter, three models, which were successfully taken up in Homiletics in the 20th century, will be outlined, and their significance for the task of the preacher's self-perception will be highlighted.

### a) The Structure of the Personality.
### On the Homiletic Reception of Impulses of Sigmund Freud

Within the framework of his psychoanalytical work, Sigmund Freud became convinced that the varying, often inconsistent, expressions and behaviors of humans are due to particular parts or *functions in the structure of the Ego*. He therefore distinguishes the *Ego* of a personality structure from the *Superego* on the one hand, and from the *Id* on the other.

The *Superego*, interpreted by Freud himself as the "conscience", is the place of morality, both of moral standards and moral feelings of guilt.[107] This is formed and activated in the course of the individual's biography, whereby persons in authority play a special part: even during the course of education and development of a person the Superego increasingly takes the place of parents, teachers and other persons in authority. The Superego is the place where *standards and maxims* the person was confronted with from outside are internalized. "The poor Ego"[108] is frequently put under pressure from the Superego, which serves as "heir" and "legal successor" of earlier authorities. The Superego demands standardized self-observation and, at the same time, holds

---

**107** Cf. on the following S. Freud, 1964, 57–86.
**108** Loc. cit., 61.

up to the Ego an unattained, ideal self-portrait: "The Superego is [...] the representation of all moral restrictions, the advocate of the strive for perfection, in short, that which has become psychologically available to us of the so-called higher things in human life."[109]

In contrast to this relatively strong category of consciousness, the Superego with its principles, the *Id* is characterized as the *area of the unconscious,* compulsive and uncontrolled. In the "apparatus of the person's soul" the Id is that part which seeks well-being without consideration of what is good or bad. It is a potential of energy which can only be controlled with great effort by the Ego – with the Superego breathing down its neck, so to speak.[110] In order to understand this element of the structure of the personality the mundane linguistic usage can serve as orientation: We are in the habit of saying "it's brewing within me", "it's bubbling within me" etc.[111] By contrast, it is unusual to say "it's thinking within me", "it's judging within me". The "Id" signifies impulses which are only partially controllable through ratio; empirically, they affect both the motivation behind attitudes and actions – and they belong to the emotional conditions under which a change of will is in the offing.

The Ego appears by implication as the true *location of the formation of human authenticity.* The Ego is the authority which must be strengthened. A person's capability to find and maintain their own identity is defined by their Ego's sovereignty – at least relative sovereignty – over both the Superego and the Id. In Freud's view, the dynamism and drama of a person' psychological personality consists in the fact that their Ego, although it cannot serve two masters (Superego and Id) simultaneously, must struggle with "three severe masters"[112]: with the outside world, the Superego and the Id. All psychological dysfunctions (anxiety, depressions, obsessions etc.) are correspondingly traced back to this internal conflict-constellation of the Ego between the Superego and the Id.

Based on Freud's model, it is a person's individual relationship of the Ego to the Superego and to the Id which determines the ethics, feelings of guilt, repressions, ideals, etc. that will become apparent in this person's sermon. *That preachers can only preach under the conditions of their person* also means that it is impossible to hide their very own biography and fortunes, for the structure of a personality is not defined anew every day. It is the basic position which people have taken up because of various experiences in the course of their lives, in order to reconcile external expectations, internalized norms and their own needs in such a way that they can do them justice and come to terms with them. Personality structures are therefore expressed particularly in specific fundamental attitudes people have towards their surroundings – to their fellows and to God – and to themselves.

---

**109** Loc. cit., 66f.
**110** Loc. cit., 71–73: "The ego's relation to the id might be compared with that of a rider to his horse. The horse supplies the locomotive energy, while the rider has the privilege of deciding on the goal and of guiding the powerful animal's movement. But only too often there arises between the ego and the id the not precisely ideal situation of the rider being obliged to guide the horse along the path by which it itself wants to go" (loc. cit., 77).
**111** In German we are in the habit of saying: "Es brodelt in mir" ("it's seething within me"), "es rumort in mir" ("it's rumbling within me") or "es kocht in mir" ("it's boiling within me").
**112** Cf. S. Freud, 1964, 77.

Against this background, the significance of the subject for the sermon was initially defined as the question of the actual effect of the preacher. The focus is no longer on a vague, and also problematic appeal for "more personality" and individuality in the pulpit; instead, it is on the analysis of one's own person as a homiletic task. *Working on the sermon implies working on and with one's own person.* Performing the task of the sermon is impossible if preachers are not aware of three things: firstly, they need to be mindful of who they really are, and, secondly, of their own role when they enter the pulpit. The third aspect is the knowledge of one's own tendencies in communicative behavior without the correcting influence gained through reflecting on oneself, Scripture, and the congregation.

### b) The Self and the Entirety of the Person.
### The Homiletic Reception of Impulses of Carl Gustav Jung

The beginnings of the reception of personality-psychological aspects in Homiletics are not conceivable without the impulses of Freud's psychoanalysis.[113] Yet the ideas of C. G. Jung are the primary source used in Homiletics for the understanding and expression of unsolved homiletical problems, and to characterize personal competence.[114] For this purpose, the *contact of a person with their "self"*, or the re-establishment of this contact, play a special part. The basis for setting this focus is the observation that preachers frequently know themselves less well than they know the theological doctrine which they attempt to reformulate in the sermon. Indeed, and even more problematic, it is overlooked in the theory and practice of the sermon that theological truths can find their adequate expression only in a personality-specific concretion.

In Haendler's Homiletics, the "self" represents the balanced *entirety of the person of the preacher.* While Freud so firmly separates the *Ego* of a personality-structure from the Id and the Superego that he declares it to be the true partner of debate with the therapists (for it is only worthwhile to enter an alliance, to treat and to work with the "true" Ego), Jung explained the self to be a state which is relevant to the *entire* personality structure, but remains to be fulfilled. The "self", as he sees it, is "more extensive than the Ego" and stands for the concrete

---

113 Otto Haendler worked out the models and methods of psychoanalysis not only in theory but also in practice. Parallel to his work as a pastor in Neuenkirchen near Greifswald, and while he was a lecturer at the Ernst Moritz Arndt University of Greifswald, he underwent an educational analysis at the Psychological Institute in Berlin under the Freudian Werner Kemper in 1935–37.
114 Haendler received important stimuli for his work from the writings of C. G. Jung and through correspondence with him. Cf. on Haendler's biographical background M. Meyer-Blanck, 1999, 395–405.

individuality of a person in the sense of an "innermost, final and incomparable uniqueness".[115] The self comprises the unconscious as well as the conscious. For the constitution of the self, emotional impulses, rational insights, standards and ideals are equally constitutive.

"Self-realization"[116] consequently describes a process in which people analyze their emotions and moral concepts to the extent that a coherent relationship and inter-communication arises between the diverse areas of a personality structure. Through this, preachers should be enabled to interact and deal with all the areas of their person, as well as to access their total wealth of expression.

This kind of human "self-realization" (in German originally: "Verselbstung") is also described as *"Personification"* or *"Individuation"*[117], and it is assessed as an expression of personal presence and competence. "Individuation means becoming an 'in-dividual', and, in so far as 'individuality' embraces our innermost, last, and incomparable uniqueness, it also implies becoming one's own self. We could therefore translate individuation as 'coming to selfhood', or 'self-realization'."[118] In Freud's terminology, this would mean: the Id and the Superego are no longer factors pressurizing the "poor Ego", but they are refined and integrated functions of a person who – in harmony with himself – is in contact with all the parts of the structure of his personality. This is attended by the surmounting of a self-satisfied subjectivism, and it is connected to a new view of personality status: it is more than merely granted, which implies that a person could only become "what (perhaps) another could and should with right have been", yet not "what he should become according to his own most personal being".[119]

Thus, one possible approach is to understand the self as a task and goal of a personality. Additionally, in a more metaphysical sense, the self can also be understood as a basic motive of a personality. In this view, the self is something archetypal, passed forward to the individual, a kind of inner-personal programme of direction and guidance. In Haendler, this second sense is taken up as part of a theology of creation. He sees self as corresponding to the archetype which the creator has devised for the individual. The self is identified with the person as meant by God: "The self is [consequently at the same time] the factor which points the way and leads the person in the direction of the archetype presented at the beginning."[120] The formation, or regaining respectively, of the self is, according to Haendler, comparable with "a clearing-up operation on the place on which one intends to build a new house".[121]

---

**115** C. G. Jung, 1972, 173.
**116** Ibid., cf. on this O. Haendler, 2017b, 339.
**117** Loc. cit., 338f.
**118** C. G. Jung, 1972, 173.
**119** O. Haendler, 2017b, 339.
**120** Cf. loc. cit., 340.
**121** Loc. cit., 341.

Transferred to the preacher it is a matter of taking stock of the premises, contents and forms of expression which characterize his own work on the sermon. It means dealing with homiletic inventory, which one hitherto has considered suitable simply because it was thought to be correct in terms of dogma and exegesis. This is not accepted: theology in general, and work on the sermon in particular, require dogmatic patterns of interpretation to be continuously referred back to the background experience and comprehension of the self, as well as the reformulation of its contents through the ability of the self to communicate.

The inventory mentioned here applies not only to the examination of terminology and concepts which a preacher may have taken over directly from the theological doctrine they learned. It also applies to the ideas which have developed in the preachers themselves on the basis of particular impressions (e.g. images of God) and experiences that have become established in their subconscious, or their conscience, and have become opinions.[122] These may stand, without the preachers necessarily realising this, contrary to the dogmatics of their theology. As a result, obedience to, or belief in, authority finally leads to the omission of one's own experiences and ideas. The consequence is that the sermon is alienating rather than helpful – an effect which in this case is "accounted for in the unconscious alienation of the preachers from their own conviction".[123]

Looking back on decades of teaching Homiletics, Haendler observed that students are often still unpractised in the reflection of their own personal, theologically perfectly relevant, everyday experiences. Consequently they tended to reformulate, without further ado, the yield of their exegesis as a sermon. Likewise, curates would clutch at "dogmatic formulations" in the preparation of their sermons, as if they were "lifebelts", because they were afraid to bring their own spiritual experience in a verbal form. This is also true for the experienced preacher: because they do not believe that they are able to draw from a living theology that is fused with their person, they prefer to fall back on stylistic solutions and practical generalizations.[124]

A convincing sermon – for which the self shares the responsibility, and which the self shapes in regard to content and expression – requires preachers to avoid

---

122 "A sophisticated manner is frequently [...] not a sign of security but of hidden insecurity. If we desire to help here, it is not enough to cite God's demand in contrast to the demands of the Ego; we must also find the true, hidden being of the person in order possibly to change their escape into confidence" (O. Haendler, 2017b, 323).

123 Loc. cit., 351. Cf. also my remarks on the problems of the preacher's professional language, which today – far more than in Haendler's day – have to do with the discrepancies between the language of dogmatics, the repertoire of religious expression in our time and the pastor's ideas of faith (W. Engemann, 2006b, 87–91).

124 O. Haendler, 2017b, 293f.

becoming completely caught up in abstract, excessive assertions. Instead, they must have the courage "to lower one's word to the expression of that which we have earnestly experienced and are prepared to represent totally, [... for] we can only proclaim the gospel in a lively way as it has become alive for us."[125] Such statements are not an expression of a false modesty. They formulate an important conclusion which comes from the insight that a lively sermon is mostly given by those preachers "who can address the creed of the church [in their own words] as an adequate expression of their personal conviction"[126] because they are in contact with their self.

In this context Haendler developed the concept of *assimilation*: "The effect of the preacher is inevitably [...] restricted through the fact that only the assimilated parts of his proclamation can bear fruit."[127] We use the term "assimilated" if the sermon brings forward something that is related to the self and therein is a *genuine testimony*. A *genuine* testimony – unlike an *inventive* testimony – is always creative, even though it may be expressed simply and in an unoriginal manner. Yet doctrines are not assimilated by placing oneself qua decision "under them" and by approving them; they must be connected to and hence form an organic unity with one's own being.[128]

Accordingly, assimilation can be understood as an act of personal hermeneutics for the success of which theological insights and individual experiences are equally relevant. Writing a sermon on the basis of an "assimilated creed" then means bringing theology and biography into a reciprocal relationship of perception, under the concrete conditions of a person. The sermon which thus emerges does not allow the separation of dogmatic truth and personal experience. They have become amalgams of the sermon. They are an interpretation of Scripture and an adequate expression of one's own conviction at the same time. The sermon is thus both *in one*, a testimony that *brings up* before God the person's truth and that allows preachers to express themselves.

Haendler notes that *meditation* is one decisive measure for the support of that assimilation, and the associated process of self-realization as a form of personal competence. This, for him, is not one homiletic step among many, comparable to personal reflection in addition to the exegesis, but a lifelong process of analysis and development both of one's own self as well as of the gospel.

---

125 Loc. cit., 331, 400.
126 Loc. cit., 394.
127 Loc. cit., 333.
128 Loc. cit., 338.

"Meditation is the art of entering the characteristic layer [of the person] and receiving insights in it."[129] With the help of a therapist's knowledge or relevant literature, the perceptions thus made possible can be reinforced and communicated through dreams, myths and fairy tales but also through parables and Christian symbols. Meditation is supposed to support a) attaining *a deep truth from the information contained in a single text*, or attaining a deeper understanding of the self from the initially superficial awareness of personal impressions respectively, and b) recognizing basic impulses and anxieties; in order to c) finally realize the weight and significance of a *"meeting of the entities, gospel and subject"*[130]. Successful meditations are characterized by allowing for advancing from individual perceptions, both in relation to one's own person and to the text, to an integral understanding of the self and of the gospel – which goes beyond the approximation towards the concrete task of the sermon.

It is part of such meditation that one becomes aware, in relation to conscious and unconscious attempts at reception, of "the whole work of understanding the gospel which fills the years and decades of a life". In as far as a concrete text and a concrete preacher are "factors within living history", the authenticity of both can indeed be marred.[131] Mistakes can be made not only in the interpretation of a text; the effect of a sermon can also be impaired by preachers inserting their own person into the communication of the gospel under inadequate premises.

### c) The Ego States and the Integrated Personality.
### The Homiletic Reception of Eric Berne

*Transactional Analysis*[132] is one of the more recent theories about the development of the human personality structure, which, taking up Freud to some extent, have been made fruitful for Homiletics and were developed further in this context. In practice, it is primarily used for the analysis and therapy of interpersonal (communication-)relationships in different social contexts (partnership, family, business). Transactional Analysis is, first of all, based on the general assumption that a person's biographically distinctive and specific personality structure strongly predisposes the course of communication processes. Hence, the failure of communication is attributed less to specific external conditions of communication, but rather to dispositions and disproportions in a person's

---

**129** Loc. cit., 441.

**130** Loc. cit., 431.

**131** Loc. cit., 432. It is therefore comprehensible that Haendler used the term "auto-psychotherapy" to describe meditation from which a purifying and healing power is expected (loc. cit., 454).

**132** Eric Berne's work *Games People Play*, 1967, still remains representative in this field of research. On the theoretical debate cf. W. Engemann, 1992a, 5–7, 109–111. For a comprehensive representation cf. W. Engemann, 2003b. The theses developed in these works were taken up by, among others, Michael Thiele within the framework of his rhetorical reflection (cf. M. Thiele, 2005, 104–122).

personality structure. In principle, anyone who initiates a communication process tends towards "transactions" (cf. in Latin: transigere), i.e. to *transference* of sensations and emotions, through which, *on a relationship level*, they make another person assume a particular attitude, or prompt them to find themselves in a very specific position.

In the literature on Transactional Analysis there is a differentiation between three basic types of transactions.[133] I am applying these types directly to the person of the preacher:
1. In the analysis of *passive transactions* a central question is the genesis of the preachers' personality structure. The question is raised as to what, in the course of their lives, has been "transmitted" to them in the form of patterns of behavior, worldly wisdoms and with respect to the evaluations of their sentiments.
2. *Interpersonal transactions* describe the process of stimulation and reaction as it takes place between preacher and listener, corresponding to their personality structures' dispositions. During this process, methods of transmission are uncovered, with which the communication partners maneuver themselves into specific patterns of behavior and put each other under the pressure to act, potentially assigning the roles of the "winner" and the "loser".
3. Finally, within the framework of *therapeutic transactions* the focus is on finding ways to undo destructive formations in the personality structure to such an extent that preachers can express the message as themselves. This includes the ability for authentic communication, which does without the concepts of "winners" and "losers", and which is not determined by the participants' egoistic benefits.

These assumptions and analyses are based on two models of personality psychology: *ego states* and *life positions*. The model of the ego states[134] differentiates between three ego sates, in each of which a human's feelings and actions unfold. The Parent ego state (P), the Adult ego state (A) and the Child ego state (C) – there is some analogy to the Superego, Ego and Id in Freud – describe *autonomous functional systems of behavior, ideas and feelings*. They are, in other words, a person's "conditions", which are activated as soon as the person begins to communicate.

When people open a communication process or enter into it, as a rule, they do so in a way that their stimulation and reaction are each shaped by one of the ego states. In relation to preachers, the ego states illustrate an entirely individual mixture of principles, standards, values, forms of expression etc. These do not derive from the concrete text, or from the analysis of the situation, but have been established *before* the work on the sermon begins. They influence the approach to

---

**133** Cf. Systematizations in W. Engemann, 1992a, 33–35.
**134** E. Berne, 1967, particularly 23–28. The hypotheses on the life positions will be referred to in connection with questions on communicative competence (II.2.3.4).

the sermon's task from the outset. The resulting model of the human's personality structure[135] resembles of traffic lights (cf. Fig. 2):

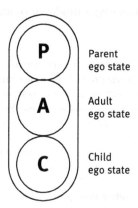

**Fig. 2:** Graphic scheme of the personality structure, illustrated on the basis of its ego states

The *Parent ego (P)* depicts the rules of conduct, prohibitions and warnings which a person has learned, particularly in their childhood. When people act in this state, they invariably draw on something which their parents and other authority figures have imparted to them. According to Muriel James the P "is like a videotape in the brain that contains laws, admonitions, and rules about thinking, feeling, and behaving"[136]. Depending on the content of the stored potential, the Parent ego can be either *nurturing* or *punitive*. The former is oriented towards 'rewarding' one's communication partners, while the latter generally views them as 'bad children'. Finally, an authoritative, *decisive* Parent ego can be recognized by its regard of traditional values, competences and internalized norms as the basis of its authority.

The dominance of a particular ego state manifests itself in the sermon, e.g. in recurring, stereotypical pictures of God, in the topics of the sermon and in significant linguistic expressions.[137] A pronouncedly authoritative P, for example, speaks of God as the great *rewarder of good deeds* or as the rewarder of faith. Correspondingly, the listeners are accused of *self-satisfaction and smugness*. In a linguistic respect, the Parent ego favors *speaking in absolutes* and uses assertions rather than argumentation.

---

**135** On the theological difficulty of the anthropology underlying this model cf. W. Engemann, 1992a, 109–111.

**136** M. James/L. M. Savary, 1974, 6.

**137** Cf. W. Engemann, 1992a, 37–49.

The pattern of behavior marking the *Child ego* (C) comprises, first and foremost, expressions of feelings, desires and needs. Modes of expression of the Child ego are: judgments being made out of an immediate feeling, well-being or disquiet that are directly connected with the fulfillment of one's needs, childish (verbal and non-verbal) 'statements' in form of a spontaneous expression of pain or joy, rage or happiness. The *free, natural Child ego* enables spontaneous, creative and uncensored behavior. If imagination and enthusiasm are restricted by a punitive P, the child possibly develops either the habit of passive adaptation, which leads to a broken existence (*broken Child ego*), or, in the case of spoiling by a nurturing P, the children retreat into sulking rebellion whenever they face any demands (*rebelling Child ego*).

Depending on the development of this ego state the preacher speaks of God as their *fate*, deals thematically, above all, with *patience* and prefers to speak of *surrender to what exists*. If the Child ego is more strongly pronounced as a status of freedom, God appears in the sermon as the generous one, whose kindness is discussed and shown clearly in an *anticipatory language*, perhaps also in fictitious dreams.

Finally, the *Adult ego* (A) is the state of rational reflection. In the A, people only keep to normative propositions from the P area of their personality structure when these correspond with their own understanding and support their own autonomy. The intact Adult ego deals with facts, clarifies connections, works out solutions, and makes decisions. "Whenever people act in reasonable ways, we say they are acting in their Adult."[138] It is a declared goal of Transactional Analysis to integrate parts of the Parent ego and the Child ego into the Adult state, as it is only from this ego state that one can expect the assignment of positive functions to the P and the C, which in turn enables a person's becoming and remaining themselves.[139]

A sermon preached in the mode of the Adult ego usually offers a lot of *information*. In correspondence with the Adult ego's strive for autonomy, God is described in particular as a humane God, who demands *nothing unreasonable*. Such a sermon is normally delivered on the level of *discussion*. Dysfunctions in the Adult ego as the true or ideal command center of a personality structure are always interpreted as interferences from the P or the C: in the case of a dominant Parent ego (Fig. 3a), which simultaneously implies an exclusion of the C, the person tends towards a *dispassionate, seemingly objective view of things*. If, on the

---

138 M. James/L. M. Savary, 1974, 12.
139 "Parent, Adult, and Child is entitled to equal respect and has its legitimate place in a full [...] life." The Adult ego in particular has the task "to regulate the activities of the Parent and the Child, and to mediate objectively between them" (E. Berne, 1967, 27f.).

other hand, the P is switched off and the disruptive interference comes from the Child ego (Fig. 3b), the measuring, opinion-forming element of the P changes into *arrogated autonomy and decreed judgments.*

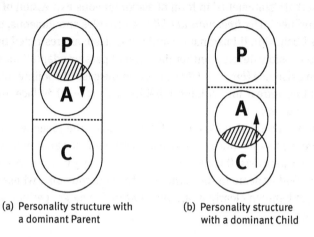

(a) Personality structure with a dominant Parent

(b) Personality structure with a dominant Child

**Fig. 3:** Examples of personality structure dysfunctions according to Transactional Analysis

In Transactional Analysis, the idea that a person's behavior *categorically* takes place in various ego states or "functional systems" is modified by the so-called *Egogram:* Assuming a person's behavior potential is 100%, the P, A and C do not simply hold a share of 33.3% each. Corresponding to an individual's biography, one ego state will become dominant and will dictate action and communication. Here, the principle of complementarity is presupposed: the growth of one ego state can only take place at the expense of the others. A person whose manner and speech were determined to 60% by their P would have perhaps only 30% available for rational, reasonable actions (A) and correspondingly only 10% for spontaneous impulses and reactions (C).

Eric Berne's Transactional Analysis is not concerned with bringing a person's personality under the control of the Adult ego. By autonomy, he understands a person's ability to be oneself in *every* ego state. Accordingly, a personality structure's disproportion or the ego states' "dissociation"[140] is confronted with the model of their "integration": depending on the communicative situation, the "balanced", integrated personality is capable of activating the appropriate ego state as functional system of the whole person.[141]

---

**140** E. Berne, 1966, 366f.

**141** Cf. E. Berne, 1967, 182f. On the conceptual differentiation in the characterization of the Adult ego in Transactional Analysis cf. W. Engemann, 1992a, 22f.

On the basis of this model one can specify some problems and criteria of competence in one's own style of preaching: by understanding homiletic (mis-) conduct also as a reflection of a particular personality profile, the examination of this profile can be seen as implicit work on the sermon. For example, one cannot enter into a dialog about only theological questions of the sermon and the corresponding hermeneutics of the gospel with a preacher who (from his P) can only speak of God as a normative authority and who ties his listeners down to their spiritual and moral deficiencies. This preacher also has the opportunity to take a critical look at the character of his Parent ego or the blocked functions of his Child ego and recognize them as internal personal conditions of a possibly negative sermon strategy.[142]

Before these possibilities are further developed homiletically – in the context of the perspectives elaborated –, attention should be drawn to some significant *convergences* between the presented models. They do not only affect the tripartite structure of the conceptions outlined, but also its content. This includes the basic insight that a person who says or claims, fears or expects this or that, is by no means simply determined by practical constraints (which include, as a rule, text and situation), but also acts from an internal disposition: from the unconscious and from repressed memories, from experiences that have been taken over impetuously or have been acquired through fear. The parallels between the above mentioned models are as follows:[143]

---

[142] On the basis of a transactional-analytical analysis of sermons H. Heyen investigated what the preacher "does with himself" while preaching. The study reveals in particular personality-specific dispositions for a "life-affirming and life-negating attitude in the pulpit" (1995, particularly 12–16, 135–138).

[143] Cf. on this Fig. 4, p. 54.

## Models for the description of personality structure

| Psychoanalysis (S. Freud) | | Depth Psychology (C. G. Jung) | | Transactional Analysis (E. Berne) | |
|---|---|---|---|---|---|
| Terminology | Function | Terminology | Function | Terminology | Function |
| Superego | **Superego:** Representation of internalized rules and norms which in the course of growing up step into the place of earlier influences and authorities. Expressed, among other things, as conscience or in feelings of guilt. | Self | **Self:** On the one hand an archetypal leitmotif, on the other the goal of personality formation and expression of personal competence. Makes coherence between rational and intuitive thinking possible. | P | **Parent Ego:** Reservoir of rules and norms for thinking, feeling and behavior, like a "video-tape in the brain" with persons of authority playing the leading parts. |
| Ego | **Ego:** Not an entirely delimited but constantly "tackled" area. A sort of autonomy manager. Basis of the individual's authenticity and sovereignty. | Conscious / Image Layer | **Consciousness:** Layer of rational thought, the use of which is intuitively guided by the unconscious. Medium of communication with the unconscious. | A | **Adult Ego:** State of rationality, makes judgments on the basis of evaluated experience. Responsible for the reorganization and integration of P and C. |
| The Repressed / The Subconscious / Id | **Id:** Area of the unconsciousness. Potential of energy and drive; oriented towards gratification. Only indirectly controllable e.g. through being made aware of what has been suppressed. | Unconscious | **Unconscious:** "Deep layer" of the human being, "core" of the impulses and fears which lead them. Location of internal psychological processes. Makes preliminary decisions for processes of the consciousness. | C | **Child Ego:** Facilitates spontaneity. Basis of emotional "statements". Can mobilize creative resources but also degenerate to the element of adaptation in a personality structure. |

**Fig. 4:** Models for the description of personality structure

1.  According to all three models, whether people enter into a communication as themselves depends on the *human ability to be aware of themselves*, which is assumed possible. Although this ability is differently rooted in every person's personality structure (cf. the Ego, the Self and the A), it ultimately comes down to the double determination of *authenticity* as something which is both *given and to be achieved ever anew*.
2.  Not everything that people bring into communication can be controlled. *Unconscious expectations and motives* are always in play and establish their positions even against the meaning of individual sentences, at least on a relationship level. As the control entity responsible for this (cf. the Id, the unconscious and the C) constantly questions all too "rational solutions" and introduces new stimuli which can switch from constructive to disturbing from one moment to the next, it cannot be ignored.
3.  A large part of the convictions which guide a person and determine his attitudes do not result from carefully weighed reflection, but from *assumed attitudes to life, God and morality* (cf. the super-ego and the P). Due to the influence that this part of the personality structure can have in its role as an internalized authority, it is important to see to its "equipping" and to replace self-destructive instructions with ones that are helpful for living.

*In summary, we can state:* the origins of a sermon always include the concrete preconditions of a personality structure, the constitution of which is influenced by a person's biography. This can neither be excluded from the preparation of the sermon nor can it be deliberately switched off for the duration of the sermon. When preachers approach the text, or step in front of their listeners, this occurs under the conditions which determine their personality. Preachers can become aware of these conditions and possibly change them as they are not irreversible.

### 2.3.3 Personal Competence and the Function of the Sermon

Homiletic possibilities which arise from a better understanding of the preacher's personality structure can be seen from two points of view: (a) from a conceptual and (b) from an analytical standpoint.

### a) Conceptual Aspects

The inclusion of self-perception in the work on the sermon is of conceptual significance, as the different parts or states of a personality's profile can be related to particular functions of the sermon. The deficient development of certain inner-personal functional systems is consequently accompanied by the limitation of a sermon's expressiveness, and can result in some of its functions being impaired. Conversely, it would benefit the sermon's successful outcome as an act of communication, if preachers *could support the sermon's plausibility on the basis of their selves or of an integrated personality structure* in the sense of the personality models developed by C. G. Jung and E. Berne.

As the Adult ego's competence shows itself in a person's ability to represent various communication subjects realistically, it serves the *representational function* of the sermon: a sermon always has *teaching* aspect to it. A sermon which does not have anything to discuss or is incapable of arguing logically, fails to provide information and arguments to its listeners. As "insignificant self-evidence"[144], as a dogma detached from the experience of being challenged, as a mere airing of theological material; a sermon of this kind offers no teaching but merely groundless theory. However, by connecting the Adult ego to the other personality parts, the preacher can clearly define the necessary information in a personal way and thus facilitate the listeners' comprehension of what is represented[145].

This in turn means: the "message" that a preacher wants to convey, the content and their statements only become *evident* for the listener in the *expressive function of the sermon*. The state particularly predestined for this is the Child ego, as a person's resource for "self-revelation"[146] traditionally lie in this functional system – or in the corresponding areas of the other two personality models respectively. It corresponds to the Child ego's expressive function or to the sermon's function of testimony, if the sermon does not only consist of intellectual language in the style of a lecture, but shows that the preachers themselves are affected by the gospel.

*Paraclesis* as (implicit or explicit) *presentation of consequences* also forms part of the sermon's scope of duties. A sermon which only offers information and testimony and does not address or question the listeners on a behavioral level, would miss a crucial point. A sermon's goal always includes an element of appeal, the explication of which – in the language of Transactional Analysis – would come

---

144 Cf. O. Haendler (2017b, 392f.) on the problematic nature of a sermon unconnected with the self.

145 The tripartite functional description of linguistic communication as *expression* (symptom of the sender), *signal* (appeal to the sender) and *representation* of content (level of symbols) goes back to Karl Bühler's Organon Model (cf. K. Bühler, 2011, 34–39).

146 In Bühler's earlier works the expressive function of language was still named (self-)revelation. Cf. on this Bühler's commentary, 2011, 34.

from an integrated Parent ego. In this sense, the sermon is a signal to the listeners aimed at consequences.

Christian paraclesis[147], however, does not consist of appeals only, but expresses itself in a comforting or generally "pastoral" way of preaching. In this respect, we must point to the differentiation previously made between the nurturing and the authoritative Parent ego. As integrated functional system they can prevent dogmas and rituals from taking the place of arguments or suppressing creativity, and can become forms of "spiritual hygiene"[148] instead.

Such tripartite function designations or dimensions, converging with models for the preacher's personality structure, are often found in Homiletics, even though without this convergence being stressed explicitly. In Figure 5 I have applied the above-mentioned basic functions of a sermon to the model of Transactional Analysis and Bühler's theory of language on the one hand, and to analogous homiletic explanations in Otto Haendler[149] and Hans v. d. Geest[150] on the other hand.

| Personality Structure *according to Transactional Analysis* | Functions of the sermon *from a theological point of view* | Basic functions of speech *according to Karl Bühler* | Functions of the sermon *according to Otto Haendler* | Functions of the sermon *according to Hans van der Geest* |
|---|---|---|---|---|
| **Parent Ego** | Paraclesis | Signal or conative function | Boundary | Guidance |
| **Adult Ego** | Teaching | Reference to content or representational function | Question | Reality |
| **Child Ego** | Testimony | Expressive function or self-revelation function | Expression | Comfort |

**Fig. 5:** The basic functions of the sermon in relation to personality structure of the preacher

### b) Analytical Aspects

On a critical-analytical level, the examination of one's own personality profile leads to a clarification of the factors involved when working on the sermon: those

---

147 Cf. e.g. παρακαλεῖν in Acts 13:15 and Rom 12:8.
148 According to Haendler – following C. G. Jung in this respect – dogmas can serve the "spiritual hygiene", if the preacher is able to locate at least parts of the experience-based background of dogmas in his own reality (O. Haendler, 2017b, 391).
149 Cf. loc. cit., 394f.
150 Cf. H. v. d. Geest, 1978, 40–42.

who have become aware of their suppressions or imprint in the different ego states, and who to some extent are familiar with the background of their favorite topics, will more likely be able to avoid falsely attributing their own problems to the congregation as "God's inquiries". The characteristics of disproportions in the personality structure can help describe, at least hypothetically, and consequently understand particular forms of inappropriate homiletic behavior.

Hence, the *isolation of an ego state* can compromise the credibility of a sermon. A preacher who primarily expresses theological knowledge and only accepts what seems to be rational, who is unable to establish a stable relationship level, and who talks of peoples' fears and hopes simply as "objects of reflection" (pronounced A), could detect elements such as suppressions, or severed contact to his self or the exclusion of his Child ego state, in an analysis within the framework of the aforementioned models. The decrease in expressiveness or malfunctions in self-revelation (necessary for reciprocal communication) are – in a homiletic sense – *a restriction of the sermon's function as testimony*.[151]

Dysfunctions in self-perception and communication behavior can also be the result of *decontaminations* of one area of the personality by another. Such an "obfuscation" exists, for example, when people consider parental principles which they have internalized as children to be a result of their own rational reflection, and regard them as self-evident rules: "To be liked by others one must be capable of being ruthless with oneself". Such obfuscations can result in particular sermon functions ceasing to be effective, a constructive question (A) being perceived as an accusation (punitive P), or in the paraclesis (P) deteriorating into mere information.[152]

Example: On the occasion of Thanksgiving and with reference to Luke 12:13–21, a pastor intends to motivate his listeners to share more generously. To achieve this, the pastor desires to highlight the over-abundance of God's gifts in all areas of life, and to make the listeners see that objectively more than enough is available. According to him, it is a matter of accepting everything that God in his kindness and benevolence has in store for humanity with an *attitude of thankful composure*. Yet instead of giving room to their Adult ego and elaborating on the difference between possession and existence, for example, the whole sermon is left to a punitive Parent ego, which continually discusses the *ingratitude of the listeners* and treats them like egoistic children.

The *faulty homiletic positions* described by Hans-Joachim Thilo are connected to the profile of personality structures.[153] He finds that *personal competence* is a prerequisite and a part of *homiletic competence*. According to Thilo, an analysis of inappropriate homiletic behavior is barely possible without an examination of

---

151 For further connections between disproportions in the personality structure and faulty homiletic behavior see W. Engemann, 1992a, 49–52.
152 Cf. the scheme of sermon-functions above.
153 Cf. H.-J. Thilo, 1974, particularly 114–119.

oneself, which is best conducted in a dialog with others. Hidden, unconscious and partially destructive sermon motifs, detached from the self or Ego, can thus become visible. Thilo describes *three fundamental phenomena* which express and demonstrate these motifs: (1) the "orality of the preacher", (2) the "fear of conflict situations" and (3) the "aggressiveness of the preacher".[154]

1.  *Orality*, the preacher's "desire to be fed", is an expression of an unfulfilled and unreflected wish for recognition. Preachers tend to flatter their listeners with their sermon content and communication method, demanding nothing from them and avoiding problematic matters – without any awareness of their deep-seated experience of rejection.[155] This attitude's tragedy, for the preachers, lies in the fact that the listeners are all the more likely to have a disinterested attitude towards such a woolly, pointless, "purring" sermon, which increases their distance from the preacher even more.
2.  The same is true of *fear of conflict situations*: a preacher declares that "we are all in the same boat" and pleads that therefore one should bid farewell to reciprocal claims and demands, that one should not allow differing opinions to degenerate into a quarrel, and that one should "look only to God's righteousness".[156] The preacher is not aware that he is denying the congregation the chance to accept him, with his personal convictions they may not agree with. Yet it is this very lack of acceptance which hurts him.
3.  If the fear of conflict in a sermon leads to the suppression of one's own subjectivity, and to a trivialization of one's own needs, it can turn into *aggressiveness* and express itself in reproaches aimed at the listeners. "We are destroying the image of God revealed to us humans and adopting the bestial human image of the naked ape exalted to an idol in its stead. In doing so, we are opening the door for all our unbridled sexuality, right up to the most shameless perversities."[157] When preachers say "we", do they really mean themselves and the congregation? In this example, it is more likely that the preacher has become aware of his own problems, but attempts to transfer them to others, so that he needs not tackle the difficult situation himself.

When extant basic impulses of the preacher's personality structure are suppressed or denied, they appear in the sermon as an unacknowledged opposite standpoint that constantly asserts itself. They have direct influence on the communication process between preacher and listeners. In the end, this is why the sermon's subject cannot be examined without considering *personality-specific communication strategies*. These are expressed in particular forms of how a people treat themselves as well as certain topics and the listeners – which leads us to the next chapter.

---

**154** Loc. cit., 114.
**155** Personalities with a broken Child ego or a nurturing Parent ego are particularly prone to such an attitude.
**156** Cf. H.-J. Thilo, 1974, 115.
**157** Example given in H.-J. Thilo, loc. cit., 113.

### 2.3.4 Communicative Competence and the Preacher's Comprehensibility

#### 2.3.4.1 Basic Patterns of Sermon Communication. Two Analysis Models

The question of the homiletic significance of the preacher as a person implies the question of his communicative competence to a certain extent: some particular styles of communication are closer to a preacher's specific personality structure than others. The form of a communication process does, however, reflect more than specific personality profiles. The interaction with others, in its capacity as foundation of communication, is also the expression of a *self-definition*, in relation to the communication partner, as well as an expression of a constant positioning and of a basic communicative attitude which may not be equally suited to all messages.

A basic position acquired through communication, and played out in communication, has characteristic features, including its specific merits and impediments, which can promote or undermine the sermon's comprehensibility. Consequently, it is not enough to simply describe such basic positions. It is rather their *determining function* for an implicit understanding of the sermon which has to be examined. This means dealing with a preacher's personality-specific basic positions, which invariably lead to very specific, stereotypical productions of sermons, regardless of the text, the context, or ecclesiastical calendar.

Remarkably, in the investigation of such basic positions, time and again the number of types in various typologies has been four, and even though they are based on diverse and independent academic insights, there are clear analogies between them: e.g. between the classic "four temperaments", the "four forms of thought" and the "four forms of neurosis", to name three of the best-known. "This suggests a regularity for which we still have no satisfactory explanation today."[158] Yet for the following examination, which is, again, based on four types, it is not important to insist upon a regularity, which may even be thought of as rooted in genetics. It is enough to observe that there are constantly recurring *specific forms of references* to oneself on the one hand, and to the listeners, to the text, as well as to God and the world on the other hand. These modes of behavior correspond to particular images of God, favored topics, characteristic expressions etc.

In order to clarify the communication practice of preachers, we shall attempt to connect the perspectives and components of two complementary models. These are (1) the model of the four life positions of Transactional Analysis[159], and (2) the typology of the preacher's four basic impulses and anxieties according

---

**158** F. Riemann, 2009, 61.
**159** Cf. W. Engemann, 1984 and 1992a.

to Fritz Riemann's depth-psychology model[160]. While Transactional Analysis provides a comprehensible terminology[161], which is nevertheless rooted in a broad academic basis, Riemann's model already contains homiletic reifications. These, however, can be deepened with regard to the preacher's communication practice.

1.  The terms "Okay" and "Not Okay" are characterized in Transactional Analysis[162] as basic positions of human existence, as lifestyles which are rooted as far back as in infancy and early childhood. The terminology of "Okay" and "Not Okay" has a more extensive meaning than the Okay-jargon typical to our everyday life, of course. Being "Okay" or "Not Okay" respectively means *a person's basic feeling as an expression of his relationships* to his surroundings (to other people, to the world, to God). Therefore, it describes a life position which can be characterized, in various degrees, by a positive or negative attitude to life, by tolerance or intolerance, by confidence or despair, by feelings of security or isolation etc.

Consequently, according to Transactional Analysis there is a kind of conclusion about life that people can already draw at the beginning of their lifetime. Otherwise they could not establish any relationship between themselves and their surroundings: I am not okay – you are okay: The toddler who is frequently "corrected" and is "forbidden" many things, and who is occasionally punished without being able to comprehend these oppositions, gets the impression – on the relationship level – that they are "not okay". Such conclusions and verdicts are of course not irreversible. As much as they can become firmly established and not simply experienced passively but lived actively, they can be influenced therapeutically – e.g. by creating awareness and making appropriate counter-decisions.

Yet when a person assumes a position, this is akin to making fundamental decisions based on a position shaped by particular values: it is not reformulated day by day. It results from the attempt "to make sense of himself and the world in which he lives"[163]. In this process, the following positions can develop: (1.) I am okay – you are okay. (2.) I am okay – you are not okay. (3.) I am not okay – you are okay. (4.) I am not okay – you are not okay.

---

160  F. Riemann, 1996.
161  A particular advantage of the neutral terminology of Transactional Analysis lies in the fact that, in contrast to other typologies, it does not raise the impression that personality analysis and communication analysis always result in implying neuroses.
162  This refers to I.2.3.2 c).
163  T. A. Harris, 1973, 60.

2. Without referring to the factual analogies to Transactional Analysis, Fritz Riemann, from a depth-psychology point of view, distinguishes four fundamental positions. Each is – "biographically–genetically" speaking – traced back to a stage of development in early childhood.[164] Accordingly, Riemann develops four personality profiles (schizoid, depressed, obsessive and hysterical), in which extreme forms of phase-specific development impulses (closeness, distance, persistence and change) can be noted.

It cannot be pointed out often enough that neither Riemann's model, nor the models of other present-day representatives of depth psychology state that every person suffers from a disorder of some kind. The terms *schizoid, depressive, obsessive* and *hysterical* are heightened terms of *essential impulses* such as closeness and distance, persistence and willingness to change. Without these impulses a person cannot find their way around everyday communication, nor can a preacher speak about love or sin appropriately and intelligibly. In the case of a one-sided intensification of one such impulse, however, there is an atrophy of its opposite pole, which is then experienced as a 'fear of...': if the impulses to closeness and security are dominant, for example, a fear of distance is experienced. If the impulse to persistence is dominant, every change and alteration is felt as a threat, and vice versa.

In order to understand the relevance of both analysis models, it is important to recognize life positions and basic positions as parts of the determining factors of a particular preaching style. The basic positions outlined above are part of the fundamental basis of *any* communication process. It is inherent in the logic of such positions, or in the expectation of a person about to enter into communication respectively, that *in the course of communication the adopted life position is confirmed.*

In the following chapter I shall connect the examination of the individual life positions and their depth-psychological characterizations with the *problem of the comprehensibility of the sermon.*[165]

### 2.3.4.2 The Significance of the Preacher's Attitude to Life for the Plausibility of his Words

#### a) Preaching that Creates Distance and the Incomprehensibility of Love

A style of communication which creates distance is typical of preachers who predominantly structure their lives from the position of "I am not okay – you are not okay". People with this life position have an equally disapproving and harsh attitude towards themselves and others. They have the impression that they spend

---

164 F. Riemann, 2009, 61f.
165 Cf. also Fig. 6, p. 71.

their lives avoiding "punishment [...] of others"[166]. In actual fact, however, they seek affection and desire a positive reply to their attempts to experience recognition. As they have been unable to achieve such experiences, they retreat in order to avoid further disappointments. "There is nobody to turn to and, therefore, the child is seen by others as a nonresponsive person."[167]

From a depth-psychology point of view, the genesis of this impulse arises in the infant's *sensory stage*, up to the third month of its life. The completely dependent child experiences his surroundings or mother not as such, but as the fulfillment or – e.g. in momentary absence – as the disturbance of his needs.[168] Through such disturbances, the experience of dependency can turn into a latent fear of dependency, so that the child retreats into himself as a means of protection and thereby develops an impulse to isolating distance.

When this motive of self-isolation has become the leading basic impulse of communication, one can speak of a *schizoid personality*. Since people with this personality type cannot overcome their inner loneliness and insecurity by opening themselves to the outside world (*that* they cannot do so is their very problem), they attempt "to become self-sufficient, not to need anyone" and "not to be reliant on anyone"[169].

Preachers whose basic position has a schizoid tendency are correspondingly biased in the structuring of their sermon – as long as they are not conscious of their "tendency": they give preference to *topics which imply distance* – "being a Christian in the face of the world's hostility", "nuclear congregation and non-active Christians" – in short, everything which appears to be suitable to illustrate a strong personality and individual power of endurance. At the same time, these preachers will attempt to dissociate themselves from the mass of listeners and will insist that each person must find their own way in order to be accepted by God – who for his part did the same thing. Yet no indication is given that a person can ever achieve this. God is not spoken of in terms of relationship. On the contrary, he is presented as somebody with whom – last but not least because of his unpredictability – one *cannot* have a relationship; we humans are at his mercy. Only the *painful realization of the truth* (of God and the world) can serve as an adequate orientation for faith.

What preachers with this basic position tend to accomplish better than others is the effective, i.e. understandable *confrontation with unwieldy, awkward truths*. Such preachers frequently "have their fingers on the pulse of time and are

---

166 M. James/L. M. Savary, 1974, 80.
167 F. Hedman, 1974, 45.
168 Cf. F. Riemann, 2009, 62–64.
169 Loc. cit., 64.

opponents of both sentimental or false piety, and rituals and customs which have become fossilized and meaningless"[170]. It is obvious that a preacher with such a position will find it virtually impossible to construct the event of preaching as participative act of communication. They will not be able to convincingly convey the fact that God desires to relate to humanity *out of love* and that not even people's sins can make God keep a distance or turn his back on them.

This is their impediment, not only to preach without a relational character, but also to break off relationships during preaching and to use the sermon to scandalize; and this impediment will eventually make these preachers appear as the strong lonely men at the head of the congregation. The indignation felt by the listeners as a consequence – as well as the congregation's possible approval – will only increase the distance which causes these preachers' suffering. Yet it is not only the preachers who suffer from their own communicative strategy; they can also cause "ecclesiogenic damage" in the congregation by pushing the listeners too hard with "overly subjective and utopian ideas or demands" and by leading them to steps "which they are not able to cope with yet".[171]

As far as the preachers' share in the situational power ("Situationsmacht"[172]) is concerned, they will claim "authority", motivated by their drive for self-sufficiency, and they will not hesitate to express this with gestures, facial expressions, hodology[173], and in other ways. Preachers with a pronounced punitive Parent ego state are more liable than others to such representations in the sermon.

---

**170** Loc. cit., 65.

**171** Loc. cit., 64f.

**172** Heinrich Lausberg expands the numerous ways of looking at a communicative situation in a very instructive way by taking into account the specific social constellation of the communication partners (exam, medical consultation, job interview, pastoral counseling etc.) and asking which of them belongs to those in a position of power in the situation ("Situationsmächtige") and which of them belongs to those interested in the situation ("Situationsinteressierte"). Cf. H. Lausberg, 1967, 4–8, 15f., 22f., 64f., 67, 70.

**173** The term "hodology" (from Greek ὁδός = path) relates to the symbolic repertoire available in a space through fixed or chosen paths (procession in the central aisle of a church, interpretation of the "liturgical ways" by moving between pew, altar, pulpit, lectern etc.). Hodologic codes provide preachers with the possibility to make the audience or congregation understand certain things through the use and manner of just walking these paths. In his lecture on liturgics, Karl-Heinrich Bieritz speaks of a preacher who only remained in the nave when he acted himself. Whenever the congregation sang or was involved in any other way, he withdrew from the congregation's sight and disappeared into the sacristy. Whoever desires so little contact with their congregation will hardly bring across the idea of the community of the body of Christ. Cf. also K.-H. Bieritz, 2004, 43–45, 95.

### b) Preaching which Embraces and the Incomprehensibility of Conflict

"I am not okay – you are okay" – this is how Transactional Analysis denominates the basic position of people who have developed a predominantly negative view of themselves and who simultaneously tend to see others as unattainable examples, admirable "lucky ducks" who are more fortunate and always at an advantage. Because they do not believe that they themselves are lovable, they continually see themselves obliged to earn the respect and affection of others and of God. If they don't succeed in that, people with this life position may withdraw physically and emotionally from others and refuse to assume responsibility for their own feelings and behavior.[174]

In depth psychology, the basic impetus for closeness and attachment is formed primarily in the *oral stage* of development in early childhood – in the course of the first year of people's lives. The child, gradually distinguishing between "I" and "you", experiences life above all in the form of the attachment to his mother. A successful, overall undisturbed relationship between the infant and the mother provides the child with the basic emotional equipment necessary for his own still developing ability for attachment.[175] Disruptions in this phase do not result in the child not developing an attachment impulse, but in this impulse dominating the development: the lack of closeness makes the child fixate all the more on attachment figures; the child clings on because he is not "sated". If, on the other hand, the child is spoiled because the mother keeps him dependent in order to be loved herself, the natural process of the child's maturing and becoming independent will be accompanied by feelings of guilt. To evade these feelings of guilt and the possibility of the mother's withdrawal of love, the child will not choose the path of becoming himself. Instead, the child will strengthen the attachment which causes his suffering.

Depressive personalities are often people with a disturbed sense of self-worth. They doubt that they can cope with their lives on their own. To avoid this danger, they are prepared to accommodate the expectations of others to a large extent. In order for their desire for security not to be disappointed, they have a great willingness to ignore the guilt of others or to interpret it as their own error. There is hardly any expression of disappointment or inner protest about the behavior of others: these feelings are suppressed and stored away as tensions in their own personality, which is thus 'undermined'.

Preachers with a fundamentally depressive structure tend to discuss *love and suffering as the perfect example of Christian life*. However, they do this without addressing the possibilities of changing sorrowful situations, unless perhaps by self-abandonment or by a radical renunciation of the ego, in the hope of winning other people's acceptance at this price. "God" appears in their

---

**174** Cf. M. James/L. M. Savary, 1974, 51.
**175** Cf. F. Riemann, 2009, 66f.

sermons as someone who does not make demands, does not expect anything, but accepts everything and is concerned with nothing other than imposing his love on others.

In trying to attain approval and recognition the depressive preacher avoids conflicts and *evades confrontations with guilt*. Still, similar to the situation described above, these preachers are likely to achieve the opposite of what they intended: by presenting themselves primarily as selfless helpers and claiming to forgive and forget everything in perpetual abjection, they possibly lose the other parts of their profile they need in order to be taken seriously as a counterpart. The listeners will find this level of proximity oppressive and unpleasant, with the preacher in their perception pandering to them. This makes the distance that the preacher has to overcome even greater. The ego states that can best represent this basic position in communication are the broken Child ego and the nurturing Parent ego.

In a sermon presented accordingly, the situational power ("Situationsmacht") is entirely attributed to God – in fact, to a God understood as fate. Everything that happens must be understood and interpreted as a sign of his love, yet his positive power cannot be used to change a given situation. The imminent *ecclesiological damage* is obvious: if the congregation is given the impression that "reservations, doubts or criticism of ecclesiastical institutions or even of God" are blasphemous presumptuousness, they may feel that they could forfeit God's love if they experienced any kind of scepticism or uncertainty.[176]

As long as the impetus to attachment does not, through malfunctions, become a preacher's dominant program, it has a beneficial impact as well, however. It is important for the preacher's ability of identification and thus supports the pastoral care dimension of the sermon.[177] The preacher is able to convey to the listeners that they have worth, that they will be loved, wanted and needed.

### c) Compulsive Preaching and the Incomprehensibility of Freedom

The life position of "I am okay – you are not okay" is often illustrated with the example of the Pharisee in Luke 18:9–14.[178] People with this basic position appear to be arrogant. Because of their pronounced Parent ego state and their claim to authority, which comes with the former, they tend to correct others or to first perceive people and objects as something to be judged. In their presence people can only feel comfortable if they think of themselves as "not okay", if they gladly

---

**176** Loc. cit., 68.
**177** "A preacher with predominantly such a personality is often a natural pastoral carer" (loc. cit., 67).
**178** Cf. for example F. Hedman, 1974, 50; M. James/L. M. Savary, 1974, 59 and others.

participate in the autonomy and authority of others and in so doing find their own status validated – in other words, people with a depressive basic position who yearn for the attention of a strong personality.

This basic position, which aims at the submission of others and at the *standardization of life*, can be traced back to disturbances in the so-called *anal stage* (roughly between the ages of two and five). In this stage the child's independence develops; they employ their own increasing abilities more and more to achieve what they want. They acquire an idea of their own power. If the child is hindered in this development by parents who abuse their factual predominance, who drill the child or teach him blind obedience, the child will, out of fear, consider the compulsive observance of regulations as vital and adapt himself to the current "laws". If, on the other hand, the parents attempt to negotiate everything in a power struggle with their child and thus overburden the child's developing emancipation, the result may be opposition at all costs.[179] It can be assumed that, without such disturbances, the *basic impulse for self-assertion*, which is important for survival, is established in this stage.

Influenced by the disturbances mentioned above, the constructive drive for self-assertion can develop into a compulsive basic position. As a result, people will categorize their emotions, thoughts and behavior as "permitted" or "forbidden" expressions of life. *Insistence on predetermined rules and traditions* is considered to be vital, since deviations from the norm will be avenged with punishment or love deprivation. People with such a character will find it difficult to summon up the courage for a life determined by their own wishes, convictions and decisions. They will scarcely be able to give in to the weak impulse for a free life formed on the basis of their own insights.

As preachers, such people will favor topics in which they can present their own standards. These are topics which can be connected to a particular life philosophy and which confirm corresponding rules, e.g. the respect for "higher decrees" such as the Ten Commandments, the *development of faith as an act of obedience*, or the insistence on the ability to measure up to the commandments respectively. In this sense, compulsive preachers are at the same time *lawful preachers*, who tend to point out the difference between existence as it is and as it should be to the listeners to stress the deficits in fulfilling God's expectations, and to represent the coming judgment as the main motive for repentance.

The intolerance towards the alleged deviations from God's list of norms which such preachers experience is viewed as necessary self-protection against their own striving for freedom. Correspondingly, they talk of God as of a "moral principle"[180] without which there would be chaos. It is certainly true that persistence, especially in combination with an appropriate sense and

---

179 Cf. F. Riemann, 2009, 69f.
180 Loc. cit., 71.

awareness of responsibility, is of great importance whenever it is necessary to demonstrate concepts of universal validity. The compulsive preacher, however, is hardly able to show for which risks and for which freedom this persistence is required.

As compulsive preachers consider innovations equal to chaos, and because they take traditions more seriously than situations, their sermons are of an *aggressive-instructive character*. Such sermons are problematic in as far as they reduce the gospel to commandments and prohibitions, and do not highlight the freedom that the sermon is supposed to serve. The latter would probably be considered a relinquishment of part of these preachers' situational power ("Situationsmacht"), which – from their point of view – stands and falls with the need for guidelines on the part of dependent congregation members.

The dilemma of this basic position lies in the fact that the listeners do not feel the strong tendency towards persistence as a protective impulse for freedom, flexibility and living environment. Instead, it leads to even greater disappointment with regard to obeying the law. The listeners are not likely to grant the preachers the authority that they claim from their decisive Parent ego.

### d) Unlimited Preaching and the Incomprehensibility of the Law

The life position of "I am okay – you are okay" is based on the conviction "that people can change and grow and that everyone is capable of higher and higher levels of self-actualization"[181]. Limitations or boundaries are difficult to accept for people with this basic position. They will scarcely allow a project that has been developed with vision and imagination to be played down. Freedom and autonomy rank right at the top of their scale of values; they do not perceive any determinism at all and know no absolute, unfounded limitations. They are highly self-assured and led by an understanding of an inexhaustible reservoir of possibilities placed at their disposal. This feeling is also conveyed to respective communication partners. A conversation with people in this position often leaves others with the desire to change something – not out of a feeling of guilt, of course, but as a result of expectations that have arisen.

It is evident that the foundation for this impulse can be traced back to experiences in the so-called *phallic stage*[182] (ages of five to six). The child begins to cultivate his own identity

---

181 M. James/L. M. Savary, 1974, 69.

182 Even though the stages of the human psychosexual development up to puberty can be analyzed in a more sophisticated way today than in Sigmund Freud's Psychoanalysis, his terminology is still widely used. This also holds true for the "phallic stage", which from time to time is erroneously referred to as the "genital stage". The "genital stage", however, is the sixth and last stage of the psychosexual development (taking place after latency stage which begins

and looks towards role models for this purpose. The search for a satisfying role or identity is carried out through trial and error, and this temporarily becomes the child's decisive attitude to life. In the case of disturbances this attitude can, in the long run, turn into a dominant life-long impulse. If there are only "unreliable or immature parent models" without a clear profile available to the child, further attempts to find his own identity may not be carried out. Instead, the child will rather concentrate on more attractive but unrealistic models from the world of his imagination. A similar effect can result from parents confronting the child with excessive, egoistic identification guidelines.[183] The child experiences acceptance only at the price of giving its all. On this basis, a "hysterical personality" with an unstable sense of self-esteem may develop, which sometimes expresses itself in feelings of inferiority, other times in over-estimation of one's abilities. A person who receives too little acknowledgement in one moment and too much in the next, might develop into a *virtuoso of adaptation*, so as to win the others' respect and benevolence. Determined by the impulse to change, and accompanied by the fear of finality, the hysterical personality plays certain roles without being anchored in his own ego or self.[184]

Preachers with this basic attitude like to present themselves as a *tolerant friend of their listeners*. Their sermons tend to not deal with specific themes or topics; instead, the preachers take up the expectations of their respective counterpart. This leads to a certain exploitation of content issues: their main function has become to present the preacher as someone who can live up to the listeners' expectations. These preachers "value their personal impression above the content"[185]. They are not focused on a particular canon of themes for their sermons; the general tenor is the "freedom of a Christian". Irrespective of sermon content, these preachers will speak of God, and people's relationship with him and one another, in a way to inspire hope, joy and affirmation of life – as much as they as preachers possibly can.

Preachers with this basic position have a certain advantage over others: their ability to convey that life is more than a challenge imposed on us in which we have to try and evade the temptations of sin as well as the threat of a God who is

---

approximately at the age of six or seven, in which sexual impulses are repressed and in which environmental demands are internalized). The genital stage lasts from the age of eight until puberty. The "phallic stage" owes its name – according to Freud – to a detail in connection with the child's discovery of his or her sexuality, which *equally affects boys and girls*: penis envy on the part of the girls; castration anxiety on the part of the boys. Decisive for understanding the relevance of this period is that it coincides with the differentiation of the child's relationship to mother and father as same- and opposite-sex attachment figures leading to the experience of rivalry with the same-sex parent, the learning of how to deal with competition, the seeking for being recognized as a (small) man or (small) woman, the child's search for norms of orientation for successfully acquiring this role etc.

**183** Cf. F. Riemann, 2009, 73f.
**184** Cf. loc. cit., 73–75.
**185** Loc. cit., 75.

watching us. They would never simply judge sorrow or distress as a consequence of sin. Resolute resistance to what is perceived as fate, and rebellion against unnecessary suffering can, in their view, be genuinely Christian expressions of faith. Their impediment lies to a high degree in *only apparent communication*: anyone who preaches like this is deceiving oneself and others with something that does not hold out against reality. Moreover, it would not be able to withstand reality, because what is being preached has no root in the listeners' real-life experience. This sermon strategy, which borders on a *denial of reality,* can increase ecclesiological neuroses and lead to the listeners' disappointed withdrawal from the church service.

In these cases, the preachers' Adult ego state is so strongly clouded by their Child ego state, that their personality will give a naive rather than a free impression. Their own understanding of the law ignores the real world[186], and therefore they will hardly succeed in making listeners see their own lives' realities: The "law" is not taken into account as an necessary limitation of a person's possibilities, nor as a essential criticism of deceptive, narcissistic self-images. Consequently, the sermon is unable to attain a dimension of pastoral care, an influence on lost life perspectives, to speak of latent guilt, or to reflect upon the "communication of the gospel" in this overall context. The audience as those interested in the situation ("Situationsinteressierte") will experience their preacher as a shallow, frivolous character rather than as someone in a position of power in the situation ("Situationsmächtiger"), and hardly consider his situational goals ("Situationsziele") to be worth striving for.

At this point, if not before, it is evident that the quite convergent models of Transactional Analysis and classic depth psychology cannot be absorbed into one another. While Transactional Analysis characterizes the life position "I am okay – you are okay" (attributed here to the hysterical type) as a desirable ideal position, depth psychology points out that a certain part of *all* four basic positions or impulses is necessary to cope with life (with or without religion). Consequently, in depth psychology it is only the disproportionate growth of particular drives and anxieties which leads to a deformation of the personality structure and thus also to disturbances in a person's communication behavior. It is certainly true that such a balance of necessary impulses and inhibitions could, entirely in line with Transactional Analysis, be identified with the position of "I am okay – you are okay". This stance, however, ignores those psychological ("hysterical") disturbances which result from the latent imperative for the use of all potential possibilities. It is therefore important to establish the two models in a convergent relationship so as to be able to explain the preacher's psychological profile and disclose his strategy of communication.

---

186 Cf. III.1.3 and III.3.2.

| Aspects of Differentiation | Communication Profile / Strategies of Preaching | | | |
|---|---|---|---|---|
| Type of communication | distant | embracing | compulsive | unlimited |
| Life position | I am not okay – you are not okay | I am not okay – you are okay | I am okay – you are not okay | I am okay – you are okay |
| Depth Psychological type | schizoid preacher | depressive preacher | compulsive preacher | hysterical preacher |
| Basic impulse | distance | closeness | persistence | change |
| Basic anxiety | fear of dependency | fear of separation | fear of change | fear of finality |
| Understanding of existence | to avoid threats | to bear one's fate | to defend rules and regulations | to use opportunities |
| Understanding of faith | struggle | devotion | obedience | self-realization |
| Self-concept | lonely witness | selfless helper | reliable guardian | tolerant friend |
| Concept of God | unpredictable power | unconditional love | guarantor of order | guarantor of freedom |
| Image of the listeners | people, who think themselves safe | people, who must not be disappointed | People, who fail at keeping God's law | people with wasted opportunities in life |
| Thematic "cantus firmus" / focus | hostility of the world | patience in suffering | security through obedience | life in freedom |
| Problem of clarification | love or affection | conflict or quarrel | freedom or autonomy | responsibility or law |

**Fig. 6:** Synopsis of the communication profiles and of the effects of typical preaching strategies

Irrespective of internal divergences in classifying basic positions and life positions, a symptomatic communication in preaching is to be expected, along with corresponding forms of dealing with the listeners, specific ideas of faith and God, and characteristic disturbances in plausibility. Preachers who are aware of the dominance of a typical communication pattern in their sermons have the chance to take counter-measures and to analyze the content of their sermons critically with respect to their theology, linguistic characteristics, their view of the audience etc.[187]

---

187 An introduction to the ways and means of sermon analysis will be provided in part II.

In the table above (cf. Fig. 6), the results of a convergent view of Transactional Analysis and depth-psychology are summarized.

### 2.3.5 Confessory Competence and the Credibility of the Preacher

The heading "Current Angles of Reflection" is not meant to imply that earlier homiletic approaches paid no attention to the preacher as witness, of course. It has certainly been advocated at times. In a number of these instances, however, there was nothing more than a reference to the special opportunities for a personal testimony, or a plea for a clearer attestation. The function of the preacher as witness was often identified simply with the "ceryx" in the sense of a "herald". Only in the Homiletics of the 20th century was the preacher recognized and understood *as a subject* necessary for the development of confessory competence. For the first time, it was acknowledged that a preacher's personal credibility or incredibility is an overt foundation of his testimony. The preacher as a subject was finally recognized as a theological theme.

Christian Palmer certainly had a very sophisticated concept of confessory competence. According to him, "the secret of the preacher's position as witness" was founded in the witness being "the whole person which has become one with the truth."[188] Theodosius Harnack's argument was more cautious, but he too assumed a similarly earnest trust in the preacher's ability as witness, stemming from a personal ability to conform to his message. For Harnack, the preacher is "not simply an envoy but a living witness who vouches with his own person for the message which he has become a part of."[189]

Even Alfred Niebergall[190], in his book "Der Prediger als Zeuge"[191] [The Preacher as Witness] misunderstands the examination of the preacher's person as a mere echo of a "*psychological* demand for self-discovery"[192]. He does not take into consideration that the examination of the person is a *theological task* which is carried out for the sake of the communication of the gospel. In Niebergall's work, the witness appears virtually as the *product of church authority and biblical text* – as if Haendler had not demonstrated the homiletic absurdity of this assumption in

---

188 Ch. Palmer, 1857, 554.
189 Cf. more context in T. Harnack, [1878] 1978, 222.
190 Compare the difference between Alfred Niebergall (1909–1978) and his father Friedrich Niebergall (1860–1932). Alfred Niebergall was appointed to his father's chair in Marburg in 1959, did, however, not take up the latter's concept of Practical Theology based on empiricism and interdisciplinarity.
191 A. Niebergall, 1960.
192 Loc. cit., 19. Emphasis W. E.

his criticism of the "non-congruence between person and bearer of the gospel"[193] propagated in dialectical theology. Niebergall considers the preacher's ability to give witness sufficiently constituted in "Christ's position as king", and in the preacher's baptism, vocation, ordination and mission, and the contents of his preaching as determined by the New Testament.[194]

Haendler's counter model depicts the personal subject not as an obstruction but as a *prerequisite of the witness*. A. Niebergall judges this to be a mere "elimination of the concept of the preacher's office and position as they have been determined by the New Testament and the theology of the Reformation"[195]. Instead of theologically reflecting the prerequisites which the sermon, as personal communication, shares with other means of communication, he substantiates the sermon's function of testimony with the assertion "that its essence can only be understood from the New Testament". He does not recognize that the sermon is *demanded* as the testimony of a person[196] – not least in accordance with the New Testament and the Reformation. Thus A. Niebergall arrives at the short-sighted conclusion that it is "the commission alone"[197] which qualifies the preacher as a witness.

If this were the whole truth, one would indeed have to demand of the preachers that, as witnesses, they must "retreat behind their testimony"[198]. The question whether they *can* do so must certainly be answered in the negative.[199] Particularly in view of the classification of the sermon in the context of personal communication established above, it would be illogical to raise this question anew. In the same way, the question as to whether they even *should* has been settled.[200] The issue which remains to be addressed, however, is what it could mean *not* to try and bring oneself as a testimony of one's own. This would mean, among other things, a denial of confessory competence in as far as it pertains to a preacher's personal repertoire of expression. Only after lengthy homiletic examination and discussion could these misunderstandings be analyzed sufficiently, both methodically and theologically; and it has finally become a homiletic maxim to link *confessory competence* and the question of the *person of the preacher.*

---

**193** O. Haendler, 2015, 344.
**194** Cf. A. Niebergall, 1960, 59–74.
**195** Loc. cit., 23.
**196** Cf. below III.4.2.
**197** A. Niebergall, 1960, 24.
**198** Wording probably by D. Bonhoeffer, 1965, 247.
**199** Cf. H. Barié's study (1972). The author proves, on the basis of the behavior of various listeners, that the testimony is in no case received as a "testimony itself", but always received in connection with the person's perception. "Whether he desires it or not, in every case the witness positively or negatively contributes with his own personality to 'the Word itself'" (loc. cit., 27f.).
**200** In Barié this question is "temporarily set aside" (1972, 37).

The homiletic reception of insights into the contribution of personality-specific elements to human communication has been further developed by Manfred Josuttis, among others.

"On the one hand preachers must be rediscovered as determinants of the preaching event. They are not simply a mouthpiece or an interpreter in the dialog between text and situation, Bible and congregation, but rather personal and biased witnesses. They must [on the one hand] learn to recognize that they always influence their proclamation through a range of factors such as their personal problems, their social background, their academic education, or their own emotional constitution. And they must [on the other hand] learn to discover that all this cannot be suppressed or even eradicated; instead, they are appointed, as free witnesses of the gospel, to include their own ego in the sermon."[201]

This is Josuttis' theological argument why the person is necessary for the testimony of the gospel. He also shows the extent to which a preacher's reluctance to position himself as a person in the sermon arises not only from theological misunderstandings but also from a general social taboo with regard to the ego.

The construction of pedagogical and political theories has changed greatly since 1974.[202] Yet the phenomenon of a certain self-denial, as soon as the level of religious communication is reached, still exists in the practice of homiletic seminars. The tendency to adapt to what is supposedly expected is great, and there seems to be little desire to take up the stance of a sermon's critic or to even contradict a group. Anyone who dares to say "I" "upsets the balance of a group, plunges it into an identity crisis and demands a change of its structure"[203]. Anyone who says "I" comes into conflict with the interests of others and questions existing positions. Nevertheless will stabilizing the I in the pulpit most probably lead to a stabilization of the confessory competence of the preacher, too. The following aspects[204] play a particular part in this:

1. Anyone who says "I" makes space for necessary positioning. They do not hide behind authorities; they become open to attack; they risk rejection and *provoke responses* as prerequisites for the opening of a dialog. The congregation is thus enabled to compare the preacher's testimony with their own experiences – of which they may only become aware through this testimony.

2. Anyone who says "I" forgoes conjectures or insinuations concerning the reality of the life and faith of the listeners, but at the same time demonstrates

---

201 M. Josuttis, 1972, 134f.
202 Initial publication of the text referred to here (cf. M. Josuttis, 2003).
203 Loc. cit., 87.
204 Loc. cit., 91–96.

how one can talk about difficulties and perspectives of life and faith (in relation to his own person). The "I" in the sermon *makes it more difficult* for the preacher *to project* on the congregation, and it is conducive to the congregation's identification with the preacher.

3. Anyone who says "I" also becomes a witness in as much as they *relieve the gospel from the suspicion of being an ideology*. While ideologies and ideologists commonly present their teachings as objective and claim that they can monitor and check themselves, the witness identifies himself outright as personally involved. Especially in cases of a proclaimed "renunciation of the 'I'", there is the likelihood of "an ideological concealment of one's own interests". In contrast, the deliberate and overt inclusion of one's own person can ensure "that the gospel as such remains more than its interpretation by this person"[205].

Manfred Josuttis examined and defined various ego functions with regard to both a comprehensive theoretical analysis and the practicing of a preacher's appropriate relationship with their ego. According to him, *learning to say "I"* is essential for a preacher's confessory competence as described above.[206] It is important for a preacher's ego not to experience theological statements "as threats to one's own existence" anymore, and not to misuse these statements to defend oneself; it is equally important for a preacher not to misunderstand criticism of their theological position as personal denigration[207]. The extent to which these two aspects can be achieved, equals the extent to which preachers will become visible as *themselves* and will find a way of "presenting themselves"[208] as neither aggressive nor defensive but simply as a witness.

Josuttis has outlined specific *forms or profiles of the "I" in the pulpit*[209] for practicing the use of the first-person pronoun in a justified and responsible way. These profiles show the manifold ways in which a preacher can say "I"

---

**205** Loc. cit., 95.

**206** Although in Josuttis' explanations the "confessory I" appears to be one possibility among others for the I-presence (cf. Fig. 7, p. 77), his argumentation reveals that it is important to him that the preacher relinquishes "the pose of the omniscient person" as well as adhering to abstract concepts and, in saying I, finds his way to a proclamation, in which, as it were, "the spirit of the sermon [...] comes together with the person of the witness" (loc. cit., 82).

**207** Loc. cit., 97–100. In this context Josuttis takes up Freud's understanding of the Ego and refers to his suggestion of working on "strengthening the Ego against the powers of the Id and the Superego".

**208** Cf. the respective concept of "religious self-portrayal" in F. D. E. Schleiermacher, 1850, 205 (no English translation available for this part of the book).

**209** M. Josuttis, 2003, 100–103.

and how they each suggest different manners of understanding. Almost all "I" forms are equally suitable for making a life in faith plausible, and require preachers who know who their "I" in their sermon refers to. The exception is the *verificatory I,* which is in danger of wishing to document the truth of the gospel with references to one's own successful life, or of limiting the truth to these references.

A preacher may say "I" in order to discuss diversity of experience relating to the surplus of promise in the gospel (*confessory* I), or they may say "I" to address the listeners' questions and doubts in their own daily lives (*biographical* I) – depending on the function assigned to individual statements or the sermon as a whole. They may say "I" in a representative function – i.e. using themselves for a pointed illustration of basic experiences of human existence and questions of faith (*representative* I); in other cases, their "I" may be used to put the significance of the gospel in concrete terms by referring to personal consequences from one's own understanding of the message (*exemplary* I). Finally, it is possible to use the image of a specific frame of reference (e.g. oriented on the sermon's relation to issues and the text) in the sermon and thereby create a sphere in which the I's fortunes illustrate what the gospel amounts to and what may happen if the sermon achieves its goals (*fictitious* I).

The boundaries of these "forms of the I in the pulpit" can certainly be blurred at times: it is hardly possible to imagine a confessory I without any biographical touch. In a similar vein, the exemplary I bears features of the representative I. Such possible intersections do not, however, disprove the factual multifunctionality of the I in the pulpit but rather highlight the necessity of a more conscious interaction with it.

In the interest of a more precise differentiation, the ego profiles can be juxtaposed by their respective functions, connections, and opportunities or risks (cf. Fig. 7).

| I-Form | Functions | Reference | Opportunity/Risk |
|---|---|---|---|
| **Verificatory I** | Verification of the truth of the text and of the reality of God | One's own experiences interpreted as confirmatory experiences of faith | Life is instrumentalized as evidence for truth (e.g. of the text); risk of hubris |
| **Confessory I** | Highlighting the surplus of promise as compared to human experience | Experiences of diversity, situations of doubt, reasons for a "despite" of faith | Gap between what can be testified and what is promised is taken seriously; high credibility |
| **Biographical I** | Making plausible the relevance of biblical traditions for basic questions of life | Experiences, questions and doubts in the biographical context | Clarification of the text's relevance for life instead of confirming the text through life |
| **Representative I** | Personal illustration of the general validity of the message; concentrates the sense of "we" of the listeners | The preacher takes up basic experiences of life and faith without having to refer to his own biography | Immediate identification with the I is possible for the listener since it representatively stands for other "I"s, due to its lack of biographical limitations |
| **Exemplary I** | Exemplification of the significance of the message by referring to the preacher as its first addressee | Concretizations regarding particular personal consequences of the message | The exemplary I of the preacher is to be considered as an act of translation and thus implies a certain model of understanding |
| **Fictitious I** | Perspectival clarification of the gospel within a specific frame of reference | An e.g. narratively created context with its own scope of action and understanding | Possibility of verbal anticipations of the impacts of the gospel on the lives of people |

**Fig. 7:** Features and functions of the I in the sermon

The inclusion of the category of "confessory competence" does not postulate that there is nothing *more* to say about the "dawning of the reign of Jesus Christ" than what is suggested in the testimony of a preacher who says "I". One of the defining characteristics of confessory competence is that preachers cannot illustrate the perspectives of living by faith without expressing, in a fragmentary yet equally authentic manner, in how far they themselves are affected by these perspectives and what consequences they expect if they believe what they say.

At this level we must also discuss the connection between the preacher as witness and the credibility of the sermon as a whole. The person of the preacher is quite significant for the persuasive power of the "Good News". It is undoubtedly true that the revelation and the experience of faith, according to the understanding of the New Testament and the Reformers, is "grace" – and thus not necessarily the result of a successful sermon. Yet this faith can only be communicated and attested to as the *faith of a person,* and therefore the credibility of the sermon will be promoted or indeed impeded, depending on the level of the preacher's awareness of the crucial (sermon-) testimony as related to his own person. For the sermon to become a credible testimony for others, the preacher first and foremost has to frame it in the context of his own existence. He must not attempt to disconnect its message from the horizon of his own issues, weaknesses and conflicts. Otherwise he will find it virtually impossible to demonstrate *that preachers themselves are reliant on the gospel.*

A preacher's exemplary life, or their ability "to meet the demands of the law", are therefore not the first, or even second, most important aspect of the testimony which pastors owe to the members of their congregations. If these were the decisive premises of credibility, then "a particular structure of the organization of church offices would stand in the way of the message of the forgiveness for the sinner"[210]. Anyone who demands perfect conformity of doctrine and life, of gospel and testimony, contributes to the distortion of the gospel and to the incredibility of the sermon. It is, then, firstly, "*normally the case* that pastor preaches what he himself can only fractionally fulfill in his own existence; secondly, the reason for this is that he preaches the gospel rather than the law, and the gospel presumes the inability of *all* the members of the congregation to fulfill the law; and thirdly, the pastor therefore always preaches to himself, too."[211]

The endeavor to say "I" is therefore not merely a rhetorical attempt but theological work. It is the effort to clearly show the *personal requirement of the life-testimony of Christianity.* For a credible sermon, it is necessary to abandon false, ideal self-portrayals which only reveal the person one would like to be. It would not harm the credibility of preachers but rather serve it to present themselves as no other person than who they really are. And the plausibility of the address would not be spoiled but rather reinforced by preachers recognizing their own "shadow"[212] and showing that they themselves are dependent on grace and forgiveness.

---

**210** D. Stollberg, 1979, 46. In contrast, for A. Niebergall the "personal contribution" of the witness consists in "the conclusions from the ‚new being' into which that testimony has called and placed him", as well as in the ability "to translate and convert the witnessed reality and truth of God [...] as a binding truth" (A. Niebergall, 1960, 48). The witness must stand by his testimony "with his whole person and being in order to help the truth achieve victory in this way" (loc. cit., 29).
**211** D. Stollberg, 1979, 43; original emphasis.
**212** On the necessity of accepting one's own "shadow" and how to deal with it cf. O. Haendler, 2015, 250f., 345f.

H. Barié's[213] "hypotheses" on a preacher's credibility give interesting insight in this context: according to him, (1) the (pre-)judgment on the preacher's testimony depends on the extent to which the image which the listeners have of this person meets their own ideal picture of being a Christian. (2) A sermon's judgment will be the more positive the more unquestionably the listeners have the impression that they are taken seriously and are understood by the preacher. The listeners' opinion of the preacher's testimony is (3) influenced by their knowledge of "the harmony or dissonance" between the words and the behavior of the preacher. Barié finds that the listeners' judgment is positively affected by a supposed "harmony of word and behavior". If, on the other hand, there are known dissonances between the words and the behavior of the preacher, the impact on the judgment will be correspondingly negative.[214]

The aspects discussed in this chapter are directly relevant to each of the hypotheses on the credibility of the preacher formulated by Barié: People who allow themselves to be seen as personal subjects with their own ego identities, and who both dare to position themselves and provoke others to do likewise, get the chance to be seen as a human counterpart rather than as projection screens for ideal images. It is the preachers' taking themselves seriously, and not denying their own issues, dilemmas or embarrassments, which determines the extent to which the listeners will feel taken seriously in turn.

Somewhat more difficult is the thesis that the credibility of a preacher is *not* based on the congruence of doctrine and life. First of all, it must be stated that this tension only seemingly reveals a real inconsistency: honesty in addressing problems, sincerity in assessing difficulties of life and faith, or the admission of one's own limits etc. – these are by all means part of a worthy *behavior* and a certain ethos. Such honesty is valued highly by the listeners. Barié's third form of credibility, however, tacitly implies that behavior which corresponds to the teaching or the message means a *morally irreproachable life*, and that "doctrine" means *law*. On the very contrary, it is important to note that a preacher can be a witness and a role model for their congregation exactly by *personally challenging this concept of sanctification*, which the listeners may also struggle for in their own lives.

We must therefore agree with Dietrich Stollberg when he reminds preachers: "You may be an example by dealing with your weakness differently than is usually done in the world [...] The pastor can be a role model in unvarnished self-awareness – including its blind spots."[215] This does not mean that preachers have to present themselves as a difficult, morally depraved, ethically undemanding

---

213 Cf. H. Barié, 1972. In spite of the empirical foundation of his arguments based on a successful experiment Barié continuously speaks only cautiously of "hypotheses".
214 Loc. cit., 27, 35f.
215 D. Stollberg, 1979, 49, 53.

people, or as someone who is simply particularly weighed down. They should only appear as they are, and orientate their sermon neither towards their own ideal nor to the ideal image which the congregation might have of them. "No pastor [preaches] credibly [...] if he demands achievements from his congregation which he cannot deliver himself."[216] Admittedly: preachers are not supposed to effect a performance themselves but should rather help their congregation attain self-awareness in the light of the gospel. Through their sermon they can contribute to each individual – still encumbered by self-reproaches – experiencing himself as appreciated, lovable and taken seriously.

## 2.4 On the Category of the "Personal Sermon"[217]

### 2.4.1 On the Problem of Defining a "Personal Sermon"

Bearing in mind the highly relevant findings in the introduction to the current angles of reflection, it must be noted again that the personal sermon, from a homiletic point of view, is not an imperative in the first instance but an indicative. It is not a command but a description of a segment of the sermon's factual communication requirements: since preachers can only face their congregations "in person", they *always* speak as subjects, as individuals with particular personality structures. Even when they 'seem detached', or are experienced as rather as distant and cold, they are still personally generating that coldness and detachment.

This "indicative of the personal sermon" must certainly be discussed for at least two reasons: firstly, to counter the impression that it is possible to give *a theologically objective sermon without any personal touch.* Secondly, a sermon is not to be justified from a homiletic standpoint simply because listeners describe it afterwards as somewhat personal. A sermon is not good simply because it was "somewhat personal". Nevertheless the personal sermon does exist as a homiletic category, and it denotes the sermon as an expression of personal, communicative and confessory competence. A personal sermon in this sense does not need necessarily be an *overall* successful sermon that inspires and sparks belief in the listeners like no other, that is theologically elaborate, rhetorically

---

**216** Loc. cit., 48.
**217** I put terms such as "biblical", "rhetorical" or "pastoral sermon" in quotation marks in order to signal a certain distance to these phrases. Such terms cannot be used for certain preaching styles or alternative sermon definitions, but are *fundamental dimensions or categories* of the sermon as such.

convincing and motivates action. It is a category of sermon with its own criteria; it is no less important than the "biblical sermon"[218], for example. These designations do not signify alternative or competing approaches but rather qualities which are important for every sermon.

Axel Denecke has collected relevant homiletic impulses from a range of different approaches, and has put them in the context of his own understanding of a "personal sermon". For him, to preach personally means: 1, "saying 'I'"; 2, "preaching without fear"; 3, "speaking unambiguously"; 4, "preaching freely, openly and objectively"; 5, "preaching in a both tangible and vulnerable manner"; 6, "preaching democratically"; 7, "being in solidarity with the listeners"; 8, "establishing a dialog with the listeners"; 9, "encouraging the listeners to say 'I' themselves"; 10, "yielding oneself to the listeners"; 11, "preaching modestly".[219] Observing the conceptions formulated here can by all means generate a personal sermon in our sense. Many of them, however, *presuppose* a high level of personal competence and can easily be misunderstood as tautological. "Preaching freely, openly and objectively" is not suited as an objective. One can, on the other hand, certainly strive to "speak unambiguously" (if one has the required knowledge of the functions of language), or to "take the listeners seriously" – which demands understanding the homiletic situation methodically.

This is not to suggest that Denecke's differentiated deliberations should be called ill-considered claims. Yet I plead for a clearer definition of the category of the "personal sermon" which explicitly distinguishes it from a (seemingly) friendly, tolerant style of communication. For if the various homiletic angles of reflection all produced a "personal sermon" when considered appropriately by the preacher, it would lose its plausibility as a category of its own. In the same vein, the criteria of a "biblical sermon" are quite congruent with Denecke's characteristics of the "personal sermon": courage for debate, a position of vulnerability, a stance of solidarity, modesty, directness, etc. The same could be said for the "rhetorical" and even for the "political sermon". Such attempts run the risk of losing themselves in debates of semantics, i.e. boiling down to ideological disputes about the "true" criteria for a sermon, or about the most important homiletic principle.

To avoid this, no list of wishes relating to the form and effect of the personal sermon will be formulated in the following chapter; instead, the fundamental requirements arising retrospectively from the question of the subjectivity and personality of the preacher will be outlined.

---

218 Cf. I.3.
219 Cf. A. Denecke, 1979, 47–50.

## 2.4.2 Prerequisites of the "Personal Sermon"

### a) Self-perception as a Basis of Inner Congruence

A personal sermon requires the *self-perception of the preacher*. The preachers themselves are, as persons, a specific factor in the process of the sermon. This means that they not only have to deal with the text and the situation of the listeners, but must also enter an "intrapersonal" dialog. The focus is on an inner harmony of feelings, thoughts, speech and action, which is experienced as coherence in one's own address, amongst other things. It is a matter of a preacher's experience of congruence in feeling, appearance and argumentation, which in turn makes the argumentation more easily comprehensible (coherence) and plausible to others.

"Self-perception", in this context, is more than a simply receptive act; first and foremost, it shapes identity. There is a continuous change process, which is implied in mechanisms such as becoming aware of one's hidden fears, revealing concealed motives, reflecting on one's self, analyzing one's own wishes, clarifying one's own intentions, etc. The personal sermon is not primarily a matter of good will, much less of merely choosing from various options of identification.[220] Above all, it is an expression of the preachers' awareness of what moves, encourages, worries, or frightens them.

A deepened self-awareness can hardly be achieved without the assistance of others: the personality structure of a person is moulded in relationships in particular, and people only become aware of their own "position" through the presence of others. Speaking about the listeners' relationships with God, themselves, and others requires an awareness of oneself in these relationships.[221] For this purpose, all forms of analytical and therapeutic communication – including everyday communication – can come into consideration: seeking pastoral care for oneself,

---

[220] Bernd Düwel expects from the analysis and provision of certain guiding principles or offers of identification (clouds, snow, mountains, cockerels, ravens, dogs, cattle) "aids for today's preachers in their challenge to build up a specific identity for themselves" (B. Düwel, 1992, 56). "As a cockerel", for example, the preacher could perceive himself "as taking on the role of someone who initiates communication with the listeners and draws their attention to 'God' in a way that cannot be ignored" (loc. cit., 413). However, reducing the help for achieving a personal sermon to identification offers in the form of a catalogue of different terms and concepts is problematic in that it again implies projections of the self: it relies on homiletically dubious "ideal preaching types", on illusions and wishful roles, which could in fact prove to be an obstacle to a really authentic sermon.

[221] Cf. in this context also the programmatic title of W. D. Edgerton's book: "Speak to Me That I May Speak. A Spirituality of Preaching" (2006), in which the homiletic work is described as a process inevitably and desirably connected to the life of the preacher as a whole which also involves transformations within the context of his ideas and principles of faith. Otto Haendler's was the first Homiletics to argue from a theological as well as psychological perspective and to emphasize

personal conversations with other preachers, feedback discussions after the sermon, or individual supervision.[222]

## b) Individuality as a Basis of Originality

According to Otto Haendler "becoming one's self", "self-realization" ("Selbstverwirklichung") or "individuation" is a basic prerequisite of a personal sermon. It also guarantees its "originality" in the true sense: it is a sermon whose practical communication source is a specific subject – which is the very reason for its unmistakably unique and individual character. Haendler presents his own understanding of "self-realization" with regard to the category of the personal sermon as the preacher's attempt *to stand before the congregation as himself* once he has personally occupied himself with the biblical tradition, also in the context of his own feelings and behavior. Having talked to people whose perception he takes seriously, and having gained a certain distance from his own homiletic work through critically re-reading his own sermons, as well as other forms of "meditation", he must still – unmistakably – finally appear at the pulpit as the individual he has become in the course of his hours, months and years of studies.

This endeavor is both demanding and modest at the same time. It is demanding inasmuch as the category of originality suggests that preachers say something *which only they can say in this way*. On the other hand it is modest because it does not demand a sermon which is particularly original in terms of its language, kerygmatic force, or rhetoric accomplishments. The originality of the sermon goes along with a *perceptible, reflected subjectivity* of the preacher. Anyone who is trained to disregard "himself", will tend to deliver an "impersonal" sermon, because it cannot be more than a copy, an imitation, perhaps even a forgery of an authentic testimony.

Accordingly, Axel Denecke calls for *modest preaching* in the context of personal sermons: "I abstain [...] from a sermon which is as self-contained and as rounded-off as possible, which treats the listeners as ignorant people [...] by announcing carefully edited religious truths which arouse reverence. On the contrary: I let myself be known to others with my experiences of faith [...] which definitely do not demand reverence. My faith is quite mediocre, incomplete, [...],

---

the close connection of homiletic work and questions of self-perception, lived spirituality and an "assimilated", coherent theology. Cf. Otto Haendler (2017b [1941]), e.g. 374–379, 436–465).

**222** A refusing attitude of the preacher towards his own role or the impression of lacking own space in the face of the text, the expectations of the congregation, the mission of the church etc. are, among other things, significant for a disturbed inner congruence (and consequently for a sermon which sends out corresponding signals of irritation). In this context cf. I. Kuttler, 2008, particularly 57, 74.

characterized more by defeats than by victories. I consider it useful that this faith is communicated to others. [...] The listeners [for their part] gain the ability to express their own personal modest faith."[223]

### c) Reference to Experience as a Basis of Authenticity

The theological depth and homiletic quality of a personal sermon depends to a high degree on the preacher's level of awareness regarding the necessity of a personal and linguistic reformulation and appropriation of the general Creed of Christendom. Klaus Winkler generally uses the term "personality-specific creed"[224] in analogous contexts: A believer should be able to believe, think and express their belief according to the conditions of their own existence. This is generally a self-evident, unobtrusive process, but it can be disrupted by the preacher's linguistic subordination to particular formulations offered in the history of Christian dogmatic theology. Otto Haendler's comments on the necessary "assimilation of the creed", Klaus Winkler's observations regarding each person's individual manner of expressing his faith, and the considerations presented above on the connection between personality structure and faith, suggest that the personal testimony is of fundamental significance for the authenticity of a sermon.

The same rule applies in this context as before: "authenticity in itself" does not guarantee that the category of a personal sermon is taken into account. A sermon which is carelessly prepared or delivered with a cynical undertone, can still express "authenticity" as to what the preacher thinks of faith, God, himself and the listeners. Personal faith is beneficial to a sermon if it is *experienced and reflected* faith, that makes it possible for the preachers to have a critical look at their own idea of themselves[225], and that has helped them to accept themselves.

---

223 A. Denecke, 1979, 49f.

224 On the "personality-specific creed" cf. above p. 31 and K. Winkler, 1997, 267–269.

225 Marinus Beute's (2016, esp. 55–96) study provides an informative overview of the homiletic impulses of the 20th century that imply an examination of the preacher's self-concept ("zelfbeeld"). In view of the complex debate in Homiletics on the acquisition of an adequate self-concept (which is, among other things, influenced by psychological as well as anthropological aspects), the attempt of recommending the self-concept of Paul as a learning model is, however, less convincing. For the homiletic problems that arise in connection with the preacher's self-concept are hardly ever the result of a lack of guidelines for orientation or role models, but of the motives, reasons and intentions out of which preachers constitute their self whereby they (for example) frequently refer to Paul. In other words: Paul's self-concept served the plausibility of his message in many ways; but the challenge that preachers are faced with consists in finding a self-concept that is – according to C. G. Jung's ideas – conditioned by their own self, since one can only preach under these, i.e. one's own (and not Paul's) conditions.

In conversation, particularly with older pastors, I am occasionally told that young people today have had less experience of faith because they do not know "real hardship" – e.g. the disaster of World War II and the post-war period – in which faith has a function important for survival. Such argumentation is problematic because existential distress – in which one perhaps reflects upon faith more than in other situations – is not only a question of external circumstances. I am, however, aware of how difficult it is for students to express their own life events as experience *at all*. They are rather timid, for example, when they are asked to reflect or comment on experiences of attaining freedom (or experiences of lack of freedom) relating to their own faith. In the sermons which I have examined, two substitute solutions can be found: firstly, to avoid having to involve one's own reflected experience, preachers use the cliché that perceptions such as "flower in the crack of the concrete", the "smile at the window" and the "ray of sunshine in the tea cup" are encounters with a *deus ex machina* (cf. I.6.1.6). The second strategy is the radical abstraction of experiences in faith, often connected with the category of the extraordinary. If such ideas of experience in faith – which are on the one hand banal, on the other hand obscure and anemic – are conveyed to the listeners, they will feel either overwhelmed or bored.

If these fundamental prerequisites of a personal sermon (congruence, originality and authenticity) are fulfilled, or at least accepted as expedient, the acquisition of specific communicative and confessory competences can become an issue of homiletic training. Preachers who are experienced in self-perception, who know the repertoire of their own pattern of communication, who have gained insight into their own "life position", and who have examined this position, can practice saying "I" without succumbing to the danger of projecting their own problems onto the congregation.

The argumentation compiled and systematized in I.2 certainly does not exhaust the range of issues concerning the person of the preacher in the framework of Homiletics. This chapter has dealt with those aspects of the sermon which result from the human structures of the preacher's being as a subject and a person. The competences demanded from a preacher, however, go beyond being able to deal professionally with one's own person, having the appropriate distance from one's "self", standing by one's own identity, etc. The sermon is based on competences which pertain to the entire process of communicating the gospel, which includes occupational competences specific to the preacher's office. We will get back to this in the context of a theology of preaching[226], whose range of questions include the following: to what extent is the sermon to be understood as an *assigned communication*, what qualifications allow such an assignation, and why is it that not everyone preaches even though the Churches of the Reformation argue that all people are priests in a sense.

---

226 Cf. particularly III.4.2 and III.4.5.

# 3  Preaching with a Text. On The Question of the Sermon's Reference to Tradition

By referring to a text the sermon establishes *thematic continuity* between a piece of biblical tradition and contemporary communication of the gospel. Our initial understanding of the sermon as a process of tradition and communication (see I.1) already highlights, among other things, the importance of such continuity: The sermon is *one* sequence within an infinite process of exchange and comprehension; in this process the gospel is mentioned in the respective contexts of specific situations, which in turn means that the communication of the gospel is continued or revived. Referring to a text always implies asking what people in the past thought and believed *when they encountered comparable challenges and had similar experiences. Understanding* these challenges and experiences that once led to the emergence of biblical texts is an essential part in the attempt to place oneself in their "tradition".

This goes beyond and is indeed a different matter than merely taking over or affirming certain core statements of the tradition. Precisely because a sermon's task is not about striving for one particular *understanding of the text* and passing on the results to others, text reference as such can never be the goal of homiletic efforts. A sermon should *not introduce* its listeners *to texts*. Instead, its goal should be to *accompany them in their lives by referring* to the old testimonies of faith, and to thus help them mediate a "life lived by faith". This implies allowing the text to become historical in the course of the sermon to the effect that eventually the listeners are not confronted with a text which they either accept or "do not believe", but become involved in a lively discussion which allows them an examination of their own life lived by faith.

Certainly, if in the preparation of the sermon, preachers do not examine the text thoroughly and introduce it, as it were, somehow sheepishly, by means of frequent quotations ("our text tells us")[227] there is a risk of its misuse as a passe-partout for any kind of arbitrary statements and any desired message in the sermon. Accordingly, in the next chapter some of the most common problems in dealing with biblical texts are highlighted. The vital aspects of a homiletically responsible integration of the text in the preaching process will thus become evident.

---

[227] Cf. in particular the observations on the "ruined text" and the "auctor ex machina" in the study on text examination by Wilfried Engemann, 2003e, esp. 108–112.

https://doi.org/10.1515/9783110440256-003

## 3.1 Snapshots. Empirical Indicators of Problems

### 3.1.1 Exegesis without Focus

The failure or success of a sermon does not only depend on specific homiletic abilities. It is further influenced by key qualifications in theology. These include competence in dealing with texts from the Old and New Testament, which requires a basic knowledge of the corresponding original languages. This competence should, however, not just aim at *exploring the origins and development of ancient texts* by means of historical-critical methods. It also involves the skilful use of the repertoire of traditional exegesis and other approaches from literary studies in order to explore and truly understand the *meaning* of a text. In the process of sermon preparation, exegesis is a tool which turns the text into a doorway allowing access to experiences and convictions which have marked the history and character of the Christian faith.

But no matter how conscientiously the individual steps of the historic-critical text analysis are performed, many sermon outlines, submitted within the framework of theological exams, still fail to provide an answer to the question of *what this all means for the understanding of the text*, why this text was *needed* at that time, what it was able to *clarify* in what kind of situation, why, for what purpose, *with what intent* it was written. Hence, respective résumés often consist of dogmatic platitudes, which are so generally applicable that one can neither categorically deny them, nor really believe them. In fact, they are often positions which could have been reached even without the complicated approach of exegesis, or which thorough, goal-oriented exegesis would have averted:

"And in conclusion this is what Rom 8:31–39 wants to tell us: You, man, are accepted and redeemed just as you are. [...] We can assume that the exclusiveness of Jesus Christ and his deed emphasized in the scope of the sermon text is basically accepted by all members of the congregation – otherwise they would not have attended the service. [...] Hence the sermon text is of fundamental relevance for all its listeners. [...] Correspondingly the sermon must respond to the realms of humankind, point them out their situation as rejected (court of justice), contrast this with the Bible's message (grace) and show them a way."[228] Frequently what is stated under the headline "synopsis of the text message" merely refers to the *structure* of the text, but is, however, misinterpreted as "a core message". "The text's content refers to the authority of Jesus by using the form of a farewell speech to depict 'the receiving of the Spirit' and the 'conflict in the world' as two incidents prophesized by Jesus."[229] Another sermon considers "the promise of the Spirit and its effect regarding the concrete, historical situation" as one of the text's "core messages".

---

228 From the preliminary work on a sermon manuscript on Rom 8:31–39.
229 From the preliminary work on a sermon manuscript on John 15:26–16:4.

But what exactly *is* promised when the Spirit is promised? And why is this promise significant? What is it good for? What could it save us from – then and now?

There is another side to this problem: If exegesis does not additionally aim at developing a *communicative intention,* it is not only hard to address certain experiences and situations of life today in the light of this particular text; preachers moreover deprive themselves of the possibility to see their own convictions, ideas and intentions questioned by the text – or to "see" anything at all which they had not already anticipated. Hence, working on the sermon fundamentally implies methodically approaching the text's experiential core, its resulting communicative intention as well as the text's communicative interest *in the sense of a "situational goal".*[230]

## 3.1.2 Exegesis in the Pulpit

If a preacher's exegetical effort to understand the text is not completed *before* their work on the actual sermon, this becomes strikingly manifested in the incorporation of exegetical findings in the address. Consequently, the listeners are confronted with such things as the "Gnosis in Corinth", with "editorial interventions on the original form of the text" or with speculations on the ideals "of its true author" without these omissions contributing in any respect to the better understanding of the text's intention.

The preliminary work on the sermon doubtlessly requires preachers to consider all the relevant exegetical aspects of text analysis and to explore the different ways of understanding the text (which could also lead them astray) before relevant points come into view. But once this process has been completed, it is no longer necessary to repeat all the exegetical problems and aspects considered to the congregation. Exegetical processes belong to the preparatory phase of the sermon work and what has been achieved in the separate stages of this phase cannot simply be handed on to the listeners as a "message". Hence, "we should never lecture on the text but simply say what is there...No exegete should stand in the pulpit wondering whether a word is to be understood this way or that... The congregation should be presented with the results of this careful preparatory work."[231]

---

**230** On this cf. in particular I.3.3.3.
**231** K. Barth, 1991, 128.

Three-quarters of a Whitsun sermon on 1 Cor 12:4–11, for example, are devoted to the mere explanation of the event at Pentecost as contained in Acts and the situation of the Corinthians. In the course of this sermon there is a substantial report on what the disciples are thinking, what they become aware of, what they intend to do and what they confess. The same is repeated for the Corinthians: "The Corinthians, to whom Paul has written the letter in which today's sermon text is found, have also experienced enthusiasm through the Spirit [...] Paul confirms them, [...] the Corinthians thought [...], the Corinthians intended [...]. But in thinking this way they are massively in error, which Paul tells them very clearly in his letter. He desires [...], Paul understands [...], Paul knows [...]."[232]

The only case in which exegetical details are allowable in an address from the pulpit is when they are imperative for the understanding of the sermon itself. After all, a sermon is not – as opposed to other ways of dealing with biblical texts – concerned with providing an understanding of the text in its historical horizon *at that time*. It is a matter of communicating the gospel in the horizon of life today. This means: A sermon is not about contributing to a historical understanding of a text by means of all the available resources of scientific theology and maybe arbitrarily constructing some corresponding scenes from "life today" afterwards out of a merely illustrative interest. It is the other way round: The text is relevant in its significance for understanding our lives today before God, before ourselves and in co-existence with one another. It *becomes* historical in the act of its interpretation and reception.[233]

### 3.1.3 Misunderstood Text-Sermon

It is widely believed that the mere fact of constantly recurring to what a certain "text says" provides sufficient evidence for the sermon's continuity with the text's thematic content. Its function as a reference text is, however, entirely misunderstood if we assume that the sermon's textual appropriateness already results from the intensive *use* of the text, i.e. from the repeated recitation of individual text passages or from an amalgam of one's own rewording and biblical quotations.

A preacher entitles the first section of his sermon "Motivating Entry" and integrates in merely 14 lines all of the text's characterizing terminology: "Unity", "Unity in the Spirit", "Unity of the Spirit", "one Body", "one Hope", "one Lord", "one Faith", "one Baptism", "one God", "New Testament", "Old Testament", "Indications of Unity", "Church Unity", "the Concept of 'Church'", "the

---

**232** Sermon manuscript on 1 Cor. 12:4–11.
**233** For more detailed explanations cf. I.3.3.3.

Concept of Christianity", "one Body", "Body of Christ", "Worldwide Christianity", "Baptism", "Body of Christ", "Christian Unity".[234]

An analysis of various sermons based on one and the same text reveals that the explicit presence of a text by no means guarantees a consistent orientation on a particular message or intention of this pericope. After equating some of the text's leading theological terms and concepts with supposedly existential human problems, "our lives today" seem to match up with the text like "needle and thread" – as if it was written precisely for this one sermon on this particular day. The text, which in the first place always says the same thing, "corroborates" all the more the less one has bothered to work out its possible intention. As a result such sermons are "pure text-sermons" as they were in fact *developed along the text from the very start*, so that in the end everything appears to go together – even though under questionable premises. These sermons give the impression that their purpose is to serve the text, rather than to serve the congregation with the text. The following is an example of this:

"In the wealth of meaningful and closely-packed statements of our sermon text I see two points which illuminate the relationship of the Christian congregation from different sides. As for the first point, you might still remember the catchword 'divine service' [followed by a *quotation from the text*] and I imagine it already offended you when you first heard the sermon text [*Quotation from the text*]. But we should not misunderstand Paul here. When he speaks of the body that we should surrender to God he does not mean *our bodies* but our whole existence. Let's take another look at the beginning of the text [*Quotation from the text*]. And then there is the second point [...]. Following the exhortation to true divine service we read: "And do not be conformed to this world"[235] [longer *quotation from the text*]. In the further course of the sermon the text will basically only be aired without the preacher being able to decide on hermeneutical grounds to move away from Paul as the logical subject of his sermon, to realize that he himself is (at least temporarily) the "traditioner", the one who "passes down" and correspondingly needs to speak more precisely.

The sermon quoted shows that the tradition in which the preacher believes that he is placing himself cannot simply be inserted into the sermon by means of quotations. *Continuity to tradition* is above all a *hermeneutical* demand and hence needs to be striven for *at the level of content,* which requires approaching the text at a much deeper and more fundamental level than its superficial structure. This means that a narrative sermon, for example, which neither draws on the text's wording nor intensively uses its terminology can stand in quite firm continuity to

---

**234** Sermon manuscript on Eph 4:1–6.
**235** Sermon manuscript on Rom 12:1f.

its reference text and be eminently shaped by its core positions.[236] Such a sermon requires, however, looking closely at where the text is coming from and where it is going in order to achieve a thorough, deep understanding that allows for an equally "free" and "true" dealing with the text. When the term "text-sermon" is understood as describing a sermon which stands in theologically responsible continuity with the tradition that has originally given rise to and interpreted its reference text, "faithfulness to the text" is *not preserved through a particular form* of the sermon, but practiced *through theological* (exegetical, systematic, hermeneutic) *text examination*.

### 3.1.4 Minimizing the Message

What is conveyed as "Good News" to the sermon's listeners, under closer consideration often proves to be a sequence from the reservoir of the little comforts of daily togetherness: a smile, a friendly glance, the question about one's welfare. Yet, *transforming the idea of living by faith into some kind of alleviating moment in everyday life* has nothing to do with modesty or thankfulness for the unexpected small things becoming great. By "Minimizing the Christian Message" I understand the thoughtless trivialization or episodization of what the gospel stands for, of what is worth hoping for and what is to be expected. Minimalizing the possibilities of living by faith usually goes along with *playing down* both, "life in the world" and "life before God". In an abundant number of cases, nothing more than romanticizing talk is achieved, restricting both what is to be feared and "the Good News" itself.

> "Jesus is such a good shepherd for humankind. He has directed his attention to each of our souls. If we gave him the chance to speak to us we could hear his voice as clearly as if he was standing just beside us. When we lose hope, he makes the sun shine and shows us the beauty of a meadow full of bright flowers, the wisdom of an old tree and the fascinating starry evening sky. And when we are sad, he lets us meet a friendly person who gives us a warm-hearted smile which makes us forget our problems for a while. In my mind I see Jesus standing among us, opening his arms kindly to show us that we are all invited to find acceptance, comfort and communion in mutual trust with him."[237]

From a theological point of view, such persistently trivializing hermeneutics will hardly be able to clarify what preaching the gospel could possibly have to do with

---

**236** For more details cf. I.4.3.2.
**237** Sermon manuscript on John 10:11–16.

existential processes such as insight, repentance, change or dispute. Hence, the fact that the communication of the gospel implies personal change processes and confronts people with the possibility of becoming different beings is scarcely taken into consideration. The practice which is criticized here does not necessarily reveal, however, *homiletic* inability, but rather the lack of a refined *systematic* competence that aims at theological argumentation and includes the awareness and reflection of personal experience. How else could we explain that on the basis of large-scale exegesis sermon goals are defined so vaguely that one could extemporize them any time without even reading the respective text: "It is not the purpose of Christianity to exclude each other in faith, but rather to embrace one another."[238] Despite extensively quoting dogmatics, the quotations' underlying (at times controversial) positions often remain unconsidered. Instead, in order to justify even the most simple, in one way or another always "correct" statements, whole approaches such as those of e.g. Paul Tillich, Karl Rahner or Karl Barth are employed – as if this would settle the argument.

From what I have observed, the platitude of a sermon's content often corresponds with its linguistic abstractness. It is quite telling that the banal is also often described as that which has deteriorated into a phrase, into insignificance. Conversely a sermon's degree of relevance rises with the degree of its perspicuity.

### 3.1.5 Pragmatic Hermeneutics

A sermon should always *clarify* something for its listeners and, as a consequence, amplify their understanding. This is achieved to a great extent already during the sermon's preparation phase, when preachers come to realize – in view of their own understanding of the text as well as the congregation's circumstances of life – what they wish their listeners to comprehend. No matter which of the different concepts of understanding (e.g. understanding as consent, as interaction, as construction etc.[239]) preachers adopt, they need to develop a methodical will to understand the text as well as the topic the sermon is dealing with. Without an awareness that there is, in fact, something to understand which requires a particular method or approach of understanding, the "homiletic realization" of the preaching idea comes to nothing.

Within the context of sermon preparation or homiletic seminars hermeneutic reflections are often replaced by declarations of intention. The very resolution to

---

238 Sermon manuscript on Rom 6:19–23.
239 Cf. I. Reuter, 2000, 54–116.

say this or that in one way or another is then considered to be a sufficient basis for these or those effects to be achieved: "By initially questioning the text and raising doubts on what it says, I would like to right from the start awaken the congregation's attention for the message of the text defended in the last part of the sermon." How does the preacher know that one gets the listeners' attention through problematizing a biblical text? And why come up with defending of what is vital only in the last part of the sermon, embedded into the rhetorical gesture: "I bet you didn't see that coming!"? Certainly the listeners are not confronted with such clumsy practice, through which in the end everything appears to seamlessly fit together, for the first time.

The following example reveals several principles of an all too pragmatic hermeneutics, all of which are, from a homiletic perspective, doomed to failure. The text's "fictitious I" represents a disciple, a point of view which is intended to make the listeners experience the emotions of this specific disciple themselves. As a consequence the listeners – as the author sees it – "might not only be able to understand, but also feel the healing power of Jesus the same way the disciple did, when his life [...] took a salutary turn by the appearance of Jesus of Nazareth. The story meets the listeners exactly where they are stuck in their everyday lives [...]. By finally returning to her own interpretation in the sermon's concluding section the preacher is able to place emphasis on the dogmatics she considers appropriate in the context of the corresponding pericope.[240] The introduction and conclusion of my sermon can serve as invitations to the listeners to join me in my exploration – if I succeed in triggering the appropriate mood in them. I do, however, not attempt at confronting them with some sort of ready-made content, as this would deprive them the opportunity of developing their own thoughts on how they can possibly experience or have already experienced the Holy Spirit. This is the reason why no concrete examples should be used in the final section of the sermon. After having listened to the sermon the listeners should be given the chance to think further in the 'premonition of freedom' and the security of the promise of the Spirit, and go forth into the week."[241]

These remarks on the sermon's impact neglect the essential question *under which premises it can be expected* that a "first-person report of a disciple" might in fact achieve the intended effect of a "shared feeling of the agreeable presence of Jesus" instead of leading to the potentially awkward impression of participating

---

**240** It should be precisely the opposite. A sermon is not delivered in order to introduce its listeners to the fundamental questions of dogmatics and teach them the theological phraseology they should apply to most suitably express their experience of life and faith. The sermon must, on the basis of theological insight, endeavour to translate from the language of dogmatics *into the language of everyday life and faith*. Relating it to the models of Systematic Theology should not occur *in* the sermon but rather *in the preliminary homiletic work*. This facilitates the development of a sermon which does not require the belated, explicit incorporation of dogmatic linguistic patterns of Systematic Theology because it has accrued from the working with them.
**241** From the preliminary work on a sermon manuscript on John 14:23–47.

in a "Sunday School Hour". Neither do they explain *in what way* the sermon's intended "effect of meeting its listeners where they are stuck in life" is to be attained or why the sermon's theological profile should only appear in its concluding section. They do not specify why remaining *unspecific* should prompt a higher degree of reflection on the part of the listeners than taking up a clear position, nor do they point out any reasons why the conclusion that it is precisely the omission of examples that allows for further thought seems permissible – particularly since research into sermon reception comes to a contrary result.

In terms of the congregation's comprehension of and consent to the sermon, hermeneutical problems frequently arise when preachers rather allusively hint at the relations between text and situation instead of clearly pointing out the analogies upon which these relations are based and in which (limited) connections they hold true. This becomes even more serious when preachers lavishly operate with fundamental concepts of Christian Soteriology and tacitly insinuate that in doing so the gospel is handed down virtually unadulterated, as, e.g., in this sermon for Good Friday:

"God himself speaks to us in the crucified Jesus. In Jesus' cross God experiences human misery, desires to be with humanity, wants to suffer with humanity. God has become human in Jesus Christ as we celebrate each year at Christmas. But this humanity of God is expressed most of all in the healing ministry of Jesus, in his cross which disappoints all human expectations. [...] Jesus hangs on the cross, remains human in his doubt. [...] God knows my suffering and is not far away in the most difficult phases of my life. God suffers with me. This insight can give us great consolation. Certainly, our suffering remains painful, does not become more bearable for the moment, but God is with those who suffer. [...] I must seek out these places, endure my crises, and make the disappointments of my life bear fruit, for God knows my afflictions."[242]

In this sermon the death of Jesus is simply transferred, without any further hermeneutic reflection, to the "totality of the world's suffering". Yet, the reason why it should be comforting that God experiences the same as I do remains untold. Would equalizing "suffering here" and "suffering there" not have the opposite than intended effect and lead to a schizoid rather than trusting attitude towards life and faith, particularly when God can do nothing other than suffer, too? "I am not well – and God is also no longer who he once was. Why then should I turn to him?" Although, from a theological perspective, it is reasonable to establish a *certain connection* between the suffering of Jesus and the suffering of humankind, no understanding whatsoever is gained by means of such equations (see above). In non-ecclesiastical counselling no one ever doubts that crises are meaningful either; one can even read this up in more detail in relevant self-help books.

---

242 Sermon manuscript on Matt 27:33–50.

But if the suffering of God or Jesus should contribute to a deeper understanding of living by faith, a hermeneutics is required which goes beyond the mere *assertion of the significance* of this suffering and dying.

### 3.1.6 Text- and Concept-Fetishism

In many cases, pragmatic hermeneutics is paired with a kind of text fetishism which almost evokes magical practices. Even the tiniest of problems appearing as hazy shadows on the horizon of the sermon, are immediately "resolved" by means of using the text as a sort of weapon. The questions touched upon in rapid succession may be so cryptic, the crises hinted at appear so irrefutable, the "so-says-the-text" is inserted into the sermon in various stereotypical language patterns like an incantation.

This strategy reveals the preacher's more or less conscious conviction that the mere use of *quotations* is enough to ward off every harm without any theological argumentation, without any awareness of the listeners' doubts or "temptations"[243], or the tensions the text produced in its own time. The linguistic and theological syntax of many sermons appears to be based on constructing a subject-object relationship between text and congregation. Common signs of such practice are – to quote from a sermon – expressions such as: "The text will show us", "the text will open our eyes", "the text draws our attention to", "the text wants to encourage us", "the text wants to tell us", "the text addresses us directly three times."[244] But how can a text address us *directly*? Quite apart from the logical linguistic problem, in view of such a sermon the question arises in what way *God* plays a role - if we have this attentively caring text.

"It is easier to build fences between each other than to seek unity. [...] We experience this particularly [...] in situations of disagreement between two people, married couples, parents and children, neighbors, work colleagues, groups, nations, above all when they are at war. If, in spite of all differences and arguments, the text calls humankind to unity in the Spirit of God, this *must* mean that as humans we are capable of actually achieving it. *The text does not leave us alone* with its claims and demands but explicitly specifies certain qualities which support us in achieving this unity."[245]

---

**243** Cf. E. Lange, 1976, 25. By temptations ("Anfechtungen") Lange means e.g. the doubts arising to the *listeners* when, equipped with the promises of the gospel, they need to relate what they have heard and what has been promised with their actual, daily experiences. Likewise – and possibly to an even greater extent – preachers entertain their own doubts: "*In view of the facts*" they may well be "left speechless" (ibid., 25).

**244** Sermon manuscript on John 15:26–16:4.

**245** Sermon manuscript on Eph 4:1–6. Emphasis W. E.

By *text fetishism* I mean the paradoxical effect of expelling God's Word from the sermon by means of God's Word, and preventing 'it' from saying what 'it' could actually tell us today by constantly referring to its documentary condition (i.e. to what 'it' once *said*). The same holds true for a constant overstraining of certain theological concepts: for example, a preacher is convinced that there is only one way of pointing out to a congregation of hospital patients that they belong to the community of the others, and that is by explaining the term "concept of the Spirit", for it is this term (sic!) which will show the path "into the community of believers."[246]

The lesson is clear: The above-problematized approach fails to notice that any kind of understanding (of what is read or heard) is based on the fact that the reader or listener adds something to the *form* of the word that is *not* read or heard, which is *content* and *meaning*. Such supplementing effort – which is at the core of every comprehension process – needs "guidance" through the sermon itself. The key factor in the comprehension of a text is for a listener to be able to "go beyond" the sermon they have heard: if they were asked to reproduce its contents, they should be in a position to do more than quote individual phrases. The listeners must be able to place the meaning of these sentences within the context of their own lives.

## 3.2  Indicators of Problems in the History of Homiletics

In order to track down the different *reasons for referring to a text* in the church's tradition of preaching one can either turn to explicit directives in sermon instructions. Alternatively, these reasons can be deduced from the way biblical tradition is implicitly included into the practice of preaching and homiletic theory.

When dealing with the question of whether and how a sermon must refer to the Bible or not, we need to bear in mind that *every personal testimony* which arises from the communication of the gospel is part of a process of tradition: by expressing what is binding for themselves, people inevitably refer to what has been passed on to them. It is hence the result of a complex acquisition process in which it is not simply a matter of affirming or rejecting the tradition but, additionally, of analyzing, processing, translating and transforming tradition. The lack of an explicit interpretation or scriptural reference can therefore not be equated to a "break with tradition". Instead the question has to be raised for what reasons a sermon should in fact refer *to the individual text,* beyond its actual relation to tradition.

---

246 From the preliminary work on a sermon manuscript on 1 Cor 12:4–11.

### 3.2.1 On the Scriptural Accuracy of Text-Free and Text-Based Sermons

As the practice of preaching in the Christian church shows, scriptural sermons have not always been understood as text interpretations followed by a meditation of the "text's message". Taking a look at the initial motives for referring to the Scriptures in the biblical books themselves reveals that the first traces of communicating the gospel in Early Christianity can certainly not be considered as text interpretations. Instead they clarify – *within the horizon* of Scripture and by *taking into consideration the existential circumstances of the listeners or readers* – what it means to live in the presence of God or to belong to Christ.[247] They intend to encourage believers in their present lives before God, to remind them of the requirements and consequences of their freedom – and to prepare them for changes in view of the coming of the kingdom of God.

Hence, the source of such testimony is not a single text; instead it partly refers (1) to the biblical records as a whole, i.e. to the Old Testament, partly (2) to the unwritten traditions of experience of the Christian communities and partly (3) to the concrete experiences of the respective community itself.

Already in the letter to the Hebrews such reference to various sources becomes apparent, as it uses all the above-mentioned forms of referring to tradition.

On 1:   The "sermon" provided in the form of the Letter to the Hebrews is delivered in view of the Old Testament as a whole. It is not only concerned with one particular text but refers to greater connections regarding the Christ event. Thereby the Old Testament is not simply quoted but various event levels are interwoven with one another. Christ is revealed as high priest who fights for us "to receive mercy" (4:16) by sacrificing himself (9–10). The listeners should identify themselves with God's wandering people led no longer by Moses but by Christ as the "pioneer and perfecter of faith" (12:2).

On 2:   Frequently it is not the biblical word of the Old Testament which the author refers to, but rather the experiences of the *community* which have given rise to the testimonies of faith later put down in the form of texts. Hence to come up with, e.g., the whole "cloud of witnesses" (11:1–12:1) serves the purpose of encouraging the readers on the way of discipleship.

On 3:   Finally the author attempts to provide a theological interpretation of the present and, as it were, uses the circumstances of potential recipients as a "text" which he then interprets: "Endure hardship as discipline" (cf. 12:7–11).

Throughout the centuries there have always been *text-free, yet scriptural Christian sermons*, which often referred to other testimonies, such as e.g. hymns, catechetic

---

247 Meanwhile they are regarded as confessions having provided as texts for later sermons, a traditional practice which, as we shall see, has repeated itself throughout the history of preaching.

texts or creeds[248], i.e. to texts *already containing an interpretation* of the Bible. Likewise there have always been topical sermons which dealt with e.g. the practical impacts of Christian faith on particular areas of (social) life, the meaning of particular church holidays for Christian spirituality, contemporary questions of life etc.

Some of the best-known text-free, yet scriptural and situational sermons are M. Luther's Invocavit sermons, preached in 1522[249], which aim at repairing an "out-of-control situation". In Wittenberg there is turmoil: a new decree released by the town council condemns believers to follow a Protestant way of life. Suddenly they are e.g. faced with the idea that young people should not live celibate lives as this is not provided for in the Bible or that receiving the communion under only *one* kind is sin. By referring to the displaying of images in church as idolatry, over-enthusiastic zealots destroy sculptures in the town church. In view of the importance particular expressions of reforming piety had gained in the public consciousness, Luther's admonition to show consideration to the weak represented a form of political action.

Luther's Invocavit sermons are exemplary in that they remain sermons, despite their thematic focus. Luther resists any temptation to explicate the 'proper position' on the basis of the public discourse; instead, he takes up the urgent questions in the light of the gospel in order to proclaim the "freedom of a Christian" again, from which no (new) law can be made.[250]

In view of the specific function of the sermon as a Christian public address it is highly important not to reduce it to a prophetic-critical impulse or to a certain political dimension, particularly when it comes to topical sermons. Neither its dimension of pastoral care (priestly function) nor its promissory potential (kerygmatic function) should be neglected. Without doubt this is equally practicable when it comes to preaching on current issues. "There are topics which certainly belong in the pulpit, for which it is, however, hard to find suitable texts. I consider it useful, even necessary to preach on problems such as abortion or euthanasia, but I think it would be wrong to evolve such heated questions, presumably controversially discussed by the congregation, on the basis of only one text – e.g. the Fifth Commandment. By attempting to unveil pressing contemporary problems

---

**248** Nicolaus Selnecker, for example, held a sermon-cycle on the Formula of Concord in 1581, which is exceptional in that Selnecker himself was involved in the composition of the Formula (cf. N. Selnecker 1577). Given the confessional character of this text Selnecker's sermons are actually to be regarded as sermons on a sermon (cf. N. Selnecker, 1581a and 1581b).

**249** Cf. the Introduction to the Invocavit sermons and their critical edition by H. Junghans, in: Martin Luther, 1982, esp. 520–529.

**250** In this context it is interesting to take a look at the controversies Luther does *not* touch upon in the Invocavit sermons: he leaves it to the municipal authorities to sort out the church finances, ban begging and the practice of usury, take care of the problem of prostitution etc. (cf. M. Luther, 1982, 523).

against the background of the *whole* Scripture, particularly text-free sermons can meet the Reformation's scriptural principle."[251]

Errors and oddities have occurred at all times, both in case of text-based and of text-free sermons. There were, for instance, sermons on biographies which – often in total failure to spot these men's and women's actual achievements for the Christian self-understanding – amounted to the mere appeal for emulation or resulted in a virtual glorification of individual heroes of the faith.

In this respect *Cyriacus Spangenberg's Luther sermons*[252] became famous, in which he preached on Luther before the miners' congregation of Mansfeld, presenting him as a miner, foreman, face-worker and wagon-boy. In this context we should also not fail to mention the sermons on political issues of industry and welfare such as agriculture, re-forestation and smallpox vaccination at the time of the Enlightenment. The *Enlightenment sermon's* wish to be contemporary and to deliver important issues for the listeners' everyday lives is certainly not done justice if one merely highlights the oddities of this period in the history of preaching: a sermon in Advent on the stealing of wood (with reference to Matt 21:8), Christmas sermons on the toughening of shepherds, on the (dangerous) use of fur hats or on feeding in stables, and Easter sermons which examine the problem of being buried alive or address the topic of rising early. Even a more moderate approach such as that of J. Spalding[253] reveals the extent to which the moral educational principle dominated the purpose of the sermon. And finally we need to point to the *Revivalist sermon*. Even though it is commonly based on a text, it tends to stray far off course, away from the text's own message. The text is often merely used as the starting-point for the "call for repentance" actually developed from a specific topic. Claus Harms stated that freeing preachers "from the shackles of the text" would have a positive effect on the church in general[254]. Instead of preaching the gospel the preachers struggle unnecessarily with historical questions.[255]

Harms' criticism of the sermon's text relation reveals that a sermon's scriptural accuracy cannot be traced back to the mere use of a text but to a *particular way*

---

**251** J. Ziemer, 1990, 213. Emphasis W. E.

**252** C. Spangenberg, 1589. This work has been published and edited more than 40 times. J. Matthesius' (1883) collection of 17 sermons on Luther's life has become equally renowned.

**253** In his work "Über die Nutzbarkeit des Predigtamtes" [On the utility of the preaching office] Johann J. Spalding continually returns to the idea that the sermon should improvingly impact both, society and the individual and therewith bring about a blissful effect (cf. 1791, 63–76). Consequently a preacher must know "above all other things" that "in order to become happy people have to become good" (334). In his dedication, which rather resembles a preface, Spalding emphasizes that what matters in preaching is "to keep in sight the cause of improving and comforting Christianity" in order "to lead many people through this to their happiness" (loc. cit., XXV-XXVIII).

**254** C. Harms, 1837, 53, 67f.

**255** Similar arguments can be found in Alexander Vinet. He considers allowing the text to dominate the sermon in such a way that the Word of God is no longer perceptible as a living witness irresponsible. Cf. A. Vinet, 1944, 98–100.

*of using the text.* Both, Vinet's accusation that by biting into the text, sermons often resemble an "enforced execution of the Word of God"[256], and Harms' recommendation to shed the "shackles of the text" reveal great homiletic helplessness. Apparently it was hard to imagine that there could be any other academically justified and reasonable way of dealing with texts. Thus the – actually in no way compulsory – alternatives seem to be to *either* "ride the text"[257] *or* "to free oneself from its shackles". It is therefore required to take a closer look at the issue *which* model of dealing with the text does justice to both, the *individuality of a concrete testimony* and the *necessity of a new testimony.*

Acknowledging the scriptural accuracy of text-free sermons should by no means be misunderstood as an advocacy for preaching without a text but instead aim at intensifying the issue of the specific function of text reference. Certainly, it should be easier to preach in accordance with the Scriptures by referring to a text than to do so without a text. A sermon without a text *misses out the opportunity of getting involved with the concrete form and a certain (interim) result of the communication of the gospel.* In other words, it lacks a resisting "opponent"[258]. A text-free sermon is composed without any dialogic confrontation, without the resistance represented by a different position – which could be provided by engaging with a text. Such practice surely increases the temptation of randomly searching for certain passages or aspects matching one's own individual concept of God. It furthermore involves the danger of ideologically misusing testimonies of faith or striving for getting one's own view of things confirmed by the Bible.

Frequently, a topical or text-free sermon's general reference to the Bible results in the following problem: they preach the "law" and refer to "the Bible", they demand decency and courtesy and refer to "the Bible", they call for thoughtfulness in everyday life and, again, refer to "the Bible". However, the individual testimonies of the Old and New Testament cannot just simply be ascribed to some random ideas of faith and God or used for any kind of, albeit noble, purpose. In order to understand them and integrate them into a sermon it is not enough to refer to a representative collection of some of the Bible's key core statements and combine at whim. Proceeding in such a way bears the risk of overlooking the fact that each biblical text expresses what faith means in its very specific way and intention.

---

**256** A. Vinet, 1944, 99.
**257** The illuminating concept of "riding the text" originates with Harms, 1837, 68.
**258** Andreas Horn vividly and powerfully describes the manifold difficulties and possibilities in dealing with texts (cf. A. Horn, 2009).

From what has been said above, some of the most important aspects that have always played an important role in the relationship between sermon and Scripture or text should have become obvious. What has, however, gone unmentioned so far are those arguments which consider texts, above all, as the "Word of God". Though neither reflecting on *how to deal* with a text nor on its *function within the frame of the sermon process* but, instead, relating the text's importance solely to its being the Word of God, they have had a strong influence on the methods and practice of preaching. Thus they are to be considered in the following chapter.

### 3.2.2 Traditional Arguments for Text Reference

The theory and practice of communicating the gospel distinguishes between three traditional arguments for referring to biblical tradition. Text reference is considered (1) as an argument for the truth, (2) for the reliability and (3) the credibility of the sermon's message. To some extent, this distinction corresponds to certain aspects which also apply to the effects of language or the functions of the sermon in general[259]:

- The *argument for the sermon's truth* is related to the *content* of the text or message; it is used to reinforce, among other things, the sermon's *objectivity* which is gained from the text (representational or teaching function).
- The *argument for the sermon's reliability* is provided for by the *meaning* the text has for its addressees; it refers to the sermon's *relevance* for the faith, thoughts and actions of its listeners (signal or paracletic function).
- Finally text reference can be linked to the preacher's *credibility* and contribute to the sermon's message appearing as plausible (function of self-revelation, expressive function and function of testimony).

#### a) The Text as an Argument for Truth

Scriptural reference in this sense is to be considered as a reaction to the difficulties arising from the fact that preachers frequently regard their *own* awareness of God's – never immediate – redemptive work as too meagre. In the same way the listeners, too, may be wearied by the constant challenge of having to recognize the "signs of the coming of God's kingdom" in their everyday lives or the course of the world and to interpret them as being salutary or helpful. Occasionally such worrying experience leads preachers to the assumption that their

---

259 Cf. the three functions of the sermon (teaching, paraclesis, testimony) in I.2.3.3.

own testimony may not be sufficient to set a convincing example.[260] Hence, calling upon the truth of a text and using it for substantiating the credibility of the promises cultivated in Christian tradition seems to be the obvious consequence.

The historical comprehensibility of the events portrayed or narrated in the text plays only a minor part in adducing it as a reference for the truth of the message. No one, for example, is interested in the situation of the one who once bewailed his faith as he prayed in a Psalm (cf. John 19:24 with Ps 22:19) or the circumstances in which Moses and Aaron set out the order for the Seder (cf. John 19:36 with Exod 12:46). When the texts of the Passion narrative are called upon as testimony, all that matters is the *truth of the message* of Good Friday in all its details – right up to Jesus' descent from the cross: "The man who saw it has given testimony, and his testimony is true. He knows that he tells the truth, and he testifies so that you also may believe. These things occurred so that the scripture would be fulfilled: 'Not one of his bones will be broken'" (John 19:35f.).

Basically there is nothing wrong with the attempt to let the proclamation's plausibility benefit from the authority of texts: Already in the New Testament the truth of the message is emphasized by referring to the Scriptures. The news of Jesus as the love of God made flesh to redeem humanity is e.g. repeatedly testified by "scriptural references" like a *cantus firmus* in John's description of the Passion. The stereotypical expression "...so the scripture would be fulfilled" intends to underline the fact that it really happened like this. By means of the authority of the Scriptures the author guarantees, so to speak, that the readers and listeners can trust their eyes and ears: "It *is* finished" (John 19:30). The preceding references to "what is written" also have an authenticating character and serve as pieces of evidence. Thus, on the one hand they are part of a specific strategy of communicating the gospel, on the other hand they are part of the message itself, for it is good news to learn that a part of the promise has been fulfilled.

This strategy presupposes, however, that a text is considered to be relevant by its readers or listeners just because it comes from "Holy Scripture", because the Bible represents an unchallenged authority which is just not questioned.

A preacher attempts to move his congregation to a stronger sense of community by virtue of the authority of the Scriptures. After repeatedly connecting his appeals with several quotations from the text he recapitulates: "According to our Bible text Christianity should [...] get it together and sit down at one table to make the God-given unity of the church visible. This is how I understand our text. [...] Otherwise its writer would not have picked up the term 'unity' seven times."[261] Another preacher, referring to Scriptures, advises his congregation to give up their doubts about

---

**260** Many preachers are left frustrated in face of their engagement regarding the sermon by the slight (perceptible) resonance their homiletic endeavors meet (cf. K.-W. Dahm, 2005, 236).
**261** Sermon on Eph 4:1–6.

the resurrection of Jesus Christ in order to obey God's will and, in doing so, experience the power of the resurrection. Reduced to a formula, truth through obedience: "When the disciples obeyed Jesus' orders to cast their net on the right side of the boat, they were rewarded with a great catch – and realized that it is the Resurrected One whom they have to thank for it. This delivered them from of their lethargy. The text shows us: We, too, can participate in the fullness of life if we let ourselves into the will of God – and in so doing we shall also be freed of our doubts."[262]

The difficulties of this kind of text reference are obvious: To contemporary sermon listeners "it is by no means any longer evident why it should be any good and useful to have biblical texts interpreted and explained." They ask: "Why should that interest me? [...] It is not a basic instruction [...] on the authority of the Bible that can help me but only the personal experience that this was good for me. I really needed that."[263] Anyone who endeavours to use a biblical text predominantly for its "authoritative function"[264] runs the risk of lapsing into attestations to the authority of the text instead of experiencing the reassurance of this authority for themselves together with their listeners.

The problem suggested above is further intensified if the authority of Scriptures allegedly brought into the sermon by means of a text is not addressed with respect to the *listeners* but, above all, in order to suppress the preacher's subjectivity. In this case referring to the text is understood as a precautionary measure against an all "too personal" sermon. In this context, Hans Joachim Iwand reflects on the sermon's loss of relevance by stating that today's preachers are obviously no longer patient enough to listen to the text and "not needy enough [...] to approach the text", that they "always [...] bring something along" and thereby stand in the way of the truth of the text.[265] With ever-new formulations he describes the necessity to-disregard-oneself and to-rely-upon-the-text as cohesive, mutually interacting homiletic virtues. This attitude has brought him the somewhat ambiguous title of a "text-homiletician"[266].

For Hans Joachim Iwand, there is a good reason for studying the text in the phase of the sermon preparation: "To meditate means to seek truth in the *Word* and not in ourselves, [...] means searching for the gospel in the text, to hear the *viva vox* in what is written and the Spirit in the letter". "The letter of the Scripture is the place where we may, and must, knock." In regard to the impact of the text's authority on the preacher, the assumption is: "How the Word of God comes to us and how it appeals to us lies with itself, even when it is 'used' by us."[267]

---

262 Sermon on John 21:1–14.
263 K.-P. Hertzsch 1990, 16.
264 Cf. M. Josuttis, 1983, 387–389.
265 II. J. Iwand, 1979, 489f., 493.
266 Cf. J. Henkys, 1990, 48.
267 H. J. Iwand, 1979, 490, 494f.

In a similar way Hermann Diem demands relating a sermon to a text particularly because "the triune God in his unity" desires no other testimony than "making the testimony of his action heard which is given in Scripture". Anyone who preaches without a text must unavoidably "answer the questions of truth given in the testimonial character of the text in a different way", namely by means of his "human self-understanding".[268] In an earlier work Diem argues that the "the sermon's power to testify [is based] on the canonical text which is preached".[269]

The "objection of secularization", which has been raised by Klaus-Peter Hertzsch and others, can certainly not be swept aside with reference to the "self-disclosure mode" of biblical testimonies. But then, why should it be argued away, anyway? It only becomes problematic when text reference is linked to the demand that preachers should "make room for the text". In the preaching process it is *the preacher* – not the text! – who is the "ultimate witness", the last link in the chain of the communication of the gospel until the listener *in turn* becomes, through the sermon, the (again temporary) "ultimate witness" of living by faith. But in the act of delivering the sermon the preacher (in awareness of his own personal communicative and confessory competence) as the ultimate witness comes to speak of the gospel as his own concrete, distinctive, individual, by no means arbitrary, testimony.

In a recent approach to Hans Joachim Iwand's Homiletics ("Denn wenn ich schwach bin, bin ich stark…" ["…for when I am weak I am strong"])[270] Norbert Schwarz attempts to show that Iwand's homiletic significance cannot be reduced to his role as a text-homiletician. In order to reconstruct Iwand's understanding of the significance of the person of the preacher, Schwarz portrays Iwand's homiletic anthropology "between the two poles of the Word of God and subjectivity".[271] In doing so he attempts to prove that Iwand's argumentation perfectly fits the domains of a communication science-oriented Homiletics.

But, with all due respect to his achievements, especially regarding his comment on Iwand's understanding of the ministry and the task of the sermon, Schwarz' endeavor rests on shaky legs. On the one hand the reasons he gives for Iwand's listeners orientation are largely hypothetical: certain positive effects of Iwand's sermons – which Schwarz obviously deemed desirable – are transferred to the listeners at the time; they are simply assumed, based on the words used in Iwand's sermons. In doing so, Schwarz fails to account for the fact that he naturally handles the sermon manuscripts differently than a listener in the '40s would have done.

---

268 H. Diem, 1971, 281f.
269 H. Diem, 1939, 207.
270 N. Schwarz, 2008.
271 Loc. cit., 49–94. Admittedly this seems to be indeed a legal matter: What preachers have to achieve in order to expose themselves to the "antinomy of the self-relation and thereby to keep open the place where Christ proves himself to be the basic determinant of life" (19) is enormous and conforms with the author's elsewhere stated own justification-theological criticism of the over-estimation of the role of the preacher.

On the other hand the evidence Schwarz provides for Iwand's interest in the preacher and listener shows that the *reasons* for this interest do not result from a differentiated understanding of the particular characteristics of these homiletic "objects", i.e. do not rest on an examination of the corresponding perspectives of reflection. Instead, it *derives from an agenda which is based on certain premises,* connected to questions which are motivated by a particular homiletic preconception of the "Word of God" and "the text", and which clearly favor a specific notion of "text-Homiletics". Consequently Norbert Schwarz's examination lacks a sufficiently critical distance towards the crown witness for the "receptivity and productivity of the subject of faith"[272]. One indication of this is the inclusion of the concept of kerygma, which Schwarz uses in reference to Iwand, to point out: "By no means the preacher must place himself between God and the congregation and attempt at guiding the 'arrow of the Word of God' to its target."[273] As Iwand put it: "The moment preachers begin to rule over souls, they run into the sword of God."[274] Certainly, this caricature of a homiletic position is not an alternative to refraining from characterizing the preacher as "keryx".

The debate on Iwand's "text-Homiletics" shows: It is not decisive for the theological-conceptional understanding of a homiletic approach whether it mentions preachers and listeners or not. (No teacher of preaching would ever have dared to say that preacher and listener could be *ignored* in the homiletic process.) What is in fact crucial for the homiletic process is the question as to *why, with what interest and with what kind of theology of preaching* particular sermon issues are made key points of the comprehension of Homiletics. As concerns Iwand, this means that it is simply not necessary to retrospectively try and understand his insights as a sort of anticipation of modern Homiletics. Iwand – here we must agree with Henkys[275] – certainly deserves the title of a text-homiletician. Even if the reasons he cites for the necessity of a sermon's text reference manifest both, methodical and theological problems, homiletic discourse owes him a deeper understanding of the resistance of biblical testimonies and the corresponding questions on truth.

## b) The Text as an Argument for Reliability

Preachers frequently intend to emphasize, or even just establish, their sermon's reliability when they refer to biblical texts. Basically there is nothing wrong with this argument for text reference either. Both, the argument for reliability as well as the argument for authority have their place in the theology of preaching.[276] The particular reliability a sermon achieves through referring to a *text* has to do with the fact that the examination of it – and of the sermon – cannot be reduced to reflexes of acceptance or rejection. Hence, within the sermon process the reliability of the Holy Scripture becomes apparent in two different ways: through the fact that the preacher – as an interpreter – is forced to expose himself in the

---

272 Cf. the subtitle of N. Schwarz's examination, loc. cit.
273 Loc. cit., 122.
274 Ibid.
275 Cf. J. Henkys, 1990, 48.
276 From a theological point of view this will be accounted for in ch. III.4.4.

testimony of Scriptures on the one hand, and due to the listeners' understanding of the preacher's testimony as a challenge and support for their own faith on the other.

This function of text reference, too, corresponds to a New Testament way of turning to the Scriptures. Particularly in the Pauline Epistles the messages' reliability is often substantiated by referring to the Scriptures and thus ensuring that their content is not misunderstood simply as a matter of opinion (which may be approved or rejected) but heard as the gospel.

By referring to the Old Testament, Paul shows his listeners, for example, that Christ wants to remain in communion with them (2 Cor 6:16b) and that it is part of their faith to take the saving righteousness of God for granted in their own lives (Rom 1:17). In his Epistles the Scripture is cited particularly often when it comes to bringing across difficult matters and at the same time attempting at enhancing the messages' reliability. This is the case when Paul e.g. addresses the question of guilt (Rom 3:9–20). In the so-called Sermon on the Mount the reception of certain passages from the Old Testament serves the purpose of substantiating Jesus' message and the message of the Old Testament itself. Obviously the audience have fabricated their own, rather harmless, interpretation of what is to be expected from God and what lies before them in their lives, when all of a sudden and unexpectedly a far-reaching, yet immediately relevant, prospect of life opens up for them. At the same time they are confronted with a strong reliability, contributed to by the newly interpreted Old Testament text, which they cherish as a rule and norm for their lives and faith. Of course, the Sermon on the Mount in Matthew is not to be considered as a "text-sermon". It is, however, a biblical sermon in that it links the current circumstances of its addressees (e.g. being persecuted from Jewish and Roman side, threat to their faith through heretics) to the communication of the gospel by taking up texts rich in tradition (Deuteronomy, the Psalms and Prophets).

The argument for reliability is – seemingly paradoxically – torpedoed if the function of text reference is reduced to a measure against the preacher: According to such a view a sermon must above all refer to a biblical text in order to eliminate the preacher as "a potential source of friction in the course of the preaching event"[277]. If the preacher just interpreted the Bible or, even better, merely repeated what it says in the text, it was more likely that God himself would be heard. Hence Alfred Dedo Müller grounds the homiletic maxim of the "sermon's scripturality" on the fact that without referring to a concrete text the congregation would be offered nothing but "the preacher's private opinion": "The church must guarantee that the sermon does not become an access point for unbridled subjectivism or rigid intellectualism." The text as the "original Word" is equated with the "voice of God", which means that it is actually two

---

[277] Cf. M. Josuttis' analysis and critique of the one-sided emphasis of the normative claim of the text (1983, 386f.).

functions that are attributed here to the explicitly text-related "connection of the sermon to the scriptural Word": The sermon's reference to the biblical text is both, a necessary *prerequisite* but also the *provision* of "an opportunity for hearing God". According to Müller, connecting the text to the sermon may free the listeners' ability to hear "from literally everything" that would usually impede their hearing.[278]

Because "everything is already there that has to be said", Karl Barth also claims that preaching means, above all, to "maintain obedience to the text": "Scripture should purge all our own opinions, desires, and thoughts. In strict discipline we must stay with the Word and be ready to hear only what the Word says, not what the great public, the smaller congregation, or our own heart might like to hear. [...] I have not to say something, but merely repeat something. If God alone wants to speak in a sermon, neither theme nor *scopus* should get in the way. [...] Our task is simply to follow the distinctive movement of thought in the text."[279]

In view of such theories and hardly practical instructions it is not surprising if the desirable reliability of the communication of the gospel is frequently considered *neither* in relation to the person of the preacher *nor* in relation to the listeners but is often merely reduced to the existence of a text. Consequently we may hear in a sermon: "How does that concern us today? It *must* have something to do with us because the text is there in our Holy Scripture, in the New Testament, in Matthew's Gospel. Don't we assume that every word in the Scripture is important for us, for our lives? So let's start out and get to know the text step by step, and allow it to become a piece of our own lives."[280] This view of the text's significance for the sermon is a homiletic dead end. In fact, it even falls behind Müller's or Barth's theses on the text's significance. However, categorizing the concept of text the way they did is problematic, and leads to similar misunderstandings as becomes apparent from the just mentioned sermon.

Being a homiletic (not simply theological) category, reliability of the text is assigned a function which cannot be proclaimed but results from a process and therefore must prove itself: The text *becomes* reliable in dealing with it, i.e. in the context of sermon preparation, of preaching or listening. It will, however, be reliable to the extent to which it – in the sense formulated above – *becomes* historical and entails the testimony of preacher and listener.[281]

---

278 A. D. Müller, 1954, 196.
279 K. Barth, 1991, 49, 92, 95f. Emphasis W. E.
280 From a sermon on Matt 12:1–8.
281 Cf. Phase III and IV in Fig. 1 in I.1.

### c) The Text as an Argument for Credibility

Scriptural reference does not only serve the purpose of substantiating the message's authority and reliability, but moreover of supporting its credibility. This is expressed e.g. in the expectation that, through its reference to a text as a tried-and-tested testimony of the faith of Christianity, the sermon shares in the solidity and validity of Holy Scripture.

This sort of scriptural reference is already found in the New Testament's reception of the Old Testament, particularly in the context of the Promises which 'by their very nature' were considered as rather improbable. This applies, for example, to the Pauline proclamation of resurrection in which not only Jesus' raising from the dead is testified as happening "in accordance with the Scriptures" (cf. 1 Cor 15:1–11) but also *one's own* resurrection is, through referring to the Scriptures, presented as reliable fact: In taking up accounts from Genesis as well as from the Psalms and Prophets it is shown with ever new arguments that there is actually no reason to doubt the credibility of the message of the resurrection of the dead and of eternal life (cf. 1 Cor 15:12–58).

According to the argument of credibility, referring to a text ensures that even the most unwieldy and risky testimony can be trusted just because it is connected to other outlandish-seeming (text-)testimonies which have already revealed themselves to be trustworthy. Because the text says "it" is true the sermon is true.

Admittedly, according to the rules of its own logic the argument of credibility remains ineffective when preachers do not reach a testimony of their own and a correspondingly clear theological position but restrict themselves to an abstract, paraphrasing repetition of what the text says or the mere airing of the text. For this reason the attempt to use this argument precisely for the preacher's sake seems highly dubious: According to Hans Urner referring to a text is no less than an act of obedience that should prevent the preacher from providing their congregation with anything other than the Word of God. The problem with this sort of argumentation is, however, that it fails to see that a sermon's credibility is greatly influenced by the relationship level between preacher and listener.

"When a sermon simply consists of such obedience it must consist in an interpretation of Scripture first and last and nothing else." The interpretation of the Scripture is conducted "in the certainty of faith that [in the Scripture] God's Word itself is speaking to us". And therefore "proclamation" should be "nothing else than spreading the Word." Anyone who comes along without a text withholds God's Word; and anyone who refers to a text but adds their own, personal dimension does not deliver God's Word to their congregation either, as they replace it with 'profound insights' and 'personal fantasies'. "What God has to tell us is to be found in the text and nowhere else."[282] – *The question is: How was "God's Word preached" when the faithful could not yet receive it from a duplicated text?*

---

**282** H. Urner, 1961, 69, 71, 73f.

Looking back at the text fetishism at the end of the epoch of dialectical theology reveals to what alarming extent the significance of personal experience, personal emotions and – last but not least – personal thought has been sustainably tabooed for the acquisition and communication of faith.[283] We experience who God is for us through the Scriptures *on the one hand*, but *on the other hand* (and in a different way) also through our own lives and the lives of the of people around us – just as did the people who once wrote the biblical texts. Hence text reference is by no means simply a matter of differentiating the reliable "Word of God in Scripture" from the unreliable words of humans. Thus Homiletics has to pay attention to the text in that it testifies to the reliability of God in the lives of people through the words of people.

Anyone who, for reasons of truth, reliability and credibility of the message, stereotypically demands that nothing should be added to the text, that instead only the very written word of the text should be passed on, is to be accused of not having given sufficient thought to the hermeneutic requirements of the sermon process.

### 3.2.3 Hermeneutic Problems of Text Reference

The fact that the sermon communicates the gospel by referring to Holy *Scripture*, which testifies to the "Word of God" in print, raises the question of what distinguishes the *reception of texts* from *verbal communication*. The fundamental-theological "Sola-Scriptura-principle" should not be unconditionally applied as a maxim for interpretation and preaching as "interpreting and preaching the Scripture" unavoidably also implies to speak *about* the Scriptures. In doing so, the words of the Scripture are necessarily embellished with words which are not "the Scripture".

Certainly, to say "God speaks to us in Scripture" is a theological statement. It should, however, be understood *symbolically*; for basically nothing is spoken "in Scripture" – it is a written record. Taking the Scripture seriously in this sense (*sola scriptura*) and accepting the challenges of understanding it, requires – for methodical as well as theological reasons – dealing with the *conditions of the*

---

283 As H.-O. Wölber already recognized in 1957, this would certainly not do justice to the apparent claim to security and reliability: "The preacher [...] as a rule keeps strictly to the specific text. He does not say 'God speaks' or 'I think' but 'the text says', 'this text overcomes us' etc. The text becomes a quantity of its own. But the preacher does this to have a safeguard; he is theologically, materially and basically prepared for such protection. [...] He brings in the arsenal. [...] He misunderstands the sermon as a theological system" (H.-O. Wölber, 1971, 368f.).

*written form of these testimonies of faith* and with what it needs to understand them. It can be assumed that no special conditions are required in this process of understanding the Bible. Just as incarnational theology must cling to the idea that God revealed himself in the person of Jesus under the conditions of human existence, it applies to his Word that it enters the conditions of a text and discloses itself in terms of its conditions.

In the following sections three problematic models of text reference, frequently encountered in the practice of preaching, shall be reconstructed. Though not regarded as recommendations for the sermon work, they facilitate a detailed discussion on the reasons and perspectives that need to be considered in this context.

### a) Unmediated Interpretation and the Conditions of Literature

"Unmediated interpretation" basically disregards the conditions of the text's writtenness and applies to all sorts of text use that fail to draw any consequences from the aforementioned asynchrony of the situations of author and reader (I.1.2). Unmediated interpretation means drawing an arbitrary line from what is written in the text to what it means *today* – without having asked what it could have meant *then* and what it can effectively say today.

This criticism is not directed against a "Second Naïveté" in dealing with the Bible, as this is what it takes – particularly in case of theologians – to be able to read a text "just because" or "solely" with the objective of taking pleasure from and being uplifted by it. It is important not to lose this ability of meditating on the text's overall context without exegetically anatomizing it, in order to find parallels to other, similar texts, or let oneself be led to prayer while reading. Rudolf Bohren rightly demands that such way of reading should find its place in one's personal sermon preparation. This chapter, however, deals with the question of what it means *to reach an appropriate text interpretation and to incorporate the text into one's sermon work in a methodically expert way.*

In a certain sense unmediated interpretation follows a "method", too: As a rule individual phrases of the text are picked out, offered as a solution to current pending questions and used for labelling certain experiences of life and faith.

The final sentence of the pericope of the "laborers in the vineyard"[284] is, for example, frequently used to infer that "today, too, everyone gets a chance before God". Whether the text could possibly have another, theologically seen, more concrete meaning – which could be easily spotted if one has not failed to notice that this sentence is a later addition – remains unquestioned. This

---

[284] "So the last shall be first, and the first last" (Matt 20:16).

strategy of immediate (i.e. un-mediated) text use is particularly problematic if such an act of arbitrarily relating the text to an apparently obvious facet of the listener's life is explained away as an attempt "to take the text seriously" or as the desire to "merely allow the text to be effective".

Unmediated interpretation often refers to passages of (literarily created) direct speech, to the "voice of God", the "words of Jesus", to prophetic sentences etc. – i.e. to the level of quotations offered in the text itself. However, what actually happens to the characters appearing in the text, what decisions they have to make, in which way they could be considered as role models for the reader etc. often remains unnoticed. Torn out of the concrete situation such individual phrases lose their contextual relevance and become universally applicable, groundless allegations about God's doings.[285]

*In this way* the text is certainly not taken seriously; in fact the reader or listener is actually deprived the opportunity to encounter its earnestness by way of feeling inconsistencies, facing a different opinion and – instead of being exposed to grandiloquent adages – being confronted with the experiences and convictions which have initially given rise to this text. Taking a text seriously means understanding it as a *result of dispute* instead of misusing it as a supplier of key words. Unmediated interpretation overlooks the significance of the text's situatedness. This is the reason why literary studies point out the asynchrony of author and reader in order to show that texts must always pass through a translating process of mediation before they can actually be comprehended.

In the *spoken address* simultaneity, as a rule, provides clarity: "Tomorrow" means "tomorrow", "this evening" means "this evening". If, however, such phrases occur in a *text* which is received at a completely different time, the reader – due to the asynchrony – must think of them as "at that time" or at least as "the day before yesterday". This act of reframing is required on other levels, too: regarding certain cultural practices which no longer apply today as well as regarding religious customs, world views and future expectations. Therefore, it is, for example, not enough to explain the listeners the Last Judgement as being an event in which they will be read from the book of good and evil deeds and give them the prospect of a final general commendation or punishment. We must rather ask what this address meant back then and in what way we can talk about its concerns today.

---

285 In the analysis of a series of sermons referring to Gen 28:10–19a I noticed how tempting it actually seems to be to make a phrase such as "I am with you and will keep you" (v.15) the rather abstract and general "theme" of the sermon. Texts containing confirmation or marriage motto-like sentences are obviously hardly understood in their specific, tension-filled relation to concrete day-to-day life. Relevant "key sentences" are frequently used as starting points for uttering commonplaces without resulting in a deeper understanding of their part in the light of the whole pericope.

This brings us to another thought which also urges us to refrain from the tempting practice of unmediated interpretation. Authors are not only writing from *their own* situations; in writing they equally take into account their addressees who will read the text *in another situation.* This means that to a certain extent they must detach from their own concrete circumstances in order to prevent misunderstandings. In doing so they expect their text to be *accepted for interpretation* and assume that their readers will reach adequate, analogous concretions of *their own.* One-sided fixations on the "text's Sitz im Leben" undermine the author's attempt to give meaning to their text, to plant an idea into it which goes beyond the scope of their own situation. Unmediated interpretation works with passepartout-like abstractions of the text instead of raising the question how it could be made fruitful for the realms of the listeners.

Naturally there are contexts of spiritual life – e.g. the morning prayers at the beginning of a team meeting or the meditation on a biblical text – in which an immediate and associative text interpretation is appropriate, in order to transfer the word from the situation at the time to the modern situation. But this implies to know exactly what you are doing: In both just mentioned cases, preachers resort to forms of Christian spirituality in which it is part of the rules *precisely not* to academically dissect texts but to immediately receive them for the sake of one's own edification. This (alone) can and certainly should not achieve what can be expected from text analysis according to the rules of exegesis and hermeneutics in the preliminary stages of sermon preparation. For this reason the earlier tendencies in dialectic-theologically shaped Homiletics of remaining sceptical about the achievements of exegesis and instead resorting the traditional arguments for text reference outlined above are hardly convincing.[286]

### b) Historical Interpretation and the Problem of the Historical Author

Basically all the aforementioned traditional arguments for text reference proceed more or less emphatically from the idea that "determining [...] the text's original meaning" frees us from the need of having to "give the text a new or different meaning than the one ascertained"[287]. Even though – because of human short-sightedness – this means to lower one's sights and content oneself with "approximate accuracy"[288] there always remains the explicit or implicit demand to get down to the meaning the author once gave it, through a "receptive", "tentative", and "objective", i.e. "impersonal" attitude in the examination of the text.

Historical-critical interpretation is, in a certain sense, the counter-model to the principle depicted above. It is determined by the expectation of coming as

---

**286** Cf. here Manfred Mezger's criticism of Rudolf Bohren in: M. Mezger, 1989, 92, 104.
**287** H. Urner, 1961, 70f.
**288** Loc. cit., 72.

close as possible to the text's original intention. This implies taking into account literary and historical contexts, recognizing additions and deletions made in the course of the processes of its transmission and edition in order to be finally able to state what the "purified text" or the "best ascertainable version of the text"[289] most likely once meant. Even though the methods of historical-critical exegesis were not yet available and refined in previous centuries, this form of text interpretation has been considered as basically possible and advisable as long as it has existed.

Even the great interpreters of the Early Church appeared to "naturally" refer to personal targets of the biblical authors. Augustine, for example, speaks of "propositum" when referring to Moses' intention in writing Genesis. At the time of Scholasticism and stimulated by Thomas Aquinas, the premise of "the main sense which the author intended" circulated. The European Humanists, e.g. J. Clichtove believed in methods of interpretation according to which "things are to be understood as their authors intended". And even the hermeneutics of the early and middle stages of the Enlightenment is still characterized – as regards the interpretation of biblical and other ancient texts – by the conviction that historical authors can be considered as "aequi", simultaneous.[290]

In the current practice of preaching the aftermaths of this perspective frequently result in a casual recourse to "what Paul wanted", "whom he was aware of as he was writing", "what he clearly had in mind", what "he most likely anticipated and expected" etc. This, however, implies a similar effect as occurs through unmediated interpretation: The text itself, the text as a whole *with its specific structure of generating and refusing sense*, the text in its individual characteristic of mentioning something in a way no other text does, no longer plays a role. It is no longer needed. For the preacher it is enough to know what the author of the biblical text wanted or what the text meant historically. However, through the supposed clarification of its historical function a text's expressiveness can in fact be boycotted.[291]

To prevent misunderstandings here, it is important that we point to the legitimacy of historical-critical exegesis once again.[292] Today we know so much

---

**289** According to M. Mezger in doing so the interpreter takes into account the text's "verbal reliability" (1989, 98).

**290** Cf. my own examination, 2003e, 109 and the literature cited there.

**291** Correspondingly, we read for instance in the preliminary exegetical work on a sermon draft on 2 Sam 12:1–15a: "The text reveals why Solomon becomes David's successor." In another résumé the yield of the exegesis is summed up as follows: "The pericope attempts to contribute [to the unity of the church] in kerygmatizing the story and figure of Paul and thus characterizing him as the prototype of the redeemed sinner" (Sermon draft on 1 Tim 1:12–17).

**292** For more detailed explanations – including a text example – see Ch. I.3.3.

more about the historical circumstances regarding the genesis and function of individual texts and the books of the Bible than any generation before us did. Anyone who disregards the text's *Sitz im Leben* lacks certain imperative requirements for its interpretation. But whoever accepts "the author wanted to say" as a result of interpretation fails to see the conditions under which the author once wrote.

At this point we need to extend the above-mentioned conditions of literature by another one: *Anyone who writes allows the text to speak in his place.* The text takes the place of the author. Roland Barthes speaks in this context pointedly of the "death of the author"[293]. In literary studies this is the *terminus technicus* for the simple fact that an author, once his text is written and circulated, steps back behind the text and is no longer available as an aid to interpretation in the dawning process of reception. It is part of the act of reading not to fixate on the historical world 'behind' the text but to integrate the world *portrayed in the text itself* into one's interpretation.[294]

For the time being it is crucial to stress that it contradicts a *lively production and reception of texts* (which is actually a tautology since text production and interpretation are equally *creative acts*) to subject them to a historicizing author's meaning. The "death of the author" requires us to accept the text for interpretation and strive for an understanding which the author, who knew neither me nor my circumstances, could certainly not foresee but which he was nevertheless able to *make possible* through his text. Understood as the explanation of the author's meaning the interpretation of biblical texts would imply, taken strictly, the possibility of writing a definite book containing unchangeable, historically-critically established final interpretations of these texts which henceforth should be in circulation as a supplementary volume to the Bible.[295]

To make matters worse, historical analysis tends to overestimate the ability of the interpreter to "de-historicize" himself. Anyone who desires to

---

**293** "La voix perd son origine, l'auteur entre dans sa proper mort, l'écriture commence" (R. Barthes, 1994, 491).

**294** In I.3.3.1 the manifold possibilities of this approach will be highlighted.

**295** For this reason there remains doubt of the realization of an optimized exegesis such as M. Mezger obviously renders possible: "Anyone to whom *the central ideas of the sermon* have jumped out *already in the exegesis* will not achieve any more in meditation. [...] Whoever knows one's craft will fairly faithfully find the world, humanity, the congregation and oneself in the text" (Mezger, 1989, 105; emphasis W. E.). From exegesis to the central ideas of the sermon – precisely here lies one of the key problems. That an interpreter "does not know his craft" if he is not able find these basic ideas faithfully reflected already in the exegesis is not only untrue – it would even be dubious if this were so. Wishing to get hold of the text in this way could pose serious threat to the text's meaning.

understand a 2000-year-old text written in a foreign language in his own language and to strive for an interpretation in his own language cannot simply abandon his specific life situation which is, however, *de facto* assumed and demanded within the framework of historical analysis. No interpreter can ever achieve an objective historical interpretation, for this would be a contradiction in terms.

A preacher who is attempting to reformulate a foreign text and its foreign message without taking into account his own personal convictions and expectations would greatly affect his interpretation's usefulness for his own and his congregation's current circumstance.[296] Dealing with texts in such a way entails further problems: How do we deal with texts which can be traced back to great authorities (as, e.g. the Jahwist) but have been treated so normatively without any interest in the *intentio auctoris* that we are actually faced with the question as to *which* of the authors and authorities involved in the development of the text we are inclined to respect. Harold Bloom points out the danger of seeking the author whom one needs.[297]

### c) The Kerygma-Model and the Ambiguity of Texts
It would certainly be more elegant to speak of the "kerygmatic model". However, this could raise the unwarranted suspicion of denying the kerygmatic interest of certain other forms and attempts of text interpretation. Talking of "kerygma" in the preparatory phase of the sermon means a particular understanding of textual interpretation: The interpreter should examine his text until he becomes able to summarize the text's "kerygmatic content" as its "scopus" by means of "using the conceptual framework of the author or editor and taking into account the homiletic situation of its readers",[298] i.e. the readers of the author then. Certainly, in the course of time there have been some grades and variations regarding this method.[299] Nevertheless they all agree on the fact that through the kerygma the text's proclamatory content can be compressed into one single sentence: The "exegesis necessary for the sermon" is achieved as soon as I

---

**296** In this context cf. Ronald J. Allen's reflections on the hermeneutic challenge of interpreting the gospel, R. J. Allen, 1998a.

**297** Cf. H. Bloom, 1989, 9f.

**298** From L. Fendt, 1970, 64f.

**299** W. Marxsen, for example, thinks it imperative that in the scopus not only speaker (according to J. Schieder God is always the subject [1957, 65]) and listeners are named but that what is said is inserted into the situation of the historical listeners (W. Marxsen, 1975, 54).

"have figured out the following three things: I. What is the text's *main point*? II. Through which *supplementary scopoi* is this main point [...] supported? III. How do the individual verses of the text serve the main scopus or the supplementary scopoi?"; whereby, as a general rule, supplementary scopoi "which contradict the main scopus [may] be left unconsidered in the further course of the sermon work"[300].

It hardly needs saying that it is important not to allow the efforts for a theological understanding of the text to run aground. Correspondingly, one must keep a firm hold on the results of the text analysis, on what it has yielded and what has become clear in dialog with the text. Only in so doing can one give direction to the next steps and set up markers for the homiletic work, erect signposts to prepare the ground for the upcoming theological analysis. But is it really necessary to put already the results of the exegesis into *one single* kerygma-saturated final sentence? Wouldn't it do more justice to the text if one initially kept in mind all the statements it facilitates, the ones it opposes and to what extent it mentions the experience of faith? Here the problems of the "kerygma-principle" come into sight:

1. Taking a look at the sermon's extent of relation to reality and experience reveals why it is problematic to attempt at obtaining the *sermon from a distillate* instead of referring to the text as a whole for reasons of perceiving it as being too profane. Kerygmatic concentrates prevent us from seeing under which circumstances, through which doubts and with which expectations a text was created as a testimony of faith. It could leave an insipid taste if the "kerygma" – like a stock-cube diluted with water – is offered to the listeners as a sermon.

2. Due to the fact that on the way to the "kerygma" significant focus is placed upon working out a text's "main meaning" while at the same time avowedly blanking out any possibly interfering "supplementary scopoi", the *interpretation's arbitrariness* dangerously increases. This becomes not least apparent from the fact that those theologians who called for "the kerygma" as an answer to the question of a text's proclamatory content came to proclaim entirely different kerygmata when preaching on the very same texts.

3. Inserting the kerygma into the day-to-day reality of the listeners involves the danger of causing *short circuits*: Is there anything to which such text distillates, frequently verbalized as theological proclamations or as general remarks, could *not* relate? Proceeding in such a way certainly pays too little

---

300 L. Fendt, 1970, 65.

attention to the hermeneutic question of the analogy between the experiences which once resulted in the text's creation on the one hand and the lived experiences of people today on the other hand.

4.  A final problem is that the disclosure and temporary taming of a text's meanings by way of breaking them down into one *main meaning* are often presented as exegetical necessities. This problem is intensified in view of the demand to formulate this main meaning using the text's own conceptual repertoire. How can such a demand be justified if the text is expected to point beyond itself and to be relevant for us today? It would therefore be more plausible to assess, after having completed the exegesis, the various possible meanings of the text, to reflect on its embedding in the lived reality of the listeners and to carry out a homiletically and didactically founded reduction on the basis of hermeneutic considerations.

In view of these problems, it seems advisable to recall the objections raised by classical interpreters: "to single-mindedly go for the text's main meaning"[301] does not do justice to the text. Jerome and Origen admit without regret that reading the Scriptures causes the impression of having to wade through an "infinitam sensuum siluam"[302] or a "latissimam Scripturae silvam"[303], of having an "ocean"[304], a "sea", an "inexhaustible current" before them which constantly creates new meanings as it flows.[305]

With his basic distinction between literal and spiritual sense Origen wanted to encourage "freedom from the letters by obedience to the Spirit." "The cause [...] of the [...] ignorant assertions about God" comes from the fact that "Scripture" is read "to the mere letter". Therefore one should rather pay attention to *quod significatur* than to *qualis verbis significetur*.[306] As it was "extremely difficult" to find the "things" [conveyed in a text] – particularly when the Scripture speaks to us in "riddles" or "cryptic words" – it was not our task to examine the body of this piece of Scripture until it would finally give us a possibly plausible answer as to how things might have been. Since under certain circumstances texts do not contain any plausible literal or historical

---

301  L. Fendt, 1970, 63.
302  Jerome, 1910, 609.
303  Origen, 1989, 156.
304  Jerome, 1964, 677.
305  Further sources are cited in W. Engemann, 2003e, 127.
306  Cf. Origen, 1976, 21, 23, 700, 799 (English translation in: Origen, 1995, 357, 378). This distinction can admittedly not serve as a model for the highly closely postulated correspondence between historical truth and kerygma since the latter is always comprehended (by the representatives of this approach) as an obvious actuality of the historical sense. Even M. Mezger still regards the sermon as a matter of simply "providing the congregation with what is recognized in exegesis and clearly desired in the text" (1989, 105).

meaning, we need to strive for a figurative, "spiritual" interpretation, i.e. to decisively ask *what does that which we read in the text stand for.*[307] If at all, the meaning "quem auctor intendit" can only be determined in relation to the literal meaning. Accordingly Thomas Aquinas[308] insists that in addition to the author's intended meaning other possible meanings should be given serious consideration, too. Augustine assumes that the authors were not aware of the far-reaching spiritual meanings of the texts and that they wrote through the Holy Spirit, which is why the texts of Scripture say more than their authors intended.[309]

Melanchthon controverted at first two, then three, then four meanings of Scripture[310] according to which the Middle Ages were accustomed to interpret, and instead – similarly to the insistence on the kerygma – propagated *one spiritual meaning.* However, to follow this view naturally means to burden oneself with the entire difficulty of this hermeneutic approach of having to put a slant on the unwieldy literal meanings[311] with the help of theological commonplaces.

It is surely no accident that no one has come up yet with the idea of writing a book on Central Meanings in which preachers could look up the one definite kerygma of each and every text. And it is neither possible nor necessary to give it a try. The Reformation's sola scriptura principle does certainly not stand and fall with the unambiguity of ascertained scriptural meanings.[312] Even those

---

**307** Cf. Origen, 1995, 358f., 361. For Origen this discovery unfortunately came a little late: Some years before his idea of supposing multiple meanings of Scripture when interpreting the Bible the so-called eunuch-quotation (Matt 19:12) prompted him to let himself be castrated "for the sake of the kingdom of heaven".

**308** Cf. Thomas Aquinas, Summa Theologica, I, q. 1, 9 ad 2.

**309** Cf. Augustine, 1962a, 24–27 and 1962b, 96–102.

**310** The teaching of the fourfold meaning of Scripture is usually attributed to Nicholas of Lyra: "Littera gesta docet, quid credas allegoria, moralis quid agas, quo tendas anagoria." Quoted from E. v. Dobschütz, 1921, 1.

**311** Cf. H. Sick, 1959, esp. 24–28, 43–47, 49–51. Recently Paul S. Wilson attempted to counteract those approaches to biblical texts, which – in his view – focus too strongly on historical-critical aspects, by recalling the category of the literal or spiritual meaning (P. S. Wilson, 2001). In doing so, he takes up a classical conviction of homiletic hermeneutics according to which exegetical-historical knowledge alone is not enough to grasp and comprehend the personal relevance of particular texts for one's own life lived by faith. Quite rightly, Wilson questions the frequently encountered reduction of biblical texts to their historical informative content. In order to surmount such – homiletically fruitless – practice it is, however, not sufficient to apply the category of spiritual or literal meaning, which then – just like a revelation – may only be either affirmed or rejected. Those who preach can certainly not avoid *to cooperate* with highly headstrong texts and to acknowledge that their authority lies in their quality of being testimonies of faith. For more detail see below under I.3.4.2, p. 141–145.

**312** In his preaching practice Luther himself only occasionally subordinated himself to the strict principle of searching for the one meaning of Scripture – a hermeneutical process, which,

hermeneuticians of the Enlightenment, who for a long time had taken up the cause of identifying the one, original meaning came to see in their later works that "every text" is "inexhaustible as regards its possible interpretation", so that "every interpretation, even if it is correct" can "be improved" and in fact be improved to the extent that the reader possibly achieves a better understanding than the author of the text did himself.[313]

In fact, the historically or kerygmatically constructed alternative between authorial intention and readers' interest, disregards the fact that both, the comprehension as well as the interpretation of texts *are creative acts which cannot be accomplished without adding something to the written words which is not in the original text.* That this does not necessarily mean to abandon the text becomes obvious by contemplating a third way which goes beyond the rivalry between a historical or kerygmatic meaning of the text and reader's intention: the co-operation between text and reader.

## 3.3 Current Angles of Reflection

The issues discussed above raise the question: How can a preacher refer to the text in a responsible way and get beyond historical ascertainments, yet avoid being taken in by hasty applications? When we speak in what follows of the sermon's "text reference" we shall for now restrict ourselves to the text's function in the sermon's preparatory phase in which – through close text examination – a sermon manuscript or outline is created.[314] In the third and fourth phase of the preaching event, the *sermon and the text combined* take the place of the text. Whether and how the text *reappears* in the sermon itself is above all a question of the sermon's structuring. But the decisive steps regarding text interpretation and reception are taken at an earlier stage. There are a number of factors which influence this process and which have to be taken into account.

---

of course, comes close to his own theological principles. Instead he often trusted, as his vivid language, rich in associations and his references to several biblical texts in one and the same sermon show, in "reliving the content" or in his own "inspired instinct" and – for the rest – relied on the Holy Spirit. Cf. on this K. Holl, 1932, 578, 569.

**313** L. C. Madonna (1994, 35), referring to the hermeneutics of Christian Wolff.

**314** In the aforementioned scheme of the elements, phases and situations of the sermon process (cf. Fig. 1, p. 4) this act belongs to Phase II or the "Situation I of the Preacher".

### 3.3.1 The Cooperation Model

**a) The Model of the Textual Worlds and the Different Instances of Author and Reader**

Highlighting the problems of primarily historical or kerygmatic approaches to the meaning of the text does not mean that preachers are left to themselves in the attempt to interpret a text. The historical author remains available to the reader as "the text's internal author" *under the conditions set by the text.* This means that in the process of reception, readers encounter various accompanying instances which support them in exploring the fictitious world portrayed and narrated in the text, in becoming a witness to conversations and observing certain events.[315]

This, however, presupposes that readers are prepared to get involved with the reading behavior demanded by the text, i.e. are not merely seeking for certain hidden theological conclusions or posing historical questions to the text. Just as the author takes on various roles in the text, the reader and interpreter are equally expected to take on different roles. The following synoptic overview (c.f. Fig. 8) introduces the terminology used in this context.[316]

---

**315** In Fig. 9 (p. 124), the Model of the Textual Worlds, I refer to and summarize concepts that were originally developed for the analysis of narrative texts (cf. e.g. W. Schmid, 1973, 23–29). In the meantime models of this kind have been used in various forms for other genres (e.g. letters and reports), whereby the author is *always* assumed to have an "idea" of his readers and to adapt his text accordingly.

**316** Cf. p. 122f. On the origin and differentiation of the concepts referred to above cf. W. Engemann, 2003a, 121–126. The explications on the author and reader mainly refer to the works of W. Schmid (1973), H. Link (1976) and W. Iser (1976).

| 1. Text-external level | | |
|---|---|---|
| **Historical Author** | **Historical World** | **Historical Reader** |
| Actual author as a historical person/group of people | Real world in which the author is writing his text | Real reader as an empirical person/group of people |
| **2. Text-internal levels and their respective instances** | | |
| **Authorial Instances (A)** | **Worlds of the Text (W)** | **Reader Instances (R)** |
| **A 1: Implied Author** | **W 1: Portrayed World** | **R 1: Implied Reader** |
| Literary version of the writer; an abstraction reduced to the authorship of the text | A draft by the writer; an abstract situation of communication connected to a reduction of reality; reveals values and standards of A1. It is about the world as it can be historically *portrayed* on the basis of academic research. <br> *Examples:* A world in which particular roles are assigned to Romans, Pharisees, tax collectors, in which there are groups of followers or disciples and certain, constantly recurring social and political conflicts etc. | Imagined reader, in today's language one could also speak of a "virtual" reader. The act of reading preordained in the text, the structure the text needs in order to be realized. |
| **A 2: Narrator** | **W 2: Narrated World** | **R 2: Fictitious Reader** |
| A creation of the author; voice of the author; fictitious author | A fictitious situation of communication; a world in which everything that is narrated is possible. Other than the "dead" portrayed world, in which nothing takes place (yet) the narrated world is dynamic, it is "alive". <br> *Examples:* A world in which the different disciples have their own individual story, catch fish, walk on water, breakfast with Jesus etc. | As counterpart of the narrator a virtual representative of those to whom it is narrated and to whom particular points of view and judgments are suggested. |
| **A 3: Observer** | **W 3: Cited World** | **L 3: Witness** |
| Literary tool of omnipresence; the omnipresent observer of events who is always there when something happens or someone says something. | A world created through the speaking of the individual people; the world in the text. <br> *Examples:* The disciples at Emmaus in conversation with one another, Jesus' prayer in Gethsemane. | Role, which allows for simultaneity with the event together with the observer |

**Fig. 8:** The levels and instances of texts

1. *Historical Author:*
A real, historical author (also referred to as the "text's external author"[317]) living in particular circumstances has composed a text and structured it according to certain specific aspects. In the text itself he appears only implicitly and abstractly. The only conclusion which may be possible is to his state of mind at the time of writing.

2. *Implied Author (A 1) and the Portrayed World (W 1):*
The "implied author" is the historical person reduced to their function as author of a text – the literary version of the historical author. Through them the reader is confronted with a particular depiction of the world.[318] This portrayed world represents everything that has to be said about the time and situation then and refers to such things as customs and traditions, social roles and hierarchies, self-perceptions and taboos – in short to a variety of cultural rules.

3. *Narrator (A 2) and Narrated World (W 2):*
On the basis of the portrayed world the narrated world arises in which the omnipresent *instance of the narrator* (A 2) rules and circulates stories relating to real or fictional characters and events.

4. *Implied Reader (R 1) and Fictitious Reader (R 2):*
As part of this construction of a narrated world, the narrator imagines potential readers or listeners, which are correspondingly referred to as "implied readers" (R 1). The narrator takes them by the hand and leads them into a world in which everything tellable exists. This enables the implied readers to a level of *simultaneity with the persons acting.* Hence the readers are faced with the same decisions as the text's characters.

5. *Observer (A 3) and Witness (R 3) on the Level of the Cited World (W 3):*
Accordingly as a third authorial instance an observer can be figured out in the text (A 3), who is always present when the story's characters speak or think. *Through the observer the readers become fellow-observers or witnesses* who see everything the observer allows them to see (R 3). Thus, one can finally distinguish a cited world (W 3), the traces of which are occasionally inserted into the narrated world. Such a world appears when e.g. two of the characters talk about something which lies beyond the world portrayed or narrated in the text itself.

Fig. 9 illustrates the hierarchy of the above-mentioned textual worlds and of the different roles of authors and readers:

---

**317** H. Link, 1976, 16.
**318** H. Link. 1976, 21f., 34.

**Fig. 9:** Hierarchy of the textual worlds in relation to the instances of author and reader

## b) Example for Explanation of the Textual Worlds and Instances of Author Respectively Reader

In what follows, the nature of these textual worlds and instances shall be illustrated with an example from the Old Testament: Isa 40:1–11, a sermon text for the third Sunday in Advent. I deliberately choose what is not a particularly narrative text in order to show that the above-mentioned categories apply in principle to all sorts of text.

*Level 1:* The *historical world* of the text is Israel's period of exile at the end of the second half of the 6th century BCE. "Jerusalem" is an epitome for everyone who was deported from the city in 586 BCE. But to "Jerusalem" also belong those who – after 586 – fled from the city and are now oppressed in other parts of what was once their own country.

Imminent change is heralded to the exiles – their return from captivity. In order to understand the text in its historical significance, one must know of Israel's general issues with what home actually is, as well as the significance of the "Promised Land" and its history. The text is spoken at a time long after the expulsion. The exiles have perhaps come to terms with their situation to a certain extent. Many will have given up hope of returning home from captivity. From a historical perspective the text is thus to be comprehended as the encouraging appeal of Deutero-Isaiah not to lose hope of an intervention by God and a liberating return.[319] The prophet encourages the people in exile (and this might be the resume of a sermon based *solely* on this insight) to count on God's intervention and – as a consequence – on their return. This prospect is experienced as consolation.

*Level 2:* The *world portrayed* in the text is the world Deutero-Isaiah built against the background of the historical situation. It represents his perception of reality and contains the components the author needs to create the meaning of the text, to build up the stage for the actions and utterances of its characters:

To this world belong (1) a God who forgives sin, (2) a people who is described as "his people", (3) the preparing of a highway as was usually done for the journeys of high-ranking personalities or troop movements, (4) "all people" (in older versions and in German the reading here is "flesh"), obviously an epitome for referring to other nations, (5) "withering grass", (6) "the everlasting Word of God", (7) a "shepherd" who takes care of his lambs and much else. – On the level of these components we can explain what the text actually describes and the means by which the writer stages his representation. He needs a reader who is prepared to engage with this "scenario". In order to grasp the meaning of this world "conceptual exegesis" proves particularly fruitful. It reveals how the text is illustrated and what it shows: That God is like a shepherd who gathers his own people like lambs and desires to protect them from further threats, and that the Word of this God, unlike "flesh" and "grass", lasts forever.

The *narrated world* reveals in detail *what* actually happens on the stage set up at the level of the portrayed world and *how* it happens – in short, everything possible: The hope of "forgiveness of sin" and of an "end of bondage" circulates and catches on. Yet what is required is something which is literally "trail-blazing". In sharing the deportees' feeling of feebleness whilst reading, our own courage might equally sink.

---

**319** I am well aware that by deciding on this interpretation I can capture only *one* of the obvious historical meanings. One could, of course, relate the historical significance of the text more emphatically to the difficult question of the author ("Deutero-Isaiah").

But according to the narrator it is God himself who prepares that trail – ignoring every mountain or valley. (From this I must conclude that we – the people in the text and myself – merely over-hear what the prophet hears, and that, therefore, it is not we who are the recipient of God's "command"; it is only narrated as an 'arrangement between heavenly beings'.) The prophet hes-itates, and so do I with him, finding it hard to understand all of this. Meanwhile, it turns out that the perception of the intended use of the road was wrong: it is not, as is customary, meant for the use of the ruler but for the people. The homecoming – under the eyes of a large number of spectators, including enemies (verse 5b) – appears to be a safe project soon to be realized.

*Level 3:* The third text-internal level, the *cited world*, contains words spoken by different 'persons': "Comfort, comfort my people [...]." In verses 1 and 2, both speaker and addressees appear to be heavenly beings. In verses 3–5, another voice is heard: "In the wilderness prepare the way of the LORD [...]." In verse 6, the prophet realizes that he himself is directly addressed. Verses 7–8 appear to be part of the response to "the voice." Finally, the prophet himself bursts out: "Have you heard, Zion, herald of good tidings [...]." (9–10) The reader comes to witness a conversation which takes place on several levels and in several places.

The readers can, for instance, "overhear" the voices calling out in heaven; they can witness the appointment of the prophet; they can observe the prophet's entrancement in Jerusalem: their role as an observer allows them this privileged view. Unmediated interpretation can as "easily" be applied to this text as to all other sorts of texts. It will latch onto the text's best 'nuggets'; it will declare "comfort, comfort my people" to be the text's volition, and it will cut straight to "the many great and small crises in our everyday lives in which we require the comfort brought by this text." Yet is it really necessary to use this 'exotic' text to recount any number of day-to-day distresses and thus the multifaceted situations of comfort in our lives, in order to attain a more precise concept of living by faith?

## c) Conclusions

Now, what are the consequences of these considerations for interpreting the text? First of all it is imperative to point out that the text's meaning cannot be sought on merely one of the mentioned levels *alone*. The textual worlds outlined represent a symbiotic whole. Only *together* they determine the unique individuality of the text and the inner distinctiveness of its meaning. The hermeneutic approaches outlined in I.3.2.3 represent various forms of the problematic attempt to get by with only *one* of these textual worlds. While unmediated interpretation often contents itself with looking at the cited world, historical interpretations tend to explain all texts on their historical level and the rather constrictive perspective of kerygmatic solutions often merely refers to what is depicted in the text (images of God, values and norms etc.). From what I have observed, it is the level of the *narrated* world, which arises in the narrative process in the first place and which is of great importance for the text's functioning and the internal plausibility of its assertions, that is most often neglected in the process of discerning the text's meaning.

If, however, we intend to understand the text on more than *one* level it is not enough to – after having recognized the *intentio auctoris* – verbalize a kerygma or choose a suitable catchphrase from the cited world as the motto of the sermon. Cooperation with the text first and foremost requires allowing oneself to be accompanied by the text while working on the sermon: Preachers must read the text several times (particularly when they think to know it) in order to rehearse the expected roles. Those who engage with the text, and whose past and future exegetical work does not impede their ability to draw from the text itself everything which is necessary for their comprehension, will find that their reading is de-automated. They are prepared to *read a new text*, anticipating *what they have not yet read* and retrospectively correcting *what they have already read*.[320] "Those who fail to re-read are obliged to read the same story everywhere."[321] Considering the many stereotypes appearing in Christian sermons (Christ in the function of representative, justification by faith etc.) it is important to pay careful attention *to the text itself* in which God's relationship to humanity is precisely not treated stereotypically.[322]

This, however, is not yet a sufficiently adequate description of what the act of cooperation actually means. Cooperation presupposes that particular precautions are taken as for text and readers becoming equally involved in the process of interpretation. For instance, it implies repeated reading as the repeated encounter of text and reader, by means of which the "text's intention" and the "reader's expectation" give rise to a meaning which can neither be read already in the text itself nor be drawn straightaway into it by the preacher. In order to prevent us from falling prey to our initial understanding of the text, Klaus Weimar recommends confronting the text with somewhat "foolish" Why? and What for? questions and answering them in our own words – i.e. precisely *not* in the language of the text.[323] This could reveal certain important aspects which can be traced back both to the text and to the reader's initiative.[324]

---

**320** Cf. K. Weimar, 1993, 166–168.

**321** R. Barthes, 1974, 16.

**322** The popular *Sermon for the Year* publications in the 17th and 18th centuries, to mention only one example of the leveling down of biblical texts, dealt with one and the same subject a whole year long, Sunday after Sunday, and – without fail – referred to the predetermined Early Church readings (cf. M. Schian, 1912, 16f.). Needless to say, with such interpretation the text had hardly any chance to play a part of its own in the sermon, let alone to contradict the *intentio lectoris* (i.e.the attitude and expectation of the reader).

**323** Cf. K. Weimar, 1993, 170–177.

**324** Cf. the "Dialektik von Protektion und Protest" [The dialectics of defense and protest] as regards the preacher's attitude towards the text, in W. Engemann, 1992d, 169f.

Let us get back to Isa 40:1–11, and let us ask ourselves what it means not to instantly demand from it a message which we can pass on or turn into a directive. What does it mean (1) to ask the text those questions which relate to the motives, to the argumentation, and its objectives, and (2) to look for answers which may be given in today's language and which may be located in our contemporary world, yet which can be viewed as a result of text examination and which would not be possible without it?

### 1.  What is the text talking about?
The text tells us about a gigantic, unstoppable move. We read a story about coming home. As readers we shall become witnesses of a grandiose return which affects the people as well as their God. They come together again. It tells us about a 'reunification'. But the narrator also presents us with a skeptic, a prophet who doubts change, who seems to wearily wave this aside and expresses objections (verses 6b-8a) in which the dubious nature of political promises seems to be reflected. The text confronts us with the encounter of a utopian dream and reality and how Utopia is favored in the end: The homecoming-fever in which the text appears to be written corresponds to a reality. The reunion of God and his people is underway. The text holds fast to this as a perception of reality.

### 2.  Why does this text exist?
This text exists because the time is ripe, because the one who has the power to change the situation no longer wants to look at the sorrow of the people. This text exists because similar events actually happen: oppression, deportation, exile. This text exists because someone feels concerned, because someone raises his voice and does not withhold what he sees coming.

### 3.  Where could working on this text lead us?
While reading we might wonder why people care *so much* for their home. And we might wonder why God for his part appears to fixate on certain locations for living together with his people. At first we might not be able to understand this; but through repeated reading we encounter "exile in our own lives", are reminded of the necessity of a repeated "departure back", back from a world of estrangement from ourselves and from God, from a world in which we must always be the ones whom others expect us to be etc.

### 4.  Why should we confront today's congregation with this text?
Referring to this text presupposes that the analogies we have 'seen' in the course of repeated readings can give rise to a sermon dealing with our day-to-day reality within the horizon of a specifically Christian tradition. A sermon on this text can make the listeners become aware of further, more concrete analogies regarding the "exile in their own lives" as well as "returning home" and "living together". Consequently, we will look for correspondingly structured stories on the topic of "returning home from exile" in the Bible[325] and, above all, in life.

---

[325] The "Prodigal Son", too, does not believe that he can expect his father to respect the person he assumes to be. His path into the foreign land was also a path of estrangement from himself and from his father. His skepticism about his being-able-to-return-home is thwarted. Cf. also Jesus' statements about the "many dwelling-places" (John 14:2) and, more generally, the inner coherence of the aspects "stranger", "dwelling", "homecoming" and the God – humankind relationships they reflect in the Bible.

The manner of reading which develops through repeatedly going through a text does not, however, always result in the same understanding of the text. In our endeavors to understand the text in our time we are well aware that we approach it with images from the world we live in, with our own experiences and our personal way of believing and hence read it as if through a film. An interpretation that is likewise relevant and understandable in the respective present presupposes that the text facilitates as well as requires various ways of looking at it.

The preacher as the interpreter of biblical texts is consequently not only faced with the task of tracking down what the text says *explicitly*; the exegete's efforts to create sense through their own interpretation furthermore involve bringing to light in their own words what has been necessarily (!) concealed in the text. The author, who naturally had to limit himself in the selection of what to write down, has thus arranged the text and its respective worlds in a way which allows the reader to infer what has remained unsaid – but nonetheless been touched upon in what has been written.[326]

In this context R. Barthes speaks of the "pleasure in the text"[327] which transforms the reader into an "ideal reader". U. Eco states that – in view of the potential wealth of meaning which is to be expected from the encounter between text and reader – it would be best if readers suffered an "ideal insomnia", for then they could question the text in re-reading *ad infinitum*.[328] This wish strikingly resembles the biblical version of the likewise sleepless, never finishing, ideal reader: "Blessed is the one [...] whose delight is in the law of the LORD and who meditates on his law day and night" it says prominently in Psalm 1.

Therefore to cooperate with a text has fundamentally to do with being prepared *to portray the different reading roles* required on the various levels of the text. Only those will be able to bring to light what is hidden in the text, who – as a rule on the level of the narrated world – confront the indistinct passages in the text and fill them with elements of their own world of life and faith. Usually a text contains "a whole spectrum of possible fillings for the hazy passages" which is why "interpretations that suppress the plurality of the concretisations [...] are rightly criticized for missing the point of what has been recounted"[329].

As a consequence, understanding a text requires tentatively occupying the enclaves provided in the text with one's own questions and expectations. These enclaves or empty places are to be assessed as being the "central elements of exchange in the interaction of text and reader". They "regulate the reader's

---

**326** Cf. W. Iser, 1994, 264f.
**327** R. Barthes, 1974, 20.
**328** U. Eco, 1987, 35.
**329** W. Schmid, 1973, 35f.

imaginative activity, which is at this point employed within the terms set by the text"[330].

In the interpretation of Isa 40 above, these activities expected from the reader were only hinted at. A further attempt would have to consist in occupying the text – on the basis of the understanding already obtained – with further, analogously structured life situations and subsequently in looking at how they appear in the text, which perspectives they develop,[331] how they possibly change, which roles they open up for the reader. The implied reader is supposed to act as an agent and assumes a new appearance as the present-day historical reader. The structure of the text corresponds comparably to the structures of actions or events which are indispensible for the realization of the meaning of the text in the time of the reader.

A successful reinforcement of the aforementioned arguments is provided in Georg Lämmlin's study, "Die Lust am Wort und der Widerstand der Schrift"[332]. This study, which focuses on the homiletic significance of the reception of biblical texts, reveals on the example of the "re-reading of the Psalter" that the insights outlined above are not only relevant for the understanding of the Jewish-Christian tradition on a text level. A cooperative handling of texts is likewise important for the understanding of situations, for the sermon's situational relevance comes into play not least because of a particular way of dealing with the text itself. This certainly presupposes that the preacher respects the text's own requirements of reception and enters into the process of reading the text's construction- or anticipation-space which is nurtured from and geared towards situations. Lämmlin states that through the specific mode of text-reader-relationship described by Wolfgang Iser, interactions might be set in motion, which allow the sermon process to become an equally text-related and situationally appropriate event. As a result of his analysis the author presents a "model of reading" which aims beyond text comprehension and coping-with-situations in as much as it challenges the believing subject in the course of this cooperation to react to what they have perceived, so to speak 'make themselves topical' and possibly to develop themselves further. "The subject wins themselves from the text [...] whilst reading by directing their intention to understand to the significance of the text rather than to themselves."[333]

### 3.3.2 The Analogy Model

In the previous explications we have spoken of "analogies" in various ways – of analogies the reader recognizes between textual structures and structures of

---

**330** W. Iser, 1994, 266.
**331** W. Iser considers texts to be able to make the reader the bearer of their own (i.e. the texts') perspectives. In exposing themselves to the textual worlds "readers are provided the opportunity to occupy the viewpoint which has been established in the text" but does not appear in the text itself (cf. W. Iser, 1994, 61–63).
**332** Cf. G. Lämmlin, 2002.
**333** Loc. cit., 139f.

events and actions in their own life, of analogies for "exile", for the "return" and the "living again in unity", for the experience of being allowed to exist without having to justify or explain oneself. Anyone who talks of analogies with regards to the significance of ancient texts for the present age, assumes that similarities, commonalities and relationships actually exist between the situation or experiences which gave rise to the texts on the one hand and the situation or experiences of the reader on the other.[334] In order to see or establish analogies, questions such as the following are helpful:[335]

1. On the *level of the historical world*: Is there any common ground between the situation addressed in the text and the situation in which my sermon will be delivered?
2. On the *level of the world portrayed in the text* we have to ask: Are there any similarities regarding the attitudes to particular issues, problems, life, or to oneself? Is there any correspondence concerning the conditions or disruptions of the relationship to God between the text on the one hand and the experience of today's recipients on the other?
3. Questions *relating to the narrated world* might be e.g.: Is the basic pattern of the story which the text tells repeated in the present? Which people, which conflicts, tensions, prospects of solution must in this case replace the corresponding references provided in the text?
4. Finally in respect of *the cited world* we have to ask: What meaning do the spoken sentences (promises, warnings, confessions etc.) assume if they are repeated "untranslated" in the analogous context? Is this meaning in continuity with the text's intention I have previously worked out? If not: How would I have to remodel it so that – given the limited analogies – something *appropriate is said* which in turn corresponds in its effect with the effect described in the text?

*The construction of analogies has nothing to do with equalization,* which is why the above-mentioned questions can be equally effectively applied when asking for respective *differences*. It is precisely because of the differences between the two units of the targeted comparison that searching for analogies becomes necessary. It is a matter of the fact that, in spite of all their variedness, situations, actions, attitudes are comparable and reveal common ground *in some particular respect*. The characteristics, attitudes, or stereotype actions, which are found to be similar in a contrasting juxtaposition of the respective units, are called *analogon*.[336] In the course of such juxtapositions, however, not only analogies between

---

334 I use the terms "analogy" and "analogous" here deliberately in their usual meaning in everyday language, i.e. denoting "equivalence" or "equivalent" and "similarity" or "similar". In a homiletic context such analogies appear to be particularly relevant when they are established between *situations* and in connection with *relationships* (esp. interpersonal relationships but also between people and "objects", events and conditions, between humanity and "God").

335 On this cf. the Synopsis in Fig. 8 (p. 122).

336 For example in a sermon on Isa 40:1–11 the "identity crisis" (along with the corresponding theological and anthropological implications), which is equally experienced both, by the people of the exile as well as by today's readers, represents such an analogon.

the "historical situation behind the text" and the "historical situation today" are expected to be explored, but also between the world portrayed, narrated, or even merely cited in the text and the day-to-day reality of the congregation.

Furthermore, the Analogy Model is to be clearly distinguished from the two other strategies of interpretation: focusing on a kerygma, on the one hand, is to be considered in some way as an act of "digital" disclosure. The meaning of a highly complex text is represented in the shape of an abstract sentence. It thus focuses (merely) on the *result* of the preceding textual work, on a truth, so to speak, filtered out rather than on how the text as a whole can become an aid to faith and comprehension for the reader. Analogous interpretation needs the text – to remain with the metaphor – in an unfiltered condition; for the text reveals how, for what reasons, in what situations people come to what convictions, and under what conditions "God" can reach them, or under what conditions they begin to inquire about him. The parameters of the text are not insignificant for the plausibility of its message. Consequently we have to search for reasons, circumstances and attitudes in the text and in everyday life today which expose – at least to a certain extent – similarities regarding human self-perception as well as regarding people's life with others and their existence before God.

Attempts of unmediated interpretation, on the other hand, which largely ignore what is portrayed and narrated in the text, frequently result in pseudo-analogies. In such cases correspondences between the textual worlds and lifeworlds are not based on common features concerning a conflict situation or comparable possibilities of conflict resolutions[337] but are achieved through the isolated transfer of individual text passages to quite arbitrary life situations.

One particularly significant example for the forming of analogies which arise from cooperating with the text is what Scholasticism referred to as *analogia proportionalitatis*. This form of analogy it is not based on a mere, frequently rather short-sighted, parallelization of certain isolated statements or even only single terms occurring in the text with Christian *common sense*. It is a matter of "a relationship between two relationships"[338]. The interpreter consequently has to ask, for example, whether and in which way – I return to the previously introduced text of Isa 40:1–11 – one can speak, in view of the people's relationship to God or their attitude towards their exile (or to an imminent return), of *correspondences* regarding the listening congregation's *relationship* to God or regarding other factors which determine their current situation. This form of analogy construction has two advantages: First, since it is always a matter of a "relationship between relationships", "God" and "congregation" usually appear as constituents of an analogous relationship, and on the conditions of the text or the current situation, which always has to do with *concretions*. Second, this

---

**337** On the relevance of the category of conflict for the homiletic work (inter alia for the purpose of accentuating particular problems) see also D. Buttrick, 2007 as well as respective indications in this volume (p. 23, 59, 65f.).
**338** J. Track, 1978, 628.

form of analogy construction is based on adequately considering and hence bringing into sight *the particularities* of the contrasted situations or relationships, where required even in respect of their irrevocable differences.

Any attempt to establish a cogent sequence of text examination, situation analysis, analogy formation etc. will sooner or later reveal that those steps are hardly delimitable in practice– particularly for a theologian well experienced in text comprehension, who, as a rule, already knows the historical background of the individual texts and is not studying them for the first time. It seems, however, advisable to take particular steps before others, even if this implies having to adapt previous decisions in the face of new discoveries which potentially lead to corrections in the process of text interpretation. Against the background of the problems previously discussed in this chapter I suggest the following way of proceeding[339]:

*Step 1: Repeated Reading of the Text:* One should not immediately proceed to exegesis after the first reading. Instead, the text should be read a second or third or more times in order to approach it with as 'little previous knowledge' as possible. I ask the text what it has to say, why and what for I should know this, what it has to tell me and allow *it* – not a commentary or a dictionary, not a sermon meditation – to answer these questions while I am reading it. This is how cooperation with the text begins.

Naturally I do not have to deny my exegetical knowledge in this process. When reading a text, theologians are always "primed" by their training. A sound basic knowledge of the conditions of the authors and addressees of the biblical texts makes it easier for them to answer at least some of the 'Wh'-questions: e.g. "Who is speaking here?" It is, however, important not to stick to the very first answer ("Paul") but to continue to dwell on the "Who?"-question for a while. This shows for instance: Someone who is in prison is writing here, reckoning apparently with his execution but nevertheless feeling himself "self-sufficient" etc. (cf. e.g. Phil 4:10–20). Anyone who does not perceive the reading of the text to be their own task or even reads it up in the commentary along with the corresponding explanations will hardly be able to see the facets of text comprehension which lie beyond the scope of the exegetical commentary, which mainly focuses on the historical and portrayed textual world.

---

**339** In the following I will neither describe a "way to the sermon" (which can certainly not be achieved in the course of dealing with the text alone) nor will I offer another detailed method of text interpretation in addition to those already established in the framework of historical-critical and social-scientific exegesis or developed as psychological, empirical or creative methods (cf. the overview provided in J. Ziemer, 1990, 225–235). The following rather describes a *way of dealing* with texts, which should, in principle, always be applied, regardless of the actual method of text interpretation applied, and refers to tasks and questions one always has to deal with in interpreting a text.

*Step 2: Taking on the Reading Roles required by the different Textual Worlds*: I attempt to specify the results of my reading and extend them where appropriate by studying the various textual worlds and by distinguishing between the historical, the portrayed, the narrated and the cited world. The aim of this approach is to become aware of what has been left open in what the text has said, too, and to occupy its enclaves tentatively with observations, experiences, expectations and questions arising from the reality of my own life.

The text presumes *my initiative* which I have to take *under the conditions set by the text*, for the text itself is not going to change. This enables me, for instance, to become aware of how a fragment of the story of my life is retold in the story of the text, how a spoken sentence from the cited world becomes audible as a 'word for myself'. This process opens up wholly new possibilities of understanding which go far beyond the answers initially found when posing the "Wh"-questions mentioned above.

*Step 3: Historical-Critical Exegesis and other Academic Forms of Access to a Text:* As a rule, this step allows for exploring *one* of the textual worlds more precisely. Historical-critical exegesis deepens particularly the historical and portrayed level of the text. Psychological or bibliodramatical methods are ideally suited for the better understanding of what happens *between* the characters of the narration, how they feel, what moves them and the extent to which the 'solution' becoming apparent in the text is connected to the experience of freedom. The goal of this step is *to further deepen* the understanding of the text in a certain area, *to gain* new aspects of interpretation, but also to *reject* previously proposed ideas, perspectives and analogies because they run entirely contrary to the scientifically ascertainable data for reconstructing the text's meaning or at least do not agree with them.

*Step 4: Sounding out the Lines of Interpretation:* Steps 1–3 represent a process of discovering, deepening and rejecting interpretations which are in fact different from one another but nevertheless correlate to the extent that they are actually all possible *under the conditions set by the text*, exegetically plausible and theologically appropriate. It may not be possible to attain the *one* kerygma from the study of a text, but it is still vital for the further process of text examination, particularly in view of the *different lines of meaning*, to establish a 'temporary focus' which is conceivable under the conditions set by the text. On this understanding it is not only permissible but even necessary to provide statements such as "In this text we are told that ...", or "The text deals with the experience of ...", or "Reading this text one is confronted with the insight that ..."

*Step 5: Sounding out the Analogies:* Readers will hardly be able to fight against devising analogies from the first moment of receiving the text. As they move on the various text levels, certain pictures, scenes and events will immediately surface. First, the analogies which had initially been formed associatively were in part consolidated, in part rejected and in part expanded (steps 1–3); then they were put into correlation and focussed under convergent perspectives (step 4). Now it is essential to examine *the relevance* of the analogies taken into consideration so far in regards to the contemporary context of the listeners' day-to-day reality.[340]

### 3.3.3 Functions of the Text in the Homiletic Process

#### a) The Confronting Function of the Text

The term "confrontation" takes on meanings such as "encounter", "resistance", "dispute". Since this term is used to denote a certain function of the text, we shall first of all take a look at analogies to those experiences which initially gave rise to the text: In the events and encounters which in biblical times were interpreted as an "experience of God" and understood as "revelation", people were obviously confronted with a reality which affected their existence in a fundamental or earth-shaking way and which stood in tension with their habitual everyday experiences. Their ideas of God, their future expectations, their self-appraisal and moral concepts were all of a sudden called into question, shattered and changed. This is what the texts testify to. They have emerged through such a confrontation and are to be viewed as attempts to express the unsought encounter with God in stories and songs, in letters and parables, with pictures and metaphors. Readers of biblical texts face an alien reality, which, paradoxically, is presented to them as if it could be their own; and in the course of the reading experience it turns out that in one or another aspect it actually *becomes* their own.

Confrontation in this sense implies the challenge to take position: on a yet unknown reality, of which we perhaps disapprove, which probably causes us to amend our judgements and actions. It is the examination of the text which forces us to subject our own standpoint to critical inspection, and to attend to questions and perspectives which would not have come to our attention without the text.

Manfred Josuttis speaks of a text's "creative function" in this context: "The confrontation with the alien text provides the challenge as well as the impetus for the preacher's own speech. The

---

340 The criteria, which are to be taken into account in this final step of homiletic analogy formation, will be dealt with in more detail in the context of the question on the listener as well as the sermon's situational relevance (cf. I.6 p. 259–329).

hermeneutical act is consequently in fact to be understood as a dialogical encounter, in analogy to the open conversation with a living dialog partner. If this conversation amounts to more than a reciprocal exchange of acknowledged values, [...] a creative extension of both, the life-horizon and the linguistic competence as a critical surmounting of previous barriers to awareness and expression occurs."[341]

By referring to a text while preparing a sermon, preachers increase the probability that the confrontation with the "conditions of God's kingdom" expected in the communication of faith benefits from the concreteness of a situation. For the text does not simply ventilate theological concepts or ideas; it formulates *faith under the conditions of a specific situation* and may aim at very specific *changes* of a situation. In texts we are frequently confronted with models as to how situations and the acting people might change. Without a text, the preacher would probably only consider answers for constructed situations which he is familiar with – without having the chance to encounter the 'real' questions.

### b) The Creatorial Function of the Text

A discussion of the various elements of the text's creatorial function can be based, for the most part, on the reader's task of *cooperation with the text* as discussed above: the text creates, in a certain sense, its reader. Dealing with the text is a creative process – not only because it requires both expert knowledge and imagination on part of the recipient. The text's own creatorial function is manifest in the way it causes its readers to become aware of themselves as another.

Basically this is always the case when we read 'good literature'. What makes biblical texts so special is neither their structure nor their 'design'; this is what they share in various respects with other letters, songs, stories, parables, prayers etc. The specificity of biblical texts lies much more on the level of their special, entangling contents, their intentions, their claims, their radical orientation on humanity's relation to existence. This means that biblical texts can *also* be read like other texts, in order to gain aesthetic pleasure and *an enjoyable reading experience*. Their ethical values can be studied and be corrected in one's own opinion, making the reader a *learner*. This is, as mentioned before, also part of the intention of other literary texts.[342] Biblical texts – and naturally the tradition of their interpretation – have a specific claim: the reader must to some extent become a witness to what is reported, and the cooperation with the texts ought

---

**341** M. Josuttis, 1983, 389.
**342** On the controversy on the function of biblical and other literary texts cf. W. Engemann, 2000a, 233–238.

to be experienced by the reader as comforting, liberating, encouraging, etc.[343] The recipients are supposed to view the texts as existentially pertaining to themselves; the texts' purpose is to help them to better understand what is at stake with regard to their own lives.

The definition of this function of the text as "creatorial" is not to be confused with what Josuttis refers to as "creative function". There are, however, parallels between the "creatorial function" examined here and the "authoritative function" discussed by Josuttis.[344] The idea that the reading or hearing of a text 'qualifies' the listener or reader in some respect is warranted. However, justifying the text's authority in this way is an *intratextual argument* which does by no means substantiate the *extratextual premise* – rightly criticized by Josuttis – according to which the text gains authority from the mere fact of its existence.

### c) The Confirming Function of the Text

Reading biblical texts also means reassurance. Certainly, many readers of the Bible would name this their number-one function. By reading those texts, people find themselves affirmed in what they believe and eagerly hope for. Through the "written word" their doubts can be dissipated, and skepticism be eliminated. In the text someone bears witness to their conviction – together with the reader or interpreter, albeit not simultaneously – that their faith has helped them.

The reader does not need to be able to repeat the witness, or to duplicate the experience in the exact same way. The purpose of the text is not to make them a follower of the author. A confirming effect merely requires, or implies respectively, that readers recognize *common identity markers* between themselves, the author of the text and those who have familiarized them with the text. Anyone who reads Scripture learns that finding answers to their questions, overcoming their problems, or gaining a sense of orientation can be based on answers which have already been found and on the experience of an overcome affliction.

Such a definition of the text includes certain aspects which, according to Josuttis, belong to the "communicative" or the "identity-establishing" function of the text. Josuttis' description of the latter refers to the socio-psychological argument that "in our culture, human communities" are constituted "through their reference to written documents."[345] Initially he explains the communicative aspect of the text in the same way: "It [the text] creates community." At a later point, however, he states more precisely: the text proves to be a "platform" of communication "on

---

**343** A. Horn (2009) suggests some "hopefully relieving" exercises for dealing with the text which make sure that these claims are, in fact, implemented. Cf. especially his remarks on the "Prediger als homo ludens" [The preacher as homo ludens] in: A. Horn, 2009, 148–150.
**344** M. Josuttis, 1983, 387f.
**345** Loc. cit., 392.

which the homiletic act as an endeavor to communicate the topical relevance of the Christian faith can develop"[346].

### d) On the Question of Introducing the Text in the Sermon

In the preaching event itself the text fulfills the above-mentioned functions only in *combination with the sermon*. It is therefore indispensable to examine the question of how it should be included in the sermon address.[347] Reading out the text at the beginning of the sermon, as is usual, reduces its functional repertoire to a minimum, particularly when it comes to difficult texts, the essence of which is only understood after repeated reading. Merely heard once, such texts tend to not even fulfill an informing function; rather, they are perceived by the listeners as an *opening ritual to the sermon*.

A text's explanatory function for the content of the sermon as well as its comprehensibility is increased by using it later in the sermon by carefully elaborating on the situation for the later location of the text, by plausibly going over the questions which are touched upon by the text – or expounding the answers questioned by the text.

If the listener is prepared for the text in the course of the sermon, the text immediately begins to speak and becomes "useful" in the sense that it takes up a place in the listener's understanding and becomes capable of guiding his actions. Placed at the very end of the sermon it can all of a sudden illuminate the spiritual horizon of the sermon and take on an *assuring* function by accompanying the listeners in their everyday lives. An easily comprehensible text, such as, for instance, a narrative text, can certainly stand at the beginning of the sermon or take on different functions within the sermon, respectively. If it is comprehensible, standing at the beginning of the sermon it often obtains a *confronting* function. A text's *creatorial* function is particularly fulfilled when different points of view are applied for analyzing the text in the course of the sermon. It is then that it can convey to the listeners their own respective conceptions of the role(s) it suggests to them – on all its different levels, as it were, or through insight into the connections of its 'worlds' (see above, 3.3.1.a, p. 121–124).

This does not mean that there is a set of laws simply to be followed. However, every preacher should be in a position to make the text multifunctional through purposeful contextualization. It does not suffice to merely cite the text at some

---

346 Loc. cit., 390.
347 Cf. two examples for bringing the text into play at the end of the sermon and respective homiletic considerations on the text's function in: W. Engemann, 2001b.

point or other in the sermon, hoping that the text itself will provide its own desired reception.

## 3.4 On the Category of the "Biblical Sermon"[348]

### 3.4.1 Requirements of a Biblical Sermon

How is text reference to be defined for a sermon which should correspond to the category of a "biblical sermon"[349]? From what we have seen above it is not enough to settle for the rather vague answer *"that the biblical text should take center stage in the sermon"*[350], not even if we add "to make the biblical text the site of insight in the sermon, waiting to see what may come from it"[351].

According to J. P. Grevel's assessment, "Bible-oriented sermon theories"[352] only include the approaches of Christian Möller, Horst Hirschler and Friedrich Mildenberger, which, incidentally are all based on similar misunderstandings. He states that what has been concluded from Ernst Lange's approach for the practice of preaching is "to give up exegesis of the text as a critical distance in sermon composition" (38) – a grotesque allegation. The semiotic method is even considered to be in danger of becoming the "deus ex machina in the guise of theological power interests" (54) – to mention merely two instances which direct the author to deny his seal of approval which is "Bible-oriented Homiletics". Based on his preconceptions of "Bible-oriented Homiletics" the author mourns – with reference to the aesthetic-of-reception discourse in Homiletics – the alleged "questioning" of the authority of the text by corresponding approaches.[353] He thus does not do justice to this discourse's subtle differentiation, and its enthusiasm for and attentiveness to the text. Grevel identifies a "relativization" of the text through the homiletic impetus of reception's aesthetic. He thinks that it is possible to overcome this "relativization" by the use of Karl Barth's doctrine of light ("Lichterlehre", cf. 56). This suggestion is fundamentally faulty: Grevel construes homiletic oppositions (e.g. a "relative", or an "absolute" understanding of the text) which do not apply to the discourse he refers to. He fails to scrutinize his own premises, which bar him from regarding the *theological grounds* of a culture of dealing with biblical texts that includes aesthetics-of-reception and semiotic approaches. The accusation that the biblical text is relativized is not least the result of an unsolved relationship between the *kind of authority* of biblical texts as literary texts, the talk of "God's Word" and the kind of authority of a contemporary testimony of faith in the form of a sermon (on this see below, 3.4.2).

---

**348** The following comments shall provide a summary and presuppose the reading of I.3.2 and I.3.3.

**349** Cf. my critical remarks on such definitory attempts above, p. 80f. (esp. footnote 217).

**350** This is what H. Hirschler regards as "a sharpening of the homiletic task" (1988, 18) to preach biblically; original emphasis.

**351** Ibid.

**352** J. P. Grevel, 2002, 30–37.

**353** Loc. cit., 41–51.

Where the text – as in Hirschler – is flatly proclaimed as the focal point of the sermon, the sermon runs the danger of becoming a more or less informative per-egrination: Just as a guide who leads Christian pilgrims to the holy sites in the Holy Land and informs them in a more or less expert way of what once happened there, the listeners are referred to this and that particular detail of the text – and thereby remain so far remote from everyday life as if they were actually on a real journey to the Holy Land.

If *the text* is simply declared to be the "site of insight" it is elevated to the true location of the homiletic event. The pivotal point and site of understanding, however, is, as has been repeatedly argued above, the day-to-day reality of the listeners. *Through the sermon* which *refers to a text*, they should be enabled to mediate afresh between tradition and (their own) situation.

In order for this to happen a different definition of the relationship between biblical tradition and sermon is required. The goal is not to make a text the focal point of the sermon, but to highlight the Bible as a resource for life. The sermon, therefore, does not run up to a text but is based on biblical tradition. What does this mean in detail?

1. First of all we need to point to a seeming paradox: *A biblical sermon must be a situation-related sermon,* for referring to biblical texts is a process which orig-inally starts out with the testimony of people in a particular situation which is only appropriately interpreted in the context of a specific situation and is again directed at experiences (of faith) in concrete situations (cf. Fig. 1, p. 4).

2. A sermon is "biblical" neither *already* nor *first* through referring to a text in Scripture but through reviving the communication of the gospel and by calling upon this tradition. This includes that people take a step into freedom, expe-rience that they are loved and valued, can joyfully and confidently turn to others and their own lives and are strengthened in their own self-esteem.[354]

3. A sermon is biblical if it situates the text in history: the preacher's testi-mony succeeds the testimony of Scripture, and the preacher's testimony – the sermon – is a result of his encounter with the text. Contents, intentions, aspects and perspectives of the text are brought up in a new form and usually also in different concepts and images.

4. A sermon is biblical if it places itself deliberately in a process of tradition and interpretation and draws on experiences preserved in tradition as a source, corrective, and an assurance of its witness. It is not the aim of this way of relating to tradition to experience precisely *the same* as the authors and first addressees of biblical texts did or to be enabled to repeat their confessions

---

354 Cf. III.2.2.

verbatim but to reach *analogous* insights and experiences in the continuity of this tradition.

5. A sermon is biblical if it respects the special *conditions of the literary form* of the "Word of God", which – in the case of sermon texts – is presented to us in the form of written testimonies. A sermon which, for example, is based on only *one* of the aforementioned levels of the text[355] runs the risk of becoming unbiblical, despite extensive quotations, despite a kerygmatic reduction and despite all its historical discoveries.

6. A biblical sermon does not simply repeat what is written in the text. Its "biblicity" arises in that it speaks of the text's blank spaces, of what is necessarily withheld in the text but still granted to the readers. A biblical sermon consequently demands highly independently-reasoning and "headstrong"[356] preachers, who know precisely what they want to say and achieve, and why, with their concrete sermon on a particular Sunday.

## 3.4.2 The Authority of Scripture – a Hermeneutic Category

### a) Observations on the Experience of Authority

It is one of the biggest challenges of theological hermeneutics to do equal justice to both, the authority of tradition as well as the homiletic requirement of relevance. It is part of the homiletic art to deliver a sermon and deal with the text – which was neither intended to serve as a sermon text for this particular Sunday nor written at all for us today – in such a way that it becomes clear why this text from past times is just as relevant to the respective congregation with their experiences of the here and now.

This challenge becomes apparent already in the debate over the very *nature* of the authority of biblical texts: while students and pastors are certainly enlightened when it comes to the genesis of a letter, a hymn, or a parable, this is often later contrasted in the sermon, when single sentences of the text are "proclaimed" as the "Word of God" without any form of mediation or hermeneutic confrontation; proclamations they believe they must conform to, regardless of whether they make sense to them or not. Frequently it is the conviction that, in obedience to Scripture, one must "give an unvarnished account" of "what is written", which dominates the work with the text. This allegiance is readily justified with psychological assumptions and such as are to be found in the theory of communication

---

**355** Cf. above, Fig. 8 (p. 122) and Fig. 9 (p. 124).
**356** Cf. K.-H. Bieritz, 1998.

or with human deficiencies: "I dare not mention only the things which please me personally." "It is wrong to select only what is pleasant from God's Word and withhold what is unpleasant." "Faith doesn't exist to make us feel good." "Where if not in the worship service must one be allowed to do some straight talking?" In discussions of the background of such positions, corresponding premises become apparent, such as the view that the Scripture's authority is ultimately proven by the fact that it does not have to be relevant but "lays down the law" instead. (And the rules of evidence or relevance do not apply to the law, of course.)

In practice, of course, the act of experiencing and acknowledging authority usually echoes the experience of relevance. Authority arises, among other things, as a side effect of experiences of communication when something becomes accessible to us through someone else and is henceforth important to us. Experience shows that where authority is not achieved in the act of the communication event itself, it is all the more proclaimed, demanded or tentatively enforced, which may result in gestures of seeming obedience. In addition, authority loses its true character under force or pressure: the generally recognized result of its own effect.

It is a common and recurring misunderstanding that Scripture's significance is entirely and most importantly dependent on measures of updating the historical texts. This misunderstanding partially accounts for the interrelations between the appreciation of scriptural authority and the ways of dealing with its texts. However, hermeneutic procedures – like, for example, analogy formation– are, as was described above, far more complex. Having grasped the point of a biblical story does not just mean to affirm it or to simply do or think the same or to identify with the story's hero or heroine or even with God. What is decisive is whether preachers have grasped their text to such an extent that they can "leave" it with a changed view of things, can go beyond it, and are enabled to address the pressing questions of living by faith with the knowledge gained through the confrontation with the text – a text which has become their own, is coherent and hopefully relevant. This is something fundamentally different from the results of text "updates".

More generally speaking, to understand a biblical text means to come to see it *as a testimony of a particular concept of life and faith* – and in this sense naturally also as a wilful authority. Whether approaching the text in such a way, however, results in a salutary uncertainty and questioning, in an inevitable distancing, a surprising confirmation or whatever else varies from case to case. But whatever the case may be, a text does certainly not lose its authority if we disagree with it or if it shows us a way of coping with life which we today no longer wish to accept for ourselves.[357] It is precarious both for the authority of Scripture as well as for the relevance of the sermon if the essence of biblical texts is not understood as a testimony of faith of humans

---

357 As an example the call for practicing more radical or rigorous discipleship could be mentioned (Luke 14:25–35).

coping with life, as this makes it impossible *to see their authority in the credibility of their testimony*. Yet, biblical texts cannot achieve any theological significance, never mind become relevant to life, if it has not become plausible to what they witness as human texts, why they were written and what they were needed for, which core of experience, what faith determines them. This is the ground water of their authority. If one does not drill deep enough to get to this point, one can try to squeeze out all kinds of meanings from the texts without coming upon anything relevant.

### b) The Authority of Scripture as a Concept of Communication and a Hermeneutic Category

What constitutes the authority of biblical texts? Considering the origin of the term *auctoritas*, biblical texts have authority because they come from authors whose texts have proved to be credible and relevant. *Auctor* and *auctoritas*, author and authority do not only share the same linguistic root, they are, above all, substantially interconnected with each other: The term authority originally refers to an author who can be quoted, an author upon whom one falls back in order to substantiate one's own statements or interpretation. Such authorities were referred to particularly in political and judicial debates in which propositions as well as counter-propositions were supported by arguments *ex auctoritate*.[358] In political and legal day-to-day business this has remained the case ever since.

But the authority of what is cited turns out to be effective only if the voice of the author has already proved to be credible, relevant and well-founded in previous situations of communication. Consequently authority is, at heart, a phenomenon of communication and hence a hermeneutical category. It is an unenforceable *echo of the experience of respect* which can only be attained in communication processes, when listeners or readers not only comprehend *something* but *attain a new understanding of themselves in relation to something*. In this function, authority must constantly prove itself, otherwise "it loses itself", it "diminishes" and is only perceived as an arrogated authority upon which one must insist – because one does not "possess" it.

How does an understanding of Scripture's authority arise from all of this?[359]
1. The authority of biblical texts is the result of a hermeneutic process. In that its testimony is examined, found to be credible, understood and thereby *recognized in its relevance* it gains in authority.

---

**358** Cf. H. Lausberg, 1990, 102, 234–235. Here the terms "author" and "authority" are indiscernible. *De Auctoritate* means both, "on the basis of an authority" as well as "witnessed to by a well-respected author".
**359** Cf. also the summarizing theses in W. Engemann, 2014, 125f.

2.  Authority and relevance is ascribed to biblical texts all the more when they become comprehensible *as existentially relevant testimonies of human life and faith* instead of documents postulating rules or maxims which humanity just cannot adopt as their own. This applies particularly to communications which entail life-opening, liberating implications and, in consequence, become important and existentially relevant.

3.  Believers receive traditional texts and pass them on because they have good reasons for giving them a credit of trust and recognizing them as an authority. In the act of receiving and interpreting them, however, *they maintain the tradition and thereby become themselves a potential "authority"*.

4.  The authority of biblical texts is not achieved by approval, consent or merely accepting them as true. In the course of sermon preparation they claim to be recognized as a credible testimony, to be discerned as a valid pattern for living by faith. *As human testimonies of faith they are due the highest possible authority.* They still wring a statement from today's readers and listeners. This process, however, does not exclude but rather includes coming to one's own conclusions in the language of tradition, to a confession regarding one's own life lived by faith.

Consequently the testimonies written down in the Bible are, with all their authority, an "intermediate station" in the process of handing down faith. Greatly simplifying the many-facetted process of the tradition of faith it could be summarized as follows: After a story-teller has told a story (pre-biblical tradition), an author has written it down (biblical tradition) and someone has given an interpretation of this (homiletic tradition), it is finally the listeners' turn to take up their part, to specify the relevance of what has been heard for their own lives and thereby to become "doers of the Word". The purpose of the sermon is to support them in this process.[360]

It has nothing to do with questioning the authority of God, to not think of the collected testimonies which bear witness to him as the "Book of God" but rather as a literary securing of evidence of the Christian culture of faith and freedom which makes the Bible a unique "vademecum" for a living by faith and thus gives it authority.

Referring to the authority of Scripture in the homiletic process means taking into account the fact that in the end it is not texts but subjects which are under consideration, people who live by faith should be strengthened in a life which is to be determined to a great extent as a life in freedom. From time to time, however, in working on texts, concepts of authority appear which feature elements of paternalism,

---

**360** This process is described in detail in the explanation on Fig. 1 (cf. p. 3–13).

which are based on bossy intimidations or even put on a somewhat inquisitorial tone. In these cases Scripture is misunderstood as a tool of power which is always right – and this is the most important thing the reader or hearer must comprehend.

To hold on to the category of a *conferred* authority in biblical hermeneutics, an authority that is *conceded* in the process of comprehension, demands relating the authority of Scripture to other premises of the homiletic work. One of these concerns the relationship of authority and freedom: It is an expression of freedom to bind oneself to principles whose relevance one is convinced of. In relation to the biblical texts this means that they achieve their authority for us above all because we have "grown to value" the way in which they take people and their lives seriously and have allowed us to understand ourselves – and this not least because we personally benefit from them by an increase in freedom. The freedom *to bind myself to particular grounds* and *allow my judgements to be influenced and conditioned* by an authority such as a biblical text is an expression of an understanding of authority based on communicative resonance. If, however, it is only asserted and rhetorically "enforced" authority loses its communicative power. Rationale, and therefore plausibility, are required in interpersonal communication, and this also applies in regard to authorities.

A further, homiletically crucial relation is the relationship between the authority of Scripture and rationality on the one hand and ideology on the other. Effective authority arises from open-ended communication processes, and in communicative practice it takes on the form of advanced trust; it was therefore very soon obvious that ideological arguing with authorities was dangerous. It is not just since the Enlightenment, but already since the ancient times that people have warned against the danger of a "belief in authority". This attitude is not recommended in the devotional reception of a text in the preparation of a sermon. If the authority of biblical testimonies lies in the content to which they testify, i.e. if their import stems from quite comprehensible, irresistibly clear, often surprising positions and points, then their authority does not contend with the principle which says that understanding a text is the indispensable requirement for its relevance and effect.

### 3.4.3 Christian Preaching with the Old Testament – Normal Case and Special Case

**Preliminary Remarks**

After intensive discussions in congregations and synods, and because of numerous national church statements on the relationship of "Christians and Jews"[361] in the '80s and '90s of the 20th century, we are in a different situation

---

[361] This is also the name of the Association of German Protestant Church Congresses ["Konferenz landeskirchlicher Arbeitskreise Christen und Juden"], established in 1961, which has published many articles on this topic.

today than back in the period after the Second World War. Not only has the awareness of the Christian congregations changed: church laws, too, have been altered
and rewritten to take into account fundamental insights. In accordance with the
(revised) vote of the Conference of the Regional Church Workgroup 'Christians
and Jews' of the Evangelical Church in Germany ("Konferenz landeskirchlicher
Arbeitskreise Christen und Juden", abbreviated as KLAK) there is agreement that
all worship services and sermons should contribute to appropriately expressing
that Jews and Christians confess one and the same God, that God's covenant
with his people uninterruptedly continues to exist and that Jesus preached his
message as a Jew,[362] i.e. without renouncing the Jewish tradition with his faith,
but rather with the intention of continuing it in his own way.

This agreement has contributed to the fact that – at least in theory and in accordingly designed liturgies of the Regional Evangelical Churches in Germany –
there is no longer space in our worship services for any kind of triumphing over
the Jewish faith and its distinctive divine revelation. Certainly the respective
statement of the Union of Evangelical Churches ("Union Evangelischer Kirchen",
abbreviated as EKU) and the United Evangelical Lutheran Church of Germany
("Vereinigte Evangelisch-Lutherische Kirche Deutschlands", abbreviated as
VELKD) is – as its critics aptly notice[363] – interested almost exclusively in dogmatic figures of argumentation without taking exegetical, religious, historical etc.
aspects into equal consideration. As a result, the old, tortuous ways of dealing
with the Old Testament are not named clearly enough which leads to the fact that
basically all the models problematized below still seem possible.

The little that has been said in the statement of the EKU and VELKD on the important and complicated issue of hermeneutics has a strongly apologetic character and offers hardly any constructive hints for dealing with the Old Testament. It advocates for a christological reading of the
Old Testament and states that the Old Testament together with the New make up the Christian
Bible and that, as a consequence, there are "two [potential] endings of the story of faith witnessed to in the Old Testament", one according to Jewish and one according to Christian understanding. With regard to the decisive question of a *justification for the Christian interpretation of
the Old Testament* it refers to the existence of "the specific horizons of interpretation of Jews and
Christians". It fails to explain, however, why it is sensible, or even necessary, "to understand
each traditional statement [also] in its original meaning"[364].

---

362 Cf. "Lobe mit Abrahams Samen" ["Praise with Abraham's Seed"], 1995, 3–5. This basic
agreement – with quite varied degrees of interpretation – has been adhered to throughout the
debates that followed. Cf. the numerous papers in: "Streit um das Gottesdienstbuch" ["Disputes
on the Order of Worship"], 1995.
363 Cf. e.g. F. Crüsemann/W. Romberg, 1995, 30.
364 Cf. the statement of the Theological Committees, 1995, 18f.

The arguments presented in connection with the scriptural sermon above naturally hold true for Christian sermons with texts from the Old Testament, too. In view of the necessity to pay attention both, to the content and form of the text and to read meticulously what has been written on the one hand, and to "proclaim Christ" in every sermon on the other hand, we are faced with a specifically hermeneutical problem: How do we deal with texts "which do not know the One whom we wish to proclaim in our sermon"?[365]

From my point of view, in the history of Christian interpretation of the Old Testament three different models can be distinguished, which attempt to answer this question but which, in so doing, in fact, create new problems. I suggest referring to them as the retrospective model, the opposition model and the dynamic model. In the following sections, these models will be outlined briefly before discussing the benefits of applying a fourth model – the analogy model already mentioned above – to sermons on the Old Testament.

### a) The Retrospective Model

This model assumes that a true understanding of the Old Testament is possible *only in retrospect*, i.e. from the New Testament. The basic pattern of this hermeneutic approach is the relation between Promise and Fulfilment, whereby the Bible represents an apparently coherent referential context. According to such a reading, the main interest of which lies in hints on what is yet to come, what is written in the first part of the Bible latently refers to the second part and appears, above all, to be worth reading because it can be related to the New Testament testimony of Christ.[366]

The problems of this model are obvious: It is (1) *ahistorical* since it rests on a selective coupling of the story of Christ with selected, seemingly relevant scenes from the salvation history of God and the people of Israel. (2) It implies that the authors as well as their first readers had an *inadequate understanding of their own texts* and reduces the prophets, who fought for true faith, to fortune tellers.[367] (3) It overlooks the fact that there is *fulfilment* of the Promise *also in the Old Testament* and that questions, doubts, unsolved expectations and new promises that await fulfilment (cf. e.g. the expectation of the parousia) have their place

---

365 K.-P. Hertzsch, 1997, 3.
366 Wilhelm Vischer, in particular, championed this point of view (cf. idem, 1934). Strictly speaking it is, of course, inappropriate to speak of a promise-fulfillment-pattern, since the hermeneutics outlined here does not start at the promises of the Old Testament but at the accounts given in the New Testament, for which clues are *then* sought in the Old. In correspondence to this hermeneutic strategy one should rather speak of a fulfillment-promise-pattern, in order to mark this inverse perspective.
367 Cf. K.-P Hertzsch, 1997, 9.

in the New Testament, too. (4) The retrospective model does not lead to a new understanding. Such a reading does not disclose anything, as it only requires acknowledgement or identification without reflection on the text's relevance for one's own life.[368] One reads to learn what has been long known – and to discover if that which one knows about Christ has also already been testified in the Old Testament. Therefore Horst Dietrich Preuß quite rightly asks: "I see! So?"[369]

## b) The Opposition Model

This model is based *on equating the Old Testament with "law" and the New with "gospel"*. One of the best-known and most effective representatives of this antithetic approach to the two biblical Books is Rudolf Bultmann. According to him the Old Testament shows people "under the law", while the New Testament puts them "under grace". The Old Testament relates a "tale of failure". Anyone who draws on it does so with good reason for "the situation of the righteous" becomes apparent "only on the basis of failure". For the Christian believer, however, "the history of Israel is past and done with".[370]

This model, too, holds numerous problems. Let us begin with a practical one: (1) provided that every sermon de facto refers to law and gospel, one would have to – strictly speaking – come up with two texts in every sermon in order to show the listeners, first by reference to the Old Testament, how to understand their existence in relation to the "world kingdom" and then to clarify, by referring to the New Testament, how to live in the "kingdom of God"[371]. Such a comparison is, however, not only impractical but, above all, exegetically wrong since neither the Old Testament nor the New Testament view the Holy Scripture[372] simply as a story of failure. There is not only tension but also continuity between the two biblical books[373], for the God of the New Testament is worshipped as "God of the forefathers".

---

**368** I do not think this holds true for the so-called "reflection quotations" (German: "Reflexionszitate", in English still referred to as "quotations of fulfillment" or "fulfillment quotations") in the Gospel of Matthew. While in the history of their reception they have almost always been degenerated to some "scriptural evidence" or used in order to back the call for a retrospective reading of Scripture, they actually serve the writer of the gospel to make his readers understand, that they (too!), may regard themselves as belonging to the people of God.

**369** H. D. Preuß, 1989, 128.

**370** R. Bultmann, 1964, 333; 1969, 193–196, and 1972, 185.

**371** This "distinction" stems from Emanuel Hirsch's work "Das Alte Testament und die Predigt des Evangeliums" (1936) [The Old Testament and the Preaching of the Gospel].

**372** Within the Bible this term is restrictively used for "Moses and the Prophets" or the Old Testament respectively.

**373** Cf. Heb 1:1f.: "Long ago God spoke to our ancestors in many and various ways by the prophets, but in these last days he has spoken to us by a Son."

The opposition model is, furthermore, (2) ahistorical: The early Christians attended both, the traditional Jewish services in the temple and the Christian services in house churches. (3) Additionally, the New Testament offers just as much "world kingdom" as the Old Testament does, in order to make God's act of salvation visible in the context of actual history. The necessity of the gospel does not only arise from the Old Testament or the law it contains. The New Testament itself clearly brings up the subject of the law and also knows the story of failure just as God's mercy and grace are not foreign to the Old Testament. (4) As in the Old Testament the "first covenant" was terminated and broken, so too, in the New – and also today – the "second covenant" is terminated and broken by humanity. God still proves to be the only faithful one. The fact that this faithfulness – compared to the Old Testament – now has another basis, namely in Christ, must, however, not lead to the conclusion that the experience of God's faithfulness through the people of Israel is irrelevant.

### c) The Dynamic Model

The dynamic model postulates an *intensification regarding the clarity and abundance of divine salvation* from the Old Testament to the New. God makes (salvation-) history with his people who in reports, narrations and songs attempt to interpret such action and connect it to their own experience. "The story with God", however, does not stand still but is a dynamic process which, "as a story of salvation, is brought to fulfilment"[374]. Besides, it corresponds to the vividness of God's Word that it implies an inexhaustible *surplus of promise* which finds expression in constantly new texts which testify to this. The interpretations of these texts are superseded by God's continuing action on the one hand and by constantly new attempts of interpretation "until this continual movement reaches its goal and purpose in Christ"[375] on the other. Only in Christ does God's saving will, which includes all peoples, become fully apparent and effective, as the New Testament testifies.

The problems of this model are easily found: (1) If the fullness of salvation is only visible "in Christ" or the New Testament, and the Old Testament on the other hand represents hardly any more than a barely convincing *supporting-act*, it would be a waste of time to take a look into the Old Testament at all. (2) The reductionist question about the *eschatological conclusion* of the Testament ignores all that we have established above regarding the cooperation with the text and its functions.[376]

---

[374] G. v. Rad, 1958, 131, 342.

[375] W. Schütz, 1981, 84.

[376] No notice is taken here of the fact that the biblical texts, for example, are an indispensible help for obtaining self-perception and self-awareness, that they allow us to participate in the hope and certainty of other believers and can help us with our own decisions (cf. H. D. Preuß, 1989, 134f.).

(3) The dynamic model threatens to rob the history of faith of its dynamics when it plays down the *eschatological difference remaining* post-Christ for the fulfilment of salvation. In Israel as well as in church, the dynamics of faith result from God's showing himself time and again in the face of ever new questions and doubts.[377]

### d) The Analogy Model

With regard to *method*, there is no difference for the preachers whether they are working with an Old Testament text or interpreting texts from the New Testament. The analogy model presented in I.3.3.2 is therefore also relevant for approaching the texts from the Old Testament: in both cases they are dealing with testimonies from an *ancient time*, in a *foreign language*, expressed by someone in a *particular situation*.

The texts both from the Old Testament and the New belong to *two situations* – that of the author and that of the reader. Consequently we can neither read the writings of the Old *nor* those of the New Testament as if they were written for or to us today. If we nonetheless read these texts as "texts for us" in both cases we accept that the situation today and the situation at that time can show *common structural features*: There are "basic experiences of reality, a basic pattern of interpreted experience"[378] with faith and God which are indispensible for understanding our own experience as well as for the renewal, reinforcing and questioning of our own faith. We read the texts of the Old and New Testament expecting that they can meet us in a situation similar to the one from or for which they were originally written.

On the one hand, this expectation seems reasonable due to *anthropological constants* in the history of humanity: What makes people suffer and doubt God, what makes them hope and the ways that help them find confidence and assurance can – although narrated in tales from long ago – all of a sudden reflect and change *our own* story. This expectation is further supported by the conviction that the God of the people of Israel is the Father of Jesus Christ. Potential analogies are above all proportional[379] i.e. they refer to the comparability of the *relationship* between Israel and their God on the one hand and between church or individual believers and their God on the other. Hence the analogies are based on the comparability of religious convictions, defined as attitudes towards a relationship to God.

---

377 "There is the question of John the Baptist: Are you the one who is to come, or should we wait for another? There is uncertainty in the Second Letter of Peter: The fulfillment of the world has dawned and yet everything remains as it was. Here, too, there occurs to us the promise which is still unfulfilled: [...] 'God, the Lord, shall wipe the tears from all their faces', an expectation and promise which in Revelation 21 is continued unchanged" (K.-P. Hertzsch, 1997, 10).
378 H. D. Preuß, 1984, 121.
379 Cf. above, p. 132f. on *analogia proportionalitatis*.

As a consequence, the analogy-model is not concerned with the creation of more or less arbitrary object analogies (Promised Land = goods of salvation in Christ) but with analogies referring to human existence[380] before God, i.e. referring to people's daily lives, to their fears and hopes, to their questions and experiences which they identify as "experience with God" and such like. The fact that texts from the Old Testament can *additionally* show us "how much we are in need of Christ"[381] – namely precisely as much as Israel was in need of Yahweh's intervention – is not based on an arbitrary re-interpretation of the texts but rather on a reading of the ancient stories that was already common in Israel. Re-reading and re-telling them is always an act of reviving them in a new present which is, of course, characterized by a wider horizon of knowledge: narrators and readers of the Bible know more than the narrated story's characters are aware of, and it is a good tradition to read and understand these stories with this knowledge and relate them to one's own experience.

"And this is just what we experience, too, when we tell the stories from the Old Testament. We know the end. I find my experience reflected in their experience and yet I know more than the characters of the story do. It is my story and yet an alien one. I recognize myself in the running Jonah but at the same time I know: It is pointless that he runs away from his task. I sympathize with Israel's fear of the unknown, and yet I know: There is no reason for fear because God is already waiting for them there. I have a new perspective, from which I now view the familiar situation critically, or possibly as encouraging."[382]

Analogies are not to be equated with identifications. Where "historical relations"[383] are respected the differences between God's people wandering in the wilderness and the history and fate of the church are maintained. To talk of analogies presupposes an awareness of the difference between the respective situations. For Christian readers this includes the "situation post Christum". This is why it is important in each case to determine anew, from text to text, the type and content of possible analogies between Old Testament and New and current history. Early Christianity – itself living from "Scripture" – formulated its witness to Christ, too, anew, referring to these writings, instead of simply identifying themselves with the traditional experiences handed down to them.

Thus e.g. in 1 Cor 10:1–11 Paul assumes that the stories of "our fathers", particularly the narration of Israel's wandering in the wilderness, amounts to more than the mere recounting of an event which happened at that time. With his knowledge or his eschatological expectation, respectively, he encounters something in these texts (Exod 13–17; Num 11–21) which affects himself and his

---

**380** H. D. Preuß speaks of "Existence Typology" (1989, 135).
**381** H. D. Preuß, 1989, 136.
**382** K.-P. Hertzsch, 1997, 9.
**383** H. D. Preuß, 1989, 135.

readers: the possibility of missing the kingdom of God as the goal of the wandering. This problem was found to be pressing precisely in consideration of the new covenant. Correspondingly he makes the narratives about the events in the time in the wilderness topical and warns that a fall from faith, similar to the one that happened at the time of the fathers, might occur. This argumentation does not express any superiority of later interpretations but clearly points to the relevance of Scripture in a changed situation, also and particularly under the premise of belonging to the "eschatological generation"[384].

The previous chapter mainly addressed the general question of the possibilities and arguments for dealing with Old Testament texts in sermons without insinuating that the attitude of Jewish believers towards their Bible is in any way improper. That contents might be changed in the case of structural analogies is obvious. When Christians interpret biblical texts, their findings will always pertain to questions of the person of "Jesus Christ for us today".[385]

For the purpose of copying with this task, sermons on texts from the Old Testament are not only allowed, but are even highly desirable. Frequently these texts are formally even better suited for the creation of relevant structural analogies than the partly abstract texts from e.g. the Epistles of the New Testament. What characterizes many pericopes from the Old Testament is *the reference they bear to the reality of human life*. They address human life before God in revealing humankind as being a part of creation, involved in economic connections and political actions, searching for a partner, running away from pressurizing family situations, on the battle-field, or facing death. All of this counteracts insubstantial, pneumatic, bloodless and thus all in all inhuman interpretations of the biblical testimonies to faith.

Quite apart from all of that, we might be able to understand the 'spiritual' or 'pastoral' texts of the New Testament even better if we have previously attended the 'language-school' of the Old Testament.[386] "Christ, true Israel, faith, sin, kingdom of heaven etc. are Old Testament words. The Old Testament has the hermeneutic function of teaching a language in which Christ's fate is stated as an act of salvation; [...] it testifies that God began to prepare salvation in the Old Testament."[387]

---

**384** Cf. N. Walter, 1997, 63.

**385** Cf. III.2.1.3 and III.3.

**386** In this context cf. particularly the significance of the Psalms. "The Psalms can [...] be understood as help of the Jewish-Christian tradition to acquire sober knowledge about the having-become life history in the successful and sorrowful" (P. Deselaers, 2004, 166). In his text, Deselaers additionally points to a revelation-theological aspect of psalm sermons (loc. cit., 159–161).

**387** H. D. Preuß, 1989, 127.

# 4 Preaching with a Structure.
## On the Question of the Form of the Sermon

**Preliminary Remarks**

With regard to the conditions required for the process of constructing a sermon, it is naturally not enough to work on the *text* and to examine one's own *person* against the background of homiletic challenges. This fourth chapter, dealing with the structure of the sermon, immediately follows the chapter on the significance of the text. There are systematic reasons for this, which emerge from the description of the preaching event: In the model provided above[388], which represents a process of tradition, the biblical text is formally and chronologically followed by the preacher's manuscript. Therefore the following chapter deals with structural questions of sermon composition.

In the last chapter we noticed: We can make considerable progress in the understanding of biblical texts, and yet these insights gained through text examination are not enough in themselves to create a sermon. The phase of dealing with a piece of biblical tradition nevertheless contributes in laying a trail, finding clues for the content or the main focus of the sermon still to be worked out. From this moment on the text becomes involved in the question of *what* should be preached – without being able to answer this question on its own. To further pursue this question it is additionally necessary to conduct a similarly thorough examination of the *situation* to which the actual sermon is targeted, an examination of the *experiences* which should be addressed as well to consider possible *ideas regarding the potential changes* for which the sermon will aim, as well as other similar steps.[389] Such content-related questions, however, already bear in themselves components of *a sermon structure*:

1. *Why* – from what necessity, on the basis of which observations do I wish to say this or that? What 'drives' me to say what I say? This 'Why'-question points at the sermon's 'from where'; it relates to the sermon's *motivation.*
2. *What* do I want to say? What do I want to clarify? Which position do I take in which matter? The 'What'-question refers to the *content of* the sermon, to its message.
3. Inherently connected to the answer to question 2 is the question about the reasons and arguments for what one has to say: *How* do I arrive at my

---

**388** Cf. Fig. 1, p. 4.
**389** Cf. I.5–7.

https://doi.org/10.1515/9783110440256-004

message? The 'How' question concerns the *rationale* for the sermon's core, its central statement.

4. Finally, one has to face the 'What for' question, regarding the *purpose* or the *intention* of the sermon. *For what reason* do I speak? What do I aim to achieve when I speak, especially when I deliberatly speak from a pulpit?

These four questions – Why? What? How? What for? – form the core of every plausible speech structure. When taken seriously they provide the preacher with a helpful guideline for developing a coherent line of argumentation. They define a logical basic structure, which is easy to follow for everyone and does not require any additional explanatory headings or captions that interrupt the flow of words.

The order of these questions is only to a limited extent interchangeable. Anyone who sticks too long with the 'What'-question at the beginning of a sermon without giving account for the 'Why' will only confuse their listeners, who will barely understand why, on a lovely Sunday morning, they should, for example, attend to the exegetical discoveries of a theological scholar. The 'How'-question, i.e. the reasons for the preacher's position, on the other hand, may just as well be discussed at the end of the sermon in order to finally unveil its main point or a new perspective. This is especially the case when a sermon is primarily designed to change the listeners' *judgments*.

In I.4.3, four angles of reflection[390] are presented, which shall serve the purpose of refining the sermon structure, which has so far only been sketched with the help of questions. Before that, however, we have to (once again) take a closer look at a few selected problems regarding the construction of sermons.

## 4.1 Snapshots. Empirical Indicators of Problems

### 4.1.1 Disintegrating Argumentation

Sermons generally tend to consist far more of assertions than arguments. In such cases it is frequently the 'What'-question that stands in the foreground, sometimes combined with the question of 'for what reason', i.e. with prospects to potential consequences which are expected to appear through the mere visualizing

---

**390** For a detailed discussion on the linguistic and stylistic aspects of sermon composition see I.3.5.

of factual issues. The all too often lacking illumination, however, of the "why" –
i.e. the lack of argumentation – casts doubt on the intended effects the preacher
has in mind. Homiletic argumentation is not only indispensable for the *comprehensibility* of an address but also for its *credibility* as well as for its *convincibility.
Argumentation generally forms the basis of every speech composition* because it
implies the consistent sequence of structural components which are coordinated
to one another and coherent.

Anyone who, for example, wishes to explain how to deal with a specific problem should, for
instance: (1) be able to make understandable why this really is a problem (the 'Why'-ques-
tion), (2) explain by means of referring to already existing attempts of "solving this problem"
where the limits of these attempts lie (part of the 'how' question), (3) be able to explain wherein
their ideas and approaches differ from others ('What'-question) and towards which attitude or
behavior their suggestions possibly lead ('What for'-question), (4) give reasons why the solution
presented is best suited to answer the problem addressed ('How' question), (5) provide future
visions of how the world could be if their ideas and suggestions were actually implemented
('What for'-question).

Of course this order of questions is not compulsory; one could just as well begin with
future visions and then come to speak of the empirically perceptible "deviations from reality",
ask for the reasons for such deviations, thereby focus on a particular problem etc. It is, however,
quite obvious that *the outlined components of an address need one another in order to be able
to function each for themselves.* A sermon limited to the double structure of providing "hypothetical solutions" for "hypothetical problems" is hardly beneficial for the communication of
the gospel.

Naturally it is easier to repeat in various expressions particular dogmatic doctrines of Christianity in the sermon than to deduce, by force of argument, what
they *mean* for the reality of our lives or to what extent it is at all *relevant* to deal
with them. The fact that these dogmatic doctrines are the foundations of Christianity does not mean, at the same time, that they can be considered as plausible
arguments for answering questions as to what living by faith means today.

*Dogmatic doctrines* – whether in New Testament literature or in the Confessions of Faith – are always the *result of previous discussions.* We cannot
even properly understand them historically if we do not know under which
circumstances and on what premises they came into being. It is therefore all
the more problematic when they are quoted in contexts which are shaped by
entirely different questions, experiences or situations than those assumed
from the point of view of the history of dogma. It is not enough to simply
declare by means of stereotype proclamations that there is a relation between
theological insights and the modern-day experience of life, as can be frequently found in the last quarter of many sermons, when they state that this
all holds true "also for us today". In such cases the sermon ends precisely
where it should actually begin.

An example of this: "God becomes man in Jesus Christ. Unbelievable. God becomes man and takes the blame for us! In Jesus Christ God takes the consequences of the law upon himself in place of us and goes to his death. The certain judgement of death is enforced. Not on us, on God himself in Christ. God is dead. – But God does not remain in death. He overcomes it. – God would not be God if he remained in death. 'Christ is risen from the dead' is the message of Easter eve. Death has lost its sting. Now God sends his ambassador into the world, his messenger-boy, to tell the people: Listen! God has fulfilled the law in your place! He has filled the void between us and himself, once and for all, through his Son, Jesus Christ. [...] This holds good for you and me, too, for all of us. Believe that God in Jesus Christ has settled the outstanding score, that God has put things straight again. Believe that we are God's partners again because God himself has fulfilled the law. [. . .] In Jesus Christ God has made us his counterpart again. And who knows, perhaps we shall one day, at the end of time, when we are with God, sit together with him and gaze together into the starry sky" [end of sermon].[391]

A sermon which in such a way closely follows the Reformation theology – with a substantial focus on argumentation – leaves open the question as to what the listeners are to do with the things which "God" appears to deal with on his own. The congregation receives no answers to obvious questions. For providing answers in this case would not mean to explain God but to learn *how the preacher arrives at what he says* – i.e. for what reasons he thinks the way he does. Instead the listeners watch their preacher climbing up the Rocky Mountains of Dogmatics and airing, from up there, the connections between law and faith and works and grace and justification. This sermon gives rise to, among others, the following critical queries:

1. Why is the preacher in this location?
2. And, above all: Why should the individual attend to *God's* dilemma "not to lose face"[392], and *therefore* have to insist upon the fulfilment of the law?
3. Why is there a void between me and God?
4. Why must God in Jesus take the blame for me?
5. How does "a life in freedom" emerge from this for me?
6. Why is God's partnership placed before my eyes as something *almost forever missed* – and then all of a sudden offered as something "given"? Perhaps I should like to have nothing to do with a God who needs such an elaborate justification for the execution of his "messenger-boy"?
7. What does it help me that God helps himself by fulfilling the law?
8. What does my life have to do with the "outstanding score" which had to be "settled" then? Do I not have the grace of the "late birth"?
9. Are there still any effects of that law today, which make a sermon that proclaims freedom from the law still relevant for me?
10. How can I be sure that I am God's partner? Are there no other clues for this apart from the starry heavens?

---

391 Sermon manuscript on Rom 3:21–28.
392 Ibid.

These questions are by no means to be misunderstood as accusations against the preacher; they should be viewed as taking on the listeners' *mandate*, as their advocate as it were, in Ernst Lange's sense.[393] Such questions are part of the endeavor to reformulate common dogmatic loci in ever-new linguistic attempts, connect them to lifeworld experiences and process them, on basis of argumentation, for their intended purpose: being heard and understood by the listeners.

### 4.1.2 The Problem of Problematizations

One of the most common strategies for structuring sermons – mostly their openings – is that either the text or the world is rendered problematic. The rest of the sermon then serves to handle these problems. With regard to this homiletic pattern attention should be paid to the following:

a) *Problematizing the text* in the sermon can be useful where the text (as *sermon text*) appears in fact to be a hindrance rather than help for the communication of the gospel. In such cases it can be, for example, appropriate to speak *"against"* the text in order – paradoxically – to preach *according to Scripture*. It seems to me, however, that rendering the text problematic is in most cases a scarcely credible ritual to command attention. Quite often this strategy has the function of postulating an argumentatively comfortable, apparently diametric difference between text and situation in order to be able to come after all to the "surprising result" that precisely this text fits better than any other for the people of today:

"Paul behaves as if we were school children. [...] Paul, you have not struck the proper tone for us people of the 20th century. After all, you are not our superior. If you have something to ask for, please do so in a matter-of-fact way, consult the relevant people in the congregation. The way in which you behave here you have nothing to say to us. [Stage direction of the preacher to himself:] (Here I close the Bible in a way everyone can see and put it aside.) I am a little uneasy. Perhaps I have acted too rashly? [...] I thank you, Paul, that you have said this in this manner."[394]

This strategy is not very illuminating because it is a "ruse"[395] which is easily spotted. The listeners are confronted with a – even theologically barely plausible – hypothetical problem and yet sense that there are more authentic problems pertaining to life for which they have in fact come to church.

---

393 Occasionally it may be useful to stage the appearance of an "advocate of the listeners" within the framework of follow-up discussions or sermon analyses. Cf. W. Engemann, 2009c, 422f.
394 Sermon manuscript on 1 Thess 4:1–8.
395 Cf. the discussion of the "strategic pseudo-antagonism" in W. Engemann, 1993, 122f.

b) But the *ritualized problematization of situations*, too, implies the danger of being nothing more than a peg on which to hang unworldly sermons which do not lay themselves open to the questions arising from the actual life of the listeners but merely refer to particular emergency situations in order to indicate a certain awareness of problems. Listeners are then often swamped with long lists of crises, catastrophes and disasters which no sermon – not even the most ambitious ones – could examine in enough detail, arguing all the related questions and issues.

"What a bitter situation this is: [...] A cry rings out for someone who can put an end to the misery and bring salvation, and ever and again the bitter realization: In this world there is no one. This cry is well known to us ourselves. Our life today now and again holds situations where the question of the one who brings salvation must for the moment remain unanswered. [...] Bad things can happen. The illness or death of a beloved person can very quickly lead to the cry for the end. War, suffering and injustice stand around us like a big question mark in the world. [...] Precisely in such a situation John gives his congregation the confirmation: Yes! There is someone."[396]

Successful problem orientation is certainly not expressed in terms of numbers, i.e. the number of troubles listed in a sermon, but by the attempt to address actual, concrete – and this always means: a restricted number of – experiences, facets and problems of human life. These are not alien to the listeners; on the contrary they bring them with them to church, are aware of them, because in certain circumstances they prevent them, for example, from experiencing freedom even more extensively. Such problem orientation does not amount to pulling a fine rhetorical solution out of the hat at the end of the sermon – like, for example: "If only we – then [...]!" Problem orientation is successfully implemented in a sermon when it mentions a piece of authentic world in a way that the listeners are enabled to see its relevance, which is the necessary precondition for the listeners to take an interest in what the sermon has to say about change or a new way of looking at that world we live in.

### 4.1.3 Pseudo-Dialogs

Dialogical preaching does not necessarily require delivering a so-called *dialog-sermon* in which two speakers appear or in which the preacher enters into a conversation with the congregation. A sermon *becomes* dialogical already when the listeners really appear in it, i.e. when they are not only regarded as a case of

---

**396** Sermon manuscript on Rev 5:1–5.

text application or a container of theological knowledge but when their presence has become *constitutive* for the questions and problems which have led to the respective sermon.

Mere dialogism, based on previously prepared mock questions and mock answers, can hardly be seen as convincing evidence that the listeners played a part in preparing the sermon. Staged dialogs with a co-preacher or the congregation frequently turn out to be mere *monologs with assigned parts*: the partner in the dialog only serves to communicate a predetermined approach and solution.

A preacher envisions dialogically approaching her self-posed question as to whom one "can entrust oneself and one's whole life without being disappointed"[397] as follows:

| | |
|---|---|
| *Preacher:* | "Whom can I trust completely? Have I not been disappointed all too often? We know this mistrust from our own lives. Mrs. F., for example. The diagnosis after seeing a doctor was definite: Multiple Sclerosis. |
| *Speaker 1:* | Should I tell my husband? What if he leaves me? And yet – whom can I trust, if not him? |
| *Preacher:* | Or there is Mr. K. His colleagues all agree: |
| *Speaker 1:* | A nice guy, always in a good mood. |
| *Preacher:* | But no one knows how unhappy and lonely Mr. K. often feels. |
| *Speaker 1:* | I yearn for someone to whom I can entrust myself. But who will love me when the mask has fallen off? [...] |
| *Speaker 2:* | Let yourself be helped – Yes, I would like to. But who will help me? |
| *Preacher:* | Jesus says of himself: |
| *Speaker 1:* | I am the Good Shepherd. I am the real, true shepherd. I am the only shepherd who really means you well. |
| *Speaker 2:* | And I am supposed to believe that? Everybody wants that. [...] Politicians, company directors, sect leaders [...]. And next I shall risk entrusting myself to someone in my personal life, too, who then watches as a shepherd over me? No. Not on my watch. I better remain my own master. |
| *Preacher:* | We are frequently let down by other people. But maybe Jesus also feels let down by us? By our mistrust of him although he even gave his life for us? And yet: Jesus stands by our side as the one who loves us."[398] |

With the solution offered that "full trust" can be "justified only in Jesus" the problems touched upon and instrumentalized earlier are swept aside and *precisely not* integrated into the sermon. True to the motto "Everybody only cares about themselves, but Jesus only cares about you – and that is all you need" the potential doubts and temptations of the listeners remain unconsidered. The sermon opens a void between what people can experience and what Jesus wants to do for them. In the example above, the "mock questions" of the "mock listeners" in

---

**397** Preliminary work on a sermon manuscript on John 10:11–16.27–30.
**398** Sermon manuscript on John 10:11–16.27–30.

fact appear so fabricated that this mock dialog loses all the tension it requires in order not to collapse as a dialog. If one were to assemble the lines of the different speakers, there would be no indication that the text as a whole involves the individual experiences or viewpoints of different people.

Such a sermon can hardly withstand the questions of its listeners. It has tempered with the genetic material, as it were, which makes up human questioning; it has tempered with it to an extent that is no longer useful for authentic questions but appears to be appropriate for the answers given in the sermon. People who experience disappointment and do not succeed in leaving the "darkest valley" are themselves to blame because they are lacking faith. And yet the "darkest valley" definitely belongs to the sphere of the Good Shepherd, from which he emerges as the one who he really is. The "valley" is then, however, not a mere ornament of the sermon, like in the example above, but the sermon's basis.

As a rule, successful dialogs are characterized by dynamic argumentation in which thesis and antithesis, pleas and objections, assumptions and convictions etc. are blended into a kind of 'thinking aloud' and thus provide a path which the listener can follow easily.[399]

### 4.1.4 Non-Specific Examples

Examples should be the insertion of concrete segments of either perceived or desired reality into the texture of a speech, exemplary snapshots of particular facets of life as the preacher sees it – or how it could be under changed conditions. As a rule they take time and require a particular setting. They are precise. Examples indicate that there is something which requires clarification or action, or they are a step towards clarification, i.e. they are able to "demonstrate" possible attitudes or actions. It is rather immaterial whether here something invented or something truly seen, heard, experienced or fictitious is mentioned. What is important is that the example does not consist in merely juggling with metaphors or synonyms but opens a window, throws open a door through which a surprisingly new view into the reality of one's own life is gained.

In order to explain to his listeners what it means to fulfil the mission to bear witness, the preacher tells them: "I wish that we all allow the little witness in us to speak out more often in that we ask ourselves in all possible contexts, be it at one's workplace, in one's family or within one's circle of friends, in politics, on the street or when shopping, whether it were not necessary or

---

**399** For further details on the creation of the dialog-structure of the sermon cf. below under I.4.3.3. This chapter (I.4.1) primarily deals with indications or signs of problems.

useful to give clear or little witness to our LORD. The shape and form of your witness is up to you. Whether quietly in a hidden place [...], whether in words or actions, there are no limits to our imagination."[400]

If "there are no limits to our imagination" why then does the preacher himself not make use of this anticipatory power through which people are being enabled to see something which belongs to that which is "not yet" and is thus more than the mere reflection of the status quo? This, however, requires examples in the sense of imaginative impulses through which "the promises in the Bible" are not merely explained from the past but appear as present and future reality. In its far too open and ambiguous argumentation the sermon above gives neither a concrete indication of the problem nor a clear perspective, so that in the end it provides no room for identification, no reference point for orientation to its listeners. In doing so, the preacher entirely delegates the act of discovering the potential consequences of the presented perspective to the listeners.

Here the difference between *factual openness*, which basically applies to all forms of verbal utterances, and created, staged, associative *tactical openness* – a characteristic feature of every kind of artistic creation – is ignored: While the former holds true for even the most diffuse utterance, the latter demands taking into consideration the by-no-means arbitrary *form* of the message and structuring it in a way that potential recipients are enabled to deduce its *meaning*.[401] In the sermon cited above it could, for example, have been explained what happens in a workplace when someone begins to practise their faith as a form of acquisition of freedom, or what situation comes to our minds when someone in a family is enabled through their faith to take themselves seriously and restructure existing relationships: What sort of confusion would this trigger? What changes could be initiated?

Examples draw their illustrative – i.e. their "illuminating" – power from their details. Something seemingly peripheral can be of vital significance in characterizing or depicting the circumstances of a particular scene and thus greatly influence the appropriateness of the example. As a consequence successful examples are often "contingent": they are unique, they surprise us by deviating from clichés, so that in the end every action, speech act or experience focussed on within the depicted overall situation obtains a specific point through all its details.

---

**400** Sermon manuscript on John 1:29–34.
**401** For more detailed information on a sermon composed according to the principles of the "open work of art" see I.4.3.4.

Even in the instructions for pre-formulated sermons – in German: "Lesepredigten" that serve as aid for lay readers who conduct church services without having completed full theological training – the false conception prevails that examples should be kept as general as possible in order to be relevant for as many people as possible. "Think of occurrences or events which apply to any congregation."[402] An advice obviously taken all too seriously in the following sermon: "Structures, institutions and human behavior linked to guilt and being guilty are the result of sin. An example of this would be the widespread inability to form relationships, which can be blatantly seen in families the individual members of which can hardly speak to one another: They talk past one another, do not understand each other, have nothing to say to each other. Other examples may be inserted here."[403] – There is hardly any "input" here. How the "results of sin" actually affect people's social lives and what it would be like if this changed, is not mentioned.

The hermeneutic power of an example is not achieved by referring to incidents which might happen to *each* of us *every day* and *everywhere*. Novels, tales and films etc. frequently confront us with experiences which are most certainly not part of our own reality (as, for example, an odyssey in space). What is portrayed in these examples, however, becomes important for our own experience if in their reification they become *translatable* and thus *comprehensible* for our own lives. Mere lists of examples in which nothing more than the very first available associations are enumerated, on the other hand, will hardly contribute anything to the clarification of experiences, mindsets and attitudes problematized or intended:

"I don't know how it is for you, but for my liking everything goes far too quickly today. In fact, we are constantly confronted with new pieces of information [...] on the radio or television, in the newspaper, by our neighbors: senseless wars, human rights flouted, the hole in the ozone-layer, nuclear weapons testing, Neo-Nazism. Added to this, my own small personal wishes on which I daily founder in my dealings with my partner, my children, my friends, my work-colleagues etc."[404]

Such lists of putative "examples" are all the more disastrous the more tragic these rapidly presented life situations are: "Things can be bad at times: the illness or

---

**402** From the leaflet Ag 459–23–84 "Hinweise zur Gestaltung der Lesepredigt" [Basic notes on composing sermons for reading] handed out to authors of the read sermon series, "Er ist unser Friede" ("For he is our peace", published by Evangelische Verlagsanstalt Berlin) in the 1980s. "A sermon is to be preached, not to be read. It is first of all a specific type of speech and may only in a secondary way be considered as a text which may be good for reading. So in some respects Lesepredigten (scripted sermons for public oration, to be presented not by the original author but by somebody else) are a contradiction in terms and should be considered as a special homiletic genre. The term has been invented by the German Confessing Church where lay preachers, who were on call, needed pre-formulated sermons to read in the pulpit. Today, reading sermons is common practice in the Protestant Churches in Germany not only in services with lay preachers" (M. Heymel, 2013, 38).
**403** Sermon manuscript on John 1:29–34.
**404** Sermon manuscript on Phil 4:4–7.

death of a beloved person can very quickly lead to the cry for the end. War, suffering and injustice stand around us like a big question mark in the world."[405] Instead of anchoring the irrefutability of *one* such "question mark" in *one* situation in which it cannot be argued away, the preacher takes it up with the whole world. But will it then be of any interest to the listeners what conclusions their preacher comes to when actually he deals above all with "God" and in the end, in fact, only defends him against humanity?

In another sermon the preacher refers to "for example, the many sleepless nights of a woman suffering from cancer" who is unable sleep because of her pain. "Or I think of the old man in the old age home who can't find peace because he is so lonely and lies awake all night long. [...] But also the fear of losing one's job is ubiquitous and makes us lose sleep."[406] At this point the preacher could discuss the "thoughts", "wishes" and "doubts" of those affected on the basis of *one* case. Why does he not do so? Is he afraid of real, substantial objections? Does he need his "examples" only to prepare for his offering of a solution? Thoughtful listeners could gain such impression when at the end of the sermon it says – in view of such a huge mountain of fears – unintentionally cynically: "Sleepless nights can be salutary nights, my dear congregation. Nicodemus is one of those people whose life was fundamentally changed by a conversation at night. [...] Anyone who comes to Jesus and truly becomes involved with his Word does not remain the person he once was."[407]

Examples should show clearly what it could mean when somebody – in case the sermon cited above did not give an exaggerated depiction – after a sleepless night starts the day *as a new and changed person* or how *one particular* day in which hope prevails over the fears of the night looks like, what distinguishes this particular day from all others.

## 4.2 Indicators of Problems in the History of Homiletics

The perceptions mentioned above already provide an indication of some of the most vital aspects of sermon composition. It should have become *clear to what extent questions on the sermon content are connected with questions on the sermon's structure.*

As pointed out in the introductory remarks to this chapter, the question of content is not already settled by working out the text's meaning. The embedding of structural and linguistic aspects between the large chapters on text and situation has formal reasons. On a specific point during the work on the concept of his sermon, the preacher is faced with the question as to how and with which means

---

**405** Sermon manuscript on Rev 5:1–5.
**406** Sermon manuscript on John 3:1–8(9–15).
**407** Ibid. The last sentence quoted is, in fact, the end of the sermon.

he can say what he has to say – on the subject he is dealing with, on the faith he, in so doing, is concerned with, on the perspectives which arise from his understanding of contemporary Christianity and of living by faith today.

The import given to questions of sermon *structure and design* has fluctuated throughout the history of Homiletics. Since, however, the understanding has won through that (in an address) questions of content always also arise as questions of structure, a comprehensive, interdisciplinary discussion of the sermon's formal aspects has become part of the standard of Homiletics. The preceding dispute centred in particular on the assessment of the role of rhetoric in the communication of the gospel. Hence, the following chapter provides an overview of the controversial issues of this debate.

### 4.2.1 On the Dispute about the Rhetorical Tradition

The attempt to bring the content of an address more strongly to people's awareness through a carefully considered structure is, of course, older than the homiletic discussions of this matter. Throughout centuries many ideas and suggestions of how to structure a formally successful sermon came from rhetoric. This circumstance considerably contributed to the fact that the seemingly obvious question as to whether the formal principles of an address are to be kept in mind when preaching a message as unwieldy as the gospel was consistently argued about.[408] Behind this dispute was a biased picture of the principles of the "Art of Eloquence", caricaturing the self-understanding of rhetoric, that considered rhetorical skills as a kind of strategy of persuasion demanding from the preacher manipulative interest, self-will and a lack of respect for the work of the Spirit.[409]

This instrumentalized understanding of rhetoric rests on a selective reception of the rhetorical tradition, which tends to overlook the fact that this discipline is not merely concerned with teaching skills for the effective use of speech *but rather an art determined by content and ethic responsibility.*[410] Its aim is, above

---

**408** As an example of the many contributions on this matter cf. Michael Thiele's comment on "Rhetorikverachtung der Theologie" [The defiance of rhetoric in theology] (M. Thiele, 2005, 15–22).

**409** This is how e.g. H. M. Müller emphatically expressed his appreciation of the efforts "to abandon rhetoric in Homiletics" and to keep firmly in view the "nature of the matter" and the "task of the speaker" – statements which unfortunately are not explicated in more detail (cf. H. M. Müller, 1996, 559). Cf. also Gert Otto's criticism of Müller (G. Otto, 1999, 95f.). Cf. also James F. Kay's (2003) theological criticism of the neglect of rhetoric in, among others, Karl Barth's Homiletics.

**410** On this cf. G. Otto's fundamental work, *Die Kunst, verantwortlich zu reden* (1994) [The art of responsible speaking]. No matter whether Otto refers to Plato, Aristotle, Cicero or Augustine, to

all, *to enable dialog through the structuring of language* in which the listeners can provide qualified statements on a particular matter, the relevance of which the speaker himself is convinced of. Certainly the classical rhetoricians also sought to establish specific rules according to which the speakers' intended goals can be successfully reached, so that rhetorical efforts always also imply the basic impetus for effective speech.

Cicero considered an important requirement for carrying off the "victory of the address" – as was the common terminology at that time – to establish among the listeners "goodwill", i.e. a basically favorable attitude towards the speaker in order to be able to guide them more efficiently and win their approval.[411] "Anyone who speaks in the Forum and in civil actions by giving proof, in an entertaining way and by dominating the will of the listeners" may, according to Cicero, call himself a good orator. For "to give proof is necessary, to entertain is agreeable; but the one who knows how to determine the will of the listeners carries off the victory"[412].

Augustine ties in with this idea and explains to the speaker in church: anyone who wants to achieve something with their address "must not only teach so as to give instruction, and please so as to keep up the attention, but he must also sway the mind so as to subdue the will"[413]. Bearing in mind Augustine's overall conception of rhetoric shows, however, that he did not adopt Cicero's approach lock, stock and barrel: the choice of rhetorical means is determined by the content of the address and by the preacher's responsibility before God. Neither the question of content nor the question of responsibility can be explained rhetorically; they arise from the content of the communication of the gospel, as well as from the basic functions of the sermon already discussed. With Augustine's homiletic reception in mind Gert Otto summarized: "Augustine's *praedicator* differs from his *orator* in that, in fact, for both is true: the speaker refers to the listeners – but it is the *praedicator* alone who is simultaneously a hearer of his God. This is a new understanding of the orator, emerging from his relationship to the revealed Word and its all-surpassing quality."[414] In this respect the "victory" for which the preacher struggles is certainly not a victory for himself as a speaker, and even less a victory over the listeners, but a victory of the gospel.[415]

The subsequent question about the criteria for the structuring of an effective speech was based on the basic insight that the goal of an address needs to be aimed at in the very context of its *"Sitz im Leben"*. In line with this, the ancient

---

positions of the Baroque period, the Enlightenment or to current theories: he strives for pointing out the insoluble connection of rhetoric, aesthetics and ethics and in, in doing so, for searching for possibilities to escape from the instrumentalization of rhetoric in theory and in practice (cf. esp. G. Otto, 1994, 72–130).

**411** Cf. Cicero, 1976, 316. 323.

**412** Cicero, quoted in G. Ueding/B. Steinbrink, 1994, 35.

**413** Augustine, 1887, 584 (IV, 13, 29). Cf. also 583 (IV, 12, 27).

**414** G. Otto, 1999, 66f.

**415** As a consequence Augustine asks: "Who will dare to say that truth in the person of its defenders is to take its stand unarmed against falsehood" (1887, 575 [IV, 2, 3]).

genres of rhetoric were referred to as *genera causarum*[416], oriented on the very cause or cases the speaker attended to in the interest of their listeners.

The classifications suggested as for the most important "types of cases" have never been truly consistent; following Aristotle, Cicero and Quintilian above all, there was an initial propensity towards a classification consisting of *three* categories with comparable basic content structures. The main ideas linked with this rhetorical program are most easily grasped through not only considering the *case* a particular genre relates to, but by additionally looking at the *matter* which is to be discussed, the particular *function* of the address, the *competence expected from the listeners* and the *overall goal* of the address.[417]

**Classification and function of the ancient Genres of Speech (genera causarum)**

| Genres / in Relation to: | the Case | the Subject | the Function | the Audience | the Goal |
|---|---|---|---|---|---|
| **Judicial Speech** (genus iudiciale) | prosecution and defense in court | assessment of what has already happened | *docere:* to enable judgment formation | judgment formation | a just verdict |
| **Deliberative Speech** (genus deliberativum) | need for clarification in (politically) difficult situations | recommendation for future action | *movere:* to weigh-up opportunities for action | capacity to act | a well-founded action or attitude |
| **Epideictic Speech** (genus demonstrativum) | praiseworthy and objectionable behavior | public praise or public criticism | *delectare:* to grant entertainment | enjoyment of the speech | successful entertainment |

**Fig. 10:** Classification and function of the ancient genres of rhetoric

---

**416** The oftentimes vague reception of rhetorical aspects in Homiletics resulted in terminological diffusion, whereby frequently inaccuracies were put into circulation due to an all too unthinking citing of quotations. So it is, for example, misleading to use the term *genera dicendi* as a correlate or in lieu of *genera causarum*. While the latter refers to *specific needs* of a polis (see above) the former dates from a later epoch in which rhetoric was just one of many art forms and no longer belonged to the key qualifications of a politically involved member of the educated class but was understood rather as a cultural occurrence or used for religious reasons.

**417** The following illustration (Fig. 10) attempts to provide a synthesis of the ideas of Aristotle, the Auctor ad Herennium, Cicero and Quintilian on this matter which – regarding the genera – do neither display a common classification, nor a consistent terminology.

It should not be inferred from this classification of speech into three genres that there has ever been a rhetorical practice strictly following such a blueprint.[418] This would indeed be hardly presumable or achievable, since every successful address contains *elements of all three genres*: for it is difficult to imagine a speech which does *not* in one way or another contribute to judgement formation, which does not *also* discuss different opinions and perceptions, gets by without evaluations and does not *also* provide an impetus for future action.

According to Quintilian there is, in fact, no rhetoric genre in which we do not – at least implicitly – also have to "praise or blame, advise or warn against something, strive for or ward off something. They also have in common the fact that at times they all win, narrate, teach, intensify, weaken and, through arousing or soothing passions, determine the listeners' state of mind. [...] For everything is based, as it were, on reciprocal aid: Even when praising, the issues of justice and benefit appear, just as does kindness when advising, and one can seldom find a judicial speech which does not, in one section or another, contain some of the things mentioned above."[419]

Aside from that, the vagueness or pragmatism regarding the description of the functions of the genera becomes apparent in determining the expected effort of the listeners, too: thus a speech which should result in judgement is classified as belonging to the *genus iudicale*, but at the same time the one who hears an epideictic speech is called "a critical judge" (aestimator).[420] Likewise the epideictic speech, by containing praise and blame, competes with the principle of representation of the classical judicial speech.

From this we can, however, not infer that generic theory is irrelevant or negligible, but must rather ask wherein the *actual achievement of ancient rhetoric* consists:

1. Ancient rhetoric discovered the rhetoric triangle of speaker, listener and topic.
2. It revealed that the effectiveness of an address greatly depends on the extent to which the interdependent relationships between the individual elements of this triangle are considered.[421] It would therefore be overhasty to take over the ancient rhetoric genres into Homiletics by simply specifying – in parallel to the genera – individual sermon genres and demanding stylistic purity.

Consequently, preachers should not be advised to decide between a "cognitively" shaped "teaching sermon", an "emotional", "ceremonial sermon" or an action-oriented hortatory

---

**418** J. Engels, 1996, 702.
**419** Quintilian, 1995, III, 4, 12 and 15f.
**420** Martianus Capella, 1983, 154f.
**421** "For every speech is composed of three parts: the speaker, the subject of which he treats, and the person to whom it is addressed, I mean the hearer" (Aristotle, 1935, 33 [1, 3]).

sermon instead of offering a "'balanced' mixture".[422] It is precisely such "mixtures" that form the heart of rhetorical efforts, the effectiveness of which is not diminished but rather increased by the *simultaneity* of information, impetus to action and expressive power. Within the framework of the discussion of the three basic functions of the sermon (representational function, paracletic function, expressive function or function of testimony) it has already been ascertained that it is precisely the interdependence of the different rhetorical functions that prompts a linguistically effective sermon. It is, however, a quite different matter to approach this from the perspective of the Speech Act Theory: to reflect which "act" should stand in the foreground of the sermon and by what content or witness the intended speech act situation should be determined (cf. below, I.5).

Even the young Melanchthon, who meticulously studied and initially conspicuously applied classical rhetoric in his first fragmentary basic outline of Protestant Homiletics,[423] soon realized the inadequacy of this strategy in view of the complexity of the homiletic task. He attempted to introduce as a fourth genre the *genus didascalicum* which should strengthen the instructive character of the sermon.[424] Although the later Protestant school rhetoric and Homiletics did not tie in with this terminological suggestion, Melanchthon significantly marked the continuity and relevance of rhetorical questions in the homiletic context when he reformulated the insight that an address must be geared towards its listeners in order to obtain situational suitability. Its goal cannot be determined without speaking of a hermeneutic effort, of "learning" on the part of the listeners[425]. The question is how this goal can be achieved not only in terms of *content* but also through the *form* of the sermon.

In view of the entirely changed situation – compared to the heyday of classical rhetoric – of public speaking in general and the sermon in particular, the cases of ancient speech situations are to be regarded as the general *dimensions of speech*. Provided that *every* sermon is about, among other things, (1) motivating the listeners to listen, i.e. to engage their attention, (2) representing a content and revealing its significance and (3) providing impulses for specific actions or attitudes, it stands to reason to adopt the genera in this way – particularly since they describe basic linguistic functions. Regarding the question about the form of the sermon this basically means to be able to relate its functions to the (again classical) structure of introduction, main part and conclusion:

---

422 Cf. M. Meyer-Blanck/B. Weyel, 1999, 69f.
423 Cf. the chapter "De sacris concionibus" in Melanchthon's textbook, *De Rhetorica libri tres* (1519).
424 P. Melanchthon, (1531/1542) 1963, in particular 423–425.
425 This position is taken up by the *psychology of learning* model introduced in 4.3.1.

| Basic Speech Structure | Classical Genres | Speech function | Sermon function |
|---|---|---|---|
| Introduction | genus demonstrativum | Enhancing the willingness to listen | Function of establishing contact |
| Main part | genus iudicale | Presentation of a case | Teaching function |
| Conclusion | genus deliberativum | Demonstration of consequences | Paracletic function |

**Fig. 11:** Basic speech structures and functions of the sermon

**Notes:** Because the sermon is a process of communication, it is rhetorically imperative to reflect on how *the communicative situation itself can be established* and to ask what could encourage people to listen and what could increase their motivation to follow the sermon. *Communication-conducive contact*[426] even at the beginning of the sermon, for example, means that the introduction already conveys some solidarity with the listeners in regard to a particular (basic) situation and resists the impression that the preacher himself is not also part of the circumstances in view of which the sermon is delivered. Benefitting from this initially established relationship, in the *main part* of the sermon its topic and theological doctrine can develop argumentatively towards the sharing of *humanistic life skills*. As a consequence of the plausibility of its teachings, the course of the sermon argument is followed by *paracletic impulses* which can lead to specific actions or attitude changes.

It is evident from this table that there are distinct analogies to *Karl Bühler's* linguistic-theoretical *sign model*, according to which *each* of the three basic functions of an address occurs simultaneously (though to different extents) in *every* linguistic utterance. This means that every linguistic sign – e.g. a spoken sentence – is *at once* a (self-)revelation of the speaker, an impulse to action and a representation of content. According to Bühler this is the case because *every* linguistic expression (1) is presented by someone, (2) refers to something and (3) has to be received by someone else. As a consequence, each *part* of a speech has an *aesthetic function*[427] substantiated in its form, a *representational function* related to its content and a *signal function*[428] in reference to the listeners, with each function potentially playing the most important part at a time.

---

426 This contact has considerable influence on the achievement of a positive, buttressing level of relationship between preacher and listener.
427 Cf. the aspect of entertainment in the *genus demonstrativum* in the classical genera.
428 Cf. K. Bühler, 2011, 30–39.

| Part of the Address | Semantic Functions of Language | Sermon Functions |
|---------------------|-------------------------------|------------------|
| **Introduction** | **aesthetic function** | **contact** |
| | representational function | teaching |
| | signal function | paraclesis |
| **Main Part** | aesthetic function | contact |
| | **representational function** | **teaching** |
| | signal function | paraclesis |
| **Conclusion** | aesthetic function | contact |
| | representational function | teaching |
| | **signal function** | **paraclesis** |

**Fig. 12:** Exemplary model for the shift of main and secondary functions of language in the course of a sermon

One should not, however, construct a rhetorical straitjacket out of this model. A well-structured sermon is capable of going *in medias res* immediately regarding its content *and* "of moving" its listeners. It may raise enough attention to succeed in *both*, delighting the listeners *and* provoking them to certain assessments or stances. It can, for example, refer to aspects of justification with argumentative precision *and*, in so doing, strengthen the contact between preacher and listener by presenting the church's doctrine as a personal, credible testimony etc.[429]

Remarkably, it is precisely among biblical texts – the mere *content* reproduction of which mattered so much to Karl Barth – that there are numerous examples of the coincidence of the above-mentioned different functions of the address: In his sermons – e.g. before the people in Jerusalem (Acts 22:1–21) or before Festus and Agrippa (Acts 26:1–32) – Paul revealed a great deal about himself, partly in order to justify himself, partly referring to God's grace. Finally, after long and very personal "introductions" he comes to the "point" when he states "Christ is risen from the dead" (Acts 26:23). Even without any specific appeals to faith he sets such a strong impulse with his testimony that King Agrippa finally says: "You almost persuade me to become a Christian" (28). In other words: Introductions are perfectly capable of saying something essential and of anticipating the main points of the sermon. Theological doctrine may precede or indeed succeed a personal testimony, and both are related to one another at all times.

The restructuring of the genera into linguistic functions originated from the development of rhetoric itself. Consequently the rhetorical outlines of the 20th century

---

**429** Karl Barth vehemently opposed both "introductions" and "parts" or "segmentation" in the sermon. Admittedly he justified this with arguments which run counter to the specific and well-founded interest of rhetoric in introductions and parts: When Barth states that introductions are "a waste of time" and the "segmentation" of a sermon is no more than a scripturally inappropriate addition and application of doctrine (*explicatio* and *applicatio)*, he is unjust to the semantic and pragmatic relevance of the interrelations discussed above. Cf. in contrast Barth's particular manner of focusing the homiletic work on the text (K. Barth, 1991, 122, 126f.).

do not see themselves faced with the task of revitalizing the ancient genera.[430] Instead they describe and discuss the personal and situational conditions under which the content of a speech can expected to be *comprehensible*, its impulse for action to be *responsible* and its position to be *credible*. Naturally particular functions may be dominant, depending on the individual case; but each of them achieves its effectiveness in the address only in its correlation to the others.

### 4.2.2 On the Correspondence of Content and Form[431]

The question of the relation of correspondence between the sermon's content and form is not only concerned with the contentwise plausible and formal logical disposition of the sermon, but just as much with individual words, metaphors, parables and sentences as with the sermon as an organic whole. Both, its individual pieces of semantic content as well as its overall message are effects of linguistic composition. What is to be communicated is in every case tied to particular (symbolic) forms. Consequently the success of the communication of the sermon depends largely upon whether its content is represented in an appropriate form, i.e. whether it is offered significantly enough for the listeners to be able to locate what has been heard in the context of their own experience of life and faith.

In theology there is an abundance of formulae and basic principles which put straight certain views of the interrelationship between God and humanity, of faith, of life and death etc. and thus become "open for discourse" for theologians. The more strongly preachers, particularly in the sermon itself, draw from this repertoire of views, conceptions and formulae the more standardized their language becomes and all the less would people notice if they were replaced by someone else who acted in exactly the same way. If preachers read their texts focusing above all on which dogmatic or moral standards goes best with the 'most significant' concepts of the pericope (grace, sin, love, hope, neighbour) their sermons would become more and more interchangeable due to their monotony and irreproachable theological correctness.

---

**430** "None of the three main schools of the 'New Rhetoric', neither the psychological-communication scientific rhetoric, nor the philosophically oriented theory of argumentation and communication, nor the linguistic or semiotically-oriented rhetoric regard the theoretical-textbook separation of the genera of speech as an urgent field of action" (J. Engels, 1996, 270).
**431** Cf. the introduction to the topic based on two source-texts in W. Engemann/F. Lütze, 2009, 189–194.

This problem is linked to the irrevocable correlation of content and form. It is not enough for the preacher to just become clear of what he wishes to say in the run-up to the sermon and have his "message" in mind as a sort of theological conclusion. Anyone who desires to motivate the congregation and prompt them through the sermon to understand more than what can be put on a four- to five-page manuscript – and this is decisive for the sermon's receivability in the everyday lives of its listeners – must closely relate the question of its content with the question of its structure and form.

In this context one can learn a lot from the unique biblical texts which say what they have to say in a way most other texts do not: they have, just as unbiblical texts have, too, a distinctive structure of their own which allows for, as it were, studying them on their own conditions and, in doing so, extracting quite different, yet by no means arbitrary, interpretations. Thus it is, for example, not by chance but rather in the 'nature of things' that traditionally sermons on the kingdom of God are preached in parables. Parables, in their just as puzzling as revealing way of speaking, obviously represent a particularly suitable and appropriate form for the message of the coming of this kingdom. Parables, on the one hand, are immediately clear; on the other they leave much open – and above all they captivate us and prompt, once understood, self-reflection. Through their pictures, metaphors and stories they compel us to appear in them ourselves and take on the roles provided. The sermon can benefit from these observations. We come back to this below (4.3.4).

In the 20th century, Friedrich Niebergall was the first to reintroduce to Homiletics the idea that questions of content can only be adequately discussed in connection with questions of form. His ideas on sermon composition are at the same time to be understood as a sort of funeral oration on what he considers the last attempts to impose a scholastic rhetoric upon Homiletics.[432] With satisfaction he notices:

"How far has it [i.e. sermon composition] departed from the old rules of homiletic scholasticism! Torture yourself on your text until you find a topic; then, by sweat of your brow look for a structure, but take care that it follows the course of the text precisely according to the law of the analytical-synthetic method! Exhaust this text if possible! Then assemble the parts, but make each the same length as the others – two, three, even four, none of them should be much shorter than the others! [...] It was the old ideal of German essay writing, the form of which was dictated, for it should later be filled with content. Or it was the drama, the content of which had to be forced into five acts. Or the house, the facade and walls of which were first built, an outer shell into which the rooms were forced only afterwards. In this way one built from the outside to the inside and filled forms

---

**432** Later attempts to re-introduce the genera and rhetorical rules of scholasticism no longer played much of a role in the homiletic debate: W. Trillhaas in the third edition of his *Evangelische Predigtlehre* (1954) [Protestant Homiletics] still insisted on the "iron rules" of a (topic-)sermon: "All parts must be of equal value, [...] all the must be mutually exclusive, [...] all parts must be contained in the overall theme" (1954, 147). At the end of the '50s, H.-R. Müller-Schwefe – likewise unsuccessfully – proposed returning to the *genera iudicale, deliberativum* and *demonstrativum* (1958, 247–249).

with content rather than allowing the content to adopt its very own form. – In the arts, many things have since changed. Many times the old four-act structure is broken up; some plays even consist of stations or tableaus. Today houses are built from inside out, starting from purpose because we are tired of the tyranny and falsehood of the form. In the furnishing of rooms we have given up the previously sacred law of symmetry. [...] To look at the development of the form of the sermon this way, too, does not seem too bold. [...] One could say, to use another comparison from art and literature, that the sermon has moved from the era of form-oriented Classicism to Expressionism."[433]

F. Niebergall seeks for an "order which corresponds to the matter", for a flexible and easy-to-handle "model"[434], for a way of structuring the sermon based on a reflection of its content. In his view the mere division of the sermon into "introduction, main part and conclusion" is not sufficient as it is too formalistic and leaves open what should be contained in those parts.[435] In search of a basic structure which is usable independently of whether one desires to compose a classical teaching-sermon or an emphatic ceremonial address, Niebergall develops a basic model along four specific content elements, which entails certain structural consequences:

A sermon should (1) contain an explanation of the "requisite circumstances" in terms of a problem analysis. In a second step (2) the "norms", guidelines, principles which influence these circumstances shall be recalled.[436] Next (3) the "objective aids" through which a change of situation can be achieved shall be discussed. Here everything should be brought into play "that has happened, is happening and will happen through God", as well as everything that humanity can do.[437] (4) By "subjective aids" Niebergall means on the one hand the communicative repertoire that is available to the preacher; on the other hand he assumes that the success of a sermon largely depends on "making [the listeners] receptive"[438].

Hence, he advocates a sermon pattern
- in which the communication of the gospel is located in the midst of real living conditions because the Word does not need "empty air" but the "solid ground of reality"[439],
- in which those living conditions are not simply repeated but are confronted with the rules of play of the kingdom of God[440] since otherwise it would lack a goal,

---

433 F. Niebergall, 1929, 211.
434 Loc. cit., 168, 212.
435 Niebergall was not familiar with the above classification of the functions of address and sermon.
436 Cf. F. Niebergall, 1929, 176–182. Niebergall argues here less from the promises of the gospel than above all with the "content of Christian Ethics" (loc. cit., 168).
437 Loc. cit., 169, 182.
438 Loc. cit., 169, 188.
439 Loc. cit., 176.
440 Cf. e.g. the Beatitudes in the Sermon on the Mount according to Matt 5:3–16.

- in which God's actions in the past, present and future and everything humanly possible regarding those "conditions" and "norms" is discussed, so that what has been promised can be distinguished from pious hopes and wishful thinking, and
- in which the existing relationship to God of those engaged in the sermon[441] is taken into consideration.

Moreover Niebergall attempts to show, by means numerous examples, how the listeners' comprehension can be aided by using "these very elements not only in regards to content [but] also for the basic pattern of the address."[442] As a consequence, the following modification of the models presented above arises:

**Basic aspects regarding the structure and content of the sermon according to F. Niebergall**

| Structural Aspects | 1. Requisite conditions | 2. Expected changes | 3. Objective possibilities for change | 4. Subjective possibilities for change |
|---|---|---|---|---|
| Aspects of Content | Analysis of an individual's situation; factual circumstances of life | Examination of the rules of the "kingdom of God"; texts from the Old and New Testament | Recollection and anticipation of God's action; conclusions for human action | Consideration of the sermon's personal dimension or its relationship level |
| Allocation to the Sermon Functions | "Sitz im Leben" | Representational or teaching function | Paracletic function | Function of contact or testimony |

**Fig. 13:** Basic aspects regarding the structure and content of the sermon according to F. Niebergall

---

441 F. Niebergall, 1929, 169.
442 Loc. cit., 211f. On this cf. the chapter "Die Gestalt der Predigt", loc. cit., 197–212. Many of these templates would almost certainly not be appealing for today's listeners anymore, which is probably mainly due to the linguistic conventions of the sermons quoted as well as their topics or contextual descriptions which are rather far from our minds today. What I regard as questionable is F. Niebergall's idea that the listeners' cooperation in action or thinking is more difficult to achieve in country parishes than in an urban environment. To say much in a few words is only "possible in a congregation which is used to thinking while listening" (loc. cit., 206). Against this one should remember that any sort of comprehension (not only in the sermon) is a compositional act in which what is heard (here: verbal expressions) is supplemented by attaching meaning to the words spoken before they can actually achieve any significance for the individual.

As this table shows, the four structural elements resemble the aforementioned conditions that are vital for an effective sermon. What makes Niebergall's approach, however, so distinctive is, above all, that it takes account of the situation ("requisite conditions") towards which doctrine, paraclesis and testimony must be geared. A further characteristic feature of sermons created in accordance with this model or pattern is their goal orientation. In reference to the previously conducted situation analysis, the second and third step are concerned with the *changed* situation. This, however, means that in fact *every sermon is case-related* by referring to the circumstances under which people live, to conditions which are in need and capable of change, which in turn sets people free to get involved in the co-creation of their own life and the relationships determining it.

Creating awareness of the necessity to clarify the given situation in the course of sermon preparation and, in so doing, to focus more strongly on the sermon's goal[443] are some of the most important achievements of the homiletic discussion of the rhetorical tradition. This is notably reflected in current angles of reflection.

## 4.3 Current Angles of Reflection

### Preliminary Remarks

Today, the "art of speaking responsibly"[444] is no longer discussed only within the context of linguistic theory and pragmatics but is conceived as a task which of course still includes language, yet goes beyond linguistic arts. An appealing address undoubtedly requires linguistic knowledge and skills. Language is and will remain the decisive medium of rhetorical communication. Therefore the subject of language usage in preaching will be dealt with in a separate chapter (I.5).

Those who desire to speak because they have something to say, who desire to speak because they want to set the wheels of change in motion or warn against something, those who desire to teach something and wish for their listeners to

---

**443** The rhetorician H. Lausberg, demands that, in analyzing a speech one must always pay heed to "the speaker's desired intention to change the situation" which determines every address (1967, 14f.). Against this background he thinks it appropriate to describe speakers as "those in the position of power in the situation" ("Situationsmächtige"), listeners as "those interested in the situation" ("Situationsinteressierte") and the purpose of the speech as the "situational goal" ("Situationsziel") (ibid.).

**444** Cf. the corresponding title of the book by Gert Otto (1994).

remember what they have heard should, however, also know about the *character-istics and conditions of successful communication*. They should know what pro-motes and what impedes the process of comprehension.

In the homiletic context this involves, among other things, the question of what it means "to preach decisively[445]. In view of the previous chapter it should be clear that this does certainly not mean to adopt a snappy, loud and rigid style of preaching which leaves no room for questions. The necessity for decisive preaching is in fact an irrefutable, elementary condition of the art of speaking responsibly.

In this context Michael Meyer-Blanck formulated the following, quite remarkable, answer: "Hence to 'preach decisively' does not mean to provide listeners with predefined decisions (or even to impose such on them) but to put certain decisions up for debate or make them possible in the first place. It means exactly the self-critical stance of consciously keeping one's own decidedness as a possibility of chosen freedom – and of being innocently open to everyone and everything, unconsciously suppressing approval of one's own personal views. [...]. Preaching decisively means to preach purposefully and in a goal-driven way, and thus, self-critically. But this self-criticism must be firmly implemented rhetorically. Otherwise one's speech will lack personal involvement and cause performative damage. Anyone who, while running, constantly thinks about falling is in danger of actually doing so; and, when dancing, ruminates on the sequence of steps will step on their partner's toes or arouse their pity but certainly not dance properly with them. There is a time for everything: Self-criticism of one's own goals has its time, as has decisively speaking up for them. The same holds true for preaching."[446]

Composing one's sermon in order that it becomes a responsible address, through which the addressees come to know about the speaker's intention on the one hand, and realize what all of this could mean for themselves on the other is one of the bigger challenges of Homiletics. Faced with this challenge, there are several approaches the preacher can turn to in order to connect the aspects of content and form in a way that facilitates sermon communication.

In what follows, four of these approaches will be presented: These include (1) the psychology of learning perspective, (2) the narratological perspec-tive, (3) the dialog perspective and (4) the semiotic perspective. This order should by no means be understood as a reflection of any order of priority

---

445 Cf. M. Meyer-Blanck, 2009a, 8–12.
446 Ibid., 8f. Cf. on this Gottfried Voigt's text: "Die Predigt muss etwas wollen" [The sermon has to aspire for something], in: W. Engemann/F. Lütze, 2009, 33–42. Cf. in this context also Katie G. Cannon's homiletic didactics, which aims at following one of the main principles of the Meth-odist theologian and preacher Isaac R. Clark: "If you ain't got no proposition, you ain't got no sermon neither" (K. G. Cannon, 2002, 14).

these perspectives are given in homiletic discourse but rather corresponds to a growth in complexity from the psychology of learning model to the approach of fundamentally looking at the sermon's sign character from a semiotic point of view.

### 4.3.1 The Perspective of the Psychology of Learning: The Sermon as a Process of Learning

Taking up the observations and insights of the psychology of learning into Homiletics means considering the preaching event to some extent as a learning process. From this point of view *the goal of a sermon is regarded as the result of a learning process.* It takes into account the very fact that the communication of the gospel was already in the New Testament conceived as a learning process: the verb διδάσκειν (teaching) belongs to the most important terms of describing a process which today we refer to as "preaching".

That Jesus *taught* – and when he preached appeared like a teacher – runs through the gospels like a *cantus firmus*: people gather round Jesus and follow him *to hear his teaching* – "and [he] as was his custom [...] taught them"[447]. Jesus' teaching encompasses getting acquainted with ideas, pictures and comparisons which must not be believed and followed blindly; his teaching consists in making them understandable, making something clear, i.e. in teaching them something which the addressees as a rule have not "seen" or thought of in this way, never mind understood, before. The content of his teaching affects the addressees existentially and their comprehension of reality substantially. In the course of this certain rules are revealed and connections uncovered, as e.g. in the Beatitudes, in the Lord's Prayer or in his remark that the one who "first strives for the kingdom of God", i.e. who knows what he wants to live for, will almost certainly cope with the rest. These statements can neither be reduced to a liberating message and nor should they be followed as law but are held up to the view of the addressees as relevant for and capable of changing their lives.[448]

By this way of looking at things, neither the working of the Holy Spirit should be made superfluous nor should the coming of the kingdom of God be reduced to a lesson. The psychology of learning model rather assumes that listening to a

---

**447** Mark 10:1. A selection of further relevant passages include Matt 5:2, Matt 7:29, Matt 13:54, Matt 21:23, Mark 1:21f., Mark 2:13, Mark 4:2, Mark 6:2, Luke 5:3, John 8:2.
**448** On the teaching dimension of Jesus' proclamation and the problem of dismissing this dimension in certain approaches of Homiletics and pastoral care cf. W. Engemann, 2004, 885–889 and 2006a, 28–32.

sermon implies (or at least potentially implies) *relearning* or *further learning.*[449] It is based on a comprehensive, integral concept of learning which is not merely targeted at factual knowledge but refers to humanity's total repertoire of behavior, i.e. their thoughts, feelings and actions.[450]

That listening to testimonies of faith is capable of initiating learning processes can be illustrated by means of numerous texts from the Old and New Testament in which people are confronted with "revelations" or with the coming of the kingdom of God. Whether one thinks of the "shepherds in the field" who must learn that their king presents himself other than they expected, or whether one thinks of the fleeing, unhappy Jacob who, in the open, against his expectation, experiences God's company, or whether one thinks of the cry for repentance of the Baptist or Jesus: it is always related to messages which, in order to be understood, require rethinking, which in its turn entails far-reaching changes in almost all areas of life.

The interrelation of content and form demands – viewed from the psychology of learning perspective – taking into consideration certain individual stages within the course of the address. Processes through which people change their attitudes, are motivated to action or, in the sphere of the emotions, have new experiences, manifest a recurring basic pattern. Anyone paying regard to this pattern will attempt to structure the content of what they have to say in a way that (1) a certain *interest* for the subject matter can be expected on the part of the addressees, that (2) the *core content* or basic problem of the subject matter addressed is clearly transmitted, that (3) their *arguments* are formulated in reference to potential counter-arguments, that (4) the message is brought forward in relation to the problem addressed and suggests a *'solution'* and that (5) the sermon itself demonstrates, i.e. verbally anticipates, the reliability of its message. Hence, the respective distinctive functions of an address or sermon are linked to five specific stages or steps[451], which can be identified as the following:

---

449 H. B. Kaufmann goes even one step further when – advocating the psychology of learning model – he states: "Faith is not a once for all established, pure phenomenon of consciousness but must be regarded as a Christian, continuing experience, as a process of living and learning." From the introduction to: P. Düsterfeld/H. B. Kaufmann, 1975, 10.
450 W. Schütz' criticism of this model is based on an outdated concept of learning according to which learning consists in the cramming of knowledge. He esteems the worship service as having degenerated into a "school event" (1981, 216) and overlooks both the didactic and theological premises of this homiletic approach (cf. the summary at the end of 4.2.1) as well as the corresponding impulses of Luther or Melanchthon mentioned above.
451 The first homiletic works including this position stem from H. Arens (1972, esp. 125.138) and H. Arens/F. Richardt/J. Schulte (1975, 41–81). A detailed examination of the psychology of learning model is found in P. Bukowski (1995) who highly appreciates this approach (ibid., 31–35).

| Phase | Function | Exemplary Sketch |
|---|---|---|
| **1. Motivation** | The listeners are motivated to take on a questioning attitude; they should perceive the topic as relevant for themselves or be able to recognize themselves in the situation described. | The sermon visualizes a situation in which one perceives one's lack of freedom as burdensome. The listeners are reminded of the difficulty of living in coherence with their thinking, feeling and action. They listen because they wish that this would change. |
| **2. Delimitation of the Problem** | The established question is focused on a problem; the topic addressed receives a particular profile and thereby becomes concrete. The situation is structured. | The sermon refers to the fear which can prevent people from living their freedom appropriately. Here the fear of their own responsibility and weakness plays a special part. It can be described as the fear of living *as oneself.* |
| **3. Trial and Error** | Possibilities of solving the problem are revealed, illusionary solutions are highlighted as such. The need for another, new solution which could actually change the situation becomes clear. | The sermon describes forms of substitutions or compensations for a life in freedom: Arrangements with rotten compromises, reinterpretations of existing obligations as "imposed crosses", renunciation of the experience of a liberated life etc. |
| **4. Offering a Solution** | Introduction of an offer of a solution which is no illusory solution – i.e. does not need to dread counter arguments. The solution to the problem is in the offing. The new situation comes into sight by way of apprehending the biblical text. | The sermon brings into play the fact that the resurrection of Jesus is without compromise: The women on Easter morning – making a pilgrimage to his grave – who had prepared themselves for the end of a once promising story were then confronted with the fact that they no longer had a place in their own graves but should live instead (cf. Mark 16:1–8). |
| **5. Reinforcement of the Solution** | Clarification of the suitability of the solution offered by depicting how it proved successful in various other situations. Here it is a matter of encouraging those present to render the solution offered possible and to act correspondingly in their own situation. | The continuation or new beginning of this life is envisaged under difficult circumstances: For this re-awakened life the "heathen Galilee" becomes the preferred place of proving itself and that among morose fishermen and failures: Because God desires to be there, the life of these people, too, is given a new chance. |

**Fig. 14:** The psychology of learning model from a homiletic perspective

That the "offering of a solution" is not addressed until the fourth stage of the learning process does not mean that the biblical text only plays a minor part in this model.[452] The relevance of the text for the sermon is secured above all in the course of its *preparation with the text*. This preparation process implies that in working on the text – and demanded by it – questions are addressed which relate to the day-to-day reality of those who will hear the sermon. In a certain sense such questions are themselves the result of approaching the biblical texts as, among other things, a form of coping with life. Consequently it appears appropriate and perfectly "biblical" to start out from questions posed by "life".[453]

Using the psychology of learning model involves taking into consideration that the individual steps (named in Fig. 14) appear in a quite different order in the *preparation* of the sermon: As a rule it is step 2 (delimitation of the problem) and 4 (offering a solution) which must be treated first.[454] Questions about the listeners' motivation, analyses of apparent alternatives and considerations for solution reinforcement will follow as soon as it has become clear what the sermon shall be all about, which problem it shall address and which communication objectives it shall meet. Since these questions have already been discussed in some detail above, I shall confine myself in the following further explanation of the psychology of learning model to steps 1, 3 and 5:

In working on the *stage of motivation* (step 1) we must ensure that the sermon actually reaches the horizon of experience of the listeners or the area of existential experience respectively and thus addresses what truly *concerns* the listeners so that they can find themselves caught up by the sermon or the situation it depicts. This is achieved through factual knowledge as well as a relationship which emotionally supports the message that what I hear is, in fact, a *sermon for me*.[455]

The thoughts and ideas one has at the *stage of trial and error* (step 3) are especially important. After all, this stage is about looking critically at one's own mistakes and failures, which are in part the cause of the problem. A sermon which

---

**452** Cf. the first such reproach in A. Mertens' critical comment on the psychology of learning model (A. Mertens, 1975) and later in different statements on the significance of the psychology of learning in Homiletics (e.g. in H. W. Dannowski, 1985, 144). What is disillusioning about this criticism is not its scepticism regarding the reception of a psychodidactic model but rather its implicit understanding of the biblical sermon.

**453** On the criteria of a biblical sermon see I.3.4.

**454** We have already addressed the difficulty of establishing a precise chronological order when it comes to approaching situation and text, problem determination and solution possibilities (cf. I.3.2).

**455** As regards the preacher's communication behavior, all the principles summarized in Fig. 7 (p. 77) come into effect here.

constructs artificial problems at this point is easily figured out as being irrelevant or dishonest. In such a case the stage of motivation has failed to keep its promise. Another problematic approach is the attempt to smooth out real problems with theological concepts. The listener should be able to follow the argumentation introduced by the preacher at all times.

Step 5, the *reinforcement of the solution*, should not be any less concrete than the motivation stage. Descriptions of the situation, delimitations of the problem, going through possible solutions, offering a solution – all of this remains ineffective and, seen from the psychology of learning perspective, leaves behind frustration if it does not offer a vision for one's own life, if what was said only *appears* to be true without its being experienced or proving its worth in one's own life.

These considerations possibly remind the reader of those voices which turned against rhetoric in the attempt to keep away everything manipulative from the preaching event. Indeed, the advertising industry, too, benefits from the psychology of learning by making use of its research into problem and uncertainty creation and expectation formation in order then to offer a suitable product as solution and at the same time – through the "delight in the white washing" or the "baby's laughter" etc. – come up with a reinforcement of the solution. Whether attending to somebody's – your neighbor's, to be exact – problems is actually a favor to them, however, certainly depends to a large extent on two aspects: if they actually have these problems, and if the nature of your interest is rooted in solidarity, Protestantism, charity, etc., or merely in self-interest. "To preach decisively" and, in so doing, not only to promote one's own a particular "view of things" but above all a certain experience of life is part of the basic principles of an ardent communication of the gospel. From a homiletic point of view it is vital to bear in mind: a thoughtless sermon or sermon which allegedly just follows the text is not immune to trotting out artificial problems such as are encountered all over in the world of advertising. Such a sermon runs the risk of promoting religious products (e.g. particular images of God and oneself) the preacher favors for reasons probably even unknown to himself. Someone who thinks about *how* to get things done usually also thinks about how to get them done *effectively*. What is decisive here is the *responsibility* preachers accept when they rise to speak to the best of their knowledge and belief. *This is* what preachers must consistently account to themselves and their congregation for – irrespectively of the method they use in order to come up with a sermon that is comprehensible and meaningful to their listeners.

In addition to that, there are several other aspects in the theory of the psychology of learning that seem worthy being considered in Homiletics. These particularly arise from the relationship between learning and faith: the images and concepts people have of God as a child change as they grow older. This is a learning process for which the sermon is able to provide crucial impetus. In listening to the sermon Christians learn, among other things, that the existing conditions are change-worthy. They learn to translate the gospel into the context of their own lives. The sermon also teaches how account is rendered for Christian hope and how Christian freedom can be practised and thus proves to be a guiding principle for living by faith.

### 4.3.2 The Narratological Perspective: The Sermon as an Engaging Story

There is a fundamental difference between *discursively explaining* and *narratively evolving* a particular content. The former involves, above all, a stringent discussion of facts, a systematic presentation of information, a logical weighing of arguments and counter-arguments. The latter, by contrast, consists in depicting, within the frame of a story, to what extent the content matters to a person's everyday life, under which living-conditions an individual is faced with and needs it, what this content practically means for taking a decision etc. In the field of Homiletics this means: a sermon delivered in narrative shape can make clear what living by faith really means, which developments, which consequences must be taken into consideration. A sermon can, in a way, have an effect through the fiction of a story, which – ideally – is created in the act of hearing it.[456]

People who preach *by narrating* bring their listeners *in medias res*. They open up before their audience a world which is just as complex as it is true in detail and rich in facets, a world in which "a situation exists" which can change over the course of the story and the sermon. People who preach by narrating create a world with a before and an after, a world of events and experiences in which the actors of this *narrated world* experience what the gospel can mean for the listeners in their *real world*. The congregation participates in *both* their real world *as well as* in the narrated world.[457] While listening, they become involved in what happens in the story. Following the sermon demands from the listeners and – at the same time enables them – to become "doers of the Word"[458]. In listening to a narrative sermon, the Lutheran *fides ex auditu* attains a pragmatic touch: because such a sermon "generates consternation among the listeners" it turns them into "doers of the Word", which "in turn allows them [the listeners] to become the subject matter"[459].

---

456 Cf. the fundamental difference of "discussed" and "narrated" worlds already discussed in H. Weinrich (1964, 44–50).

457 In a way the detailed model provided above in order to describe the processes occurring in the production and reception of literary texts (cf. I.3.3.1 and Fig. 8 and 9, p. 121–124) applies to speeches as well. The main difference between the relationship of author and reader on the one hand and speaker and listeners on the other consists in the fact that the latter, as historical persons – other than author and reader – find themselves simultaneously in a common situation of communication.

458 Cf. Jas 1:22.

459 H. Weinrich, 1973, 333.

The participatory fulfillment of a story which has been heard does in fact not automatically lead to a better understanding[460] or to "religious consternation succeeded by faith". But "good stories" certainly do facilitate a more intensive participation in the communicative event of the sermon. Good stories are the kinds which truly reach a narrative level, which bring the listener into a "narrated world" in which they can play a part, stories which do not merely insert a few little anecdotes for the purpose of illustrating bold assertions. What the theologian and author Wolfgang Hegewald writes about the reading of tales most certainly also applies to the hearing of good stories: "Every successful story entertains its readers in several ways; as an aesthetic pleasure and as a resource for life. The narrator is able to entertain me, his reader, because he devises a structure for the complexity of his material which seems to me at one and the same time intangible and conclusively obvious."[461]

Basically the *homiletic legitimacy* for the use of a narrative style in preaching or the narrative sermon respectively arises from the character of the biblical message itself. Whether one thinks of the reception of the great stories of the Old Testament or of the much shorter parables, the "Historical Books" or the gospels: what "God" means for believers, how it stands with the relationship between God and the individual or humanity in general, which future awaits us "with God" or "in his kingdom" etc. – all of this is preferably described in the form of stories. Even at the high point in the liturgy the celebrant begins to narrate: "In the night in which our Lord, Jesus Christ was betrayed, he took bread [...]."[462]

The "mysteries of faith" can only be adequately spoken about in stories. Christianity is "not primarily a community of argumentation and interpretation but rather a *narrative community*"[463]. When it comes to content, however, the Judeo-Christian stories are everything but harmless chitchat. They are subversive. In this respect, too, there is a strong congruence between form and content. Anyone who considers taking up the Bible's narrative tradition and continuing

---

**460** Otto Haendler, who primarily starts out from the person of the preacher in his Homiletics – to point to only one of the blind spots in the homiletic discourse at that time – expects something decisive from narrating in the pulpit. The connection of form and content requires to cultivate in the sermon the "true narration of stories" because this "activates the pictorial level" of the listeners as the "location of true understanding" (2017b, 557; cf. also 629f.).
**461** W. Hegewald, 1998, 39.
**462** On the "event character of the sermon" cf. the introduction to the contributions of M. Nicol and H. Weinrich in W. Engemann/F. Lütze, 2009, 231–234.
**463** Here J. B. Metz (2009, 221) takes up a concept from Walter Benjamin. H. Weinrich considers that Christianity might have "lost its narrative innocence [...] through its contact with the Hellenistic world". Just as "reasoning philosophers" increasingly replaced the "narrating mythologists", theology, too, evolved into a science, whose objective appeared to be "changing the handed-down stories into non-fiction as quickly and entirely as possible" and thus reducing them to (possibly abstract) factuality (H. Weinrich, 2009, 247).

with it from the pulpit should be aware that this is a traditionally 'dangerous' business[464]: Biblical preaching[465] through narrating on the basis of the Bible entails bringing to mind stories of liberation and effecting change of existing conditions from within if these conditions involve the suppression of freedom, recklessness and conflict, and are life-threatening. Anyone who preaches in narrative form puts counter-stories into circulation,[466] which, though told to their end in the worship service, are further continued in the stories of the listeners.

These prerequisites cannot hide the fact that actually very little is narrated in the pulpit. According to a study conducted by Andreas Egli the linguistic form most frequently used in preaching is the "discussion" of texts, situations, topics etc. Nonetheless, according to Egli's findings, narrative language makes up 26% of a sermon on average.[467] This figure needs, however, to be treated with caution. For estimating, as Egli's study does, the narrativity of a sermon only quantitatively and stating solely on the basis of individual sentences and sections that sermons consist "on average of a quarter of narrative sentences"[468] does not say anything about the *quality of the narrative*, let alone about whether a real story was achieved or not. In part, the examples mentioned by Egli are nothing more than empty phrases inserted into assertions, explanations and theological conclusions. They offer hardly anything of what has been understood since the middle of the '70s as "narrativity in preaching".[469]

"Narrative theology" was firstly outlined and given its name to by the already mentioned (Protestant) literary theorist Harald Weinrich. In the '70s of the 20th century this approach was systematic-theologically reflected and subsequently linked to relevant dogmatic discourses. This certainly involved the risk of playing narration off against argumentation.[470] *The argumentative achievement of a narrated story* should, however, not be underestimated and can scarcely be overestimated. Narrated with a particular situation in view, a story cannot only take on an argumentative function as a whole, but – due to its concrete details – also serve as an ideal basis for abstract argumentation.

---

**464** According to J. B. Metz stories from the pulpit imply "dangerous memories" (1973, 336f.).

**465** On the biblical sermon cf. I.3.4.

**466** Cf. in analogy the counter-model of K.-H. Bieritz, 1983, 153–158 as well as a current series of volumes of sermons which attempt to consider narratological aspects (e.g. H. Nitschke, 1981).

**467** A. Egli, 1995, 118.

**468** Ibid.

**469** What is in fact narrated if, for example, the congregation is told: "Yet one thing is clear: A person who does not hide his misery from Jesus but confesses this before him, receives his forgiving Word. Jesus has the right to forgive sins, to cleanse us, for he has fulfilled the Law doubly" (loc. cit., 97).

**470** Cf. e.g. D. Ritschl/H. O. Jones, 1976.

In a situation in which Jesus' audience – according to Luke – increasingly harbors the expectation that "the kingdom of God was going to appear at once" (Luke 19:11) one might probably have expected a clear statement from Jesus. Instructions regarding the Last Days, an explanation of the "already but not yet", an elucidation of appropriate and inappropriate attitudes and hopes – in other words: plain language. Instead Jesus tells them a parable in which he addresses the passive religious observer-mentality of the present crowd and engages them in a change of perspective. Without the expected future being denied, the present emerges as an eschatological place in which people are challenged and enabled to reckon with the coming of God's kingdom, and to live accordingly.

In this context, it is essential to bring the respective imagined communicative situation to mind. Naturally, this does not mean that the use of argumentation and, as a consequence, the possibility of logical reasoning or definitions should be abandoned in the science of theology.

Yet the preaching situation, with its task to encourage and strengthen belief, particularly requires an experience-based language: a language which benefits from the fact that experiences can be used as analogies and that such a process engages the listeners, giving it the character of argumentation, as it were. It is to be doubted that for the listeners, theological arguing has the quality of arguments merely because what is being said is logical and stringent (only) to experts. A sermon's argumentation – be it abstractly or narratively designed – stands and falls with the comprehensibility of the individual elements of its line of argumentation for each and every listener. But fact is that they can follow it more easily if the sermon's chain of reasoning contains narrative elements.

Significant impulses for narrating on the basis of biblical records, which, however, have not yet entirely found their way into Homiletics, are offered in the narrative models developed by Dietrich Steinwede and Walter Neidhart in the context of religious education.[471] The authors show that a narrative based on a biblical text initially demands the same theological preparatory work as an "explanatory text sermon". While Steinwede's concept attempts to integrate into the narrative specific analogy-laden elements (e.g. the sequence of scenes in a parable) in order to reveal the binding character of the text as a *prime*-message, Neidhart strives for a way of narrating that introduces the text's understanding of faith in the light of questions of contemporary life.

There are different ways for achieving a narratologically composed sermon. Manfred Haustein enlists the following: 1. The "recounting of biblical texts", 2. the "biblical story as a prototype of the story of one's own life and time", 3. the "recreation of a biblical text in a way that is relevant to the present times" and 4. the

---

471 Cf. D. Steinwede, 1981 and W. Neidhart, 1989.

"biblical narrative, passed on in a creative, topical manner".[472] These narrative forms, however, closely resemble one another and thus can only be in a limited way delimited from one another, particularly since all of them are modeled, in some way or other, on *the form of the biblical text itself*. This is, however, in no way compulsory, since the narrative composition of a sermon does not depend on the form of the text. Most of all, it is important to be aware of the effects of the different narrative structures.

1. *Narrative elements at the beginning of a sermon* can – provided that the usual clichés[473] are avoided – contribute to a *condensed view on the reality of life* and make the situation addressed in the sermon plausible as a genuine, true-to-life situation.[474] Experience has shown that in case they succeed – i.e. they are narratively well-made – narrative elements are associated with an increase in the audience's willingness to listen.

2. If narratives take on the *function of examples* in the sermon, they should not purely illustrate what has already been said but *strengthen, deepen and specify the intention of what has been said towards a particular direction*, in order to further intensify the "decisiveness of the sermon"[475] and allow it to become unambiguous.

3. Whether a sermon which considers itself above all as the *retelling of a text* is more comprehensible than the – perhaps difficult – text itself depends on a number of aspects, one of which is that no "text explanations" are put in the mouths of the characters appearing in the narrative, i.e. that they act as authentic subjects with whom the listeners can identify. The "presupposed

---

**472** M. Haustein, 1990, 464f. When he speaks of "recreation in a way that is relevant to the present times" Haustein actually means the recreation of *biblical texts*. Many sermons from the period when narration from the pulpit was rediscovered proceed in a similar manner (cf. e.g. H. Nitschke, 1976 and 1981). In view of the reinforcement of the function of the text referred to in I.3 this is not compulsory. It is perfectly legitimate to tell a story, indeed even in a *biblical* way – i.e. in the spirit of Jewish-Christian tradition – without, in so doing, aiming for the recognition or comprehension of a particular text. Likewise, the biblical text can play its own "supporting role" within the narration and, in this way, can serve its overall understanding in a special way. Cf. the examples in: W. Engemann, 2001b, 12–24.

**473** Cf. I.5.1.5 and I.6.1.6.

**474** "Those who tell stories pledge themselves to what Ingeborg Bachmann once named 'high-voltage current of the present'. Their curiosity about everything that is the case is scarcely satiable and they are well advised to take an interest in the signs of their own time" (W. Hegewald, 1998, 38).

**475** Cf. the preliminary remarks to I.4.3, p. 175–177. Those who narrate "should make no secret of their opinion". They are, after all not presenting 'googled' knowledge from the Internet, that monstrous model student "who retains everything and understands nothing, the swellhead of the global village, a useful idiot. Its idiom is prattling indifference" (W. Hegewald, 1998, 38).

identity of past and present history"[476] should not only be assumed; it also needs to be shaped.

4. The homiletically most consequent narrative form is the *sermon as narrated story* in which no additional explanations are required because its communicative intentions are apparent, its purposed position is discernible, its impetus for action is clear and its offer of identification is comprehensible. In terms of the aforementioned criteria for a biblical sermon it is perfectly possible in *one* coherent story to achieve both, a clarification of the theological point of the text as well as representing the existential interest of the listeners – even without speaking *expressis verbis* of the "text then" and "us today".[477]

It would defy the homiletic reception of narratological principles if one were still to conclude finally that it is not "possible [...] to compose an entire sermon as a narrative", that a "subjectively authenticated and verified interpretative pattern"[478] must be additionally included into the sermon. It is precisely the advantage of a narrative communication of the gospel that the listeners can understand the "interpretative pattern" developed by the preacher through systematic groundwork on the basis of a concrete case; that the listeners themselves must appear in this story or at least can translate it for the context of their own lives, for their own "case".

A sermon in the shape of a story is capable of being a "testimony" in the double sense of the word: on the one hand, in a theological respect, as the frequently dogmatically deviating talk – composed in *personal language* – of the motives, convictions and expectations of one's own faith, on the other, in a narratological respect, as a quasi professional ethical duty of the writer, speaker or narrator who has to turn to his neighbor *in a narrative form*. Anyone who does not take care of their message's form, i.e. who does not know their craft, "bears false witness" and, according to the American author Ezra Pound,[479] breaks the 8th Commandment.

---

476 H. W. Dannowski, 1981, 153.

477 Cf. W. Engemann, 1993b, 25–29, 123–129 and 2001, 71–78, 116–127. Some new suggestions for the practice of narrative Homiletics are given in Janet K. Ruffing's book "To Tell the Sacred Tale" by pointing to the relevance of not only biblical but also of current stories of faith. She emphatically advocates the "sharing" of "sacred stories" for the purpose of continuing God's story with humanity to the present day, which, according to her, is at the same time a privileged form of spiritual accompaniment (J. K. Ruffing, 2011).

478 H. W. Dannowski, 185, 156.

479 One of Pound's most often quoted thoughts, above all in literary-critical essays, though in the texts I have studied always without source reference, as for example most recently in W. Hegewald (1998, 40).

### 4.3.3 The Dialog Perspective: The Sermon as Conversation

#### a) Premises of a Dialogical Culture of Conversation and Speech

With reference to a common homiletic misunderstanding[480] it has already become clear above that it is not the dialogic form which finally bestows dialog-character onto a sermon. Dialogicity is first and foremost a *contentual dimension* of the sermon.[481] Its key component is the inclusion of the listeners' situation, which means dealing with the realities of life of contemporaries. Of course, this maxim is easier proclaimed than accomplished. In the philosophical, rhetorical and theological history of dialog, including the relevant theories, successful dialogs have been characterized by certain features which cannot be covered by the customary demands on a good speaker. Anyone who sets out to dialogical preaching should be aware of the basic premises of such a venture.

1. With a dialog one enters into a current and interactive event that is reciprocal in nature and *lives from the active participation of all involved*. This intentional and expected mutual engagement is the *one* premise, the factual frame and abstract aim of any dialog. One enters into dialog because one expects something from exposing oneself to the ideas and thoughts of *another one*.

2. The *structure of the dialog is triadic*. With regard to the sermon this means: preacher and listener act *jointly* in terms of a shared frame of reference (in the language of ancient rhetoric: the *Logos*), "which may, but does not have to, materialize as a common topic"[482]. In terms of a dialog sermon this may, for example, apply in that it relates to a piece of common tradition (e.g. a text) and contributes to coping with a shared concern (e.g. "living by faith").

3. The dialog models of antiquity and mediaeval scholasticism are neither to be considered as makeshift solutions nor were they devised for the sake of bringing change into an otherwise dominant monolog culture. These dialogs had their *Sitz im Leben* in actual situations which awaited attention. The *ars dialogica* was strongly connected with the clarification of legal issues or biased statements; it served establishing the truth in scholarly disputes and – last but not least – maintaining a culture of conversation which was, in a deeper sense, "witty", pointed and original.[483] This means: in a dialog "there is always really something at stake", not least the relationship between the

---

480 Cf. I.4.1.3., p. 158–160.
481 The level of the content is preceded by the anthropological: Every communication has its origin in the human need for a life in relationships ("social intercourse"), the essence of which is dialog.
482 E. W. B. Hess-Lüttich, 1994, 607.
483 Cf. C. Schmölders, 1979 and K.-H. Göttert, 1988.

dialog partners. People who "preach in dialog" should thus be aware of the reason why they – in the best sense of the word – wish to struggle with others for knowledge and understanding. They should have resolved for themselves whether they intend to defend the listeners (e.g. *coram deo* or against their self-recriminations), whether they want to approach and come closer to the truth out of doubts regarding a particular question etc.

4. Every dialog – except for those taking place for the mere purpose of conversation – *essentially follows an argumentative structure* for which the Socratic Dialog[484] is still exemplary. To open a dialog homiletically means in this respect to plunge into the world of rational reasoning, logical thinking, questioning and allowing oneself to be questioned. Through conversation (διαλέγεσθαι) the dialog partners attempt to come closer to the truth. If they succeed it is not due to the amount of knowledge (e.g. of a preacher) brought into the conversation from *one* side of the preaching event but rather the result of a successful dialog *between* the communication partners in which accountability is demanded and rendered (λόγον διδόναι). The obligation to give good reasons is a core element of dialog.

5. The theological-philosophical requirements on a homiletic culture of dialog go – following Schleiermacher's concept of the encounter of subjects in the *communicatio* of a conversation as well as the dialogists F. Ebner, M. Buber and G. M. Martin – beyond an elaborately composed structure of thesis and antithesis: it focuses on the overall sense which develops *between* the communication partners and characterizes as well as determines their commonalities, rather than on individual, as speech acts analysable and mutually related, monolog sequences. This implies a specific concept of communicating the gospel, from which new perspectives can be gained to understand this kind of dialog as the foundation of a congregation.

6. Making such a dialog succeed – and the willingness to be open for the insights it leads to – is more important than the immediate usefulness of its results and in any case is to be valued more highly than (apparent) solutions which do not withstand the dialog. The fact that dialogs are capable of leading from opinion to knowledge implies that they also lead to experiencing the current limits of knowledge.

Beyond such far-reaching premises we must address the following question: Can appropriate structures give additional support to the dialog ideally already

---

**484** Cf. Plato, 1982, particularly the dialogs in Vol. I of this edition.

implied in the contentual reference of the sermon, in order to reinforce the congregation's participation in the preaching event?

### b) Dialog Sermon with and before the Congregation

Basically there are two forms of a dialog-sermon imaginable: on the one hand, immediate and direct dialog with the congregation itself and, on the other hand, a dialog which is carried out by two people in front of the assembled congregation and thus involving the listeners only indirectly.

A sermon developed in dialog with the congregation primarily requires the same preliminary steps as a sermon delivered as a monolog – which includes the attempt to give an account (if possible in writing) of one's own position. This also implies being, already in the run-up to the actual preaching event, a considerate interlocutor who has questions that bother himself, questions that move him particularly in dealing with certain texts and situations. It is imperative already in the preparation phase of an explicit dialog to bear in mind the arguments which usually come up and are discussed in relation to particular questions.[485]

It is certainly not necessary for those who preach in dialog to pretend that their choice of sermon form, the dialog form, is a direct consequence of their perplexity or insecurity in view of the particular text. The decision to opt for a dialog-sermon could, however, rather be based on the insight that a dialog reveals the experiential background of certain questions, positions and expectations to a much greater extent than a monologic preaching style. The congregation possibly recognizes in dialog more clearly than in monolog *how the preacher has arrived at*

---

485 Cf. in this context the homiletically promising and inspiring principle of "other-wise preaching" by John McClure (2001) – developed in analysis of Levinas' deconstructivism –, which refers to "a constant going forth to the other, [. . .] an endless journey of solidarity and affinity" (151). A corresponding Homiletics would take seriously the challenges of preaching under the conditions of life and comprehension of the other so that the sermon becomes meaningful for them. This not only requires a contemporary engagement with the biblical text, but also approaching the way and premises of life of potential listeners in an unbiased manner, which is certainly not achieved by way of resorting to merely rhetorical solutions of theology, above all, if these solutions allow for nothing but affirmation or rejection. Hence, deconstructivist reflection in the run-up to the sermon is to be considered neither as an expression of a lust for the annihilation of approved means of orientation nor as a confusion of the congregation in a know-all manner, but as a necessary consequence of questioning "total" explanation-, plausibility- and authority structures, which, in communicative practice, cannot deliver what they promise. New and consistent patterns of argumentation can only be developed if they are, from the listeners' point of view, applicable and can be integrated, expanded, further continued and transferred into their own lives.

*this opinion or that open question.* Through dialog, preachers, on the other hand, may realize whether they have really touched upon the questions and positions of the listeners with their sermon idea, whether their understanding of faith finds a place in the lives and experiences of the congregation. As a consequence, such a dialog can result in changed ways of looking at things and shifts in positions on both sides. After all, a sermon is always also about one's own personal way of believing. Accordingly, dialog sermons frequently have a somewhat more open, more risking and "revealing" effect and thus particularly emphasize the pastoral care dimension.

Dialogic communication in and with the congregation, by means of which the gospel is recalled both by the congregation as well as the preacher, stands or falls with the ability of the dialog partners to overcome the latent expectation that listeners pose questions which the preacher answers.

Strong impulses for sermons structured also formally as dialogs were provided by the structural reform movement in congregations at the end of the '60s and beginning of the '70s, whereby democratic considerations in a certain sense were the driving forces: Franz Jantsch suggests to invite members of the congregation "to ask questions in the next sermon, the subject of which has been announced to them in advance"[486]. But why is it only questions? Why should members of the congregation not additionally express in the worship service how they as Christians deal with the issues announced and what "faith" means for them in this context? What kind of dialog is this when the congregation merely prepares for questions while the preacher prepares for all the answers?

Dialog-sermons make clear to the congregation that preachers, too, have questions, and it must become obvious how and what they believe in the light of this. Further, the congregation is to be addressed with regard to their experiences of living by faith. Here the dialog could take on a maieutic function: through dialog it emerges anew what people day in day out insinuate with regard to their lives, what they are actually searching for, what they really want, what they live upon, their expectations, what they for various reasons refrain from doing etc. They will (once again) become aware of what they live for, of what they regard as essentially significant and what as irrelevant.

In order to prevent a sermon composed as dialog from merely airing answers to which there are no questions, the congregation – to be taken seriously as a dialog partner – should be included into the hermeneutical processes of searching for life situations and text apprehension. In doing so, one could follow the basic pattern outlined below:

---

486 According to M. Haustein, 1990, 468; without source reference.

1. *Introductory Phase: Motivation and Information*
Setting the stage for a dialog implies providing the congregation, in all due conciseness, with all the information they need about the text and its "Sitz im Leben", in order to grasp its point.

Analogously, one can start out by skilfully and briefly approaching the lifeworld focus of the sermon that sparks off questions regarding the relevance of faith, the acquisition of freedom etc. In either case this stage is essentially about throwing light upon the text or a particular way of looking at a certain problem to such an extent that the congregation can get involved in the text or the topic.

2. *Consolidation Phase (Dialog I): Consolidating Problems and Perspectives*
   *together with the Congregation*
The linking of problem outline and text knowledge ideally prompts the perception of tensions, parallels and convergences. It is practically unavoidable – and should in fact not be avoided anyway – that linking text and topic in a certain way when opening a dialog already reveals a certain positional stance and at least suggests a particular interpretation.

From then on it is up to the congregation to establish connections between the (outlined or other) problem areas and the tradition that has grown into the text and, in doing so, broach personal concerns regarding their day-to-day reality. In the following conversation, preacher and congregation may come to an understanding about wherein the main point, the core issues, the "root" of the answer or question provided in the text might have consisted at that time. In further consequence new problems appear, which the text obviously does not address, but which can nevertheless be discussed in dialog and be related to the respective pericope or other texts, hymns, works of art of the Christian tradition.

3. *Confirmation Phase (Dialog II): Expression of Convictions and Expectations*
It is important for a real dialog to occur that preachers also express what they personally believe in respect of a particular matter, what they hope for, what they doubt. They should conduct the dialog, as discussed at the beginning of this chapter, "decisively". This not only implies to allow for *queries* on the part of the congregation. The dialog should furthermore bring to light experiences *which reflect the personality-specific creed of the members of the congregation* and thus become an impetus for articulating one's own faith.

The same holds true in a figurative sense for *a dialog that is carried out between two dialog partners before the congregation*: it is inappropriate and will easily be conceived as insincere if the – possibly particularly serious – problems of the one speaker are magnificently mastered by the prepared answers of the other. In such a case the dialog partner becomes the puppet of ostensible solutions – another case of "bearing homiletically false witness against one's neighbor" and an offence against the 8th Commandment.[487]

If the sermon is composed as a dialog between two members of the congregation, the two of them should already have completed a real dialog before: in

---

[487] Cf. above at the end of I.4.3.2, p. 187. Further investigations on dialogical character of preaching are to be found most recently in Marlene Ringgaard Lorensen's dissertation Dialogical Preaching (2013).

advance of their first meeting, they should have worked on the text for themselves and have taken a look on their own current life situation in the horizon of a concrete understanding of the text. They should have clear ideas of the extent to which it deals with specific conditions of human existence, of how the sermon is capable of contributing to understanding and changing these conditions, of the attitudes it advises. The conversation, which the two dialog partners subsequently meet up for in order to conduct a first dialog, should be recorded. This allows for composing the actual dialog sermon on the basis of this record. In the course of this it also should be clarified in what context the text shall be mentioned in the sermon, which of the problems and relations to life previously discussed in private should be focussed on in front of the congregation, in which manner the "personality-specific creed" of the two dialog partners should be expressed and much else.

### c) From Polylog to Bibliolog

Since the beginning of the '70s Homiletics has developed greatly regarding the question of an appropriate form of the sermon through the inclusion of perspectives relating to communication science and the social sciences. This becomes particularly apparent when we look at two specific forms of dialog, which in a rather exemplary way represent two basic, yet widely divergent, understandings of the dialog dimension of the sermon.

According to Heinz Wagner's concept of the *polylog sermon* the preacher first of all (1) in relation to the text gives "an impetus for reflection or provides access to the text in the frame of a situation analysis. This introductory part is the basis for (2) a conversation which the pastor holds in the nave of the church. Their stimuli trigger off reactions, their questions encourage for statements, experiences of members of the congregation substantiate the message and critical comments deepen comprehension. [...] What follows is an 'interlude', usually in the shape of songs from the choir or congregation. (3) For approximately 10 minutes the pastor retires to the sacristy in order to sort out and go through the contributions received from the congregation. (4) After this the pastor appears in the pulpit and delivers an in some sort premeditated but regarding its form still improvised sermon"[488].

Apart from the one triadic element of a shared frame of reference, which is the bible text and Christianity itself, very few of the aforementioned premises of a dialog speech event can be discovered here. By means of a quite distinct focus on the text, the preacher simultaneously provides a matching point of view on the world today. Precisely *this* – i.e. the problem areas the preacher is familiar

---

488 Cf. H. Wagner, 197. Quoted in M. Haustein, 1990, 469.

with – is what the congregation should ask questions about and comment on. Hence there is a great danger of cutting down the congregation's potential range of experience in order to make it fit the preacher's theological range of questions and of entering the stage with a repertoire of prefabricated answers. (The idea that the pastor should "hold"[489] the dialog *in the nave of the church* and then, of course, preach *from the pulpit* what has already been thought of and prepared to some extent in advance[490] is quite telling.) The underlying basic idea of this rather meagrely staged dialog being the mere a *warm-up* for one's own monolog instead of giving more weight to consulting the faith of the congregation is additionally questionable. Instead pastors withdraw into the sacristy (which was once their place of preparation for "mediating" between God and the congregation) to exert themselves in finding solutions on their own.

The model of the *bibliolog-sermon* described by Uta Pohl-Patalong is based on a quite different approach. She takes up the thoughts of Peter Pitzele[491], who seeks for a dialog *with* the congregation similar to Bibliodrama. Here again the shared frame of reference in the shape of a text plays a decisive role. The members of the congregation are "led to the text in a way that they are enabled to make their own discoveries and draw their own conclusions"[492]. In detail, this approach is commonly based on the following structure:[493]

1. First of all, the preacher – in Pitzele's words: a "facilitator" who opens up the dialog-space – provides methods or rules for approaching a text.
2. The preacher introduces the situation of the biblical story to the listeners and attempts to activate their imagination.
3. "At a certain point she [the preacher] opens the Bible and reads out a sentence or a short passage. From this sentence she [...] allocates to all those present the role of a biblical character and subsequently addresses them as such."[494]
4. Those addressed say something if they wish to. Perhaps they remain silent and meditate; in any case they react in a way which is significant for the progress of the bibliolog.[495] The

---

**489** One can at best *conduct* a conversation, but certainly not *hold* it, and in order to conduct it one must *enter into* a dialog with others – without being able to foretell exactly how to *come out* of this dialog.

**490** What is striking here is not only that the ideas and thoughts determining this sermon are already specified before the worship service but also the change of venue totally unnecessary for mutual understanding: What is talked about with and said by the congregation in the nave is obviously considered to be merely 'ho-hum'. According to Wagner's point of view the real matter is clearly yet to come from the pastor, from above – and in the form of a monolog.

**491** Cf. P. Pitzele, 1998 and 1999.

**492** U. Pohl-Patalong, 2001, 259.

**493** Cf. U. Pohl-Patalong, loc. cit., 258–268. Numbering added by W. E.

**494** Loc. cit., 260.

**495** Cf. the examples ibid.

listeners should put themselves in the shoes of the text's different characters and understand them in the context of their own experience.

5. The preacher takes up what is said, possibly quietly and bashfully, by the members of the congregation and repeats it loudly and clearly before the whole congregation (by Pitzele referred to as "echoing"), intensifies what is said, when needed, whereby emotional and thought contents are considered equally important. Another way of reinforcing the bibliolog is the use of ask-back questions on the part of the preacher (in Pitzele's words this is called: "interviewing").

6. Repeating steps 3–5: After a while the preacher "carries on with the story and reads the following sentence or passage. The congregation is again assigned a role which can either be that of another character ('You are Mary. Mary, you have heard the message of the angel. What is the first thought that comes to your mind?') or the same character at a later stage ('You are Gabriel again, on your way back to heaven now: What do you think of your encounter with Mary?'). Once more the congregation provides comments, again followed by echoing and interviewing"[496].

7. After several such sequences "the facilitator concludes the conversation, releases the congregation from their roles and leads them back into the present. The individual statements are allowed to stand for themselves instead of being turned into a coherent message"[497].

The fact that this form of dialog remains rather close to the text itself arises from its origin in Bibliodrama: instead of approaching the text in an exegetical-intellectual way, it is enacted in a bibliodrama with those present; they play the parts designated or discovered in the text and in doing so arrive at a deeper understanding of the text and the situation as they experience the character's conditions, troubles and sorrows firsthand. Involved in such a preaching event, the congregation experiences, feels and reflects upon what is at stake in this text or in this story.

Compared against *polylog*, the advantages of this approach are obvious: the congregation is really needed for understanding what this is all about. They *participate* in the endeavor to discover the main focus of the text. The "answers" are not distributed from the sacristy but are achieved in dialog. *What happens interactively is what can happen. There is no need for completion or improvement on the part of the preacher.* So much for the theory. Skillfully mastered[498] a bibliolog can certainly result in a lively and memorable approach to the text and life for those involved.

---

496 Loc. cit., 261.

497 Ibid.

498 According to Pohl-Patalong it is advisable to lead bibliologs not only "on the basis of theoretical knowledge or participating experience but to attend advanced training on this method" (loc. cit., 259). Methodically convincing ideas and instructive examples are found in: U. Pohl-Patalong, 2009 and U. Pohl-Patalong/M. E. Aigner, 2009.

One weakness of this method, however, is that it deliberately refrains from the attempt to come to an understanding of the text's *overall meaning*, of its main point and profound position, its striking arguments – of the text's "clou" so to say. After all there is often something truly decisive at stake in texts that are meant to be experiential reports. The people and characters appearing in the story are – in a way – only means to an end: they should bring something to light, draw attention to something. Acknowledging that the *dramatis personae* want *something quite particular* that is worth discussing would certainly not do any harm to the dialog approach to the text.

A further disadvantage is the abandonment of *dispute and positionality*, general characteristics of any dialog, which are determined by a *struggle for truth and clarity* and imply the weighing up of pros and cons, affirmations, rejections, objections etc.[499] For a dialog is precisely not about everyone sharing their momentary view of things just because they make sense to them at the time of speaking. It rather serves the purpose of jointly examining whether the views expressed are useful, how substantial and well-founded they are, which of them hold true and which do not. It is this nonchalance regarding the *result* of the bibliolog that seems questionable: the listeners should "be able to find their personal interpretations (or slightly modified forms of the same) in the sermon"[500]. Wouldn't that mean, one might ask, that everyone should just stick to their first thoughts, to what they worked out in a few minutes? "An unambiguous message will no longer be provided."[501] The fact that texts do not allow for being moulded into an unambiguous kerygma does not rule out but rather presupposes that preachers act decisively, that they know what they want and – above all in the dialog – can explain how they have achieved this.

What is more, stubbornly clinging to the roles offered in the text can become a problem as these parts usually fit only a few of those present. If particular parts or characters from thence are to be filled with the experiences of listeners today, this of course presupposes that it is in some way worthwhile playing, for example, the part of the angel Gabriel. That this *works* is beyond debate; that thereby particular aspects of the text come to light more clearly than through traditional exegesis, too. It seems, however, doubtful whether in this way a new perspective on one's own life can be achieved.[502]

---

499 Cf. I.4.3.3a, p. 188–190.
500 U. Pohl-Patalong, 2001, 263.
501 Ibid.
502 The above-mentioned principle according to which we resort to biblical texts in preaching in order to understand and conduct our lives (before God) and not primarily seek for stories and experiences from our real lives in order to be able to understand biblical narrations must surely be neglected now and then in using this method: Only before the 7th and final step (see above) does "the preacher release the congregation from their roles and leads them back to the present"

These critical remarks, however, only address the possibility of expecting too much from the bibliolog. Here, too, misuse and manipulation are basically possible, just as they are with every other form of preaching, e.g. through a particular way of presenting the text, through latently suggestive questioning etc. Furthermore, the preacher's theological understanding of the dignity of the biblical text seems to have an impact on the openness or the predictability of the bibliolog. That said, Pohl-Patalong's further developed "Grundformen des Bibliologs"[503] (Basic forms of bibliolog) shall still be strongly recommended for reading. It is obvious that this way of preaching is accompanied by different expectations than those usual in the homiletic process. Nonetheless the bibliolog as one specific form of the communication of the gospel has its own right and in the manner developed by Uta Pohl-Patalong is to be regarded as a milestone in the sermon's dialog culture.

### 4.3.4 The Semiotic Perspective: The Sermon as an "Open Work of Art"

#### 4.3.4.1 The Listener's Involvement

Speaking of the Sermon as an "Open Work of Art" has occasionally led to the misunderstanding that this was about a homiletic structural principle that leaves everything open in preaching, that in terms of understanding the sermon's contents and crucial points everything is left to the listener's ability and willingness to comprehend. These false conclusions result from transferring the common meaning of the term "open" to a semiotic context in which "open" actually means precisely the opposite. In semiotics "openness" is not regarded as a deficiency in determination or the acceptance of uncertainty concerning the communication's contents or addressees. Here "open" is, in fact, a sign of quality of a particular communications medium or artefact (a picture, a sculpture, a text, a speech etc.) that demands an intensive, so to speak, entangling interpretation through its specific structure; listener or observer are supported in their interpretation by the structure of the open work of art.[504]

---

(loc. cit., 261). Were the listeners not there earlier – i.e. in the present? It remains rather unclear, though, how this could do justice to Ernst Lange's claim for speaking to the listener about their life; a claim that U. Pohl-Patalong, too, declaredly supports. It seems at least not unlikely that in the course of a bibliolog the congregation learns more about the text's subliminal aspects than about themselves.

**503** U. Pohl-Patalong, 2009 and U. Pohl-Patalong/M. E. Aigner, 2009.

**504** For more detailed explanations see W. Engemann, 1993a, particularly 153–176; 1998b, 312–317 and 2000, 138f.

To follow structures and to create structures by adding something we do not perceive (i.e. content) to what we actually perceive (i.e. forms) is the essence of all communication and understanding: we understand something in that we assign particular *meanings* to specific *forms of expression* (a word, an attitude, an object, an event etc.). Without such permanent completions it would be impossible to obtain an understanding awareness and perception. The openness of a text, a sculpture or a gesture is thus nothing other than the semantic power of potentially *meaningful* forms and structures awaiting interpretation. They encourage us to deal with what there is to see or hear. They inspire us to establish connections between expression and meaning, form and content, between what has been perceived and deduced. In the course of this process signs emerge: elementary structural connections between signifier and signified, between the forms these signs take and the concepts they refer to.

Accordingly, integrating semiotic aspects into Homiletics means dealing with the question what it takes to preach in a way that what is said in the sermon does not remain unresolved but is continued, expanded and put in concrete terms by the individual listeners in relation to their current life situation. Sermons to which nothing can be added because of their fomenting redundancy, their abstract claims, their linguistic dullness, their ideological platitudes etc. are, as a rule, also badly *constructed*.[505] Including the model of the open work of art into Homiletics is linked to the expectation not only of making such constructive and co-operative work on the part of the listener possible but also of prompting and guiding the listeners' understanding through the very structure of the sermon itself. It is, thus, vital to provide for the listeners' participation, their work with and on the sermon instead of rendering their additions unnecessary. The "open work of art" does not allow for common expectations of reception; it de-automates perception, resists obvious interpretations and prompts dispute instead, and thus teaches its viewers to reconsider their initial understanding.[506]

As a consequence artwork has to be characterized in a dialectic manner as "open" and "closed" at one and the same time: it is open to the extent that it remains unfinished until an observer, reader or listener perceives it, interprets and understands it. In its completed form, however, in its perfect presentation, in its aesthetic quality it is far from being arbitrary but rather powerful and

---

505 On the "redundanten Exzess" [redundant excess] cf. W. Engemann, 1990, particularly 790–792.
506 Cf. U. Eco, 1989, 3.

"convincing".[507] The open work challenges confrontation and is appealing. It is open *because of its wholeness.*

This capacity of a text or sermon is based on a *qualified equivocalness,* technically speaking referred to as *ambiguity.* Something is ambiguous when *on the one hand* it bars obvious and foreseeable meanings and thus leads the observer, reader or listener into a *crisis of interpretation.* The ambiguity of the respective work *on the other hand* consists in the fact that this crisis of interpretation can be overcome with the aid of the very same structure that has initially caused it. Consequently, the ambiguity of the open work of art results from the dialectic tension between its enigmatic form and its demonstrative character, between its disturbance of and its aid to perception.[508]

It is at this point at the latest, when we discuss causing and overcoming crises of interpretation, that the question of the theological and homiletic legitimacy arises, and whether such a perspective is indeed essential.

If the preacher knows what he wants to tell his listeners – as one argument against the model of the open work of art goes – why then not *straightforwardly* so? First of all we must point to the fact that this question starts from an apparent alternative: from a semiotic point of view, too, one can of course speak "straightforwardly" to the listeners. But whatever one says, it will certainly not be able to remain as the "last word" which the listeners only must, so to speak, preserve and "keep" in order to benefit from it or receive an impetus for action. If what is said straightforwardly should catch on with its listeners and make a difference in their lives, it needs to be linked to concrete meanings, be provided with interpretants. Only in this way what is said can become relevant, can the words of a sermon – in which the individual life of each person, of course, scarcely appears *expressis verbis* – find a place in the lives of those present. The listeners must, by using what they have heard, mastering it and making it topical etc. become "doers of the Word". This supplementary work is the *modus operandi* of all understanding hearing.

At first sight the idea of delivering a sermon which is not "self-evident" and does not entirely meet the listeners' expectations might appear as some sort of

---

**507** In his explications on the "open work of art" U. Eco points out that it should not be mistaken as "an amorphous invitation" to any kind of intervention. The structural openness implies a neither compulsory nor unambiguous invitation to engage in the work of art in a way that is oriented on the work itself, an invitation to insert oneself into a world which nonetheless "always remains the world intended by the author" (1989, 19).
**508** In my opinion U. Eco's remarks on ambiguity allow for the conclusion that its character can be described as the dialectic of self-reference (autoriflessività) and referentiality (riferimento). Cf. U. Eco, 1985, 329–331.

gimmick or a special kind of manipulation. Yet, in fact, this maxim aims at doing justice to interactions of content and form. One example therefore is the theological particularity of "revelations" in which God himself – as e.g. in the testimonies of faith in the Old and New Testaments – communicates with his people. They all have in common *that they defy previous patterns of perception*. They, too, are often communicated in an unconventional way and are of unusual content. They are open because they are not self-evident, and they are not self-evident because they bear witness to something unexpected. Anyone who risks the attempt to understand them accepts challenging one's own as well as generally accepted conceptions (in semiotics: codes) of God and the world, becomes aware of other ways of looking at things and experiences changes of attitude within themselves.

From the multitude of examples which could be mentioned in this context I shall limit myself to the signs Jesus set through his appearance, speaking and actions: his dealing with sinners and those cultically impure, his parables, his way of speaking of the kingdom of God, his appearance in the Temple, his naturalness in the presence of women etc. were signs which expressed *offensive contents* in an *offensive form*. Already during his lifetime they resulted in a wealth of interpretations. "A glutton and a drunkard, a friend of tax-collectors and sinners" (Matt 11:19), a political rebel (Mark 15:26 par), a lunatic (Mk 3:21), an eschatological prophet etc., are only some of the customary interpretations. The reason for these diverse interpretations lies in the openness of a message, the content of which cannot be finally determined and filed away but then, of course, has never been incomprehensible or arbitrary. People did not conceive Jesus' message as provocation because they did *not* understand it but *because* they understood that here their images of the world, of themselves and of God were at stake. Jesus confronted them with a message to which they had to react somehow by understanding it.

The "people who demand for a sign" (Matt 16:1–4) do not wish to expose themselves to such an understanding because they feel that their own images of world, of themselves and of God are at stake. They do not want any open, self-entangling, demanding signs but a sign which meets their expectations and confirms their point of view. However, the sign the shepherds are confronted with in Luke 2:12 – "a child, wrapped in bands of cloth and lying in a manger" – is one which neither corresponds to expectations nor corroborates anything: that an infant in bands of cloth in a feeding site is capable of signifying the "savior of the world", or even the "Messiah", puts everything upside-down that one had learned about power and rule and the significance of "top" and "bottom". Through this sign the shepherds were – in semiotic terms – familiarized with a new code. They were first led into a *crisis of understanding*, then out of it again. They understood because the disruption of an accustomed way of looking at things at the same times opened up a new view on their reality.

### 4.3.4.2 Dialectic Considerations

In view of this background, doing homiletic justice to the symbolic character of a sermon requires taking it seriously as a creative and perceptual process with its *own dialectic.*[509] First we must bear in mind that preaching *always* demands providing one's address with a clear structure. As, however, mentioned above: even the most clearly and precisely formulated sermon will never lose its fundamental openness for *multiple possible interpretations.* This could be referred to as the sermon's *factual ambiguity.* The next step, from factual towards *tactical ambiguity,* requires the readiness to view a *certain openness* as a quality and to continue the line of thoughts towards a wide range of different options in continuing interpretation. It implies a kind of staging of this openness.

In both cases the objective is the same, which is to promote the constructing process of reception required on the part of the hearer. This involves a sermon which denies particular possibilities of comprehension to its listeners and suggests others, a sermon which – delivered between the poles of the denial and generation of sense – guides the listener towards the construction of meaning. The sermon should thus be an address the listeners are able to make use of, through which they are led to a reality which has as yet not been addressed in this way, an address which the individuals put to the test in their various life contexts and which they can develop further along these lines.

The listener apprehends the sermon in a similar dialectic tension to preachers experiences when referring to a text in composing their sermon: on the one hand it is the preachers' task to protect and defend the text, to "follow" the text and control its factual ambiguity. Preachers have to ensure that the text is not interpreted in any possible way. It is part of their duty to protect it from being dumbed down and interpreted in an arbitrary manner. On the other hand preachers have to quest for and finally come to a sort of clear and distinct interpretation in the course of the sermon's preparation. In protecting the text from arbitrary interpretations – not least through their own particular interpretation – they surely impede or obstruct certain other possibilities of comprehension. For every time we interpret a text, i.e. transfer it into our present times and put it into a context in which it no longer has the same meaning it had 2000 years ago, we find ourselves involuntarily and inevitably in conflict with the meanings this text generated in its original context etc. Dealing with texts thus always implies a *struggle for interpretative faithfulness and the awareness of granted freedom.*

With regard to the listeners' reception of a – semiotically speaking – "open" sermon we can accordingly speak of a *dialectic between application and consumption:*[510] What the listeners get to hear must first be *applicable,* i.e. immediately comprehensible and suitable so that with the help of the sermon they can understand more than what is explicitly said and formulated in the sermon

---

**509** Cf. W. Engemann, 1992d, esp. 167–173. On the "generating quality of texts" cf. also M. Thiele, 2005, 136–139.
**510** More detailed explanations in W. Engemann, 1992d, 171–173.

itself. In this sense a sermon may be "headstrong"[511] in that it suggests a surprising way of looking at things to the listeners, which challenges or sharpens their own view of God, the world or themselves. If this is the case, the listener – just like the observer of the open work of art – discards certain interpretations and opinions in the course of wanting to understand or having to interpret the sermon, and thus *consumes* preconceived ideas. If the sermon in the end does not draw the listener's attention to itself but proves, as it were, as a medium (for insights beyond the sum of its explicit statements), one can speak of the sermon to use itself up to the degree in which it is needed.

Pointing out the sermon's ambiguous dimension and advocating the cultivation of such ambiguity has nothing to do with being ashamed of the gospel or deliberately concealing something from the listeners. These remarks merely highlight the fact that, from the moment they begin to preach, it is not longer the preachers alone who are involved in the work that unfolds. They can, however, set a process in motion that motivates the listeners to make use of the signs of the sermon – a process which delights them as well as comforts and instructs them.[512]

With that said we have to revisit the question of how to actually compose such a sign-like sermon. Corresponding to the model of an open work of art, one of its characteristics would have to be that it unfolds an "idiolect"[513] in the proper sense of the word: a "language of its own" which distinguishes it perceptibly from all others. This means a sermon which has something distinct or unique. An idiolect encompasses *all* the levels of composition and means that – for example in a speech – vocabulary, sentence structure, metaphor usage and articulation match up. The fact that we can clearly distinguish pieces of music or works of art from one another, that we can easily distinguish Beethoven from Chopin, Bach from Mozart, Renoir from Klee, van Gogh from Dürer etc., despite them all using the same notes and primary colours, is due to their individual idiolect: these people were capable of expressing something in a unique and distinct manner which no one else could have done in the same way. This is what makes others sit up and take notice. The same holds true for texts, whether they are written or spoken: they are capable of expressing a particular content in a unique way and, in doing so, can mediate something which could not have been mediated as such in any other way.

Hence it is not enough to just insert a few fascinating images into the sermon, to include or banish foreign words and technical terms – or to fit a masterly tale

---

511 Cf. K.-H. Bieritz on "the headstrong sermon" (1998, 29–40).
512 Cf. the functions of the sermon in I.2.3.3.
513 Cf. W. Engemann, 1993a, 186–198.

into an otherwise linguistically tiring sermon. Is it a matter of creating a piece of art – new every Sunday – then? Yes and no: there is neither a need for bringing one's sermon close to particular rhetoric genres nor for modelling it on literary works of art or entering the pulpit with poems or polished short stories. No matter how helpful such an attempt may occasionally be: the basis – no more, but also no less – of a homiletic idiolect is the "personal sermon" as was described in I.2.4. It is most closely linked to the preacher's individuality, and those who do not know as who they are speaking will never acquire an idiolect, a personal manner of referring to biblical texts and life as it is lived.

Respecting the criteria of the "personal sermon" does not yet automatically lead to an interesting, convincing structure but, without doubt, will facilitate the search for further possibilities of composing a consistent sermon. These include a quest for effective images (each and every one has their own imagery, rich in concrete ideas!), the development of creative metaphors, the discovery of authentic stories, the use of suitable concepts and fresh formulations. All of these are linguistic forms which achieve on a small scale what is expected from the sermon as a whole according to the model of the open work of art: they surmount common perceptual habits in order to lead to a deeper perception. They violate the rules of language in order to reveal something in a new way. They are, in a way, iconoclastic in order to prevent the listeners' personal images, thoughts and impressions, which they need to create in order to be able to discover and express themselves what they believe and hope for, from being rendered superfluous by the densely packed picture-gallery of Christian faith for which theology provides an almost complete catalogue.

In their textbook, "Im Wechselschritt zur Kanzel" (Two-stepping to the pulpit), Martin Nicol and Alexander Deeg attempt to adapt some of the principles of the open work of art for a kind of "dramaturgical Homiletics".[514] They suggest locating the homiletic work – like several other Practical Theologians since Schleiermacher have done, too – within the sphere of the arts.[515] Accordingly they recommend composing sermons less in the style of a lecture or discursive essay but rather constructing them like a film or a play.[516] They refer to pieces of art whose effects mainly rest upon dramaturgical endeavors. The sermon's

---

**514** M. Nicol/A. Deeg, 2005.

**515** Here rhetorical impulses and aspects of contemporary Homiletics are taken into account which deal with communication practical, semiotic and reception's aesthetic aspects of the sermon. On the theoretical deepening of this approach cf. Martin Nicol, 2005. Cf. also the volume, published in 2008, on the challenges of "performing" a sermon, which include, among other things, aspects of physical demeanor as well as of the musical contextualization of the sermon (J. Childers and C. J. Schmit, 2008).

**516** In a separate study, Jana Childers addresses the question of what preachers could learn from the principles and methods of dramatic arts, which, in the end, could also contribute to an increase in creativity in the phase of sermon preparation (J. Childers, 1998).

realization is imagined as a lively speech-event; the dynamic composition of its individual sequences ("moves") together with their arrangement ("structures") is given special weight.[517]

In order to illustrate what kind of sermon they have in mind, the authors give numerous examples of well-made sequences from lively and vivid sermons from the preaching tradition of the 20th century. All of them show how a moving, enlightening, interesting and "revealing" address is designed and indicate what is actually possible in the craft of sermon composition. The "two-stepping" metaphor used in the main title refers to the "dance-like lightness of sermon composition"[518], which can certainly not be achieved without recognizing the unity of content and form, of theology and hermeneutics, of theory and practice. The linguistic mastery of the sermon preparation does, of course, not only consist in the mere rhetorical surmounting of dogmatic depths – as for example that one cannot talk of God but yet one must. The authors focus on homiletic exercises comprehensible to everyone who is prepared to deal with their own language, with alien texts, with speaking and listening.

"In a worship service within the framework of a homiletic seminar a student no longer talked about the matter but allowed the matter itself to take place. Her sermon was about the story of Mary and Martha (Luke 10:38–42). Though the student had as well informed her listeners that in Judaism at the time of Jesus the repeating of someone's name was a sign of special familiarity, she did not leave it at that. She made it manifest, allowed us to experience it for ourselves: not 'Martha, Martha' (with a wagging finger), but 'Martha, Martha' (with love and affection in her voice). The preacher did not talk about the repetition of the name but repeated it herself. In doing so, she managed to create an impressive scene, the staging of a little piece of film or theatre so to say. During the feedback session it turned out that it was precisely this little scene that had remained in the memory of many of the listeners as particularly impressive. It can be so impressive and yet so simple: to make things happen. That seems to be all it takes in practice to bring about conceptional change from the sermon as a lecture to the sermon as a piece of art."[519]

In this concept it is the literally actual *connection between word and gesture* that plays a special part and allows the sermon itself to appear as a "moved gesture" through which "the movement of the biblical Word" shall continue.[520] Under the key words "biblical Word and address from the pulpit" the authors discuss the interaction between quoted (biblical) and one's own language[521] and, by analogy,

---

**517** Cf. D. Buttrick, 1987.
**518** M. Nicol/A. Deeg, 2005, 6.
**519** M. Nicol, 2009, 242.
**520** Loc. cit., 21.
**521** Cf. the example given in the previous paragraph.

outline, in a separate chapter on "artistic word and language of the pulpit", the criteria of a productive multi-faceted contextualization of borrowed words. In addition to this they describe the interdependencies between liturgy and sermon as independent yet related genera of a dynamic, eventful religious communication.

*Excursus: The Virtual Perspective: The Sermon as Construction of the World*

Finally there is the *category of virtual reality* that has to be mentioned in the context of sermon composition.[522] Virtual reality, in the broader sense of the word, is the reality to which people react. The "virtual world" is the world as it is *perceived or imagined, wished for or believed in.* It is a reality as a necessarily insinuated, effective field of reference of our existence. In this sense our world- and self-views, too, are an expression of a virtual reality co-determined by ourselves. But virtual reality also arises by virtue of our ideas, by virtue of our faith and our ability to think of tomorrow and to anticipate the future

Virtual reality does not, however, rest on human fantasies alone: it is additionally won through a confrontation with the material world, with "hard reality", learned through mistakes and, thus, in the end a world acquired. It is permanently in a state of progress and flux. It is consistently enriched with new pictures and ideas while others disappear from its scene as soon as they no longer reflect anyone's thoughts, wishes and hopes. But the prevailing structures, rules, connections, pictures, visions and traditions of virtual worlds in turn also release forces and thus rebound upon their "users", which illustrates the relevance and importance virtual worlds have in terms of the individual's or a group's identity formation. Constructing virtual worlds is thus to be regarded as a way of the developing and acquiring one's own identity. Whenever people talk about their identity they draw on, inevitably by means of *constructing* it, their "virtual reality" by explaining, e.g. what they consider as given in their lives, with which world they are reckoning, how they adapt to this world, how they try to fit into this world. Sermons should contribute to the construction of this world or to its listeners "ability to arrange themselves" in the virtual world of faith.

To visualize the challenges this view poses in a model: Anyone who preaches has to deal with *three different worlds*, which partly overlap but can, at times, also be competing one another: There is (1) the "real world" as the sum of all material

---

522 Since this is currently just yet another homiletic perspective which has neither been analyzed nor specified in a methodical structural way so far, it is presented in the form of an excursus here.

and incorporeal factualities, the world as it is, the world we stumble against, which just does not get out of our way, the world as it meets the individual – with heat and cold, day and night, violence and war, with unforeseeable events. While preaching (2) pictures of another or changed world come into sight: a sermon can break "new grounds", show pictures of a renewed world, draw the "kingdom of God" into the world as it is and thus advance into the virtual world of faith.[523] Brought into play by the individual listeners (3) is their own personal cosmos, the world as it has become for the them in the course of their own life, the world as it "exists" for them through particular experiences, values and expectations, the world which comes along with a certain "conception of the world", the world they have established for themselves.

Against this background the sermon is charged with the task of participating in the extension of that virtual world in which the faithful orientate themselves. Although faith certainly is a power which should provide help to the individual in their "real" life (and thus be more than a mere pattern of thought), a resource regarding the experience of real and concrete freedom, it also implies living in a virtual world in that faith not only consists in what we actually see but also in what we do not see. Faith has to do with living under God's possibilities, with an imaginary and nonetheless certain "whereupon". To exemplify this on the basis of a single weekday, on the basis of significant encounters, concrete experiences and visions could lead to the blueprint of a new "conception of the world".

In an extensive study Ilona Nord has depicted the consequences of such an approach for Christian religion in general and for the worship service and the sermon in particular.[524] She takes up the principle of many biblical texts to confront the real world with bold conceptions of a forthcoming or already opening new world, which involves not only ideas but also real consequences. Viewed in this light, biblical texts are frequently experimental texts in that they manipulate the virtual world of those who read them, meditate upon them or hear them by enriching it with new options and becoming constituents of that particular world

---

**523** In this context cf. the worlds of reality and faith created by individual preachers and reconstructed by C. Usarski (2005) within the framework of his research into the history of preaching on Matt 15:21–28. It is illuminating to see how particular theological ideas are linked with gender-theoretical premises, typical conceptions of faith, stereotypical images of God and the world and corresponding views of life, how analogue salvation-historical frames of reference are constructed and corresponding election-theological patterns of argumentation are developed. In the course of this, virtual worlds arise in which the preachers travel – and which they also encourage the congregation to pursue. The "sermon typologies" analyzed by Usarski could actually apply as a *leitmotif* to the virtual world (of faith) created in these sermons.
**524** Cf. I. Nord, 2008, esp. 258–332.

the reader or listener reacts upon and which they insinuate in everyday life. (The "communion of the saints, too, is not only the congregation gathered together for a worship service but also a "virtual community"[525] with whom the individual knows to be connected beyond the co-ordinates of space and time.)

As a consequence, preachers should have in store images and stories, imaginative conceptions and dreams about the world they postulate, anticipate or "see" because they believe. For I. Nord the detailed description of the virtual dimension of faith is an indispensible extension and correction of a Practical Theology and Homiletics otherwise rather one-sidedly oriented on processes of perception. She therefore looks out for certain impulses for the homiletic structuring of opening sources which are capable of becoming connected to the virtual world of the listeners. The sermon's virtual dimension, which obtains validity, among other things, through productive metaphors or visionary tales is an expression of the "reality of possibility"[526]. Working on this dimension means to preach "constructively", to lead beyond the speculative diagnoses of the real world, not to persist in the pictorial biblical world, but to participate in a newly illustrated imaginative world in which the individual can try out new and unfamiliar roles, a world upon which they can react already in listening to the sermon and in which they can experience themselves as another.

According to I. Nord, the preaching event is, among other things, "an opportunity to re-structure one's own life situation [...]. Thus, the sermon creates a possibility space for the communication of the gospel. It is not unless this space is actually entered and used in terms of personal experience by the participants of the sermon process, that the preaching event becomes real for them. Only through such participation the possible proves to be real"[527].

## 4.4 On the Category of a Sign-Like Sermon

Reflecting on working on the sermon's sign character necessarily requires bearing in mind everything which previously has been held to be relevant with regard to the structuring of sermons. Consequently the semiotic perspective can be reasonably applied to the psychology of learning model[528], as well as to a narrative

---

**525** Cf. loc. cit., 31–36.
**526** Loc. cit., 92. Cf. also the philosophical background in I. Kant and S. Kierkegaard referred to by I. Nord, loc. cit., 88–100.
**527** Loc. cit., 286f.
**528** Cf. particularly those works in which learning is not characterized as a reproductive process, but rather as a process of re-learning and further learning.

sermon, in the context of an open dialog as well as under dramaturgical or virtual points of view. In like manner one could detect elements of learning or dialog in each of these approaches.

And yet do these various approaches not simply have the same thing in mind in terms of structuring of a sermon. What they share are certain basic assumptions regarding the temporary significance of the sermon delivered within the process of communication with the listeners as well as their interest to do justice to the content of the sermon through an adequate form. What differentiates these four approaches of crafting a sermon, on the other hand, are their respective frames of reference used for making the coherence between the form and content of the sermon plausible, which are always to be presupposed and, at the same time, always to be newly realized. There are connecting criteria for these different frames of reference.

In the '70s and '80s of the last century some of these were dealt with under the term of the "symbolic sermon"[529]. Symbols are ambiguous, a kind of *open work of art en miniature*. They cannot be reduced to *one* interpretation. Provided that they are created within the context of experiences symbols are capable of invoking these experiences whenever they appear and of triggering cognitive processes in the observer, reader or listener. This is the reason why a symbolic or symbol-related sermon does more justice to the language of faith than a sermon merely consisting of thetic propositions.[530] A symbol is capable of engaging the listeners in the process of meaning construction, of calling upon their own experiences, without which faith would lack its necessary existential basis. The symbol "is situated in a referential context", it "provokes thinking about its deeper meaning and brings about a process of communication with others"[531]. These expectations run very close to the premises of a semiotically oriented homiletic approach.

---

**529** Cf. H. Albrecht, 1985, 36–44. The symbolic-theoretical approach of Homiletics harks back particularly to J. Scharfenberg's suggestions and concepts. Cf. most recently J. Scharfenberg, 1992.

**530** In a reflective article on the language and theology of preaching, Roman Roessler, who was in charge of editing the "Predigtstudien" (Kreuzverlag) for decades, points out the necessity of a symbolic manner of speaking in preaching: "We speak in metaphors and allegories about what we cannot say in another way. If we do not hold on to the brokenness of symbolic speech, two realities emerge which are no longer reconcilable: there an over-worldly, biblical-dogmatic autonomous reality determined by its own causalities, and here our present-day awareness of reality. Where these two fall apart there won't be any chance of building bridges between the biblical text and day-to-day reality. This is the core problem of today's sermons" (R. Roessler, 2001, 64).

**531** J. Scharfenberg, 1992, 251. Scharfenberg intends to homiletically link what he considers the major symbols of the church year (light, darkness, cross etc.) with the individual stages of human development and maturation (cf. loc. cit., 253f.).

The debate on symbols has quite often led to false conclusions in practice and frequently blurred the theoretical horizon of the motto "living with symbols":[532] The concept of the symbol was, for instance, used to substantiate the authenticity of religious experiences, to derive from the historicity of the form of the symbol its claim of truth, to believe that a direct access to the reality of faith could be gained by means of symbols.[533]

The consequences of such practice can be observed e.g. in sermons in the form of "Bible dreams"[534] (in principle indeed worthy of approval) in which the concepts of "symbol" or "symbolic" and "sign" or "sign-like" are regularly encountered. The individual is constantly reminded: Attention, a symbol! Attention, an emblem! The permanent apostrophizing of the symbolism of symbols, does, however, not exactly contribute to symbolical preaching. Providing the listeners not only with the symbol itself, but supplying them with its meaning and practical everyday conclusions at the same time will rather impede than facilitate the necessary bringing-them-selves-into-play on the part of the listeners. Instead of making the "spark of hope" easily inflammable through the sermon the preacher explains that this spark is waiting "for us to kindle the flames and make it true as a momentum in our lives"[535]. Mistaking the useful *power* of symbols for an *appeal* to realize them would certainly lead to a maldevelopment of the symbolic approach which set out with the claim to contribute to a deeper understanding of biblical texts and human existence.

Due to this development (and the fact that in theology the concept of the symbol has become overgrown with vastly varying functions) it seems advisable to proceed from semiotic (rather than symbolic) categories in the analysis, description, critique and form of the preaching event as a process of communication and comprehension. From the perspectives presented in this chapter the following principles arise:

1. A sign-like sermon makes the listeners not only understand what a preacher has to say. By its specific structure it helps them to translate what is given into the context of their own lifeworld.
2. What is said in a sermon is sign-like in that it enables the listeners to continue what has been heard in their own situation and thus promotes the acquisition of a "personality-specific creed"[536].
3. The sign character of a sermon is not only a communication-theoretically necessary and required but also a theologically relevant criterion. It strengthens the dialog form of a sermon which does not merely aim for approval or

---

**532** J. Scharfenberg/H. Kämpfer, 1980.
**533** For a critical comment cf. W. Engemann, 1992b, 19–21.
**534** O. Schmalstieg, 1991.
**535** Loc. cit., 85.
**536** Cf. I.2.2.1.

reckon with rejection but which expects from and grants the listener a role of their own in the sermon as well as in their own lives.

4. A sign-like sermon is neither confusing nor vague, neither arbitrary nor tentative. It awakens and guides the listener's attention by means of a structure in which it gives shape to concrete contents which cannot be depicted and act as stimuli in any other than such sign-like way.

5. A sign-like sermon inevitably implies processes of learning. This, of course, does not aim at the schoolification of the congregation, at exegetical lessons or at instructing speech acts. It is, however, part of the intention of the communication of the gospel to evoke change regarding people's rigid and "frozen" ideas and distorted images of themselves, God and their relationships to others.

6. Dialog, narration and learning processes can be forms of an "open" sermon. They strengthen the sermon's sign character by defying zealous solutions and hasty conclusions and by enabling the listeners to become participants in the "virtual" construction of the prospects of a renewed world.

7. The idea of a sermon which requires supplementation and is amendable, and thus ambiguous, does not imply an unnecessary complication of homiletic principles. It takes into account the dialectic character of the communication of the gospel which, among other things, is determined by the fact that on the one hand it conflicts with existing patterns of expectation but on the other hand provokes, presents and introduces new ones which enable the listeners to a reorientation.

# 5 Preaching under the Conditions of Language. On the Medium of the Sermon

## Preliminary Remarks

If we consider the didactics of Homiletics as indicated in guidelines and instructional literature on Homiletics and in the examination requirements of the established Protestant churches, we find that linguistic considerations play a comparatively minor role. Exegetical, theological, situational, liturgical and homiletic discussions tend not to go beyond the familiar territory of questions on content, rationales and the structural implementation of a particular *preaching intention*. The disturbing appearance of an "advocate of language"[537] is *one* possibility of integrating into sermon practice the resources of language, which are often left unutilized. Apparently minor linguistic modifications can effect an entirely different, clearer, and more convincing impression of the overall intention of the sermon, to the surprise of many. This may result in experiences which have been described by Walter Benjamin as the "magical aspect of language". This means that meaning can be disclosed in an unexpected moment – just as an optical illusion all of a sudden reveals something that has previously been concealed. Benjamin regards language as a "medium" in which things do "no longer [appear] directly, [...], but in their essences, in their most transient and delicate substances, even in their aromas."[538]

In the course of the previous chapter we already had to refer to the medial effect of language in numerous instances in order to be able to describe what is meant by "homiletic competence", "a credible sermon", "dialogical communication" and "structures promoting connections". Language is the most important medium of the preaching event[539] and thus a factor and indicator of quite different, yet concurrent processes. The question of the language of preaching as a medium arises, however, first and foremost from the multi-perspective approach to the sermon process itself: The communication of the gospel – up to and including the construction of an Auredit[540] on the part of the attendant listeners – relies

---

[537] In the debriefing sessions taking place after a sermon within the framework of seminars the "advocate of language" has, among other things, the function of pointing to linguistic possibilities which may have been squandered. Cf. W. Engemann, 2009c, 425f.

[538] W. Benjamin, 1999, 697f.

[539] The medial presentation of a sermon naturally also includes other (sign-)languages, too: postures, movement patterns, clothing (cassock), facial expression, gestures, spatial categories (distance to the listeners), "co-preaching" objects that surround the preaching event (pulpit, the open Bible) etc.

[540] Cf. above, p. 11.

https://doi.org/10.1515/9783110440256-005

on the fact that a *process of interpretation and appropriation* is set in motion by the addressees. While ideological speeches communicate primarily through an instrumental use of language or by using "rhetorical tricks", sermons work on the basis of hearing and understanding.[541]

"Theological considerations aside, a sermon is a linguistically-constructed speech which desires to reach and influence the listeners, people with a body and a soul and also a brain. A sermon is a linguistic form, a structured speech aimed at specific people. This is what we should be focusing on. It is not theology but language that comes first. [...] The conclusion is not, of course, to turn the preacher into a lay poet or semi-littérateur. [...] But to become sensitive for linguistic possibilities, to test the flexibility of one's own language, to risk leaps – in short: to use as little academic terminology as possible in the sermon – that will do; there's no need to compete with the poets."[542]

Before we consider some of the basic rules in dealing with the medium of language we must address some of the problems which often obstruct the function of language as a medium of the sermon.

## 5.1 Snapshots. Empirical Indicators of Problems

### 5.1.1 Theological Stylistics

As other sciences, too, theology has its own technical terminology, a professional jargon. This level of speech is very useful for agile communication among specialists. Obviously, most theologians will also preach at some point and, in preparing the sermon, are certainly faced with questions similar to the ones they have dealt with in the framework of theological discourse. It therefore often seems natural to them to use this repertoire of abstract concepts in their address from the pulpit as well.

---

541 Cf. the foundations provided in I.1 as well as the classification of particular aspects of preaching summarized at the end of each of the previous chapters. Anderegg also distinguishes between an instrumental and a medial use of language: "If a particular use of language prompts people to ask after the meaning, it is not this use of language itself that we are ultimately concerned with, but language usage offers itself as a medium for the construction of meaning, which goes beyond itself; what we are ultimately concerned with, what should be comprehended and realized through meaning-construction can only be approached by way of getting really involved with this use of language, by taking it seriously as a medium for our meaningful comprehension" (J. Anderegg, 1985, 51).
542 G. Otto, 2009, 259f.

As useful as technical terminology may be in lectures and books, in the sermon the sophisticated use of dogmatic terms and expressions has an excommunicating effect. The language of dogmatics serves the purpose of discussing and communicating theological issues, but it is hardly advantageous for the *address to the listeners*. "Our life in Christ", "the relevance of justification for the discipleship in faith", "the transsubjective power of sin which all too often predetermines us" and the "permanence of our self-centeredness as a boycott of God's merciful action" are phrases which do not quite increase the plausibility of a sermon. When preachers demonstrate how skillfully they can move in this world, the signal they send to their listeners is that this whole thing is "out of their league". Such a preaching style may appear unkind, careless or indeed thoughtless:

"*In Jesus Christ* God has become human for humanity. Not a totally unknown, alien, celestial being [...]. Right up to the *final consequence of his death* on the cross he *lived and gave trust and reconciliation.* By raising him from the dead God confirmed the *rightness of his way,* the exemplary nature of his life. The Apostle Paul was himself brought to this way, experienced the life of Jesus as a guiding principle for his own life. [...] We are *invited to a communion with God* and our fellow human beings in the discipleship of Jesus *in terms of the law of Christ,* in terms of mutual love, compassion, gentleness and peace. For Paul and ourselves, Christian cooperation has limits, when we are induced to action which is not in the spirit of Jesus and at the same time denies our responsibility before God. [...] But the spirit of Jesus can only develop among us when we try *to live in the discipleship of Jesus.*"[543]

Such language is in danger of losing itself in *religious phraseology* and no longer revealing any pattern of argumentation. The rationales and points of the overall intention are then lost; the real *goal* of the sermon, *the reason why* the listeners should become involved, and *in what way* remains unclear:

"All flesh, no matter how powerful, perishes! An experience which history teaches us time and again. *Now something which is permanent is put up against this transitoriness, this impotence: The Word of God!* It is permanent to all eternity. *This is the beginning of comfort.* [...] From this we gain trust and comfort for ourselves that *we* can anchor *ourselves* with our helplessness and transitoriness to the power of God and to his love and affection for us. *This is why God's Word is not an empty promise,* but real comfort and support. *For he is our Good Shepherd. This experience of Deutero-Isaiah, of course, holds true for us Christians, too,* since in Christ we have a Good Shepherd for our lives. [...] In this good experience of the love of God we can *prepare the way for Christmas* in our congregation."[544]

---

**543** Sermon on 1 Cor 9:16–23. Emphasis W. E.
**544** Sermon on Isa 40:1–8. Emphasis W. E.

Such style is characterized by "semantic noise". Though it certainly pretends that there *is* something to understand, it makes it actually quite difficult to understand something concrete or precise. It goes without saying that such a manner of preaching sooner or later leads to frustration on the part of the listeners, who, in view of such listening experiences, will find it hard to discern how they could benefit from listening to a sermon.

### 5.1.2 Dysfunctional Speech Acts

Linguistic utterances cannot only be classified as correct and false, rhetorically successful or clumsy ones. They can furthermore be defined according to the *action* they imply. As a basic principle, through speaking, people always "accomplish" something: reality is formed and created and something happens for (and through) those addressed.[545] With *words of thanks* we can achieve a positive effect on someone and thereby *encourage* him. We can *promise* help to someone in times of disaster and thus *relieve the pressure of a situation*. We can indulge in *assertions* and thereby *put up* certain facts *for debate*. It has been observed that in sermons assertive speech acts are predominant.[546] If this is true, it means that other speech acts are subordinate, for example speech acts that make something plausible (explanatory speech acts), that mobilize (advisory speech acts) or that express one's own feelings (plaintive speech acts). It is not uncommon that after hearing a sermon, the listeners are at a loss as to what the address was actually about. In these cases one can usually find that, in terms of speech acts, there was little to be found beyond a series of statements or assertions.

"God alone has permanence in this world and so has everything, and only that, which belongs to him like for example his Word. And that certainly does not mean that God's statements will persist as timeless truths. [...] The Word became flesh. Here God's Word revealed in a special way its effectiveness. [...] If we remember this it gives us hope for the future. In the meantime Jesus Christ has not left us orphaned behind but we can meet him in his Word because he himself is that Word."[547]

*The sermon withers away as an act of communication* if it resorts to mere assertions and does not integrate into its language the whole range of human communication. This is certainly not about paying more rhetorical respect to the address

---

545 For more detailed information on "speech acts" cf. I.5.3.1 – I.5.3.2.
546 Cf. H. W. Dannowski, 1975, 174.
547 Sermon on Isa 40:1–8.

from the pulpit. A sermon reduced to a "confrontation with facts of salvation" in the form of propositions and assertions is justified neither from a theological point of view nor from a homiletic perspective. Existentially relevant questions, demanding dialogs, engaging narrations, the articulation of experiences, personal creed etc. – none of these dimensions are achieved through the mere utterance of assertions.

Sermons, as a genre of speech, furthermore feature in their practice specific forms of language and speech which are hardly ever encountered in everyday language and are closely connected to the favoring of assertions. Many sermons, for instance, contain speech acts which – though formally corresponding with a particular sort of speech act – do not fulfill their corresponding functions. This particularly applies to expressions connected to *concepts of permissions*: most of the times the, as a rule, euphorically articulated message *that something may be allowed or allowed to happen* belongs to situations in which restrictions are enforced or laid upon oneself – restrictions which one actually wishes did *not* exist. A permissive speech act in the sense of a *declaration*[548] thus establishes a new reality and unleashes in the situation portrayed *possibilities that are desired or longed for*. Restrictions and limitations are finally overcome.

When the listeners "are permitted" something in a sermon, however, in the vast majority of cases morality is preached. If the congregation is finally allowed something, as a rule, particular ways of behavior are advised. The following examples demonstrate this:

- "Perhaps we are able to become witnesses for others. [...] Simply through something we do, a conversation, our presence. We are *allowed* to live in this hope. And we *are allowed* to ask for this."[549] Was it ever a problem for fictitious or real listeners *not* being allowed to ask *for this*? What the preacher actually aims for is to heighten the congregations' awareness of how to become a witness for others and to ensure that they become aware of the responsibility associated therewith. Why doesn't the preacher just say so?
- Another sermon stresses: "That is why I regard the Pharisees as well as the tax-collectors as our opposite number who should give us a wake-up call! This should encourage us perhaps to think more often about ourselves. For sometimes it is salutary to ask sincerely 'Who am I?'. We *are permitted* to show such honesty before God."[550] The preacher desires to encourage the listeners "to reflect upon themselves". That the listeners (supposedly) do so too little is certainly not due to the fact that they think it is forbidden. To divulge a false self-portrait requires

---

**548** According to J. R. Searle (1975) "declarations" (appointments, vocations, marriages, permissions etc.) serve to create a qualitatively new reality.
**549** Sermon on John 15:26–16:4.
**550** Sermon on Luke 18:9–14.

courage and a non-frightening prospect of the person one has to expect to get involved with. Being given the "permission" to do so would be of little help here.

- "We may feel that we are adopted through God's becoming human in Christ; God has assured us of this in Christ."[551] The problem the author wishes to address is once again not that people do not *dare* – although they *would* like to dare – "to feel accepted through the incarnation", but that it is just not *plausible* for them that the birth of Jesus should have anything to do with their own acceptance. So in the end, this again is nothing more than a mere assertion, albeit covered by talk of *being permitted*.
- In view of this widely disseminated manner of preaching, one final example: "If we are *allowed* to feel that we are part of the Body of Christ we can be sure of being connected with him."[552] This, too, is of course an appeal which yet again does not fail because people think that they *dare* not feel that they are part of the congregation. Furthermore, this suggests a condition for the connection with Christ, namely an emotional state which is yet to be achieved by the listeners. The problematic nature of this manner of speaking could hardly be more evident.

Such formulations can be found in their hundreds in literature on and in the practice of preaching. While the words *"permitted"* or *"allowed"* are uttered, the message clearly concerns what one *"ought to"* or *"should"* do. Apparently aware that one should preach the gospel – and not the law – the possibilities of life revealed in the gospel are represented as a result of endless chains of permission. This is a (poorly performed) form of a typical sermon on the law: it is characterized by concealed assertions, questionable assumptions and vague appeals. Such a sermon leaves – with regard to its demands on the individual – the impression behind that, in the end, it is simply a question of trifles to which one can easily do justice with a little good will.

Perhaps the numerous "permissions" are the symptom of a certain self-understanding on the part of the preacher. For who can say "you may"? Being in a position to give permission presupposes authority. This speech act has its "Sitz im Leben" above all in the authority of parents over their children, of public authorities over citizens etc. It is not, however, an appropriate basis for the relationship between preacher and listener. Moreover the attempt to conceal moral appeals through the linguistic gesture of giving permission contributes to the fact that genuine and necessary appeals, which should clarify to the listeners wherein their part actually consists, are overheard. Through the use of phrases such as "perhaps we should", "now we may finally" etc. the earnestness of a compelling address is lost.

---

551 Sermon on 1 Tim 3:16f.
552 Sermon on Eph 4:1–6.

### 5.1.3 The Homiletic Lassiv[553]

This expression indicates a special use of the verbs "to let" or "to allow" something (to) happen, frequently encountered in sermons. Although formally and grammatically recognizable as indicative or imperative, the actual semantic function of the statements in which something should be "let" or "allowed to happen" is considerably more difficult to determine.[554] "The mercy of God accompanies our life. [...] Paul *encourages* us to accept God's mercy, *to let it do the work* in ourselves so that it can be experienced by other people."[555] Similar, frequently recurring formulations are: We only need "to let peace to be given" to us, "we should let our eyes be opened", we only need "to let Jesus into our lives", "merely let ourselves to be inspired by God's spirit" etc.

In order to give the sermon a Protestant character and in order to avoid – because they are obviously perceived as disturbing – such things as appeals and calls to action, the advice to just let God's gracious work happen has spread into the addresses from the pulpit. As a result the life promised in the gospel and in the sermon will set in automatically. Such a "Lassiv" is more (or less) than a form of an unsuccessful communication of the gospel, since the attempt to actually follow what has been heard as instructions inevitably leads to frustration: For – to come back to the quotation above – how do you do that? To *let* God's mercy work in you? Isn't it capable of achieving this on its own? Is someone who has already experienced mercy really faced with the choice of "letting it work now" and that "in himself"? Are "mercy", "kindness", "noblesse" and "love" not quite joyful experiences in the face of which deliberation is no longer needed, which always come at the right time and for which one hopes without special invitation? Through the ideology of "simply letting things happen" the listeners – as is the

---

553 In German the coinage "Lassiv" is grammatically connoted with passive as well as active qualities, which automatically prompts one to think of a third way of acting (in addition to passively or actively). The "homiletic Lassiv" has an ironic undertone, which is connected to an inner contradiction of meaning that results out of the fact that the main verb "lassen" means to "to let sth. be, to leave sth., to not care about sth.". However, [ironically,] when used within the sermon, the verb "lassen" is always used as an appeal for a certain conduct [to do something.]. The verb "lassen" then exclusively functions as a modal verb, that is, with the intention to motivate the listeners to accomplish something – in terms of imagination, emotional readiness or the like. Oftentimes this also goes hand in hand with the expectation of a sacrificium intellectus. 554 This does not only refer to statements which, *expressis verbis*, speak of "allowing something" but also to comparable passive stereotypes which – as a rule in connection with the little word "only" – are intended to emphasize the triviality of our own action: "We *only* need to..." etc. 555 Sermon on Rom 12:1–8.22. Emphasis W. E.

case with certain advertising strategies – are pushed into the position of customers who are being talked into buying a shelf warmer.

This manner of speaking has a trivializing function: as a rule, the contexts in which we are told that we only (sic!) need to let or allow this or that to happen involve delicate questions of human life and faith. Contrary to the apparently passive style of speaking, here, too, we are dealing with a particular form of a "sermon on the law"[556]: "You will surely also cope with this difficult situation: just let it happen." The homiletic Lassiv insinuates that Christian faith is at heart no more than an *act of affirmation and consent*, an implicit assertion which, however, does not do justice to the practice of dedication and acquisition of faith.

"Christ says: 'Behold, I stand at the door and knock.' [...] He does not kick the door open in a threatening manner but knocks quietly. He does not storm the door but leaves it to us whether we wish to open up for him or not. [...] He invites us to hold the supper with him. Hence we must do nothing more than to open the door for him in   order to sit with him at the table. In coming to us and knocking he attempts to heal all our insensitivity, disinterest, self-satisfaction, the worry about our own essential being which we have locked away and surrounded with walls. We only need to let him in."[557] But how do we do this?

Such a manner of speaking obscures the indicative of the gospel, plays down the power of the communication of the gospel which requires taking a stand and leads into confrontation. The homiletic Lassiv particularly conceals appeals or calls to action. In contrast to the wording ("to let" or "to allow") it is not a matter of happenings in which the astonished listener might participate in Christian calmness and tranquillity; in fact *they are demanded* to make what is decisive happen: "We are allowed to use our talents trustingly and self-confidently. In this way we allow the Holy Spirit to be effective among us."[558]

The above criticism of the "homiletic Lassiv" does, however, not imply calling into question that theologically we should hold on to "letting things happen", to the happening of the story of Christ in human lives and to the calmness of faith. Yet the experiences associated with such calmness and happenings are not created by the appeal to let something or other happen, but are a fundamental homiletic challenge: the sermon has to clarify how a person, independently of constant initiatives – and also independently of a passivity made into a virtue – is

---

**556** In a similar context M. Josuttis points to the "legal falsification of the sermon on the law": "Sin is played down and its elimination is presented as a human possibility" (M. Josuttis, 1995b, 121).
**557** Sermon on Rev 3:4–22.
**558** Sermon on 1 Cor 12:4–11.

related to an event which influences and affects the conditions of his life in a positive way.[559]

## 5.1.4 The Gift-Imagery

What is a gift about? A gift, particularly one that has been chosen with and out of love, is always welcome. To receive gifts certainly belongs to the bright sides of life, not only for children. No one will come up with the idea – at least not without risking being accused of hypocrisy or considering morbid modesty a virtue – of debating about the acceptance or non-acceptance of a well-planned and lovingly-chosen gift. While phrases such as "You shouldn't have!" or "You really didn't have to!" can appear polite, they also may appear offensive at times. They have their Sitz im Leben in situations when, for example, a waiter is given a generous tip or someone is honoured for services which he was only partially obliged to perform. But no one needs, in fact, to be persuaded to accept a real gift which connects giver and recipient anew. On the contrary, we are highly delighted, perhaps taken by surprise, but certainly not averse to receiving a gift – as long as they are not infamous gifts (bribes) which place us under the obligation of returning the favor.

The gift-imagery used in sermons, however, hardly ever addresses these concomitant circumstances of being presented with a gift. Instead, one encounters in numerous variations, the stereotypical demand to finally make up one's mind and accept the immeasurable gift of grace, of forgiveness, of life, of hope, of redemption, of justification etc. It is only then that we can learn to appreciate it. "God for his part has done everything to deliver us from death. He even sacrificed his son and in doing so gave us the gift of life. We only need to accept this gift."[560] Frequently this demand is combined with the accusation that the acceptance of this gift has been notoriously refused due to base motives.[561]

Sermon-gifts are offered like lemons instead of being proffered like a coveted present. It is again mostly a matter of contention that what is presented is indeed a *gift*. In case of "real" gifts, however, significance, value and implications of the

---

**559** This question will be considered from a linguistic as well as theological point of view in 5.3 and 5.4.

**560** From a sermon on Rom 8:31b-39.

**561** In this context the fundamental question arises what a person would have to do in order *not* to accept a gift – with an immediate effect on his reality and existence ("forgiveness", "mercy", "care") – from God. We will come back to respective homiletic premises in the context of the theology of preaching.

gift are usually self-evident. They arise from the evident possibilities, perspectives and chances the recipient is enriched with – and which he unquestionably knows to appreciate.

Perhaps the common *reference to the high price that God paid* (without the *significance* of this gift being "unwrapped" with the same intensity) is an unconscious indication that preachers themselves notice the problematic nature of their offer. Gift metaphors are often used to deliver moral appeals – which are just as often likely to provoke resigned reactions because they are difficult to follow and comply with. "God has given us three strengths, first humility [...], and we are required *to allow the humility which has been given to us to develop.* Along with humility God has also given us gentleness, *being able to silently look beyond ourselves.* God's third gift to us is patience, the *union of forbearance and generosity* which grows out of love." [562] Who could just "simply accept" these "gifts"?

Of course it is legitimate to retain, theologically, the gift-character of the salvation enacted in Christ and to make God's presence for the sake of humanity plausible as the basis of a successful life, which does not need to be earned. Whether the gift-character outlined above actually appears in the communication of the gospel depends on the *plausibility of the gift* as being something desirable that opens up opportunities. Consequently preachers who argue by means of using the gift-metaphor should at least have found an answer to the following questions: What is the purpose of such a gift? Do I myself experience this as a gift? What would I be missing if I did not receive this gift? What pleasure can I get from this gift?

The sermon itself, too, should feature some of the characteristics of a gift that preachers give to their congregation. This presupposes that they knows what they "need" or what they "lack", what could do them good, what they must deal with in their daily lives. But a gift should not only be useful; it should also be carefully prepared, packaged and tied up, which in a homiletic context implies earnestly striving for a linguistically thoughtfully created sermon – e.g. for a narration.

### 5.1.5 Broken Narrativity

In a sermon narratives may fulfil a variety of different functions.[563] For one thing, through stories it may become clear where the sermon emanates from, what it insinuates and implies and for what "reason" it is held. On the other hand, a

---

562 Sermon on Eph 4:1–6.
563 Cf. also I.4.3.2.

narrative may anticipate intended consequences. This means that what the preacher desires as an effect of his speech can take place paradigmatically in the narration. Within the frame of a story it is therefore already anticipated where the sermon may, as it were, "lead", or at least, what it should refer to. This is something entirely different than scenically glossing over a sermon that is basically composed in the manner of a lecture, in which what the preacher wants to say anyway is put into the mouths of various characters and figures that are only ostensibly connected to one another. Appearing here and there in the sermon, these characters then speak or think so "well-worded" that a search for good quotations is rendered superfluous. As a result a real narrative context fails to be established. Nothing is revealed which could not also be delivered with the help of explanations or assertions. After the sermon text has been read out, one hears for example: "For Miriam it was as if God himself spoke to her: 'Do not be afraid – See! I shall be the foundation of your hope, I will show you what it will be like when I finally establish my kingdom. Even now this should affect your life, this has the power to change you and your reality!'"[564]

*Narration in the sermon is something fundamentally different to having assigned parts utter dogmatic sentences.* Quite often what preachers themselves find to be too stereotypical, is put into the mouth of a hypothetical person in order to make the sermon sound less clichéd and bland. Another widespread attempt to make the sermon appear livelier is to fictitiously set it in temporal proximity to the time of Jesus and let his disciples or contemporaries appear as witnesses. The resulting texts can scarcely be distinguished from usual sermon language:

In one sermon a disciple ponders: "Jesus was sent by God. What he did and said convinced us: He comes from God. And that is why his Word was so important to us. We knew: if we wanted to overcome the injustices, the cheating, the hate among us, [...] in order to create better living conditions for all people sometime in this life [...] we had to remember precisely all that he told us. [...] Very powerfully and insistently Jesus told to us again and again that we should not be afraid. We should not stop loving him, then we would also love his Father and he would love us, too, [...] his Father and he himself would live with us if only we kept a firm hold on his Word. And also he would return and take us with him to his Father."[565]

Finally, we need to refer to sermons in which initially there is a real narration, but in which subsequent explanations obstruct the impulses given through the narration and bring its continuing effect to a standstill. The clarifying achievement of a narration can certainly be diminished when, at the end of the sermon, one

---

**564** Sermon on Isa 35:3–10.
**565** Sermon on John 14:23–27.

offers "a moral from the story" instead of trusting in the "translation" of the story which has long been under way among the listeners anyway. In such a case the reception of the sermon through the listeners is undermined:

"The ring of the telephone interrupted her thoughts. 'Ulrike Fiedler', she answered. 'Hello, Ulrike, how are you?' asked her friend, Pia. [...] Pia was fascinated: 'That sounds as if you *have had an experience of God!*' 'What makes you think that?' contradicted Ulrike, 'things like this only happen to Jacob or to people who go to church every Sunday, like Mrs. Jürgens.' Pia broke in: 'But you heard this voice. *I don't believe things like that happen to everyone in this way. But one can experience this kind of encouragement through other people. You don't need to be particularly religious for this.*' [...] Slowly Ulrike found that the idea no longer seemed so disconcerting. '*You mean that I have been assured that God accompanies me?*' she asked sceptically. '*Yes, God has promised this to everyone of us.* [...] Particularly when we are in a difficult situation' Pia attempted to explain. 'In a difficult situation...,' Ulrike thought. 'Could this possibly help me to finally talk to my boss?'"[566]

Good narratives on the other hand bear in themselves the quality of arguments. They deal with cause and effect, with backgrounds and intentions, with the foundering of hopes as with fulfilled expectations. In this way they stand for a particular "way of looking at things", for a particular idea of God, they reassure the listener in terms of particular attitudes and render others problematic. In case such aspects appear in the address from the pulpit, no further "solutions" need to be added to a consequently narrative sermon, for they are already contained in the story itself.

## 5.2 Indicators of Problems in the History of Homiletics

Dedicating the following pages primarily to the *pragmatic dimension of the language of the sermon* has, above all, a practical reason: In I.4 important *syntactic* (regarding the linguistic structure) and *semantic* (referring to the creation of meaning) aspects of the communication of the gospel were discussed.[567] Pragmatic aspects, on the other hand, have only occasionally been addressed.

The research into the possibilities of touching and stimulating people through language and speech, to move them and influence their thoughts and actions has had a long-standing place in the field of rhetoric. What is new in

---

566 Sermon on Gen 28:10–19a. Emphasis W. E.
567 Cf. also the linking of the basic functions of language and the dimensions of the sermon (I.2.2.3) and the interdependence of aspects of content and relationship in the sermon communication (III.4.1).

the so-called field of "pragmatics" is that this effect is not – as in Classical Rhetoric – primarily discussed in the context of polished structures of speeches and texts but examined on the basis of everyday language. Pragmatics deals with language and speech as a basic form of behavior, addressing the question of "how to do things with words"[568]. Its research interest is geared towards the capability of particular forms of everyday communicative behavior, linguistic interaction, the cooperation between speaker and listener based on their common use of language. The semiotic approach[569] developed, above all, through the works of Charles Morris, John L. Austin and John R. Searle, attempts to explain *how and under which conditions language achieves what it intends* – and how intentions communicate themselves altogether. The speaker's actual intention cannot simply be deduced from the wording or external form of a sentence.

Against this backdrop I shall now outline *three problems in Homiletics* which are associated with certain basic assumptions concerning the effect of language and speech.

a) One of the basic problems concerning the understanding of language in the history of Homiletics has to do with the fact that *language was not actually understood as a medium* but as a quasi-mechanical instrument, as a means of conveying objective truths. As a result, the corresponding homiletic concepts ignored the fact that preaching is a *process of mediation* which may fail even though what is said is, in fact, true and correct. They overlooked the fact that language does not only convey facts, but also information *about* these facts, information *about* the speaker, *about* the addressees etc. – and that all of this influences the sermon's effect. If in preaching the impact of these linguistic conditions is ignored, there is the risk that the actual effect of the sermon is understood as an expression of faith or disbelief or reduced to humble consent or disdainful rejection. Correspondingly, Eduard Thurneysen demanded the whole sermon to be set on "the one thing necessary", "that every mouth shall be stopped and the whole world were guilty before God [...] so that, where everything human is silent, God can speak again"[570].

---

568 The title of John L. Austin's Speech Act Theory, 1962.
569 Semiotics is not just one of many perspectives of reflection applied in linguistics but is a "fundamental science" which "provides indispensible terms and comprehensive concepts for the examination of speech" and consequently is considered an umbrella term also for action-related approaches to language (cf. A Linke et al., 1996, 7).
570 E. Thurneysen, 1971, 116.

Because the sermon must aim for an *interaction* with the listener, in order to be able to *communicate* the gospel[571], the theological justification metaphor of the "stopped mouths" (cf. Rom 3:19) can certainly not be a homiletic maxim. In order to understand, the listeners must be enabled to "take part and have a say", or else they won't be able to connect their own ideas with what is said and expressed in the sermon. If one demands that "nothing alien" is to "intrude" into the communication of the gospel,[572] one deprives the "Word of God" of its necessary relationship to the world of human experience – the world in which it should take effect after all.

b) Another problem arises from the *religious and theological idiomatics*[573] of the sermon's language, at times referred to as the "language of Canaan". The vocabulary and phrases of this "speech-code" emanate, among other things, from the texts of the Old and New Testaments, the translation of which was last revised before the middle of the 20th century. This oftentimes results in a cliché-ridden way of speaking about God, faith and humanity which may appear formulaic and out-dated today. Therefore Hans-Rudolf Müller-Schwefe summarized already back in 1957: "It is quite telling that the language of Canaan is used for the most part by people who have not really accepted the modern world. This may not only be considered an act of treason against the people but also against God, for God wishes to be alive in our time."[574]

What is plausible and admissible within the framework of theological systems can be entirely incomprehensible outside this system. Such language, too, does not remain without effect; it can, in fact, lead to an excommunication of the sermon's listeners and thus take on a disturbing, antisocial tone.

In his Homiletics Karl Barth does not go into detail about the various creative possibilities of language but instead discusses "the *problem* of language". He dismisses the objection taken up from hearsay[575] against "abstract", "theological" sermons by arguing that the sermon is, after all, concerned with "something very serious"; reason enough for him to warn against deviant, individual language. "The danger is especially acute when we present personal experience.

---

571 Cf. the preconditions outlined in I.1.
572 Cf. K. Barth, 1991, 127.
573 Cf. the signs of problems already outlined in I.5.1.1.
574 H.-R. Müller-Schwefe, 1957, 46.
575 The problems of the language of the sermon – above all its lack of compatibility with the modern world – have been thoroughly discussed in theology and church since the 1940s. Cf. e.g. the quite enlightening extracts from the general debate of the Lutheran General Synod (cf. Lutheran Church Office, Hanover, 1957, 59–78).

We must also be careful not to intrude into the lives of the listeners."[576] He does not consider the positive effect it might have on the sermon "if our individuality and our location are mentioned"[577]. Gert Otto, on the other hand, pointed out that the notorious nonchalance and methodical abstinence of Barth, Thurneysen and others with regard to linguistic efforts – contrary to their own theoretical maxims – could, in fact, result in a most individual and "expressionist rhetoric"[578] in practice.

c) The *theorem of the self-efficacy of the Word of God* for a long time suppressed other theological premises of Homiletics to such an extent that hardly any attention was paid to the language of the sermon as the distinct mode of expression of an individual. There was even the notion that a sermon could do without any hint of "personal taint". Instead, preachers were advised not to jeopardize the "intended efficacy of the Word of God" – as it emerges from the biblical texts – with their own intentions but to rely on the fact that this Word "looks after itself"[579] – also in the preaching process.

The issues discussed in I.2, in the context of the person of the preacher and their communicative competence, deserve to be regarded again in this context, now from the perspective of linguistics: looked at from the outside it is first and foremost linguistic features which cause a sermon to appear distant, embracing, compulsive or unlimited. This does, of course, not mean that a particular effect can be achieved solely by applying a few rhetorical tricks. What is, however, possible is to enhance the sermon's *comprehensibility* through the use of certain linguistic means and devices, which, in turn, contributes decisively to its *effect*.

It is a question of the use of linguistic means to attune content and form, style and structure of a sermon with one another in order that the actual effect of the address from the pulpit does not run counter to its intention but is in line with it. On the other hand, anyone who considers the irrelevance of the speaker to be a necessary constituent of the communication of the gospel[580] and the preacher's lack of intention a virtue, runs the risk of speaking incomprehensibly and, consequently, of acting uncontrolledly in the pulpit.

Against this backdrop, Albrecht Grözinger's demand for a "theological grammar"[581] seems understandable. He regards it as a task of theological anthropology

---

576 K. Barth, 1991, 128f.
577 Loc. cit., 180. For Barth, such individual marks imply "making great detours to avoid the detours of the text" (ibid.)
578 G. Otto, 1999, 73f.
579 H. J. Iwand, 1979, 494f.
580 On this and other homiletic myths cf. W. Engemann, 1993a, 142–149.
581 Cf. A. Grözinger, 1991, 233–235.

"to discern and preserve human language in its individuality". Anyone who does not strive for "the language of human beings" eventually runs into danger of theologically super-elevating it in a wrong way.[582] To prevent this, the following chapter presents some of the perspectives from which the language of the sermon can be observed.

## 5.3 Current Angles of Reflection

### 5.3.1 Preaching and Acting Behavior

Homiletic behavior is to a large extent behavior through language. Because this behavior is driven by a particular interest and aims at *effects* one could also call it a *behavior* in terms of verbal action: anyone who preaches acts by speaking. Pragmatics asks how people act through language use. Accordingly, Homiletics asks about the consequences resulting from the insight into the relationship between speaking and acting for the assessment and structuring of sermons.

#### a) The Basic Thesis and its Terms and Concepts

A widespread model for the development of homiletically relevant maxims of linguistically successful preaching is the Speech Act Theory. Its most influential work, John L. Austin's book, *How to do things with words*[583] starts out from the observation that whenever they say something people perform a certain kind of action.[584] An utterance can thus be understood not only with regard to its *content* or labelled as *either true or false*. One can furthermore determine its *function* by examining how what is said *affects* one's communication partners and constitutively *influences* particular situations. In this sense one can speak both of utterances and of actions. They are performed at the moment of speaking and – because the speaker is the one acting – are usually composed in the first-person present indicative active: "I accept my election as Bishop of the Evangelical Lutheran Church of Saxony." "We declare the defendant guilty." "I hereby appoint you Minister of Foreign Affairs." "I'm letting you have my room for the next four semesters." "I hereby order you to pay €3,500 in compensation."

---

582 Loc. cit., 234.
583 This text is the transcript of a lecture given by Austin in 1955 (published in 1962). The Speech Act Theory became known and effective above all through John R. Searle's book, Speech Acts, 1969.
584 Cf. J. L. Austin, 1979, 112.

Where such sentences are uttered, decisive actions take place. Something fundamental changes for the person affected as well as for other affected parties. Their reality – at least in particular areas – becomes another. A significant point of Speech Act Theory consists in the conviction that action through language is not only performed when certain words, such as *herewith* or *hereby* or a particular verb (to appoint, to declare), announce the action. Verbal actions *always* occur when people step into a relationship with one another through the medium of language. This reveals the insoluble interconnection of relationship and content level in human communication: those who speak nolens volens start interacting with other people. In this context three aspects can be distinguished:

1. *Locution or locutionary act*: According to Austin the "locutionary act"[585] describes the circumstance that something is expressed in words *at all*. The term locutionary act thus refers to the actual physical utterance itself.

2. *Illocution or illocutionary act*: Utterances are always performed with a particular *intention* in mind. This intention does not necessarily become evident from the sentence's wording but can be deduced from the situation in which it is uttered as well as from particular features such as, for example, the tone of voice or the type of sentence (question, wish, order etc.). The illocutive aspect thus reveals how the statement is actually *meant*.[586]

3. *Perlocution or perlocutionary act*: When something is uttered with a particular intention and, in consequence, understood, a certain effect is achieved, which has an impact on people. Communication always takes the others' reaction into account.

These three levels do, however, not refer to three different speech acts but are partial acts which, taken together, constitute a speech act in the first place and thus occur simultaneously. It is, however, illocutionary acts which influence the course of a communication most strongly. In a certain way, they define the actual interests of the communication. As a rule, people firstly react to that what they

---

**585** Cf. J. L. Austin, 1962, 91–99, 101–107, 113, 122–124.
**586** Cf. J. L. Austin, 1962, 101–107, 108–119 and J. R. Searle, 1972, 153f., 159. This basically refers to the general semiotic fact that an act of understanding (provided this means understanding through the use language) is based on linguistic signs as physical entities, i.e. on the level of signifiers. Understanding takes place through combining the forms of expression perceived (in this case the words spoken) with something which the locution itself does not provide (therefore *il*-locutive act) and which, in further consequence, has to be deduced or supplemented with the aid of codes.

comprehend (on the illocutionary level) as the intended motives of their conversational partners, and only at a later point to the subject matters treated on the level of content.[587]

In this context we must pay attention to one last important aspect which is frequently represented in its relation to the illocutionary act. This is the so-called proposition or propositional act: Within the framework of an utterance, particular contents are addressed. A person who says something refers to particular subjects or topics of the speech. This act is called "proposition" because it is about "putting forward" facts and circumstances in the conversation. The relation between the content (p) and the function (F) of an utterance forms the basis of the definition of speech acts: a speech act is a verbal expression which manifests an object-relation with a communicative function: F(p). These are to some extent abstract classifications, which, in the sense of a working hypothesis, can be viewed in the following manner:

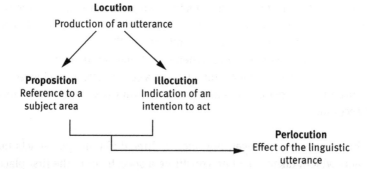

### The Individual Acts of a Speech Act

**Locution**
Production of an utterance

**Proposition**
Reference to a
subject area

**Illocution**
Indication of an
intention to act

**Perlocution**
Effect of the linguistic
utterance

**Fig. 15:** The individual acts of a speech act

An example should help us visualize the different functions of the individual parts of the act: someone who says "Jesus is coming" initially performs an utterance (*locutionary act*) and, in doing so, takes part in a particular discourse. The sentence has a definite subject area, a concrete content which can be specified with the aid of theological textbooks and lexica (*propositional act*). Once this content is not only established as a fact (e.g. in a book or in "private") but is furthermore introduced into lively communication – i.e. incorporated into a "speech

---

**587** Cf. A. Linke et al., 1996, 201.

to someone"[588] – its intentional character comes to the fore. It becomes clear how the sentence "Jesus is coming" is actually meant (*illocutionary act*). Even without further verbs of action this sentence can warn, comfort, raise hope or lament: "I testify: Jesus is coming." "I warn you: Jesus is coming!" "How thankful I am that Jesus is coming." "Take into consideration: Jesus is coming." "I set my hope on this: Jesus is coming!" "I lament: Jesus is coming – and no one is aware of him." "I tell you, Jesus is coming, and that's that!"

*It is the illocutionary act that is setting the course in communicative action.* It sets the *direction* of the utterance, decides how what is said is to be understood. The final partial act, perlocution or the *perlocutionary act,* refers to the continuing influence the utterance may have on the addressee, which no longer lies entirely in the hand of the speaker. The leeway between the illocutionary and perlocutionary act is the area of interpersonal communication. As a rule – this dare not be overlooked in view of the critical analyses which have also been carried out in Homiletics with the help of the Speech Act Theory – an utterance is understood under the terms of its *actual* intention[589], which means: the way *it is expressed in the illocutionary act.*

Problems of differentiation which have been overcome: Austin's attempt to divide spoken sentences into (merely) *constative utterances* and *illocutionary acts*[590] could not be sustained. For (1) it is not *sentences* that are *in themselves* either constitutive (true or false) or illocutive (action-oriented) but the *utterance* of such sentences *in particular situations* is decisive for their assessment. (2) A person who performs an action can at the same time also state something: The observation "They are preaching without a manuscript" may – on the unspoken illocutionary level – for example, signify: "They are obviously too lazy to prepare carefully for the service." At the same time this statement can express admiration for the mastery of the art of speaking without notes. "They are speaking without a manuscript" can also be a confirming or ascertaining statement – as a rule, the context of the communication provides clarity in this respect. In these cases, it is neither praise nor insult but merely an observation which is either true or false. (3) Conversely one can embed every statement into an illocutionary act in that all one says may imply praise or reproach, a request or a warning etc., depending on the context of the speech situation. When saying something true or false about the world, I can at the same time make a judgemental statement about the addressees of the utterance.

---

**588** In his reception of the Speech Act Theory, B. Casper distinguishes between the locutionary act as "speaking as such" and the illocutionary act as "speaking to someone" (B. Casper, 1975, 53).

**589** This has been confirmed for the preaching event through several pertinent surveys. Cf. K.-F. Daiber/H. W. Dannowski et al., 1983, 184.

**590** Cf. J. L. Austin, 1962, 144–146. Austin speaks of "constative utterances" and "performative utterances" in this context, a differentiation which, of course, broadly corresponds to the differentiation into locutions and illocutions.

Accordingly the significance and function of an utterance cannot be entirely grasped by merely determining its content and judging it as to be either false or true. This is not only due to the fact that there are numerous sentences which have a rather vague propositional content (as e.g. a greeting or congratulations – linguistic utterances which are highly important in forming human relationships) but, above all, due to the fact that an utterance needs to be *understood* before it can become *effective*.

By analogy to the four partial aspects mentioned above the assessment of speech acts can be conducted on four levels:

**Functions of Speech Acts according to their Individual Aspects**

| Individual Act | Level of Assessment | Question |
|---|---|---|
| Locution (The statement as such) | Level of composition | How does what is said attract attention? |
| Proposition (Relation to content) | Level of truth | Is what is said true or false? |
| Illocution (Orientation towards action) | Level of intention | What is intended by the utterance? |
| Perlocution (Effect) | Level of effect | What kind of behavior or action does the utterance lead to? |

**Fig. 16:** Functions of speech acts according to their partial aspects

First homiletic conclusions from Speech Act Theory imply the insight that preachers do not only have to be aware of *what* they have to say (proposition) and of *how* they intend to convey the corresponding contents to the congregation (locution). They must furthermore ask themselves what they intend *to do*.[591] In other words: They must clarify and examine the *function of their sermon, how to deal with the listeners* (illocution), *what form of continuation their sermon* may receive *in the actions of the congregation* (perlocution).

Provided that when we speak, we create a particular reality which always also affects those addressed, the question of an adequately *justified intention of speech* arises. When preachers speak from the pulpit, they should be aware that

---

[591] According to Henning Luther the incomprehensibility of many sermons is caused by the fact that preachers are oftentimes not aware of the function and effect of the speech acts used or intended (cf. H. Luther, 1989, 227).

they, in fact, *"intervene" in stories and events* and perhaps even *influence some-one's fortunes*. In one way or the other, the sermon's illocutionary act will always leave its mark on the listeners.

### b) On the Classification and Homiletic Relevance of Speech Acts

At this point we must first of all clarify the unit of speech which the Speech Act Theory refers to: is it just about individual sentences or may it also be applied to longer linguistic units? Could even the sermon as a whole be regarded as a speech act? The answer given by Speech Act Theory is fairly clear: "Speech Act Theory derives from the sentence and always centres approximately on the sentence."[592]

This conclusion may, of course, be criticized.[593] For, from the standpoint of rhetoric it is, in fact, possible to target the linguistic form of a sermon as a whole. This occurs, for instance, when in working on or analyzing a sermon e.g. learning psychological, narratological, dialogical strategies etc. are taken into account. One should not, however, expect *one single* theory to be able to provide solutions to all questions arising in regard to the linguistic form of the sermon. In view of the limited issues addressed in each of the corresponding models, it is certainly more sensible to use the specific potential of the individual models for an analysis and solution of particular problems of linguistic communication.

On another level, the question arises as to whether in a chain of linguistic utterances, as there is e.g. in a sermon, hierarchies and dominances can be detected in respect of the important illocutionary types of speech acts which characterize the communication event as a whole. The acceptance of this is part of the prerequisites of a sermon analysis on the basis of speech acts.[594] A sermon is, among other things, to be characterized as behavior through speech, by means of which the listeners are provided on the illocutive level with an overall picture upon which they react.

---

**592** A. Linke et al., 1996, 188. "It still remains difficult to describe the communicative function of longer utterances with the tools of Speech Act Theory" (loc. cit., 195). Due to its strong orientation on concrete situations of communication it is only possible to a limited extent to transfer the methods and insights of Speech Act Theory to written texts (as e.g. sermon manuscripts). In fact, the application of the Speech Act Theory in Homiletics requires an awareness of the original speech situation. Given the complex embedding of speech acts into a whole ensemble of linguistic signs and conventions of interpretation we can, however, at least look at some basic patterns or stereotypes in homiletic practice concerning speech acts.

**593** O. Fuchs (1978, 124, 132) is among those homileticians who criticize Austin's and Searle's manner of dealing with speech acts on a merely sentential basis.

**594** Cf. II.1.2.

Another controversial subject regarding the reception of the Speech Act Theory in Homiletics is the question as to whether one should postulate particularly religious speech acts[595] or at least should hold fast to a "speech act of proclamation"[596]. I consider both views problematic.[597] The actual division of linguistic forms of action into religious and profane collides both (1) theologically with the essence and informative nature of the sermon as an event of communication as well as (2) linguistically with the core of Speech Act Theory. On 1: The communication of the gospel is no more based on "special linguistic requirements" than is the communication with God: anyone who preaches or prays does so, for example, in acts of pleading, thanking or recounting, i.e. in acts which generally belong to the human repertoire of communication. On 2: One of the advantages of Speech Act Theory is that it is able to reveal universal types of action which, independently of their content, point out how people deal with each other, themselves – and "God". In consequence one should not talk of religious speech acts but perhaps of *speech acts with a religious dimension* (as e.g. a plea within the framework of personal prayers) and *in religious contexts* (as e.g. a public lament[598] in a political evening prayer).

After these preliminary remarks we can now turn to the question of how to categorize speech acts. Various attempts have been made in order to classify the different speech acts used in human communication. The resulting typologies again relate to the respective *illocutionary functions* of speech acts. Thus, the question of how to classify the different speech acts actually focuses on the *action scope of the speaker*.

In the course of the development of the Speech Act Theory it was mainly the typologies of John R. Searle[599] and Jürgen Habermas[600] that won through. In Fig. 17 the respective classificatory systems suggested in these two models are related to one another.

---

595 Cf. e.g. B. M. Kaempfert, 1972.

596 Cf. J. Kleemann, 1973, 101f.

597 I. U. Dalferth, too, offers criticism against the differentiation discussed above: "Religious speech acts [...] are not to be declared as concrete realizations of a religious speech act patterns but as *qualified realizations of the speech act patterns* of assertion, command, questioning etc." Their religious character "cannot [...] be specified on a *linguistic level*" (I. U. Dalferth, 1979, 108; emphasis W. E.). But independently of this, it is certainly useful to describe the special condition of possibility of religious sentences and to determine the function of the speech acts which thereby are shown to advantage, as S. Gärtner has shown in his illuminating study on "divine speech" (cf. S. Gärtner, 2000, e.g. 213–221). Appropriately Gärtner does not speak of *speech acts* in this context but of "elenctic, paraenetic" etc. *forms of speech* (220).

598 Cf. the basic considerations on the relevance of lament in liturgy and preaching in S. A. Brown, 2005.

599 Cf. J. R. Searle, 1979, 1–57.

600 Cf. J. Habermas, 1971, 101–141; 1972, 214–216 and 1976, 246.

| Types of Speech Acts according to J. R. Searle | Speech Mode | Classes of Speech Acts according to J. Habermas | Use and validity claim |
|---|---|---|---|
| **Assertives** Underlying assumption of the communication: *The speaker assumes that p*[601] *is the case.* | to say, to ask, to answer, to agree, to oppose, to quote etc. | **Communicatives** allow for the continuation and structuring of communication in the first place. | pragmatic use of language with the purpose of making the speech recognizable as such |
| | to assert, to report, to relate, to explain, to affirm, to doubt, to deny, to insure etc. | **Constatives** bring content into play by e.g. asserting something. | cognitive use of language with the validity claim of truth |
| **Directives** Underlying assumption of the communication: *The speaker desires to get the hearer to do p.* | to request, to beg, to appeal, to urge someone to do something, to advise something, to recommend something, to ensure etc. | **Regulatives** define the relationship between the communication partners in the sense that these either comply with or violate particular rules. | interactive use of language with the validity claim of rightness |
| **Commissives** Underlying assumption of the communication: The *speaker commits himself to do p.* | to promise, to apologize, to forgive etc. | | |
| **Expressives** Underlying assumption of the communication: The *speaker expresses his sentiments or internal state in relation to p.* | to think, to reckon, to dread, to want, to desire, to admit, to confess, to praise, to moan etc. | **Representatives** serve the purpose of self-revelation on the part of the speaker. | expressive use of language with the validity claim of sincerity and incredibility |
| **Declarations** Underlying assumption of the communication: The speaker is involved in institutions and *creates a new reality through p.* | to nominate someone, to appoint someone, to baptize, to marry somebody, to convict somebody etc. | | |

**Fig. 17:** Classification of speech acts according to Searle and Habermas

---

**601** As explained above, "p" refers to the content or proposition of an utterance.

There are two fundamental ways of expressing speech acts, which specify the *illocutive level* mentioned above:

*Direct* speech acts formally denote their intention through verbs which express action, through the mood of the expression (optative, imperative, interrogative etc.) or through a certain word or phrase (herewith, hopefully, please etc.). *Indirect* speech acts, on the other hand, are speech acts which have an effect on the addressee that differs from the one suggested by their formal indicators: They may sound like an advice but are actually meant as a threat: "I advise you not to mess with me." They seem to be a polite request or question, but are, in fact, a categorical prohibition: "Could you please mind your own business?" Here the action intended, the illocutionary act, does not correspond with the indicators of illocution. These indirect speech acts are – especially in terms of sermon analysis – of particular interest in Homiletics, as it is on the basis of such speech acts that we can understand why some of the statements uttered in the sermon are comprehended differently than their propositions actually suggest.[602] Taking stock of Speech Act Theory from a homiletic point of view, three observations can be made:

1. There is a wide range of different possible speech acts, which, however, does not mean that this is necessarily reflected in common preaching event. On the basis of extensive individual studies[603], H. W. Dannowski notices "a strong dominance of 'assertive sentences' in current preaching". Other acts (such as questioning, hoping, lamenting, confessing etc.), which would be just as important for the communication of the sermon, are, however, scarcely used. "The overstress of constatives to the detriment of regulatives restricts the sermon's scope of action."[604]

As a result, the communication process of preaching gets into serious trouble. Not only because communication and comprehension, personal testimony and necessary impulses for action can only to a limited extent be based on mere assertion (not to mention the pastoral-psychological implications of a compulsive-dominant address from the pulpit) but also because a mature congregation deserves an *insight into the rationales for* such assertions. Remarkably even those preachers, who conducted a speech act-theoretic analysis of their sermons, were frequently unaware, as they testified themselves, of the extent to which they had communicated in an assertive style.[605] In consequence the speech acts intended by the preachers do not necessarily correspond with the ones perceived by the listeners.

---

602 The same phenomenon is described as "disguised transaction" in Transactional Analysis (in jargon referred to as: "Gallows Transaction"). Cf. W. Engemann, 1992a, 66f.

603 Cf. K.-F. Daiber, H. W. Dannowski et al., 1983, 124–186.

604 H. W. Dannowski, 1985, 122f. "The fewer questions the members of the congregation have about the proclamation, the more *is asserted* in the sermon. But assertion then becomes self-assertion" (loc. cit., 122).

605 Cf. K.-F. Daiber, H.W. Dannowski et al., 1983, 184.

2. As a communication event, the sermon cannot be mastered on the basis of assertions alone. Instead, it *requires the whole spectrum of speech acts* in order to be able to show clearly the varying communicative intentions in relation to the people, subjects and situations in question. One can find in the texts from the Old and New Testaments – which, just as the sermon, deal with the communication of faith – numerous examples for the quasi-homiletic use of many different speech acts.[606] Here the expressive speech acts are given particular significance because they serve the function of the sermon's testimony to a special degree.[607]

3. As an *institution-specific speech,* the sermon is a communicative situation which displays specific habits of reception on the part of the listeners. This can complicate in individual cases the implementation of a sermon's whole spectrum of speech acts.

Surely, the sermon as a whole cannot simply be labeled as an "institutional speech act"; this would presuppose that the sermon qua institution (1.) *always* brought about something particular, which (2.) could not be achieved in any other way than through ordained clergy. On the other hand, it is certainly true that a reality-creating effect is expected from the sermon,[608] and that preachers tend to promote this effect by means of using a correspondingly declaratory language or that listeners sometimes also perceive non-declaratory sentences as assertions just because they are uttered by an official. In view of the actual institutional grounding of the speech acts of the sermon it is particularly important to become aware of one's own understanding of one's role and self-image.[609]

---

**606** Cf. particularly those Psalms, in which just as much doubt as confidence is uttered, lamentation as well as praise, warning as well as encouragement is expressed etc. Though in this book particularly instructive speech acts are in no way dominant it has – astonishingly enough – also been used as a "Book of Instruction and Edification" (cf. H. Seidel, 1980, 60). In this context we must also point out that the praying, reading out and meditation on the Psalms was performed by the persons praying deliberately as a "speech act" (cf. idem, 1980, 45–47).

**607** Here we can certainly see points of contact between Speech Act Theory and Karl Bühler's Organon-Model discussed above in the context of linguistic signs (I.2.3.3–I.2.3.5). Cf. also H. Luther on the connection between expressive speech acts and the credibility of the preacher (H. Luther, 1989, 234).

**608** Cf. G. Hornig, 1982.

**609** Cf. K.-F. Daibler, H. W. Dannowski, et al., 1983, 91. *Sociolinguistics,* which has been hardly considered in Homiletics so far, examines, among other things, the connection between the "role-relationships" of the communication partners and the speech acts which are established between them. Thereby particularly "underlying power and status relations" play a special part as could be shown especially for directive speech acts (cf. G. Hindelang, 1978, 106). Hence, reflecting on the one hand on the latent, on the other on theologically appropriate role definitions can surely be an act of communication hygiene. In this respect, Ernst Öffner's (1979) homiletic work is still to be considered a relevant sociolinguistic examination.

In this context it becomes clear how strongly extralinguistic aspects influence the linguistic effect of the sermon.

The theologically as well as linguistically describable effect of the sermon on human existence is neither enforced by the institution of the preaching office, nor by the church, but can only be striven for as an *aim* of the communication of the gospel. This emerges already from the definition of the perlocution as being part of a complete speech act: without the interest and engagement of the listeners for what should be understood on their parts, the sermon disappears into a void. This means that e.g. promising or confirming speech acts are not fulfilled until the listeners let themselves become encouraged "to new and different action or behavior", the future of which is anticipated in the promise.[610]

### c) On the Question of the Success of Speech Acts

Against this backdrop we must now ask for the fundamental preconditions of *successful* speech acts. These imply, above all, the fulfillment of the following rules[611]:

1. *Proposition Rule*: Successful speech acts presuppose that the content (proposition) of an utterance fits its execution (illocution):

A promise must refer to something in the future, judging something which has already happened, a piece of advice to an action which has not yet been considered. In many cases sermon communication suffers from the fact that the *contents represented* do not correspond to the linguistic *acts performed*. Thus it is e.g. hardly communicable when statements which should serve as a promise and affirm expectations are in no way anticipatory, but only relate to what has already happened and provide no prospect of what it means for the future to live by faith today – even if they only assure that the future is in a positive sense open, the present is thus not frozen.

2. *Initiation Rule*[612]: Successful speech acts are furthermore defined by their effect – the speaker sets something in motion, makes something happen which would otherwise not have taken place.

---

**610** Cf. R. Wonneberger/H. P. Hecht, 1986, 149–194, 207.
**611** My own compilation created on the basis of various different suggestions (cf. e.g. A. Linke et al., 1996, 190 and H. P. Grice, 1979b, 16–52).
**612** The common, somewhat misleading (translated from German) term for this precondition is "Introduction Rule"; cf. A. Linke et al., 1996, 190.

This requires specific personal, institutional as well as communicative skills. The initiation rule is broken when a preacher, as one says, "promises the moon" ("Anyone who entrusts himself to God will find the gate of heaven open") or every Sunday demands a new "Yes to Jesus" from baptized members of the congregation: "If you speak the 'Yes of your life' today your name will be recorded in the Book of Life." In contrast, it is both linguistically and theologically appropriate if preachers speak about concrete hopes which open up a prospect, visions which could have the character of a creed because they demand courage and reveal a particular, well justified attitude which is capable of motivating the listeners to action.

3. *Relevance Rule*: Successful speech acts presuppose that the speaker says something relevant that truly matters to those addressed.

If you choose speaking as your form of action, you have to hold yourself accountable for the connection between the envisaged speech act and a corresponding demand – or for an awareness of the sensibility of such action. Anyone who mainly refers to biblical texts within the framework of discussions acts as if listeners came to church to hear sermons primarily out of an interest in the theological depths of the Jewish-Christian tradition. If this is not the case – which, as a rule, has to be assumed – listeners will experience this act as ill-fated communication. Anyone who, for example, with the best of intentions promises a patient in hospital: "Next week I shall celebrate Communion with you" could possibly trigger off dismay in the patient if he thinks of Communion above all as a "medicine of immortality" in the face of imminent death. In case the relevance supposed by the speaker as it were "fails being conveyed" to the hearer, the promise contained in that sentence can, as a matter of fact, even assume a threatening element.

The list of such rules could be extended further in order to catch a more precise view of the particular conditions of the individual speech acts. Karl-Fritz Daiber, for example, has dealt in detail with predominantly *proclamatory* sermons which pass on the gospel to the listeners by promising them the forgiveness of sin. In terms of communication a sermon's success depends, among other things, on whether "the legitimacy of this kind of religious speech remains unquestioned within the framework of established institutions". This in turn means that "wherever religious institutions lose their legitimacy, or at least no longer have any self-evident plausibility, the trustworthiness of the [...] preacher gains special significance"[613].

But to conclude from this that preachers should make an increased use of "the authority given to them by their hearers" for "speech acts of a proclamatory preaching" is not good advice. The fact "that a dogmatically testifying sermon [...] may be experienced in a positive

---

**613** K.-F. Daiber, 1991a, 249, 251.

way by its listeners"[614], can, after all that has been discussed here with respect to the problem of personal competence, hardly be interpreted as a call for an increase in proclamation.[615] In addition, when it comes to being involved in speech acts it has to be assumed that particular effects and changes are not always achieved by the same speech acts. This means that, for example, the experience of forgiveness does not follow exclusively from an officially pronounced declaration of grace. People can also gain another view of themselves and experience forgiveness in a conciliatory and clarifying conversation or through a narratological sermon.

Those who listen to a sermon do not only notice *what* is said but also *why* this is said: in order to explain something to them, to comfort them, to move them to do something. This is usually deduced from *how* something is said, i.e. from the illocutionary act. The *why* of the utterance, which the preacher has to find an answer to in the run-up of the sermon, involves an assessment of the hearers and defines the preacher's relationship to them. In this respect Speech Act Theory facilitates more concrete elucidations on the sermon's effect. It allows the comparison of a preacher's conscious intentions with his de facto executed actions; discrepancies or correspondences respectively can then be attributed to a disregard of, or compliance with, individual speech act rules.

The knowledge of relevant speech act-theoretical backgrounds can and should lead to more effective preaching. This means that when a preacher's intended message is received and understood, the sermon is a successful act. In this context, Henning Luther raised the question as to whether, in view of the possibilities of manipulation, there should be additional speech act-theoretical rules in the sense of homiletic virtues. He answered this question in the affirmative by stating that the communication process which is the sermon "calls for the insight and approval of the hearer [...] from which the intended and desired reaction of the hearer may follow"[616].

### d) On the Effect of Homiletic Patterns of Acting Behavior
The fundamental principles for a homiletic application of Speech Act Theory described in the last three sections can be further deepened and specified in various directions. One of the most productive ways, however, in pursuing homiletic pragmatics seems to be the research on the sermon's effect on the basis

---

614 Loc. cit., 253f.
615 M. Josuttis' objections concerning this matter have remained valid until today (cf. 1988a, 81–87).
616 H. Luther, 1989, 230f.

of specific "patterns of action" which appear in sermons. In linguistics the term "pattern of action" refers to sequences of speech which are marked by a standardized sequence of specific speech acts in typical situations, linked with particular intentions and topics, additionally often so with stereotypical terms and concepts and a significant mode of speaking. Patterns of action are essential in everyday communicative situations.

Anyone, for example, who asks for help sticks more or less to the following pattern, here in a somewhat more detailed form:

1. *Expressive speech act*: Friendly small talk with polite questions about the other's welfare.
2. *Assertive speech act*: Account of the plight, occasionally followed by giving assurances of one's attempts to solve the problem alone, which have, however, foundered.
3. *Directive speech act*: Explicit request that the other might help with solving the problem.
4. *Commissive speech act*: The one requesting promises to help the other in another situation or reminds the other (*assertive speech act*) that he also helped in a similar situation.

In his foundational study on the intention and effect of the sermon[617] Frank Lütze recorded about two dozen patterns of action typically used in sermons which have gained acceptance and became prevalent in the history of preaching and which can also be detected in current sermons. He deals with the question of whether particular patterns do correspond better than others to the claim of the Protestant teaching on preaching – i.e. not simply to speak *about* justification but to understand the preaching event itself as a sort of implicit communication of justification. Lütze doubts the homiletic achievement of patterns of argumentation which continually make use of concepts such as justification, grace, freedom etc. however, pragmatically, for instance, merely persist in the venting of accusations, break the simplest rules of successful communication or amount to nothing but an ordinary moralizing lecture.

To examine the problems and possibilities of such Homiletics, Lütze analyses the patterns of action of various different sermons dealing with the same theological *topoi* (particularly the *topos* of justification) and shows how, independently of the preacher, the same rhetorical structures and speech act-theoretical patterns recur. In this process it became possible for the first time to prove, on a linguistic level, the linguistic regularity of the games played in the pulpit[618] already regarded

---

**617** F. Lütze, 2006.
**618** Cf. below, II.2.1.2.

from a homiletic angle as well as to describe in detail and theologically comment on their modes of action. Through the enumeration and subsequent assessment of patterns of action such as "murky scenery", "let's not fool ourselves!", "God would be willing", "almost a gift", it becomes clear how firmly particular stereotype patterns are associated with theological clichés about God and humankind without linguistically corresponding to those functions which, according to their content, they wish to fulfill.

Thus, for example, the homiletic pattern of action "But the Bible is right"[619] shows how a sermon's argumentation-strategy is entirely geared to the antithetical juxtaposition of biblical testimony and modern , which results in the listeners apparently only being able to be blessed if they are willing to free themselves somehow from this world, which might, of course, be accompanied with painful experiences. Such a pattern of action could, in a given case, have the following structure:

1. Constative speech act: Thesis on the importance of X (e.g. the Doctrine of Justification)
2. Regulative speech act: The preacher insinuates that the listener (other than himself) does not really know X.
3. Constative speech act: The preacher explains how wrong people are who don't know what to do with X.
4. Constative speech act: The preacher points out the consequences of not knowing what to do with X.
5. Expressive speech act: The preacher affirms how important X is for himself.
6. Directive speech act: The preacher challenges the congregation to consider X important.

What is entirely missing in this pattern is, above all, a vision of what it meant if X had real significance, which would imply anticipating a reality in which X would be really important for the listeners – or perhaps already is. In this way "there is frequently a pseudo solution offered, which, however, fails to live up to the task of a justificatory sermon"[620]. In the further course of the analysis, reasons for the lack of surprise or the predictability of corresponding sermons are stated.

In this context, Frank Lütze introduces an instructive differentiation of homiletic speech acts into "interrupting" and "opening patterns of action" which, however, ought to be understood as more of a theological rather than a linguistic differentiation. It is based on the premise that a reformed sermon implies a communication culture of justification. Homiletic endeavors, in which life is dealt with under the law, are classified as "interrupting patterns

---

**619** F. Lütze, 2006, 163–168.
**620** Loc. cit., 122.

of speech", whereas "opening patterns of action", on the other hand, describe certain attempts on the part of preachers refer to life from the perspective of the gospel.[621]

The analysis and interpretation of these patterns shows how the idea of justification can be brought to fruition, both linguistically and theologically. Here, for example, the significant difference between the linguistic patterns of "God would be willing"[622] and of "breaking the spell of sin"[623] becomes clear: the latter operates strongly with anticipatory statements which do not tie the listeners down to a particular attitude in the past but help them see their present lives in a new light, discover their own faith and remain curious about themselves. Presupposing they are Christians, this linguistic pattern allows the listeners to see *the* reality in which they are already living. Such a sermon linguistically aims for a "counterfactual attribution of faith"[624]: "The listeners are imagined as Christians – and are enabled to *discover* themselves as such as if through a mirror; a process which Isolde Karle reveals to be a 'self-fulfilling prophecy'[625] in that the linguistic anticipation of a possible future can already change the present. To hear who we already are in God's eyes opens up the possibility of perceiving ourselves as this very person."[626]

Linguistic insights in the area of homiletic pragmatics are reformulated and continued in the context of sermon speech-patterns, which also opens up new possibilities of sermon analysis, as discussed in Part II.

---

**621** Cf. loc. cit., 131–209, 211–290.

**622** The basic structure of this pattern consists of abstract indicatives and subsequent vague appeals: Indicative: "God would like to give you something." Appeal: "He can only do so if you accept his gift," or "the gift is only useful if you unwrap it" (loc. cit., 226). The same holds true for the pattern of "justification paired with the need for encouragement" which is structured in a similar way: First a series of assertions in the sense of "God has done X" is put forward, which is then followed by the appeal: "Make X your own!" (Loc. cit., 221).

**623** Loc. cit., 284–290.

**624** Loc. cit., 288. The extent to which one argues "counter-factually" when one encourages the congregation to have some trust in their *own* faith ("Your faith has helped you" is a key statement in the communication of the gospel of the New Testament), however, deserves a detailed theological discussion. We shall return to this matter in a chapter about the anthropology of the sermon (III.2.2, p. 445–451).

**625** I. Karle, 2002, 340.

**626** F. Lütze, 2006, 288.

### 5.3.2 Argumentation and Anticipation

#### a) Preconditions of Argumentation-Based Sermon Language

The effect of a sermon, as follows from the knowledge on the functional principle of speech acts, can be deduced neither from its content nor from its form. It is produced through the speech acts actually performed in the delivery of the sermon. Thus, the sermon's true effect is determined in the "Phase of Realization" (cf. Fig. 1, p. 4) or in the perlocutive sequence of linguistic action, respectively. Through this act the listener enters into the communication event structured in advance by the preacher, enters into interaction and, in a way, follows the preacher. Hence we have to ask: under which circumstances and conditions do the listeners take part? In what way can their interaction be taken into consideration in the preparation of the sermon?

Interested in analogous questions in the field of rhetoric, Josef Kopperschmidt tapered the Speech Act Theory in that he regards persuasion as the (to him) decisive dimension of human communication. If the conditions mentioned above were the requirements for being able to grasp and comprehend *illocutions* as such, Kopperschmidt now is concerned *with the speech act as a whole, including its perlocutive function.*

Consequently he describes the speech act as a whole as a "persuasive"[627] act, *as communication which desires to convince.*[628] To prevent misunderstandings, however, Kopperschmidt stresses that rhetorical instructions in this respect should never lead to manipulation, i.e. should certainly not teach the art of persuasion. For common convictions never result from a decreeing form of communication but arise in the course of a process guided by argumentation and reasoning: "The binding nature of successful consent lies in the persuasiveness of arguments of which one can approve."[629] In the following table (Fig. 18), Kopperschmidt's deliberations[630] are summarized.

---

627 From *persuadere* or *persuasio*, here exclusively used in the sense of "to convince" or "convincement". In Latin one can only infer from the respective context whether it means "to convince" or "to persuade".

628 Cf. J. Kopperschmidt, 1976.

629 J. Kopperschmidt, 1977, 215.

630 Cf. J. Kopperschmidt, 1976, esp. 87–95.

| Requirements on the Part of the Speaker | Requirements on the Part of the Addressees |
|---|---|
| **1. Aptitude for Collaborative Communication** | |
| A speech act can turn out successful if the speaker is willing and able to accept the addressees as equal subjects capable of making their own decisions, who may only be influenced on the basis of argumentation. | A speech act can turn out successful if the addressee is able to deal with the arguments put forward and if he is in principle convincible, i.e. is capable of learning. |
| **2. Willingness to Participate in Consensus-Building Communication** | |
| A speech act can turn out successful if the speaker himself is convinced of the plausibility of his arguments and is ready to enter by way of what is said into a communicative process guided by argumentation. | A speech act can turn out successful if the addressee is subjectively interested in consensus and ready to allow himself to be convinced on the basis of the arguments provided, should the occasion arise. |
| **3. Respecting Argumentation-Based Convictions** | |
| A speech act can turn out successful if the speaker shows that he will also accept the outcome of the communicative interaction even if the addressee does not agree with his argumentation. | A speech act can turn out successful if the renunciation of non-persuasive means of communication on the part of the speaker corresponds (on the part of the addressee) to the commitment to act accordingly in the case of a convincing speech. |

**Fig. 18:** Requirements for successful communication

These deliberations are of direct importance in Homiletics. A sermon which is successful to the extent that it deals with the listener responsibly and "knows what it is doing" is not simply a speech *about* this and that. It is a speech *to someone*. The communication of the gospel must not have the character of a decree, which prohibits dictating;[631] instead, what is implied is a dialog structure, albeit formally constructed as a monolog. This dialogical structure is all the more perceptible the more considerately the preacher – on the basis of argumentation and reasoning – strives for the listeners' ability to agree with what he says. The listeners should not be turned into the puppets of an institutional address but should rather be put into a position to react to and engage with what is said. The arguments provided in the sermon should enable those listening to act in the freedom of faith.

---

631 Cf. G. Otto, 1994, 108.

However, the rules provided by Kopperschmidt pose *specific challenges*: The fact that the sermon as a public speech is also an institutional speech can easily lead to conflicts with rule 1 (the principle of collaborative communication). An exaggerated understanding of the ministry on the part of the preacher or unreasonable role expectations on the part of the congregation may impair the will to a sermon based on argumentation and reasoning. "The *failure* of a sermon – in the sense of dialogical communication based on understanding and agreement – may oftentimes be caused by the preacher's inability to accept the listener 'as an equal subject, capable of making his own decision'."[632] Likewise, difficulties may arise in carrying out rule 2 (the principle of consensus-building communication): as the credibility of the communication of the gospel highly depends on the authenticity of the preacher, this rule opposes the already repeatedly mentioned concept of excluding the person of the preacher from his own address.

The fact that, as experience shows, it is often difficult after a sermon to agree on its intent as well as content, is no doubt also linked to the theologically dubious maxim discussed in I.2 that one should "keep away any personal influence from the 'Word of God'". In such cases it is impossible to make plausible why what is said is an integral part of one's own conviction, because it *is*, in fact, all to often *not* an integral part of *one's own* conviction. In everyday communication, on the other hand, we are easily capable of discerning that somebody tells us something they themselves find supremely urgent, necessary or momentous. We allow ourselves in certain circumstances to be convinced by a message which we are somewhat skeptical about, just *because it is brought up by a certain person*. This experience is reflected in expressions such as "Because *you* say so" [I let myself be convinced by this].

In spite of the essential role argumentation plays in the sermon, the category of "conviction" is not *per se* the *non plus ultra* of this craft. Just think of sermons in which hardly any efforts at persuasion is required because they refer to the faith of the congregation beyond approval and rejection and thus confer it to them anew, as it were. It would, thus, be more sensible to speak of the sermon's effect to consist in an "*agreement* with the listener" (rather than in *convincing* the listener) in which "the freedom of the opposite as a subject is taken seriously and called upon".[633] In order to make this agreement possible at least two conditions must be fulfilled: The listener must know and understand the intention (i.e. the purpose of the speech) of the speaker or preacher respectively. The preacher must know and understand the expectations of the listeners.[634]

---

**632** K.-H. Bieritz (1990, 81) referring to J. Kopperschmidt.
**633** H. Luther expects the listener to be able to handle the following questions: "Which potential interpretation does the preacher offer? Does it suit my life? What kind of action is demanded by the sermon? Based on which reasons?" H. Luther, 1989, 233.
**634** Loc. cit., 231f.

At this point one last differentiation that is frequently encountered in Homiletics, has to be mentioned, which is the differentiation between a "successful" and an "effective sermon"[635]. The characterization of speech acts as "successful" and "effective", which goes back to J.R. Searle, implies that a speech act *succeeds* if the illocutionary act is recognized as intended on the part of the listener, and that it is *effective* when the intended effect of the address actually comes into being. A sermon, too, should be able to be analyzed as to whether it is effective in the sense that it actually *achieves* its communication goal (comfort, encouragement, self-awareness etc.) – instead of having the opposite effect. It would therefore be improper to speak in the context of the preaching event only of "effective communication" if the underlying intention is *approved of*, if *consensus* is achieved and an *agreement* is reached[636]: According to Dannowski a sermon is successful "when the listener has understood what the preacher was concerned about. [...] It is effective when the listener can inwardly relive and integrate this. An effective sermon allows them [i.e. preacher and listener] to progress further together. The sermon's success is not attainable; it is – in theological terms – a work of the Holy Spirit."[637]

This conception implies two problems: For one thing, (1.) some sermons deal with something other than particular lines of thinking and believing, which should, *above all, be taken up approvingly*, on the part of the congregation. A sermon can lead to insights, which even the preacher himself is not fully aware of when delivering his sermon. The sermon can engage the listeners in a story through which they (re-)experience parts of their own biography, perhaps in a slightly new way, and make discoveries the preacher could not have foreseen.

For another thing, (2.) it has to be made clear that particularly in the preaching process the listeners should be taken seriously as subjects whose freedom may manifest itself, among other things, in that they do *not* approve of the sermon's conclusions but are still moved by the sermon as such and have, through listening to it, progressed a bit further in their acquisition of faith.

The terms "successful" and "effective" are in fact often used in the sense of "feasible" and "unavailable", which may have some merit, and is – theologically seen – innocuous. It remains unsatisfactory, however: How can a speech act performed in the course of the sermon possibly be described as *successful* if it is not realized on the perlocutive level, i.e. remains without the expected effect? Or asked from a different perspective: couldn't it be considered a "success" if the

---

**635** Cf. e.g. K.-F. Daiber/H. W. Dannowski, 1983, 125; H. W. Dannowski, 1983, 125.
**636** Here following the ideas of K.-F. Daiber/H. W. Dannowski, 1983, 91, 124–126.
**637** H. W. Dannowski, 1985, 124.

perlocutive intention of a sermon – e.g. the listeners' readiness to get involved and participate in the congregation – may perhaps not be fully realized, however, on the illocutive level of the sermon, listeners may still experience some sort of connection with themselves, which restructures the dynamics of their relationships?

### b) Imagination for Reality

In view of the significance of language for the actual "creative character" of the sermon[638] we have to ask what it means, in regard to the use of language, that the communication of the gospel is expected to provide impulses for the renewal of people in their current situation as well as for keeping open their future. The testimonies of the Old and New Testament hold on to the interconnection of both of these perspectives by linking their future expectations to the experience of faith in the present. For this purpose they draw on the anticipatory patterns of speech already discussed above (I.5.3.1.d).[639] On the basis of accumulated experiences and by referring to the images in which promises of a life lived by faith are manifested, it is also vital to linguistically anticipate in the sermon what is to be expected and what can be hoped for. In this context, particularly those aspects prove to be useful that were reflected within the framework of the virtual perspective of the preaching work.[640]

Anticipatory speech does not necessarily rely on the use of the Future Tense. Stories that take place in the present and relate how oppressive situations might change, dreams which are often narrated in the Past Tense, but offer visions of how the kingdom of God takes on a concrete shape under the conditions of this world, little scenes highlighting a "before" and "after" through which the transformation of conditions is understood – these are all linguistic attempts to communicate what may be expected as a distant or close effect of a sermon.

---

638 Cf. below, III.4.3.

639 This anticipatory structure is of fundamental significance for the Jewish-Christian tradition. What will happen "when the LORD restored the fortunes of Zion, we were like those who dream. Then our mouth was filled with laughter, and our tongue with shouts of joy. Restore our fortunes. May those who sow in tears reap with shouts of joy. Those who go out weeping, bearing the seed for sowing, shall come home with shouts of joy, carrying their sheaves" (from Ps 126). *Experience and imagination at one and the same time* characterized the faith of the early Christians: Their daily deeds and actions were determined by something which is described as "imminent expectation" and was geared to a future for which they developed visions. On this question cf. also W. H. Ritter, 2000, 162–168.

640 Cf. the excursus on "The Virtual Perspective: The Sermon as a Construction of the World" inserted after chapter 4.3.4.2 (p. 205–207).

Two examples of this: "If God loves you – why don't you do so, too? Don't shy away from yourself: the convinced egoist who is happiest when he can use his life all for himself – that's not you. The egocentric, whose greatest pleasure is to revolve around himself – he is not your role model. Christ, your brother, has rendered it useless a long time ago. It no longer works."[641]

"Let nothing keep us from living our lives *looking back at death*. This also means a life in which we look back at some form of God's judgment, dreaded or conjured up in speech. We can look back at this because we have left it behind. To lead a life in the power of the resurrection and looking back at one's own death means to be no longer tied down to stories of defeat. We find ourselves on a new path. That apprehensive life which very much resembled a pilgrimage to our own grave has come to an end. The cover of the tomb into which we had retreated in our frustration has been rolled back. Jesus says: Because I live, you also will live. Live as I do, live as people resurrected, live looking back at death. Do not raise the old days as if your present was not a time of salvation. Rejoice in the morrow, ask yourselves what it will be like. Do not hold back your life: You can no longer lose it."[642]

Anticipations are seldom found in the spectrum of argumentation of sermons. More often they retrospectively refer to the situation of the text then or a rather abstract present. The attempt to put into words what could be the case "if the sermon was successful", by contrast, is less often found. But anyone who is unable to develop a concrete idea as to where the oftentimes-required changes in attitudes and habits should lead, leaves the listener in the dark as to whereupon it is (according to the sermon) worth living. The congregation should also receive a sermon for the sake of concrete ideas, images and patterns of speech which help them to adopt certain expectations as their own. They rely on future prospects in order to be able to exist and act. Independently of whether these verbally expressed expectations are fulfilled in detail later or not: they are important for the *present*.

A further significant implication of anticipation is its power to transform situations. Detailed pictures put abstract options in concrete terms and give them the appearance of *prospects* which play a vital part within the framework of motivational processes. In other words: the verbal anticipation of particular conditions can, in fact, contribute to their actual *realization*.

Friedrich Niebergall's suggestion to first address in the sermon the "presupposed conditions" prevailing in a congregation and then turn to the quite different objectives ("norms") provided in the gospel while at the same time enumerating suitable "objective and subjective aids"[643] appears, at a first glance, to correspond to structuring the sermon according to the consecutive pattern of law and gospel. One could, however, also look at these thoughts from a different angle

---

**641** From the final section of a sermon on Phil 4:10–13.
**642** From the final section of a sermon on John 5:39–47.
**643** F. Niebergall, 1929, 170–191.

and correspondingly present the "norms" of the gospel not simply as an intervening message which either abolishes the law or makes it superfluous, but as a linguistic construction of the altered basic conditions of life. Looked at in this way, we do not only have to deal with two, as Niebergall recommends, but with *three situations* in Homiletics: The listeners are not only interested in the message against the backdrop of the *situation of the text* (which primarily the preacher should know about), neither should the listeners get pinned down to the *present-day situation* (which they should, however, be made aware of as being the *given frame of reference*); the point is to put into words the *situation which is opening up or emerging.*

Accordingly Albrecht Grözinger regards "visualizing humanity in the possible horizon of God"[644] as the "sermon's task". There is nothing new in this notion of imagination. In literary studies, the philosophy of language and psychology imagination and anticipation are described as having partly interchangeable functions. It in view of the thesis that the verbal anticipation of future conditions and situations in the sermon can lead to an impact on actual conditions and situations it becomes clear why anticipations or imagined scenes and pictures are commonly deemed subversive: They are – as Jean-Paul Sartre put it – *temporary nihilations* in the face of things as they are.[645] They set a new world order, and are in this respect necessary "acts of freedom"[646]. How else could we come up with a sermon which does not only have a past history but also an impact history?

In a similar context Grözinger tackles the possibilities of an "appealing speech": The sermon does not simply state the story of God but makes the story of God *visible* for us. So we ourselves can get into it. But we do not have to. Appealing language knows no compulsion, but wishes to move people to let themselves in for this story. [...] Yet appeal is not shapeless. As formed speech it contains an enticement, an invitation, sometimes perhaps even a demand. [...] Appealing means: A sermon wants something from those who listen to it – but not in the form of an asser-tion, a forceful argument or even an order. The sermon opens a particular speech area which invites us to think and to speak for ourselves. Appealing language consequently adds something to reality – a new picture, an unfamiliar perspective, an unexpected turn. The parables of Jesus are in this sense a language-school of appealing speech."[647]

---

644 A. Grözinger, 1995, 98. Cf. also the role of imagination in the homiletic concept of Paul S. Wilson (1988, 16–18) – not least for the faith recommended by the sermon.
645 Even though, according to J.-P. Sartre, what is imagined is – even if not verbally expressed – part of a quite *individual* process of imagination, it represents – as a "néantisation" of existing conditions – some sort of effective *reality*. Cf. J.-P. Sartre, 1949, 161.
646 R. Warning, 1976, 220.
647 A. Grözinger, 2004, 238f. and idem, 2008, 239–242. On the specific aspects of sermons refer-ring to parables and the opportunities of parable-like preaching cf. D. Buttrick, 2000 (including numerous examples).

*Excursus: Hearing Acts of the Sermon. On the Auditory Dimension of the Medium of Speech*

In order to comprehend language as a structural component and medium of the communication of the gospel, we frequently returned in chapters I.4 and I.5 to the process of communication and understanding *between* preacher and congregation. A further homiletic deepening of the medial use of language on the part of the listeners, however, requires not only to ask about the effect of *speech acts* but also to additionally understand the *hearing acts* of a sermon.

Accordingly, Thomas Nisslmüller has taken a closer look on sermon listening from a media aesthetic point of view and formulated relevant consequences for the linguistic shaping of sermons.[648] His reflections are to be understood as a comprehensive representation of the homiletic model of the "Auredit" in which the hermeneutics and interpretational performance of hearing is shown to advantage in terms of the inevitable process of updating, supplementing and acquiring the sermon.

In the blurb of his book, he explains his approach as follows: "Hearing becomes the anthropological cornerstone in determining the purpose and meaning of our existence, and there is an inner hearing stage on which the network of human behavior and life preferences develops. It is one of the distinguished aspects of this study to advance the awareness of hearing from theological-philosophical, psychological and aesthetic perspectives, and to thus provide a forum for hearing quality. It focuses not least on [the sermon as a] sort of audio play coram Deo."

The scope of this introduction does not allow an examination of this approach which is equal in breadth or depth to the analyses of speech act and conversational theories in this chapter. We should, however, at least mention the contours of this approach relating to auditory experiences. Nisslmüller considers "hearing as [a] 'cornerstone' of life"[649]. He thus regards hearing as an anthropological dimension. From a theological point of view he asks what "listening into the Scripture" or "bringing God to our ears"[650] means. The attempt to explain sermon listening on the basis of audio play concepts and thereby to establish a connection with "New Testament listening experiences" and "biblical audio plays" proves to be a deepening in respect of homiletic methodology. On this basis, an "auditory" culture is outlined, which includes a homiletic reflection of the tasks permanently performed by hearing, i.e. providing orientation and interpretations. They are

---

648 T. Nisslmüller, 2008.
649 Loc. cit., 37–40.
650 Loc. cit., 90–94, 131–133.

specified as "simulations", as "fictions", as "sculptural activities", as "incarnations of the Word", etc.[651]

In a certain analogy to the classification of the speech acts, yet more subtly differentiated, Nisslmüller analyses a total of 95 ways of hearing, which are to be understood as particular forms of meaning construction, which include, for example, "participatory hearing", "reflexive hearing", "calculating hearing" or "eucharistic hearing".[652] Through this cartography of hearing a sequence of the sermon process, which has largely passed unheeded in the homiletic discourse so far, is comprehensively illuminated.

Hence, previous findings on sermon reception are extended by pointing out "sermon listening as stage experience", by defining the homiletic position of the "hearer as a translator" and by establishing a "hearing theory of faith".

## 5.4 On the Category of the Conversational Sermon. Language-Theoretical Consequences

### 5.4.1 The Sermon as Latent Conversation

Linguistic reflections in Homiletics are concerned with the development and application of rules for a successful communication of the sermon in which not only are messages understood but the members of the congregation – which of course include the preacher – also relate to one another in the horizon of the gospel. The *terminus technicus* for a communication *based on* and *aiming for* a common basis and mutual understanding is *conversation*. It implies aspects of content as well as the relationship aspect of human communication. In terms of the rules that must be followed in this respect one can speak of "conversational maxims" or – with regard to the analysis of these rules – of "conversation analysis"[653].

It is no accident that the term *conversation* shows direct semantic correspondences to (Lat) *sermo* and (Gk) ὁμιλία.[654] For centuries the understanding of

---

651 Loc. cit., 141–214.
652 Loc. cit., 215–376.
653 A. Linke et al., 1996, 196, 259.
654 The term "conversation" (Fr.: *conversation* or Ital.: *conversazione*) has its direct model in (Lat.) *conversatio* (contact, communion). Since the Renaissance "conversation" has served in use and meaning as an equivalent translation of *sermo* or ὁμιλία. On the many-facetted history of this term cf. K.-H. Göttert, 1998.

"preaching" has been shaped by and discussed in relation to these terms. They do not strictly differentiate between "address" and "conversation" and consider the communication event as a form of "getting together", of "interaction" or "social interplay". In a historical respect, too, the "conversation" between believers may be regarded as a prototype of the communication of the gospel: it is obvious that the story of the life of Jesus of Nazareth was not passed down through public lectures but that it initially spread among the early Christians through animated, certainly ardently conducted, conversations.

The category of conversation stands for a *comprehensive communication* which is not merely concerned with effectiveness and clarity in order to exert a particular effect upon the listeners. A sermon oriented on the conditions of conversation cultivates *practices* that presuppose an interest in one another on the part of the communication partners which goes beyond a mere interest in particular topics of life or questions of faith. A process of communication which promotes showing and forming interest in a sense of community is one of the most decisive impulses which lead into the preaching situation. So, what constitutes such a process?

Homiletic conversation implies:
- striving for a real *contact* with the communication partners, i.e. to "devote" oneself to them when addressing them,
- *not being untactful* and treating the other in his uniqueness or otherness with respect and appreciative attention and politeness,
- paying regard to the principle of *equality,*
- *not appearing self opinionated* when displaying one's own position – particularly when it comes to *important* questions over which people have racked their brains for centuries,
- attempting to achieve the *maximum of clarity* for the sake of the other and making sure that one's conversational partner is able to keep up with what is said,
- *being open* in the search for truth for the discovery of the uncertainty of one's own views and opinions,
- taking heed of the *well-being of the other,* their "edification", freedom – i.e. not to aim for coming out the superior winner or fountain of knowledge in the end,
- keeping the *balance* between, on the one hand, general questions of societal, social, religious and other areas of public life and, on the other hand, questions of deep interest for the other as an individual.

Even if – as shown in the discussion of the dialog structure of the sermon above – we have to assume that due to the actual distribution of roles in a speech situation we can only speak of conversations to a limited extent, we must not make any compromises regarding the homiletic relevance of the *attitude* and *language* which make for successful dialogs and conversations.[655]

It would go beyond the scope of such an introduction to homiletically reformulate the whole spectrum of conversational linguistics here. This would, among other things, require to contrast the conversational principle of "reference" (or of "complement") with the above-mentioned problem of "scolding the listeners" and imply – as the term *reference* already indicates – appreciatively acknowledging the presence, faith and life of the other. This has, of course, nothing to do with gushing praise or with dropping a few trite "positive" statements here and there, but above all with showing a committed, courteous awareness of the listeners. Likewise the meanings of *leisure* and *sociability* as concomitant circumstances of conversation would have to be reflected on homiletically. It is not by chance that the sermon is held within the framework of a ceremony and on a Sunday. The fact that the sermon should in consequence be experienced as "effortless" to some extent does not, however, mean that cutbacks should be made regarding its earnestness and disputability but arises from a homiletic principle already discussed above: a sermon among Christians does not serve the purpose of bringing "faith" or "the Word of God" (which they otherwise would not have) to the congregation within a time span of 20 minutes but of communicating anew *in the light of* this faith, in which preacher and listener face one another, about living by faith.

### 5.4.2 Linguistic Cooperation with the Listener

The basis of the principles of communication sketched above is abandoned if the listeners – in spite of their fundamental interest – are more or less "excommunicated" by the linguistic obstacles of the sermon. Consequently the idea of a sermon as successful conversation (on questions of life and faith) involves that preachers now and again check the linguistic repertoire of their sermons for its communicative suitability.

---

**655** Since its first edition (cf. W. Engemann, 2000, 353–360; 2011, 248–251), this volume has presented and discussed a preaching model that is oriented on the principles of conversation, which is discussed in a similar way in American Homiletics, though integrated into the didactics of Homiletics under slightly different premises (cf. O. W. Allen, 2005, esp. 3–15 and 38–57). In her volume "Sharing the Word", Lucy Rose introduces several vital aspects of a nonhierarchical sermon and finally summarizes: "In such a nonhierarchical context, where power, leadership, and authority are shared, conversational preaching describes the whole of preaching as an ethos that surrounds the pulpit, traditionally a place of power. This nonhierarchical ethos perhaps leads those who are ordained to resist monopolizing the pulpit and to reenvision their role as ensuring that preaching occurs. This ethos perhaps leads the community of faith regularly to invite others, particularly laity, to preach. The term preacher, then [. . .] refers to the one whose function [. . .] is to offer the sermon as one exchange in the ongoing conversation of the community" (L. Rose, 1997, 123).

In Fig. 1 (p. 4) which shows the communication process of a sermon in its inner connection, language proves to be the medium within which the production and reception of the sermon intersect. Through *one* sermon address *two* users of language are joined together, preacher and listener; their mutual understanding rests, among other things, on the fact that they draw from a common stock of linguistic signs. What we have discussed within the framework of the semiotic perspective and with regard to the category of a sign-like sermon requires further clarification here: That the individual is able to connect the linguistic forms of expressions of the sermon with the intended meanings and to perform the necessary interpretational achievements presupposes that both, preacher and listener, participate to a certain extent in a common conversational code.[656] Some *differences* between the respective codes of the communication partners, preacher and listener, are generally to be expected, and they must be overcome again in every single sermon.

Sociolinguistics had for a long time described this problem with the aid of the so-called deficit theory[657]. According to this theory, communication difficulties can be traced back to the use of *class-specific codes,* the differences of which result from the speakers' belonging to different social classes, each with their own level of conversation and discourse. While the educated upper or middle class uses an *elaborated* code, rich in linguistic possibilities of expression, the lower class employs a rather *restricted,* less complex code which is scarcely suitable for coping with abstract questions because it consists in the use of very concrete language. Even though the attempt of explaining communication barriers through social stratification is certainly outdated and has at least been amended by other theories,[658] the problem investigated by Bernstein is still relevant, albeit under changed conditions: The fact that today it is the *milieu of experience*[659] rather than the socio-economic class in which particular codes of conversation develop does not alter the fact that *different codes circulate simultaneously* in one and the same culture. The language of a sermon, which is frequently abstract and empirically looked at belonging to the "pattern of advanced civilization"[660] is not particularly suitable for entering into a communication about life in the light of the gospel with listeners from highly different social and experiential milieus.

Against this backdrop it is still appropriate today to bear in mind Bernstein's basic differentiation between "elaborated" and "restricted" code.[661]

---

656 Cf. above, I.4.3.4 as well as the models presented in J. Kopperschmidt, 1976, 158f.; E. Öffner, 1979; 82, G. Schüepp, 1982, 44 which are similar to each other in many respects.

657 The main representative of this theory is Basil Bernstein (cf. B. Bernstein, 1972).

658 The deficiency model experienced significant corrections through the concepts of difference ("Difference Hypothesis") and variety ("Linguistics of Variety"). A. Linke et al. provide comprehensible introduction to this subject, 1996, 298–323.

659 Cf. G. Schulze, 1993, 169–217, esp. 174f.

660 Loc. cit., 142f.

661 In the following table Bernstein's (1979, 216–231) central basic principles are summarized.

| Levels of Differentiation | Restricted Code | Elaborated Code |
|---|---|---|
| Syntactic level | Short, many unfinished sentences. Use of the active verb form predominant. Direct speech predominant. Determinant speech mode: indicative. | Complex sentence constructions based on nouns. Many conjunctions and subordinate clauses. Frequent use of indirect speech and conjunctive. |
| Level of abstraction | Low level of abstraction. Statements relate to concrete topics and facts. High level of clarity. What cannot be seen is scarcely communicable. What is concrete remains without transparency or transcendency. | High level of abstraction. Statements are frequently condensed into concepts. Knowledge of complex interconnections is presupposed. Statements achieve transcendency through the networks of relationships in which they stand. Restricted relation to concrete reality. |
| Argumentative structure | Refers to concrete situations and contexts, shaped by emotions. Low level of general validity. Subjectivistic argumentation. | Flexible speech patterns. The relation of argument and situation or context is oftentimes hardly discernible. Distanced, objectifying reference to facts is possible. |

**Fig. 19:** A comparison of restricted and elaborated codes

In the – as far as I know – first homiletic reception of this basic differentiation between restricted and elaborated codes several interesting examples from the practice of preaching are given.[662] By means of a juxtaposition of "laborer" or hearer on the one hand and "academic" or preacher on the other the "problem of communication" should be revealed as "the church's problem *per se*"[663]. Although the one-sidedness of this perspective, fixed as it were on social classes, has now been overcome in sociology and – as already mentioned – in sociolinguistics, too, Öffner's conclusions are just as relevant under changed conditions as Bernstein's analyses. They do not lead to the short-circuited consequence that a preacher dare not express himself in an "elaborate" way. The hearers *need* preachers who are able, if necessary, to abstract from a particular situation or concrete facts and get down to questions which point "beyond today". This medial quality of language is, as a rule, preceded by a homiletic struggle for the alleviation of communication barriers. In doing so, the following points should be taken into consideration:[664]

---

662 E. Öffner, 1979, 65.
663 Loc. cit., 57. "Anyone [...] who desires to promote faith, who wants to make the gospel a εὐαγγέλλιον, a healing message which holds true for everyone, comprehensible for everyone, must first and foremost express himself in an understandable way. *That is why* the problem of communication is 'the church's problem *per se*'" (loc. cit., 87).
664 Cf. also loc. cit., 86–110.

a) *Experience-based language*: The language of the sermon should refer to or be gained from the potential of common experience. Common language grows from common experience.

b) *Narrative language*: Stories can verbalize experience in a specific way in that they clarify something on the basis of a specific case or problem which points beyond the story itself. In narrations, restricted and elaborate language supplement and interpret one another reciprocally. The combination of firsthand experiences and interpretations in a story can result in new experiences through the narrative.

c) *Dialogical basic attitude:* By addressing the listeners' questions and, in so doing, joining them in their experiences of reality, the preacher takes on a dialogical attitude. Thereby the discussions before and after the sermon, in which the members of the congregation come forward with their opinion, play an important part in promoting the sermon's lasting comprehensibility.[665]

d) *Translating language*: The language of the sermon can obtain a translating function and itself be understood as an aid to comprehension if it – instead of using the terminology of an elaborate code – draws on pictures, metaphors, parables, symbols, and, in certain circumstances, also on dialect.

Linguistic cooperation is a prerequisite for the communication of the gospel. Tied to this is the task of preaching in a comprehensible manner and of conveying to the congregation a dialogic attitude which makes preachers themselves "living witnesses". Mutual understanding does not remain without effect: The verbalization and interpretation of common experience is an intended and desired form of influencing a life in faith.

### 5.4.3 Consequences for Cooperative Acting in the Sermon

The just-mentioned effect of the sermon is not an effect which – once "programmed" – henceforth adheres to the sermon wherever it might be delivered, but is, if everything goes well, achieved through linguistic cooperation with the congregation.[666] Hence, in the following section some of the consequences shall

---

**665** "If the listener does not get the chance to comment on what has been said by the preacher, i.e. to reassure himself as to what has been said, he is very likely to mishear or misunderstand certain things – and remember them in this way." In a survey "Protestant churchgoers were asked after the service what they had retained from the sermon they had just heard: only 4% could give a correct answer, 69%, however, only a false answer or none at all" (loc. cit., 94).
**666** Cf. also H. Luther, 1989, 229.

be mentioned that are to be taken into consideration for cooperative acting in the sermon.

The table below (Fig. 20) points out, on basis of H. P. Grice's conversational maxims[667], the convergences between the prerequisites of successful speech acts, stimuli for action on the part of the speaker and indispensable demands on the qualities of verbal utterances.

| **Maxims of Cooperative Speech Acts** Basic maxim: Be cooperative | | |
|---|---|---|
| **Maxims** | **Value** | **Conduct** |
| Quantity | Information | Say as much as is necessary, and do not say too much. |
| Relation | Relevance | Make sure what you say is relevant. |
| Manner | Clarity | Bring what you say into an appropriate form and be concise. |
| Quality | Truth | Only say what you assume to be true, or make clear the level of probability of your statement. |

**Fig. 20:** Maxims of cooperative speech acts

For the communication of the sermon it is not sufficient that the preacher's utterances are (merely) felt to be truthful. If the sermon is to succeed as a cooperative act all the maxims mentioned above must be fulfilled *simultaneously*. This requires:

1. *Congruence between communicative intention and the speech act chosen:*
   All too often the questions uttered in a sermon prove – on the illocutive level – to be, in fact, reproaches or accusations towards the listeners which clearly impedes a favorable response. Requests are irresolutely expressed as possibilities or even granted as permissions instead of being formulated as what they are: appeals. Imperatives are not a taboo in the sermon.
2. *Checking one's attitude towards the listeners:*
   Anyone who thinks lowly of their listeners and appears before them with a self-understanding of being, in fact, "spiritually superior" or regards "reading them the riot act" as the main task in preaching should not be surprised if the e.g. supposed sermon of consolation is not received well.
3. *Analyzing the speech act repertoire of one's sermons:*
   Becoming aware of hierarchies and dominances in the use of particular speech acts is a vital aspect in the examination of one's own preaching

---

**667** Cf. H. P. Grice, 1979b, 16–52, and A. Linke et al., 1996, 199.

style. This includes searching for the reasons for the potential lack of specific speech acts. The clarity of an address depends to a high degree on the harmony between propositional content and illocutionary intention.

4. *Being aware of the special function of expressive speech acts:*
   This corresponds to the aforementioned necessity of saying "I" in the sermon. For it is – seen from the speech-event – the preachers who take the action with their witness. If in so doing they withhold their "I" from the congregation they prevent their listeners from taking a stand on the sermon and from "cooperating" in any way.

5. *Rationales for the sermon intention:*
   In order to prevent a reception that is driven by the mere faith in institutions (i.e. considering the sermon as true or correct merely because of its "official quality") preachers should make clear that they do not only say *qua office* what they have to say. This includes the attempt to provide the listeners with an insight into the reasons for the intention, or proposition, of the sermon, i.e. to strive toward argumentation also in this respect and to thus grant the congregation the distance without which an act of genuine processing is impossible.[668]

6. *Accounting for relevance and informative content:*
   The maxim of relevance does not apply to church life *intra muros* but refers to the suitability of the sermon for a life lived by faith on a daily basis. The same holds true for the information maxim, which addresses the question of how the information provided in a sermon could be used in the life of the individual.

7. *Variety in terms of speech modes:*
   With respect to their speech patterns, many sermons aim, above all, for an agreement on a particular view of things. This has little to do with "communication" of the gospel. The listeners become "doers of the Word" (cf. Jas 1:22) through a broader range of linguistic practices rather than when merely used as a container for holding pieces of theological information.

---

**668** Michael Brothers' examinations on the sermon as a "room to speak" and a "space to listen" (cf. the subtitle of his volume, M. A. Brothers, 2014) provide an important addition to phenomenological discussion of the effect of the sermon. His volume, "Distance in Preaching", offers an instructive discussion of the fact that understanding (in the sense of linguistic-hermeneutic cooperation) is promoted through the methodological-conceptual granting of a critical distance, which, of course, also holds true for the field of sermon composition.

# 6 Preaching for the Individual. On the Question of the Sermon's Reference to Situation

## Preliminary Remarks

Having outlined the structure of the preaching process above (Fig. 1, p. 4) – with its main emphasis on the text, the person preaching as well as the form and language of the sermon –, there now appears a further area of importance: the listener and their individual situation as an integral part of the communication event preaching. The title of this chapter – "Preaching for the Individual" – implies not only the aspiration that what is said serves the reality of a person's faith and life circumstances. "Preaching for the individual" likewise serves as a maxim and a plea for a *humane sermon*, created with individual people in mind and which expresses respect and an esteem for those listening. This includes a critical analysis of existing attitudes towards faith and life. A "humane sermon" draws its premises not solely from Soteriology, Christology, Dogmatics or a "Theology of Revelation" but also to a significant extent from contemporary Anthropology.[669]

The lack of sermons that are – in this sense – *ad hominem* has been a matter of complaint for many generations as it has been regarded as one of the greatest deficiencies in the communication of the gospel. Nevertheless, has the scarcity not instigated a fundamental change in culture of preaching: "No form of preaching deserves to be called a sermon, if it is not ad hominem, if it does not direct itself towards people. One of the most severe theological misperceptions of today is the peculiar trend towards a so-called 'objective' manner of preaching. Therein a great theological inconsiderateness is revealed which is only surpassed by its ineffectiveness."[670]

The purposeful, *ardent visualizing of contemporary life* and the examination thereof must bear fruit both in the preparation as well as in the communication of the sermon itself; especially if the sermon as an address "for a person" is not simply to remain an intention.[671] All homiletic skill is futile if the individual cannot derive anything from the sermon communication which might be significant for their existence. Sooner or later they will no longer expose themselves to this event.

---

669 More detail in III.2.2.

670 H. Lilje, 1957, 22.

671 What Wolfgang Hegewald describes as a "chorus" in the poetical-didactic way of writing is anologously relevant as a homiletic maxim: "Literature is, as is art in general, '*a virtuosity of visualizing resp. realization*" (W. Hegewald, 1998, 43. Emphasis W. E.).

https://doi.org/10.1515/9783110440256-006

This has nothing to do with the competition of the modern media: Uwe Pörksen shares a charming dialog from the beginning of the 1950s: "In my parents' house there was a washerwoman, Aunt Hedwig. Once, asked by my mother: 'It's true, isn't it, Mrs. Hinrichsen, that you don't go to church?' she replied: 'I can't make anything out of it.' My mother was somehow amused by this answer – by the expression."[672] One can find a far more differentiated assessment in Kim Apel's "Predigten in der Literatur" – an informative work on the multifarious documented connections between the effect of the sermon, self-perception of the listeners and their behavior. In the resulting criticism from his work regarding the sermon – in this case it concerns Karl Philipp Moritz' novel *Anton Reiser* – the emphasis is "not on the intention or content of the sermon but on its actual effect" in the life of the people who listen to a sermon.[673]

Based on this, the situation and context of the listener is marked as an area[674] which stretches beyond the sermon as an act within the worship service. The listener is not merely in a setting through which he is connected with the congregation and the preacher for a certain amount of time. The worship service is only a segment, a particular area of life and experience within a complex life situation which is specific for each person. A person who attends a worship service, among other things, to hear a sermon, comes with certain experiences and convictions, but also with fears and questions relevant to their current life – which, as can rightfully be expected, are to be addressed in some way through the liturgy and sermon.

In the history of Homiletics this standpoint has time and again been associated with the name of Ernst Lange. This is correct to the extent that, at the end of the 1960s, the apparently easily understood theses which Lange trenchantly presented sparked off far-reaching theological debates concerning the *way of perceiving* the listener within the sermon. Because of the fixation on Ernst Lange's theses other impulses are certainly easily overlooked which are no less relevant for the homiletic discussion of the situation in which the sermon is held.

To these belong Manfred Mezger's[675] precedence-setting works, the present homiletic findings on this subject by Alfred Dedo Müller[676], the impulses given by Tillich's Theology of Correlation[677] as well as the questions raised by Otto Haendler in the 1950s: "The questions and conditions which particularly put pressure on our time and therefore on the congregations [must] be discussed in detail with regard to their effect upon the structuring of the sermon. Every age is determined in its inner life by fundamental questions and fundamental conditions. [...] How one copes with life [...] is one of the *fundamental questions* of humankind. [...] A person who

---

**672** U Pörksen, 2006, 93.
**673** K. Apel, 2009, 448.
**674** Again cf. Fig. 1, p. 4.
**675** M. Mezger, especially 1959, 1970, 1971.
**676** A. D. Müller, 1954.
**677** Cf. P. Tillich, Vol. I, 1967.

preaches must] regardless of the answer – or for the sake of it – address and live the question of how to cope with life – just as the thousands – as a question of day and night and lead, as a witness, to the solution. Only then it becomes clear how far from reality a sermon is, that proclaims and builds up a construct of unrelated and timeless (instead of convincing) truths over the present-day people."[678]

Before we discuss these impulses for a homiletic approach to the existential dimension of being human, the highlighting of some problems shall make the urgency of the connected perspective clear.

## 6.1 Snapshots. Empirical Indicators of Problems

### 6.1.1 The Dismissal of the Realities of Life

The listener to a sermon is – in theological terms – at one and the same time a citizen of the kingdom of God and a citizen of the world. Their existence cannot be divided in percentages in two worlds, whereby their "spiritual existence" could be considered as having a greater share than the profane existence. Consequently, sermons must in general be related to *worldly experiences.* Anyone who preaches cannot be satisfied with a "spiritual superstructure" but must take the word in the light of matters as they are or how they are experienced. This presupposes a perceptive ability, expertise [on the subject] and – in the interest of concretisation – Sunday after Sunday a reduction of complexity. As far as the "relation to the situation" is concerned, what matters is to work out a relevant and thereby also significant *detail from the spectrum of human experiences of reality* and make this the "vanishing point" of the sermon. Anyone who vaguely speaks about *all possible* unpleasant, inferior, unfortunate and sad things and then goes on to talk of all that is good, pleasant and desirable and which – with a little faith – would be open to access, risks not saying anything substantial whatsoever.

The necessary examination of the actual life realities of the people for whom the sermon is held is frequently misunderstood as a task which concerns only Homiletics or Practical Theology.[679] But it is the task of theology *as a whole* – and in a *specific* way it is also a concern of Dogmatics and Ethics – to consider

---

**678** O. Haendler, 2017b, 529.
**679** "Practical Theology relieves the other theological disciplines from the special historical responsibility of repeating the Word of God today" (E. Jüngel, 1968, 44).

the question which Dietrich Bonhoeffer positioned as the central question of all theological reflection, namely "who Christ actually [is] for us today"[680].

Dietrich Bonhoeffer discussed this question in a context, by problematizing the accomplishment and efficiency of "theological and pious words". He doubts that one can speak of God understandably with people who are "no longer religious" (even if these people were to dispute this) by naturally presupposing a "religious a priori" of the western "Christian preaching and theology" in people. On the contrary, it is a matter of overcoming a "religious terminology" and a language which immunizes against the world and turning to the question of "how [...] we [can] speak [...] in a 'worldly' way about 'God'".[681] Therefore, Systematic Theology has to – within the framework of its own reflections and perspective – achieve its part in what is usually readily left to Practical Theology in the sense of a division of labor. This, then, is not a question of discussing who Christ is *per se* – Christ cannot be spoken of in this way – *but it is a question of who he is for the individual,* since his presence, speaking and action always took place in relation to those whom he encountered.

Correspondingly, a contemporary theology must explain and make plausible *who we today are in relation to Christ,* what this relationship means for us at the beginning of the 3rd Millenium and how we, in the midst of the fates and stories of our lives, might become aware of, experience and testify to the coming of God's kingdom.

By placing the problem of the fading-out of the reality of life from the sermon at the beginning of this chapter, I would like to draw attention to a *general problem of sermons* or a popular understanding of what a sermon is: In comparison with the numerous exegetical discussions offered as well as the faithful reproduction of standardized theological rhetorical figures of argumentation, the consideration and perception of the real life of the listeners occupies a strikingly meagre space. Frequently the dimension of the experience of the human existence is reduced to the *life in the congregation* or even the *questions of the worship service:*

"Our congregation would give a far better impression to those outside if we could succeed in approaching one another more openly and not leave practical help and counseling to the social state. We should see ourselves more and more as a family wherein one bears responsibility for the other."[682] "Has the form of our worship service, which has developed out of tradition, still anything in common with the service of the early Christian congregation in Corinth? Are the Charismatic congregations in Africa and here in Germany not much closer to the ideal of the early Christian worship in their yearning to experience a service with their ecstatic spiritual gifts? These questions constantly move me anew. [...] Perhaps these are also your questions, brothers and sisters."[683]

---

680 D. Bonhoeffer, 2010, 362.
681 Loc. cit., 364.
682 Sermon manuscript on Gal 6:1–3.7–10.
683 Sermon manuscript on 1 Cor 12:4–11.

Far too seldom the listeners are seen as people who, out of the 168 hours of the week, spend one and a half at most at church, who have to endure arguments, want to raise dissent or have to give in. They know what zest for life is but could also write their own psalm of lamentation. Instead in the sermon they are too often confronted with "little exegetical discoveries", with topics and problems of interest to theologians which, naturally, the preacher must consider *in the preparation* of the sermon but should not overtax the congregation with, especially when they simply "air" the ideas connected them.

"What is God? When I am asked that question, answers only occur to me after some hesitation and reflection: God is the Creator. God is the Almighty. God is the final Judge before whom we must accept responsibility. God is higher than our reasoning, he is the completely "Other" [...]. God is Lord of the heavenly hosts [...]. God is love – only three words, but these words contain a powerful message, the explosive force of which is immense. Are we still aware of this? [...] John assures us that God is love. What he means is that our Father in heaven loves us, indeed that his being itself is love. The Creator loves his creatures, God loves humanity. [...] We can be told: You are loved. God loves you. God is love. [...] When we reflect on God's acceptance we can draw courage from this and overcome fear."[684]

When listening to some sermons, even with increased attentiveness, one cannot establish which question or problem, which necessity of life the preacher has brought to the pulpit because he has not asked himself a fundamental question: *Why am I going to the pulpit today?* The need for further clarifications arises from this question: *Which* conditions of actual human existence and the Christian faith do I assume when I preach? *What* have I to say about these? *What must be the case* if my sermon is to be significant – and what could the sermon achieve in this context?[685] Such contents can scarcely stand up to such questions:

"How does the communication between a man and God function when each speaks a different language? Paul speaks of the Holy Spirit who intercedes for us with silent sighs. The Holy Spirit acts as an interpreter so to speak. The Holy Spirit translates for God what human beings are unable to say to God. In the present Age of Technology, one could also, with some exaggeration, say that God's Spirit is given to the human heart 'as a transmitter' and keeps 'radio contact' with God which they cannot do by their own efforts. Yet, it is not quite so easy. [...] The transmitter cannot be adjusted but adjusts itself. The person cannot set 'the frequency'. [...] Words which I utter in my prayer only reach God through the Holy Spirit [... end of sermon:] Dear congregation, whether you give thanks or lament, praise or rebuke, confess or remain silent – none of us knows what we should pray, as is only proper – every word spoken or not spoken reaches God's ear only through the Holy Spirit."[686]

---

684 Sermon manuscript on 1 John 4:16b-21.
685 Cf. the function of the similarly arranged core questions (Why? What? How? What for?), p. 153f.
686 Sermon manuscript on Rom 8:16f.

Frequently Bible passages are discussed for only one apparent reason, that is, when the text has "its turn" in the course of the Ecclesiastical Year: "Since today is Pentecost, the Feast of the Holy Spirit, I should like to speak of the Giver of Gifts, the Holy Spirit in the sermon."[687] But even a church service on Pentecost is a "service", is to be for the benefit of the listeners. It is held for their life's sake and not (in the first place) for their dogmatic instruction and certainly not to pacify the trinitarian godhead. Every church service represents a form of God's service towards his church. Consequently, the *anthropological dimension of the Ecclesiastical Year* and its liturgical variations should also be perceptible in the context of the sermon.[688] A person who attends the church service should not hear about the Holy Spirit in the perspective of biblical tradition for an entire Sunday morning "because it is Pentecost". Rather, they should hear about it because the tradition on the subject of the "Holy Spirit" affects their everyday life and opens up a central dimension of religious practice or a Christian way of life. (The reverse perspective, in which everyday life would only be spoken of here and there and even then, simply to explain theological concepts in the text, would ultimately be *inhuman*.)

Rudolf Bohren uses the concept of the "inhuman sermon" to characterize another problematic sermon strategy:[689] A sermon is "inhuman" when the listeners – searching for "links" to the Word of God – are confronted with everyday problems from the pulpit and in then merely reminded of their own troubles. Bohren does not cite any examples of this way of preaching, but it is obvious what he has in mind here: Those resolute lists of problems, beginning with A for "*Arbeitslosigkeit*" (unemployment) by way of L for "*Lieblosigkeit*" (inconsiderateness) among humans to Z for "*Zerstörung* (destruction) of the environment". However, these topics are not presented to the listeners in any way that differs significantly from the newspaper. They are thrown before their feet in such a way that – after the sermon – they are seemingly unchanged and appear as they did before. The inhumanity of such a sermon does not consist in the fact that it relates to problems but that it ventilates *all possible problems* without considering them from a changed view of one's own existence, let alone opening up a more complex understanding of reality or a broader perception of reality through the communication of the gospel.

Besides this form of inhuman sermon, which one could name Type I, there is also the aforementioned Type II; this type is manifest in those sermons *which immunize themselves against any connection or relation to real life*. They provide

---

**687** Sermon manuscript on 1 Cor 12:4–11.
**688** More detail on this in I.7.3.1.
**689** R. Bohren, 1971, 446.

information about the text as well as details of what should be avoided theologically when contemplating "our pericope". This type of inhuman sermon can be encountered at least as often as that of Type I.

"Our text reminds us that faith is a gift which we only have to accept. Paul puts great significance on the fact that we ought not desire to achieve any success with faith or wish to compete with one another but should understand faith as a favor. We cannot impress God with what we do, only faith counts."[690] Apart from the cliché-ridden characterization of faith and the human capacity for action it remains entirely open how faith relates to what a person ultimately can do or cannot do (at any rate one "must accept a gift"), and what consequences this faith might have for the life of the listener, which the person themselves must *lead*.

Such a manner of preaching marks a basic homiletic problem which cannot be reduced to an overly stereotypical approach to a supposed reality of life. When the uncomfortable sides of life are cited simply as links, as a "plug" in order to then linger by this or that aspect of the text (instead of, conversely, considering various situations and experiences of human life in the light of the gospel and possibly in relation to the text) the task of the sermon has fundamentally been misunderstood.

The talk of "points of contact" initially had a negative connotation within the history of Homiletics. It was assumed that *after* one had briefly considered the human situation one could finally come to the "true concern", to an interpretation of the text "freed from those points of contact", to the Word of God.[691] The context and situation of the sermon, which has been degraded to a mere sidenote or point of contact, substantially belongs to the practice of communicating the gospel. A theologically human sermon – to remain with this conception – requires the conceptual integration of the everyday reality of life which demands no less attention than the exegetically engaged reading of what the text holds. It is a matter of turning away *from using the reality of life as an instrument to illustrate the text* to a *respect for the reality of life as a world of experience* from which the listeners emerge to hear a sermon and for which they likewise need the sermon.

In a similar context Gerhard Ebeling related the effect of the Bible – that it does "not pass by but enters into life"[692]. Correspondingly he emphasizes, with reference to Luther's "sola autem experientia facit theologum"[693] that dismissal of experience is not something inherent in theology but is *an expression of bad*

---

690 From a sermon on Rom 3:21–28.
691 A detailed commentary on the homiletic topos of "point of contact" follows in I.6.2, p. 279–283.
692 G. Ebeling, 1979, 42.
693 M. Luther, 1531, WA TR I.16.10–13 (no. 46).

*theology*: "If the Christian Word does not relate to experience and the Christian faith is not lived in a way that it impacts everyday life, then there is cause to concern as to whether theology does its due part in connecting Word and faith with experience and the reality of life."[694]

### 6.1.2 Ignoring Christian Existence and the Faith of the Listener

Many sermons appear to treat their listeners – whom, as churchgoers, one must generally consider as among the religiously socialized – like candidates for Confirmation who should become acquainted with the basic questions of the Christian faith. This often happens by way of a very low level of information which would perhaps be suitable, with regard to its statements, for the blurb on the dust-cover of the Bible. The examination of questions relating to faith are sometimes conducted on a level which does not do justice to the awareness of problems nor the degree of maturity of a congregation assembled for worship.[695]

"The Good Shepherd knows his sheep by name. Just think of that with a flock of 100 sheep and more! And he also knows precisely: The sheep with the short tail is Bertha. And Florian, that's the sheep with the black ear. He takes care that not one sheep runs in one direction and another somewhere else. [...] Jesus invites us to test whether he is the Good Shepherd. [...] He wants to take away our fear and give us a life which, despite the threat of the wolf, can begin here and now [...]. The shepherd, Jesus, he pleases me. But when I see these other sheep around me [...]. Actually, it is good that each person can have a unique relationship to Jesus [...]. Should I have the courage to speak to Jesus about this? I shall say to him that I would very much like to belong to him and his congregation."[696]

The aim of the criticism expressed above it is not to completely dismiss a sermon which discusses basic aspects of the Christian faith nor that it cannot contain any existential dimension. On the contrary, the constantly recurring readings from the gospel and Epistles for the individual Sundays are chosen precisely for this reason – because they are of elementary significance for the connection of existence and faith. However, contrary to the sermon just quoted they deal with life and death, with guilt and forgiveness, compulsion and freedom, with doubt

---

694 G. Ebeling, 1975, 16.
695 Preachers do not speak to the congregation e.g. on the basis of a more experienced, stronger, greater or more proven faith but inter alia on the basis of a tested *theological* competence and because the congregation, from a declared need for the communication of the gospel, expressly wishes "that the Word comes in vogue". On homiletic competence cf. I.2.3, p. 38–80 and on the understanding of the commission to preach cf. III.4.5.2 and III.4.5.3, p. 504–515.
696 Sermon manuscript on John 10:11–16.27–30.

and hope – in short, with an everyday reality for which a simple diet of "milk" does not suffice, but for which people need "solid food" in order to persevere (cf. 1 Cor 3:1f.).

Especially given the fact that many older people attend the church service who, in the matter of their spiritual maturity – however one defines this – are not to be considered inferior to the preacher, the plea to, at long last, try life with Jesus seems arrogant and bizarre. After all, those addressed here are people who – in part looking back at a World War – can imagine something very concrete with the "descend of the wolves" and who, in the most difficult situations of life, had to see how far their faith would carry them. Yet, instead of encouragement and companionship for the way they have already followed, far too often the congregation is chided for choosing comfort over the "path of discipleship":

"By nature, we humans seem to have something against discipleship. We much rather do what we want or what seems to be rational: We consider obedience to be a virtue from past centuries. But anyone who does not follow wherever God calls bypasses one's life."[697] In this sermon several, in part contradictory stereotypes are used, which we cannot discuss in detail here. Above all the concept of discipleship is problematic. Discipleship is not only interpreted as directionless obedience but is also played off against achieved insights. In contrast, discipleship can also be an expression of an achieved insight (e.g. in the sense of repentance) and lead to the acquisition of freedom. The sermon sample is also fatal in its radicalism which denounces the possibility of the congregation having positive experiences *without* carrying out special exercises of obedience.

In this context, another quotation: "To the core-congregation, first and foremost, one must preach the earnestness of discipleship. [...] Therefore we should challenge the individuals to make changes in their lives." Such declarations of intention are then translated into sermons as follows: "The foundation on which we build our lives on is important. If we live according to the Sermon on the Mount we shall be saved at the Last Judgement. [...]. If I wish to obey Jesus I must begin to make changes in the little things of life."[698]

That the congregation could already have experienced both the earnestness and the freedom of discipleship and is therefore relying on affirmation and "edification" is not considered in these two sermons. Even if critical words should be uttered, the congregation is entitled to expect that the sermon reaches a level of argumentation which corresponds to its listeners' competence in life and faith.

A preacher who avowedly turns to an evangelical-missionary congregation in which "numerous events", "Bible study groups", "home groups", "open evenings", and even "Saturday services" supplementary to the Sunday worship service et al. are a matter of course, preaches to the congregation: "We have no idea of who this Jesus really is or what he is like. [...] We should understand that Jesus Christ came into this world to relieve us of our sins, our burdens and troubles.

---

**697** Sermon manuscript on Luke 14:25–33.
**698** Sermon manuscript with preliminary work on Matt 7:24–29.

[...] I don't know what is perhaps preventing you as individuals from recognizing Christ, to come to him. I don't know what barriers stand between you or why they are there. [...] If we truly earnestly become engaged with Jesus we shall then ourselves [...] become witnesses for Christ."[699] So the preacher expects that the members of the congregation become "witnesses for Christ" only if – after the sermon – they finally "become earnestly engaged with Jesus". This must be contradicted inasmuch as the members of the congregation have gathered for the church service *because* they have already taken this step.

Friedrich Schleiermacher repeatedly demanded that, when preaching, one should take into consideration that every individual believer participates in the priesthood of all believers, that is, has a part in the "independent exercise of Christianity"[700] This requires not only a more dialog-based communication instead of a hierarchic sermon structure, but makes the further demand that when preaching one should weigh up in the content of the sermon what the congregation really needs in order to "exercise their Christianity" in their day-to-day lives.

### 6.1.3 Scolding the Listeners

The lack of analysis of one's own person in the run-up to the sermon or of one's own subjectivity in the sermon process frequently comes with the inability to take the listeners for their part seriously as subjects. After all, it was them who confronted themselves with the preacher *as a person from their midst*.[701] Within the framework of this "counterpart-function" a sermon that *challenges* its listeners does have its place, however, never by ways of scolding them. A reprimanding preacher treats the listeners like ill-bred children, so that they – at least for the duration of the sermon – become victims of a dim education in faith: They have to listen to inquisitorial, moralizing homilies and are misused to exemplify all that which the preacher is commonly offended by. Such scolding of the listeners is usually accompanied by vague assumptions and conjectures.

"We intoxicate ourselves with consumption. Wishes, wishes, wishes. I ask myself: Who needs Heaven when the earth fulfils every wish? We speak of 'heavenly pleasures', of the 'seventh heaven of love' or a 'gift from Heaven'. Heaven seems to be established in the midst of the great and small pleasures of everyday life. [...] The 'Heaven' which we can acquire in this way is an illusion. What have we made out of Heaven? We have drawn it ever closer, ever closer to our

---

**699** Sermon manuscript with preliminary work on John 1:29–34.

**700** F .D. E. Schleiermacher, 1988, 126.

**701** On the theological background of this way of looking at things cf. III.4.5.2 and III 4.5.3.

daily pleasures; we have made it calculable, payable, purchasable, and precisely in this way we have lost Heaven."[702]

Such generalized allegations appear all the more out of place the more one deliberates who the preacher is actually talking to: a comparatively small group[703] of Protestant Christians who gather together at Sunday services throughout the country and who not only wish to "keep a sense of proportion" but also consider themselves to be members of the church. Thus, the preacher has before them the already committed who, as Martin Luther expressed it, "earnestly want to be Christians".

"The pictures of the terrible end of a Christmas Midnight Service in Frankfurt-Sindlingen are still ingrained in my memory. A woman goes into the church and, in the course of the Christmas service, kills herself with two hand-grenades. Here, too, there was great consternation and dismay and yet it did not last long. Soon everyone went back to their daily agendas. [...] We, too, have quickly filed this incident away. [...] Sorrow is a place where God wishes to reveal himself. The life of the assassin in Sindlingen was such a place, and we as fellow human beings must confess: We have failed in this case, we have not sought after this place of the cross, have not discerned it."[704]

Certainly, with such a diffuse argumentation much remains in the dark in a logical respect. But nevertheless, it is clear that it is implied that the listeners lack sensibility for sorrow. But how does the preacher know this? Perhaps those who sit under their pulpit have come to the sermon to be reassured and supported in *their* sorrow as well as in the face of their dismay over another's sorrow. It is not only theologically problematic but also inept when considered in terms of communication skills to reproach these people that they could neither comfort – "Who can comfort? We ourselves are helpless!" – nor be ready to admit their own need of comfort because it sounds "far too much like helplessness"[705] to them. Instead

---

**702** Sermon manuscript on 1 Pet 1:9.
**703** Anyone who preaches on Sundays in a Protestant church is dealing with people who belong to the approximately five million people (out of 81,189,000 inhabitants in total, cf. census figures 2011) who hear sermons on a regular basis. "In Germany, 808,000 million people take part in a Protestant worship service every Sunday" (Church Office of the EKD, 2016, 14). In addition, 3,546,000 Catholic Christians (15% out of 23,76 million Catholics living in Germany) attend church every Sunday, cf. Kirchenamt der EKD, 2016, 14, https://www.evangelisch.de/inhalte/113471 (last accessed on April 18, 2017). Moreover, around 600,000 Christians "follow the television broadcasts of Protestant as well as ecumenical worship services on Sundays, which corresponds to a market share of 6.4%" (ibid.). Taken together – and that is without those attending worship services in retirement homes and hospitals - this is 6.12% of the total population, a quite remarkable rate for a weekly recurring event.
**704** Sermon manuscript on Matt 27:33–50.
**705** Sermon manuscript on Isa 40:1–11.

of authentically and comprehensibly examining various facets of personal experiences with sorrow in their congregation in a way that speaks of solidarity and cooperation,[706] the preacher sneers at not having witnessed a deeper sense of consternation after an assassination with hand-grenades. It seems, however, that the misdeed on the part of the listeners attending the service is only marginally connected to what took place at the scene of the crime, the ca. 600 kilometres removed city district of Sindlingen, but is rooted in the of insufficient perception of lives characterized by suffering within a radius of five kilometres on the part of the preacher.

### 6.1.4 Dubious Offers of Identification

Preaching – inter alia – has to do with suggesting "offers of identification". The concept of "offers of identification" (German: "Identifikationsangebote") is in this connection the *terminus technicus* for the confronting of the individual with a new self-understanding through the communication of the gospel. The expression "offer of identification" is not to be taken literally, that is, as if the way of existing and living expressed is like a kind of special offer from a catalog of Christian options with an editorial deadline in the 4th century C.E. which one could fall back on from time to time in order to master certain situations. The term describes exemplary concepts of desirable human existence, outlines of a particular way to understand oneself, to see oneself in relation to God and the world, to lead a life that is one's own and to appear as a human being.

No offers of identification are presented in a sermon which simply cites particular leading concepts of Christian existence as expressed e.g. in the body of various Epistles in the New Testament. One needs additional hermeneutic efforts.[707] Nevertheless, there are of course also Christian offers of identification in the biblical tradition itself, for instance in Jesus' Sermon on the Mount. There he speaks of the "meek", of people "pure in heart", "those who mourn" and "peacemakers". Those addressed in this way were given to understand themselves *as other*, i.e. as other *than those whom they believe themselves to be.* They were not encumbered with who they were and certainly not thrown back in it but appeared, as it were, as human beings for whom the Beatitudes (to remain with this example) are paradoxes of a successful life. It is important to orientate a sermon towards reasonable, worthwhile and promising offers of identification and not to offer living

---

**706** On further criteria of the sermon – which concern the preacher – cf. I.5.4, p. 250–257.
**707** Cf. I.6.3.3, p. 290–296.

by faith as an alternative to a fulfilled life. Still, many sermons founder on the challenge of the homiletic imagination connected to this.[708]

A sermon follows negative descriptions of identity with a massive plea for sanctification, whereby the listeners should find their true identity. "We cannot, like Max and Moritz, lie replete and self-satisfied in the grass. We must hear God's call, which comes to us every day anew – and hearing means to answer in faith to the promise God gave in Christ, and to love God with our whole heart. Amen!"[709] It is not made clear in the course of the sermon what – if not repletion and a break on the lawn – is then "allowed", what could "refresh" them, what prospect for life would be desirable, what perspectives should be opened for them in the course of the communication of the gospel – in short: *who they could be.* Not only is the experience of repletion and contentedness with life made off-putting for the listeners but as the only alternative a vague, bitter-sour discipleship is promised in which what is most important is to be prepared for the regular call of God, not to miss answering it and on top of this to experience it as an expression of love.

In some sermons temporary offers of identification, only relevant for the duration of the sermon, are presented to the listener, which are related to a somehow inferior character or a pitiful figure in the passage of the sermon. In this way, they should be shown problematic attitudes and ways of behaving. The listener then sees themselves in a particular respect as "one standing on the edge" or as "poor" or "rich", "leprous", "alien", "crippled", "blind", "lame" etc. These in principle legitimate temporary offers of identification[710], however, lose their predominant function of arousing awareness in the listeners if the listeners become quasi frozen in these roles, i.e. when no *change of roles* can be observed

"Strictly speaking *the foolish man* did not really listen. If he had understood what the offer of discipleship means he would not refuse to act in an appropriate way. The proper listening to the words of Jesus includes obeying. But obedience is always something concrete. [...] There are many little things which I constantly avoid. I believe everyone here can spontaneously think of something where he should make a change in his life. We must take this seriously, draw personal consequences and not just play with the thought. [...] As long as we Christians live in this town like all everyone else, no one will notice that there are Christians here at all. Even if someone

---

**708** Konrad Müller recently (2015) pointed out the relevance of the *category of imagination* as a supplement to this or *contrapuntal to the category of experience.* Even if this dissertation goes too far in playing the virtue of imagination against the principle of experience in the homiletic process (cf. ibid., 365) its plea for a language in the sermon which calls for imagination, devises pictures and in that respect, anticipates reality is greatly to be welcomed. On the relevance of the Sermon on the Mount for the understanding of the task of the sermon see also D. Buttrick, 2002.
**709** Sermon manuscript on Rom 8:26–30.
**710** Many stories, novels and films use this strategy when their protagonists find themselves in all kinds of difficulties and have to endure great misfortune, characters whose lives are so mixed up that we can recognize our lives in the story of these people although it takes place in quite different coordinates of time and space.

notices that we call ourselves Christians he will justifiably ask what differentiates himself from us."[711] Naturally, the listeners will ask themselves all the more what rewarding prospects will open up for their lives if they live as Christians. The permanent appeal to be an example and the latent reproach that one does not manage this is, in this combination, a rather unsuitable offer of identification.

In this context, we must also refer to the problematic habit of emphasizing certain characteristics of a form of the text, or the negative attitudes or vices which it describes, as a prototype for the "modern man"[712], who then has to serve as a scapegoat for all that is said to be bad or negative in our time. A preacher addresses obedience to God and God's claims on the person and in so doing brings the "modern person" onto the stage as follows: "The one who requests something of us is God [...] But, it is not difficult for us – because we are modern people – to push this claim away immediately."[713] After all, Jonah and other prophets could do this too without being "modern men". Has to be claimed by God not been one of the human difficulties since Adam and Eve?

Such attempts at identification give the impression that the relevance of a text on each occasion depends upon the listeners being adequately reflected *in a character in the text*. Apart from the fact that such offers of identification all too often border on scolding the listeners, in their short-circuiting analogies they overlook the listeners' actual experience of deficiency. This is all the more problematic when the vagueness of the offer of identification implies the refusal of an offer of a solution, when the *gravamina* on "man and his time" mentioned are simply left hanging or at the most are tackled with quotations from biblical texts.

Even though the sermon should certainly not be understood primarily as a socio-therapeutic opportunity, one can and should expect the communication of the gospel to participate *in the creation of a picture* of modern society *which corresponds to Christian ideas* by developing visions as to how it could look like.

### 6.1.5 Recommended Feelings

Like other forms of vocalizations, sermons reveal the emotions of the person speaking which simultaneously trigger feelings on the part of the listeners. However, there is *not necessarily a consistency* between the semantic content of a sentence and the emotion which it produces in the listener which could be *forced through the content*. The ambiguity of human communication on a *level of content*

---

711 Sermon manuscript on Matt 7:24–29.
712 Cf. on this W. Engemann, 1996 and "Sermon Clichés" in I.6.1.6, p. 273–276.
713 H. Lindenmeyer, sermon on Rom 6:16–23, in: Kirche in Rundfunk, 1965, Nr. 33.

on the one hand and a *level of relationship* on the other leads to the fact that something apparently comforting in the content by no means always comforts. The "Good News" by no means always delights nor do texts drafted for encouragement necessarily encourage.[714]

The frequency with which particular feelings are suggested to the listeners from the pulpit and are unexpectedly derived from the speaker's own address suggests a common misunderstanding; namely, that a sermon can *qua* statement or appeal result in an identical simultaneous response on the emotional as well as on the contentual level. Correspondent remarks are all the more problematic the more they are formulated as an appeal: "I would like to encourage you to hope conjointly and to spread joy."[715] "We should feel it as a great relief that we don't need to do anything in order to be able to experience the love of God."[716]

Nevertheless, the criticism of the attempt to produce emotions among the listeners on the basis of recommendations and appeals should not lead to the conclusion that feelings and emotions should be kept out of the sermon or are not suited as a topic of Homiletics. On the contrary: since they are always present we must ask how one can integrate their effect. Generally, the desired feelings are not felt due to a fitting instruction – since sentiments are always *a result of perceptions on the relationship level*– it is important to know some basic rules of the reception of human speech and to be aware of the relationship gap in one's own style of preaching.[717] The structure of a person's personality influences his basic disposition such as how he mainly prefers to communicate with others, in which emotional state or prevailing mood he lives in and which "vibes" he radiates when speaking to others. We must therefore consider whether there are criteria and controlling mechanisms which prevent the preacher from always diving into the same basic mood (e.g. depressive, compulsive or euphoric) – regardless of the texts and topics he is preaching on.[718]

### 6.1.6 Sermon Clichés

The old *cliché of the modern man* which arose in the period of prosperity after the Second World War is still alive in the present-day sermons. Just like "the modern

---

**714** On the double aspect of content and relationship cf. I.2.3.3, p. 55–59, and on the communicative character of the sermon III.4.1, p. 485–487.

**715** Sermon manuscript on Rev 3:1–6.15.

**716** Sermon on John 3:16.

**717** Cf. the description of problems in I.2.3.4, p. 60–72.

**718** More detail in W. Engemann, 1992a, esp. 37–56, 77–84.

man" at that time put his trust in "our good sense, our science and technology"[719] and put all this in the place of God, so also today he is used when preachers need a "culprit" or an "antagonist" to their model of solution.[720]

According to many sermons, human beings are – to this day – "obsessed with the idea, [...] that everything is possible."[721] Everything for which one can blame a person – and that through all the ages of human history – is blamed on the "modern man". He is – and has always been – discredited as "having become a slave of the *Zeitgeist*" and the preferred manner of this contemporaneity is in general diagnosed as a dangerous conformity:

The "modern people today [...] are confused by the countless deserts made by humanity, by wars, terror, climatic catastrophes, economic exploitation and hunger. They roam through the deserts of their own lives which are isolated and lonely, purposeless and worthless. They roam [...] through the deserts of their own frustration and their rebellion against God"[722]. "The modern person believes only in himself. He has forgotten how to trust and is even proud of this. He basks in his independence and only takes on commitments if they gain him some profit."[723] "The modern man has long ago done away with God as Creator of Heaven and earth. He believes in evolution, i.e. in an upward development 'from below'. He attempts using technical means to turn the logic of creation to a supposed 'better' one."[724] "The modern man and the western lifestyle are driven by the enjoyment of life to the full, by the experience of as many facets as possible and the enjoyment of the days as if there were no end."[725]

Clichés develop from stereotypical observations, whereby the perception of real events and occurrences are just as valuable as the medial-prefabricated and suggested observations. There is reason to believe that most clichés cannot develop if – at least for a time – they are not generated through direct observation. Observations only become clichés when they *take the place* of one's original awareness of reality and *become rigid as stereotypes*. They are then no longer the result

---

719 T. Knolle, Sermon on John 3:1–5, in: Das Zeugnis der Kirche in der Gegenwart, Nuremberg 1951, 370.
720 On the analysis of the topos "modern man" in the sermon cf. W. Engemann, 1996, esp. 448–453.
721 G. Kugler, Sermon on Isa 5:1–7, in: Kirche im Rundfunk. Ev. Ansprachen im Bayerischen Rundfunk, 1994, 76.
722 P. Heribert Graab S. J., Sermon on 1 Cor 19:4–8, http://www.heribert-graab.de/texte/predigten/jahreskreis (last accessed on April 7, 2006).
723 Sermon on Heb 10:35–36(37–38).39. Looking back at the two previous quotations from sermons we must on the one hand object that they address perceptions and problems which have been part of the life of believers at *all* times in the history of humanity. On the other hand they pay homage to a caricature of how people make relationships and underestimate their need both to give love and also to receive it.
724 M. Widl, Sermon on Gen 11.1–9, http://www.predigten.uni-goettingen.de/archiv7/050516-2.html (last accessed on April 7, 2006).
725 J. Block, Sermon on Gal 2:16–21, 2006, http://www.predigten.uni-goettingen.de/archiv-8/060827-3.html (last accessed on April 7, 2006).

of one's own perception but take its place. They then strengthen a particular ensemble of prejudices about reality, circumstances and the world. The moment perceptions have passed through this extended process of self-repeating observation and have become clichés, they frequently no longer correspond with the reality which they wish to bring to the point. The specific cliché about human faith in technology and science can no longer be taken up in this way in *post-modernity*. The values and expectations of people living today, their idea of the world and of themselves as well as their "illnesses" and "addictions" which are persistently diagnosed in the sermon lie on *other* levels. The "post modernity" of humankind is expressed, among other things, in saying that it is well aware of the problems of the modernity; but it no longer expects that a solution can be achieved through a more consistent implementation of its ideals or through technical progress etc.

In the sermon, the "modern man" frequently performs a function of a kind of easing the strain, of a scapegoat. This eases the strain on the preacher who otherwise would have to adopt the insignia of the modern man but this way can direct their dressing-down "out of the window" to the "people in general". The conspiratorial tone in which the topic of the "modern man" is dealt with before the congregation, usually *in the third person*, also takes the strain off the listeners who may possibly come to the conclusion that they are not thought of as belonging to "modern humanity": These allegedly do not go to church and do not listen to God's Word.

Here two quotations for comparison, an older and a newer one: "Who among us is not time and again gripped by the horror of what faces us today? Who doesn't battle with the temptation to despise humankind when we [sic!] on the one hand see people [sic!] in their uninhibitedness and in their dull covetousness which only demands eating and drinking? [...] Jesus is quite different."[726] In a recent sermon the complaint is made that "many people do not feel attracted to the church today because it no longer inspires them." The consciousness of the Holy Spirit and the Feast of Pentecost threatens "more and more to be lost" because "we as modern people" no longer have any idea about "the third article of the Creed"[727].

The reverse side of an unreflected application of stereotypes is a disguised perception of recent developments in cultural sociology. Corresponding sermons not only disregard the current "Zeitgeist", whose existence cannot be denied for any era, they also show no interest in the listeners. For them it is sufficient to view the world in familiar stereotypes and thus to repeatedly offer the same solutions. To this stereotypical way of preaching also belong the clichés of the "little things" and the "small steps".

---

**726** B. H. Forck, Sermon on Matt 9:35–38, in: Das Zeugnis der Kirche in der Gegenwart, Nuremberg 1951, 301.
**727** Sermon manuscript on Rom 8:26–30.

"Were there also moments in my life when I experienced something of God's contact with the earth and humanity? [...] I mean times in which perhaps something very small and inconspicuous happened whereby I experienced a sense of God's nearness. [...] I admit that one mostly *fails to notice* the times when God is in one's own life. Only when the others [present] told of quite mundane, everyday occasions I remembered some little things and moments in which I had noticed something of God myself. These were [...] the moments in which I unexpectedly started a conversation with a person and he became a good friend to me."[728]

Why must it only be the things that are felt to be *pleasant* and are referred to as *little* – a good conversation, a flower by the wayside, a friendly face opposite at mealtimes – that are built up as an *encounter with God*? The frequent reference to the "little things" in sermons is often a sign of great abashment: one has clearly *not* had a good look at the little things, the concrete details of human existence and religious experience. Consequently, without further ado, one passes off *everything* as an encounter with God.

We should "set off together with Jesus, go farther along the way, forwards, beyond death into life – and not backwards. [...] We can follow this way with many small steps. When we learn of starving people in the media and, not only on Christmas Eve, dutifully put some money into the offering bucket for 'Brot für die Welt' (Bread for the World), when in summer we are once again plagued by ozone and hear horror stories about the forests dying and don't boast in the fact that, this time, we did not use the car to go to the baker, when at Christmas for once we do not succumb to the temptations of commerce and [...] find time for friends and family [...] we have then always come a little further on the way to life."[729]

The "little steps" prove to be a cliché at the latest when they are nothing more than the mere application of stereotypes and self-evident matters of middle-class Christian decency towards the "great step" of the resurrection of Jesus. Here, too, the literally frightened steps arising from the Easter event[730] which must first find their way are not mentioned. In these cases, the "little steps" are a great step beyond the potential Easter experiences of the listeners.

## 6.2 Indicators of Problems in the History of Homiletics

In the chapter on the task of the sermon and the approach to biblical texts we have considered the question of the sermon's situational context. By making this question a central topic we are taking into account that the examination of situation

---

728 Sermon manuscript on Gen 28:10–19a.
729 Sermon manuscript on Mark 16:1–8.
730 Remarkably the Easter Gospel in Mark closes with the women at the grave experiencing a disruption of their conception of the world and running away appalled.

and context in the sermon process has not only contributed to the differentiation of various kinds of approaches to sermons in the history of Homiletics but is also of fundamental significance for the discussion of new homiletic standpoints. Moreover, since about the middle of the 20th century the "contextual relevance" has developed into its own homiletic perspective of reflection, which seems to make a separate treatment necessary.

### 6.2.1 The "Situation" in the History of the Sermon and Homiletics

If one is dealing with the character of homilies in the biblical texts, with the beginnings of the communication of the gospel in the Early Christian Era and with the homiletic premises of reformed preaching according to Martin Luther, one might inquire as to why a problem ever arose out of the question whether and to what extent the context of the listener should be considered a matter of Homiletics. After all, the biblical texts stand as it were under high tension because of their situation. They speak into concrete life situations. *They formulate convictions relating to concrete situations and contexts.* The context is of imperative importance in understanding the biblical testimony; in fact, one can only grasp the meaning of most texts, if one has understood for which context they were (originally) intended.

The reasons which induced *Martin Luther* to call for an understandable Protestant sermon for "John and Jane" should be understood as significant signs of problems in this matter. When the worship service and sermon lose their communicative character and therewith their relevance, they degenerate into events without any 'benefit'[731]. Then they no longer correspond to *God's service to humankind* and miss their purpose. Accordingly, Luther argues his plea for the addressee-oriented catechism-sermon: "Christ, because he wished to move human beings, had to become human. If we wish to move children, we too must become children with them."[732] In another place we read: "In the pulpit, one should pull out the teats and soak the people with milk, for every day a new church grows up, *quae indiget primis principiis.* I don't want to acknowledge Dr. Pomeranus, Jonas, Philippus with my sermon for they already now know much more than I do. I also

---

**731** According to Martin Luther the worship service is not a *sacrificium hominis*, a sacrifice which the person brings into play to pacify God, but is a *beneficium dei*, a favor and act of blessing from God to believers.
**732** M. Luther, Deutsche Messe, WA 19, 78.

do not preach for them but for my John and Jane, *illos observo*[733]" – all my attention should be given to them. This *"illos observo"*, the attentive observation of the contemporary circumstances is the homiletic self-commitment to the awareness of the addressees of a sermon, a consideration for the context of the listeners *as a hermeneutical interest.*

Already in the *Era of Lutheran Orthodoxy* it became clear that Luther's instructions on preaching had only partially been passed on and put into practice and were lacking at the most crucial points: "Of Luther's fundamental concerns only the dogmatic-educational is adopted."[734] The sermon concentrates on the dogmatic elaborations of supposed truths of salvation. Their position on, or connection with experience is generally not taken into consideration. A differentiated systematic-theological pattern of explanation and the experienced reality of life and world stand opposed to one another. In the practice of preaching, theology and religion fall apart.

To mostly reduce the concept of situation to the cases of daily life corresponds with the wide-spread understanding of the task of the *Sermon in the Age of the Enlightenment.* To the extent in which one understands that the human existence itself is no longer considered a problem one looks – with a bit of effort and good will – at the apparently avoidable problems which unnecessarily weigh down human existence: The troubles of daily life as well as difficulties in following good principles are quasi elevated to the rank of situations. The sermon should be useful in that it teaches how one can cope with the incidents and especially with the moral temptations of life. In this way – so the general expectation – the sermon makes a contribution to the building-up of the congregation and to the improvement of society.

The *sermon in the Age of Pietism and the Revivalist Movement* primarily considered the inner state of mind, the condition of the "soul" or "heart" of the listener as "situation". What determines the content of the sermon is the worry about coping with such situations in which the soul of the listener is threatened with the renunciation of faith: "You souls tell me how I can win you? Are the lures of the Gospel not stronger on you than the threats of the Law, more moving the

---

733 M. Luther, Tischreden, WA TR 3,310, 12 (Nr. 3421). Emphasis W. E. Luther's maxim for translating the Bible is to be understood in the same way: "Listen to what the people really say" is not a pseudo-rhetorical maxim which enables the preacher to sneak into the listeners to be recognized as one of them. The gospel should be opened up in the language of "John and Jane" because only in this way can they understand their own reality – their reality under the conditions of freedom and the love of God. Cf. on Luther's understanding of the sermon in the matter of comprehensibility M. Doerne, 1940, esp. 40.

734 A. D. Müller, 1954, 180.

descriptions of virtue than those of blasphemy? Tell me."[735] If in Orthodoxy the empirical world and the world declared to be theologically relevant fall apart, in Pietism – against the declared intention of the corresponding preacher – everyday experience and religious experience frequently stand unconnected side by side. Without dealing with the realities of existence, with real life conditions or with a disappointed or overtaxed faith, one counsels the listeners to simply leave what divert them behind: "Brothers, so let the resolution be secured today: We want less time in the company of people and more with God! – This will also be a blessing for our attendance at church. You will see: A heart that's not diffused, brought into the house of God usually brings out with it a treasure from God."[736] Preachers who elevate this to a maxim and consider it a virtue to see the listeners merely in the "situation of the congregation" and to perceive them only as church members or visitors in worship service do not need to concern themselves with the "situation otherwise". They do not need to connect with the experiences, questions and problems of their congregation.

In the *Era of Dialectical Theology* one had even declared this as taboo. The preacher, according to Karl Barth, is failing in his mission to pass on the divine message if he looks for points of connection for this message because "the revelation itself creates of itself the necessary point of contact in man."[737] The dialectical-theological phase of Homiletics brings forth a one-sided conception of "situation": the listener is perceived as a being that simply stands in the situation to be addressed by God's Word – and then must react accordingly. A person's complex reality is reduced to a hypothetical, constantly repeating situation of decision between 'Yes' and 'No' in response to God's call.

### 6.2.2 The Quarrel over the Point of Contact ("Anknüpfungspunkt")

Although the quarrel over the point of contact ("Anknüpfungspunkt") did not only concern the field of Practical Theology it was constantly sparked off anew by the question over the task and purpose of the sermon. If today one reads the relevant polemic writings side by side one could wonder over such a painstaking misapprehension. The term "Anknüpfungspunkt" was introduced by Friedrich Schleiermacher. With this expression, he wished to encapsulate the necessity that one must know of and concern oneself with the situation, the expectations

---

735 C. Harms, quoted from E. Winkler, 1990, 602. Cf. also the complaint of August Tholuck about the "diversions" which often have "easy game" in the hearts of believers (loc. cit., 605).
736 A. Tholuck, quoted from E. Winkler, 1990, 605.
737 K. Barth, 2009a, 28.

as well as the developments in the life of one's contemporaries. One should be a thoughtful contemporary when one moves in the field of pastoral action. Behind this conception stands, among other things, the understanding that humans are created as responsive beings who carry around with them significant questions that are directed towards dialog.[738] However, it was not Schleiermacher but Emil Brunner who – like Rudolf Bultmann and Paul Tillich later – declared the question of the "point of contact" to be a fundamental question of responsible theology and thereby made it popular.

E. Brunner does this by bringing a creation-theological argument into play: as created beings, humans are essentially *open to conversation*. This readiness to converse demands entering into its (e.g. linguistic) conditions and concrete situations.[739] In that the sermon links into things which exist, including experiences of failure and the dubious nature of one's own life, the idea of the transforming power of the communication of the gospel becomes more concrete.[740] Consequently for R. Bultmann "man in his existence, taken as a whole, [is] the *point of contact*"[741]. The Word of God is thus always related to the life context "in which the one who understands and what is understood belong together". Here the sin of which one becomes aware or the experience of failure serve as a "*point of contact* for the contradictory word of grace" ("*Anknüpfungspunkt* für das widersprechende Wort von der Gnade").[742]

It is thus no contradiction to deal with the world of the listeners, to analyze existing concrete realities in the interests of a concrete sermon – and at the same time to question this reality. Those who represent the idea of the point of contact assume that a person to whom one wishes to reach must be seen as a creature in space and time. After all, those who listen to a sermon are not beings without history, and, likewise, the communication of the gospel is not a revelation event outside of history.[743] On the other hand part of the expectation of the sermon is God making history within the history of the listeners. Anyone who does not see *this* history does not see the future history of God among humanity.

Measured on these premises the criticism of dialectical theology is mistaken when it assumes that the idea of the homiletic "*point of contact*" aims at replacing the communication of the gospel with the ventilation of life realities.[744] It is just

---

738 Cf. F. D. E. Schleiermacher, 2016, § 108, 5, 6.
739 Cf. E. Brunner, 1932. W. Trillhaas later takes these thoughts up homiletically (cf. I.6.3.1, p. 287).
740 Cf. E. Brunner, 1932, 510.
741 R. Bultmann, 1955, 137.
742 Cf. R. Bultmann, 1969, 315 and 1955, 137. For Bultmann this signifies the "point of contact" in contradiction (ibid.).
743 On the "rediscovery of linking in the sign of the historicity of the revelation" cf. H.-R. Müller-Schwefe, 1993, 748f.
744 E. Thurneysen, 1971, 113.

as incorrect to equate the endeavor to find links by ways of "digging and delving" which is intended to "[force] the revelation from the other side"[745]. This stereotypical critique of dialectical theology allows us to recognize that the – occasionally harsh – misrepresentation of theological impulses is connected to the insistence on a small number of revelation-theological premises. This always leads to a rejection of insights which are based on other premises.

Georg Merz takes the field against the idea of the "point of contact" in the sermon after he has re-interpreted this principle as a psychological discovery of the point of the "persuasion of the listener". The rejection of any linking – in spite of the relation of the situation in the text – is justified by the fact that, after all, the gospel has nothing to say about "why this or that person was particularly receptive to the Word of Christ as a result of certain prerequisites, but it makes it known that all nations have experienced salvation". Consequently, it is false to believe "one has to speak to people who are particularly receptive, receptive nations, receptive (social) strata, receptive times. With all this I should like to stipulate an act of God while I have only the task of repeating God's great actions"[746]. This does not need to be put right *en detail* after what has already been said. The glaring misunderstandings are obvious: The biblical texts are neither a space- nor time-less "repetition of God's great actions" – a contradiction in itself – nor does "linking" mean looking for particularly receptive listeners and to persuade them to something which has no relevance for them.

It is proof of far-reaching misunderstandings in the reception of the practical-theological discourse by kerygmatic theology[747] that Karl Barth justifies his strict rejection of introductions to sermons – which he considers merely a point of contact – by referring entirely to the "link from *above* through the miracle of God". Correspondingly he emphasizes: "The theological damage of sermon introductions is in any event incredibly extensive, and it is usually an error when preachers use them. For what do they really involve at root? Nothing other than the search for a point of contact, for an analogue in us which can be a point of entry for the Word of God."[748]

How exhaustively and for how long this problem (naturally *also* triggered off by the question of introductions) of refraining from a point of contact was felt is made clear by a speech of the regional Bishop of Hanover, Dr. Hanns Lilje, in 1957: "Anyone who preaches without an

---

**745** Ibid.

**746** G. Merz, 1992, 125f.

**747** On this cf. also the analyses by H. Leipold, 1993, 745.

**748** K. Barth, 1991, 124. The only thing which is correct in this way of looking at things is that links – obviously! – are often connected to analogies: Here it is admittedly not a question of crass equations (e.g. of pictures, characters or incidents in the texts at that time with situations today) but of analogies between the *relationships which become clear in the texts* which people have to one another or to God on one side and *corresponding relationships in situations today* on the other. On the function of such analogies cf. I.3.3.2, p. 130–135.

'introduction' and in so doing thinks that he is not obliged as preacher to construct a bridge between the text and the listener, who forgoes the *applicatio*, the genuine attempt of putting what is said into concrete terms and [offering an] application, renounces the sermon. [...] The wooden inhibition which one encounters in some sermons is the unavoidable consequence of a theological way of thinking which only knows the theological 'school' and its vocabulary but has long lost sight of the world in which we live in."[749]

Against Barth's critique we must first put something right: The question of the "point of contact" is, according to the subject, not a formality which concerns the beginning of the sermon nor a desperate pragmatic temporary solution but relates to the basic understanding and central interest of the sermon in general. In the question of linking it is a matter of finding relevant starting points for opening a dialog in which those listening can enter against the background of the reality of their own lives. Without this, the understanding of the basis which contributes to the construction of the sermon, the communication of the gospel degenerates into a fatal one-way traffic in which one speaks but no one hears.

Some of Hans Joachim Iwand's efforts in the context of the debate over the point of contact are worth reading. They certainly mark a gradual change in views about this matter. In them we discern a whole spectrum of "academic, spiritual and political reality"[750] and make selective reference to "the special historical situation"[751]. Remarkably, this reference is connected to the construction of a double reality: *The true reality* appears for Iwand to be that "in Jesus Christ"; the *other* reality is at most "a dream world". The true reality is only entered by those who believe – in that they live e.g. from forgiveness. "Who lives from this, [...] lives from reality." Anyone who does not do so falls into the "unreality, into *the merciless world of their own plans and ideas*."[752] But the sermon is not aimed at *this* reality but at *that*. This means that experiences are made in the reality of the world in order "[...] to grasp God's Word and reality"[753] – and not the other way around.

In the formulation of his homiletic principles Iwand does not distinguish between *necessary awareness* of human reality and an *unscrutinized trust in reality*. Congruently he demands: "This false trust in reality which one 'sees' and which is always a hopeless, deceptive reality which is not grasped by God and his word must then step by step retreat from our hearts."[754] The threat

---

**749** H. Lilje, 1957, 22f.
**750** H. J. Iwand, 1984, 419.
**751** Idem, 1979, 240.
**752** Loc. cit., 458, 479. Emphasis W. E.
**753** H. J. Iwand, 1984, 419.
**754** Loc. cit., 122.

herein lies in the countering of the given and experienced reality of life on the one hand and the experienced reality of God on the other. There is the risk that the reality of life is misunderstood as a kind of "reality of resistance" against the reality of God, through which in turn the experience of the grace of God "stands in contradiction to reality and to all human experience"[755]. The tinkering with such alternatives of reality and experience is an expression of an insufficiently clear understanding of the homiletic topic of "point of contact".

The separation of the *reality of God* and the *reality of humanity* which frequently recurred for a variety of reasons in homiletic history corresponds to a certain extent to the ancient idea of a world divided into 'above' and 'below'. It "leads to a split existence, to a conflicting sermon, to a double-bottomed pulpit. One has the absurd onus of demonstrating to the listener that there is for the moment a reality for each case: that which is loosely at hand with everything humanly attainable; but then, beyond this, a second one that transcends the former, the real world which signifies all the desired 'someday' for which we yearn. How can the listener bring these together? He is, after all, one person and not two. He tries to do so in a continual to-ing and fro-ing, is in this way never himself and thinks that it is exactly the Christian thing to do – to switch from one level to another just as one wishes. On the one hand, there is the workday in which everything is a matter of cause and effect, motive and deed; on the other hand there is the Sunday, in which incredible things are possible which – because of this dynamic – have no influence on the workday."[756]

Having considered the aforementioned issues in the history of Homiletics we now stand before the question which angles of reflection we must consider in order to surmount the homiletic restraint against the daily reality of life and understand it as a place for an encounter with the reality of God.

## 6.3 Current Angles of Reflection

The homiletic-hermeneutic backgrounds of the endeavor to relate to contemporary life as it really is in the sermon process and to see the context of the individual will, in the question of the "point of contact", will first be shown in a systematic-theological advance.

---

**755** J. Hermelink, 1992, 46. Cf. also the subtly differentiated critique of Iwand's understanding of the sermon, loc. cit., 31–95.
**756** M. Mezger, 1970, 216f.

### 6.3.1 The Principle of Correlation and the Regaining of the Situation

It was particularly Paul Tillich, who established all theories that present the "point of contact" ("Anknüpfungspunkt") as alternatively based on *either* the Word of God *or* the human situation as theologically misleading. His work illuminates to what extent understanding the communication of the gospel in such a way that it *takes the context of the listener into account*[757] and considers it as a fundamental part and source of potential questions for preaching, is the purpose of theology. Accordingly, Tillich developed a sound theology for the "point of contact". He assumes that "points of contact" which connect the Word of God with the context and situation of the listener do not need to first be constructed but already exist and must only be discovered. "Theological answers" which do not stand in a *correlation* with "existential questions"[758] cannot claim to serve the purpose of theology. "Theology formulates the questions implied in human existence, and theology formulates the answers implied in divine self-manifestation under the guidance of the question implied in human existence."[759]

This self-assured thesis can still be traced in the ductus of dialectical-theological argumentation: For Tillich, it belongs to the daily business of theology to be able to tune into the "divine self-manifestation" in order to virtually answer human existential questions from a divine viewpoint. Problematic here is not only the threatening overestimation of *academic theology*: What Tillich is considering here extends far into the area of *religious experience*. Remarkably, this implies the claim for superiority on the part of theology when it comes to the understanding of the human existence. On the level of the academic discourse a stronger convergence of the humanistic disciplines would have been evident. 'In principle' Tillich was aware of this, however in the appeal to "God's Word" the principles of argumentation won in this connection – as with other systematic-theological concepts – repeatedly fall into the background.

For the sermon, the principle of correlation brought into the theological discourse by Paul Tillich means that, in the communication of the gospel, it is questions which provide *the situation* and not questions which were constructed by the preacher's favorite theologian that should be incorporated. Otherwise there is the danger of simply airing answers to self-posed questions which the individual – without any clue of the situation or context – can "not receive" because he "has never asked" those questions.[760] With a similar concern Gerhard Ebeling made clear that one cannot pursue responsible theology when one sees humanity abstractly as "people before God". To perceive the person in his "general

---

**757** For further information on this thesis cf. W. Engemann, 2007b, esp. 161–170.
**758** Cf. P. Tillich, 1967, II.13–16.
**759** P. Tillich, 1967, I.61.
**760** Loc. cit., 65.

situation" means that one should always "perceive him in his controversial and consequently desperate situation".[761]

Against the background of the continual explicating correspondences between the questions arising from the context on the one hand and the potential of theology for answers and argumentations on the other, Tillich speaks of the *method of correlation*. Provided that correlations, i.e. the interrelations between the gospel and the situation or between religion and culture must not only be established but should also be taken for granted one should – also taking under consideration the vague precision of the "methodical" elements of correlation Tillich has in mind – speak in a less ambiguous way of the *principle* (instead of method) of correlation.[762]

Although the model of correlation cannot solve all the problems which are connected to the question of the situation of the listener, it has given decisive impulses to Homiletics. Nevertheless, we must analyse the thesis supporting this model that a person should not be bothered with answers to questions "which he/she never asked"[763]. In explicating this position, it should be indicated that one of the tasks of the sermon is to expect and encourage a questioning attitude of the listener: Sermons can be a contribution to the learning or the *appropriation of a questioning attitude* in that they sensitize people for the dubious nature of their lives and thereby help them to perceive "more complex" situations. Tillich would probably counter this objection by saying that this is precisely what is meant with the phrase "questions agreed *in* human existence" as a task of theology. That this existence can nonetheless be confronted with questions – not simply with answers – which are brought to attention from the *outside* is not discussed with the same clarity.

The idea of a homiletic work structured correlatively in this respect was taken up decidedly among others by Alfred Dedo Müller: "This hope for a connection can never mean that the empirical person should be made the *content* of the sermon and put in the place of the Word of God. It is far more a matter of the marvel that God [...] hears his questions [i.e. of the person] – and unceasingly answers. [...] In this respect the preacher must be aware of all the questions which are vivid in his congregation and in his time. It must be perceptible in the sermon that God is a listening and answering, a speaking God – and not a mute idol or abstract concept. The congregation asks, the sermon answers. That is right and proper."[764]

---

761 G. Ebeling, 1979, 189f. Many illustrative examples for the implementation of this principle can be found, for instance, in the practice of "Black Preaching". Cf. in this context Cleophus J. LaRue (1999, 2010).

762 Incidentally, Tillich views the correlative identity of culture and religion as an expression of "theonomy". If one or the other side of this exchange-relationship is ignored, society would sink either into an uncontrolled striving for autonomy or a disastrous heteronomy (cf. P. Tillich, 1962, 60–65).

763 P. Tillich, 1967, I.61.

764 A. D. Müller, 1954, 202.

In Müller's work the limits of such a sermon-model based on question and answer became already evident:

1. Paradoxically, it can lead to a narrowed view of the situation of the listeners if one always attempts to sound out their questions for which the sermon then delivers the solutions. The risk to select nolens volens and, in doing so, tailoring the world of the listeners in accordance to the answers theology can provide, should not be underestimated.

2. Placing the sermon in a situation of answering does not do justice to the multi-layered functions of the "sermon" as a type of speech. A sermon is not just significant for the individual because it primarily answers questions but also because it explores questions which give him a new understanding of the faith which he already has, because it mediates serenity and helps in strengthening his confidence etc.

3. Finally, the perception of the sermon situation as a great receptacle of questions hides the latent danger that both the preacher and theology will be stretched too far.[765] These are questions to which – although in Tillich's sense they grow out of human existence, are incredibly interesting and forceful – neither a preacher nor any kind of theology can give satisfying answers simply because it is Sunday and a sermon is due again.

Furthermore, one must make it clear that *situations, insofar as they are incorporated reflectively into the communication – i.e. comprehended, constructed* by particular perceptions and situations *worked out* with a particular (homiletic) interest – are *interpretations*.[766] A person who refers to situations hermeneutically, theologically and communicatively necessarily takes up a *construct* of the real situation. Correspondingly we must differentiate between abstract and real situations. This differentiation can help to not view the overall situation one has constructed for the sermon and wishes to address and relate to in the sermon as an adequate "likeness of facts". At best, one has achieved a fitting *approach* to the real situation.

---

**765** In this connection, we should once again remember the principle which was (already) explained in the chapter on the person of the preacher. Preachers are not ordained because they have a deeper faith or because they cope with life better than the non-ordained. What qualifies them for the office of preaching is, among other things, a tested and certified theological-hermeneutic competence, knowledge of the rules of interpreting biblical texts etc., the usefulness of which must prove itself from case to case. What "advantage" they have on the basis of their theological education over the un-academically educated members of the congregation in certain circumstances is not a superiority in the life lived by faith but frequently a greater competence in discovering and formulating the *questions* which arise or are asked in living one's life.

**766** Cf. J. Barwise/J. Perry, 1983, 1–7, 56f.

The most important gain from this debate is a changed homiletic awareness: "There is no timeless sermon". Anyone who preaches must "speak in time"[767]. For Müller, a prophetic dimension of the sermon was connected with this demand. Accordingly, the sermon should not "preach *the time*" but "speak *into time*"[768]. Part of this is the "no" to a misunderstood adaption to Modernity, to what one might call "Zeitgeist": a confused jumble of indignation, standard opinion and taboos. A contemporary sermon will nevertheless recognize this mood and must take it into account as the general circumstances or a common consciousness of life.

The deliberate inclusion of the concept of situation through a theological *point of contact* in the narrower sense and the reality of life connected to it in the theological and homiletic work has gained a greater theological depth in various ways. Initially it was considerations from a *creation-theological standpoint* from which established the necessity for a situational and contextual sermon; the theological legitimacy of the salutation in any sermon is consequently seen as based on the fact that man is a creature of God. Trillhaas understands the link to the createdness of humanity as *a link to the situation of the individual*.[769] When the sermon relates to the createdness of humanity it also relates to their experiences, including the experiences of being guilty and of failure, to experiences which express the presence of the law.

A sermon which does not relate to the situation in this sense will struggle to make clear as to why it tells its listeners of the "freedom from the law". A sermon, which does not relate to the situation of those listening is one which does not recognize the "law" as a dimension of human reality and is consequently an "unevangelical" sermon. If, however, real situations are the places in which people experience *both* their failures *and* become aware of God's saving acts in their lives – if, that is, the world in its concrete reality is where God meets them – a preacher cannot be committed enough to deliberating this world and communicating his reflections with the best interest of the listeners in mind, and by doing so, practicing "virtuosity in visualizing resp. realization" ("Vergegenwärtigungs-virtousität").

---

767 A. D. Müller, 1954, 202.
768 Loc. cit., 202f.
769 "The person is addressed in his createdness and in all what follows out of this – all the conclusions and facts – and since humans are created beings, a certain order is set which commits them unto God, and the non-observance of which makes one guilty before God. And thus, we shall be addressed as creatures – and even as creatures who will be guilty or have become guilty before God – by the sermon" (W. Trillhaas, 1954, 50f). Cf. supplementary to God's image III.2.2, p. 445–451.

### 6.3.2 The Overcoming of Divided Reality in the Sermon

The regaining of awareness for the situation as a point of reference for the sermon was initially hardly connected to methodical and conceptual consequences. First, however, we must consider the reasons why relating to actual life realities and experiences – even when one has developed an awareness for the necessity of the sermon preparation to relate to the situation – is often difficult to determine. The description of the problem presented by Mezger and others[770] refers to a problem which has constantly weighed upon the establishment of the sermon in the world of the listeners: It is a matter of the burden of the already mentioned theological and homiletic "division" of the respectively presupposed reality.

A sermon which merely picks up human reality in order to pass a negative judgement upon it instead of supporting the individual in living a life by faith under the concrete conditions of reality misses its target. A sermon which fails to use a language fitting to the reality of the listeners' lives and instead tinkers with theological ciphers that ultimately hinder its comprehension, perpetuates the fatal division of the reality of the sermon into a dogmatically ordered model world and an empiric reality which must be endured. In this case "reality" is only used to attest to the achievement of the explanation of the model world in a linguistic laboratory experiment called *sermon*. And yet, it should be the other way around: Human experiences are not the material on which one falls back on for the *purposes of demonstration* but represent the real challenge for theological reflection or for the theology of preaching. Mezger, however, observes an apprehension of changing or revising "leading biblical concepts" in many preachers[771]. Apparently, many are afraid of inevitably also having to give up the concept and the reality connected to it.

In the continual division of the reality of sermons and in the resulting incomprehensibility Mezger sees a frequently unconscious adhering to "ancient ideas". Consequently, a situational sermon first requires "honesty" which does not desire to push the listeners into a metaphysical world of probability. Preachers should not entice them into "vacant rooms" in which e.g. the laws of physics do not appear to function completely, but should surrender themselves with the listeners to the *one* reality.[772] "'There is only *one* reality, not, say, a reality of God plus a reality of the world or, let alone, one of the devil'... With the incarnation

---

770 M. Mezger, 2009.
771 Loc. cit., 19.
772 Loc. cit., 20. Cf. also Mezger's insistent remarks under the title "Das Problem der Profanität: Die Gemeinde in der Welt" (The Problem of Profanity: The Congregation as part of the World), in: M. Mezger, 1971, 402–406.

of Jesus, it has become forbidden for us to divide God and humanity, divine and secular, holy and profane, supernatural and natural, Christian and unchristian into dual domains. [...] There is no higher and lower court of truth; there is only truth and untruth, represented in the things or events as they really are."[773]

The listeners are not taken seriously in their faith and knowledge if the sermon lacks an understandable, relevant content and thereby refuses to be grounded in the situational points of reference. It would be like a relinquishment or watering-down of the sermon's relation to the situation if of all things "scientific absurdities and miraculous special events" were moved into the centre of interest in such a way that in the end they might become "actually almost as good as possible, even – who knows – might become 'facts'". To act in such a way means to invest "the greatest energy into the wrong place" and to persuade the listener that "the text is right – in aspects in which it does not even want to be right"[774].

This in no way means that the sermon should make it 'easy' for the listeners. If it earnestly deliberates the reality of the individual it inadvertently includes "the discussing of societal taboos"[775]. However, the power of the gospel does not serve the justification of God against existing conditions or the defence of ancient philosophies but can be seen in the alteration of oppressive conditions, and in the creation of situations, which lead to and initiate the emergence of freed human beings.

Jan Hermelink emphasizes Mezger's hermeneutic interest and stresses that contemplation of the situation of the listener does not guarantee the perceptibility of the Word of God.[776] The impulses of preaching which is oriented on human reality are often misunderstood and contemptuously discredited as merely "situational Homiletics". Yet, the attempt to relate to the human existence does not automatically guarantee particular effects of the sermon, as, for example, an experience-as-if-addressed-by-God or not-able-to-do-anything-other-than-believe. As part of an event of communication the reception of a sermon does not lie under the control of the preacher. Preachers can, however, do something so that the condition of a successful communication and existential understanding are taken into consideration for the sermon to the best of their knowledge and belief.

---

**773** M. Mezger, 2009, 21f. The first part of the quotation (in simple quotation marks) is attributed to Dietrich Bonhoeffer, cited from G. Schnath, 1982, 52. As far as the subject is concerned – especially what the criticism of dualism contained therein is concerned – Schnath and Mezger are naturally correct. But the quotation actually reads: "There are not two realities, but only one reality, and that is God's reality revealed in Christ in the reality of the world" (D. Bonhoeffer, 2005, 58).

**774** Loc. cit., 25.

**775** J. Hermelink, 1992, 99.

**776** Loc. cit., 100.

Such a view of the situation also has consequences for the understanding of faith, which characterizes a sermon. Heinz Zahrnt expresses this aptly in his contribution "Glauben unter leerem Himmel"[777] ("Faith Under the Open Sky"): "From now on there are no longer dual, opposing worlds – an other-worldly-supernatural 'above' and an earthly-natural 'below' – but simply one undivided world in which we live. [...] Belief in God is consequently not a matter of adding a second, divine reality to the existing reality of the world – far more, faith includes the visible, existing reality of the world in its depths: that it is God's world and should be evermore. We either experience God in the reality of the world here – or we do not experience him at all."[778]

### 6.3.3 The Listener's Reality of Life and the Homiletic Situation

It is no accident that Ernst Lange's ardent plea for a sermon filled with a witness of the gospel and anchored in the everyday reality of the listener was formulated at a time when the institutionalized proclamation of the church was exposed to massive attacks from a theological protest-generation. The sermon, so to the critique, simply upholds the governing theological system. It does not lead to any kind of change and consequently should be done away with. Ernst Lange does not come down on the side of those defenders suspicious of conspiracy nor does he agree with the demands to abolish the office of preaching. He puts himself between the conflicting parties. Jürgen Henkys aptly sums up Ernst Lange's achievement at the time: "He tries with ever new attempts to bring together experienced reality and promises of faith in such a way that a church which isolates itself against the world and a theology which closes up against the social sciences are equally challenged to take a risk and open up."[779]

One must first get into Ernst Lange's style of argumentation in order to understand him adequately. His line of thought is like a path which is laid out around a mountain, climbs higher slowly in ever new spirals and finally leads to the peak. We can conclude from the numerous misinterpretations in homiletic seminar-papers and occasionally even in specialist literature[780] that Lange's texts are not read enough. His theses appear to be popular and his arguments simple, so that, if reference is made to Lange, we frequently read only something

---

777 H. Zahrnt, 2000.
778 Loc. cit., 31f., 35.
779 J. Henkys, 1990, 50.
780 I shall speak about R. Bohren's (R. Bohren, 1981) misunderstanding – which is often quoted and which after 35 years could be called 'classic' – later.

of the "rediscovery of the importance of the listener in the event of preaching"[781], whatever that may mean in detail. Consequently, it seems appropriate to look at his approach in more detail.

### a) On the Foundations of a Situation-Related Sermon

I begin with the question as to why Ernst Lange demands Homiletics which considers the listeners not simply for reasons of a kerygmatically plausible *applicatio,* but which should lead to a deeper understanding of their life. To be sure, others before Ernst Lange have declared the situation to be theologically relevant, but "never before [has] the challenge been emphasized with such determination that the work on the sermon flourishes if the sermon really desires to conduct the dialog with its hearers. For such a dialog, where the sermon holds an implicit conversation with its hearers, to develop and to make this perceptible, preachers must endeavor in quite a different way to that which earlier Homiletics demanded from them."[782]

"Only when what I say *concerns* the listener, it also concerns him that what I say (and to what extent that which I say) has its basis in the Holy Scripture, is in accord with the tradition of faith, is consistent with the orders of my church and based on my personal conviction. [...] For the listener the relevance of the sermon is decided according to the clarity and stringency of its relation to the reality of his life, to his own specific situation. Here the term '*relationship* to reality' is actually too weak. The true subject of a Christian address is not, in fact, a biblical text or another document from the history of faith but nothing other than the day-by-day reality of the listeners themselves – in the light of the [biblical] promises. That is why the homiletic pattern of *explicatio* and *applicatio* is so unsatisfactory. It raises the impression that first come the text and understanding thereof and only then the question of how the understanding of the text should be related to the life of the listener. However, this idea is not only hermeneutically false as there is no understanding without being affected. [...] It is also homiletically false: It makes the sermon a popular theological lecture, the preacher a history teacher or the authoritative administrator of a codified truth. It gives the sermon the false task."[783]

---

781 Ch. Bunners, 1990, 144. In Bunners' remarks we are recommended to "use the possibilities of special investigation of the listeners [...] for sensibility in each 'homiletic situation' diligently and committedly" (loc. cit., 170). Here the *existential point* of the concept of the homiletic situation is lost. As if the "homiletic situation" were for the moment alien to the preacher but familiar to the listeners. According to Lange the necessity for clarification of this situation arises to a large extent *from the preacher's own "temptations".* It is not a well-intentioned empathizing act for the sake of the other (cf. E. Lange, 1976, 25).

782 W. Gräb, 1997a, 499.

783 E. Lange, 1976, 57f. The text from which this is quoted bears the title "Zur Aufgabe christlicher Rede" ("The task of a Christian address"). It was first published in E. Lange, 1968, 78–94.

The fact that, here, the talk is of the "subject" of the sermon with regard to the listeners has often been misunderstood as if what is meant by this is the précis. From the quotation cited above it emerges that what is meant is not the content but an act of reference, an address – in short: the *orientation* of the sermon.[784] Through the sermon the "light of the Promise" should be directed at the "daily reality" of the listener. It is now a question of not simply airing the reality theologically, sacralizing it religiously or defending it against an abstract darkness. The reason for the sermon to relate to a situation is consequently not out of doubt over the trustworthiness of the Word of God, nor out of helplessness because the promises of the gospel have failed to materialize or an apathy towards tradition. The reason why the sermon should relate to a situation lies in the practice of the communication of the gospel itself: It cannot take place without an intentional, desired and thought out relation to the concrete world in which contemporaries live. Preachers should concern themselves with situations in order to be able to communicate to the individual the extent to which "the God for whom Jesus speaks is the Lord of his specific life situation"[785].

### b) On the Task of a Situation-Related Sermon

After we have (a) dealt with the reasons why a sermon should relate to a situation, it can now (b) be discussed how far these ideas correspond to the premises of the New Testament, the main foci of the Reformation thinking and the requirements of a *publice docere*[786] whereby the task of the sermon comes into view:

"Preaching means: I speak with the listener about his life. I speak with him about his experiences and opinions, his hopes and disappointments, his successes and failures, his tasks and his destiny. I speak with him about his world and his responsibility in this world, about the threats and opportunities of his existence. The listener is my theme, nothing else; admittedly, the listener before God. But this does not add anything to the reality of his life; rather it uncovers the real truth of this reality." This means: "I speak with the listener about his life, not from the rich fund of my experience of life or my higher education. [...] I speak with him in the light of the promise of Christ as it is witnessed in Scripture. And that means: I speak with him on the basis of biblical texts. [...] The listener should understand that the God for whom Jesus speaks is the Lord of the situation, the Lord of his specific life situation too. They shall understand how trust in this God and his present lordship frees them from the spell of the 'law', that is, from the compulsory power of the [...] so-called 'reality', from guilt and despair (*Absolutio*)

---

**784** When Ernst Lange talks of the *content* of the sermon he always has the "gospel", "the promises", "the Word of God" or "tradition" in mind. In one place he also uses for this the concept of "object", and that again in relation to content: "The object of this endeavor is the *Christian tradition in its relevance for the current situation*" (1976, 20).
**785** Loc. cit., 62.
**786** Cf. III.3.1 – III.3.3, p. 461–484.

and fills their life with promise and thereby makes their future certain (*Promissio*) and tangibly empowers a person to a new life in love and hope (*Missio*). That is the aim of the endeavor of the sermon. [...] The sermon cannot bring faith in the promise into being. But it must show that – and why – the promise 'deserves' faith, and how the reality in faith changes the situation of the listener."[787]

This understanding of preaching clearly takes up the practice of proclamation in the New Testament to which belongs the insight that the communication of the gospel raises the question of power. Against this background a sermon should plausibly make clear to the individual that "the God for whom Jesus speaks is the LORD of his specific life situation", so that the experience of heteronomy, of the force of the system, of being inferior and impotent must not be basic motifs of life. The basis and point of reference of such a sermon is the "promise of Christ as it is witnessed in Scripture". This promise-potential is, however, not a collection of abstract dogmas but has consequences right into the individual's reality of life: Similar to the way in which Luther declared the acquisition of the *pro me* as a decisive point in the reception of the testimony of Christ, Lange stressed that the individual in his specific situation should be empowered to life, which includes the communication of forgiveness and making the promises plausible.[788] Accordingly, a sermon is more than an act of mere "proclamation of what they [the people] have to hear from God himself"[789]. It is the concrete continuation of the work of salvation in our time.

Lange takes up the question discussed at length in II.2.3 about the public character of the sermon to the extent that he analyzes the threatening loss of relevance and public nature of the sermon as a problem of communication within the church and makes it the starting-point of his considerations on the task of the sermon. It is Lange's impression of a lack in contemporaneity in preaching, which makes him question the "homiletic situation": "The preacher cannot make himself understood. He cannot break through the glass wall which [...] separates him from his contemporaries. The words which he speaks stir up neither a 'yes' nor a 'no', neither the emerging of the congregation nor the breaking-off of unsuccessful relationships to it. Within and without everything remains as it was, as if one did not speak."[790]

---

**787** Loc. cit., 58, 62f.
**788** The extent to which preachers are aware of this challenge is to a high degree determined by the direction in which the culture of preaching is developed. In his contribution on the necessity and lasting relevance of the "communication of faith" Heyen discusses "why the sermon will survive the 21st century" (H. Heyen, 2007).
**789** K. Barth, 1986, 30.
**790** E. Lange, 1976, 18.

This observation now leads directly to the question of the understanding of the homiletic situation.

### c) On the Understanding of the Homiletic Situation

The determination of the "homiletic situation" is the key to understanding Ernst Lange's theory of preaching. While the term *situation* in everyday language usually means the "state of things" in the sense of existing conditions, the *homiletic* situation is qualified by specific tensions which must be discerned (at the latest) in the preparation of the sermon, interpreted and understood in their consequences for living in this world. Such tensions sometimes lie on the surface of human experience and can be attended to in a few words. However, they can also exist unconsciously and latently mark everyday experience, they can be denied and made taboo.

The aforementioned potential for tensions arises particularly from the divergence between certain expectations and actual happenings, from the sequence of hope and disappointment, from the experience of having wished with one's whole heart, and as time passes, to feel that not only does the expected feeling of happiness not materialize but also that also the will which once permitted a wish to influence one's action no longer exists. In theological terms, it is the *tension between promise and experience*, a tension which not only plays a part in generally determining the fundamental situation of faith but also finds expression in concrete individual experiences. A sermon must enter into this potential of tension in order to be able to give the communication of the gospel a concrete connection to situations. Ernst Lange considers the homiletic situation as follows:

"Under homiletic situation one should understand that specific situation of the listener or group of listeners through which the church, bearing in mind its commission, sees itself challenged to preach, i.e. to a concrete act of preaching which corresponds to this situation. And the task of this homiletic act is, seen from this point and formally expressed, the *clarification* of this homiletic situation." Characteristic of the situation is "that in it and because of it, fate, experiences, expectations and conventions […], the mission of the church, the relevance of the Christian tradition in this situation must be witnessed to provide a certain *resistance* but also to open up certain special […] chances of communication."[791] Consequently, the homiletic situation is *"the situation, which is specific for every case,* one with resistances and chances of communication […] and which represents the *real challenge of the sermon"*[792]. "Resistance" here means "the ensemble of disappointments, fears, missed decisions, lost chances, […] the refusal of freedom and obedience". "It embodies the resignation of faith in the face of the lack of promise in everyday

---

791 Loc. cit., 22f.
792 Loc. cit., 23. Emphases W. E.

existence [...] – the capitulation of faith before the inevitability of facts. [...] At heart the homiletic situation is then, in biblical terms, the situation of contesting" especially "for the preacher who wishes to talk relevantly of God *in* this situation."[793]

Only on the basis of the analysis of the homiletic situation can the "task of comprehensibility"[794] of a singular sermon be put in concrete terms. To take up this task means to question specific experiences from the "ensemble of disappointments, fears" etc. which correspond to the no less specific experiences which are expressed in a biblical text. It is thus a matter of resistances and experiences which make the concrete sermon just as *necessary* and allow it to be *relevant*. In Paul Tillich's terminology, it is formulated as follows: What matters is that the fundamentally alleged correlation between the questions and answers *of life* – which naturally are questions or could lead to questions – is made concrete, sermon after sermon.

Lange made a special contribution by taking a crisis of faith, i.e. when faced with contradictory experiences, seriously and *as a point in itself* and did not moralize or trivialize it with "facts from another world". In his view, a sermon has the task to testify to the relevance of faith in the face of *temptations*[795]. His plea for the genuine awareness of what can make it difficult for a person to live, to believe or to live by faith finds support in the certainty that these difficulties are the genuine place where the communication of the gospel can flourish in its effect in a way that even circumstances may change.

Considering Ernst Lange's differentiated illustrations on the foundations of his understanding of the task of the sermon, Rudolf Bohren's assessment of the therewith connected approach turns out to be a gross misunderstanding: Bohren concludes that Ernst Lange's homiletic principles are marked by a "kerygmatic consumption"[796]. Anyone who "begins with the situation" – so claims Bohren – makes himself "its prisoner".[797] Incidentally, Rudolf Bohren proclaims his own interest in the sermon as follows: "I am not so interested in me as a listener that I'd want to listen to a sermon on my own account. As listener, I am an all too miserable topic."[798] But based on the aforementioned text his objections can be challenged: It is not nonchalance about the "kerygma" which causes Lange to question the homiletic situation but precisely the perceptibility of the

---

793 Loc. cit., 24f.
794 Loc. cit., 22. Like Mezger, Lange also understands the homiletic act primarily as an "attempt of comprehensibility" (cf. loc. cit., 20).
795 On the personal way of dealing with temptations see the differentiation made by W. Jentsch between "contestable temptation" (which is not a temptation of faith but an expression of a "thin skin") and *"temptation* which must be fought through" by means of which the individual can grow. Cf. W. Jentsch, 1978, 52–57.
796 Cf. R. Bohren, 1981, 416.
797 Loc. cit., 424.
798 R. Bohren, 1980, 451.

gospel: *The listener should understand "how the God for whom Jesus speaks is also the LORD [...]* *of his own specific life situation".*[799] Under "kerygmatic consumption" one thinks of something quite different.[800] Bohren's presumption that Lange has a sermon in mind in which the listener must become the *content of the sermon* is likewise incorrect. This accusation was also refuted above: Lange looks at the "listeners before God" in order to be able to represent the reality of their life "in the light of the promise of Christ".

All who, like Rudolf Bohren, see the gospel in danger simply because individuals should be motivated to listen to the sermon for their own sake, for the sake of their contested faith and with regard to their own life, fail to see that God – according to Jewish-Christian tradition – has spoken *for the sake of the individual person.* For the sake of humanity God became human and speaks in ways people can hear and understand. Incidentally, the determined rejection of the sermon being connected to the situation of the listener is not always motivated by theological modesty or the virtue of humility: All who decline to hear a sermon *for their own sake* possibly also shy away from being confronted with their own perception-of-self which always also has an effect on a person's everyday life and usual circumstances. The problem of the "inhuman sermon"[801] addressed by Bohren becomes contradictory as soon as *individuals may no longer listen to a sermon for their own sake.* For whose sake should they otherwise want to listen to a sermon?

Ernst Lange was not the first Practical Theologian who saw the situation of the listener as a category of Homiletics. He was also not the last. Jan Hermelink describes, in a representative selection, the "various alternatives of the pragmatic-empirical turn to the homiletic situation" on the basis of the theoretical sermon impulses of Hans-Dieter Bastian, Gert Otto and Werner Jetter.[802] These variations implement Lange's basic theme and decisions in cybernetic, rhetorical and dialogical terms by addressing the doubtfulness (H.-D. Bastian), the historicity (G. Otto) and the linguistics of the homiletic situation (W. Jetter).

Considering these considerations, three dimensions of the sermon will be described in the following which, in the individual case, could also determine the type of the sermon and, in a special way, grow out of the confrontation with the homiletic situation.

---

**799** E. Lange, 1976, 62.
**800** Further information on the *theological relevance* of Lange's approach to the sermon can be found in W. Gräb, 1991. On the criticism of R. Bohren's reception of E. Lange, cf. H. W. Dannowski, 1985, 98, J. Hermelink, 1992, 12; W. Gräb, 1997a, 510.
**801** Cf. R. Bohren, 1980, 446 and my explications on the "inhuman sermon Type II" in I.6.1.1.
**802** J. Hermelink, 1992, 223–255.

## 6.4 On the Category of a Situation-Related Sermon

### Preliminary Remarks

At this point we must once again consider the *distinction between abstract and concrete situations*: An abstract situation could be, for example, the result of a contemporary diagnosis or arise from the analyses of the social sciences which attempt to consider particular circumstances in a society and give a structure to the complex situation discovered. Abstract situations are therefore *situations already interpreted* which point to typical prerequisites and requirements for the life of a person in society. They mark *the parameters and general framework of individual situations* in which the reality of life – even in concrete situations – manifests in a specific and contingent way. These concrete situations reflect not simply sociological textbook knowledge but *challenge to make a statement, to take sides.* They demand clear pictures, intellectual impulses and solid ideas for changing a person's situation in some way or at least enable him to take up a reasonable position to the situation. The convergence of both sides of the situation, the abstract and the concrete, is indispensable for an adequately relevant sermon. Consequently, preachers need a basic understanding of the conditions of the present world in which we live in and should know the relevant "general interpretations of the current societal situation". On the other hand, their work demands a lively interest in making abstract situations concrete in the vicissitudes of human life.

However, we must be mindful that situations do not become effective momentarily but that they determine the course of the processes of communication from the beginning.[803] As the totality of the real prerequisites of the circumstances of communication, situations – simply because of their materiality – influence how those communicating relate to one another, when and how they listen to another etc. The real conditions thus have an effect on the way in which something is understood. The "circumstances" can get around the intentions of the communication and give another direction to automated processes of understanding.[804] Among these objective conditions are the cultural and socio-political relations in a country, the relationship of the poorer to the richer, the number of those out of work in a particular region or town in which sermons are delivered, the composition of the congregation according to

---

803 Against J. Barwise/J. Perry, 1983, 19.
804 Cf. the explications on the circumstance of communication as intention, intervention and innovation in W. Engemann, 1993, 180–185.

age and gender or the fates which individuals have suffered through war, exile, personal separation etc.[805]

All this works together in the constituting of the real situation of the sermon communication and *cannot* be disregarded in the process of preaching. Of course, it makes a big difference if this reality – in the case of a sermon with a pronounced distance to reality – simply disrupts the process of understanding, boycotts it or lets it founder, or whether this reality is intended in the sermon itself, whether it is *dealt* with literally and in this way, contributes to the relevance and veracity of the communication. The following three chapters serve this matter of concern about the sermon in respect of delusion and fear[806] as well as neediness.

To clarify the "situation, which is specific from case to case" Ernst Lange points to the requirements of the "casual speech". To him a specific case can be described for every sermon. In this, he has "special situations in which the church, for whatever reason, [is] called upon to act and speak"[807] in mind. When, in the following, the discussion turns to the categories of "political", "pastoral" and "diaconal" sermons, no such concrete constellations of problems will be specified so that one could talk of particular "situations"; however, they represent three perspectives of reflection which naturally imply a strong relationship to a situation and demand clarifications which should always precede the approach to the individual case.

### 6.4.1 Preaching in the Face of Delusion. Political Aspects

#### a) Prerequisites and Problems
Various points of view have asserted themselves in the debate about the legitimacy and range of a political sermon. Here I should like to summarize and bring to the point the discussions connected to this based on three aspects.

*The Aspect of the Creation Character:* A sermon is initially political because of its creation-character. In biblical terms: Where God speaks, a word of power is uttered.

---

**805** Leonora T. Tisdale virtually pleads for "exegeting the congregation" (L. T. Tisdale, 2008) which implies different social, cultural as well as ethnographical aspects and requires that preachers are as well acquainted with their congregation as they are with the biblical texts. "Congregational interpretation is a necessary 'first step' (as well as an ongoing process) through which the pastor can listen attentively on order to deepen his/her understanding of the congregation on its own terms" (L. T. Tisdale, 1997, 25).
**806** The two terms "fear" and "delusion" describe two classical possibilities of focusing on abstract situations. A historical stimulus for this is, among other things, Martin Luther's attempt to be aware of "along with fear also of delusion as an elementary point of reference in Christian proclamation" (cf. M. Josuttis, 1986, 40).
**807** E. Lange, 1976, 22.

From this religious experience which has been handed down there arise certain expectations of the sermon: Should not conditions change – including conditions of power – where a sermon is delivered? Does the sermon not have a part in the event of creation in that it makes history in the space and time of concrete human existence, when it has an effect on human history, when it accomplishes what it says?

Giving a sermon is inseparably connected with the attempt to make the Word of the Creator heard in the language of the creatures and in ways relevant to their existence. It is vital to speak the "Let there be ..." (cf. Gen 1:3ff.) anew. The listeners should be witnesses of how, under the circumstances of their existence, leeways for life arise and how new prospects for their future open up, perspectives which also direct their actions in the present. In this sense, a sermon *cannot* be apolitical. When it favors particular options of cooperation and existence in the world and criticizes others, when it helps those created by God grasp anew the gift of creation and speaks to them about their responsibility for creation, it makes them sensitive and virtually 'susceptible' for what is political.[808] Here two further aspects are particularly significant.

*The Aspect of the Public Character*: A sermon is also political because of its public character. The church cannot propagate the *publice docere*[809], justify the task of the sermon with Christ's office as king, prophet and priest and at the same time demand from its preachers that they do not appear political. It is connected to the essence of the communication of the gospel that a sermon not only *speaks into* human reality but also – publicly – *influences, judges and incites to a change in behavior.* The reality endorsed, reflected upon, defined and assessed publicly in a worship service must not be reduced to a "pious" reality, nor to some inner truth about humanity. A sermon contributes to the publication of an external view of the world as (in certain circumstances damaged) God's creation, without trying to condescendingly teach those holding political power a lesson.

In this aspect, too, Martin Niemöller's provocative "Dahlem Sermons" are very informative teaching-materials.[810] They explicate in what sense the gospel can be seen as an "attack", namely as confrontation with the fact "that Jesus Christ is the Lord. Niemöller understood this message as a call

---

**808** S. Kuhlmann, referring to the prophetic dimension of Martin Niemöller's style of preaching, made it clear how this *unavoidability of a political sermon* can develop and make its mark. Niemöller himself never claimed that he preached prophetically or politically from the pulpit. Nevertheless, his sermons were felt to be politically relevant and prophetically rousing. Cf. S. Kuhlmann, 2008, 20, 263–276.

**809** Cf. below, III.3.3, p. 474–484 on the task of the sermon in the light of its publicity.

**810** Niemöller's "Dahlem Sermons" have been published in full for the first time by Michael Heymel (2011). This book, on the basis of Niemöller's addresses from the pulpit, introduces in

to a daily decision. Every day anew the gospel demands that we should battle and attack insofar as it proclaims the Lord over everyone and everything. This inevitably leads into conflict with the world. Niemöller sharpens this insight in the sentence: 'The Gospel is not defence, but attack.'"[811] For Niemöller, this "attack" consists not least in a commentary on political events which is simultaneously prophetic and publicly effective. His sermons show us in an exemplary way what the genre "political sermon" means and let us see that the prophetic dimension of a sermon does not lie in an accurate description of the future but in its exposing interpretation of the present.

*The Aspect of Partiality*: A sermon is also political because of its actual partiality. This partiality is not dependent on the degree of agreement with political programs. It is the expression of the partisanship of God for a person's life over against death, for their freedom over against oppression, for their salvation over against ruin and for peace over against violence. If a sermon were to try to talk around these topics without ever really addressing them, would be like the attempt to talk around God's creating, redeeming and saving works and, by that, would take away his points of reference. A person who yields to this temptation sanctions the existing circumstances "Now faith; hope and love abide; and the greatest of these is the *status quo*."[812]

According to M. Josuttis such partisanship cannot simply confine itself to basic Christian-humanistic values. In the individual case, it has to do with rendering particular political positions problematic, and making clear that others are welcome. In these instances, preachers must expect and encourage the congregation to make use of their responsibility. The congregation's ability to judge, their ability to distinguish between positions worth discussing and attitudes which are out of the question (solidarity, tolerance etc.) should also find expression in the *form* of the sermon, in sermons which have the character of "symbolic actions", in "dialog sermons" or in "public discussions at the end of the sermon".[813]

The main danger of a political sermon lies in *slipping into legalism*. The problems of a political sermon do not grow proportionately with the obviousness of its political engagement. (This would result in the fatal conclusion that a sermon which scarcely or not at all refers to political subjects *cannot* present a problem for the congregation and the rest of the public.)

---

detail the area of conflict at that time between religion and politics, church and state, creed and ideology, the priestly and prophetic functions of ministers.

**811** Loc. cit., 35.

**812** O. Keel, 1985, 254. "No one can [...] defend himself against the fact that his silence on political disputes is judged to be an agreement with the conviction of the ruling majority. [...] The sermon does not escape from partiality in refusing to make a statement on questions of politics" (M. Josuttis, 1969, 514). On the problem of the plausibility of political statements in the sermon cf. also G. Kugler, 1983, 9.

**813** Cf. M. Josuttis, 1969, 517f.

Problems always arise for the political sermon when wrongs and grievances identified by the preacher are spoken of in such a way that the political analysis as well as the solutions offered seem to be considered pure gospel. Listeners who are set before the choice of *either* being allowed to understand themselves as Christians and accept the preacher's views, to carry them out and thereby acting according to the gospel – *or* to have been misled in their faith – are now under the law[814] instead of having become involved in the communication of the gospel. In this way, the principles of the achievement-oriented society are resuscitated precisely in the one place where individuals are not needed based on their success, but should be free to be, and valued for, who they are[815] – the church service.

When sermons have a *prophetic dimension* as well as a political one, then it is due to their power of interpreting, their ability to clarify and their courage to put the finger in a wound. A sermon that resolves to interpret time and society and evaluates existing conditions does not mean that it must also present programmatic suggestions for the remodeling of those conditions or the laws and orders which make them possible.[816] "Prophecy is to be found on the side which *interprets* the situation and from there provides a foundation for society. It defends itself against the absorption of the areas which *shape* situations, frequently by turning down apparently favorable alliances: Paradoxically it must defend itself from preference or monopolization by politics in order not to become the ideological legitimation of a political founding of the community. [...] Only when people recognize – alongside God – the authority of other higher or equivalent authorities, can human actions become the topic of prophetic sermons."[817]

---

814 If the sermon attempts to lever out the "freedom of the listener to decide", it is a sermon of the "law" and not a "sermon of the gospel" (W. Schütz, 1981, 125).

815 "The true gospel, by contrast, distinguishes itself from any moral or political program for starry-eyed idealism, 'reveals...' wherein our guilt actually lies: not in our failure yesterday, but in the delusion, in spite of and with this our past being able to win the future on its ways, namely because we now finally are doing justice to the demands'" (M. Josuttis, 1973, 563 in relation to a quotation from G. Harbsmeier).

816 In view of the possibilities of a prophetic sermon, it is, for example, quite appropriate to make people aware that "nothing is good in Afghanistan" (as the then Chairman of the EKD, Margot Käßmann explained in a Christmas sermon in 2009) without at the same time being able to give a detailed explanation how in this country the problems – including the resulting problems in Germany – should be politically coped with.

817 S. Kuhlmann, 2008, 334,338. Karl-Fritz Daiber on the other hand points out that, along with the "epideictic political" (calling to praise or complaint) and the "judgement-building political sermon" there is the genre of a "political sermon which instructs to action. [...] Where in the first case it is a matter of authorization to speak in complaint or praise, in the second it is about understanding the situation. Only within the frame of the third possibility is it a matter of political action in the narrower sense. [...] The demand for action in each case needs congregational discussion" (K.-F. Daiber, 1991b, 176). An attempt to mediate between the positions of Daiber and Kuhlmann can be found at the end of section c) in this chapter.

A further danger of the politically ambitious sermon lies in that it is *inappropriate for the audience present*. Political sermons which above all take to task, with an air of indignation, those who are not present, upon whom all the blame for existing conditions is put, can perhaps reckon with the approval of a larger number of those present. But a fostered agreement as to where "the true trespassers" sit misses the opposition-structure of the sermon situation[818], which, particularly in the case of a trenchant political address from the pulpit, dare not be surrendered: The political sermon should orientate, encourage, motivate, warn and comfort *the congregation present* with regard to existing political conditions.[819] In a political sermon one discusses what the implicitly or explicitly addressed political questions mean for the life and faith of the individual who – as Ernst Lange expressed it – is called "to serve Christ in the world"[820]. There are many forms of failing to reach the addressees. They stretch from a preacher's distorted picture of the congregation, who does not trust his congregation to perform "Christian service in the world" and counts them amid the "cosmos of the world as it is, in opposition to God and religious ideals"[821], to a rash and "overtaxing concretions" of political sermons in which "the change of the whole of society is demanded from the individual"[822] and the bringing about of the kingdom of God is expected.

Finally, we must refer to the problem of the *ideological infiltration* of the communication of the gospel, the insertion no longer observed by the preacher of things opportune from a particular political view with the respective message of a text. Just as "equality", "sensitivity", "non-violence", "responsibility for the world", "gender equality" etc. all played a special part in particular contexts of the old and new history of faith, the *selective reception* of these values is always an expression of that scale of values which is connected to a time in a society and which has developed "in the course of the ecological and technical crises of society"[823]. These values and achievements have their *own* right and do not need to be "already contained in the biblical texts", which have in part quite different, also contrary, socio-cultural premises.

The basic political relevance of the biblical texts does not lie in the fact that they surpassed our current ideas of a just world in every way, but because they

---

**818** More detail on this in III.4.5.2.c, p. 505f.
**819** W. Engemann, 1993b, 7f.
**820** E. Lange, 1976, 82.
**821** Ch. Burbach, 1990, 167.
**822** Loc. cit., 108f.
**823** Loc. cit., 84.

consistently clasp the world of faith with the real world and do not reduce it to an "island of the blessed". *They are political in that they mention God's relation to the individual in its consequences for other relationships.* With this we come to the question of the function of the political sermon.

### b) On the Function of the Political Sermon
Political preaching takes into account a person's *responsibility* for the world. It is an expression of hope that it is necessary and promising to take on responsibility in this world. Even if or precisely because the promises[824] handed down in the Scriptures of the Old and New Testaments are built upon a person's responsibility and are not aimed at the bringing about of the kingdom of God but address the consequences of witness and service in the world, they are political. The project of bringing heaven on earth, which overtaxes both the individual and the congregation, is not the issue. But the individual, like the congregation, can be approached about the consequences which result from faith in God or from the anticipation of the coming of the kingdom of God. One who lives from this faith and this anticipation can and should refuse to comply with ideological manipulations, can and should put up the necessary nonviolent resistance to injustice, can and should stand up for peace and justice even if this brings disadvantages and sorrow.

In connection with the question about the Christian's responsibility for the world, the reception of Luther's doctrine of the Two Kingdoms played a special part. Only a simplistic interpretation can reach the conclusion that this model transfigures political conditions and serves the interest of "upholding the *status quo*"[825]. To this one must object that the one who has to pass on the Word of God explains this Word not only in the "kingdom of God on the right" (the church) but – because God rules over the two kingdoms – has also to represent this Word to the "earthly kingdom on the left". *That the church should not be part of the authorities does not mean that it should be indifferent to what authority does.* On the contrary, the church should uphold God's law against the earthly kingdom. The assertion that Luther envisaged a peaceful, amiable co-existence of the spiritual and the earthly kingdoms contradicts the reformatory option for resistance in all questions which corrupt the *conscience* of the individual believers.[826] However, this resistance should not be implemented with violence, not with "worldly means". The two basic forms of the church's resistance are the *word* and – which the risky communication of the gospel might entail at all times – *suffering*[827]. What this means can be made clear not least from

---

824 Cf. e.g. the demands of the Beatitudes, Matt 5:3-11.
825 Cf. A. Schönherr, 1990, 385f.
826 On this cf. the prefaces to the *Augsburg Confession* and the *Apology of the Augsburg Confession*, 1959, 24–27, 98f.
827 Eivind J. Berggrav has particularly impressively set out wherein the task of the church consists, "when the driver is out of his mind". In his book *Man and State* he discusses what the sentence "One must obey God more than human beings" means from various perspectives (among other things, from legal philosophy, from the social sciences, from the history of the church). In

Luther's own biography.[828] *His theology and preaching*, with regard to their content and effect, are also *socio-political occurrences*, aggressively formed analyses of questions of life and time.

Looked at in this way the political maturity of responsibility in a sermon is not gauged from the degree of indignation and outrage[829] against others or "those up there", and its political relevance does not result from the quantity or quality of the demands which it raises. *A sermon is politically effective particularly when it reaches the consciences of those present, which can contribute to a change in the "things as they are"*: The congregation should become intolerant of the delusion that one must perfect people, one could destroy creation and ever again restore it *ad integrum,* one must drive out foreigners in order to uphold our home country. A politically effective sermon is less uncomfortable for individual political parties, provided they hear about it at all; they should not expect much applause especially from the congregation. If, however, it merely repeats what appears to be accepted as a newspaper opinion it would be an act of sheer self-satisfaction.

A political sermon is capable, for example, of making clear under which crazy circumstances people are prepared to live in the present, under which conditions they tend to forget their past or put their future at stake. A political sermon sheds light on the extent of so-called structural sins of society and can speak of this as *human* guilt. A political sermon makes one aware of established arrangements with power-structures and raises questions about personal efficiency. From this we can understand why, in his statements on questions of preaching politically, Josuttis repeatedly addresses the function of the law for the sermon: One can definitely "understand" the political sermon "as a modern

---

his view, this principle of obedience demands a church and a sermon which boosts and strengthens the conscience; for a person with a comforted and sharpened conscience is aware of his responsibility to the Holy One. In the end Berggrav is concerned with the question on whom can we make the greatest demands. But the one who prides himself on having the strongest solidarity must be the first to accept responsibility. Should the state become more human, the religion must be divine. Decisive is, whether an 'either -or-christianity' is found (cf. E. J. Berggrav, 1951, 78–81, 247–284, 300–319).

**828** "Here I stand – I can do no other!" Luther's appearance at Worms is the key scene of a "political position" from religious grounds "in which the individual, in spite of all ominous consequences, follows his conscience and nevertheless remains open for reasons from Scripture and rational arguments" (M. Josuttis, 1986, 39). In a similar way, E.J. Berggrav considers the readiness to take risks of a level-headed conscience committed to the Lord and in so doing also relates to Luther's appearance at Worms (cf. E.J. Berggrav, 1951, 273–284).

**829** Due to the fact that since the period of the modern Age "outrage acquire[d] its license as a basic position – *on a raison de se révolter*" as Peter Sloterdijk (2005, 36) observes, particular restraint is necessary against this fad.

form of the exposing legalistic sermons"[830]. A sermon which perceives its political responsibility in this sense is without doubt a *moral authority*.

This does not mean that we can expect moralistic sermons from this authority. Paradoxically, a moralistic sermon always amounts to *reassurance* in that it professes that, with a little good will and a bit more involvement, one could gain control of the law. As a moral authority, the sermon has the task – contrary to the vague expectation that everything is somehow running its usual course and can be done – of pointing out the pressing difference between the world possible (as seen by faith) and the existing (dis-)order and its principles. In this connection, the sermon must "bring the moral question into the open" and "have the courage to make a justified moral judgement"[831].

Further, can the political sermon practise its *critical function towards ideologies* in opposition towards the institution of the "church". If the sermon succeeds in avoiding the aforementioned traps, it is "an act of criticism of religion – any religion which undertakes the identification of nature and history in an ideological way and thereby nips political thinking in the bud." Such a sermon is capable of exposing "official suppression of problems in its ideological function", of making people aware of "political misuse of theological statements" and to contribute to the "differentiation between God and the world, God and history and God and the church"[832].

That Helmut Thielicke warned about preaching politically and claimed that he himself as preacher knew no political motivation actually implies a disregard of the prophetic dimension of the sermon. Thielicke's practice of preaching shows, however, that he was definitely political and also followed a quite particular ideology, according to which e.g. the "German passion" in the semantics of cross and Good Friday appear as a proper analogy to the passion of Jesus Christ.[833] Such preaching runs the risk "of changing the event of the cross into the myth of German history"[834]. The difficulty in the exposure of such an ideological sermon lies in the fact that, where an ideological sermon is preached, untruths are usually not deliberately told but concepts, pictures and ideas pour in which, because they themselves are the result of a development process in society, are no longer suitable to analyse *from outside*. Nolens volens particular popular socio-political semantic oppositions and axes become frameworks of an argumentative interpretation of the present as well as for the expectation of the future, which supposedly come from the Word of God.[835]

---

830 M. Josuttis, 1973, 566. Though, admittedly, at this point Josuttis speaks of the "political bedtime prayer". Nevertheless, his argumentation has a fundamental character here as it also relates to the general function of the "sermon from the law" (ibid.).
831 M. Josuttis, 1986, 40.
832 M. Josuttis on the function of the political evening prayer, 1973, 569, 577.
833 Cf. H. Thielicke, 1947, esp. IIIf.
834 A. Richter-Böhne, 1989, 109.
835 Cf. W. Engemann, 1993, 127–135.

Therefore, an important, yet not exclusive model of a political sermon is the *prophetic address* which is distinguished by the fact that it is never wrapped up in existing socio-political conditions, does not fit into them but reflects upon them critically and has an exposing character.[836] By itself it can neither establish politically just conditions nor must it explain in detail how this can happen. It can, however, constantly call attention to the aforementioned differences between the idea of order required by faith and the disorderly conditions in church and society. Hence, the demand for taking the situation into account does not mean a sermon which might flawlessly fit and disappear into the real lives of its listeners, but also shows its relevance in the specific resistance and objections which the communication of the gospel provokes.[837]

In 28 theses Sebastian Kuhlmann deliberates appropriate "criteria of a prophetic sermon"[838]. Therein we read: "A prophetic sermon is one-sided. Its concern is so elementary and fundamental that many areas of faith and also of life are not represented. Prophecy is not pedagogy: It does not give any instructions, tolerates no diversion and is as such extremely risky – for preacher and congregation."[839] "Prophetic preaching combats a lack of faith and ignorance by seeking the general public. Over and above the public present in the congregation, the sermon targets an intended public [i.e. the public as a whole who are included but are not present in the service]. In so doing it orients itself on the metaphor of the sour dough: the actual public continues the proclamation to the intended public through their daily actions. Consequently, a prophetic sermon can never be a condemnation or indictment of 'the other' but wants to change something in those present."[840]

The differentiation between the *interpreting function of a prophetic sermon* and the *structuring function of a political speech* is admittedly not absolute. It marks two poles of a continuous or unified homiletic spectrum. In the focus of the former stand the human *attitudes* addressed by the sermon (with respect

---

**836** Cf. in this sense on the function of the political sermon in G. Theißen, 1994, 117.

**837** L. T. Tisdale (2010) analyzed specific structural patterns of the profile of a prophetic sermon in which the category of a testimony plays a particular role. Credibility and integrity of the prophetic character of the sermon depend, among other things and according to the authors, upon whether the words and conduct of the preacher form an integrated whole. In the work *Preaching Fools* by Ch. L. Campbell and J. H. Cilliers (2012) particularly what is resisting and confusing in the prophetic dimension of the sermon is shown to advantage. Accordingly, it is the sermon's task – so one concludes from reading this book – to cast doubt upon existing conceptions, to confront the listeners with their consciences and at the same time put them before the choice of who they wish to be in view of the word of the cross – considering that, in the end, a liberating effect is to be expected from these words.

**838** S. Kuhlmann, 2008, 336–340.

**839** Loc. cit., 340.

**840** Loc. cit., 338f.

to people, things and situations). A political sermon therefore focuses on the self-positioning of the hearers with regard to questions of the age, to conflicts in society and to themselves. From this arise not only appeals to the ethics and consciences of the congregation. A sermon will also imagine or anticipate the behavior resulting from it, and at least attempt to articulate how human behaviour might change in the process of the communication of the gospel.[841]

### 6.4.2 Preaching in the Face of Fear. Aspects of Pastoral Care

#### a) Prerequisites and Problems

The re-defining – basically initiated by Martin Luther – of the role of the late mediaeval *priest* within the church service towards a *preacher* reveals a remarkable quality: that the possibility of experiencing redemption is no longer linked simply to the *sacramental action* of a priest but is understood as a *communication* of the gospel between preacher and listener and therewith bestows a new significance upon the office of preacher. Nevertheless, the term "preacher" did not become the real job-title or the correlate for "minister" – as occasionally happened later in the age of the Enlightenment – but Luther takes up the concept of *cura animarum* (the cure of souls), which was already common before the Reformation, and makes this a central concept of his pastoral theology. By and large, the task of the minister is understood as pastoral care.[842] The sermon is about "the souls", although not in the sense of a particularly qualified, definable, pious area in the barren land of the human being, but it concerns pastoral care as a pastoral challenge which affects the entirety of a person's life.

Pastoral care, then, is a ministry which cannot be limited to individual, private conversations. Pastoral care is a dimension of ecclesial action with manifold forms of expression. Whether I am – in passing – caught up in the narration of someone's entire life story or speak to candidates for Confirmation about the fears of failure in the course of their instruction, whether I am phoned and asked – with a tear-choked voice – for support after a bereavement or have to settle a dispute among the members of the congregation, whether I make a visit on the occasion of a birthday or sit down for a coffee break with the volunteers who just helped to clean up the cemetery – the pastoral care dimension is always present in the context of a pastor's ministry. Pastors are not

**841** On this cf. the ideas in the volume edited by Helmut Schwier, "Ethische und politische Predigt. Beiträge zu einer homiletischen Herausforderung" (2015), particularly the contributions by Manuel Stetter with an outline of concepts of an ethical sermon (ibid., 159–183) and Kathrin Oxen with considerations on the teaching methods of a political sermon (ibid., 184–195).

**842** Reformed pastoral theology follows this conception with Huldrych Zwingli: Pastoral care "occurs in every work, address and action which is set in motion by the gospel, or it does not happen at all" (S. Lutz, 1995, 71).

merely well-wishers, catechists, funeral orators or mediators but they are always also challenged and called for in their competence in pastoral care. Nevertheless, this competence, which is expressly desired and, to an extent, requested in the professionally-formed dialog and which must first be developed through specific qualifications, is not called into question by the various dimensions of pastoral care in day-to-day ministry as characterized above.

A sermon which is understandable, related to Scripture and personal in the sense of chapter I.1–I.5, which does not simply indulge in speech-acts of assertion but is inviting, encouraging, clarifying, accompanied by arguments and conceived in a dialog fashion, a sermon which relates to its contemporary listeners and their life with all the challenges which accompany them and others etc. – will doubtlessly also come closer in its pastoral task than a sermon which simply utters texts or specialist theological terms. In this context, the pastoral care dimension of the sermon should not be understood as an occasional extra bonus but as a fundamental component which results from how it relates to the situation and what this situation requires.

Considering this broad, factual horizon of pastoral care[843] it may seem displeasing to refer to a sermon with a pastoral care dimension as a "sermon against anxiety" of all things. This characterization naturally does not mean that pastoral care is, first and foremost, for people who are anxious. It is the anxiety in Kierkegaard's sense that is meant – the basic human situation of living in "fear and trembling"[844] and having to believe in spite of doubt. It is a question of anxiety as the "impertinent agitation"[845] of foundering with one's own plans and hopes or on the basic human fear of failure in general.[846]

To this corresponds the fact that the basic function of pastoral care in the Lutheran tradition is often summarized under the concept of "comfort". This does not mean the mere calming of a person in threatening times but the fundamental – and yet ever and again necessary – release from the scrupulous conscience which fears being overtaxed by the law and condemned by God.[847] Put in general

---

843 Totally unaffected by the question of the pastoral dimension of the sermon is the fact that pastoral care is a highly complex science which professionally founds, shapes and critically accompanies the practice of pastoral care. This practice, the basic paradigm of which is the dialog between two people and in which the individual is the actual focus, is a matter or research in various perspectives and is methodically mediated in relation to specific psychological, philosophical and sociological concepts (cf. W. Engemann, 2016a).

844 The title of a work by S. Kierkegaard (1843) in which the constructive function of Christian anxiety as opposed to the (earthly) fear of particular events is made clear.

845 Thus W. Müller-Lauter (1993, 726) in his interpretation of Kierkegaard.

846 M. Heidegger speaks of the experience of "not-being-at-home", the "uncanny feeling" of Angst which latently determines human existence. Cf. M. Heidegger, 1996, § 40.

847 Cf. J. Ziemer, 2015, 67–72 and – representative in the connection of anxiety and comfort in M. Luther – Luther's hymn *Nun freut euch, lieben Christen g'mein* on the surmounting of anxiety

terms one might also say: The "anxiety", the reality which the "pastoral" sermon reckons with, is the inevitable result of the experience of reality, including experiences of being guilty of the loss of relationships, of weaknesses, frustrations etc. A sermon which, in view of the situation, desires to comfort will not smooth out or trivialize this reality but must face up to it, which is impossible without a reflected relation to the situation.

### b) On the Function of a Pastoral Sermon

However, what does it mean to take such reality seriously in the sermon? Following the chronology of the topics of this introduction I should like to draw attention to some starting-points:

1. In that the preacher takes into account the requirements and demands of personal communication[848] a *relationship level* can be established in the process of the sermon. This is an important basis for the listeners to first become involved and willing to follow what is said, that is, to respond positively to the sermon and not with rejection or lack of understanding. To build such a relationship level is indispensable in order to experience the sermon – to, at the same time, name a few classical pastoral care virtues – as reliable, credible and authentic.

2. A sermon with a *pastoral care* dimension and a *personal* sermon are not in every, yet in a very particular respect correlating concepts, namely to the extent in which the listener can be uniquely encouraged to live by faith through a credible and *personal testimony of the preacher*. This demands that preachers become visible as individuals, admit to "temptations" and signify what stance they take on the experience thereof. A relevant sermon has repercussions on the listener's self-perception. It can release, sharpen, correct it etc. and thereby fulfill an important function of pastoral care.

3. A sermon can also gain "pastoral" relevance through its complex, multilayered reference to the *potentials of the Jewish-Christian* tradition to which the biblical texts belong in their confronting, creative and confirming function[849]. As textualized experiences of life and faith they can paradigmatically allow us to see how situations are experienced, borne, defined, overcome and changed. After all, the biblical traditions are about real historical situations which, within the frame of analogies, may influence the experiences

---

(Evangelisches Gesangbuch, 1996, No. 341, esp. third verse). From this, one can understand why sermons as an act of pastoral care should not only *deal* with forgiveness but should also *provide* comfort and an assurance of forgiveness.

**848** Cf. I.2.3.3 and I.2.3.4, p. 55–72.

**849** Cf. I.3.3.3, p. 135–139.

of situations today. In the process of the reception of a sermon the listeners become, so to speak, contemporary witnesses of the experiences of salvation of which the texts speak.

4. In this, they are of pastoral relevance for their potential for experiences, which are not aimed solely at an *affirmative answer* to salvation or a *certainty* of salvation but support *being able to live by faith*. Without having to instruct, without quoting the Bible and without using the Catechism, the sermon in its pastoral function always has to do with the mediation of the art known as life *as a form of mediation of freedom*.[850] In so doing it supports the listeners in experiencing themselves as subjects of their lives and of a faith which sustains them, and which accompanies the strengthening of their competence to live.

5. A sermon has as pastoral care dimension because of its *dialogical structure*.[851] Through an implicitly or explicitly conducted dialog the background of experiences which found particular questions, positions and expectations arises on the part of the congregation.[852] By forgoing the staging of a dogmatically saturated question-and-answer-game, and, indeed, through the reference to Christian doctrines, the sermon considers questions and experiences which move people, and through all that gives the congregation a part in the communication of the gospel and, in so doing, encourages them for mutual pastoral care.[853]

6. The pastoral accentuation of a sermon requires a careful and repeated approach to the *contemporary reality of life*.[854] This is not only due to the relevance and plausibility of the address. The patient, cliché-free analysis of the homiletic situation is also a sign of a necessary solidarity which neither brings about nor documents a person's basic "acceptance" by God but corresponds analogically through a particular attitude. To the perception of the contemporary reality of life in the interest of the pastoral care dimension of

---

**850** Cf. W. Engemann, 2007a.

**851** Cf. I.4.3.4, p. 197–207.

**852** Cf. in this context the illuminating case studies e.g. by J. S. McClure/R. J. Allen (2004), which clarify the extent to which analyzing concrete experiences and expectations of the listeners or the congregation (right up to conducting interviews in the run-up of the sermon) may contribute to being able to enter into a real dialog and to refer to authentic life circumstances in the sermon without having to resort to trite clichés. For more detail on the procedure adopted cf. esp. 7–20.

**853** Cf. in this context the suggestions of G. L. Ramsey, who, in his programmatic paper "Carefull Preaching", illustrates with many practical examples how this expectation may be met in the sermon (G. L. Ramsey, 2000, esp. 119–200).

**854** Cf. I.6.3.3, p. 290–296.

the sermon belongs a sharpened attentiveness to the continually evolving structural patterns in which people experience lack of freedom, loss of relationship, alienation etc. From generation to generation there are changes in the socio-psychological contexts in which people e.g. experience that they are free or not free, are living in a supportive or burdensome relationship or lead a life worth leading at all.[855]

7.  Further aspects of the pastoral care dimension ensue from the theology of preaching still to be defined:[856] The sermon accomplishes a pastoral task inasmuch as the communication of the gospel does not just take place as teaching but is connected to *healing, reconciliation and deliverance*. A sermon which is aware of its pastoral care function will consequently not aim simply to deliver information but will consider the listening to the sermon as a participatory act: People should not, first and foremost, be informed about salvation history in a sermon but become involved in the continuation of this history in their own lives.

8.  A sermon with a pastoral care dimension is, in a Christological respect, related to "Christ's office as priest", i.e. it is a "spiritual service" for the listener: In a certain way, one could say that the congregation, in ordaining a pastor, commissions him to remind them of their "salvation". Metaphorically speaking, the sermon fulfills *a regular service of religious and spiritual hygiene*.[857] It is an institution through which the congregation ensures that, for the sake of their life and faith, someone regularly inquires of how they fare. Thereby the sermon has to cultivate a language which is not the language of an academic lecture but is one of conversation[858].

Christian Möller answers the question about the pastoral care dimension of the sermon by a semantic segmentation of the biblical concept of *paráklēsis*.[859] According to him, a pastoral sermon should be expected to be a "paracletic address", to which the following three functions are attributed.

---

**855** Cf. W. Engemann, 2006b. Cf. in this context also Dale Andrews' strivings for a consistently solidary sermon and congregational practice (D. Andrews, 2002, 11, 23, 37, 43, 53, 60–67, 89–100).
**856** Cf. I.5.4, p. 250–257.
**857** Here it is not only the question whether humans can believe at all, again, or more strongly, but also the question of *how* they believe, with what perception of self and God they live their lives, what they understand as discipleship etc. On how the sermon is relevant for the image of God prompted in the listeners cf. esp. H. Schaap-Jonker (2008).
**858** Cf. on this I.5.4, p. 250–257.
**859** Ch. Möller, 1983, 72–78.

1. The sermon takes up the cry for help of "those weary and heavy-burdened, the humiliated and insulted" and takes for granted a corresponding willingness to listen on the part of the preacher.[860]
2. Through the *paráklēsis* of a pastoral sermon, "the commandment of what is necessary" is talked about in a similarly soliciting way as the pressing call for pausing and giving way. This rather pleading than demanding *paráklēsis* can both be comforting or warning. It is the same binding Word of God which makes the hardened yield and encourages those in need of consolation.[861]
3. Finally, "the consoled consolation", the assured trust as a – in principle – basic concern of preaching, is equally part of the pastoral sermon. Paracletic language should make clear "that God is the source of all true consolation". One should thus strive to show through the entirety of Scripture that one can depend upon the "God of all consolation" (2 Cor 1).[862]

The attempt to define the core of a poimenic sermon through the biblical concept of *paráklēsis* and to deduce consequences for the desired effects of a sermon from it, has much to be said for it. To take the concept of *paráklēsis* from its authoritative, subordinating and moral sanctioning constriction which it experienced through the pastoral theology of previous centuries has to be particularly acknowledged. Nevertheless, do Möller's comments fail to show any specific impulses for poimenic action. They are – in a similar fashion as the seven theses formulated above under "functions of a pastoral sermon" – more like a poimenic commentary on *homiletic* virtues such as relation to the situation (hearing a cry for help), appropriateness to Scripture (speaking the consolation found in the entirety of Scripture) and guidance (commandment of what is necessary).[863] Therefore, we must ask whether, in the discussion of the pastoral care dimension of the address from the pulpit, the question also must be considered to what extent or how concrete a sermon should be in examining experiences and problems which normally are dealt with particularly in pastoral care.

What Jürgen Ziemer develops as "life themes of pastoral care" may, in a way, also function as a thematic homiletic guideline and sensitize for the hearing of the "cry for help" mentioned by Möller: Should our expectation for a pastoral care oriented sermon not entail that it helps a person "to live in relationships", "know how to handle one's own guilt" or make headway "in the search for meaning"?[864] Like pastoral care, the sermon, too, should be helpful in faith and life.[865] H. Tacke's ideas, which Ch. Möller has adapted for Homiletics[866] may be central for this.

---

860 Cf. loc. cit., 73f. and 78.
861 Cf. loc. cit., 75f. and 78.
862 Cf. loc. cit., 76–78.
863 The three aspects of a paracletic address mentioned by Ch. Möller can also relate to the aforementioned three basic functions of the sermon (cf. I.2.3.3 and Fig. 5, p. 57): "The inviting call" relates the *function of testimony*, the "commandment of what is necessary" to the *paráklēsis*, and the "consolation of Scripture" to the *teaching function* of preaching.
864 On the following behavioral categories cf. J. Ziemer, 2015, 235–300. H. v.d. Geest also pleads *expressis verbis* for "pastoral themes" (H. v.d. Geest, 1991, 34–43).
865 Cf. H. Tacke, 1975.
866 Cf. Ch. Möller, 1983, 74.

Finally, we must ask to what extent the wide-ranging repertoire of the *principles of pastoral care behavior* are, likewise, immediately relevant to a sermon. Again, Jürgen Ziemer's suggested maxims that appear to be important at least for the act of preaching[867]:

1. *Understanding behavior* is the attempt, in preparing the sermon and in preaching, to take up an empathic attitude which distinguishes itself through the ability to empathize in concrete life situations and through the awareness and endurance of strangeness and alienation. The latter leads to the insight that one cannot understand everything and can certainly not solve all problems through preaching.

2. *Accepting behavior* in the sermon is expressed when the preacher regards and respects the listener "as an independent person", "as persons with their own worth" and "own dignity". The listeners are not the "problem". Likewise, they cannot be reduced to the label "poor sinner". They are – just like the preacher – "unique and indispensable people". A poimenic orientated sermon starts a process in which "the participation in the rituals of stigmatization and devaluation – which are more normal today than ever – is strictly refused"[868]. Embracing and accepting behavior dare not be confused with making demands on someone. The listeners dare not be forced into roles which determine the preacher's picture of humanity.[869]

3. *Encouraging behavior* means "to speak" to the listeners "according to their capabilities"[870] and not simply try to "establish a connection" based on their difficulties but also on the areas they are successful in, on what they do well (e.g. love) and in what they can be "witnesses" in the biblical sense of the word. The sermon never has to begin right at the beginning but connects to the listener's already existing resources of faith and their potentials of life. And although or perhaps particularly because these resources do not imply the ability of self-redemption, they should neither be trivialized nor combated but affirmed and developed.

4. *Authentic behavior* in the sermon was outlined above in the categories of the personal sermon to which authenticity and plasticity of one's own statements of faith and "inner concord in feeling, manner and argumentation" belong. Ziemer justifiably causes us to consider that a "one-hundred-percent agreement of what I reveal with what I feel [...] is an ideal scarcely reachable". But even without "exaggerated demands for authenticity" at the back of one's mind, should the preacher attempt "to be as real as possible. [...] Absolute

---

867 Cf. J. Ziemer, 2015, 192–201.
868 Loc. cit., 159. On this cf. also W. Engemann (1996a) on the cliché of "modern man".
869 J. Ziemer, 2015, 197f.
870 Loc. cit., 199.

authenticity, i.e. the truth itself, is, theologically speaking, a good of hope", to which even in the sermon one can "always only be more or less close"[871].

Such categories of behavior are helpful in order to stay mindful of the dimension of pastoral care in the sermon and to implement it with particular attitudes and actions.

### 6.4.3 Preaching in the Face of Need. Diaconal Aspects

#### a) Prerequisites and Problems

In the answer to the famous question John the Baptist asked Jesus – "Are you the one who is to come or are we to wait for another?" – in the end, following indications of ever growing significance, it says: "and the poor have good news brought to them."[872] This means: people who – for whatever reason and in whatever way – belong to the poor, needy and discouraged can always expect something from God. The experience of a fulfilled life is promised to them. Their lives are not lost, not in vain, not pointless. They have a future. The theological point of the talk on poverty, taking into consideration the entirety of the biblical teaching on this topic, is that the addresses in the two testaments are not directed towards the socially weakest in society. In e.g. the Psalms or the Beatitudes, the poverty which is talked about, more often means the experience of, *ultimately, always standing before God with empty hands* and of being reliant on him. "We are beggars, that is true,"[873] so summed up Luther this experience at the end of his rich life.

On the other hand, the experience of real need (physical illness, psychological pain, endured oppression, homelessness, hunger, alienation etc.) are never romanticized in the Jewish-Christian tradition of the Bible or even degraded as a symbolic reminder of a "real" spiritual need. Rather the congregations accepted and accept the challenge: The communication of the gospel to those in need in the history of Christianity is always shown to advantage in a form of concrete support. Anyone who wishes to help in such a way that people who are poor, ill and wretched can participate in life must betake himself to the places or into the situations where their lives are lived, in hospitals, nursing homes, prisons etc. The communication of the gospel takes place "in, with and under" food, clothing,

---

871 Loc. cit., 201.
872 Cf. Matt 11:2–6.
873 Concerning M. Luther's "last word", v. WA TR 5, Nr. 5677, cf. WA 48, 241.

healing, care and opportunities for conversation – sometimes even in the form of a church service and sermon.

A key text for the character of the diaconal dimension of the sermon – one could also speak of a diaconal paradigm – is the story of the healing of the paralyzed man in Mark 2:1–12:

1. Jesus is there. He is preaching, not in the Temple, not in front of the gates of the city on a hillside, but in and into the real conditions of human existence.
2. People come to him, already expecting or convinced that Jesus' teaching as a whole is significant for life, that his sermon does not simply aim for spiritual well-being but have the health of the whole person in mind.
3. At least those who accompany the invalid – perhaps we can even suppose this for the paralyzed man himself – come *as those who believe*. Their problem is not an indifferent attitude towards God but the illness of one person.
4. At the same time, the faith of those present and the high expectation of his companions provide a potential for changing the situation. Jesus takes the initiative when he "sees" their faith: At the end of the story one could also have read "your (plural) faith has helped him", perhaps also "your (singular) faith has helped you".
5. The invalid is addressed in a loving and friendly way about his need and dependence. Jesus addresses him with the word "son".
6. The essential thing is spoken first – also to clear up any misunderstandings: "Your sins are forgiven". In other words: Nothing stands between you and God. As far as God is concerned, there is no outstanding score to settle. Anyone who thinks that your illness is an expression of the fact that God has a problem with you, is mistaken.
7. The conditions of existence have changed, naturally first of all for the invalid: He goes away upright. The others – although they clearly considered that a cure was possible "in principle" when they lowered the paralyzed from the roof – were nevertheless surprised. Their view of God and the world shook. But it does not frighten them. They will come again.

The fact that the *diaconal* dimension – like the political and poimenic – is relevant for virtually every sermon has initially to do with the fact that people and groups which one could describe in some concrete respect as needy or ill naturally come to the normal church service.[874] We encounter only a small number of them in care homes, hospitals or other social establishments. The result of this is that the principle of the Good Samaritan, especially when one considers the time limit that is placed upon what he can do for the good of others, also has a homiletic component. This is particularly significant for sermons which are held in diaconal and social welfare establishments. We shall consider the challenges and consequences connected to this in what follows.

---

**874** Cf. the social welfare accent which A. Bieler and H.-M. Gutmann have marked in their considerations of the "Justification of the 'superfluous'" in the homiletic debate (A. Bieler/H.-M. Gutmann, 2010).

## b) On the Function of a Diaconal Sermon

Church and congregation owe their diaconal task a high measure of *objectivity*. This, however, not in the sense of cognition purified from personal or psychological feeling but, conversely, in the sense of a general knowledge of people as an important requirement for being able to handle human need appropriately. Correspondingly "objectivity" becomes one of the "key concepts of diaconal work and social engagement in the 20th century"[875]. This can be seen, among other things, in that the general language, including sermons, concerning social engagement and diaconal work today no longer use language such as "feeble-minded", "cripple", "idiot" or "alcoholic" but are more objective and have moved towards a somewhat un-dramatic medical manner of speaking.

With the explicitly diaconal view of Homiletics also comes – among other things – a plea for more objectivity in the sermon, which also affects the sermon preparation in that what is said should be close to the life realities of the listeners: diaconal sermons which deal with social engagement often have a similar profile to sermons on Old Testament texts regarding the *relationship to life and environmental values* which were expressly appreciated above.[876]

"In comparison with other sermons in the church" in "sermons coming out of the area of diaconal work [...] some of the following topics or questions are often addressed: living with a physical illness or mental suffering; experiences of handicapped or ill people with their environment and fellow humans; questions about being healed and/or remaining ill and handicapped; helping – and being helped; how to deal with standards such as 'achievement', to be 'weak' or 'strong'; work and wages, [...] problems of individual fringe groups, e.g. of the homeless, those suffering from AIDS, the mentally ill, foreigners, the unemployed, the poor, children; worldwide crises, hunger, war-zones; international partnerships; [...] the bases and the social esteem of diaconal work and social engagement; finance problems, hospital charges and donations; [...] borderline experiences in the professional social work [...] – all these represent topics which arise from the reality of life, from where people live and suffer, where society's structures and conditions determine the life of the individual. They arise from the direct experience of everyday life, from the confrontation with reality."[877]

Perhaps one will not always be able to communicate all these topics as directly relevant to life. Sermons that thematise the history or the self-understanding of diaconal communities must appear impertinent to people who have to live with illness or handicaps. Nevertheless, in the drafting of this spectrum of topics and

---

875 Cf. H. Wagner, 1978, 269–274.
876 Cf. I.3.4.3, p. 145–152.
877 From the preface by J. Gohde in: idem, 2004, 13.

the corresponding sermons[878] it becomes clear how strongly – and that is one of their strengths – they presume the faith of those present, connect to it, believe the listeners are capable and do not afflict them in their suffering.

One must "skip" the reciting of lists of well-known problems as well as the illustration of tiresome catalogs of afflictions – not only in the case of a diaconal sermon, but especially there. *The need is there. People bring it with them. But they also bring their faith.* The sermon takes both into account. This is, in a graded way, also true for the Sunday sermon in front of the regular congregation. Consequently, with the aid of the diaconal sermon, it is worth studying what it means to respect people's real need homiletically as a *facet of the basic human situation.*[879] In this way, the diaconal sermon focused on social engagement may broach the topic of human need – often enough suffered in seclusion, far from cameras and microphone – and bring it into view as through a magnifying glass. That is more than merely signaling the need for healing or helping interventions. The sermon itself should be understood as such an intervention.

A diaconal sermon is able to show in exemplary fashion that people – although they are to be taken seriously and called on in their need – cannot be *reduced to deficits.* It is, of course, important in the preparation of the sermon to be aware of the need for help as well as pain and various hardships, know these in detail and be able to judge their implications for the human sense of life. But that is something fundamentally different to freezing people in this reality from the pulpit or even reproaching them for a false way of dealing with this reality.

"The human need for help is not an abnormality which would give us the right to complain and cut ourselves off from God and other people. It is a part of our lives, of every single one of us. Need for help is the completion of our lives. All schoolteachers and those employed in a deaconry work know how much they can learn from those they meet. All caretakers know how much help they themselves receive from their visits and discussions. Pastors know how much encounters in the congregation help them to understand the limits of life which they frequently meet. In the first year that I was here in this congregation, I was called to a dying woman in a retirement home. I then visited her every day for a week, right up to the end. She was not afraid. She simply wanted someone beside her. In those days, I learned a great deal about life and death from this woman whom I was meant to help. Who had helped whom? Deaconry is a chance for our lives. [...] In the end we only learn how much we need God."[880]

---

878 Cf. already M. Fischer, 1957.
879 On the liturgical level this implies a particularly conscious dovetailing of the sermon with the whole of the service which should be understood and experienced as a service of God towards humans. The worship service offers, particularly in celebrations of communion as well as the blessing and commissioning, numerous elements which can take up the social care dimension of the diaconal sermon and reinforce it.
880 U. Blank, 2004, 49.

A diaconal sermon insists upon the *indivisibility and complexity of life*. Human existence cannot be divided into "merely spiritually relevant" and "merely relevant for day to day" questions. Nor can a person's life be classified by means of a healthy – ill scale as worth living or not. Living with illness, affliction and the weaknesses of age is life in the fully valid sense. To communicate this homiletically and to make life itself plausible as a wonderful gift is still a great challenge – even decades after the euthanasia ideology established long before the era of National Socialism.

The concentration on concrete, necessary questions of life, the interest in an informed analysis of painful situations and the endeavors to see the whole of life, bestow a distinctly *critical* characteristic upon the diaconal sermon.[881] The criticism of diaconal sermons is directed – analog to the prophetic dimension of the sermon – at defects both in society and in the church, and consequently relates to the practice and principles of diaconal establishments.

"Particularly because diaconal work is so strongly determined by commitment and really involves heart and soul, it must be taught ever and again to look at itself self-critically. [...] Diaconal, social action must always go through the filter of reflection. [...] This means that the *interpretation* of diaconal processes must be demanded. Above all, this includes the question of the *proprium:* What makes deaconry a concern of Jesus Christ? [...] Efforts to rush to help people are being made everywhere. The motives behind these efforts of neighborly help vary considerably. The diaconal work of the church is no longer alone in this; it has gained a beneficial 'competition'. It must prove its character all the more forcefully and win its profile"[882] – which is naturally also true for the diaconal sermon.

Last but not least does every diaconically conscious sermon mark the *mutuality of human life* and how a person's freedom is related to the presence of others. They have a part in making their freedom possible by supporting individuals in body, soul and spirit and help them to look after themselves in the particular way which is possible for them. At the same time these other people contribute to the frame of reference of areas of life and relationship within which the individual leads his life. Seen in this way, both the implicit and also – e.g. a sermon catered to the context and requirements of the employees of a nursing-home – the explicit diaconal character of a sermon contributes to leading the congregation anew to their roots.

---

**881** All the sermons edited in the volume by J. Gohde (2004) show this critical characteristic. Cf. in this context also the study by Ch. L. Campbell and S. P. Saunders ([2002] 2006), which aims for articulating the relevance of the gospel from the perspective of earnest social issues (e.g. homelessness).

**882** H. Wagner, 1978, 272, original emphasis.

### 6.4.4 Preaching in the Face of Life's Vicissitudes. Aspects of Rites of Passages

#### a) On the Debate about the Function of "Occasional" Sermons

There are two particular reasons why the question about "occasional" sermons (Kasualpredigten), that is, sermons on and for special occasions, is inserted here, in the closing arguments on the discussion and examination of the situation as a homiletic category: For one thing, looked at historically, the deepening of aspects of Homiletics relevant to the situation in the 19th century appeared with a renewed understanding of the traditional "official duties". The world in which the individual and family lived was conceived more and more as a necessary frame of reference for Practical Theology. On the other, the homiletic struggle described in the previous chapters for a proper approach to the world we live in was once again brought to a point through an explicit reference to occasional services in the context of rites of passages (Kasualien). For the starting-point of occasional services or sermons is "not an official task resulting from an ecclesiastical order or an interpretation of doctrine but the personal situation of individuals. People here are searching to be accompanied and cared for by their church and pastors. In concrete terms, it is a matter of going through transition periods in life in which people leave behind something to which they are accustomed to and must face to new challenges"[883].

Consequently, we must emphasize that everything which has been said in this chapter in the context of occasional services – those ecclesiastical ceremonies for new phases or changes in life (burials, marriages, baptisms etc. held outside the normal service) – is still valid. The fact that sermons in the context of such services are *explicitly tailored to concrete personal or family events and processes*, makes it necessary to supplement the preceding discussion in a few aspects.

To these supplements belong the implicit aspects connected with any sermon and in the Homiletics of such services often explicated as "kerygmatic", "missionary" and "ritual". In the discussion on these connected aspects, the unproductive alternative of "kerygma or ..." is often brought into play: in this case the apparent alternatives read "kerygma or ritual". Here *both* the kerygmatic or missionary *as well as* the ritual dimension of such services are shortened and distorted.

In what follows some of the positions, which have played a part and continue to have an effect in the debate of such services, will be outlined. On the basis of these observations there then result some theses for the Homiletics of such occasional services:

---

883 Ch. Grethlein, 2007, 17.

–   With regard to such services Rudolf Bohren constructs the alternative of "Word of the gospel" and "action". In doing so, he assumes that in the performance of these services the people who attend are "usually" primarily concerned with the ritual and not with the proclamation. While for the pastor it is a matter of "the orientation on the gospel", those present simply follow a sermon because what the minister says is part of the action. Here, according to Bohren, "Christ becomes Baal", "the god who blesses creaturely life"[884]. In his ironic reckoning with the practice of such occasional services in the church he sums up: "Anyone who lets himself be served by religious acts is correct; for he grows up in a Christian way, marries as a Christian and finally lies in the grave as a Christian. The ritual makes the Christian. [...] The mechanics of officiate religious acts and ceremonies continue to produce Christians who live without Christ."[885] In saying so, Bohren certainly does not wish to plead for a more resolute missionary effort in occasional services but is demanding a stronger focus on the Word of God, the same as is usual for believers. "Occasional services [...] demand the participation and contribution of Christ's congregation.[886]

–   In this respect Bohren takes up a middle position: on the one hand, he turns against such missionary expectations as we still meet in *Friedrich Niebergall* and in the practice of official services today: "What an opportunity to bring the gospel unobtrusively to a person, to at least communicate once what gospel is and how valuable it is for life."[887] On the other hand, he turns against an over-estimation of the ritual elements of occasional services. Manfred Josuttis extended this criticism of the ritual elements further and emphasized "the rivalry between ritual and kerygma" in his own way: "The ritual makes the kerygma superfluous. It achieves what the kerygma promises to achieve, it gives comfort as well as hope and the courage to face life to those who mourn, [...] because comfort, hope and the courage to face life simply arise from the performance of the religious act, uninfluenced by the character of the divine and political power in whose name the act is performed. [...] Since the ritual in and of itself communicates salvation[888], the gospel which asserts that the God Jesus is the only salvation of the world, is dissociated from the ritual, even critical of the ritual."[889]

–   Still thinking in a bipolar way and still holding the "double role" of leader of ritual and preacher in a theological tension, Walter Neidhart endeavored to achieve a mediation of these roles. One must be aware of them and accept the challenge to cross "the borders of the ritual", to meet the relatives during the ritual "as humans" and in the proclamation "as witnesses": "What he [the preacher] has to say to their situation *contentwise* must be grounded in faith and its subject and cannot be derived from the human situation. But only when the bereaved feel understood by the minister do they notice that he turns to them as a person and that he is not simply an official of the ceremonial."[890]

---

**884** R. Bohren, 1968, 18f.
**885** Loc. cit., 25.
**886** Loc. cit., 12.
**887** F. Niebergall, 1917, 23.
**888** M. Josuttis writes this from a social-psychological perspective on the ritual in which the "present sense of current salvation" is considered one of the basic elements of all rituals. Cf. E. II. Erikson, 1966, 338.
**889** M. Josuttis, 1974, 196f.
**890** W. Neidhart, 1968, 233.

From all the observations, theses and consequences developed in this book it follows that the homiletical considerations of occasional services must follow the same principles as those of the "regular sermon". These include (1.) the respect for the specific conditions of preaching as communication, which is based on the character of public speech, (2.) the readiness to appear as a person, a solidary counterpart (3.) the endeavor to "connect to and address" both Christianity's traditions of faith as well as (4.) to the situation of life and faith of one's contemporaries and (5.) a basic attitude of dialogical communication which, in particular, cannot dispense with argumentation as well as (6.) the demand of a linguistic cooperation with those present.[891]

When considering occasional services, all these points must fundamentally be specified. However, within this introduction I restrict myself to individual categories and aspects which should be of particular importance for the understanding of the character and function of such a sermon.

### b) Non-Verbal Aspects in the Communication of the Gospel

Reducing the communication of the gospel to the spoken parts in the context of rites of passages creates an artificial tension between message and ritual and is uncalled-for as it disregards the "bigger picture" and the processual character of the service as a whole. At this point, there is no need to go anew into the discussion about the concepts of proclamation and communication or – beginning with the appearance, words and deeds of Jesus up to the witnesses of faith in the 20th and 21st century – to carry out an analysis of the means and methods which "in, with and under" people can be embroiled in a communication system which, in a salutary way, is "destroying", "saving" or "confronting".

At any rate, it is not merely words that can carry meaning but also actions, gestures, expressions and touch. "The gospel" is not a substratum one may, with a few words, pour into an otherwise "unevangelical" ceremony as the necessity arises, which otherwise may "only" stir up emotions or channel them. The dimensions of freedom and love which determine the communication of the gospel are connected in the highest degree to emotions which are seen most clearly particularly in occasional services through the ensemble of language and speech, manner and action, gestures and facial expressions and equally achieve emotional, cognitive and pragmatic significance. The fact that they may also stir up emotions should not be ignored because it is allegedly not a kerygmatic effect. On the contrary – because of the importance of emotions for the experiencing of freedom and love, they are one of the central matters of the homiletic concerns over occasional services.

---

891 These points do not represent a hierarchy but reflect the individual chapters in this book.

### c) The Occasional Sermon as a Sequence within the Context of Rites of Passages

The occasional sermon is, on the one hand, itself part of the ritual, on the other hand, it is in this ritual the one element which – naturally within the scope of the rules of the ritual – may be structured freely. This means that the *total ritual* of a baptism, wedding, burial etc. legitimately takes over functions which belong to the occasional address: In a situation which is emotionally highly-charged and strained because of a birth, marital vows or a death, and for which the everyday repertoire of expressions and language seems to appear insufficient, the ritual is decisively helpful.

To mention only a few of its functions: It *relieves* one, in view of what has happened or might happen, from having to invent a ceremony corresponding to the nascent hopes and fears. The ritual *articulates* exuberant expectations and oppressive anxieties. It is able to *channel* them and to provide them with space and time. Moreover, the ritual elements of such a service have a *confirming* function: They accompany, mark and guard transitions in human life. They subdue the fear of transience and frailty and offer support.[892]

However, since the address in the occasional service is bound into the ritual it follows that, depending on the situation, it may only fulfil its function if it – somewhat safeguarded, protected and authorized through a ritual framework which "holds" it – does *not* exhaust itself in pre-fabricated patterns of speech but "risks something". The occasional sermon must make use of the provided and certainly expected leeway and room for interpretation, so that it may relate in a *non-ritualistic language* to the possibilities and limits of living by faith.

### d) Relating to the Addressees in the Occasional Services

The dispute over the unique identity of the addressees in occasional services already rings in the positions outlined above. They are highly problematical because basically they all start from the dubious premise that one could (and must) differentiate between "those who believe wholly" – i.e. real members of the congregation – and those who only have little faith (or almost none at all or only "from tradition").

Generally, quite different, even contrary interests are attributed to the "active members of the congregation" on the one hand and to "those on the fringes" on the other. While – in relation to baptism – the first wish above all to entrust their child to God, for the others it is simply a matter of a splendid celebration, which naturally entails the general public to some extent.

---

892 Cf. W. Jetter, 1986. In his article, strongly oriented on sociological requirements and consequences of occasional services, Lutz Friedrichs defines their quasi-function as a kind of "ritual exile", necessary for survival in which biographies are "lifted out of the river of time and [...][are] celebrated with the idea that life is more than the sum of biographical facts" (L. Friedrichs, 2008, 50, 53).

The expectations of the families are considerably subtler and, also in a religious sense, more widely-stretched than such short-sighted diagnoses assume. Wilhelm Gräb lists a whole range of theologically relevant reasons why those affected may desire an occasional service. He refers especially to the legitimate need for the "justification of life stories" which is definitely suitable in the church and in the public sphere of a congregation. Even those who are more likely to remain distant from the Sunday congregation, who do not combine their membership of the church with a pattern of active participation, know "that the church has reasons for recognizing the individual life" which may be deepened and unfolded in the ritual as the necessity arises.[893]

The idea that one could differentiate between believers and non-believers in an occasional service, grounds on the desire to distinguish occasional services as a missionary opportunity because there – perforce – the non-believers are present in larger numbers, directly at the borders of the congregation, so to speak. The separation of the potential addressees into Christians and heathens, which is thought to be possible, likewise underpins the demand to dispense with the idea of mission and to act as if (only) believers in Christ were there. (The others allegedly only attend because of the ritual.) Here the occasional service is moved away from the "junction-point between church and world"[894] and tailored to those who take an active part in church life.

These and other attempts to determine addressees explicitly or implicitly presuppose a clear borderline between believers and non-believers or between congregation and world: Niebergall recommends that one must use the opportunity of so many non-believers standing so close by the borderline and hope to win at least a few of them for the congregation. Bohren also sees this border but declares it to be irrelevant for the Homiletics of occasional services. Michael Nüchtern undertakes a more complex attempt in which he discusses the possibilities and limits of occasional services using the model of a "church on occasion".

Indeed, even Nüchtern assumes a "tension between the interest of growing a congregation and the attendance of occasional services out of tradition". However, he sees a specific opportunity in the selective encounters of the church with those who do not partake in church life on a regular basis. This opportunity lies beyond the alternatives of extending the radius of the core-congregation and incorporating those on the fringes or contenting oneself in missionary resignation with ritual transfer performances. In terms of occasional services, "church on occasion" means that their significance goes beyond making contact through "occasions" which may lead to the integration of those on the fringes to the congregation: *isolated, occasional encounters with the church are already useful in that people are supported in their efforts to find guidance and to act responsibly in the face of transitory seasons in life.* "This concept incorporates the calling of the

---

**893** W. Gräb, 1987, 32f.
**894** R. Bohren, 1968, 12.

church and the expectation of people in that they are taken further and led to think and hope. In this concept, the church also sees what people expect from it, the concrete relevance of its message, its images and symbols. Such a relationship of reciprocal development is the contentual requirement of 'church on occasion'."[895] In this sense, occasional services are opportunities both for the church as also for those who are – from the congregation's perspective – "believers on the fringes".

In the debate about the putative dilemma as to whether one should do justice to the "regular congregation" or to the "distanced" in an occasional service one constantly comes implicitly up against the assumption that the faith of full members of the congregation (including their religious expectations and ideas of the world as well as their "theological thinking" about concepts such as resurrection, eternal life, mercy, judgement etc.) can be *categorically* distinguished from the faith of non-members – or cannot be found at all with regard to the latter. This is neither empirically nor theologically conclusive. Experience shows that strong and weak faith, much and little faith cannot be divided equally between members of the core-congregation and those on the fringes. This analogically holds true for the question of individual contents of belief.[896] Theologically, too, it leads to aporias if one does not consider occasional churchgoers as members of a "latent spiritual community"[897] and thus treats them as those who attend or make use of occasional services for "improper" i.e. "actually false" reasons.

A far more significant role than the supposedly truer and greater faith of a member of the parish council as opposed to the allegedly confused faith of those who attend irregularly holds the fact *that in both cases we have people in quite specific situations* for whom particular questions in the experiencing, managing and leading of their own lives are important. When faced with the death or birth of a child or committing oneself to a partner etc. all face similar challenges. It is

---

**895** M. Nüchtern, 1991, 42. At a later point he sums up: "'Church on occasion' arises when the church allows herself to be challenged by the world we live in and introduces the Christian faith as an orientation and assurance in concrete life situations. Orientation means rather a rational action related to deeds and change whereas assurance is something which is emotional and stabilizing" (loc. cit., 109).

**896** Cf. on this the investigation *Was die Menschen wirklich glauben* (*What People Really Believe*) by K.-P. Jörns and C. Großeholz (1998).

**897** Cf. on this the classical position on the "manifest and latent church" in Paul Tillich (1967 esp. III.152–154, 181f., 220) on "implicit" or "anonymous Christianity" in Karl Rahner (1967, esp. 187, 190) and Edward Schillebeeckx' argumentation: Every person is created "for Christ" and in this respect lives from grace. In this sense, all of humanity has a latent "religiosity" which is independent from the relation to grace and the manifest church of the individual, which is why "the borders between church and humanity [...] are blurred" (E. Schillebeeckx, 1964, 37, 39).

a matter, for example, of situations in which people "are moved by the reality of mortality and expect answers when they ask"[898]. In occasional services and sermons ministers are particularly confronted with these basic questions of life and central anthropological themes which cannot be coped with simply or especially with a "kerygmatic awareness". A further aspect of the Homiletics of these occasional services arises from this:

### e) The Particular Reference to the Subject Matter in the Occasional Sermon
Anyone who begins to speak in the face of birth or death, lived life, crack in the future or partnership should have a theologically reflected standpoint in relation to the questions connected to this:

What does it mean that a person dies? How do I assess death theologically? What do I think about "the Last Judgement"? What does it mean to baptize a person – apart from the fact that he thereby becomes an official member of the church? What attitude do I have to the debate about the future of the children and the world? What concept, what ideal picture of partnership do I have when I prepare a marriage ceremony with a couple? What significance do I attribute to a person's happiness in my theory of the occasional services? What goes with living a life in freedom and with binding oneself – in freedom – to certain causes and on people?

Naturally, all these questions are a matter of a life by faith, however: to live life demands an "ability", a mastery of the art of living, in which Christians face the same challenges as non-Christians. Precisely in view of the "incidents" of life which usually prompt occasional services, one must remember that Jesus does not simply circulate the news of salvation and play God's messenger, but that he communicates the gospel as a *message of life* which he chiefly teaches. He appears with a teaching on how to live, which one does not simply have to believe but which one may also learn. This is extremely relevant, particularly in occasional sermons in which the borders between the core-congregation and fringe groups completely melt away. This also includes a general awareness of grave changes in view of the temporal connection of the demands of rites of passage and the ever more processual, scarcely any longer selective, "transitions" in biographies and family histories.[899]

### f) On the Question of "Mission"
Just as the sermon process does not exhaust itself in accommodating "the gospel" in one address from the pulpit but aims for individual believers living by faith in a self-determined manner, which entails a process of appropriation on the part

---

898 H.-J. Thilo, 1986, 224.
899 On this cf. Ch. Grethlein, 2007, 33–36, 74–87.

of the listener, so the idea of mission cannot be reduced to a commissioning and sending of believers to proclaim [the gospel] to half-or non-believers. Not only in the context of occasional services, but especially there it is vital to work with a concept of mission where the vanishing-point lies not in potential objects of mission but in the arrival of the individual in his own life. In the communication of the gospel, people are not casually "called to faith" simply because God or the church desires the message to be believed and that new believers would be won, but people are called *to believe for the sake of their lives* – or as believers into life. They are sent in their own age as a time of salvation (*missio*) and are in this sense themselves on their way as missionaries. They are encouraged to devote their life in serenity and curiosity and find their way – from faith, in faith. The communication of the gospel does not look for faith as an end in itself but as the specific Christian experience of being "called into life".

### g) On the Dual Function of the Biographical Elements in Occasional Sermons

To locate an occasional sermon in the appropriate context and situation is possible particularly because of its biographical elements. A baptism, wedding or funeral service[900] is a ceremony which takes places because of a significant occasion in a person's life history and marks a "transition" that is experienced in most cases. For relatives and the congregation this transition becomes the basis of which questions, problems and hopes are visualized which also stand on the agenda in other contexts of their life.

Consequently, with biographical elements within an occasional sermon it is not a matter of stylizing a journey through life as a "model" – as if the deceased or those wishing to be married have done or achieved something *fundamentally better* than everyone else. Much rather, it is a matter of an example of what it means to live by faith under the given circumstances (and in the case of an actual person) which are full of risks. By incorporating actual and authentic life situations and biographies which are true-to-life and, as such, relatable for those listening, the *plausibility* of the communication of the gospel is at stake to a high degree in occasional services.

Certainly, ritually celebrated transitions are not merely a welcome example for the congregation. It is first and foremost the actual reality of a real person's life – a life in which something is at stake and where those concerned want to consider the chances and visualize the risks before they face them. They become involved and take steps with the faith they have – without being able to be

---

900 On the canon of classical and newly-established occasional services on transitions in life cf. Ch. Grethlein, 2007, 323–328.

completely aware of what is coming or whether and how they will change as a result of what is now happening. To respect this in the form and content of an address is no gushing conforming to ritual but the central point of contact of the sermon.[901] To communicate in the preliminary discussion with those affected as well as in the sermon what it could mean in the given circumstances to expose oneself anew, in the serenity and curiosity of faith, to the gift of life is part of the "missionary opportunities" in the sense mentioned above.

### h) The Occasional Sermon's Reference to the Text

Even in a regular sermon one should not just try to "handle" a text or to view particularly perplexing passages as a welcome challenge to derive from them the exact message needed for a particular day, texts for occasional services are usually selected beforehand and befitting the occasion. As long as the people who are preparing for such a service do not themselves express the wish for a particular text, the minister must make suitable suggestions. As a rule, it is a matter of short biblical texts in the sense of key sentences which can have the character of sayings and mottos. Chosen wisely, they may suddenly appear in a new perspective which is important for the story of a person's life or for the situation of a couple, and which take those involved seriously and includes a prospect for the future.

The conversations held in the run-up to a baptism, wedding ceremony or burial offer a wealth of clues for this. Whether the texts come from family tradition (e.g. the intentional re-use of the parents' wedding-text) or are chosen by the minister, in both cases one should say, in relation to this word, what *essentially* should be said in this particular transition and in this particular life. It does not signify indifference to the actual statement of a text (mostly of a single verse) if the address goes beyond the usually very limited statement and devotes due attention to the potential of the situation for questions. Accordingly, texts for baptisms, wedding ceremonies or burials usually *bear much greater symbolic importance* – and not only through the minister – than in regular sermons: on the part of the listeners they are connected with expectations, charged with strong emotions and endowed with specific meanings which those texts possibly never had before.

Frequently there is a complaint about the exegetically unlucky choice of biblical texts which – particularly in occasional services – amounts to an unfamiliar use of the Jewish-Christian tradition. An alienating use, but still not yet

---

**901** Cf. the homiletic dimension of biographies within occasional services (along with the dimensions "congregation" and "theology") in the work by Ch. Stebler, 2006, 81–116.

inadequate, is admittedly repeated in *every* sermon.[902] *None* of the biblical texts were written so that a minister should speak to his contemporaries on them on a particular Sunday in the church year. Looking at transitions celebrated by a family the *analogy of relationships*[903] receives a special significance, i.e. the comparability with the constellations of relationships described in the old texts (between people, a person and God) with those in the current situation of those affected. Through this it is possible, e.g. in a marriage ceremony, to work with a text which gives an account of a verbal exchange between mother and daughter-in-law (Ruth 1:16–17) or stems from the everyday practice of a commercial travel-ler (Eccl 4:9–12).

### i) On the Question of the Point of Contact and Symbolization

The point of contact of the occasional sermon arises from the conversations held in the run-up to the ceremony. It is one of the unique opportunities of such a sermon that it can be *precise* in this respect and, in relation to those directly affected (who already appeared in the "preliminary talk"), mean the continua-tion of a real dialog. The frequently-quoted "connecting" to a particular situation or context is part of the concept and has already taken place. Those affected are present in and with their situation. The challenge lies in not making the rest of the family or the congregational members present spectators of an intimate scene but, relating to the actual life or lives of one or two people who are about to make a "transition", address them with the basic questions of their own lives.

Here one must pay attention to the possibilities of the "symbolization" men-tioned above. This is provoked, deepened and driven forward by the symbolic actions connected with occasional services themselves, which is why it is rea-sonable to refer explicitly to it here. These endeavors contribute to making the "analog" speech more precise, i.e. to its translation into "digital" language.[904] In this process the symbolism of the ritual should naturally not be flogged to death, however, it should be clear to everyone present what ministers are actually doing when they pour water on the head of the child being baptized, when they begin to cast earth on the coffin, when they process into and out of the church with a bridal couple, hand rings over to them during the celebration and bless them. In the sermon, one should stress the main points which set the course for the understanding of what happens in the ritual action of particular symbols. It makes a great difference whether, in the case of a baptism, merely questions of possession or membership are made clear (which, inter alia, *also* have their

---

902 On hermeneutics cf. I.3.3 and I.3.4, p. 120–152.
903 Cf. I.3.3.2, p. 130–135.
904 Cf. K.-H. Bieritz, 2004, 248–251.

own right) or whether the deeply existential significance of the baptismal ritual is seen: "Baptism is not a 'symbol' but an action: the one to be baptized descends into death; here there remains nothing but dying. And the one being baptized is 'raised out of the baptismal' and leaves the grave behind him."[905] Being baptized as a life looking back at one's death is a suitable motif for a baptismal sermon, not only for the child and his parents.

Because of the existential nature of the questions as well as the highly emotional, in part intimate, components of occasional services the preacher as subject or person is faced with a special challenge. The unavoidable confrontation with threshold situations which are concerned with death and love, fear and suffering, past and future, freedom, responsibility and life-altering decisions, may confront the preacher with themes and questions of life which he would rather avoid, and which may provoke subconscious attitudes of defense or trigger off transferrals. The fact that the attitude of ministers in occasional services often leads to confusions, sometimes even to people leaving the church is not simply a matter of false or too high expectations of officials but has to do with lack of "personal competence". What is discussed homiletically regarding the self-perception of the preacher is consequently particularly important in the context of the occasional service.[906]

An "Introduction to Homiletics" cannot inspect the whole spectrum of causes, situations and contexts. To do so it would not only be necessary to think about the sermon in the context of specific institutions (schools, hospitals, prisons, military establishments, police stations etc.) but also about preaching in worship-services with particular age-groups or in particular milieus. Initial research on these questions is at hand.[907] Thus, instead, in the following the spectrum of perspectives of reflection equally relevant for every sermon will be extended with the question of the liturgical dimension of the sermon.

---

**905** M. Mezger, 1963, 161.

**906** Cf. I.2. In this respect the remarks of H.-J. Thilo (1996, esp. 40–106) are particularly worth reading.

**907** Cf. e.g. on the sermon for teenagers M. Meyer-Blanck (2008) and M. Meyer-Blanck/U. Roth/J. Seip (2008); on the sermon for elderly people H. Schwier (2009) and considerations for milieu-respective services and sermons see E. Hauschildt/E. Kohler/C. Schulz (2010, esp. 49–85, 132–144).

# 7 Preaching in the Worship Service. On the Question of the Liturgical References of the Sermon

The function of the sermon for the inner *coherence* of the worship service and the *correlation* between sermon and liturgy has come more under consideration in Practical Theology in the last twenty years.[908] Earlier impulses were mainly focused on the "event of proclamation within the worship service" and thus primarily considered basic homiletic questions.[909] In what follows I shall consider the liturgical requirements of the sermon *in the narrower sense*. These arise, among other things, from the relationship of the Eucharist and the sermon (7.2.1), from varying situations of communication which determine the presentation and performance of liturgical texts on the one hand and free speech on the other (7.2.2) and from the fundamental tension between ritual and rhetorical communication and the change of roles connected to this within the worship (7.2.3).

First, however, the consideration of some empirical problems shall once again show clearly where the (inevitably) tense relationship between sermon and liturgy can be distorted.

## 7.1 Snapshots. Empirical Indicators of Problems

### 7.1.1 Mixing Ritual and Rhetorical Communication

The difficulties which arise from confounding primarily ritual and primarily rhetorical communication can often be seen – to name just one example – already at the beginning of the service. According to a centuries-old ritual a change in perspective is envisaged at this point of the service. For this purpose, the "liturgical agenda" falls back, among other things, on a short, significant and familiar dialog[910] with the intention of setting a collective beginning. All too often,

---

908 Cf. inter alios M. Meyer-Blanck (1997, 2006, esp.158–161); K.-H. Bieritz (2004, esp. 242–273); S. A. Brown (2005); W. Ratzmann (2006); K.-H. Bieritz (2009); K.-P. Hertzsch (2009); A. Deeg/E. Garhammer/B. Kranemann (2014); K. Raschzok (2014).

909 In order to broaden the scope of the sermon's reference to the liturgy for example speech-act theoretical questions (K.-F. Daiber, 1991a, 230f.), rhetorical observations (Ch. Dinkel, 2000, 243f.) and the "relationship between preacher and congregation" (T. Müller, 1993, 80) were considered.

910 [Pastor:] In the name of the Father and of the Son and of the Holy Spirit. [Congregation:] Amen. [Pastor:] Our help is in the name of the Lord, [Congregation:] who made heaven and earth.

https://doi.org/10.1515/9783110440256-007

however, attention is drawn, in an obsequiously friendly, chatty tone, to the lovely weather, the events of the previous and coming week as well as to all kinds of other things. Here the congregation is sometimes treated like a group of tourists who meet briefly in a church to gather information so as to be able to tick off one point among many in their program – but not to suddenly themselves become the topic, which is inevitable in successful worship services without the individual being put under pressure by this. The rather chatty, often quite entertaining tarrying in non-committal pleasantries is frequently followed by the "preparatory prayer" before the Kyrie, where the talk is e.g. that we occasionally make a mistake, are not always loving and kind to everyone etc. This has little to do with approaching the person who I am – who sometimes is completely different to what I expect, also different to what narcissistic ideals might lead me to believe.

In certain circumstances, ritual communication can do more. Provided it is used properly and on the basis of the speech patterns passed down, which are familiar through frequent usage, it may articulate something which is more difficult to grasp in everyday language, such as, for example, understanding, remorse and joy. Brief, succinct liturgical forms which put into words these facets of human experience (and which to a large extent form the structures of the initial liturgy of a worship service) contribute to the articulation and channeling of these impressions and expectations. To desire to attain this "effect" Sunday after Sunday, as it were, in free speech at the beginning of a service – without the language of the Psalms, without liturgical dialog, without Kyrie and Gloria in the form of a paean etc. – would be a difficult undertaking and, in the long term, a (too) high demand on the originality of the pastor.

On the other hand, it may also occur that the linguistic character of a sermon can hardly be differentiated from that of the liturgy. This is always the case when the terminology of the old liturgical passages which one moment are in the praising, the next in the lamenting tone of a Psalm or the monotony of a meditative, praising Kyrie-litany become dominant features of the sermon language. The sermon then raises the impression that it airs eternal truths and has nothing to add to what has always been believed and known in one way or another. This impression accompanies a high loss of relevance of the sermon.

For the sermon, however, (cf. I.5) above all the rhetorical rules of free speech, to which the whole spectrum of speech acts belongs, are relevant. While, for example, explanation, discussion and argumentation fade into the background in the language of the liturgy, the sermon does not get by without such linguistic tools. And while a sermon dominated by assertions and appeals may impend its comprehension, does the use of assertive and appealing ways of speaking occupy a comparatively extensive space in liturgical language (as, for example, in the Creed or in prayers or hymns).

## 7.1.2 Preaching in an Inappropriate "Liturgical Place"

A significant factor for the lost balance between free speech and that used in rituals during the worship service is inter alia a kind of "continuation" of the sermon in the prayer of intercession and other parts of the liturgy.

A pastor begins the intercessory prayer thus: "Lord, our God, we have heard in the sermon how much you care for us and that you do not leave us to ourselves but accompany us through the heights and depths of our lives. Our indifference to your love bears no relation to your favor. Therefore, we beseech you, open our eyes for the riches which we receive through your presence."[911] The first sentence summarizes the sermon for the umpteenth time in the service, the second begins with a confession of guilt. Only with the third does what is said become a prayer – even if it appears in the rhetoric of erudition and is formulated more as a worthy expectation directed to oneself than as an urgent cry for help from God.

Such declarations running through the service frequently extend to the adaptation of the (Aaronic) Blessing:

A preacher closes the service as follows: "The Lord bless you and keep you. – *May he be with you in all that you do.* May the Lord make his face to shine upon you, and be gracious to you. – *His eyes follow you. In God, you can take leaps of faith.* The Lord lift up his countenance upon you, and give you peace. – *As we heard in the sermon, he does not let you out of his sight and consequently you may go with composure into the new week.*"[912] No matter how correct they are theologically and well-meant pastorally, such comments may be: What they are intended to clarify has already been articulated frequently in this service. What was still missing was a ritually appropriate speech act, namely a blessing – concentrated on what is essential in the form intended for it. But precisely this is more or less missing or is unsuccessful on the level of communication. The former Practical Theologian in Kiel, Joachim Scharfenberg, reports how he was once, after a service, visited in the vestry by a lady who, according to her own words, had not been in the church for many years and consequently felt out of place during the service. "But then, right at the end, she saw me standing at the altar with raised hands, and I then said something which struck her like a lightning bolt and all at once a deep sense of peace came upon her – the feeling that nothing could happen to her. It was a feeling she had not experienced since she was a child and she would like me to write down what I said then. It was something about a 'shining face' and 'peace' – and she had to think of the Archangel Michael."[913] The use of an archaic formula of blessing rooted in the ritual of the worship service (Num 6:22–27) was able to rouse such an experience in this woman.

Sometimes one comes upon a well-meant attempt of connection between the elements of the initial liturgy and the ideas which shall later be elaborated on in the sermon. Of course, every service should have its own individual character and a

---

**911** Introduction to the Prayer of Intercession in a worship service on Sunday *Estomihi* 2014.
**912** From a service on Sunday *Misericordias Domini* 2016.
**913** J. Scharfenberg 1985, 61.

"golden thread" which, in some way, should already be incorporated in the opening welcome – following, if practiced, the liturgical greeting.[914] In any case, through the leitmotif articulated in the liturgical sections of the "proper"[915] every service receives a thematic accent of its own; a semantic field which at the same time structures the individual Sunday. If then the various elements of the "ordinary"[916] are furnished with references to the culminating leitmotif of the sermon for that Sunday, it leads to a blurring and obstruction of the individual function of these liturgical elements.

Thus, for example, the *Kyrie Acclamation* is the liturgical form of an "urgent contact". To be sure: the contact with God is not first "established" at this moment. It already existed before the service had begun. Nevertheless, here it is brought to expression by the means of speech, the way of speaking ("shocked" or "calling in despair") perhaps also with gestures (raised hands) and other signs, that one has good grounds for praying for God's mercy. It thus seems fitting that the classical Kyrie-litany is often connected with the declaration of problems, needs and defects which can also be cried out on the spot, i.e. between the liturgically preformed Kyrie Acclamation. The liturgical challenge of the Kyrie lies in the "stage-managing" of the dependence-upon-God both in words and music. This, however, is not successful if the Kyrie is homiletically breached and is introduced e.g. with the words: "As we shall hear in the sermon, many children in our country are living below subsistence level. We are asked (sic!) what our attitude is to this as a prosperous congregation [...]."[917] There is nothing wrong with social engagement in the congregation; but when, first and foremost, "we are asked" – why should we in the Kyrie bother God with this? There is something wrong here, not only linguistically; this manner of liturgical formulation is also not coherent theologically.

The text of the liturgical agendas of the ordinary are so formulated that they can basically be used in the context of any sermon on any Sunday whatsoever

---

914 Cf. footnote 916, see below.
915 The proper of the Protestant worship service is made up of the following elements – listed here in the chronological order of the liturgical event: 1. Text for the Week (or Text for the Feast- or Commemoration-Day), 2. Psalm (spoken or sung), 3. Prayer of the Day or Dedication of the Offering, 4. Reading from the Old Testament, 5. Epistle with the obligatory "Hallelujah verse", 6. Hymn of the Week or of the Feast- or Commemoration-Day, 7. Gospel, 8. respective sermon text.
916 The "Ordinary" owes its name to the regularity with which the liturgical elements combined under this name are unchangeably repeated in the service – without all these elements always being taken up in their entirety. If they are integrated they can be used in a standard version which, in principle, fits every Sunday. Following the chronology of the liturgical events – apart from the hymns and church-music contributions – it is a matter of the following parts: liturgical greeting, preparatory prayer, Gloria Patri, Kyrie and Gloria, (after the sermon): Creed, announcements, collection of offerings, prayer of intercession, the Lord's Prayer [when celebrating Communion: Praefatia, Eucharistic Prayer, Sanctus, words of institution, Lord's Prayer (which is then omitted *before* the Communion Celebration)], Commission and Blessing.
917 Kyrie-prayer in a service on Sunday *Rogate* 2009.

in the church year. In many cases one might also see a possible adaptation for these parts in the proper[918]. On the quality, one can certainly argue. When using personally formulated texts of prayers, one should take care that they have a well-thought-out structure which corresponds to the breadth of the ordinary and ties on to the entire salvation history of the church in the past, present and future. One removes something from the wide scope of the ordinary if one subordinates its individual parts to the didactically-founded interests of homiletic communication.

### 7.1.3 Ignoring and Utilizing the Liturgical Year

The tense unity of liturgy and sermon can also be damaged if the church year with its changing foci is not homiletically utilized. If on any Sunday the formative and well-known spotlights, which are thrown into a person's everyday life through the pieces of the proper, are not perceived and absorbed, the opportunity for a quasi "multi-contextual" rapprochement to the (not only religious) complexity of human existence is lost. A sign of the nonchalance regarding the church year is the total abandonment of mentioning the title of the Sunday which one is celebrating. Frequently we hear simply: "Today's gospel-reading" instead of "The gospel for the third last Sunday in the church year is ...". The fading-out of the 'Sunday program' of the church year is even more obvious when (where it *is* held) the reading and sermon text order is generally deviated from and replaced by smoother, simpler and less offensive texts. In particular cases, there may be good grounds for exchanging a text.[919] However, this should never amount to a leveling-out of the church year. If this were so, a many-voiced, occasionally contrapuntal room for resonance of the sermon, within which the voice of the preacher has its own weight, would be lost.

Every worship service has its own place in the many-branched coordinate system of the church year, embedded in diverse circles of feast days which in turn have their own high-points, *periods of preparation* (e.g. the Sundays of lent), *times of response* (e.g. the Sundays after Epiphany or Easter) and *characteristic countdowns* (e.g. the "third last", "Penultimate" and "last Sunday of the church year") to name merely a few of the substructures. The church year is an important

---

**918** Cf. e.g. the suggestions of the "developed Kyrie" in the "Evangelisches Gottesdienstbuch" ("Protestant Order of Worship") (2000, 520–527). Admittedly, the character discussed above of an "urgent contact" is scarcely observed as the *Kyrie Acclamations* suggested therein rather air 'dogmatic truths'.
**919** Cf. below, I.7.3.1, p. 364–368.

source for the liturgical wealth of the worship service and participates in establishing a meaningful context for the liturgy. Those members of the congregation who only take part in the service a few times in the year also benefit from this: It is one of the principles of the Christian worship service that it does not swear the individual to *one* ideology but confronts him with a many-voiced culture of faith. What connects these "voices" and "witnesses" can be seen every Sunday under a new stand-point, which also prompts people to make a statement of their own, without, however, forcing it.

    In a certain respect the church year ensures that the backdrops of life are drawn anew in the worship service every Sunday.[920] The pictures through which human life (not just the areas of living by faith) comes into view change. With the pictures, the colors and atmosphere of every "backdrop" change also. New (old) stories are told and staged, other pieces are continually brought forth, remarkable dialogs are quoted etc. This fund of backdrops which reflect specific human experiences show the drama and passion, the risk and the "profit" of living by faith. The preacher would do well to recall this liturgically presented world, this cosmos in a nutshell, and to use it as a backdrop for his sermon.

## 7.2 Indicators of Problems in the History of Liturgy and Liturgics

### 7.2.1 On the Relationship between Eucharist and Sermon

The ritual celebration of the Eucharist and the communication of the gospel on the basis of speaking and hearing have been a constitutive part of the worship service since the beginnings of Christianity. "The celebrations of communion were [...] always also services of the Word in the sense that no Agape was held without fervent witness and no assembly without a communal meal."[921] The unity of word and sacrament determined the worship service of the early congregations to the extent that one can (still) not speak of a division of the Sunday celebration into a part for the word and one for the Eucharist. The preaching elements of the early Christian service consisted, among other things, of the testimonies and collections of sayings initially passed on verbally as e.g. the "words of the

---

**920** A special form of focusing in the service on certain questions of life is the "theater service" in which (in the ideal case) the textbook of a drama, the text of a sermon and the prayers of the liturgy relate to comparable or analog experiences of reality. Cf. M. Hein/T. Bockelmann (2010).
**921** G. Kunze, 1955, 124.

lord"[922]. Soon, individual, partly fragmentarily available records (logia, letters) were utilized. From what we know of the relationship of ritually-developed and purely verbal communication of the gospel, we can conclude that at this time the "sermon" and the common liturgical action interpreted one another reciprocally. This can be shown clearly among others in the following features.

- Whatever is *expressis verbis* professed as gospel in the stories of and about Jesus may be sensed in the feast of reconciliation. In the receiving and passing on of bread and wine the intellectually comprehensible meaning of the "message of life" of the gospel is ritually deepened and celebrated.
- Through all forms of communicating the gospel – texts, words and rituals – the same claim arises: those present in the worship service are confronted with the unambiguous expectation that, as hearers of the words of Jesus and as participants in the communal meal they must now for their part assume responsibility for others, show solidarity with this community and in a certain sense "sacrifice"[923] themselves.
- On the basis of the emerging correlations between preaching and Eucharistic elements, the liturgy, too, gains a "kerygmatic" function. Its pictures, melodies, gestures and movements – its whole ensemble of symbols – has a part in the communication of the gospel. Conversely a liturgical component should be awarded to the sermon: It is always the expression of the praise of God, and therefore has features of a prayer. Placed before the celebration of Communion the sermon opens the way for the Eucharistic praise in that it recalls salvation history homiletically for the congregation.

The communication of the gospel through free speech, expressed according to the traditions of the celebration of the Eucharist, becomes a liturgically coherent expression of life of the congregation. By gathering with the others around the "Table of the Lord" before the sermon (according to the tradition of the celebration of communion in the Early Church), the "eldest" express their participation in the life of the congregation. What they express therewith is in a certain respect a commentary on what happens in and with the congregation, an expression of common experiences of faith. In the close connection with the Eucharistic (thanksgiving-) celebration we can again see the outlines of the latent dimension of prayer in the sermon: Every sermon is an expression of life resulting from the congregation's relationship to God and in this sense, is actually directed to God.

---

**922** The so-called "words of institution" are initially – in that they were solemnly cited and called to mind as statements made by Jesus – relevant as a *message*. They are a kind of short sermon which must be heard and understood. Nevertheless, this central text was not considered as "proclamation" before the reception of bread and wine but is set to frame a communal, satisfying meal with numerous Eucharistic sequences (e.g. prayers of adoration) as was known from the Jewish feasts of friendship and celebration (cf. 1 Cor 11:23–25; Luke 22:14–23).

**923** This side of the idea of sacrifice is (in the non-denominational sense) deeply Protestant and should be differentiated from the medieval service of the Mass in which the celebratory meal offers *Christ's sacrifice* anew.

This liturgical commentary on the sermon reminds us that the task of the sermon does not simply consist in bringing something to the congregation which they did not yet know or what they did not yet have. The preacher should speak to the congregation – and in the face of God – on the variety of life circumstances and opportunities which arise from what the congregation already "has" and how this may impact living by faith in the here and now.

A part of the structural difficulties which have led to the reform of the "Order" and to the formation of the "Evangelisches Gottesdienstbuch"[924] ("Protestant Order of Worship") resulted from the centuries-long process of the *separation of the verbal worship service and the celebration of Communion*. This process began around 150 CE.[925] Justin describes the worship service already as divided into two parts: In place of the original communal meal there comes a service of the Word, consisting of scriptural readings, sermon and intercessory Prayer. This sequence is followed by the celebration of the Eucharist.

This basic structure of the medieval Mass later developed further into *two contrary directions*: While in the Roman and Eastern traditions the Eucharist – in the sense of a sacramental, sacrificial meal – dominated the service as a whole and the sermon played a subordinate part, the services in the tradition of the reformation increasingly took on the character of a sermon-delivery with a liturgical framework. This development was certainly not in the interest of Martin Luther. Nevertheless, in many places this was soon understood to be the practical understanding of a supposedly typical Protestant service-culture in which the sermon – in reality at the cost of the Celebration of the Eucharist – increasingly gained in appeal.

Although Mass was celebrated more than once a week, the personal claim of the sacrament had already been reduced to only a few times a year in the pre-Reformation period. The widespread reserve against anything sacramental was one of the reasons why those services where the Lord's Supper was not celebrated

---

924 Under the title "Evangelisches Gottesdienstbuch" ("Protestant Order of Worship") the joint "Agende für die Evangelische Kirche der Union [EKU] und für die Vereinigte Evangelisch-Lutherische Kirche Deutschlands [VELKD]" ("Agenda for the Evangelical Church of the Union and for the United Evangelical Lutheran Church of Germany") was bindingly introduced on the first Sunday in Advent in 1999 by the council chancellery of the EKU and the church governance of the VELKD. The Order consists of two volumes, a main work (with the "basic forms", the "Ordinary" and "Proper" as well as a collection of texts on individual liturgical elements) and a supplementary volume (2002). For further details cf. W. Ratzmann (1999).

925 An important document for this is the *Apologia* of Justin which was written around 150 CE. This and other sources have been made available and commented on in a didactically outstanding way in the study book by M. Meyer-Blanck (2009b, 92–101).

were offered with increasing frequency. Nevertheless, the order of the liturgy, as far as other sections of the service were concerned, scarcely changed so that the shortened Lutheran Eucharistic service without Communion – with the sermon as high point – became more and more established. The tolerance of such "incomplete" masses was fostered by the interest in the educational potential of the service. After all, the reform of the liturgy initiated by Luther intended to contribute towards making the worship service a universally understandable introduction to the Christian faith. Luther's complaint about the lack of interest in the Eucharist on the part of many believers was connected at least indirectly with his own understanding of the service in which the word – even without any ritual context – takes on a prominent position and has a quasi-sacramental character of its own.

In the *worship services during the era of Pietism* sermon and communion were equally directed towards the fruits of faith. The members of the congregation gathered around bread and wine in order to prepare themselves through the consumption of the sacrament of the Eucharist for the way towards sanctification. The sermon had already explained what it meant to live a life directed towards eternal salvation. Consequently, address and ritual alike served to keep the personal faith of the penitent soul with its Lord. The aspects of sermon and Communion which lay outside the personal religious battle (e.g. political, relating to the theology of creation or eschatology) were faded out to a large extent. The worship services thus gained a sanctifying feature, however, frequently the beneficial character of the service could scarcely be seen.[926]

In the *Enlightenment period* the separation of sermon and communion continued, alongside an increasingly higher assessment of linguistically or rhetorically sophisticated elements in the service. This can be seen in how the numerous attempts to bring the forms and elements of the service into line with the contemporary pattern of perception and structures of expectation in the 18th century almost without exception relate to questions of Homiletics. Whereas it was scarcely considered necessary to reform the liturgy of the celebration of Communion.

In the few cases that the liturgy of Communion was reformed, it was done with the "universal bond of humanity" and not the local congregation in mind. Following the principle of immediate plausibility while forgoing all aspects of mysticism, sermon and supper were directed to the strengthening of virtues to the common benefit of all. The acquisition and deepening of personal belief was only secondary and, as it seems, was believed to benefit from the rational guidelines of a moral life.

The perspective narrowing of sermon and Communion in the time of Pietism and the Enlightenment led to certain instrumentations of the worship service in

---

**926** An example of the pattern of the narrow limitation and thematic reduction of sermon and communion can be seen in the service of the Moravian Church: Sermon, prayers, hymns, celebration of communion demonstrate in ever new images the relationship of the congregation to the "lamb" or to the "blood". The battle of the lamb for the soul of the individual is reinforced in the sermon. In the Lord's Supper, the blood of the lamb is tasted, whereby the faithful should now subjectively appropriate the mercy preached (cf. A. Peters, 1993, 137f.).

which the emphasis and main goal was either on soteriology (conversion) or on some well-intentioned social purpose (the betterment of society). Subsequently, the function of some liturgical elements and their inner dependency to the liturgy of the service as a whole was disregarded. The many facetted, dynamic structure of the service was subordinated to the realization of particular religious conceptions and theological ideas through which the sermon was in danger of losing its liturgical anchoring in the service as a whole – which in its turn overshadowed its own homiletic function. The understanding that one also needed a liturgy as well as the sermon sank more and more.

In the 19th century the elliptical double centricity of the worship service was rediscovered and the corresponding interdependency between sermon and communion seen by Luther was again reasserted. This "double centricity" became popular among theologians first and foremost through Wilhelm Löhe's picture of a path over a "mountain with two peaks". "The first peak is the sermon, the second the sacrament of the Eucharist, without which I cannot think of a perfect worship service on earth. [...] During the main service, one is always climbing until one reaches the Lord's Table where one has nothing above one but Heaven."[927] In spite of the impressiveness of this picture the practice of the liturgy in the congregations scarcely corresponded to Löhe's idea of the Eucharistic stern-weight until far into the 20th century. The evangelical worship services continued to be firmly centered on the sermon, which not only reveals that, particularly in the regions of the Reformation (particularly in Saxony, Saxony-Anhalt and Thuringia), services with a subsequently added Communion were in practice right up to the 1980s – i.e. till the beginning of the last reform movement of the liturgy.

The introduction of the *Evangelisches Gottesdienstbuch* ("Protestant Order of Worship") on the first Sunday in Advent in 1999 marks the sensibility which had grown in respect of the correlations between sermon and Communion or between the sermon and the structure of the worship service as a whole.[928] In this context, pastors were made aware that the function of individual liturgical elements can change according to how they are embedded in the structure of the service,[929]

---

**927** W. Löhe, 1953 [1844], 13.

**928** Cf. W. Ratzmann, 2006, 181–185. In this context there also belong the various attempts to hold sermons with the explicit relation to the individual elements of the liturgy or the Lord's Supper in order to show in this way the significance of the celebration of Communion for a renewed understanding and awareness of the gospel. Cf. H.-Ch. Schmidt-Lauber/M. Seitz, 1992; W. Ratzmann, 2006, 185f.

**929** Cf. the suggestions gathered together and outlined in the "Evangelisches Gottesdienstbuch" ("Protestant Order of Worship") which "show how the transition from the sermon to the Eucharist can be structured in various ways" (2000, 45).

and that Communion and sermon serve and need one another as complementary forms of communication.[930]

## 7.2.2 On the Relationship between Readings and Sermon

### 7.2.2.1 Proper and Pericopes as Frames of Reference for the Sermon

Every regular worship service has, in addition to the *Ordinary*, the unchanging elements of the service, a so-called *Proper*, a thematic accent of its own which at the same time marks the position of the respective Sunday or feast and commemoration day within the church year. Further, the *Proper* holds together the liturgical elements of the worship service like a golden thread or thematic paperclip. In the homiletic work in the run-up to the service the *Proper* serves inter alia in the thematic examination. As already mentioned, it is shaped by the text for the week, its own Psalm, the prayer for the day, the reading of the Old Testament, the epistles and the gospels, a hymn for the week and the respective sermon text. Among the aforementioned elements the gospel for the respective Sunday or feast day functions as "Principal", which means that the remaining texts can be read and interpreted in the light of the gospel. One can also allow this 'dominant' function of the gospel to be effective in an unspoken sense and give it a theological interpretation. In other words, the focus of the worship service and preaching is "the gospel" but not in the sense of a text *being talked about* but in the sense of a message which can be perceived as gospel – and in the articulation thereof one relates to the texts *with* which one preaches.

The reading from the Old Testament, epistle, gospel and sermon text belong to the – again referring to the *Proper* – "pericopes"[931]. In the language of liturgics

---

**930** This will be clarified below with reference to the complementarity of analog and digital forms of communication for which the relationship between the celebration of the Eucharist and sermon is an exemplary model. On the differentiation between analog and digital forms of communication cf. I.7.3.2, p. 374–376.

**931** This concept has performed different functions in the course of its history. In ancient rhetoric, e.g. it meant a *part of a sentence* which should be emphasized, and as such also a segment of a longer text. Justin spoke of "pericopes" as *references* for particular dogmatic statements (cf. e.g. Phil 2:5–11 as a text related to Christology). Origen already understood pericopes as *sections of biblical meaning*. On the history of pericopes as texts for reading in the worship service cf. the research done by G. Kunze, 1955, 127–166 which has still not been surpassed. In view of the difficulties which the *delimitation of the pericopes* causes in the interpretation of a text, it appears that the original meaning of "περικοπειν" has not completely lost its significance: In the ancient world περικοπειν also meant the digging out of a large lump of stone from the rock (after it had been chosen for further treatment).

the word "pericope" refers to an "extract" from the Bible which is intended for a particular Sunday or feast day as a text for reading and/or the sermon.[932] In the EKD (Evangelical Church in Germany) a revised Order of Biblical Readings and Sermon Texts ("Ordnung der biblischen Lesungen und Predigttexte" [OLP]) has been in effect since the 1st Advent of 1978.[933] This order provides six texts for every Sunday and feast day in the church year or an individual text series for six consecutive years. The selection of the texts is based on the following structure:

| | |
|---|---|
| Sermon series I: | Gospel for the Sunday. Oriented on the traditional repertoire of the "Old Gospels" Series for the sermon texts. |
| Sermon series II: | Epistle for the Sunday. Oriented on the traditional repertoire of the "Old Epistles" Series for the sermon texts. |
| Sermon series III: | Further texts from the gospels combined with Old Testament pericopes.[934] |
| Sermon series IV: | Further texts from the epistles combined with Old Testament pericopes (principally from the Prophets). |
| Sermon series V: | Further texts from the gospels (focus on John) combined with Old Testament pericopes. |
| Sermon series VI: | Further texts from the epistles (focus on Hebrews) mixed with Old Testament pericopes. |

That this *order of texts for sermons* is not compulsory is already indicated in the fact that the six series are on average extended by two so-called *marginal texts*.

---

**932** The talk of "pericopes" in the sense of series of texts for reading and sermon was first established in the Lutheranism of the 16th century. There it was a matter of the double Scripture-reading from the epistles and the gospels, as was customary in the tradition of the Mass in the Christian West.

**933** Cf. the "Lektionar für evangelisch-lutherische Kirchen und Gemeinden. Mit Perikopenbuch" ("Lectionary for the Lutheran Churches and congregations, with pericope book"), 2010, 12. The previous version, last revised in 1958, only mentions the "Order of *Sermon* Texts" (Ordnung der *Predigt*texte [OPT]). This "reduction" of the texts on their homiletic function may be considered as an expression of a programmatic theology of worship services, since, at that time, the pericopes where mostly used as sermon texts and less as a part of the liturgy. As such, the subsumption of the pericopes under the term "sermon texts" was correct insofar as all the reading pieces are at the same time also sermon texts, while not all sermon texts are presented as reading.

**934** There is no independent series of Old Testament pericopes (which would mean preaching on an Old Testament text for the duration of a church year). The Old Testament Reading which is assigned as First Reading to every Sunday and feast day appears also as a sermon text in each of the series III–VI.

Here it is a matter of texts which certainly could be considered as a sermon text for a particular Sunday "but could not have been included in the series I–VI"[935].

It corresponds to the function of the *Propria* that the elements which today determine the contents of a Sunday or feast day – including the sermon-pericopes and the marginal texts – at least appear in part to have been compiled according to the principle of consonance. When the new selection of texts for reading and sermons was put together, more attention than in the past was payed to the fact that the various texts had an inner coherence or that such a coherence or connection might arise within the context of the service. Even though the connection between two texts is sometimes only vaguely discernable, preachers should not forcibly try to produce this coherence in their exegetical work. The historical development of the readings in the old church shows that the gradual moving together of the specific Sunday or feast day readings from the gospels and epistles was determined by quite different factors, whereas the idea of consonance has only played a part in more recent times and has gained a somewhat revising role. The latest attempt to trenchantly produce an inner coherence between reading- and sermon-text and a Proper that varies Sunday by Sunday can be found in the introduction developed by Karl-Heinrich Bieritz for the *proprium de tempore*. This is included in the desk edition of the Order of Worship ("Gottesdienstbuch").[936]

Before the functions of the Proper and pericopes for the sermon can be discussed we must first outline some of the steps in the development which have led to today's thematic accentuation on the individual Sundays and feast days within the church year.

---

**935** Evangelisches Gottesdienstbuch, 2010, 15. From the conceptually "peripheral position" of these texts one shouldn't conclude that they are also of "marginal" *significance*. Marginal texts, thanks to their "un-preached" freshness sometimes prove to be particularly creative partners in interlocution. They make the mere repetition of standardized theological views more difficult and allow for new possibilities of working with the texts. To the marginal texts belong, among others, the "Baptist's Sermon" (Matt 3:1–11[12]) on the third Sunday in Advent, Paul's evidence for his office as apostle (Gal 1:11–24) on the Fifth Sunday after Trinity and the Parable of self-exaltation and humility (Luke 14:7–11) on the Seventh Sunday after Trinity.

**936** Cf. K.-H. Bieritz, 2000, 681–720. The "Liturgical Calendar" provides an excellent, didactically well-developed overview of the whole church year, made available in a common Internet-portal of the Evangelical Lutheran Church in Bavaria (ELKB) and the United Evangelical Lutheran Church of Germany (VELKD). On the webpage, all the Sundays and feast days with their texts, liturgical codes (e.g. colors) and customs are presented (http://kirchenjahr-evangelisch.de, last accessed on April 10, 2018).

### 7.2.2.2 Stages and Problems in the Development of Proper and Pericopes

The development of the Reading related to a Proper has its beginnings in the far-reaching "proprium-free" practice of the Early Church. There the custom was, according to demand, to read aloud from the Pentateuch and the Prophets, from the Acts of the apostles and the apostolic letters,[937] "as long as there was time" – i.e. until the whole congregation was assembled for the opening of the Eucharist which always followed the liturgy of the word.[938] Around 380 there is proof of four readings[939]. Two Old Testament readings ("Law" and "Prophets") as well as readings from the epistles and the gospel were now clearly part of every worship service. Psalms were sung between the readings. After the readings followed one or more sermons. All the readings were made according to the principle of the *lectio continua* as an ongoing reading. Thus, the biblical texts were heard in context and, if necessary, spread out over several consecutive worship services.

Today, the *lectio continua* usually only determines the readings and sermons on feast days or the Holy Day periods (Christmas, Easter), i.e. when it seems reasonable from the thematic content of the church year to read or preach further on a text in multiple services.[940] A modified form of the *lectio continua* is the so-called "course reading". The "course reading" also consists of consecutive readings of a biblical book or long text passages, whereby some shorter or longer sections, which are considered to be of less importance, are omitted (thus also known as *lectio semicontinua)*. For today's structure, it is the OLP ("Ordnung der biblischen Lesungen und Predigttexte"/ Order of Biblical Readings and Sermon Texts) that is above all decisive of the *lectio propria*; it takes into account the particular thematic accent or leitmotif of the respective Sunday.

An important factor in the shaping of thematic readings was certainly the Early Churches' habit of reading the story of the passion in Holy Week and Good Friday,

---

**937** It was uncommon, however, that the readings were read from all parts of the Bible mentioned for the simple reason that the individual congregations usually only had an incomplete set of scrolls and had to get by with the texts they had – texts of which they did not always know exactly who the author was (cf. G. Kunze, 1955, 122).

**938** Source for this is the *First Apology of Justin Martyr*, written around 150 CE (67.3).

**939** This emerges from the Apostolic Constitution (VIII, 57); cf. G. Kunze, 1955, 138–141.

**940** Cf. the continuing reading from Luke 2:1–20 (Christmas Eve) to Luke 2:41–52 (Second Sunday after Christmas). Already around 350–500 CE there emerged the first "church-wide" Order of Readings with a recognizable basic structure. The reports of the Passion and Death, for example, were read in the Holy Week and Good Friday, the Investiture report on Maundy Thursday, the report of the resurrection at Easter and the story of Whitsun according to Acts 2 at the Feast of Pentecost. Further aspects of order arose from the details of time and content in the texts and its connection to the church year, which was gradually gaining in outline: Luke 2:21 (the naming of Jesus) was observed on the 8th day after Christmas. Until today, Phil 4 ("The Lord is near") is read or preached on the Sunday before Christmas.

the gospel of the resurrection of Jesus at Easter, Acts 2 at Pentecost and the stories about the birth of Jesus at Christmas. Since the gospels (unlike many texts of the epistles) are often unsuitable for *lectio-continua*-readings due to the limited number of units of meaning (e.g. parables), it seems reasonable that they were "compositionally strung on the thread of the historical course of Jesus' work"[941]. In the Roman liturgy, they were soon developed into a reading-series of their own.[942] Only in the 8th century did epistle-series also emerge – in the area of the Gallicanic Liturgy[943].

It goes without saying that these series based on varying liturgical customs initially had scarcely any thematic points of contact. Until the turn of the millennium, priests used an *Evangelistar* and an *Epistolar* which had completely different structures and whose structure of the church year touched on the great feasts at the most but not e.g. on the Sundays between Pentecost and Christmas. Thus, the further convergence of epistle and gospel was at first "at the mercy of gradual agreement and custom"[944]. From the *Würzburger Epistelliste*[945] and Theotinchus' carefully worked-out Book of pericopes based on many comparisons and cautious revisions,[946] up to common lectionaries of the Early Church that circulated until the time of the Reformation, one can witness a gradual convergence of differently accented reading and sermon text orders. Only to a very limited extent this process was accompanied by organizational impulses. The consonance – or at the very least the compatibility – of epistle and gospel was largely a coincidence.

To a large extent, Martin Luther took over the pericopes of Early Christianity,[947] but criticized some of the texts, particularly some from the epistles whereby he was considering the *usefulness* of these pericopes as texts for readings or sermons. When he advocated for the deletion of individual texts from the list of pericopes he justified this particularly with the too high *degree of difficulty of the text in relation to the act of listening comprehension.*[948]

---

**941** G. Kunze, 1955, 132.
**942** Cf. T. Klausner, 1935.
**943** "Gallicanic" is the "collective term for the pre-Carolingian church areas in France, Spain, Milan (North Italy) and the Irish-Celtic-Scottish area between the 4th and 8th centuries" (A. Ehrensperger, 2005, 1).
**944** G. Kunze, 1955, 151.
**945** Cf. T. Klausner, 1935, 3–15.
**946** Cf. the *Comes Theotinchi* in E. Ranke, 1847, Appendix V.
**947** Here cf. the compilation in H. v. Schade, 1978, 29.
**948** The order of sermon texts introduced in 1978 was entirely in the spirit of Luther, and – along with the aforementioned striving for consonance – *suitability for reading and preaching* were still decisive principles of revision.

Luther also exchanged those pericopes which had only been chosen because they mentioned the name of the first apostles, for more suitable ones. His main concern was, whether a text was suitable for a missionary sermon and to what extent the pericope represented "a visible stimulation to faith". Particularly in the "*Eastertide*" he replaced the existing texts with ones which he considered to be more suitable – some of which had not yet appeared in the list of pericopes until then. The source of Luther's "*Perikopenliste*" (list of pericopes) was clearly the registers of epistles and gospel passages that were added as appendices in early prints of his New Testament[949]. Incidentally, Luther saw the usefulness of such lists in that they would prevent incompetent preachers to spread heresies.

The fact that in the morning service Luther preached from the gospel and in the evening from the epistle has established the use of the Early Church pericopes in the Lutheran Churches. Luther himself repeatedly pointed out that the *lectio continua* was an appropriate custom both for the readings and for the sermon.[950] In the following 350 some years scarcely anything changed in the system of Early Church pericopes. Nonetheless, there was constant criticism of the narrow spectrum of the pericopes. The (inner) compulsion to have to fall back on the pericopes was felt to be burdensome. Suggestions for improvement were made – sometimes with the demand for a more thorough biblical knowledge, other times the wish for more practical use or diversity in the choice of pericopes stood in the foreground. With the definite establishing of traditional feasts (e.g. the harvest festival and Thanksgiving) and the addition of new celebrations and commemoration days to the church year (e.g. feast on Reformation day, for mission or for the Gustav-Adolf-Society) the need for new pericopes arose. Nevertheless, in spite of several attempts, a generally accepted revised common lectionary on which several regional churches agreed upon could never be established in the first half of the 19th century[951].

At last – after thorough inspection of numerous proposals for a new common lectionary – the church conference in Eisenach of 1890/1896 established a five-year-circle to which the following series are assigned:

Series I:     A slightly revised series of the old gospels. Above all, the revision affected the number of verses read and only in a few cases the selection.
Series II:    A revised series of the old epistles (revised on the same principle as Series I).
Series III:   A new, second series of the gospels with the main emphasis on Jesus' Passion.
Series IV:    A new, second series of the epistles.

---

**949** Cf. M. Luther, WA DB 7, 529–544.
**950** Cf. M. Luther, *Von der Ordnung des Gottesdienstes in der Gemeinde* (1523), WA 12, 36f. and idem, *Deutsche Messe* (1526), WA 19, 78f.
**951** H. v. Schade, 1978, 34f. gives an overview.

Series V:      A series of Old Testament pericopes.
Special series: For the celebration of Pentecost and the first nine Sundays after Trinity, on the basis of regional tradition, the gospel texts are switched for more suitable texts from Acts and the epistles.

In this attempt at reform, the principles of supplementation and consonance were at least regimentally applied. In the commentaries on the new pericope book which was presented to the German Protestant Church Conference on June 5, 1896 we read: "The newly-chosen sections must on the one hand be an extension to the old pericopes, on the other they must remain related to them."[952] Since, however, the former gospels and epistles readings were themselves only partly in consonance or are at least complementary to one another, new problems arose: if one wants to use the pericopes not solely as sermon texts, but – which is scarcely considered in the Eisenacher "Perikopenbuch" (common lectionary) (1897) – also as texts for reading, new disturbances in the consonance appear. The cautious Eisenach review of the early Christian pericopes reveals the custom of reading just *one* pericope that became common in the 19th Century. Regardless of what text it was – epistles, gospels or another passage – the determining factor was usually how fitting it was homiletically. In this way, the *liturgical function* of the readings faded farther from view.

The Eisenach Pericopes have determined the culture of preaching and the textual basis of the homiletic interpretations for many decades.[953] The Proprium for the individual Sundays was strengthened – as well as through the pericopes – by the fact that influential theologians such as Theodor Knolle, Wilhelm Stählin or Hans Asmussen undertook the attempt to give each Sunday a theological motto or motif, whereby the individual texts were seen and interpreted at one time in how they were connected to each other, at another in how they complemented one another, and lastly, in how they were contrapuntally.[954] As a result, the interpretation of the Sunday pericopes themselves helped to give the synoptic view of the texts their own plausibility. It is therefore not surprising that neither the Lectionary of 1949 nor the Agenda I of the VELKD in 1955 made any fundamental changes to the text corpus. They confined the revisions to the number of verses read and revoked the few new pericopes of the Eisenach lectionary. Only the preparations for the

---

**952** Hermann Freiherr von der Goltz, Vice-president of the German Evangelical Church Conference in his paper on the reason for the new model, in: *Allgemeines Kirchenblatt*, 1896, 474f., quoted in G. Kunze, 1955, 167.
**953** Cf. e.g. Leonard Fendt's commentary on the Eisenach pericopes in: *Die alten Perikopen* (1931) and *Die neuen Perikopen* (1941).
**954** Cf. T. Knolle/W. Stählin (1934), H. Asmussen (1937), 232f., W. Stählin (1958). These impulses have led to the formulation of the so-called "models" for Sundays and feast days. So, for example, the first Sunday in Advent bears the title "the Approach of the Lord", and Palm Sunday stands under the motif of "The Man of Sorrows", the Second Sunday after Trinity is entitled "The Invitation" and the Penultimate Sunday of the church year stands under the name "The Last Judgment" etc. Cf. W. Stählin, 1958, 9, 139, 212, 382.

1958 published *Order of Sermon Texts* (second edition 1965) led to an examination of *all* texts including the old Christian pericopes with regard to their relation to the Proper. The structure of the new order now appears as follows:

| | |
|---|---|
| Series I: | Renewed basic series of the old gospels |
| Series II: | Renewed basic series of the old epistles |
| Series III: | A new, second gospel series, mixed with texts from the Old Testament |
| Series IV | A new, second epistle series, mixed with texts from the Old Testament |
| Series V: | A new, third gospel series, mixed with texts from the Old Testament |
| Series VI: | A new, third epistle series, mixed with texts from the Old Testament |
| Appendix: | Texts from the Psalms |
| | A lectio continua series |
| | Various marginal texts for every Sunday |

This common lectionary was only in use for about 20 years. The renewed revision was due to the fact that the consonance between the sermon texts and the proper for some Sundays was still felt to be inadequate. Consequently, all the readings were subjected to a careful examination and an attempt was made "through a rearrangement and new ordering of texts" to reach "a comprehensible connection or affinity" of gospel and epistle, whereby contrapuntal relations were also considered.[955] These revisions led to a trial lectionary introduced in 1972 under the title "*Neue Lesungen für den Gottesdienst*" ("New Readings for the Worship Service") to be tested in the German-speaking Churches of the Reformation.

After the trial run of this lectionary followed the penultimate revision of the basic cycle of gospels and epistles as well as the other of the sermon series. In this revision, difficult texts – i.e. above all those unsuitable as *texts for readings* – were replaced by "more readable" texts, thematic duplicates were avoided to a large degree and pericopes which were "overly long" were reduced to a length which made it easier to understand when heard. Other important texts were added which until then had not yet found a place in the spectrum of the pericopes. Furthermore, the texts were examined for their suitability in terms of the plausibility of the dialectic of law and gospel. This revised order of sermon texts became effective on the 1st of Advent in 1978 and has the structure represented above (I.7.1.2.1).[956]

---

**955** Cf. W. Schanze: *Reform der Lektionsperikopen* (1968, unpublished), cited in H. v. Schade, 1978, 57 as well as further details on the whole in H. v. Schade, loc. cit., 58–64.

**956** Michael Meyer-Blanck highlights the differences to the Roman Catholic *Ordo Lectionum Missae* (OLM): "The Lutheran sermon series I-VI and the OLM have very little in common: The Roman Catholic Order from 1969 has three readings (Old Testament, New Testament, epistles) in a three-year cycle. In each year a Synoptic gospel is read as a serial and an Old Testament text is assigned to it in relation to content and a text from the epistles also serially. The Seasons

### 7.2.2.3 Revisions of the Common Lectionary in Germany in the 21st Century

A further attempt to reform the Order of the Sermon Texts went back to the "Conference of the regional Church Association of Christians and Jews (KLAK)".[957] This model distinguished itself in that Torah, gospels, prophets, epistles and other writings were intended to be shown to advantage as of equal status. The principle of structure here did not end simply in a comprehensive series of sermon texts covering five (instead of six) cycles or years but – related to the Proper – was intended to show to advantage in an exemplary fashion on each individual Sunday. For the practical implementation of this principle two extreme versions and a "middle way" were considered:

1. In accordance with the previous rule of preaching only gospels in the first year, only epistles in series II, etc., each of the five text groupings could be made into a sermon series.
2. A maximum amount of diversity would be achieved if on every Sunday and feast day one moved from one text group to the next, i.e. on five consecutive sermon dates one would refer to Torah, gospel, prophets, epistle and writings, and then to begin again with a text from the Torah.
3. A "middle way" between those two alternatives would then consist in orienting the structure on the particular season of the church year (e.g. 1–4 Advent, Christmas 1 to New Year's Eve, ascension to Whit Monday) whereby the KLAK rather had in mind a change to be carried out "approximately every four preaching occasions, i.e. fifteen times in the year"[958], so that three sermon sequences would be dropped in each area.

It is obvious that a greater consideration of the wealth of the biblical texts would require a more comprehensive inclusion of Old Testament texts, which would be beneficial for a variety of theological reasons. Nevertheless, the perceptible increase in the share of Old Testament texts could also become a problem[959]; the requirements of the lectionary perceived by many pastors as a kind of herme-neutic burden would not be overcome therewith: (1) The exclusively thematic orientation of the church year which assumes a regular participation in the worship service, (2) texts which are hermeneutically difficult to access, which need an explicit historical and theological commentary to prevent them from being misunderstood, (3) the wide divergence of the customs of feast days and

---

of the liturgical year after Epiphany and Pentecost are uniformly numbered as 32 (33) Propria, numbered-off as 'Sundays in the liturgical year. In the liturgical year 2005/2006, for example, Matthew's gospel from Chapter 9 to Chapter 25 was read on the Sundays after Trinity; less impor-tant passages are omitted in this process" (M. Meyer-Blanck, 2006, 155).

**957** Cf. Konferenz Landeskirchlicher Arbeitskreis Christen und Juden (ed.), 2009.

**958** Loc. cit., 4.

**959** M. Dutzmann and K. Potthoff, for example, draw attention to the difficulty of elucidating "the message of Jesus' resurrection" through the "detour over 1 Sam 2, the Song of Hannah" "simply because in v.6 it says: 'The LORD kills and brings to life?'" Cf. M. Dutzmann/K. Potthoff, 2004, 56.

the choice of text[960], (4) the scarcely convincing fixation on many texts from the epistle to the Hebrews in sermon series VI alone, (5) the total relinquishment of Psalms as "orderly" (i.e. found in the six series) etc.[961]

Since the first Sunday in Advent 2014 (by a resolution of the Evangelical Church in Germany [EKD], of the Union [EKU] and the United Evangelical Lutheran Church of Germany [VELKD]) a moderately revised version of the lectionary[962] has officially been in the *testing phase*. This draft will be introduced on the First Sunday in Advent 2018 – exactly 40 years after the last reform. It is the outcome of a long-standing process of discussion accompanied by surveys and analyses, out of which significant expectations have ensued. Among the criteria developed, which have shaped the reorganised system of biblical readings and sermon texts, especially noteworthy is the *increase of the amount of Old Testament texts* (from less than a fifth to a third of the texts), a more specific and consequent *variety in the texts* regarding their origin from different biblical books[963] including the Apocrypha, a recourse to a greater diversity in genres (more narratives, wisdom literature and poetry) and a *wider spectrum of topics*. For the first time seven *Psalms* are part of the regular cycle of the six sermon texts for a Sunday or feast day.[964] In five instances in the church year the Scripture of the week has been altered and related more clearly to the Proper. Overall, more attention was paid to the principle of consonance.

With the introduction of the "the trial-draft of the new lectionary for the worship service" there is a pedagogical expectation which should not be underestimated: Considering that the coming generations of young people have scarcely any knowledge of the Bible the selection of texts was made somewhat more elementary: "We must provide an offer of elementary biblical texts for those who, as young or older members of the congregation, have scarcely any knowledge of the Bible."[965] Thus,

---

**960** Cf. the numerous examples in R. Roessler, 2004, 58f.

**961** Cf. loc. cit., 57–60.

**962** Cf. Neuordnung der gottesdienstlichen Lesungen und Predigttexte (New Order of the Readings and Sermon Texts for Use in the Worship Service), 2014, 14.

**963** According to empirical surveys the number of texts from the epistles, for example, "tended to be evaluated too highly. [...] In particular the second sermon year, in which previously *exclusively* texts from the epistles were preached" was judged to be problematic. In the reception of the Old Testament the main focus previously lay in the area of prophecy, hymn-like or poetic texts were integrated to a much smaller extent in the readings and sermon texts (loc. cit., 25).

**964** Here we are concerned with the following texts: Ps 24 on the First Sunday in Advent; Ps 46 on Reformation Day; Ps 51 on Ash Wednesday; Ps 85 on the Third from Last Sunday in the church year; Ps 90 on the Sunday before Advent; Ps 113 on Trinity Sunday; Ps 126 on "Eternity Sunday" (also referred to as "Last Sunday in the church year").

**965** W. Ratzmann, 2010, 51.

a large number of biblical texts was taken up "which belong to the core of Scripture but were not represented in the lectionary up till now, such as e.g. the instructions to Abraham, [...] the crossing of the Red Sea, Elijah at the brook Cherith, the tales of Jonah and Ruth, Judas' betrayal, Peter's denial, Jesus' struggle in Gethsemane"[966].

Further important baselines and principles of the revision: 1. The "combination of the order of texts for reading and preaching assigned on the basis of each Sunday and feast day [...] – Early Church pericopes from gospel and epistle [...] together with an Old Testament text for a Reading"[967] has been retained. To this also belongs the cycle of six annual series for the sermon texts. 2. In all six of the annual sermon series gospels, epistles and Old Testament texts alternate regularly. 3. The principle of consonance has been taken more into account, whereby attention was paid that "the spaces allowed by this for the text neither fall apart nor become too narrow"[968]. 4. Some texts have found a new place in that they have been reassigned to the reading and sermon text cycle within a Sunday (or sometimes to another Sunday or feast day) so that their own statement has more force. 5. The delimitation of the pericopes has been examined and corrected in many places particularly in the interest of the coherence and consonance of the texts and how they are understood. 6. Minimal adaptations in the structure of the church year were made to achieve greater clarity: Thus e.g. the Period of Epiphany should (always) extend to Candlemass (40 days after Christmas) i.e. till 2nd February, whereby the number of "Sundays before Lent" increase without the Propria of the earlier Epiphany Sundays being lost. 7. The orientation towards ecumenism also played a role in the new location of individual texts in the church year.[969] 8. On its webpage, the EKD announces: "The co-ordination and evaluation of the statements are made in the regional churches. After an inclusion of the regional votes and a final resolution is passed on the new texts, on the First Sunday in Advent 2018 we shall begin, EKD-wide, with a new Lectionary, a new Pericope Order, new collections of hymns for the week and new aids to preaching."[970]

From this emerges the following new structure of the Pericope Order:

| Series I | A proportional mixture[971] of texts from the gospels (no longer in all cases identical to the originally preached Sunday sermon or gospel-readings), epistles and Old Testament pericopes. |
|---|---|
| Series II | In principle as Series I. The selected epistles are no longer in all cases identical to the originally preached Sunday sermon or epistle-readings. |

---

**966** Neuordnung der gottesdienstlichen Lesungen und Predigttexte, 2014, 17.

**967** Loc. cit., 14.

**968** Ibid.

**969** For example, Col 3:1–4, previously the epistolary and sermon text (Series II) on Easter Virgil, was moved to Easter Monday since this pericope functions as an epistle in the three years of the Roman Catholic *Ordo Lectionum*.

**970** http://www.velkd.de/gottesdienst/perikopenrevision (last accessed on July 4, 2016).

**971** Other than one might expect from the Preface ("constant alternation of gospel, epistle and Old Testament texts", cf. Neuordnung der gottesdienstlichen Lesungen und Predigttexte, 2014, 15) this change between the groups of texts only occurs *in principle*. In some cases, several pericopes from the same text group follow each other within a certain series. Sometimes, a text group appears just once within a long chain of sundays.

| | |
|---|---|
| Series III | A proportional mixture of texts from the gospels and epistles and Old Testament pericopes. |
| Series IV | As series III. |
| Series V | As series III. |
| Series VI | As series III. |
| Appendix: | Serial Sequences of sermon texts: The draft integrates more than ten longer sections of the Bible as a *lectio continua* or *semi-continua* sequences[972] in the regular series of sermons and also suggests the choice of additional series which could alternatively replace the designated pericopes and their Proper for a few Sundays. |
| Appendix 2: | Further sermon texts (earlier: marginal texts) suitable for the Proper.[973] |
| Appendix 3: | A Series of Psalms, supplemented and slightly modified, but intended primarily for use in the liturgical psalm prayer. |

We have dealt with these questions in such detail because today the "New Order of the Readings and Sermon Texts for Use in the Worship Service" is used by the majority of Lutheran pastors in the German-speaking world, even though at the same time there are complaints about the resulting problems. The same is true of the clergy in ecumenism.[974] Many preachers only halfheartedly resort to self-chosen substitute texts. It remains to be seen whether the revised lectionary, which is still being tested, will actually eliminate much of the complaints and criticism and help to reduce decades of hermeneutic burden. Considering how well-balanced and stringent this draft is, such expectations or hopes are not too excessive.

Nevertheless, if one wishes to deal in an adequate way with proper and pericopes without attributing a dignity of its own to the complex corpus of the OPT, one must – along with the historical aspects mentioned – visualize some "strategic" principles for dealing with them. Additionally, it is necessary to deal with a practical problem of communication concerning the liturgical "role change" from liturgist to preacher (and back)[975]. However, before tackling this it is important to look at the challenge of preaching in the context of the sunday readings in other churches in the ecumenical world as well.

---

972 When a series of sermons follows a biblical book consecutively or with interruptions one speaks of a *lectio continua* or *semi-continua*. Another form of making the sermons on several consecutive Sundays as a connected whole is choosing the sermon texts according to the requirements of a main thematic focus. In this way one can, e.g. – foreseen for Sermon Series IV – preach from the 1st to 3rd Sundays after Trinity on John 1–4 (*lectio continua*). In the New Lectionary, there are also suggestions of texts for thematically connected sermon cycles, e.g. on the question of humanity, the experience of home and foreignness etc. (cf. loc. cit., 546–549).
973 Some of the earlier "marginal texts" have been taken up in the new order of the OLP in one of the six series of sermon texts.
974 Cf. below 7.2.2.4 and 7.2.2.5
975 Cf. below 7.3.1 and 7.3.2.

### 7.2.2.4 Orders of Liturgical Readings in the Ecumenical World

#### a) The Roman Catholic Ordo Lectionum Missae (OLM)

The Roman Catholic lectionary prompted by the second Vatican Council, the *Ordo Lectionum Missae* (OLM)[976], is an attempt to enrich the liturgical and homiletic texts which until then had been used every year and consequently contained only a small repertoire, to make more use of the variety of what is contained in the Bible and in so doing to pay more attention to the topical coherence. A model of readings constructed for three years was developed, the basic structure of which is represented below:

| Year A "Year of Matthew" | 1st Reading | Old Testament Series A – chosen to fit according to the principle of consonance with the gospel for each Sunday. During the Season of Easter, the Old Testament readings are replaced by texts primarily from Acts. |
| --- | --- | --- |
| | 2nd Reading | Epistle Series A – as consecutive readings (lectio semi-continua); apart from feast days without any planned reference to the other two readings. |
| | 3rd Reading | The *Gospel of Matthew as consecutive readings* (lectio semi-continua) In the Season of Easter, the texts from the synoptic gospels are replaced by readings from the Gospel of John. |
| Year B "Year of Mark" | 1st Reading | Old Testament Series B – chosen to fit according to the principle of consonance with the gospel for each Sunday. During the Season of Easter, the Old Testament readings are replaced by texts primarily from Acts. |
| | 2nd Reading | Epistle Series B – as consecutive readings (lectio semi-continua); apart from feast days without any planned reference to the other two readings. |
| | 3rd Reading | *The Gospel of Mark as consecutive readings* (lectio semi-continua). In the Season of Easter, the texts from the synoptic gospels are replaced by readings from the Gospel of John. |
| Year C "Year of Luke" | 1st Reading | Old Testament Series C – chosen to fit according to the principle of consonance with the gospel for each Sunday. During the Season of Easter, the Old Testament readings are replaced by texts primarily from Acts. |
| | 2nd Reading | Epistle Series C – as consecutive readings (lectio semi-continua); apart from feast days without any planned reference to the other two readings. |
| | 3rd Reading | *The Gospel of Luke as consecutive readings* (lectio semi-continua). In the Season of Easter, the texts from the synoptic gospels are replaced by readings from the Gospel of John. |

**Fig. 21:** The basic structure of the Roman Catholic Ordo Lectionum Missae (OLM)

---

**976** Ordo Lectionum Missae, [1969] 1981.

In this model, the coherence of the texts – apart from feast days and holiday seasons as well as the intentionally aimed for point of commonality between the gospel and the Old Testament readings – are not very strong. The texts from the epistles frequently dissolve the connection between gospel and Old Testament reading because – even though they change in the reading years A, B and C – they circulate as consecutive readings. The selection of Old Testament readings determined solely by the progress of the respective gospel is also problematic. The accent on theme or motif intended here demands a hermeneutical deliberation in the pattern of promise and fulfillment.[977] Here significant independent witnesses from the Old Testament are not given enough attention.[978]

In the cycle presented there are *no explicit sermon pericopes*, for in the *Ordo Lectionum Missae* there is no distinction made between texts for readings and texts for sermons. There are simply series of readings and years. Anyone who preaches in a worship service "may preach on the Old Testament text, the reading from the epistles or on the gospel (or the Psalm) or on several or all of these texts"[979].

These possibilities are certainly made use of in the Catholic practice of preaching: In the best-case-scenario the homiletic allusion to a whole ensemble of texts (or the simultaneous reference to selected aspects and facets in the readings) prevents the dogged and unproductive slaving over a single text which frequently harms more than helps the sermon.[980] Treating biblical texts in this way also counteracts the misunderstanding that the primary task of the sermon is to explain a text, to pass on "the kerygma" or to perform other questionable tasks. One can most certainly reach a point from a whole spectrum of metaphors, allusions and experiences. On the other hand, this model – apart from the rather weakly-developed profile of themes (Proper) of the Lectionary – perhaps conceals the danger of airing the spectrum of the witnesses read rather than arguing concretely with *one* position or with *one* experience more so than the new draft of the OLP from 2014.

### b) The North American Revised Common Lectionary (RCL)

Inspired by the reforms of the Second Vatican Council several churches in North America decided to reform the lectionary for the worship service based on the Roman Catholic order of readings. The "Common Lectionary" was already published in 1983, two years after the new Roman Catholic Order. In 1992 an ecumenical association of churches in the USA and Canada published the revised version which has been valid since then.[981]

---

977 Regarding this problem cf. above, 3.4.3a and 3.4.3c.
978 Cf. also A. Franz, 2013, 26.
979 A. Franz, 2010, 156.
980 Cf. W. Engemann, 2003e.
981 Revised Common Lectionary, 1992. This concept is most easily accessible in the "Handbook for the Revised Common Lectionary" (1996) edited by P. C. Bower and online at:

The North American lectionary differs from the OLM primarily in that it seeks to place the texts from the Old Testament equally alongside readings from the epistles and gospels. This equality expresses itself in Old Testament course readings whereby – apart from feast days and holiday seasons – no attempt is made to establish coherency between the readings within the individual services. The Old Testament texts which are to be brought to the attention of the congregation were divided in a three-year cycle of consecutive readings. The inner coherency of the Sunday readings has become even weaker through this. In any case, there certainly is no intertextually supported Sunday proper. The Old Testament has in fact – theologically well-meant – been assigned an independent place of its own in the system of the readings. Hermeneutically, however, nothing has been gained by this, but rather something lost – particularly if one considers the worship service as a holistic event, where understanding is not just a homiletic challenge but stimulated and fostered by all the individual elements.

In practice, the sequence of three Sundays in the liturgical year now is as follows, exemplified here on the Sundays Proper 9 – Proper 11.

| Reading-cycle for Year A | | | |
|---|---|---|---|
| **Reading in the service** | **Proper 9** | **Proper 10** | **Proper 11** |
| Old Testament Reading | Gen 24:34–67 | Gen 25:19–34 | Gen 28:10–19a |
| Epistle Reading | Rom 7:15–25a | Rom 8:1–11 | Rom 8:12–25 |
| Gospel Reading | Matt 11:16–19.25–30 | Matt 13:1–9.18–23 | Matt 13:24–30.36–43 |

That the search for a liturgically and homiletically meaningful system for liturgical readings in many cases (as in the example above) actually leads to a somewhat random collection of three readings which show no sign of a thematic connection was very quickly seen as a considerable defect. Therefore, the revised edition of the RCL of 1992 provides for the alternative of falling back on the OLM model, i.e. using the Old Testament readings which were chosen in accordance with the gospel reading. However, "switching from one system to another [...] should be avoided"[982].

### c) The British and other European Lectionaries
The order of readings published in 1990 – "A Four-Year Lectionary (FYL)"[983] – was issued by the *Joint Liturgical Group*, a forum for interdenominational cooperation

---

http://www.commontexts.org (last accessed on July 4, 2016). Further details on the development of this model in A. Franz, 2010, 158–160.

**982** A. Franz, 2010, 160.

**983** A four year lectionary (1990), easily available at: https://willhumes.files.wordpress.com (last accessed on August 1, 2016).

established in the United Kingdom in the 1960s. However, the expectation to produce an ecumenically viable lectionary used by several churches has not been fulfilled.

The model provides a *Four Year Cycle,* each year focusing on one of the four gospels in the Sunday readings. Both the Old Testament pericope and the reading from the epistles is chosen to thematically fit the gospel reading. This results in the following basic structure:

| Year A "Year of Matthew" | 1st Reading | Old Testament Series A – chosen on the principle of consonance suitable for the respective gospel for the Sunday. |
|---|---|---|
| | 2nd Reading | Epistle Series A – chosen on the principle of consonance suitable for the respective gospel for the Sunday. |
| | 3rd Reading | The Gospel of *Matthew* – on the Sundays after Pentecost as lectio semi-continua. |
| Year B "Year of Mark" | 1st Reading | Old Testament Series B – chosen on the principle of consonance suitable for the respective gospel for the Sunday. |
| | 2nd Reading | Epistle Series B – chosen on the principle of consonance suitable for the respective gospel for the Sunday. |
| | 3rd Reading | The Gospel of *Mark* – on the Sundays after Pentecost as lectio semi-continua. |
| Year C "Year of Luke" | 1st Reading | Old Testament Series C – chosen on the principle of consonance suitable for the respective gospel for the Sunday. |
| | 2nd Reading | Epistle Series C – chosen on the principle of consonance suitable for the respective gospel for the Sunday. |
| | 3rd Reading | The Gospel of Luke – on the Sundays after Pentecost as lectio semi-continua. |
| Year D "Year of John" | 1st Reading | Old Testament Series D – chosen on the principle of consonance suitable for the respective gospel for the Sunday. |
| | 2nd Reading | Epistle Series D – chosen on the principle of consonance suitable for the respective gospel for the Sunday. |
| | 3rd Reading | The Gospel of *John* – on the Sundays after Pentecost as lectio semi-continua. |

**Fig. 22:** The basic structure of the "Four Year Lectionary" (FYL)

In the time after Pentecost, when there are fewer feast days, the readings from the gospels are ordered as *lectio semi-continua.* Just like in the lectionary of the Protestant Churches in Germany, the "suitability" of the other Sunday readings may refer to a convergence in content, a harmony of motifs or a contrapuntal accentuation.

In what follows, three further orders are outlined as examples: (1) The Swedish Lectionary[984] is, with its cycle of three years, strongly oriented on the OLM and RCL but takes more trouble with the matter of consonance than the OLM and the FYL. Consecutive readings are strongly reduced. Care is taken that the texts in the series A, B and C for the individual Sundays also converge better with one another, whereby the thematic accents of the *Sundays in the liturgical year* become more evident. (2) The Lutheran Churches in Finland and Estonia also use a lectionary which covers three series and years. Series A is based on the Early Church gospels and epistles; to this an Old Testament text is selected on the principle of consonance. Series B and C also provide a thematically coordinated text from the Old Testament, the epistles and gospels for each Sunday, so that a total of nine different texts are available for every Sunday or feast day of the liturgical year. However, because sermons are held *on the gospels every other year*, the system, with three times three texts, amounts to a sermon cycle of twelve years.[985] (3) The basic structure of the Pericope Order of the Lutheran Church in Hungary is similar. What is special in the Hungarian model is the use of all the texts *as Sermon texts, but not as texts for readings*. The reader reads from the Early Church pericopes (epistle or/and gospel). The subject of the sermon, however, comes from the sermon plan which a liturgical committee draws up annually from the texts of the relevant series, whereby texts from the Old Testament, the epistles and the gospels are taken into consideration to the same extent.[986]

### 7.2.2.5 Conclusion: The Relevance of Lectionaries and Pericope Orders for the Purpose of Preaching

The unbroken interest in a feasible lectionary which is suitable for everyday life in the congregations of the Lutheran and other churches in ecumenism is obvious. This becomes evident in the ever-new efforts of reform which derive from liturgical, hermeneutical, biblical-theological, ecumenical, pedagogical and other standpoints. Where the ecclesial introduction of a pericope order is refrained from, preachers in the homiletic practice often like to fall back on models of other countries and churches.

Whether the annual cycles of biblical texts developed in this context meet grateful users or rather skeptics depends – as the discussion has shown – on different reasons, each of which may be asserted for the use of a lectionary. Those who regard the liturgical year as a suitable model for dealing – Sunday by Sunday – with a variety of specific contexts and motifs of what it means to be human in the context of our Christian faith (the main idea of the Proper) will gladly make use of the *Neuordnung der gottesdienstlichen Lesungen und Predigttexte* (*New Order of Texts for Reading and Preaching in the Worship Service*) of the

---

**984** On the "Swedish Sunday Lectionary" [1983] 2003, cf. A. Franz, 2010, 162–164.
**985** Namely: gospel, Old Testament, gospel, epistle, gospel, Old Testament, gospel etc. Cf. F. Herrmann, 2010, 189f.
**986** More detail on this loc. cit., 188f.

German Churches (EKD, UEK, VELKD). Never before in *one* order of pericopes have so many justified demands[987] been taken into account, decades-old problems been reduced and possibilities been opened to express in a harmonious ensemble of biblical texts what it means (i.e. according to how the human existence of the person is considered on a particular Sunday) to live by faith. Those, however, whose ideal sermon is some kind of *contemporarily relevant sermon*, the relevance of which results from its independence and contemporary nature of the choice of text,[988] will consider any predetermined text program as outmoded.

The alternatives – either to fiddle about with an incomprehensible framework of texts or to consider the people to whom one is preaching Sunday by Sunday – does not exist like that. The homiletic virtues, which Christian Grethlein quite rightly demands and which this "Introduction to Homiletics" likewise tries to express (the value of biblical texts cannot be decreed but can only disclose itself to the listeners; anyone who brings the Bible into play must have the listeners in view as subjects; the strangeness of biblical texts cannot be surmounted but should be preserved etc.) belong to the fundamental requirements of Homiletics. They are not the result of the fact that a preacher finally – freed from the lectionary – dares to consider a concrete situation and attempts to illuminate it with the text he has chosen.

The problem of relevance is far more complicated: Those who, Sunday after Sunday, intend to deliver a homiletic commentary on the catastrophe of the week (e.g. how someone has run amok) or on a "miracle" (e.g. the rescue of miners after many days of uncertainty) or an incident in the congregation – in order to then be able "to interpret the situation" which appears therein "according to the gospel, using a biblical text" – may inevitably overtax themselves. It inevitably leads to an overstressing of the "prophetic dimension" of the sermon when interpretations of contemporary situations[989] must become the trademark of the Protestant sermon. (With this premise, one's sermon is equally beneficial to the congregation as one with a decreeing interpretation of a text unrelated to the situation.) Incidentally, one can search for the appropriate text for as long as one wants: The Old and New Testaments do not contain a single text which was written to be used as a sermon text for a particular Sunday.[990] It is *always* a tremendous hermeneutic challenge to articulate what it means to live by faith in freedom and responsibility

---

**987** Here it is a matter, inter alia, of theological plausibility, hermeneutic stringency, intertextual convergence, homiletic-liturgical practicability, ecumenical tact etc.

**988** Christian Grethlein considers the fact that "for most people in the Sunday service the biblical readings do not pass the test of being relevant [...]. In every case in the practice of the reading today one must realize from the beginning that the biblical text is not allotted its significance by itself but gains it only if it proves to be beneficial for everyday life. [...] The parish preacher [knows] the concrete situation of the local people and can thus interpret it according to the gospel by using a biblical text [which she herself selects]." (Ch. Grethlein, 2014, 79f.). A more extensive critique, which includes cultural, sociological and didactic aspects of the new draft of the lectionary can be found in Grethlein, 2013, esp. 177–191.

**989** At this point we cannot go into the problematic postulate of an evangelical-biblical "interpretation of situations" as a task of a Protestant sermon. Cf. on this W. Engemann, 2016b, 7–17.

**990** On the topicality and relevance of historical or biblical texts cf. above, chapter I.3, esp. 3.3.1 and 3.4.1–2.

*today* with reference to a "pericope" from antiquity. After all, "today" refers to more or something other than those events which are primarily determined temporally and/or regionally or stand in relation to occurrences of the past week.

The relevance of a "sermon for today" is decided by the *evidence of its relevance to existence*, by its fundamental significance for the lives of those who hear it, i.e. by the explosive nature *understood by the individuals themselves*. By comparison let us remember the "serviceableness for everyday life" and the unique topicality of great novels, moving poetry or rousing films: The fact that such are demanded by millions usually does not depend on their successful interpretation of current events or their elucidation of a pressing situation. What makes a "good book" or a "good film" significant is that they show life from a different perspective, display it in its preciousness and uniqueness, that they – in exemplary fashion – penetrate its depths, that they illuminate human existence in a particular respect and express our lives in a contingent way.[991]

As already mentioned, this ability does not result from an appeal to seemingly current topics or (in the case of a sermon) to freshly experienced events and texts which appear to be appropriate. If – following the anthropological focusing of the liturgical year – more suitable texts are used for the articulation, deepening and intensification of the spectrum of the experiences of life and faith mentioned above, it is commensurately assumed that it is of secondary significance *in what sequence* experiences such as freedom, love, friendship, composure, loss, renunciation, limits, hope etc. are spoken of in the course of a year – since those present are not going to be driven or unsettled simultaneously by the same vital issues and questions. This means that, in a sense, each of these topics is equally well-suited to contribute substantially towards helping people to feel affirmed, challenged or assured in taking first steps towards freedom in the worship service, – as long as this happens *in a masterly homiletic way* in the sense of the criteria developed above (I.1–I.6).

Whether a sermon is found to be contemporary, relevant and beneficial for everyday life depends less on the possibility of the *personal choice of text* but is determined far more by *the way the text is dealt with*, whereby admittedly only one component of the homiletic process comes into view. In a sense, one can judge the call for the personal choice of text as thought of from only "within the church" – an accusation which is also raised against the approval of pericopes.

---

**991** Sometimes they also mark a desirable attitude, challenge with a certain position, the consequences of which each can picture for his own life. If one should desire to construct a series of sermons for the liturgical year based on fictional texts – as it occasionally happens in "literature worship-services" (cf. a representative selection of texts in J. Arnold/F. Fuchs/Ch. Stäblein, 2013) – their relevance would consist less in their direct statement about contemporary events but far more in the experience of finding in them a proverbial eye-glass for observing one's own life.

For anyone who assumes that, Sunday by Sunday, a pastor can find an accurate scriptural "word" for the state of things thinks that the Bible, as the "book of the church" is capable of more than it can do. It has nothing to say about the current state of affairs as has been expounded in detail in other places in this "Introduction to Homiletics". Consequently, the homiletic use of pericopes is not accompanied by the (false) expectation that a particular biblical text was written precisely with the next Sunday in mind. However, this does not mean that we cannot preach in such a way that it becomes evident through a certain piece of Christian tradition what it means to live by faith today.

The objection that the use of a lectionary, the structure of which is oriented on the continuous course of a liturgical year, is unhelpful considering the widespread practice of sporadic church attendance, is not effective: those who do not particularly concern themselves with the liturgical year and are unaware of the Proper are unlikely to have a problem in understanding the sermon from beginning to end and follow the service as a whole. That the sermon and readings "must have the people they are addressing in mind"[992] is an established homiletic and liturgy-didactic principle. In no way are these efforts reserved for a time after the obliteration of the lectionary. Where this principle does not come to fruition it is certainly not due to the seemingly foreign text (which may well remain foreign) but is an expression of the lack of consciousness of the reality of life of those present as the main focus of the worship service.

The recurring struggles in various churches for a coherent lectionary on the one hand, and the widespread willingness to follow it, show that preachers and liturgists thoroughly appreciate and use the resulting structure of how to use biblical texts in a *liturgical setting.*[993] While it is not necessary for the effectiveness of a model such as the OLP that every visitor to a worship service comprehends the underlying theological, liturgical-didactic and practical homiletic requirements in detail[994], it is invaluable as a multifaceted professional knowledge and as a frame of reference for people whose religious practice involves a more frequent attendance at the worship service. Calling to mind again what has already been stated in 7.2.2. I summarize the significance of such an Order as follows:

---

992 Ch. Grethlein, 2014, 80.

993 There is no need to further reiterate the fact that in the daily life of the congregation (e.g. Bible studies, pastoral care, counseling and confirmation classes) or in other institutional contexts (school) there are other forms of dealing with biblical texts and correspondingly other goals of communication.

994 As in other professions – e.g. in medicine or music – the patients, clients and visitors etc. do not need to know the underlying conceptional principles it in order to experience the success of a therapeutic treatment or enjoy a concert.

- The newly-ordered 6-year-cycle of texts for readings and sermons in the worship service (OLP) of 2014 strengthens the semantic coherence of the pericopes and thereby the profile (Proper) on Sundays.
- In the revision of the OLP the whole of the liturgical year can be seen as a liturgical model of the variety and complexity of human life. Through this the awareness for themes and texts which are particularly significant because of their uniqueness or complementary function, has grown. Without an annual homiletic "inspection" of the cycle of the liturgical year using an OLP they disappear more easily from sight.
- In the selection of the texts the following criteria were also considered important: comprehensibility, suitability for reading (for a public address), theological consonance and convergence or contrapuntal accentuation, pedagogic, didactic and ecumenical validity, a greater presence of the Old Testament, a diversity in the genres etc. These criteria as a whole have led to both a balanced and a clearly defined structure of the OLP.[995]
- The use of a lectionary in no way reduces the extent of personal initiative and responsibility in the homiletic work. Those who believe that they preach "more faithfully to the bible" by using the respective text recommendation than preaching with a self-selected text delude themselves.[996]
- Because a good sermon is not by any means the result of an ideal choice of text, even difficult pericopes (for which the criteria mentioned above only hold true in a limited fashion) are homiletically reasonable, which is why good sermons can be heard everywhere in the ecumenical world. Mind you, it would be an expression of solidarity with preachers and their congregations when an OLP with fewer theological, didactic and hermeneutical hurdles were to be put at their disposal.
- The OLP is not a dictate. Deviation from the pericope scheduled[997] can in particular cases be an expression of the homiletic competence of a preacher in dealing with such an order.

### 7.2.3 The Relationship of Ritual-Related and Free Speech

Some problems of the connection and coming together of sermon and liturgy are related to the tension which is not maintained between rhetorical and ritual communication: To confront the seated congregation with a sermon in free speech

---

**995** Cf. above in 7.2.2.3.
**996** The reasons for this were discussed in depth in chapter 1.2.
**997** Cf. below, 7.3.1.

and conduct a dialog with them about actual questions affecting life is, in the practice of communication something quite different than e.g. kneeling with the congregation, turning to the altar and speaking a confession of sin. In relation to two classical roles in religious practice one could say that in one case a more "prophetic", in the other a rather "priestly" competence is required.[998] While the "priest" has the task of speaking for the congregation and turns with them (following particular ritual customs) to God, the "prophet" stands before the challenge of taking up a position over against the congregation. This change of roles does not simply take place in the language and manner of speaking, in the choice of words, in facial expressions and posture but is accompanied by a whole ensemble of symbols. The pulpit often marks a kind of threshold between nave and sanctuary. When the preacher enters the pulpit, he, on one side, comes closer to the congregation, on the other he stands "over" the congregation and is thus somehow also far from them. Added to this is the staging of the entrance to the pulpit itself, for which the preacher (particularly in classically reformatory pulpits that are mounted high above the altar) must go a momentarily hidden, solitary way only to then appear in a new function.[999] This change is highlighted by its very own liturgy.[1000]

The integration of the sermon into the liturgy passed through a varied history which is also connected to the various demands on ritual and address. When he said that the sermon actually had its best place as a kind of "interlude" for the Mass, i.e. before the Introit, Luther had obviously understood that a sermon as a free, rhetorically lively address could not simply be accommodated in the given structures of a Mass.[1001] In this way, the sermon could in a sense be understood as a forerunner for all that followed and thus protect the liturgy or the celebration of the Lord's Supper from misunderstandings in advance. Even though this was never put into practice, the sermon still appeared as some kind of well-considered break in the liturgy in the Lutheran Agendas up to the reform in the '70s and '80s. The various attempts to recapture the sermon as part of the liturgy and yet an independent part of worship service have been based on an awareness of the entire repertoire of the liturgical composition and the codes to be considered thereby.

The sermon succeeds even better as a rhetorically outstanding sequence within the worship service the more consistently the change from ritual to address is performed on all levels of communication if and when, at the same time, the tension between the ritual and rhetorical patterns of communication is preserved.[1002]

---

998 Cf. K.-H. Bieritz, 2009.
999 Cf. K. H. Bieritz, 2009, 303f.
1000 Cf. below I.7.3.2, p. 368–373.
1001 M. Luther: *Formula missae et communionis pro Ecclesia Vuittembergensi*, 1883 [1523], WA 12, 205–220.
1002 On the following cf. K.-H. Bieritz, 2009, 306–319.

1. *The change in posture*: To stand pensively in prayer is fundamentally different to one's stance while preaching actively and free-standing which allows for gestures, seeking visual contact, turn to the side, take a step forward etc. A sermon delivered with hunched shoulders and bowed head, even bent over the manuscript, signals that this someone does not really want to talk to others but is "uttering eternal truths".

2. *The change in language*: As helpful as it can be to use the familiar pattern of speech for the joining in prayer, it is just as obstructive to fall back on formulae, phrases and clichés when speaking freely. After all, the language of the sermon should also follow current experiences of the preacher, which cannot be expressed in the formal, solemn language of the liturgy. Conversely, a linguistic originality stretching through the whole of the liturgy can prove to be an excessive demand. Intellectual virtuosity can promote the inclination to follow the address; but in the rite of praying it is frequently a matter of processes which have more to do with (self-) awareness than with subtle, argumentative discussion of problems.

3. *Complementary processes of communication*: In a certain respect, a liturgy satisfying the demands of *ritual* communication is the prerequisite for the preacher being able "to go out on a limb" in the *rhetorical* communication of the sermon: He will be both supported and clasped by the rite. He can speak freely because there is a clamp there which excludes misunderstandings to a large extent. On the liturgical level of communication, it becomes clear that the preacher is part of the congregation. Whatever he asks of them is not meant to be hostile. He stands on their side – not on God's side! – even when he "hauls them over the coals".

This complementarity of rhetorical and ritual communication is sometimes also repeated in the contrapuntal arrangement of the themes in a worship service: While the sermon may visualize human experiences and behavioral patterns in all their facets, interprets them in the context of tradition and articulates the idiosyncratic views of the preacher on possibilities of change, the liturgy always offers a reliable continuum of assurance. It communicates the constants and prevailing parameters of faith, which the sermon continues to propagate in ever new ways.

4. *Change from the general and abstract to the concrete*: It is true that the liturgy also offers elements of concretion, e.g. in the Prayers of Intercession. Admittedly, the Proper of a Sunday or feast day is determined by an "idea" or a "motto" which somehow appears in every relevant part of the service and is thus correspondingly

general and abstract.[1003] In the work on a concrete sermon with a concrete text – if one works carefully – there will naturally arise tensions between the "theme of the Sunday" on the one side and the possibly unwieldy statements of the text itself and the preacher's discoveries on the other. For the plausibility of the whole of a worship service much depends upon *withstanding this tension* so that the observed glittering snow of Christmas carols does not overwhelm the words of the sermon.[1004]

Conclusion: What held true for the cult of the old Israel is also characteristic for the Christian worship service up to the present day: "that it needs the prophetic word, ever and again also the prophetic protest so that it does not degenerate to an act of self-portrayal, self-confidence, satisfaction of one's own needs. [...] The ritually protected change of roles from 'priest' to 'prophet', which is expected of the leader of the liturgical gathering, finds its meaning here; this also includes the knowledge, the acknowledgement and the use of the rules which constitute the respective levels of communication"[1005].

## 7.3 Current Angles of Reflection

### 7.3.1 On the Function of the Proper and Pericopes in the Work on the Sermon

Anyone who has a critical look at the Proper refers to a thematic framework which is not provided by chance and is coordinated with the contents of other Sundays in mind. This framework is not only a guide for the work on liturgy and sermon. With the provision of a central idea, the congregation will find it easier to follow the worship service and, through their participation in the liturgy, to determine the inner connection between the readings, hymns, prayers and sermon.

---

**1003** Cf. e.g. the Proper for Christmas Eve ("Light in the darkness"), for Jubilate ("The old has passed away; see, everything has become new"), or for the Second Sunday after Trinity ("The boat is far from being full"). Cf. on this the *proprium de tempore* according to K.-H. Bieritz, 2000, 685, 702, 707.

**1004** Karl-Heinrich Bieritz draws attention to another danger: The supposed idea (!) of a feast, reduced to an ideology, can also hollow out the liturgy in that everything which "is said and done, perpetrated and celebrated [...] is [reduced] basically to rhetoric; the rite – which does not wish to propagate an 'idea' but has its counterpart in the experience of origin and God compressed into a mythical *narratio* – becomes language, an act of persuasive communication" (loc. cit., 317).

**1005** Loc. cit., 319.

In this context, we must once again speak of the principle of the harmony of the contents (principle of consonance). The *style* of the consonance of the pericopes for a Sunday is *not* to be understood *as thematic in the strict sense*. Certainly, there always emerges a field of mutual interpretations and associations from the compilation of texts chosen for a Sunday. However, the connections, similarities and points of contact which come to light are very seldom intended by the texts themselves. In many cases, however, they *produce* sense and are so chosen that at least they do not contradict the intention of the texts themselves. In a certain sense the Reformation principle of the *sacra scriptura* as *sui ipsius interpres* is shown to advantage, a principle which Luther also proclaimed for the reciprocal development of epistle and gospel.[1006] The confrontation with the texts assigned to the sermon text can set processes of deduction and understanding in motion and lead to surprising insights, especially if one attempts to read the pericopes of the other series *as if they were in fact an interpretation of the sermon text*.

Admittedly when one strives too hard for consonance there is the danger that the individual text with its specific conceptions and statements about God and humankind is too strongly dominated by the positions of other texts so that in the end, put more pointedly, one could deliver the same sermon with each of the six texts for a Sunday. Simply the knowledge of the "broken" consonance of the pericopes alone should counteract this danger. The fact that e.g. even according to The Revised Lectionary from 2014 the "Vita Pauli" (2 Cor 11:18–12:10) was determined as a sermon text in series 1 for the Sunday Sexagesimae simply because the Basilica of *Saint Paul Outside the Walls* was the Roman stational church for on Sexagesimae, the second Sunday pre-lent.[1007] It seemed reasonable to read a central text of Paul which summarizes his life, faith and theology in this St. Paul's Church. Nevertheless, an attempt was later made to make this text plausible according to the principle of consonance in its place on this Sunday: The text for the week reads: "Today, if you hear his voice, do not harden your hearts" (Heb 3:15).[1008]

---

**1006** M. Luther, WA 7, 97. Cf. Also WA 10/III, 238: "Hence Scripture itself is its own light. It is excellent when Scripture interprets itself."

**1007** The Church San Paulo fuori le mure (Lat.: Sancti Pauli extra muros) is one of the four Patriarchal Basilicas in Rome and simultaneously one of the many station-churches of the city. The "station churches" or "station services" owe their name to the circumstance that the bishop of Rome celebrated the central mass in these churches on a particular Sunday in the liturgical year. Hence the terms "station church" and "station service" serve two aspects: A larger part of the congregation who are on an eternal pilgrimage follow the bishop into these churches and make an "intermediate stop" with him there. At the same time the church as a building is a "station", namely one place in a whole series of churches of worship in which, in the course of the liturgical year, the mass is celebrated by the Bishop according to a detailed schedule.

**1008** For this Sunday, the new lectionary specifies that the sermon texts appropriate to the Proper may be chosen from "Wis 6:13–17 or Hes 2:1–3:3" in series II (earlier Acts 16:9–15). Gal 1:6–10

The "position" of the church in the liturgical year is in turn a statement on its higher rank compared to St. Lawrence (station church of the previous Sunday Septuagesimae) or its lesser rank than St. Peter (station church on the following Sunday Quinquagesimae, today Estomihi). This pericope, 2 Cor 11:18–12:10, can only with difficulty be combined with the other texts. *Some connections can be established; but they are above all an act of interpretation,* not a sign of wisdom in linking the corresponding texts. The exploration of intertextual coherence is therefore not an art in referring back to alleged "original intentions". Those who try to establish contexts and connections for their congregation in this manner, should be aware that they are arguing on the basis of their personal views and not on the "power of authority of the church's traditions"[1009].

In the use of pericopes, preachers will also be particularly challenged in their exegetical-hermeneutic and homiletic competence. In individual cases this can lead to a deviation from the common lectionary since (1) there can be concrete problems and occurrences *in the life of the congregation* which neither can nor should be postponed, situations for which a particular sermon on a particular matter must be held and for which an appropriate text must be found.[1010] (2) Even the preachers themselves may be personally challenged by exceptional experiences and, out of the resulting *consternation,* expound on what living by faith means to them in this concrete situation.[1011] They would possibly withhold something from the congregation if they kept quiet about an experience for which they could be their witness and instead struggled with a text which had nothing to do with their current situation.[1012] (3) It may also happen that, in spite of repeated attempts one can find *no suitable approach* to a particular text. Instead of then resorting to quoting from sermon aids or, from sheer indecision, holding an "exegetical seminar paper", one should fall back on another suitable text and in so doing attempt to keep an eye on the Proper for the Sunday.

---

has been added as a "further text" in the rank of the former "marginal texts" for this Sunday. Cf. Neuordnung der gottesdienstlichen Lesungen und Predigttexte, 2014, 148.

**1009** G. Kunze, 1955, 174.

**1010** In a city congregation, a business must be closed. 360 employees are dismissed according to various rulings. For the time being they will have less money in their pockets. The occurrence could e.g. give rise to a sermon on the question of what it means to lead a full and meaningful life, which, from the current socio-political standpoint, is to a large extent still measured on the qualities of the consumer and thereby on the income of the individual.

**1011** A pastor who loses his mother in a bus accident deals with the question of what it means to live with death and to have faith in view of (further) borderline experiences of life within the frame of a thematic sermon series.

**1012** This possibility should be chosen carefully, but is not suspicious on principle. It corresponds to the classic situation of witness which still today determines many worship services in the Pentecostal and other free churches.

Klaus-Peter Hertzsch, however, points to the possibility of a productive *tension between pressur-izing current events and the Proper provided*. With reference to the building of the Berlin Wall on 13th August 1961 (the 11th, Sunday after Trinity) or to the suppression of the Prague Spring on 21st August 1968 (the 11th Sunday after Trinity) he explains how the texts provided – if one read or heard them patiently – were suitable for appealing to people in their concrete situation as citizens of the kingdom of God, to encourage and comfort them. This, however, only works if one keeps the obvious tension between (direct) awareness of reality and understanding of the text as a suitable requirement for a sermon to be interesting and accomplishes to "make the listeners attend eagerly"[1013].

The Proper and readings for a Sunday are a challenge to deal with central questions of human existence or of living by faith in the course of the liturgical year (by working through the provided cycle of various topics of life therein). Joachim Scharfenberg considered the liturgical year – among other things – as a model for a *curriculum vitae* oriented on the life of Jesus. The liturgical year offers the possibility of "understanding" the story of one's own life "against the background of his [i.e. Jesus'] story, to interpret it anew and in this way to see its meaningfulness. Through the liturgical year, our fathers made the life of Jesus 'accessible'"[1014], and by doing so, elementary experiences and questions of one's own life can be brought up in the light of the life of Jesus or in connection with other stories of God's action. This holds true not only for Advent, Christmas, Epiphany, Lent and Easter. The "feastless half" of the church year – to which, among others, belong the Sundays after Trinity – provides clues for a new determination of one's own place in the world, to have a critical look at questions of a life in freedom, to arrange reconciliation, practice solidarity etc. The proposed series of texts help to integrate a wide range of impulses, questions and claims of the Christian tradition into a representative selection of the communication of the gospel. Such a structure of texts certainly contributes to the fact that not only the favorite topics of the respective pastor are deliberated from the pulpit.[1015]

Lastly, also a "spiritual" function can be attributed to the annual recurrence of the Proper: This kind of repetition encourages "a recognition and a new encounter [...] with a word, with a thought, in which one continues to penetrate deeper and which always unfold further. This is the secret of the profound

---

1013 K.-P. Hertzsch, 1995, 730f.
1014 J. Scharfenberg, 1985, 79f.
1015 In his book, the "Rhythmus des Kirchenjahres" (The Rhythm of the Liturgical Year), Kristian Fechtner (2007) discusses theological questions and those related to the hermeneutics of the worship service which go far beyond the text level of the Sundays. Besides the practices connected to the worship service, he discusses the cultural dimension of the liturgical year from which he draws conclusions on the challenges of preaching, which, again, render the liturgical year a good recommendation as a "house within time".

effect from which the liturgical year lives, as do all Breviary-Prayers and orders of readings."[1016] The regular encounter with certain ideas of living by faith does not simply come about with a specific structuring of the year but creates a life-accompanying rhythm in which the sermon plays a part and which in a certain way contributes to an accentuation on the life of those attending the worship service.

### 7.3.2 Preaching in the Communication Process of the Worship Service

**a) On the Reciprocal Dependence of the Liturgical and Homiletic Functions**
For an appropriate assessment of the function of the sermon in the worship service one must first recall that, according to an evangelical understanding, the liturgy is a *form of communication of the gospel*. According to Michael Meyer-Blanck the liturgy guides the service in a *dramaturgical* respect (among other things through opening, call to worship and reading) "towards the sermon and afterwards leads from the sermon (through the intensification in communion and the sending and blessing) back into everyday life"[1017]. Hence, we cannot fail to see that the sermon is simply *one* sequence within the complex event of the worship service which *on the whole* serves the communication of the gospel. This process therefore does not stand or fall with the sermon. The readings, hymns, prayers and confessions are also "testimonies". Consequently, there are worship services without a sermon but no sermon without a liturgy.

Of course, with this topic, it is certainly a question of more than the solemn conclusion that the communication of faith to the congregation is a multimedia event in which various systems of symbols (words, tones, colors, gestures etc.) are shown to advantage. Where God and a person meet in the celebration of the liturgy, where reflection and jubilation, lamentation and thanksgiving, eating and drinking take place, where reconciliation and solidarity are practiced, it is not simply a matter of an *agreement about* the basis of communion with God, i.e. of a hermeneutic task, but also of the *celebrated practice* of this communion, of the collaboration of those communicating.

The sermon is embedded in a comprehensive event of communication and participation in which individuals make themselves heard before God, in which the congregation articulates itself in the face of God and in relation to the world

---

**1016** K.-P. Hertzsch, 1995, 729.
**1017** M. Meyer-Blanck, 2006, 158.

(without two opposing "directions" being mentioned) – an event that incorporates singing and meditation, where situations are perceived and potential changes come into view. The liturgy relieves the strain on the preacher of having to achieve the whole communication with his sermon, of having to say "everything" and explain "everything". If preachers assumed that the liturgy only provided the framework for the sermon (as e.g. a choir embellishes the election- or celebratory-speech of a politician) they would overtax themselves and would most likely not even reach many members of the congregation and thus disappoint them. In the case of a pale, diffused, anemic sermon, the church would then have to regard the whole service as a waste of time.

However, it is necessary to warn against the misapprehension (sometimes developing from long-standing habit and routine), to consider the sermon *de facto* as just another part of the unchanging Ordinary of the service. If the sermon strikes up a friendly, harmless tone immediately after the greeting, continues with this and attempts above all to create a festive ritual atmosphere it will scarcely do justice to its "prophetic" dimension and the rhetorical task connected to this. The problem of the poor recollection of a sermon, mentioned frequently in the context of homiletic misunderstandings, should not be changed into a liturgical virtue: The reciprocal, functional interpenetration of sermon and liturgy is disrupted if it suffices for the congregation "to have heard what is well-known once again"; if this happens then "we [as preachers] have decisively remained in debt"[1018].

As part of the worship service the special place of the sermon is clear inter alia in that, in contrast to the other liturgical elements which *could* all be taken from the agenda and the lectionary, it is an act formed in free speech where the dialog which determines the whole service (sometimes sung, sometimes formulated as a prayer and sometimes articulated in traditional, abstract wording) now becomes linguistically and factually concrete. Through the testimony of an individual person, questions and answers become more pointed – which certainly also resonate in the songs, prayers and confessions, but may only be conveyed through the argumentative culture of the sermon in necessary positions, verdicts and decisions.

Another peculiarity of the liturgical piece of preaching is the fact that *it has its own liturgy with a fixed sequence*: In its maximal structure, it consists of: (1) A greeting from the pulpit, (2) an announcement of the sermon text, (3) the congregation rises, (4) a reading from Scripture, (5) a prayer before the sermon, (6) the congregation sits down, (7) the sermon, (8) a prayer after the sermon, (9) a blessing from the pulpit, (10) a sermon hymn. These elements, which go beyond the sermon address, have primarily emerged from the tradition of the High Medieval

---

1018 Loc. cit., 732.

predicant services. The greeting from the pulpit was used particularly in those cases in which the preacher was not identical with the person leading the liturgy. The preacher faced the congregation for the first time from the pulpit and thus welcomed them. This does not necessarily mean that one must forgo the greeting from the pulpit today. However, nowadays it has gained different functions. For example, it highlights that the congregation has now come to an important point – the point where the focus turns towards their own reifications, immersion in, and consequences of what it means to live a live by faith, which was previously articulated in the songs, prayers, and traditional texts. The greeting from the pulpit also signals that the preacher is now speaking in a distinct function, as someone who is also trained and commissioned to exemplify to the congregation, to the best of his knowledge and belief, in contemporary language, what it means to live by faith and to thereby clarify in public what Protestantism stands for today etc.

It is important to warn against a latent continuation or extension of the sermon to other liturgical elements (such as the prayers of intercession). When ritual prayers, pleas and laments, the Creed or other elements of the celebration of the Lord's Supper (beyond the inherent kerygmatic impulses) are homiletically overstrained, increased excessively and garnished with points from the sermon, their specific liturgical function loses its plausibility in the communication process of the worship service.

Such explicit continuation of the sermon is also not necessary because the individual pieces of the service are both communication and contemplation, that is, they imply – to different degrees – both a preaching and a praying dimension.[1019] They reveal both a *katabatic* (literally: descending, i.e. coming from God for the benefit of humanity) and an *anabatic* (literally: ascending, i.e. relating to God) component. Here are some examples:

---

1019 Cf. on this R. Volp, 1994, 1066–1068, also critically above at I.7.2.3, p. 361–364.

| Elements of the Liturgy | Correspondences between katabatic and anabatic elements of the worship service |
|---|---|
| Psalm | The Psalm is not a reading like t he epistle and gospel, which is why it is part of the introit to the sequence "opening and invocation" (primarily anabatic dimension) not to the sequence "proclamation and confession". Yet the psalm "preaches" to those who pray it: It shows the extent to which God is a "good shepherd" and in what sense comfort and the fullness of life can be found in him (katabatic dimension). |
| Kyrie | The same applies to the Kyrie: The congregation turns to God and asks for his mercy for particular matters of concern which – in the sense of intercessions – can also be connected expressis verbis with the Kyrie Acclamation (anabatic dimension). By doing so, the congregation also expresses its trust; it bears witness to its faith in the God who has helped them thus far (katabatic dimension). |
| Readings | Here the katabatic dimension comes initially to the fore, in that the congregation is confronted with God's acts of salvation. The renewed festive recollection of this event, however, is also an act of the glorification of God (anabatic aspect). |
| Creed | Depending on where the Creed has its place in the service the anabatic and katabatic aspects change: (1) After the readings it has the character of a confirmation of the newly revived basis of faith. Here the Creed is simultaneously a glorification of God and a testimonial confession. (2) When placed after the sermon, it expresses that – after the preacher has testified – it is now the turn of the congregation to stand and witness to the truth. In this case the katabatic dimension predominates. (3) Prayed before the celebration of Communion, the Creed is a great glorification of God's gift of salvation and has a strong anabatic emphasis. |
| Hymn | Regardless of whether a hymn is a song of praise and thanksgiving, an expression of repentance or meant as a plea – it plays a part in the glorification of God whose power, mercy, kindness, patience etc. are sung of in this way (anabatic dimension). At the same time the Church's hymns are full of educational elements, simplifying the communication of the gospel, often "little sermons" transposed into musical form (katabatic dimension). |
| Sermon | The sermon stands, as explained above, in close connection to prayer. When the Lord's Supper is celebrated, it always also serves to lead to the sharing of the bread and wine. The sermon itself verbalizes the circumstances of life which 'propel' us to the celebration of Communion or again to prayer. On the other hand, it anticipates linguistically what will be celebrated – in the Supper and in the future in general. Here, the connection of anabatic and katabatic elements is particularly dense. |

**Fig. 23:** Correspondences between katabatic and anabatic elements of the worship service

*Liturgical forms of "actualizing" of the gospel* are all the more plausible the less they are disturbed by additional 'kerygmatic remarks'. Even the "placement" and integration of the individual pieces in the overall context of a service has an influence on their meaning and function. As a rule, the individual liturgical elements imply some kind of retrospective references and anticipations, and thus stand in an inner connection to one another as we have seen in the aforementioned example of the Creed. The same could be said with regard to the prayer for the offering, the prayer of confessional and other pieces of the liturgy.

The vivid relationship of liturgy and sermon has experienced various emphases which have led to *services with specific structures*. Within these structures the function of the sermon was now and again specified. In the *Political Evening Prayer,* emerging from the area of student-congregations in the '60s, the sermon was, as it were, the aim of the service.[1020] The *Worship Services in a New Form*, which took place at irregular intervals and were usually organized by parachurch organizations (e.g. youth ministries) were an attempt to dismantle the formal hurdles of a liturgy which was incomprehensible to many people and to replace them with new forms. In this way, especially young people should be introduced to the worship service. What was special in this service did not lie in a specific orientation regarding the content but in the opening-up of the traditional parts of the service to the symbols and music of the young people. The tightening of the liturgy and the extension of the spoken part to 30 minutes and longer made the sermon a special high point in these services.[1021]

Where should the sermon have its place? In the "Evangelisches Gottesdienstbuch" (Protestant Order of Worship) it again stands in its original place after the readings[1022], only separated from them by one hymn. This makes particularly two things clear: First, the sermon – corresponding to the Protestant understanding of the relationship between tradition and interpretation – is, to a certain extent, actually a "continuation of the reading with other linguistic means"[1023]. The close connection between the sermon and the readings makes it clear that preachers

---

**1020** The Political Evening Prayer is initiated by accusation and criticism (informing those present and appealing to God), in which formally an analogy to the introit to the corresponding psalm can be seen. In the second part of the Evening Prayer the "gravamina" mentioned earlier are reinforced by meditating on texts and symbols. The sermon, which is frequently dominated by appellative speech acts, is allotted the task of making concrete suggestions for changing a particular situation and encouraging the listeners to make their contribution to the change striven for. Cf. W. J. Hollenweger, 1979, 178f.

**1021** R. Volp speaks of a liturgical "deforesting redevelopment for the purpose of feeble attractions" (1994, 1136) in relation to these services. On the other hand, it should be remembered that in every epoch of worship "profane" elements were integrated into the liturgy, or non-ecclesial signs were endowed with new religious functions.

**1022** Cf. Evangelisches Gottesdienstbuch, 2000, 43. In most churches in the ecumenical world the Creed has always had its place *after* the sermon.

**1023** M. Josuttis, 1991, 243. Cf. K. Raschzok (2014) for more information on this approach.

are dependent upon what they themselves "confess" and that – in order to speak freely – they relate to a tradition which unites them with the congregation. Second, it becomes clear that readings *and* sermons belong together and should lead the listeners beyond tradition to an independent confession of their own.

The custom of inserting the Creed between the gospel and the sermon encouraged the misapprehension that the adjoining pulpit speech more or less reflects the preacher's private opinion and *therefore* should not be universally validated by the Creed of the church. The relationship between Creed and sermon, however, is determined in another way: In speaking the Creed *after the sermon* the congregation expresses inter alia (especially if they stand up) that they *stand by their faith* and are thus themselves involved in the communication of the gospel. They are not confessing to the sermon which has just been held, but to a particular culture of faith, to which the ideals and options of the Jewish-Christian tradition belong as well as the practice of this faith in the worship service and in daily life. This does not contradict the expectation that preaching may lead to new expressions of faith and a very personal "confession" of each individual.

The question of the place of the sermon can also be related in the narrower sense to the *space* in which the worship service takes place.[1024] It makes a difference whether one preaches on the shore of a lake or in a forest, in a gothic cathedral or in a modern community center in which the space for the service is separated from the kitchen by a sliding partition. The place where the worship service takes place influences the listeners – as well as the preachers and their sermon. In a certain sense the space pre-structures the communication in that it raises certain expectations and prevents others from rising when it creates a "festive" atmosphere or allows an unobstructed view of everyday life. Anyone who ascends a two-meter high, opulently gilded baroque pulpit in a light-flooded processional church does not, however, have to cultivate the emotiveness appropriate to the Baroque Period but may make an appealing counterpoint through the unadorned clarity of their personal address. Anyone who holds a high church service in a barrack used as a makeshift church (faced by benches of which the first row is less than two meters away) and relies constantly on the Early Church formal language of the liturgy, without at least occasionally attempting adequate "more personal" formulations "in simple language"[1025] will make it difficult for the congregation to follow the process of the service.

---

1024 On the function and influence of space on the liturgy and sermon cf. the booklet on the theme *Raumerkundungen* [Explorations on space] in the periodical magazine of the Gemeinsamen Arbeitsstelle für gottesdienstliche Fragen of the EKD, Vol 21(2), 2007 and on theological questions regarding the semiotics of space cf. H. Muck (1992).

1025 The term "simple language" does not mean children's language in liturgical discourse. "Easy language exposes a certainty that is supported by traditional word combinations. In the vast majority of cases, however, the 'intermediate filter' of simple language causes texts

## b) Digital and Analog Structures of Communication in the Worship Service

A further possibility of doing justice to the different functions of homiletic communication following the rules of free speech and liturgical, ritually-related communication lies in the differentiation between analog and digital signs.[1026]

There is a great repertoire of means of expression available, the forms and structures of which have nothing to do with the "things" and facts to which they relate. Here it is a matter of "arbitrary" signs, of apparently willful connections of form and content – of combinations of particular expressions with particular meanings as they are presented through the world of concepts. In this world, one only understands properly when one has learned the appropriate combinations of words and their meanings according to the rules of a particular language. Thus, one knows what is meant when a "dog", a "car" or a "computer" is talked about. The correspondence of word and meaning is based here on a binary code which is why one speaks – simplifying the complex process of reception – of "digital codes": Particular expressions always correspond to particular contents which one can find in relevant dictionaries.

People, however, can communicate in another way. This can already be seen in particular words which reveal a similarity to what they describe; "thunder", "jingle", "hiss", "buzz", "hum", "purr", "rustle" etc. However, above all, it is the countless non-verbal signs that we invent or adopt in order to communicate spontaneously, even across language barriers: People spread their arms, making it clear that someone is welcome. They clench their fists – with which one could also strike – to threaten someone. One bows to someone as a sign of "submissiveness" or respect. Someone who ostentatiously turns his back on a person, signals that he wants nothing to do with them. One pats someone on the shoulder to assure them of their support. These gestures mark an attitude or the beginning of an action: embrace, blow, submission, departure, flight, support etc. *Something of the matter meant is present in the sign itself.*[1027]

Such signs also play a part in the worship service: the laying-on of hands in the blessing or an ordination, the spreading of arms for the greeting, the raising of the hands in prayer, the kneeling before the altar, in the pulpit or in the pew, the standing and sitting at the proper points in the liturgy, the extending of hands

---

to acquire simplicity, intelligibility, clarity, and occasionally even humility." (A. Gidion/J. Arnold/R. Martinsen, 2013, 17).

**1026** On the differentiation between analog and digital codes of communication cf. also P. Watzlawick et al., 1967, 60.

**1027** Of course, also in these cases, communication is carried out on the basis of intercultural codes in the sense of elementary rules of behavior which have developed in the course of human history.

before or after the Communion, the standing in a circle, common consumption of bread and wine, the proffering of food and drink connected to this etc. – all these signs already in their analog form of expression point to the contents of what should be communicated.

Nevertheless, one cannot divide analog and digital forms of expression into non-verbal and verbal signs: Indeed, not all non-verbal signs function according to the rules of analogy. There is a wealth of non-verbal signs the significance of which is based exclusively on more or less arbitrary agreements and consequently must be assigned to the digital area. To these belong – in relation to the service – e.g. the liturgical colors (Easter: white – not green like nature; Passion: lilac – not red like blood). On the other hand, an altar which has no decoration and has been emptied may show analogies to the event of Good Friday in its nakedness; the placing of the Reformation pulpits over the altar has both analog and digital aspects. It assigns an outstanding position to the sermon within the service which in turn is only recognized by those who participate in the world of "digital" concepts of the theology of Reformation. The same is true e.g. of an "analog" watch: the dial virtually marks – analogous to a sundial – the "rotation of the sun" around the earth only for those in the know. What this has to do with an analog watch is based on complicated arrangements. A child can never "learn" the meaning of an analog clock without guidance, but faces it with the same helplessness as with a digital one.

Both repertoires of human communication, digital and analog signs, are indispensable for the worship service[1028] as for human communication in general.

Processes of communication based on "digital communication" have a complex and logical syntax; they make a multi-layered argumentation and the reception of abstract ideas possible. "Digital" signs are more versatile than "analog" ones in that they allow for quick and accurate communication at the informational level. If one were to wish to hold a sermon which only had analog signs (and in which e.g. one endeavored in mime to give an interpretation of the Parable of the "Lost Son") one would not only need much more time but would also have to accept a high share of vague "statements". Thus, a complete "translation" of digital into analog language is not possible without a severe loss of information.

However, the recourse to the apparent explicitness of digital signs only partly fulfills the conditions of credible communication: For example, a person who, from time to time, only *mentions* to his partner that he loves her would lack credibility if the analog signs of communication – as, e.g., an embrace and a kiss – are lacking. The analog signs bring to expression the relationship between the partners in communication over and *beyond information*. Analog signs are indispensable for the practice of coming into relationship with one another through communication (holding out a hand, embrace, a reception with open arms etc.).

---

**1028** Cf. K.-H. Bieritz, 2004, 248–251. Cf. corresponding ritual-theoretic insights in the context of the church is understood in B. F. Nielsen, 2004, esp. 65–93; on the relevance of digital and analog structures of communication cf. loc. cit., 88–90.

Therefore, it is one of the standards of practical-theological education to make aware and practice digital and analog communication patterns. Much of the communication in the worship service depends on the genuinely inviting attitude of the liturgists, on the openness of their gaze (based on how open they are towards others, especially other viewpoints), on the coherence of their language, etc. Those who conduct a service and preach should be concerned that patterns of digital and analog communication are shown to advantage in order to prevent avoidable disruptions on the levels of information and relationship. It is thus also important to ensure that the information provided does not contradict the level of relationship that develops between preacher and listener.

These aspects are particularly relevant – apart from the arrangement of the sacraments in which word and action are bound together in a specific way – for the communication of forgiveness in the service, which is also a *homiletic* challenge. However, this does not mean that the communication of the gospel – presented as an event of justification – should effectively become a digitalized event of information or proclamation *about* forgiveness. Rather, "forgiveness" *is conveyed* and *experienced* in, with, and throughout the entire execution of the complex communication process of preaching as one dimension of the gospel – or it founders on the conditions of this communication, remains incomprehensible and implausible. However, it also requires those analogous signs surrounding and attesting to the words, which show themselves in the performance of the preachers, in their facial expressions and gestures, in their style of communication, in their voice, in the ensemble of the signs which communicate their esteem of those present. In this regard, we must thus agree with Michael Meyer-Blanck's objection, according to which the gospel – again according to the understanding of the Reformation – is not simply to be found in the words of the sermon but is expressed in Word *and Sacrament* with forgiveness as its aim. It corresponds to this that one should understand the production of the whole service with its merging of "digital" and "analog" patterns of communication as a space for the event and experience (also) of forgiveness.[1029]

## 7.4 On the Category of "Liturgical Conditions" of the Sermon

The detailed discussions in the previous chapter allow us now to thetically summarize the framework of a sermon in the liturgical context:

---

1029 "The prayerful and celebrating action as a whole is the form in which the encounter of God and man occurs in the liturgy. Not one particular liturgical place in the course of the service or even a particular formula, but the anamnetic and epicletical event as a whole is Eucharistic, kindling and justifying faith" (M. Meyer-Blanck, 2010, 99). Cf. in this context also Michael J. Quicke's concern to bear in mind the worship service as a whole during the act of sermon preparation, which also means paying heed to continuity as regards the content of sermon and worship service (cf. M. J. Quicke, 2011, esp. 83–102). In so doing, however, the specific functions and forms of rhetoric communication (sermon) on the one hand, and of ritual communication (liturgy) on the other, should not become blurred.

1. Sermon and liturgy hold together in an inner alternating relationship which must be taken into account through an appropriate structuring of the tense connection between "prophetic" and "priestly" roles in the service. This demands a fundamental examination of the respective independent function of the liturgical elements and includes the attempt to keep in view the Proper of a service when constructing an inner connection between liturgy and sermon.

2. The extent to which the liturgy, on the one hand, is not "prophetically" overtaxed and misused as the continuation of the sermon just in a different form, and the sermon, on the other hand, does not degenerate into an outdated ritual which maltreats external truths, the service as a whole can lead to the individual becoming the topic in the tension between departure and arrival. Existential questions are raised in the horizon of a complex understanding of life and reality. For people's experience of time the breakthrough into their own present becomes a key to seeing their own future as open in the positive sense etc.

3. The communication of the gospel occurs not simply or primarily in the sermon but determines the service as a whole, whereby "digital" and "analog" processes of understanding interlock. Nevertheless, the sermon is the sequence in the event of communication of a service in which rhetorical competence – i.e. the consideration of the principles of free speech is demanded to a particularly high degree. The traditionally-formed speech of the ritual drops into the background during the sermon and is superseded by a personal, authentic (and therein exemplary) testimony of what it means under the predetermined conditions of the present (understood as the sum of all socio-cultural factors), to lead a life "lived by faith"[1030] in an undetermined way.

4. As in the sermon it is not a question of preaching *about* a text but, among other things, *on the basis* of a text looking into the reality of the lives of contemporaries or the life perspectives which are opened for them through faith, the topics and texts of the lectionary are not to be "explained" in the course of the liturgy. Such orders provide a cycle, a recurring framework for reflection and specific experiences of faith in the liturgical and homiletic agenda of the Sundays, whereby it provides access to the whole breadth and depth of the liturgical year as a vademecum of faith within the worship service.

---

[1030] On the understanding of this formulation cf. III.2.3.

5. The liturgical context makes the sermon a common concern of preachers and congregation. The preachers stand *with and in the congregation* coram deo. Their participation in the coming experiences of life and faith as well as the expectations of the congregation which are expressed in the liturgy are an important prerequisite for the *coming before the congregation* and serving it with their personal testimony.

6. The liturgy relieves the strain on preachers of having to serve all the needs of communication or participation in the congregation with their sermon. To the extent to which they show the liturgical elements in their individual functions to advantage, they may begin to think of the sermon as a *partial aim of the service* and thus limit and concretize the homiletic task accordingly.

7. Because the liturgical elements cannot be divided into those which should only be "heard by God" (anabatic dimension) and those which are only directed to humans (katabatic dimension) the worship service cannot be simply probed according to its "achievement of proclamation" – more or less in the interest of a smooth "one-way-traffic" of the Word of God. The role of the sermon, among other things, is to adequately express the faith of the congregation (that is, the faith that the congregation has already adopted), and to continuously remind and affirm them in their faith and identity in this way.[1031]

8. All in all, it is important that sermon and liturgy each contribute in their own way to the dramaturgy of the worship service, whereby the general tension of rhetoric and ritual, of "prophetic" and "priestly" speech proceed in a very concretely defined relation to one another, which one can understand as variable ways of behaving for preachers and those celebrating the liturgy in the service: "In the context of the liturgy the sermon is the most personal, even if not private, part; it is topical even if it is related to tradition; it relates completely to the congregation even if not isolated locally but is understandable to the church as a whole. The sermon is virtually a dramaturgically necessary, a personal alien element in the context of the supra-personal liturgy. Or put in another way: The ritual element in its power and force is more easily recognizable precisely through what is individual in the sermon. That is why the ritual needs the sermon as the inherent difference to the ritual."[1032]

---

1031 Cf. below "The Sermon as an Expression of the Life of the Congregation" (III.2.1.1).
1032 M. Meyer-Blanck, 2007, 171.

Part II: **Basic Directions and Guiding Questions of Sermon Analysis and Feedback Discussion after Preaching**

# Preliminary Remarks: On Systematization of the Methodological Approaches in Sermon Analysis

Sermon analysis plays a vital part in the homiletic didactics in universities, as well as in pastoral education and training. Since the 1970s a whole series of strategies and methods for sermon analysis[1] have been developed and tested, allowing for a systematic approach to preaching as an event of communication from different points of view and varying questions.[2] In the course of this development a small number of classic models of sermon analysis have become established which can be used by individuals and groups and are relatively easy to apply. At the same time, the different questions and issues addressed by the respective methods of analysis have contributed to the academic standardization of elementary homiletic angles of reflection (on person, text, theology, language, situation etc.) New technical possibilities make it possible to further refine particular forms of analysis.[3]

Since the delivery of a sermon is such a complex process, a multiplicity of analytical attempts would be necessary if one desired to acquire a more or less complete picture of the homiletic "design" and effect of a sermon.

If it is the goal of an analysis to investigate as many factors as possible which impact the composition, content, and presentation of a sermon, it is vital to also consider, for example, *the connection between the sermon, on the one hand, and the manner of its preparation on the other*. Taking up this idea, Annette C. Müller shows in a comprehensive study conducted on the basis of individual cases which methods and strategies preachers use for the preparation of their sermons. In addition, she developed an analytical method which considers – alongside rhetorical, pragmatic, personal and theological aspects of the sermon – also the "procedural dimension" of preparation. In this way, significant coherences between the information provided by the individual respondents on their approach to sermon preparation on the one hand and the actual sermon manuscript on the other hand are revealed. The aim of such analyses targeted at facilitating the preachers' work on the sermon is, among other things, "to reduce troublesome and agonizing moments in the process of [sermon] composition" and to strengthen "homiletic dimensions which until now appear to have been under-represented in sermon manuscripts through a modification of the strategy of composition."[4]

---

1 Cf. e.g. Homiletische Arbeitsgruppe (1973); H. W. Dannowski (1973); F. Riemann ([1974] 2009); K. Götzinger (1979); H.-Ch. Piper (1976a, 1976b); H. Krüger (1981); W. Engemann (1984, 1992a).
2 Cf. the synoptic study by S. Wöhrle, 2006.
3 Cf. especially the further development of empirical sermon research through electronically-assisted processes in H. Schwier/S. Gall, 2008 and 2013.
4 A. C. Müller, 2014, 156.

https://doi.org/10.1515/9783110440256-part II

Since such complex analyses will also in the future only be realizable within the framework of extensive individual studies, the analytical focus in the everyday homiletic practice will have to be placed upon a *limited range of questions, depending on the individual case.* Consequently it is important to clarify previous to the actual sermon analysis (and also prior to the follow-up discussion with the congregation which is usually conducted on the basis of very simplified methods of analysis) which "factor", which dimension, which aspect of the sermon one should primarily focus on: The "actual" content of the sermon? The credibility of what was said? The memorability of the arguments? The "biblicity" of the sermon? Its relevance for a larger public? Its plausibility? Does it fulfill the claim of preaching in a contemporary manner? Does its pattern of speech and accordingly its rhetorical achievement contribute to the understanding of the sermon's point? Its theology?

Applying the different methods of sermon analysis presupposes the knowledge of the functions of the individual perspectives of reflection in homiletics. The analytical work on the sermon will imply for the preacher to keep reconsidering some of the points discussed in Part II of this Homiletics. This may happen, for example, by attending for a certain period of time – I am thinking of a period of about half a year – to questions of the hermeneutics of biblical texts, of one's own preaching style, of the focus of the constructed preaching situation etc.

In the following I shall only refer to *homiletically founded* – i.e. to methodically reflected – models of sermon analysis which do not approach sermons with arbitrary or global, additively compiled catalogs of questions[5] but which manifest a theory-driven interest. The sequence of the individual descriptions below corresponds to the chronological history of the development of sermon analysis after 1945.[6]

In the depiction of the different analytical attempts I proceed from the semiotic assumption fundamental to all situations of communication, that every process of interpersonal communication and comprehension is inseparably connected to the *use of signs*, especially their *significant forms*, which are what make an analysis possible in the first place.[7] For the structuring of Part II of this book this implies the following consequences:

---

5 Cf. the questionnaire of the "Heidelberger Methode" (G. Debus, 1989, 55–61). This, however, lacks one of the decisive quality criteria of scientific research, which is a critical distance towards the applied research method.

6 Previous attempts can hardly be called proper "sermon analyses". Impulses before 1945 could rather be called pragmatic instructions for examining the homiletic maxims favored back then (cf. F. Niebergall, 1929, 92–111). Cf. also the bibliography of the sermon analysis by J. Hermelink, 1989.

7 On the foundations of this approach cf. W. Engemann, 1993a.

A person who informs another of something refers to linguistic and other *forms of expression*, to the most varied facets and features a statement can have – i.e. to "signifiers" which are connected to corresponding contents. In order to detect and to understand such significant forms one must know the relevant codes. Only then is it possible to come to an adequately precise conclusion concerning the content of a sermon, its theological premises, its understanding of God, its image of humanity etc. Therefore the chapters II.1.1–1.5 are dedicated to this spectrum of questions. They describe analysis models which are linked to *the text form of the sermon* (words, speech acts, rhetoric etc.).

While these forms of analysis – due to merely focusing on the textual form of the sermon – may be applied to the sermon manuscript itself, other analytical methods (II.2) take a look at the relationship of the sermon to either its producer (preacher) and/or its recipients (listeners): Anyone who speaks, nolens volens, also reveals something about himself through which the symptom-, expressive- and self-revealing-function[8] of linguistic signs find expression. For this, *forms of analysis which focus on the subject of the sermon*[9] (II.2.1) appear to be more useful. Preachers always want their sermon to have an effect on those addressed. This refers to the appealing- or signal-function of linguistic signs. Consequently it is also possible – through an analysis of the *perception of the sermon by the listeners* – to draw conclusions about the sermon's content or its – perhaps latent – intentions, about its image of the listeners, or its theology etc. (II.2.2).

The following chapter does not include detailed presentations of specific methods for the didactic impartation of the different homiletic principles on the basis of examples of sermon analyses, because the range of possibilities arising from the approaches listed below is almost infinite. What these approaches provide, however, is a potential for the deepening of individual homiletic perspectives in varying ways. Above all, they all aim to strengthen the awareness of different concrete aspects of the sermon. One approved method of such analysis-based didactics is the "advocate model" in which previously appointed "advocates" (of the text, the listeners, the person of the preacher, the language and theology of preaching) – already before the sermon is discussed by the group – direct their analytical focus towards the corresponding aspects of the sermon and describe, whether the sermon meets the requirements of the situation, the text, theology etc., or not. These "advocates" have, so to speak, an analytical "head start". They side, as it were, with one of these aspects of the sermon and, in doing so, usually open a lively discussion which – at one and the same time – represents a continuation of the analysis and serves the acquisition of homiletic competences.[10]

---

8 Cf. K. Bühler, 2011, 34.
9 On the understanding of the term subject in this phrase cf. footnote 7 in the preface.
10 For more detail see W. Engemann, 2009c, 420–427.

# 1 Concepts of Analysis Focused on the Text Form of the Sermon

## 1.1 The Approach of Content Analysis

The development of Content Analysis is fundamentally connected to the research into mass-communication, which started in the 1950s and '60s and was strongly determined by socio-psychological and linguistic questions. Here the center of interest is, among other things, the effect of *communiqués*: *What* messages are received, and *in which way*? How do pieces of information, intentions and opinions on the part of the speaker affect the expectations and attitudes of the listeners? The basis of the analysis is a *written speech text* which provides the foundation for numerous statistical analyses. "Content Analysis is a research technique for the objective, systematic and quantitative description of the manifest content of communication."[11] Hence, the protagonists of this method commit themselves to an ideologically and theologically unerring objectivity based on statistical investigations[12] – at least when it comes to the categories of analysis. This approach restricted to the *analysis of the wording of a text* was taken up in different, text-based sciences and became known as "Inhaltsanalyse [Content Analysis]": "Content Analysis is an empirical method for a systematic, intersubjectively reliable and comprehensible description of content-related and formal characteristics of communication."[13]

Content Analysis obtains its investigation criteria from quantitative as well as qualitative categories which are further subdivided into numerous individual categories. *Quantitative* investigations statistically record what can be captured from what is written in black and white: the frequency and intensity of particular nouns, verbs and other elements of content. They are thus an analysis of "manifest content". On the other hand, Content Analysis also deals with *qualitative* categories as e.g. with the atmospheric environment, the mood, the cognitive content as well as the intended effect of the speech. This is what is referred to as "latent content".[14] In order to deduce the text's content, extensive schemata in

---

11 B. Berelson, 1956, 489.
12 We need to bear in mind that Content Analysis was developed for the analysis of *large text corpora* in the first place. The social-psychologists involved aimed at investigating whether and how e.g. trends of opinion (ideologies) of society appear in spoken language. This, of course, requires the analysis of *many* texts. Against this backdrop it seems reasonable that the only ever-published homiletic monograph on Content Analysis was designed as a large-scale project and could only be carried out with the aid of a computer. Cf. Homiletische Arbeitsgruppe, 1973.
13 W. Früh, 2001, 25.
14 Cf. the distinction e.g. in M. Schäfer, 1973, 20–22.

https://doi.org/10.1515/9783110440256-008

the form of lists are used in which the individual categories are ordered according to particular dimensions. The "content-analytic scheme of categories (codesheet)"[15] of a homiletic working group may include, for example, the following analytical dimensions and categories as well as corresponding central questions:

| Analytical Dimensions | Categories and Central Questions of Content-Analytical Sermon Analysis (Selection) |
|---|---|
| **Formal Dimension** Purpose: Recording of objective data | Number of text lines? Biblical text at the beginning, middle or end? Further quotations from the Bible? Quotations from secular literature? To whom is it addressed? Direct and/or indirect address? |
| **Dimension of Mood** Purpose: Recording of the atmospheric factors on a bipolar scale: not at all, somewhat, fairly, very much so | Serious – cheerful? Optimistic – pessimistic? Passive – active? Dedicated – indifferent? Vivid – dull? Related to the case – general? Trivial – informative? Critical – uncritical? Clear – vague? Trite – precise? Continuous – discontinuous? Helpful – harsh? With a climax – without a climax? |
| **Dimension of Function** Purpose: Recording of the effects which result from the moods. | Pastoral Counseling? Confrontation with reality? Flight from reality? Emotion? Anxiety? Striving for conformity? Dream world? Commitment? Bonding? Dissociation? Security? Departure? Success? Identification? Authority? |
| **Dimension of Experience** Purpose: Recording of the emotional qualities of experience formulated expressis verbis | Does the sermon express joy? Thankfulness? Worry? Hope? What is the main topic and to what extent is it addressed? E. g. loneliness and community, death and life, happiness, sorrow, friendship, family, occupation, success, emancipation, devotion, love? |
| **Dimension of Relationship** Purpose: Recording of the social ideas and guiding principles expressed in the sermon | Are crises considered as something rather positive or negative? Assessment of solidarity? Significance of the individual for church and society? Assessment of the roles of men and women? Consideration of political contexts? Significance of forgiveness? Evaluation of faithfulness, trust and mutual understanding? Should sacrifices be made, and if so, by whom? |
| **Dimension of Faith** Purpose: Recording of the preacher's theological statements on the case/topic | How does the preacher theologically and expressis verbis comment on: Understanding of faith? Image of God? Are there any explications on "justification", "death of Jesus", "resurrection", "sin", "kingdom of God", "judgment", image of humanity? Image of Jesus? |
| **Ecclesiastical Dimension** Purpose: Recording of institutional statements | Is the sermon's relatedness to the congregation addressed in some way? Does the sermon presuppose that the listeners are Christians? Are there any statements about the responsibility of the individual and of the congregation? Are there elements of invitation or scolding with regard to indifference? |

**Fig. 24:** Content-analytical aspects of sermon analysis

---

15 Homiletische Arbeitsgruppe, 1973, 180–187.

The development of the categories, which are indispensible for the actual Content Analysis, first of all requires the formation of hypotheses about the manifest content of the sermon examined. This is a less subjective affair than the term "hypothesis" might suggest. It is a matter of forming categories which indeed correspond to the analyzed sermon material. If, for example, funeral orations are investigated, it seems reasonable to set up categories such as death-life, future-past, despair-hope etc.[16] Interpretation of data within the framework of Content Analysis is carried out with a view to the particular project. This means:

a) If *a few or even hundreds of sermons* are statistically recorded, an initial *basic sample count* is recommended. This provides information about the frequency distribution of the different categories, and allows for detailed conclusions about the proportionate occurrence of the different categories among the examined sermons. This provides a first overview of the reality of the preaching event as represented in these sermons. As a rule, this basic sample count is followed by a *factor analysis* in which "immanent regularities and coherencies between the individual characteristics of a sermon"[17] are recorded. It has become evident that particular categories often appear together which, however, at the same time, exclude other groups of categories, which supports the conclusion that there are, in fact, concrete, differentiated basic types of sermon.

b) If only *one single sermon* is analyzed, the aforementioned process may be simplified. The first step, however, must still be determining categories on the basis of hypotheses[18] relevant to the manifest content of the particular sermon. The subsequent analysis provides material for dealing with different tasks which could be formulated as follows:

1. Point out the connection between the sermon's structure of address and its basic intention (dimension of function)!
2. Document the connection between the development of the theme contained in the sermon and the preacher's social premises (dimension of relationship)!
3. Clarify the correspondences between the preacher's image of God and the factors of the mood of the sermon (dimension of mood)!
4. Attempt to generate rules from these results (tasks 1–3)!

---

**16** This is achieved e.g. through the investigation of relevant, frequently recurring variables in funeral orations themselves, through developing a typology of funeral orations, through an analysis of dictionary entries on the topic of death and dying etc. (cf. M. Schäfer, 1973, 29f.).
**17** On this procedure cf. M. Schäfer, 1973, 32.
**18** Here the "dimensions" mentioned in Fig. 24 may act as guidance. Cf. also an example of analysis in Dannowski, 1973, 30–33.

Even if analyses like that are rarely found in the everyday homiletic practice they have proved their worth in places and in a modified form. From the double question of the pastoral-psychological approach, focusing on a complex record of the contents (cf. III.2.2.2), downwards to lengthy individual studies[19] – important insights into the sermon's world of meaning as well as its fundamental comprehension of reality[20] are gained in this way.

## 1.2 The Approach of Speech Act Theory

Since speech acts are very complex, yet at the same time concrete, spatio-temporally determinable acts, their total complexity may only be analyzed in cooperation with the present listeners. Nevertheless, available written speech texts or sermon manuscripts contain speech act signs, which provide evidence both of the manner, frequency and dominance of recurring speech patterns, as well as of their function and effect.

In his comprehensive study on homiletic pragmatics[21] Frank Lütze, for example, only deals with sermon manuscripts. He thinks it is possible "to figure out potential reception processes and effects merely on the basis of a prepared sermon manuscript". Thereby he sees the benefit of an analysis of the action-profiles of sermons above all in the following: "The analysis of the action-profile of several different sermons of one and the same person [may] reveal individual preferences and weaknesses, e.g. hidden claims to power or feelings of powerlessness. On the basis of comparative analyses of sermons with a shared theological background one can furthermore ask about connections between theological positions and dominant preaching acts. Finally, looking at the reception of biblical texts, it seems to me to be particularly rewarding to compare the pragmatics of a sermon text with the action-profile of the corresponding sermon and, in doing so, to ask for reasons for possibly arising discontinuities."[22]

When applying Speech Act Theory to homiletics, as outlined above, the basic questions in sermon analysis are:

1. *On the layer of proposition (layer of content):*
   - Which *contents* does the preacher connect his speech acts with? (Within the framework of this question it is vital to differentiate between the sermon's main content on the one hand and subordinated matters on the other.) Which basic statement does the sermon set out from?

---

**19** Cf. esp. C. Dahlgrün, 2001.
**20** K. Merten is convinced that the benefit achieved through Content Analysis is particularly profitable for the images of social reality implied in the text (K. Merten, 1995, 15).
**21** F. Lütze, 2006.
**22** Loc. cit., 292–294.

- Are the contents of the sermon put into a frame of logical argumentation and thus presented comprehensibly? Are the propositions embedded into the address in a way that
  they appear true and credible?
2. *On the layer of illocution (layer of function):*
  - Which *functions*, types and speech modes (assertives, directives, commissives, expres-
    sives etc.) can be detected in the speech acts of the sermon?
  - Is there one particular speech act function dominating in the sermon?
3. *On the layer of perlocution (layer of effect):*
  - What *effects* upon the listeners do the speech acts of the sermon intend in detail or on
    an overall basis?
  - What attitude or reaction does the preacher apparently expect as an ideal "response" to
    his homiletic action?
4. *On the congruence of the different layers (claim of coherence):*
  - How does the discernible speech act-analytical communicative goal of the sermon
    match the contents it refers to?
  - How does the intended effect of the sermon fit with the actual functions of the speech
    acts?

In the following, these perspectives shall be put into concrete terms by applying the underlying speech act-theoretical theses to individual, applicable steps
of sermon analysis:

1. Prepare a *statistics*[23] of the different types of speech acts[24] occurring in the
   sermon.
2. Arrange the different speech acts according to their frequency of occurrence.
   Identify (a) *dominant speech act(s)* as well as (an) under-represented or
   missing speech-act(s).
3. Create a *"speech-act analytical fingerprint"*[25] of the sermon by drawing a line
   from a common center for each type of speech act, the length of which should
   correspond to the percentage share of this type of speech act in the sermon.
   Through connecting the ends of these lines to one another, an irregular
   pentagon or tetragon emerges, the specific form of which reflects the *hierarchy of the speech acts used in the particular sermon.*
4. Considering the specific representation of particular speech acts, formulate *hypotheses for the problems of communication* of this sermon.
   (Are there, for example, constantly new chains of assertions, presented

---

**23** K.-F. Daiber and H. W. Dannowski (1983) recommend to initially conduct this investigation
roughly on the basis of estimations without immediately harking back to the sermon manuscript.
Cf. the corresponding evaluation grid, loc. cit., 128f.
**24** Here cf. Fig. 17, p. 233.
**25** This idea goes back to R. Wonneberger/H. P. Hecht (1986, 214).

without any argumentative basis, which create doubt about the preacher's credibility?)

5. Examine the internal sequence of individual speech acts. Attempt to identify *recurring patterns* (e.g. assertion – advice – assurance).
6. Attempt *to deduce strategies of speech* from these recurring patterns and to describe potential reasons for their success of failure.
7. Attempt to deduce the *homiletic premises* and *the preacher's self-understanding* from the recurring patterns and strategies of speech.
8. With regards to the *proposition rule*[26]: Check *whether proposition and illocution* are *in a coherent relationship* with one another (whether, for example, promissory speech acts actually refer to something in the future, counseling speech acts to upcoming decisions etc.).
9. With regards to the *initiation rule or the rule of appropriateness:* Check whether, through the dominant speech act in the sermon, something should happen or be changed *which otherwise would not happen* or be changed.
10. With regards to the *relevance rule:* Examine whether and to what extent there really is a need for the speech action which is expressed in the sermon's dominant speech act.
11. Take a look at the expressive speech acts in the sermon. If these speech acts stand for the presence of the subject, an "I", in the sermon they facilitate a response on the part of the listener and, in so doing, support the process of verbal cooperation.

What do we learn about a sermon from the analysis of its speech acts? For one thing, we obtain a specific picture of the sermon's scope of action, of what it does and leaves undone and also about its motivations which are not always evident at first sight. On the basis of the speech act-analytical approach we can furthermore discuss *why* the listeners possibly do not (and cannot) feel addressed, *why* they possibly do not feel assured or motivated etc. A successful speech act analysis – for which the cooperation of the preacher with colleagues is imperative[27] – does not only reveal specific problems of preaching but, more generally, draws attention to symptoms in the communication as well as personality structure of the preacher himself.

---

[26] On this and the following tasks cf. I.5.3.1c, p. 236–238.
[27] Cf. H. Scheler's reflections (1975, 218–222) on the integration of Speech Act Theory into the homiletic training.

## 1.3 The Rhetorical Approach

The rhetorical sermon analysis is time and again mentioned in homiletic discourse. A closer look at these instances, however, leaves a somewhat sobering impression behind that the "rhetorical" interest is oftentimes rather vague and somehow concerns everything which in one way or another is part of the preacher's utterances – the pleasant, the irritating, the content etc.[28] In accordance with the results of the debate on the rhetorical tradition[29], one could, however, ask more specific questions and in a first approach start from the structure of a sermon and thereby from the (sub-) functions it contains.[30]

- Does the sermon provide an appealing *introduction* (aesthetic function of speech) which is suitable for establishing contact between preacher and listeners as well as between listeners and topic?
- Does the sermon provide a structurally recognizable *main part*, the content of which is so useful and relevant that one can learn something from it?
- Does the sermon provide in its *closing section* a signal which offers impulses for action or pastoral orientation?

Certainly, the four perspectives of reflection we have referred to and discussed above as modern advancements of classical and medieval rhetoric[31] offer more concrete questions. One can, for example, rhetorically analyze a sermon by

- investigating its strategy as regards the psychology of learning,
- examining the function of its narratological elements,
- studying its dialogical character,
- semiotically analyzing its linguistic structures (terms and concepts, comparisons, propositions etc.) in terms of their openness or closure.

The correct implementation of analyses remains a futile undertaking if one has not already clarified in advance what should be found out through each of the individual steps and what the results of the analyses in fact *mean*. What does it mean, for example, for the rhetorical evaluation of a sermon if it uses "sloppy phrases", contains "parodic" elements or "repetitions, serializations,

---

28 As for example in R. Heue/R. Lindner, 1975, 21–25.
29 Cf. I.4.2.1.
30 Cf. Fig. 12, p. 170.
31 Cf. above, I.4.3.1–4.

accumulations" of words or phrases?[32] In order to fully answer these questions in detail one would have to – besides rhetorical – additionally apply personality- and communication-psychological categories. This would go beyond the scope of this chapter. Consequently I restrict myself in the following selection of central analytical questions to the aforementioned four principles of structuring, the specific interests of which have already been set out.

### a) Central Questions for the Analysis of the Learning Process Initiated by the Sermon

1. Does the sermon require, or at least prompt, a *questioning attitude* (motivation) on the part of the listener?
2. Does the sermon have a distinct *problem in focus* (delimitation of the problem), or is the problem merely generally "aired"?
3. Does the sermon describe any attempts which have already been made to *cope with this problem* (trial and error) and comment on their usefulness or uselessness?
4. Do *concrete options* ("offers of solution"), through which a change of the previously problematized situation or attitude might occur, appear in the sermon – options which are ready to take up counter-arguments and to "wrestle" with these?
5. Does the sermon contain any encouraging remarks on the *capability* and suitability for everyday use of its reflections or on the attitude it suggests ("reinforcement of the solution")?

Subsequent to answering these questions with the help of the listeners, it may be discussed why the sermon is possibly not perceived to be particularly helpful and beneficial for everyday life, at which points the sermon as a learning process has faltered or foundered.

### b) Central Questions for the Analysis of the Narrative Elements of the Sermon

1. Does the sermon, alongside *discursive explanations*, also develop *narrative elaborations* on its message?
2. Does the sermon mention only facts or does it also describe *events and experiences*?

---

32 Cf. the comprehensive overview of questions in G. Otto, 1999, 184–187. Unfortunately Otto does not comment on the conclusions which follow from the answers to these questions for the rhetorical *evaluations* of sermons.

3. Does the sermon only move in an historical world (the past or present) or does it also visualize *a fictitious, possible, "virtual" world,* and in a way which allows the listeners to become part of this world?
4. Does the sermon merely argue in the form of thetic phrases or does it also contain narrative elements which take on an *argumentative function?*
5. Does the sermon provide the listeners with *analogies, comparisons, pictures* which make it easier for them to transfer the sermon into their own world of experience?
6. Does the sermon only use narrative elements with respect to "the problem" or is it also able to offer its solution, i.e. its climax, in a narrative fashion?

#### c) Central Questions for the Analysis of the Sermon's Dialogical Character

1. Is the *sermon's content* or the topic addressed in the sermon an expression of a dialogical interest, or does it merely circle around dogmatic "specialissima", which are the expression of a theological monolog?
2. Which of the sermon's structural or *formal signals* (form of address, invitations and requests, direct questions, "self-proclamation" etc.) indicate efforts on the part of the preacher to develop and enter into a dialog?
3. Does the preacher take up a *position of his own* or does he keep himself out of the topic or problem which is discussed in the sermon?
4. Is the sermon composed in a way that displays a certain readiness to accept potential *objections and misunderstandings* through which it acknowledges that the preacher's intention is not self-evident?
5. In the case of a dialog-sermon with at least two preachers: do the *dialog partners* take themselves seriously *as subjects?* Does the dialog-sermon feature characteristics of a real dialog (personal commitment, divergences, tensions, emotions) or is it merely a monolog performed in play reading?

Due to its complexity, the fourth structural approach, the semiotic approach, is discussed in a subchapter of its own.

### 1.4 The Semantic Approach

The description of the semiotic analysis in this chapter only takes into account its *semantic* side, and the reason for this is the conception of semiotics itself: A comprehensive semiotic analysis would not only examine the sermon's verbal signs but would additionally have to consider its non-verbal "symptoms" and, in so doing, look at the preachers' posture, their gestures and facial expressions. Moreover, the sermon itself would have to be examined as a sign within the framework of communication between church and society. Provided that semiotics examines everything that exists in a culture *with respect to its communicative functions,* there are basically no limits to a complete analysis of signs. For this reason the following discussion shall be confined to the level of semantics.

The model of semantic text analysis has a firm place in contemporary homiletics. It has been continuously used for decades.[33] This form of analysis examines what the individual statements of the sermon *mean* in concrete terms and what overall message the sermon as a whole stands for. This is done by way of analyzing the properties of the semantic field in several different steps.

Step 1:  Analysis of basic connections between individual terms
         and concepts and their interpretants (microcodes)

In sermons terms and concepts such as "God", "man", "sin" and "salvation" refer to a large spectrum of contents, to more than what is listed in dictionaries under these lemmas. Connecting such concepts with particular correlative terms and synonyms as well as their interpretation based on examples provides them with *a specific meaning.* The analysis begins by assigning the "signifiers" – here: the nouns, verbs and adjectives discerned as meaningful in the sermon – with contextual explanations ("interpretants") provided in the sermon manuscript itself. These connections in the sermon, between signifiers and signifieds or interpretants respectively, can be depicted as follows, based on the example of a particular sermon[34] and listed in alphabetical order.

---

**33** I first presented and explained the following steps and the resulting hierarchy of coding in my post-doctoral thesis (W. Engemann, 1989; 1993a, cf. esp. 107–152). Recently Bernhard Kirchmeier described numerous analyses on various different concepts of faith in present-day sermons on the basis of this method (cf. B. Kirchmeier, 2016, esp. 127–372). Corresponding semantic considerations have been transferred from Homiletics to other areas of reflection in Practical Theology, from which, above all, (religion-)educational concepts may benefit. Cf. most recently B. Sendler-Koschel, 2016, 176–203.
**34** Sermon manuscript on 1 Cor 12:4–11.

| Signifiers | | Interpretants |
|---|---|---|
| people called by God | → | *people who simply "hear the call" every day* |
| to be called by God | → | *in fact a difficult matter* |
| to be a Christian | → | *to no longer to say "I"* |
| | → | *not to lie replete and self-satisfied in the Grass* |
| the simplest thing | → | *to turn to God* |
| Exaudi | → | *God calls you when others are in a situation of crisis* |
| the Spirit | → | *God himself* |
| | → | *someone whom one must obey* |
| | → | *enables us to respond to God's call* |
| | → | *a blank check for resurrection* |
| gift of the Spirit | → | *a community of the sermon listeners* |
| community with God | → | *a community with redemptive power* |
| creature | → | *a being with responsibility and obligations who owes God obedience* |
| saints of God | → | *people who turn away from God again and again* |
| to listen | → | *to answer God and to love God* |
| human being | → | *a being who can't get enough (5 times)* |
| | → | *desires to be seen and noticed* |
| | → | *desires wealth* |
| | → | *wants nothing but to be left alone* |
| | → | *loves him- or herself* |
| | → | *polluter of the environment, exploiter* |
| | → | *a being who has turned away from God* |
| | → | *a creature* |
| | → | *a being who does not deserve to be addressed by God* |
| humanity | → | *people who allow themselves to be led by their desires* |
| call of God | → | *an instructive appeal to turn to God* |
| to hear God's call | → | *to obey "to the voice within ourselves" (3 times)* |
| to follow God's call | → | *to take part in the worship service* |
| to be guilty | → | *to never get enough* |

**Fig. 25:** Examples of microcodes in a sermon

Step 2: Analysis of a single pattern of interpretation (structure codes)

The combinations analyzed in Step 1 (connections of signifier and interpretant) do not appear in isolation in the sermon but are components of a more extensive structure and can thus be joined together to *patterns of interpretation, to structure codes*. These decide what may appear in a particular series of interpretants and what may not (see Fig. 26).

| Concept | Structure Codes |
|---------|-----------------|
| God | Someone who calls us → someone who calls us so that we help others → someone whom we must obey → someone to whom we owe our attendance at church → someone who constantly waits for our attention |
| God's Call | "God's call" comes from a voice that calls within us → this call allows us to feel God's presence → this presence radiates a permanent appeal → this appeal concerns our willingness to love our neighbors and God → this love of God should never stop being a conscious, active turning to God |
| Human being | Someone who forgets the simplest thing: to turn to God → someone who says "I" and is egoistic because of his own needs → these needs become apparent in that the individual is not able to get enough → this means to always need attention and love of oneself → the human being is someone with an inner voice which does not tolerate self-love |
| Guilt | Can be seen upon people's faces because of its negative effects upon the body → Guilt: to be replete and self-satisfied → self-love as an expression of turning away from God → this means not doing justice to the tasks arising from Creation → which means not being able to move from "I" to "we" |

**Fig. 26:** Examples of structure codes in a sermon

Step 3: Analysis of the semantic system

The individual structures in their turn belong to an even more complex semantic network, to semantic systems which ensure that only certain particular structures contribute to the forming of meaning in the sermon. Hence it makes a difference whether one e.g., when speaking of "God", takes up structures which belong to an existential-philosophical, dialectical or a liberation theological system of interpretation. This difference becomes particularly manifest if one asks *in which delimitation* a particular concept or topic is developed. In the course of the story of faith God has been talked about in comparison to the "devil", to "gods" or to "humankind" to name only a few examples. Accordingly, "God" appears in the sermon, among other things, as a victor (over the devil), as sovereign (as opposed to dependent humanity), as a source of a human's not yet fulfilled possibilities (as opposed to an understanding of God as a self-sufficient, transcendental being).

Correspondingly, the structures shown above (2) are only the *one* side of particular polarizations, the counterparts of which vary according to the respective semantic system. In semiotics this is referred to as "semantic axes" which bring words, sentences or thoughts in line *with a certain particular direction of meaning* and thereby set them *in contrast* to other words, sentences and thoughts. By being introduced for the understanding of a biblical text or a particular situation, they lead the reader's or listener's comprehension into a certain pre-selected direction, which permits certain interpretations but, at the same time, excludes others.[35] The sermon already analyzed in the steps above shows e.g. the following "oppositions":

| Criticized Behavior | | Recommended Behavior |
|---|---|---|
| 1. Experience of happiness | *versus*[36] | living without becoming guilty |
| 2. Being replete | *versus* | being obedient |
| 3. Being self-satisfied | *versus* | having a good conscience and enduring inner hunger |
| 4. Self-love as an estrangement from God | *versus* | love of neighbor and of God as possibilities of turning away from oneself |
| 5. Satisfying one's own needs | *versus* | renouncing one's own needs |

**Fig. 27:** Examples of semantic axes in a sermon

Through the semantic axes of this sermon, "experiences of repletion", "satisfaction", "love of oneself" and "desires" are stylized as an expression of guilt; they are portrayed as the antithesis of a life as intended by the creator. Creatures can do something about their guilt and feelings of guilt by caring for God who is in need of affection and apparently easily offended, by worshipping him and looking after people who are in a crisis. *One's own* experiences of crises or the prospect of how these can possibly be overcome through God's devotion and loving affection which allows for the experience of a fulfilled, "satisfied" life is not taken into account in this system of interpretation. Thus, the motto of the Sunday, "Exaudi" ("Lord, so hear me") becomes semantically reversed. In the preachers view, with the call "Exaudi!" God calls upon people to take care of him (God) and show more commitment to others.

---

**35** Cf. the most recent reception of this analytical approach in the comprehensive analysis of semantic axes by B. Kirchmeier, 2016, 349–394.

**36** "Versus" in semantic terms denotes the "opposites" underlying or constructed in a text which result from the micro-, structural and system codes of this text. They are an essential part of the implicit premises of the author of a text or a preacher.

Step 4: Analysis of the connection between different systems

Particular theological, philosophical, anthropological, psychological, socio-logical and other systems, each with their own oppositions, always appear in a sermon as intertwined. They are the result of a selective and connective code. For the sermon analyzed here this means: Dogmatic, cultural-sociological, moral and other arguments are combined in a way that the doctrine of creation and the demand for obedience, hamartiology and a bad conscience, a particular sense of duty and fundamental criticism of people's love for themselves result in *a unified whole.* At this stage of the semantic analysis *the semantic system* comes into view according to which preachers construct their theology as a whole or their phi-losophy of life. Hence this analysis consists in capturing the preachers' complex mindscapes as far as they have left traces in their manuscripts.[37]

A sermon may reveal concrete connections of particular philosophical, psychological, social-sci-entific and other concepts (or fragments of them) with specific theological (soteriological, escha-tological, relating to creation etc.) patterns of argumentation; yet this does not say anything about the correctness of the citation or the consistency and logic of such connections. A sermon on the gospel for the Second Day of Christmas[38], for example, draws from a pool of ideas and positions, which may be falsely cited in some respect and, in part, also contradict themselves, but which nonetheless form an individual preaching theology which is also applied in other sermons by the same preacher. Here are some of its characteristics:

| | |
|---|---|
| Anthropological premise: | "Human beings have in themselves neither the interest nor the possibility to devote themselves to their neighbors out of love. For them 'neighbors' are nothing more than rivals in the battle for survival. Darwin already knew that." |
| Psychological concept: | "Because human beings are driven in their actions, above all, by their egoistic drives they only do what pleases themselves. To do something unpleasant and endure a disadvantage for the sake of others has no place in this." |
| Soteriological principle: | "Only those who are willing and prepared to allow themselves to be truly infused by the love of God, which emanates from the child in the manger, have a chance of becoming acquainted in their lifetime with a kind of love that is different to the love for oneself." |
| Eschatological expectation: | "To totally love and, in so doing, to completely abstain from one's own self-interests will surely only be possible for us in the kingdom of God." |

---

**37** A similar approach underlies the "analysis of mental images in the sermon". Cf. on this the model, which is regarded as belonging to the semantic forms of analysis, by J. Hermelink/E. Müske, 1995, esp. 230–232.

**38** Manuscript of a sermon on John 1:1–5[6–8]9–14.

Step 5: Analysis of the operative code or argumentation strategy

After having examined the semantic units of which the sermon's repertoire of argumentation consists, one is finally able to describe the sermon's overall strategy of argumentation, i.e. *to determine the angle from which what has been said amounts to a unified picture.* Here the operative code of the sermon comes into sight. To analyze this means to identify how a preacher generally approaches texts and topics and to ask, for example: Which understanding of "life" lies at the root of the sermon or which idea of existence can, according to its view, be regarded as "Christian"? How may a close look at oneself be accomplished, and what does this exercise ideally achieve? What does the sermon mean by a "successful life"? What kind of behavior would be in accordance with the sermon's message? What is the worst thing that could happen? And what is the best that could happen?

To clarify such questions one can also apply the model of "discourse-theoretical sermon analysis"[39]. Rolf Schieder regards his model as belonging to the Speech Act Theory, if anything, and this is hardly extraordinary – considering that all forms of analysis are initially related to language. Yet Schieder's suggestion of understanding a sermon also as an exemplary sequence of the totality of social discourse is constituted semantically: "It is not the one speaking who determines the discourse, but both speaker and listener are subjected to discourse. [...] Hence discourse analysis asks: From which areas of discourse does the preacher draw his 'examples'? Are there particular discourses which appear considerably often and allow one to conclude that they occupy a hegemonial position? The discourse-theoretical perspective as it were inverses the common perspective. If in the sermon a preacher attempts to speak of the 'reality' or 'situation' of the listeners, he incorporates elements of other kinds of discourses into the religious discourse and, in so doing, grants them a privileged position." In this process "certain non-religious discourses [...] are connected with the religious. The question is: Which are these? Are there typical patterns of inter-discourse?"[40]

## 1.5 The Approach of Ideological Criticism

Sermon analysis based on ideological criticism represents a special form of semantic approach, in which central insights of literary text analysis, rhetoric research, narrative research and hermeneutics are combined.[41] On the basis of an analysis of several sermons on the "discussion between Jesus and the Samaritan woman at the well" (John 4:1–12), Isolde Meinhard reveals various narrative levels and

---

**39** Cf. R. Schieder, 1995, esp. 323–329.
**40** Loc. cit., 326–329.
**41** I. Meinhard, 2003. Important preliminary work for the toolset of this analysis was carried out by Mieke Bal (1997) in the context of her critical narratology.

patterns which are understood and acknowledged as an attempt to construct a certain world.[42] If – with respect to the philosophies, roles, relationships etc. that come to light in the course of such an analysis – we talk of ideologies, however, no "negative" criticism is implied. This should rather be understood as a neutral statement: Every reader, every interpreter, every preacher approaches texts with a particular idea of the world which he "applies", modifies, perhaps also corrects while interpreting these texts. But he will never be able to abstain from finally deciding on a particular "concept of the world" and from appropriately drawing attention to the characters in the text, the listeners – and his role towards them.

In order to get sight of this way of approaching a text or a sermon, the role of the preacher and the text is examined on various levels[43] – analogous to the understanding of the relationship between author and text in the tradition of critical narratology according to Mieke Bal and, in literary studies, e.g. according to Wolfgang Iser[44]. Correspondingly, in sermon analysis the following areas are addressed: (1.) the narrative level which can be followed through listening or reading. Initially preachers appear as *narrators* or as "voices of the sermon"[45]. They inject themselves (2.) by *pointing to* something, allowing something *to be seen* from a particular point of view through which they come into play as *"focalizers"*. The listeners, for their part, are also in demand as "spectators": They "see" what is happening in a text, they are suggested a particular perspective. Finally there is (3.) in texts and sermons the level of *agents* which is determined by actions and events.

Which are the issues that should be addressed in detail in this context?
1. *The speaking*: The narration itself, its furnishing with particular characters and roles, the "transfer" of the preacher's own opinion to particular characters who rise to speak in the text or sermon.
2. *The seeing:* The level of the "viewpoint"[46] or, more precisely, the perspective from which the opinions and judgments of the narration are focused and assessed, which also displays the relationships between the different agents.

---

**42** The fact that the analytical routines suggested by M. Bal and I. Meinhard were initially developed on the basis of narrative texts does not mean that the respective levels and aspects cannot also be pointed out in other texts (cf. above on the category of the "narrated world" I.3.3.1a, p. 121–124).

**43** Cf. I. Meinhard, 2003, 98.

**44** Cf. W. Iser, 1994.

**45** Here the term "voice of the preacher" describes a *communicative function* in the event of preaching. Analogous to the "implied author" in literary studies this has to be distinguished from the preacher or author as a 'living subject' of the writing or speaking.

**46** A more explicit or more unambiguous term for this level of perspective is, in my opinion, the term "viewpoint" which I correspondingly use in Fig. 28.

3.    *The behavior*: The level of action on which the characters occurring in the text or sermon appear, become agents and become involved in the events which are held out to the listeners or against which they are warned.

In the course of the analysis each of these levels is examined under three (more) aspects through which the sermon's capacity of interpretation can be illustrated even more precisely. Here it is a matter of

1.    the *roles* which the preacher assigns to the characters in the text and, in this way turns them into those who act or those who are affected,
2.    the implicit *positions and relationships* to one another of those speaking or those addressed in the text and of
3.    grasping all the *concrete actions* of those involved in the narrative.

Particular *routines of dealing with a text* allow for obtaining a more precise picture of the sermon's construction of reality (in terms of a "narrative" about the world as it is or as it should be) as well as for reconstructing how preachers set the course through their interpretation of texts and situations. In order to give an overview of the guiding questions that are vital to this approach of sermon analysis, the following table summarizes – to a large extent in my own words – the analytical questions which Meinhard suggests in order to examine how a sermon treats listeners and texts[47].

---

47 On this cf. e.g. I. Meinhard's considerations, 2003, 192f.

| Analysis Level | Analysis Perspectives | |
|---|---|---|
| **Speech** | *Role:* | Who speaks in which role, and who is addressed in which role? How are the respective roles defined through the words spoken? Which character in the text/sermon does the preacher lend his voice to? Who speaks only occasionally or not at all? |
| | *Positions:* | Whom does the "voice of the sermon" relate to, and what defines this relationship? Do these "relationships" allow for negations or contradictions? Are they restrictive or do they give leeway? Who speaks, in what kind of tone, with whom, about what? |
| | *Actions:* | How often, and how forcefully, does the "voice of the sermon" play a part? How often, and to what extent, do preacher and listeners appear as agents? Who speaks in the biblical text (in the eyes of the preacher) or in the sermon (as concerns the characters or figures appearing in it), how often and for how long, and in which order? Whose speech has success with whom? |
| **Viewpoint** | *Role:* | Who develops the decisive perspectives? Who is able to "observe" something? Who judges, discovers, thinks? To which character in the text or sermon does the preacher's perspective appear to be transferred? |
| | *Positions:* | What is the problem, and what is its "solution"? In what position do preacher and listeners find themselves regarding the problem and the "gospel"? Who has caused this problem? |
| | *Actions:* | Who has the chance to intervene in reality? What is expected, or demanded, of whom? |
| **Behavior** | *Role:* | To what extent does the preacher – beyond his utterances – appear as an agent? Does he provide any information about the motivations for his actions? Which characters stand for which action? Who acts only rarely, or not at all? |
| | *Positions:* | How close to, or how distant from, the goal of the sermon are the listeners regarded to be? What kinds of actions are designated in the sermon? What is the hierarchical relation between the actors? Is there a central position? Who is in charge of this position, and how does this become manifest? |
| | *Actions:* | What "happens" in the sermon outside of verbal actions? Which actions are suggested to whom? Who acts how frequently, and in what sequence? How are the listeners' actions brought into focus, and how are they assessed? What kind of action is suggested to the listeners? |

**Fig. 28:** Questions within the context of a sermon analysis based on ideological criticism

The sermon analyses could reveal a close connection between the interpretation of the text and the social structures implicitly assumed by the preachers. "It seems to me as if narrations prove their theological and ideological-critical value [...] in a tension between their assuring and irritating function. Because they have an assuring effect, but always create this anew in new situations" narrations allow for "a distance not only to the prevailing reality but also among the various narrations" from which "necessary differentiations and starting-points for ideological criticism"[48] towards these narrations or sermons arise.

---

48 Loc. cit., 199.

# 2 Concepts of Analysis Focused on the Interaction between Preacher and Listener

All the approaches of sermon analysis outlined in the previous chapter primarily target the sermon's content. As a rule, they can be applied without the preacher and without a group, merely on the basis of sermon manuscripts. These analyses reveal what a particular sermon "means" in the strict sense of the word or how it "creates" its meaning.

However, as neither Content Analysis nor a speech act-theoretical, rhetorical, semantic or ideological-critical analyses of the sermon are capable of adequately capturing the sermon's significance *as an event of communication* by themselves, none of these should exclusively determine the homiletic work. That is why in the following forms of analysis shall be discussed which – with an alternating focus on preacher and listener – examine the *interactions* of the preaching event and, as a rule, require for their application the cooperation of a group.

## 2.1 Concepts of Analysis Focusing on the Subject of the Sermon

### 2.1.1 The Approach of Depth Psychology Focusing on the Basic Impulses and Basic Anxieties of the Preacher[49]

Basic impulses such as distance, proximity, persistence and change as well as anxieties of dependence, separation, change and finality are not automatically perceived as such by the individual. Oftentimes "blind spots" or "sore points" are at work here which contribute to overlooking particular corresponding personality traits, to suppressing them or reframing them. As a consequence, approaching such personality-based factors of the homiletic work and the sermon effect is hardly possible without the help and support of a feedback group.

A homiletic feedback group – which as a rule consists of people who themselves preach – does, of course, not decide on "healthy" or "ill". Nor does it – simply on the basis of sermon analyses – diagnose the preacher with potential "personality-disorders", not even if it is a "good" feedback group that is capable of giving the preacher insights into the motivational patterns of his sermon. It's just not its task. What it, ideally, should bring up, however, are *failures* and

---

**49** For more detailed information on the premises of this approach cf. I.2.3.4.2 and the "Synopsis of the communication profiles and of the effects of typical preaching strategies" (Fig. 6, p. 71).

https://doi.org/10.1515/9783110440256-009

*disruptions in communication* that are related to the understanding of existence and faith developed in the sermon, to its image of God, to the self involved and expressed in the sermon, to one-sided thematic focusing etc. Such an analysis can reveal and demonstrate, that from all the "basic attitudes" indispensible for the balance of human life, which – like the four colors in four-color printing[50] – are essential for the experience and composition of the totality of life, *one* may dominate so strongly that the others no longer show to advantage. The listeners then see, so to speak, only "red" or "yellow" and are, in consequence, provided with non-livable offers of identification which acknowledge neither life as whole nor the serviceableness of faith on people's lives.

Sermon analyses can bring to light what happens if, for example, preachers create great distance between themselves and their listeners and in so doing remain incomprehensible when speaking of the message of love – if they appear to embrace the congregation and thereby suppress the addressing of conflicts, if they compulsively adhere to particular ideas of living by faith but cannot explain what the freedom of faith is all about, or if their ignoring of boundaries and limits leads to undermining the indispensible responsibility before the "law". In an analysis referring to Riemann's basic needs (or basic impulses and anxieties) the aspects of differentiation mentioned in Fig. 7 may be taken as a basis and amended further.

1. Do the concepts, pictures and examples used in the sermon reveal a main emphasis or focus regarding the basic needs of distance, proximity, persistence and change?
2. Which are the topics and opinions that dominate in the sermon and how do they interrelate with the basic needs mentioned?
3. How can the preacher's image of God be related to the basic needs mentioned? Which basic impulse or basic anxiety does the talk of "power", "love", "order" or "freedom of God" (and corresponding predicates of God) refer to?
4. Which basic problems are the listeners confronted with and which role is given to them in this way? In what manner does the sermon deal with their need of security, of care, of experiences of failure and their wish for a self-determined life?
5. How can the preacher's self-image be located in the coordinate system of distance and proximity, persistence and change? What is the relationship between this homiletic self-concept and the preacher's image of the listeners? What does this mean for the definition of the relationship between preacher and listener which is expressed in the sermon?

Answering these questions aims at shedding light on the background of specific sermonic experiences on the part of the listeners and at providing preachers with help in understanding to what extent the reception has to do with themselves and their address. Approaching the preachers' dominant basic impulses and basic

---

**50** Cf. F. Riemann, 2009, 61.

anxieties can lead to the reduction of problems regarding the sermon's plausibility and credibility. Furthermore, sermon analyses may contribute to the detection and identification of imbalances in the practice of one's own communication of faith. Hence sermon analyses keep up the awareness that the spectrum of religious experience and human knowledge is more extensive than it might have been suggested in a particular preaching style over years or even decades.

### 2.1.2 The Approach of Communication Psychology focusing on the Preacher's Transactions and Games

Communication psychology deals with the inter-personal event-character of communication processes. Sermon analyses related to communication psychology consequently tackle the question of *what happens during the sermon between speaker and listener,* of how their communication is structured, the effects it has on the state of the listener and preacher.

Such an examination naturally is also interested in the language and structure of the sermon, i.e. in its semantic details. What is, however, truly characteristic of analyses guided by principles of communication psychology is their interest in certain *rules*, in *patterns of communication* which can be observed in the process of preaching and hearing. In the course of this, on the one hand, the sermon's content and relationship level is examined and on the other hand, complex stereotype interactions, in which questions of content and relationship are connected to one another in a specific way, are considered. There are a number of approaches which could be applied in this case. I have opted to use Transaction Analysis. Its theoretical basis has already been discussed in detail above, and it has been successfully used in the context of homiletics before.[51]

Based on the possibility to be able to explain particular stereotypes in the speech, manner and action of an individual with the aid of the models of the *ego states* and *life positions*, Eric Berne, the main proponent of Transaction Analysis, attempted to also investigate stereotypical elements in processes of inter-communication. He refers to them as "games"[52] because whenever people

---

**51** Cf, W. Engemann, 2003b and above I.2.3.2c-I.2.3.4. In what follows, knowledge of the models of the ego states and life positions introduced there will be assumed.

**52** In accordance with the varying contexts of communication in everyday life E. Berne examines, among other things, marital games, party games, consulting room games etc. which reflect the various levels and forms of social cooperation (cf. E. Berne, 1967, 67–168).

communicate, they follow certain rules according to which they can, for example, "win" or "lose"[53] in the process of communication.

Case-by-case one can observe differently motivated communication strategies which – as if following an unconscious set of game rules – determine the basic character of the communication event. In a certain way, these strategies also define the modalities of winning or losing, of triumphing or giving up. Depending on which life position is most distinctive in a preacher, and on how his ego states relate to one another, he will favor particular games and avoid others. The (limited) repertoire of the games which people open when they enter into communication with others is typical of the respective individual. This holds particularly true for people's "favorite games". They tend to prefer games which comply with their personality structure and through which their position in life is confirmed. Here the fatal downside of "winning" becomes apparent: One can win and yet lose if one e.g. with the game "I always come out the loser" manages to arouse the compassion of the others and is thus able to finally say to oneself: "I knew that the others always fare better than I do."

The "playing field"[54] of the sermon is first of all determined by the fact that the "game partners", preacher and listener, encounter one another in the preaching process within the frame of their specific personality structures and life positions. Here the preacher is, so to speak, ahead of the competition, for it is him who uses the "gaming tools" – i.e., above all, language.[55] The preacher opens the communication, has the "first move" – and, in consequence, begins *his* game. In this game only those rules apply that comply with *his* life position and with *his* predominant ego state. For this reason it has to be assumed that, in the preparation and delivery of his sermon, the preacher expects to talk to an ideal listener, presents to the congregation with offers of identification which suit his game and are suitable counterparts to his "favorite transactions" – e.g. from a punitive Parent ego to an adapted Child ego.

---

53 "To lose" can mean, for instance, to have maneuvered oneself into a situation of humiliation or to break off communication due to feeling insulted. "To win" here by no means always implies an authentic, desirable feeling of happiness but a "payoff" which results from an experience of superiority. On this problem cf. E. Berne, 1967, 56f. and the homiletic parallels in W. Engemann, 1992a, 77–90.

54 Outside the field of Transaction Analysis, this concept is also homiletically received in K.-H. Bieritz, 1983.

55 The preacher can influence the course of the game to a greater degree than the listener through the use of additional signs (through the use of the pulpit, through a particular way of moving through the place of worship, through the choice of the tone of voice etc.).

In everyday life the very *saying of "Hello"*[56] can already serve to open the game. By greeting someone in a friendly, polite, contemptuous, wrathful or deferential way, we challenge the other to react to our own pattern: in a likewise friendly, cool, distant, resentful, dismissive, obliging way. Hence our way of greeting already aims at a particular reaction and is thus part of the game. Analogously the *opening of a sermon* may be regarded as starting the game. As a consequence, already the very first sentence oftentimes provides important clues to the intricacies the listener has to expect to become involved with.

It is part of the preliminary work of the homiletic game-analysis to perceive the preacher's ego state, to discern the potential dominance of one particular ego state and to identify the life position which shapes his address.

In order to analyze the presence or dominance of certain ego states and life positions, above all, the preachers' language and communications behavior is examined first and foremost. The different speech acts, in their respective contexts, can be quite easily assigned to the different ego states: as a rule, the prevalence of admonitions, praise and scolding indicates a predominant Parent ego, whereas delivering theological lessons suggests a predominant Adult ego. And an address which is highly affective and includes strong signals of delight or aversion, tends to be articulated in the Child ego state.

Typical questions in pastoral psychology about the relationship level can be linked to characteristics of the corresponding ego state or life position, as for example in the following: Has the preacher met me like a father or mother, like a teacher or like a friend? Has he grumbled or challenged me, explained something to me or encouraged me? Has he treated me as an individual of equal rank and worth?

Answering questions like these is a prerequisite for being able to appropriately apply the scheme used in Transaction Analysis for describing and analyzing communication processes as gameplays. In the following the individual elements of this scheme shall be reformulated for the homiletic context:[57]

1. *Identifying the game thesis:* Identifying a "game thesis" means trying to determine what kind of game the preacher – as the "one in a position of power in the situation"[58] ("Situationsmächtiger") – invites the listeners to through his sermon.

---

56 Cf. the title of one of his books: "What Do You Say After You Say Hello?", Grove Press, New York 1972. More precisely this means: How do you behave when someone approaches you in a particular way and, in so doing, suggests a particular turn or move?

57 Cf. more detailed in W. Engemann, 1992a, 77–90.

58 In his "Literary Rhetoric" H. Lausberg developed a model of communication which adds to a clearer understanding of the Transactional Game Theory and the sermon – particularly as regards competitive "advantages" and "disadvantages" for the people involved in the process of communication. According to Lausberg's model the preacher might be classified as the one in a position of power in the situation ("Situationsmächtiger") as – in terms of communication – it is

A "game thesis"[59] may, for example, be a significant sentence or a catchy phrase frequently recurring in the sermon which unveils which pattern of transaction the preacher is following.[60] The game thesis usually points to the ego state or life position from which a preacher turns to the congregation and indicates which ego state or life position he expects, in so doing, on the part of the listeners and is thus used to substantiate his own thesis. In this way, the game thesis reflects the sermon's leitmotif in that it provides a sudden insight into the sermon's distinctive scheme of transaction, as, for instance, in: "You'll soon be laughing on the other side of your face!" – uttered by the preacher's punitive Parent ego to the listener's Child ego, perceived as out of control and (too) free and therefore has to be called to reason.[61]

2. *Identifying the game motif for preacher and listener*: This is about taking stock of the intentions and expectations arising in the sermon, with the aim of shedding light upon the preacher's communication-psychological motifs. Besides the manuscript itself, the listeners' impressions are also relevant sources here: with what expectation, with what attitude has the preacher addressed them? In the discussion of the sermon analyzed, both text analysis as well as the listeners' reactions resulted in the perception of the following motivation: "People are bad. My sermon cannot change anything about that. So it is better to be hard on them and, in this way, to keep them away from me". Furthermore, we have to ask about the listeners' interests or motivations to follow the sermon: in the case mentioned the listeners were "motivated" by the fact that they just did not see themselves as *questioned by the obviously overtaxing radicalism of the sermon* and thus rather felt confirmed in their being.[62]

---

above all down to him to make something of the given communicative situation, to shape it and to use it. As "the one in a position of power in the situation" he is granted certain "advantages in the game": Whether he decides to talk or to remain silent, to utter words of thanks or accusations – it is entirely up to him. The sermon only ends when he says "Amen". The situation which connects the preacher and his listeners as "those interested in the situation" ("Situationsinteressierte") is dominated – as other communicative situations, too – by the predominant tendency for "situational change" and amounts to a "situational goal" ("Situationsziel"), in this case: a preaching goal. Cf. H. Lausberg, 1967, 18.

**59** Cf. E. Berne, 1964, 48–65.

**60** Everyday games have names like "If it weren't for you...", "Now I've Got You, You Son of a Bitch!" "See What You Made Me Do!" In the analysis such theses serve the purpose of making people aware of their latent life mottos (cf. E. Berne, 1964, 7f.)

**61** Further game-analyses, conducted in connection with Riemann's aforementioned model of the basic forms of anxiety, implied, among other things, game theses such as: "So that humanity is put out of action!" "God must seize hold of humanity!" Cf. W. Engemann, 1992a, 80, 82.

**62** On the possibilities of how listeners might participate in the preaching game cf. W. Engemann, 1992a, 79.

3. *Depiction of the paradigm of content*: On the level of the sermon's contents it is examined how preachers depict reality, what they consider as given in order to be able to achieve a preaching goal in line with their motifs. Thereby preachers may, for example, turn from their Adult ego to the listeners' Adult ego (cf. Fig. 29)[63] and explain them, on the basis of "most recent scientific knowledge", how things stand for them. If, however, in the course of this an all-too-strong distortion of the empirical reality occurs, listeners – particularly if the relationship level is perceived as repressive – will search for arguments which make what the preacher proclaims as reality appear questionable.

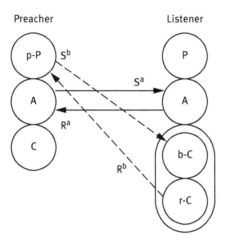

**Fig. 29:** Example of the content- and relationship paradigm of a sermon

4. *In the paradigm of relationship* the typical interpersonal transaction on the relationship level is documented: in the example given above (Fig. 29) from the punitive Parent ego (the preacher) to the broken Child ego (the listener) as well as reversely from the rebelling Child ego (the listener) to the punitive Parent ego (the preacher). Such a paradigm, however, remains hypothetical and can only be created if the analysis of the sermon and the exchange between preacher and congregation or group has led to "being able to read between the lines" and if the listeners are able and ready to also comment on an emotional level on their perception of the sermon.

---

63 In Fig. 29 "S" represents *stimulation* and "R" *reaction*. The small letters refer to the level of content (a) and the level of relationship (b).

5. *The analysis of the so-called payoff* refers to ideational advantages which those communicating are not always aware of. "Practice shows that although it is usually a particular motive that has triggered off the game, there are also other 'advantages' and 'payoffs' of quite different importance that may be connected to this."[64] Striving for such 'payoffs' has to do with, among other things, an (unacknowledged) expectation of affection, the justification of "favorite feelings", life plans and self-delusions, self-exculpations in view of morally dubious proclivities, the rejection of responsibility, the postponement of definitive, fear-evoking decisions etc.[65]

The question of payoffs is a tricky point in sermon analysis. Posing this question demands, on the one hand, the preachers' willingness to allow the idea of a "psychological benefit". On the other hand, such an analysis requires sensitivity on the part of the group not to consider their perceptions as being more important and "correct" than the preachers' own self-perception. Nevertheless the question of a sermon's "psychological benefit" should not become a homiletic taboo for it sharpens the question of the sermon's relationship level: "What does it mean for you to speak to me in this way? What do you get out of it? Does it make you feel stronger? Does this way of preaching give you pleasure? Or do you have to force yourself to it because you think this is what your mission demands from you?" Preachers who can give frank answers to these questions – at least to themselves – receive insight into their own homiletic strategy or "trick" (which need not be obsolete); and in addition they may become able to interrupt themselves, to cut themselves off, when appropriate or necessary.

## 2.2 Concepts of Analysis Focusing on the Listener's Reception

### 2.2.1 The Pastoral-Psychological Approach Focusing on the Level of Content and Relationship in the Event of Preaching

This analytical approach has been shaped to a considerable extent by influences and discoveries of the pastoral movement. It was found that particular problems frequently occurring in pastoral counseling largely resemble the difficulties which often also appear in sermon communication.[66] The differentiation between the levels of content and relationship – which has already been addressed several

---

**64** L. Schlegel, 1993, 340.
**65** Cf. L. Schlegel (ibid.) and on the different forms of payoffs cf. E. Berne, 1995, 19, 56–58, 70.
**66** Cf. H.-Ch. Piper, 1975.

times in this volume from different angles – belongs to the fundamental premises of pastoral-psychological sermon analysis: On the one hand, preachers bring up and address certain subjects *on the level of content*, on the other, they communicate *in that* they turn to the listeners *in a specific way*. They create a particular *relationship* with the listeners as well as with the subject matter of their address, and this relationship may evoke a confused, confirmative, annoyed, or other response on the part of the listeners, which is not (solely) triggered by the content of what has been said.

Pastoral-psychological sermon analysis is based on a culture of dialog between preacher and listener – more precisely, on the "feedback"[67] of actual listeners. Both, preacher and listeners, are asked to *summarize the content* of the sermon and to describe their own *emotional impressions*[68].

*Listeners* who agree to participate in a sermon analysis are requested to answer the following two questions as briefly as possible *in writing*[69]:
1. What is the message the preacher was trying to convey?
2. How did I experience the sermon and the preacher, or what kind of feelings and impressions occurred to me in the process of listening?

Correspondingly, the *preacher* is requested to answer the following questions:
1. What message did I try to convey?
2. What emotions and states (joy, freedom, trust etc.) did I wish to convey?
3. How did I experience myself? Which feelings did I have/dominated me as I delivered my address?

Here the following rules apply:
1. Initially, the listeners are not provided with *any manuscript* but depend – like other sermon-listeners, too – entirely on their hearing. Only at a later point, the sermon manuscript is distributed to all participants for the purpose of consolidation, concretization and comparison of what was heard with what was written.
2. The individual statements are addressed to the *discussion leader* in order not to thrust the preacher into a defensive role which could possibly lead to the (de-)valuation or rejection of certain perceptions.
3. The individual statements are visualized in a suitable form (panel, projector) in order to display the different *patterns of perception*, through which potential problems of the respective sermon may come to light.

---

67 Cf. the "rules for feedback", strikingly formulated by K. Götzinger, 1979, esp. 168–170 which are still worth reading. The participants of homiletically interested feedback groups are usually people who themselves serve as preachers.

68 On this questioning strategy cf. H.-Ch. Piper, 1976a, 92.

69 "The written recording is intended to prevent a mutual influencing and to facilitate the greatest possible differentiation" (loc. cit.).

This procedure is based on the pastoral-psychological hypothesis that "the problem of the sermon [...] as a rule points to a problem in the preacher".[70] Accordingly, starting from the inconsistencies between the sermon's intention and its reception (or from the failures in communication between preacher and listeners) serves the purpose of once again addressing communication problems between preacher and text and the question of how preachers deal with themselves. This corresponds with the observation that in their sermons preachers frequently unconsciously attempt to fight back their problems with the text or with the topic it contains. *These attempts catch on with the listener as "confusing signals"*[71] *on the relationship level.* Precisely that which is suppressed by the preacher will remind the listeners of unresolved issues.

Example: A preacher, who over the years has come to terms with a sort of resigned feeling of life and has scarcely any hope for any positive changes to come in his own life, deals with the topic of "hope" – wherever it appears in biblical texts – in such an uninspired and uncommitted manner as if it had nothing to do with himself. In so doing he spares himself the confrontation with the reasons for his resignation, with himself and his own anxieties and wishes which are still alive. He does not take the chance of genuinely addressing the experience of hopelessness and of dealing with it in and with the sermon, e.g. through analysis and examination of the text. He suppresses the problem of hopelessness probably well-known to his listeners, too, and which they expect to be addressed in the sermon. The address is therefore perceived as essentially inauthentic or non-credible.[72]

Pastoral-psychological sermon analysis aims for explaining the causes of such confusing signals which reach the listener as *confusions of the preacher*, e.g. regarding particular statements and positions in the text. If the reasons for such confusions are not evident to the preacher himself, associated problems will be suppressed and in further consequence also impact other sermons (of this preacher) and lead to new failures in communication. Fixing such failures, however, does certainly not mean to always agree with the listeners and to avoid any confusion. It is not a matter of constantly pleasing the listeners. But in listening to the sermon the congregation should feel *understood*; otherwise they will not be able to find the sermon to be relevant or beneficial.

---

70 Hans-Christoph Piper even states: "Disturbances in the communication between preacher and listener have their roots in disturbances in the communication between the preacher and God" (H.-Ch. Piper, 1976a, 99).
71 Cf. loc. cit., 100f.
72 Cf. loc. cit., 96–99.

The questions in Fig. 30 serve to adhere to the aspects formulated above on the levels of content and relationship for listeners and preachers. This avoids discussions focusing prematurely on strategic, hermeneutic or dogmatic questions.

| Questions on Hearing the Sermon for the First Time | |
|---|---|
| **Level of Content** | **Relationship Level** |
| 1. What have I been told in the sermon?<br>2. What is the sermon's core statement?<br>3. Under which heading would I summarize the sermon?<br>4. What could the preacher make clear for me?<br>5. Which are the reasons the preacher gives for his core statement?<br>6. What kind of action or attitude does the sermon induce me to take?<br>7. What aids of understanding and interpretation does the sermon provide?<br>8. Which offer of identification does the sermon suggest?<br>9. Wherein does the evangelical dimension of the sermon appear, i.e. in what sense can the sermon be understood as a step "into freedom"? | 1. How did I experience the communication of the sermon? Which impressions did it evoke within me?<br>2. How or as whom has the preacher addressed me (e.g. like my father or my mother, like a teacher, in a grumbling, complaining, arrogant, compassionate manner)?<br>3. How has the preacher treated me (e.g. as an equal being, as a friend, as a small child)?<br>4. How do I feel about the image the preacher obviously has of me?<br>5. Into which state has the sermon moved me (e.g. relaxation, tension, anger, wrath, sorrow, helplessness etc.)?<br>6. What would I most like to do after hearing the sermon? |

**Fig. 30:** Questions within the context of pastoral-psychological oriented sermon analysis

One particularly problematic, stereotypical preaching strategy is the clumsy attempt of setting the gospel against the conflict. The listener thus "continuously gets the impression of receiving something 'unmediated'. There is a rift through the sermon. Theological statements stand on their own, next to analyses of the situation, without mediation. Yet unintegrated theology defies communication."[73] Such homiletic malperformance is multi-faceted. H.-Ch. Piper has attempted to trace back frequently recurring communication problems to certain ways of dealing with problems on the part of the preachers themselves.

One important result of pastoral-psychological sermon analysis is the attempt of creating typologies. The typological outlines presented below were not drafted

---

**73** H.-Ch. Piper, 1976a, 103.

on the drawing board but are the result of many analyses conducted over the years by H.-Ch. Piper in collaboration with other preachers[74]. They emerged from the observation that particular psychological patterns of homiletic behavior constantly recur or are frequently encountered. In the following survey I have briefly summarized some of these typological patterns.

| Pastoral-Psychological Typologizations (Selection) | |
|---|---|
| **Typological Model** | **Characteristics/ Basic Problem** |
| 1. The worried preacher | The preacher, despite the fear of failure which often haunts him, desires to communicate confidence. His fear, however, is so strong that he cannot deal with the experience of failure in any way or form. Instead he proclaims that it is God's intervention, refusing to consider the option of changing his attitude towards his own life. |
| 2. The thankful preacher | The preacher encourages the listeners to practice a thankful, Christian life, without providing them with the rationales or motives of a grateful attitude. Although the preacher himself feels no thankfulness he wants to impose upon himself thankfulness as a Christian exercise. |
| 3. The demanding preacher | The preacher wants to relieve the listeners from the pressure of the law. Yet he measures himself, first and foremost, against his achievements as a human and as a Christian. The self-imposed pressure is expressed clearly in his sermons. This may appear to the listeners as a merciless imperative for the fulfillment of religious and ethical norms. |
| 4. The obedient preacher | The preacher wants to encourage the listeners to trust in God. Yet he constantly refers to disappointed expectations which make it difficult for him to have trust. Consequently, trusting faith is simply conveyed as a mere act of obedience. The preacher's dilemma is that while he desires to trust in God and humankind, he does not expect anything good of them. |
| 5. The distant preacher | The preacher desires to invite the listeners to live in community with God and to deepen the religious dimension of the experience of affection. However, his own experience with closeness and community has been a negative one. His congregation, the people who have been invited, are judged in an exclusively negative fashion (as unwilling to repent, godless, etc.); it therefore becomes clear that the preacher himself does not expect this invitation to have any positive effect. Thus the listeners experience a distance from the preacher and feel disinvited. |

**Fig. 31:** Pastoral-psychological typologizations in sermon analysis

---

74 H.-Ch. Piper, 1976b.

| Pastoral-Psychological Typologizations (Selection) | |
|---|---|
| **Typological Model** | **Characteristics/ Basic Problem** |
| 6. The depressed preacher | The preacher calls for a life in freedom, but is frustrated because he has experienced subjugation or a lack of freedom, which he believes is to be put up with. He accuses the listeners of constantly recoiling from a life in freedom out of melancholy or a fear of life. The listeners experience this actual self-accusation as an aggressive reproach which they are more likely to fend off than acknowledge. They do not allow problems to be imposed upon them which they do not have (as such). |
| 7. The optimistic preacher | The preacher dispassionately calls for a more optimistic attitude to life, which he himself does not have, without being able to name relevant arguments for an open, promising future, and without anticipating such a scenario in his imagination. What oftentimes hides behind optimistic slogans is, in fact, deep pessimism and helplessness. What is said remains nothing but a compulsive-like appeal. On the part of the listeners this is likely to trigger mechanisms of "missing" (Germ.: *Überhören*) what is said, or of taking on an attitude of rejection. |

**Fig. 31:** (continued)

## 2.2.2 The Empirical Approach in the Systematic Survey of Sermon Listeners

Even if – due to its complexity – this approach cannot be used by a group which only meets on isolated accounts in order to listen to and discuss a sermon, its basic idea should be outlined here since its results provide relevant and constructive suggestions for working on the sermon itself as well as for other forms of analyzing it.

The "empirical listeners survey"[75] particularly looks at how sermons are *perceived* by listeners of different ages, different social groups, milieus and levels of education. Due to the fact that it relates to concrete experiences of perception on the part of the listeners it is also referred to as "perception analysis". It takes into account the frequency of church attendances, the marital status of listeners, their moral values, their opinion as well as prejudices about the preacher in question etc. For the collection of relevant data, questionnaires were developed by a socio-statistical expert group. Apart from commenting on their overall impression of the concrete sermon, these questionnaires invite the participants to furthermore comment on their relationship with the church

---

**75** Two important studies that are available on this subject are: K.-F. Daiber/H. W. Dannowski et al., 1983 and P. Meyer, 2014.

in general, their conception of the preaching task etc.[76] The listeners' perception of the sermon itself is, among other things, recorded on the basis of the following questions:

"Please think of the sermon you heard. Do you remember any phrases or sentences from it? If so, please write them down below." There is blank space for their text, and below it, instructions on how to fill in the questionnaire: "Place an 'X' mark closest to the features listed on the right or left hand side if you agree strongly, or further away, i.e. closer to the middle, if you disagree, depending on your perception of the respective characteristic."[77]

| I perceived the sermon as . . . | | |
|---|---|---|
| monotonously presented | ( ) ( ) ( ) ( ) ( ) ( ) | dynamically presented |
| sparsely related to the biblical text | ( ) ( ) ( ) ( ) ( ) ( ) | strongly related to the biblical text |
| meaningful | ( ) ( ) ( ) ( ) ( ) ( ) | meaningless |
| not very well presented | ( ) ( ) ( ) ( ) ( ) ( ) | very well presented |
| cautious | ( ) ( ) ( ) ( ) ( ) ( ) | insistent |
| not very true-to-life | ( ) ( ) ( ) ( ) ( ) ( ) | true-to-life |
| comforting | ( ) ( ) ( ) ( ) ( ) ( ) | worrying |
| unconventional | ( ) ( ) ( ) ( ) ( ) ( ) | accentuating the office of the preacher |
| rigid | ( ) ( ) ( ) ( ) ( ) ( ) | agile |
| corresponding to my own views | ( ) ( ) ( ) ( ) ( ) ( ) | contrary to my own views |
| emotional | ( ) ( ) ( ) ( ) ( ) ( ) | factual |
| not so critical of the church | ( ) ( ) ( ) ( ) ( ) ( ) | critical of the church |
| progressive | ( ) ( ) ( ) ( ) ( ) ( ) | conservative |
| less dedicated | ( ) ( ) ( ) ( ) ( ) ( ) | highly dedicated |
| not too well | ( ) ( ) ( ) ( ) ( ) ( ) | exceptionally well |

**Fig. 32:** Questionnaire of the empirical listeners survey

Within the framework of such a survey everything is inquired that may be perceived about sermon and preacher in the context of the preaching event – everything that in some way or other may influence certain patterns of expectation in

---

76 At a later stage preachers and experts comment – on the basis of questionnaires – on the sermon as well as the listeners' perceptions (cf. loc. cit., e.g. 124–129).
77 K.-F. Daiber/H. W. Dannowski, 1983, 98f. Cf. the following questionnaire loc. cit., 99.

the perception of the preaching event. This should help to reveal connections between particular habits of perception and, in further consequence, to compare them with the intentions and goals of the preacher. In this context, the identification of "semantic differentials" plays a vital part: They reflect – in a differentiated manner and quantifiable in percentages – the whole range of perception of sermons including the conceptions which, among other things, are connected to "sermon, "pastor", "church", "Bible", "ministry", "Word of God" and impact the assessment and comprehension of sermons. The results of this method reveal a number of aspects: how differentiatedly, yet supra-individually certain characteristics of the sermon are assessed; which factors clearly seem to strengthen each other or are inter-dependent for particular groups of listeners – and which seem to be quite mutually exclusive.

In the case of the "non-professional" listeners (i.e. listeners who are not familiar with homiletic issues and topics) four factor groups can be identified:

- In a *first* factor group, the factors "good address, dynamic presentation" and impression of the preacher's "agility" and "commitment" (cf. the questionnaire above) lie close to one another: Sermons which are found by the listeners to be "good" are at the same time also perceived as "true-to-life", "meaningful" and "corresponding to their own views and convictions".[78]
- Independently of this, in the perception of the listeners the factors "comforting – worrying" along with "cautious – insistent" appear as a *second* connected group of factors: "A sermon which speaks to the listeners' emotions may be assessed as good or not so good; but even a sermon perceived as not so good may still be regarded as emotionally appealing. [...] The contrastive pairs of 'factual' or 'emotional' and 'critical' or 'not so critical of the church' hardly play any part for the listeners in the context of preaching."[79]
- A *third* factor concerning the listeners' impression of the sermon arises from how they perceive the preacher's concept of ministry, whereby the aspects "conservative – progressive" play an important part. Here sermons "perceived as 'conservative' may be evaluated as either 'good' and 'comforting' or as 'good' and 'worrying' or as 'not so good' and 'comforting'".[80]
- As *fourth* factor of assessment refers to how the sermon's text reference is perceived on the part of the listeners.

The observation that certain factors or groups of factors are perceived by listeners independently of each other means that a sermon can "be perceived as successful, regardless of its emotional content, the emphasis on his office by the preacher, or how the text is referenced and related to"[81]. For preachers

---

**78** Loc. cit., 116.
**79** Ibid.
**80** Ibid.
**81** Ibid.

and in the expert groups different dependencies or independences of certain factors can be identified. Thus, for example, a "sermon that was perceived as good by the preacher does not necessarily correspond to the attitudes of the listeners", just as experts cannot separate the quality of a sermon from the preachers' perceived authority of their office and self-image.[82] The insights of the empirical survey of listeners undoubtedly lead to an ever deeper and more differentiated understanding of problems regarding the content and form of a sermon.

Remarkably, an international study that compares the reception of sermons in the US and Germany[83] confirms many individual perceptions and implications of older studies. Peter Meyer relates the problems of preaching to their respective linguistic, ecclesiastical, religious, socio-linguistic context as well as to life circumstances and the conditions that influenced the formation and reception of the sermon. His discoveries may relieve preachers since his study worked out the multifactorial conditions of the sermon culture that the sermon has to embrace and not fight against, and within which it has to prove itself as capable and relevant to everyday life over and over again. On the basis of a field-researching approach, the sermon is analyzed as a form of lived religious practice, the meaning of which is continually formed and influenced by the corresponding conditions of life and perception. The analysis shows: Sermons are perceived all the more positively, the less they consider the listeners and their everyday life as religiously dense and theologically insufficiently thought-out and the more they are able to show how faith may be experienced and communicated in everyday life. This requires, not least, unpretentious linguistic transformations of theological contents which, to be plausible and credible, must, in a sense, "refer back to matters which are 'self-evident'"[84].

### 2.2.3 The Approach of Simultaneous Procedures in the Reactoscopic Method

With the publication of the "Befunde und Ergebnisse der Heidelberger Umfrage zur Predigtrezeption" (Findings and Results of the Heidelberg Survey on Sermon Reception) Helmut Schwier and Sieghard Gall have documented an attempt to discover *how* one can survey the reception of a sermon *in actu* in the sense of the listener's behavior regarding their reaction and creation of meaning.[85] The focus is on the exploration of the "heard sermon" – not on the basis

---

82 Loc. cit., 118, 121.
83 P. Meyer, 2014.
84 Loc. cit., 700.
85 H. Schwier/S. Gall, 2008. This work presents the results of an empirical examination of sermon reception which was carried out in 2006 in eight congregations of the Lutheran Church in Baden by the colleagues of the Department of Sermon Research during a class on Practical Theology held at the University of Heidelberg, in cooperation with the Institute REACTOS® Medienforschung [REACTOS® Media Research] (Munich).

of a survey conducted later on but on the basis of the analysis of the "immediate or simultaneous reactions of the listeners". Simultaneous feedback and
reactions of the recipients "should be submitted during the performance [...]
intuitively, independently and in a differentiated way. The production of the
individual reports should not restrict the attentiveness and perception of
the recipients; the question must be clear, the administration of appropriate
devices uncomplicated".[86]

Even though, in principle, the reactoscopic process can be applied to any sermon, part of the
exceptional features of the analysis outlined here is that the sermons which were examined were
not chosen randomly. From the outset, the whole procedure was connected to a special homiletic interest related to the comparability of particular sermon-types or -genres. Accordingly, the
sermons heard could also be divided into particular "pairs of sermons" which were chosen in
such a way, that the sermons were different from each other in a very specific respect and could
thus be compared to one another under selected homiletic aspects. Schwier and Gall decided on
the following "pairs of sermons" for comparison: (1.) a "narrative sermon" to a "text sermon", (2.)
"a theologically ambitious, instructive Easter sermon" to a "popular, more 'down-to-earth' Easter
sermon" (3) a "sermon oriented on strengthening the faith of the congregation" to a "faith-inspir-
ing, evangelistic sermon" as well as (4.) a "thematic" to "political" sermon. While, from a homiletic standpoint, it might be somewhat dubious how e.g. a "theologically ambitious" sermon
might represent a genre of its own alongside the "narrative" or "thematic" sermon; however,
from the perspective of the listener it might be perceived differently which is why those conducting the survey endeavored to reveal empirical patterns of perception, which might also be
subject to clichés on the side of the listeners.

The implementation of this method is connected to the use of an electronic,
directly adjustable sliding-controller or "reaction-transmitter" which, on the left,
is equipped with a scale A from -3 to +3, and on the right with a scale B from 1–7.
With this small handheld device, the listeners can immediately indicate whether
they, for example, feel "very affected by the sermon (upper end of the scale) or
"not at all affected" (lower end of the scale). Naturally, graded comments are possible between the two ends of scales A and B.

*During the sermon,* the listeners only have to answer to a single open question by adjusting the slide of the transmitter accordingly. "To what degree does
the sermon, which you are now listening to, affect and interest you?" The listeners are told in advance that this question relates to every possible detail of the
preaching process: length, topic, enunciation etc. In the evaluation, it can then
be precisely determined at what second, with which sentence, and through which
expression the listeners felt addressed (in a positive way) or not.

---

86 Loc. cit., 6.

This survey happening simultaneously to the sermon is supplemented by the evaluation of a – complex but easily understood – catalogue of questions which is presented to the listeners partly before, partly after the worship service.[87] On the basis of this catalogue of questions they can react to the sermons presented in a subtly diversified way, independently of one another and naturally anonymously. These questions are subdivided into various categories[88] as well as into further sub-groups which are listed below – connected to exemplary topics – in an abridged version:

1.  *Person and faith:* These questions are connected (1.1) to sociological data and personal assessments, (1.2) to the personal participation in the congregation and worship service, (1.3) to aspects of personal faith, (1.4) to the concept of God, (1.5) to the understanding of the gospels. Examples of questions: Closeness to the Christian religion: from "very close" (top) to "very distant" (bottom). – To what extent is your faith connected to hope? From "very strongly" (top) to "not at all" (bottom).
2.  *Expectations of the sermon in the worship service*: These questions relate (2.1) to the general importance of the sermon for the service, (2.2) to the preferred features of the sermon, (2.3) to the impulses expected in the sermon. Example: To what extent are the following features of the sermon important for you? From "very important" (top) to "not at all important" (bottom): a clear, understandable language, a credible and authentic testimony on the part of the preacher etc.
3.  *Perception of the sermon in the worship service*: These questions are related (3.1) to the impression as a whole, (3.2) to specific elements in the sermon (e.g. liveliness, central ideas) and (3.3) to the kind of stimuli (e.g. religious edification, practical advice on how to live).
4.  *Perception of sermons from group A 1–4 (general, standard questions)*: these questions are identical to 3, but are grouped to a separate questionnaire (4.4.), which is for a more differentiated evaluation of the sermon (length, enunciation, message, reception of the text, language, pace of speech, theological aspects). Example of a question on the sermon's reception of the text: From "The sermon should be closer to the text" – (from the center upwards) and "The sermon should be more independent, less bound to the text" – (from the center downwards) or "It was exactly right as it was" – (central).
5.  *Perception of sermons from the group A 1–4 (specific questions)*: These questions relate exclusively (5.1) to questions on sermon 1A, (5.2) to questions on sermon 2A etc. These questions are developed with explicit reference to the content and form of the respective sermon. "Was the way of the main character as told in the sermon comprehensible?" from "Very much so" (top) to "Not at all" (bottom) – "To what extent was this a sermon after your liking?" from "Very much so" (top) to "Not at all" (bottom).
6.  *and 7. Perception of sermons in the group B 1–4 analogous* to 4. and 5.

---

**87** Loc. cit., 251–261. The questions in 1 and 2 are presented *before*, in 3–8 *after* the service and answered with the transmitting device.

**88** Since two sermons or sermon groups are always compared, the question-complex 4–5 and 6–7 are to be considered as parallel to one another.

8. *Concluding methodical questions:* These questions relate to the extent to which expectations were fulfilled, to the evaluations of the use of the methods employed and to the interest in feedback discussions after preaching.

The results of the survey are relevant for almost all areas of homiletics: The study provides profound insights into the correlation of disposition and response while listening to a sermon as well as a more thorough understanding of effects of the listeners' expectations and attitudes on the perception and assessment of preaching. It is now easier to assess how certain rhetorical and theological facets of the sermon are perceived, which circumstances are beneficial in attracting the attention of the listeners at the beginning of the sermon or at which points of the sermon the listeners stop listening or "digress". "Did you find a point where you could easily 're-connect' to the sermon? What influence do language, structure or genre and theological statements have? And finally: What final impression has the sermon left on you? What can you remember of what has been said? How uniform or diverse was the impression of the listeners as a whole? Only the listeners themselves can give appropriate answers to all these complex questions."[89] To pursue these answers means to be able to turn anew to the classic questions of homiletics and to draw appropriate consequences for the structure of the sermon, how one deals with the texts, the personal presence etc.

The results of the Reactoscope procedure confirm the homiletical *common sense* in its main points. To name a few: 1. A clear reference to tradition, the concrete locating of the sermon in the reality of the lives of the listeners and a plausible imparting or crossing of both perspectives are equally significant for a sermon experienced as helpful and listened to attentively. 2. It is decisive whether the sermon also succeeds as an act of communication, for which the "liveliness" and comprehensibility of the preacher as person play a determining part. 3. It is problematic when preachers attempt to say "everything" in every address from the pulpit and consequently always say the same thing (high redundancy), i.e. when they shy away from stressing a particular point and thereby also risk something theologically. In contrast listeners expect a sermon which contains "intellectual, spiritual and theological aspects beneficial for everyday life"[90] and which also causes corresponding effects.

Since then, this procedure has also been applied to the analysis of "hearing sermons in denominational comparison"[91] The results correspond to the general

---

89 Loc. cit., 9.
90 Loc. cit., 247. "The personal statement of a participant that one leaves the church 'more cheerful and encouraged' after a good sermon has a paradigmatic value" (ibid.).
91 Cf. H. Schwier/S. Gall, 2013.

level of knowledge and insight in the homiletic discourse regarding the perception, assessment and esteem of sermons. Furthermore, it has become clear that: "Protestant and Roman Catholic listeners differ only slightly in the reception of the sermon as well as in the expectation and perception of its structure and impulses."[92]

---

92 Loc. cit., 232. In fundamentally similar survey results, certain differences between Protestant and Roman Catholic listeners can be seen in "how 'at home' they feel in their denomination and congregation", in their evaluation of individual liturgical elements, and in the "affinity to individual images of God" (237). For Protestants the sense of belonging to their domination is stronger than that to the parish. However, "those who consider themselves to be Catholics do not have an ideological but a very real home in their parish" (ibid.).

# 3 Response and Feedback Discussion with the Congregation after Preaching

To prevent the misunderstanding that feedback discussions after preaching (in German: "Predigtnachgespräche") are above all a homiletic service on the part of the congregation to improve the quality of the sermon, let it be said in advance that they are first of all to be seen as a specific form of the communication of faith and take place for the sake of the congregation – to which, naturally, the preacher also belongs. That there are such discussions is also an expression of the open, *dialogical dimension*[93] of the sermon: the communication of faith is dependent on communication and mutual understanding.[94]

That a successful feedback discussion after preaching can also always *implicitly* be seen as a sermon analysis is connected to the possibility of a comparison of the intention of the sermon and experience of the listeners. The effect and "lasting impact" of the sermon on the part of the listeners, which surface in the course of the discussion, can be compared with the intention and expectations on the part of the preacher; possible differences or other conspicuous details can be discussed. Considering the chances, a well-conducted and engaged feedback discussion after a sermon offers, it is a pity that – after its "discovery" in the '70s[95] – the culture of this special dialog is not particularly well maintained today.[96]

However, in general, churches do not find it easy to "criticize" their pastor – which is often (and mistakenly) considered the primary function of such discussions. In such cases, it is thus a matter of calm persuasion and occasionally explaining the circumstances under which a sermon is held.[97] However, since it can nevertheless happen that the level of relationship between preacher and congregation is found to be "tricky", in the discussion after preaching it is important to prevent "an unclear group-situation in a foggy atmosphere"[98]. This danger can best be met "if right at the beginning everyone agrees upon what should be discussed

---

**93** Cf. I.4.3.3, p. 188–197.

**94** On the conversational principles of the sermon cf. I.5.4, p. 250–257.

**95** Cf. e.g. G. Schmidtchen, 1973, esp. 221, Table A 64; R. Heue/R. Lindner, 1975; H. van der Geest, 1978, esp. 37.

**96** Certain reservations which were expressed also in Homiletics are clearly still latently in effect in some places. O. Haendler (2017b, 621) and M. Josuttis (1988, 164–166, 178) express a certain doubt which relates to protection of the preacher and theoretical questions of the ritual, without, however, rejecting the discussion after preaching altogether.

**97** Cf. e.g. III.4.5.2, p. 504–509.

**98** H. Schulz, 1990, 568.

https://doi.org/10.1515/9783110440256-010

and how long the discussion should last [...]. Neutral Expressions should be avoided as far as possible, personal statements are preferred"[99].

For the discussion of the sermon the simple questions about the level of content and relationship[100] might form the basis, as well as, depending on the level of familiarity within the group, questions of the "selection, overall impression and association model"[101] of R. Heue and R. Lindner:

1. With the *selection-model* the listeners refer only to a few aspects of the reception: 1. What made me happy? 2. What annoyed me? 3. What was the aim of the sermon? – Or 1. What made a positive impression? 2. What bothered me in the sermon? 3. What, in my opinion, did the preacher want to achieve in me and what has he achieved?
2. With *the model of the overall impression* questions are asked about the impressions which relate to the sermon in its entirety: 1. What did I observe? 2. What did I experience? 3. What ideas came to me?
3. The *model of association* does not provide any concrete questions but provides an open space for discussion.

The classic feedback discussion after preaching in the congregation – independently of the model chosen – is carried out in *two basic forms*. In the one – a practice widely spread in the '70s but hardly used today – the discussion comes *immediately* after preaching.[102] In the other – and considerably more frequently – it takes place immediately after the end of the service. The advantage of this second form can without doubt be seen in that nobody is forced to take part in such a discussion, and that, generally, those who participate in the conversation have something to say and desire to gain a deeper understanding of the topics, problems and views addressed in the sermon or wish to discuss questions the sermon has raised for them.

One of the most important prerequisites for a post-sermon discussion that benefits both the listeners and the preacher, is the appointment of a *competent moderator*, who, ideally, should be proficient in this matter and should not be the person who just preached. However, there are also congregational groups in which this is not always possible, so that – assuming a certain measure of

---

**99** Ibid.

**100** Cf. above, Fig. 30, p. 413.

**101** Cf. R. Heue/R. Lindner, 1975, 73–77.

**102** This quite obviously had to do with a new understanding of groups and democracy that has developed in those years. A survey conducted in Lutheran Churches at the beginning of the '70s reads: "In many congregations, it is now customary for those present at the worship service to briefly discuss once more what the pastor has said after preaching. Only after this discussion of the sermon is the service then continued. Do you think it is a good idea or not a good idea to, again, talk about the sermon after preaching?" At that time, the response was 53%: a good idea, 28%: not a good idea, 19% were undecided (cf. G. Schmidtchen, 1973, 221).

self-detachment on the part of the preacher – one should not make a law out of this ideal. If preachers themselves invite the congregation to a follow up discussion and also lead it, it will only be fruitful if *they really want to know* "how their sermons affect the listeners. It is understandable that this can present a cause for concern for them. The image that others have of us is very rarely consistent with the one we have fabricated ourselves. And yet it holds true that only through the echo which we receive we may know what we have actually said. It is important that the preacher is not left alone with the feedback on their sermon. They should get the chance to process it *mutuum colloquium et consolationem fratrum* with the group"[103]. However, certain critical and self-distancing abilities are not everything. It is important to "concentrate on a few agreed-upon questions" coupled with a "persistent style of leadership that does not involve giving grades"[104].

---

**103** H.-Ch. Piper, 1976b, 18.
**104** H. Schulz, 1990, 568.

Part III: **Theology of Preaching**

Earth Biology of Preaching

# Preliminary Remarks

In spite of its complex claims on the proficiency of the preacher – particularly regarding the hermeneutic, rhetorical, dialogical and personal competencies – in essence, the sermon represents a *theological challenge* which, in turn, reacts upon the motivation, the diversity and consistency along with the hermeneutic, rhetorical etc. elements which all play their part in the composition of the sermon. Those who preach do not only show where their understanding of the biblical traditions and their analysis of the experience of faith has led them. They also expound on why contemporary theology is necessary by putting into words what it means to live by faith under the circumstances of the world we presently live in.[1] Every protestant sermon, implicitly or explicitly, brings to the point – that is its theological aspiration – what evangelical christianity stands for today. This generally presupposes a high level of professionalism, as the majority of the conceptions of the task of preaching today show.[2]

The fact that also lay-people preach, indeed, that all Christians are in principle "called" to "bear witness" to their neighbors and, in so doing, to illustrate something of what it means to live life by faith, does not contradict this. A wide range of forms of communication and situations belongs to the communication of the gospel. The inclusion of lay-people reflects not only the fact that the story of the life of Jesus was initially passed on from direct experience, at the same time as a rumour and unregulated. Nevertheless, theology has the task of reflecting upon this process, having a look at the problematic areas, defining constructive factors and proving itself as the science of the communication of the gospel.

Theological competence is consequently an essential part of homiletic ability, which is why radical changes in theological thinking always occur with certain

---

1 Cf. W. Engemann, 2001d as well as the work of R. J. Allen, 2002, which highlights and documents on the basis of numerous sample sermons (113–128) the necessity of a personal acquisition and re-formulation of dogmatic statements in the act of sermon preparation. For the substance of the sermon a living theology of the sermon is indispensable (cf. loc. cit., 81–98). J. Kay (2007) similarly states: "This book attempts to show how and why [. . .] theology matters for preaching; and how and why preaching matters for theology" (VIII).

2 Cf. the selection of homiletic positions presented in the study book "Homiletics" by Lars Charbonnier, Konrad Merzyn and Peter Meyer. This work deduces various *concretizations* of the role of the communication of the gospel already unfolded in this "Introduction to Homiletics" in that it sets different goals: A sermon should, for example, "care for the soul" (Christian Möller), "lead into the presence of God" (Manfred Josuttis), "interpret life" (Wilhelm Gräb) etc. Cf. L. Charbonnier/K. Merzyn/P. Meyer, 2012, 34, 85, 215.

https://doi.org/10.1515/9783110440256-part III

doubts about the experience of (no longer) being able to preach.[3] If the theology of preaching is incorrect, if it is un-evangelical (in a non-confessional sense) and operates with a historical understanding of Scripture or is determined by a pseu-do-anthropology which is based on clichés and overlooks human reality, then neither rhetorical nor other methodical arts can produce a "good" sermon. The subsequently discussed signs of problems should thus clarify what it means to consider the inadequately deliberated theological premises as one of the reasons for the lack of relevance of a sermon.

---

3 The frustration caused by the homiletic principles of Dialectical Theology, which persistently discussed the *credenda* of the sermon but abandoned the preachers in their practical work, paralyzed theological discussion on the task and preparation of the sermon for years. The participants in the Lutheran General Synod in 1957 positively implored the governing bodies of the church finally to stand up for an improvement of the theological quality of sermons: "We have the impression that the aids to preaching published at present are to a large extent inadequate. We request that the governing bodies of the church consider how they can support the preachers with good aids for preaching. [...] We request the governing bodies *to do the urgently craved favor* to the preachers *that their sermon is heard by theologically well-informed advisors and talked through with them in a brotherly fashion*" (Lutheran Church offices. Hanover, 1957, 88; emphasis W. E.).

# 1 Snapshots. Empirical Indicators of Problems

## 1.1 The Cliché of People Today

Whether a sermon becomes *relevant* in the sense of the category of how the sermon relates to the individual situation of a person and actually touches upon human reality depends to a high degree on the image of humanity on which the sermon is based. If the image of humanity in the sermon is not correct – if, for example, the view of the individual is an ideological construct – the whole sermon will not agree with the listener's lifeworld. At all times, the sermon was in danger that the theses and views of the respective theological epoch or fashion were transferred to "the people of today", which brought with it a perspectivally narrowed perception of "human need", "the sin of modern man" etc. In the sermon of the prospering post-war Germany "the modern man" became, as a homiletic negative model, a popular central character in the sermon.[4] Everything which might be considered as abnormal behavior or sin was projected upon him.

"The modern man does not care about God. They only believe in themselves. In their illusion of freedom and delusions of grandeur they lose sight of their neighbors. The only love which they still feel passionately is the love of themselves. Selfishly they set goals for themselves and believe that God's world is open for conquest and belongs to them alone. Psalm 73 already speaks of these types of people, who have become separate from God and will perish on their own self-overestimation: their defiance even gives them pleasure. They boast of their lifestyle wherever they appear. They only do what they want to do – but in the end, they will stumble and fall. [...] The modern man has gone far. Unlike the time of the psalmist, today there are many technical tools at their disposal that make them believe that they can go on and on, and ultimately renounce God and other people altogether."[5]

This cliché of "modern man" or "people today" was tainted with theological problems from the start. How can one speak in one breath so indiscriminately of a person's illusion of freedom and delusions of grandeur when freedom is one of the highest goods of the culture of the Christian faith? And if the one who prayed Psalm 73 at the end of the song feels pity for inconsiderate egomaniacs who live prosperously (shocked to have considered their way of thinking as an option for themselves), to what extent can their existence be significant for "the people of today"? What has egoism to do with the virtue of "loving oneself" required in the double commandment of love? And further: Can people today so simply be referred to as "god-less" when *as sinners* they should experience justification?

---

4 On the background of the historical sermon manuscript cf. W. Engemann, 1996.
5 Sermon manuscript on Luke 14:25–33.

https://doi.org/10.1515/9783110440256-011

Furthermore, little remains of the optimism of progress of the post-war period in the late modernism that has become aware of its limitations and is critical of technology and ideologies of feasibility. Therefore, sticking to the ingrained clichés of the "people today" is all the more inappropriate.[6]

Those who deal with humanity on a theological level should not confine themselves to assembling certain soteriological, creation-theological or hamartiological positions of the history of Dogmatics ad libitum. An explicit approach to human reality such as the sermon demands presupposes basic knowledge of contemporary anthropology, i.e. here: a general knowledge of the aspects – including also those outside of theology, particularly in philosophy, psychology, sociology and medicine – under which the essence "of humankind" is reflected upon. Anyone who preaches should also know something about the socio-psychological facets of freedom and bondage in contemporary society. This can safeguard one from offering inappropriate clichés about the "striving for autonomy of today's people". An insight into the popular academic discourse of love as a basic human motivation can help to critically scrutinize the platitudes about the incapacity for love of people today.[7]

## 1.2 Contraction of the Concept of Faith to a Category of Certainty

One cannot deliver a sermon without implicitly or explicitly expressing the recommendation of a particular way of believing. In every sermon, a more or less concrete picture of what it means to live by faith appears. Whether this is in fact found by the individual listener as a recommendation depends, among other things, on the conditions in which this faith is placed before us, on the manner and the way in which the experience and appropriation of this faith is imagined and not least also on the offer of identification which the verb *believe* always implies – i.e. on what it finally *means* in the preacher's view for the individual to believe. Of course, many sermons have a tendency to reduce faith to a category of certainty, whereby the quality or strength of faith can be judged according to whether one believes particular facts *firmly, unwaveringly* and *totally resolutely.* Corresponding sermons then deal primarily with the question of what is certainly true or certainly false. In fact, however, the ability

---

6 On the special conditions of the sermon within the terms of postmodernism and the resulting consequences see also D. J. Lose, 2003, 7–29.

7 Cf. also below, III.2.2.2, p. 446–448.

to believe is then reduced to a determined verification of dogmatic statements in the guise of everyday language.

"Who can still believe today that Jesus died on the cross for his individual guilt? That sounds more than implausible. Not only because more than 2000 years lie between Jesus' atoning death and our actions but also because we, in the age of total autonomy, are completely imbued with the idea that we can accept responsibility for ourselves. As enlightened people, we are in principle prepared to accept the consequences of our actions; in any case, we would resist the fact that someone has to die for our failings. [...] But that is now the challenge of faith, which one cannot have without a minimum of humility, to say 'yes' to that which God himself allowed to happen for us. Those who fully embrace that, thanks to the crucifixion of Jesus, sin no longer stands between them and God may experience what it means to lead a life free from oppressing guilt."[8]

Is a faith which is played off against a necessary autonomy a good recommendation?[9] The partly comprehensible objections voiced by the listeners are simply left unresolved and should be overcome with humility. Who would like to have such a faith – or asked in another way: Where is the problem? In the quoted sermon, faith is reduced to the strength of one's determination to say "yes" to what has been said of a certain event, but which has hardly been adequately explained – or to the inability to summon such a resolve. "Faith" however is, according to the testimonies of the Jewish-Christian tradition – and also in historical theological discourse – much more and also different to that. Faith is above all an expression of an attitude of relationship, attendant circumstances of a person's hope, joy, confidence and courage.[10] Faith is therefore an experience *accompanied by emotions*, the prerequisites of which are not to force oneself to accept improbabilities. On the contrary: To be able to believe cannot be separated from an individual integration and adaption of religious ideas in one's own understanding of oneself and the world.

## 1.3 The Legalism of the Sermon

Preaching the gospel is an art which in practice is frequently confused with cheap calls to morality, with the firm recommendation of undisputed values, with the jargon of political and social correctness or with attempts to always stand on the proper side. Naturally, the sermon is in no way simply the opposite of values,

---

**8** Sermon manuscript on 2 Cor 5:14b–21.

**9** The seductive – but within the scope of a correct theological anthropology not tenable – countering of faith and "an internally necessary autonomy" in the sermon is a problem which has long been complained about in Homiletics. Cf. already O. Haendler, 2017a, 51; idem, 2015, 428–430, and in detail W. Engemann, 2006b, 72–74, 78–87.

**10** W. Engemann, 2009b.

morality and partiality. It has concrete ethical bases and suggests a particular ethos. In a sermon, however, these aspects are not the direct aim but rather an effect or a requirement. A sermon is a speech through which people are to understand *themselves* anew, whereby – and this is at heart a very deep ethical step in the sermon connected to moral ideas – they may take a step into freedom, rediscover the gift of their life, see their future as open again, draw hope etc. To a great extent a sermon aims at raising awareness of available, i.e. already existing open spaces and possibilities. In preaching practice, this indicative view of life is often obscured by half-hearted imperatives, which vaguely demand what one should or shouldn't "finally," "once again" or "now, really" do so that eventually one might experience this freedom.

"It is our duty not to think that the others do not matter. Let us be present in this world. We are a part of this world. We live in *one* world. We cannot be indifferent to one another. [...] We are an example to one another: 'Well, if you join in, I'll join you too.' It is this sense of community which attracts people."[11]

In another sermon it is proclaimed: "If we finally show more consideration for one another, if we no longer overlook the marginalized of society and bring them into our midst, we can reckon that in so doing more of the kingdom of God becomes visible."[12] Or to take up the theme of freedom: "If we allow ourselves to be challenged just a bit more to trust, not in ourselves, but totally in God, then we shall stop thinking only inside our limited field of vision. Even in confused situations we shall experience the liberating action of God."[13]

A sermon which makes the fulfillment of particular norms or social expectations the requirement for the experience of freedom of faith is "legalistic". This remains problematic even if the action demanded is downplayed. Expressions such as "We *only* need to...", "We *just* have to..." are often followed by problems that are universally known because humanity has struggled with them throughout the entire history of faith – problems which simply cannot be resolved by deciding one way or the other: "God is waiting for us to open ourselves to him, to give him a chance. That is the only thing which each of us must do or decide for ourselves"[14]

What would the faith of humanity look like, if it were the result of people managing to give God the opportunity to reach them? In such sermons as the last cited the old *pattern of justification through works* asserts itself. The fact that a – in this sense – *legalistic sermon* is more likely to be accepted in the discussion with the congregation after the sermon than a *sermon of the law* which confronts the individual with experiences of the "life under the law" (as e.g. with experiences of

---

11 Sermon manuscript on John 15:26–16:4.
12 Sermon manuscript on Luke 14:15–24.
13 Sermon manuscript on Gal 5:1–6.
14 Sermon manuscript on Rev 3:14–22.

failure), is connected to its downplaying tone: When the individuals are primarily addressed with the intention of making them more active in a particular respect, it is tacitly assumed "that the possibility for them to fulfill what is demanded is relatively easy". "Sin is trivialized, and its elimination [– according to the sermon –] is made a humanly possibility."[15] The intended effect of the legalistic sermon lies less in an event of disclosure (occurring *in the act of hearing*) but rather in an *action following* the sermon.

The problem touched upon here is not initially a linguistic problem but a theological one, for the overcoming of which the differentiation between law and gospel is still relevant: Protestant jargon ("Accept yourself as you are!") and the theology of the reformers are worlds apart. Through a sermon, listeners should not simply learn to accept themselves as they habitually see themselves or as the ones they would like to be. To the core of the ideas connected to the gospel concerning God's unconditional acceptance of humanity belongs the discovery that one is loved even as the person one possibly does not want to admit to, whom one believes one must deny, from whom one dissociates oneself, of whom one is ashamed of – who is sometimes sinister and alien. This is precisely what "justified sinner" means. To address the "law" in this sense in the sermon – to which belongs humankind's own autonomous laws, the experiencing of their limits and their arrangements with experiences of lack of freedom – is indispensable. In the communication of the gospel, the reality of the law is not simply brushed aside, but it becomes clear that no one's life is "frozen" and lost forever due to "legal" circumstances or fault of their own.

## 1.4 Proclamations of Compassion and Consideration for Others

Frequently the legalism of the sermon is combined with vague appeals for *more consideration of others*. Of course, it is right and proper to keep a firm hold on the idea of a "Christian" way of dealing with one another as an expression or "effect" of the Christian religion. But apart from the fact that what is specifically humane in such cooperation is hardly mentioned in the sermons and is pushed into the background by calls for more kindness, such a fixation upsets the *consecutive character of a life by faith*. We are not "nice" in order to make sure of our existence as Christians but we foster – inter alia in the form of the sermon – a culture of the communication of faith which leads to that relationships are

---

**15** M. Josuttis, 1995a, 35; idem, 1995b, 121 (addition W. E.).

viewed as a resource of granting and receiving love as well as a framework for freedom and responsibility.

All too often, in sermons, relationships are only mentioned in the context of and reduced to "consideration for others", whereby it is scarcely clear to what extent theological competence is necessary in order to reach the proclaimed insights:

"I feel that I am affected by the actions of other people. Through a gesture. Through a few words. Perhaps simply through a smile. Maybe the other does not even notice that they have become a witness for me. But it was as if I was electrified for a moment. Without having to think much about the event, I know: [...] there is someone who became a witness for me for how to act in the world. Love one another, love your enemies. And as a result, strength and confidence grows within me."[16] Similar arguments are used to reach the same conclusion in a different sermon: "Look around you! Here and now! There are people sitting around you. People who can give you something and to whom you could give something. Go out into the street and look around you and give the person next to you a smile and a kind word. Help them when they need help, not in order to do a good work but because they are your fellow human beings and deserve it. [...] I want to encourage you to pause and approach people, to hope together and to radiate joy."[17]

It is not only grotesque to ask someone "to radiate joy". Such humane pathos is also devoid of any logical argumentation. It is by no means self-evident to what extent "pausing and approaching a fellow human being" should be a *synonym of Christian existence*. Separation and dissociation can also have Christian grounds! – It is quite another thing to refer to relationships and stories of relationships for the sake of understanding and communicating faith. After all, faith is an expression of a form of relationship.[18] Therefore, by looking at the different relationships people live in, it may become clear what living by faith entails and what is at stake here.

---

**16** Sermon manuscript on John 15:26–16:4.

**17** Sermon manuscript on Rev 3:1–6.

**18** Cf. the examination of the relationship to God as a category of practical-theological formation of theories by Thomas Micklich (2009). In his theory of the practice of faith, which is grounded in sociology, the author examines inter alia the seemingly aporetic connection of how humans relate to God, to society and to themselves (loc. cit., 151–155). According to T. Micklich, faith does not arise in social connections. This, however, does not mean "that faith must not have a social side. What might not immediately be clear for faith [itself] will become clear for the church and her practices: that they are conveyed socially. The differentiation between private concerns of the individual faith and public concerns of social accomplishments by the church" does not change the fact that "also the faith of the individual" is socially mediated and otherwise" (loc. cit., 65).

## 1.5 The Moralistic Concept of Sin

The embellishment of the sermon with vices and sins has a long tradition. As dubious as the supporting effect of the catalog of sins commented on may have been for the communication of the gospel, it had a certain entertainment value.[19] If we look at the understanding of sin which underlies many sermons today, it appears as if now – in the course of the very welcome reception of humanitarian insights in Homiletics – the baby has been thrown out with the bath-water: In today's sermons "sin" is seldom explicitly spoken of; all the more often in implicit allusions: certain "human shortcomings", "the one or other weakness" or "lacking perfection" are favorites among the synonyms for "sin". Consequently God's "grace" and "mercy" are enlisted to rectify such shortcomings.

"Again and again I must discover that, in spite of all the love invested in him, a person can end up in a cul-de-sac, that in spite of the greatest enthusiasm he stands in the shadows and that little mistakes can produce large heaps of broken pieces. The most bitter discovery was the realization that I will never be the perfect person I should like to be – an experience which perhaps one or two of you can share with me. Jesus Christ, too, is aware of our failings. [...] And so, as Jesus Christ, the Son of God, understands how to deal with our mistakes which apparently never want to end, so might we attempt to cope with our failings and those of our neighbors, especially when we are – for whatever reason – once again about to slam the door before in their face. Amen."[20]

Where the existential dimension of sin is no longer in sight (e.g. in the sense of a disturbance in self-perception, of a distorted picture of oneself, of an automatic arrangement with a life in bondage or the indifference in relation to one's own life) one frequently limits oneself to *relativizing the significance of failings* and passing this off as gospel. Consequently, as "message" there remains: One must not immediately despair when one notices that one has failings and makes mistakes. The main problem with this purely moral visualizing of "sin" lies in the fact that the consequences and results of human action on the one hand are not sufficiently respected and, on the other, the offer of identification of a *person behaving almost faultlessly* replaces the one of a person living *in freedom as a sinner.*

---

**19** The voyeurism of sins cultivated in the preaching of bygone days is functionally comparable with the stirring-up of "outrageous stories" which are told to the television-viewer today in particular reality shows, combined with the comforting message: "Thank goodness that it's not me!"
**20** Sermon manuscript on Matt 25:1–13.

## 1.6 Trivial Promptings for Action

"A little smile" can – according to the sermon in which it attempts to be a sign of the penetration of the kingdom of God into the world – solve almost all the problems of humankind and everyday life. It has "a great benefit to the church of God in the world". The little smile belongs to the things which God – as opposed to "splendid, outstanding deeds" – prefers.[21] Why should the listeners attend to such a theory of smiling? Because they do not smile enough? Because they should not be confronted with essential ethical questions? Because they themselves are not capable of judging what to do or not do? The more indeterminably the "evangelical" of Christianity (in a non-confessional sense) in the sermon comes up, the more vague and irrelevant are usually the practical consequences to which the listeners are motivated. Triviality in the orientation of action, however, withdraws from the sermon that ethical dimension which it needs as a public declaration of a "corporation of public rights" and through which it claims and protects a place of its own in the life of the general public.

If a sermon addresses only matters which are self-evident – or a kind of elevated *average morality of our daily interactions with one another* – and disguise them in Christian vocabulary instead of, i.e. addressing a particular attitude, taking a position, exposing contradictions or placing causes and effects in a new connection, it loses some of its theological and political weight.[22] Instead, it falls back on the catalog of "small steps", "small signals" and "small efforts" which are more likely to defame rather than to motivate the already upstanding Christians gathered beneath the pulpit to act morally.

"What counts is to discover the hidden talents. [...] To be able to listen, to have time, to shop for the lady next door, to visit a sick person, to look after the grandchild, to comfort someone, to give your daughter the feeling that you need her and her support, to have an experience and radiate satisfaction. [...] Everyone should use their gifts for the benefit of the community."[23] In the frame of such ideas the experience of the Spirit is also simply a question of good will: "It is, then, the small signals – simply the willingness to do something together with others – which enable us to experience the Spirit of God."[24]

This kind of thoughtless lists of recommendation which, with great garrulousness, touch briefly on everything which at some point in time can be good for

---

21 Sermon manuscript on 1 Cor 12:4–11.
22 Against this backdrop C. L. Campbell pleads for a homiletic ethos which implies, among other things, an attitude of resistance and the articulation of corresponding moral visions (C. L. Campbell, 2002).
23 Sermon manuscript on 1 Cor 12:4–11.
24 Ibid.

someone, are accompanied by questionable images of God which are not only theologically short-sighted but also from a religious respect have something which deprives them of their mystique: they portray God as a – for a day passing without friction – "useful" God who can only be seen in the sum of human good works. To these images belongs the talk of a God "amputated on hand and foot" who can only be seen to advantage in relief actions carried out by human beings: "Perhaps it is a first step: first simply listen. God has no other ears than our ears, he has no other hands than our hands. In this way we, in the truest sense of the word, serve God when we put our ears and hands at the disposal of others and thereby put them at God's disposal. [...] May the Spirit enable us to change for the benefit of all."[25] Where the orientation of action in a sermon is reduced to a collective loan of arm and leg to God it will not do justice to the challenge of being a contemporary theological contribution to the ethos of Christianity.

---

25 Ibid. Emphasis W. E.

# 2 Theological Indicators of Problems in Homiletics in Past and Present

## 2.1 On the Foundation of Preaching

Why do we preach? This question of the justification of the sermon should not be equated with the prospective thematization of its task, but rather inquires after *the circumstances that virtually move us to preach*. To answer this question, it is helpful to first clarify that it is just *one* version of the basic question of why people communicate with one another *at all*: People communicate because they have to deal with one another, because they are concerned with one another. Through communication, people structure the relationships in which they live in.[26] *They also do this when they communicate religiously* and celebrate a worship service in which a sermon is delivered: In speaking and listening, people establish, form and discuss the relationships in which they live in, including their relation to objects, to the world, to God and to themselves. In the event of communication people appear as themselves, they experience themselves over against others to whom they belong and to whom they are yet different.

The discussion about the reason for the sermon – other than the question about its task – has left comparatively shallow traces in the history of Homiletics. It moves between two poles which admittedly do not represent any diametrically opposed antitheses but are mutually dependent. A sermon is on the one hand to be understood as a statement of the life of the congregation; at the same time, it is to be referred to as a consequence of the presence of God. Both aspects will be developed in what follows.

### 2.1.1 The Sermon as an Expression of the Life of the Congregation

When considering the foundations of the sermon we must start with the aforementioned *communicative dimension of human existence*: where people have faith, there is a culture of communication of faith. People communicate *their faith* – and they communicate *about* their faith. The sermon in the worship service represents, so to speak, an advanced culture-historical development of the expression of the life and faith in the congregation. In fact, however, it already contains all forms of witnesses to faith: "It is out of the abundance of the heart that the mouth

---

26 For more on this thought cf. III.4, p. 485–515.

https://doi.org/10.1515/9783110440256-012

speaks" (Luke 6:45 cf. Prov 15:28). The sermon as a verbal form of the testimony of faith is in its essence the result of experiences of faith[27] – and the need to pass it on and to talk about it.

When the congregation lives as the Body of Christ "it preaches Christ"[28] and practices the communication of the gospel. This *not being able to keep* from preaching finds its strongest expression in *having to* preach it.[29] A congregation without a sermon is unthinkable – and vice versa. "The sermon presupposes the presence of the congregation of Christ which has the Word of God; for only through that it becomes a *congregation*. The sermon ought to offer the *Word of God* to the congregation, which already possesses it, in order for them to own it and to be transformed and uplifted by it."[30] The irrevocable connection between congregation and sermon is not initially a postulate which must be kept but – with the Early Church as an unattainable example – is a given fact.

This means: the story of the contemporary congregation presses for the communication of the gospel. The primary reason for the sermon does not lie in the deficits of the congregation but in its nature to communicate Christ and in this way to be a "second home of the Word of God". In the language of the New Testament: Since "the Word was in the beginning with God" (John 1:1) it has now "become flesh" in order to "live among us" (John 1:14; Phil 2:5–11). The Word of God is handed down and reproduced in the contemporary congregation. "Christ is the primary Word of God. The apostolic word is 'word of the Word', a secondary Word, i.e. testimony of the Word. [...] But this Word of the first witnesses also [...] does not rest but drives farther by duplicating itself through the congregation and thanks to the power of the Holy Spirit remains alive in the *sermon*."[31]

Consequently, the sermon stands in both a constitutive and a consecutive relationship to the congregation.[32] Therefore, the 'Now-Let-Us-Finally' or 'Should-We-Do-More-Rhetoric' *cannot* be a fundamental tenet of a Christian sermon. Christian preaching may be critical (just as the gospel is at heart critical and often questions what counts as already explained or is regarded as normal), and yet,

---

27 Correspondingly Peter and John admit – after Peter's impromptu sermon in the Temple – before the High Council: "We cannot keep from speaking about what we have seen and heard" (Acts 4:20).

28 Cf. also D. Bonhoeffer, 1937, esp. 164, 171.

29 Cf. Paul in 1 Cor 9:16: "If I proclaim the gospel, this gives me no ground for boasting, for an obligation is laid on me, and woe to me if I do not proclaim the gospel!"

30 E. Ch. Achelis, 1899, 120.

31 W. Trillhaas, 1954, 36.

32 Cf. E.-H. Amberg, 1975, 12.

a part of it is also always the attempt to trace the saving actions of God and the possibilities of living by faith in the story of the contemporary congregation.

If now the sermon is a consequence of the fact that the congregation is alive and believes and tries to communicate the possibilities of living by faith, it has consequences for the task which must be tackled in a sermon: A preacher should not think that they have to *present* "the Word of God" to the congregation, thinking that *they* have something to offer which the church has yet to find and thus have an advantage over them.

Some sermons can leave a humiliating impression that, in the preacher's view, those gathered before him do not have any spiritual maturity worth mentioning – at least none which deserves to be called a "church". It is insinuated that the congregation has an enormous need to catch up in the way of their humane, ethical and spiritual qualities. Preaching then appears as an act to which the preacher sees himself called above all because of the *deficiencies of the congregation*.

However, preachers do not preach to their congregation because of a spiritual superiority. As a rule, they have no advantage – apart from their specialized theological knowledge – which would be relevant for the sermon. K.-P. Hertzsch asks himself as preacher: "What do I actually know more than they do? What do I really know more than those who listen to me? When I sit at my desk between all my personal belongings and all my theological books and consider my sermon, and when I then picture the people before me whom I meet on the street [...] then I become steadily more uncertain. Of course, I have a clear head start in regard to some of the information. I know more of biblical studies and exegesis than anyone in my town. I certainly know more about Gnosis in Corinth or the conceptions of the Jahwist than each of my listeners or neighbors. But what help is that for me? They are also specialists in their own fields [...]. There are the old ladies, marked by life and suffering, who have mastered their existence with tremendous courage and frequently also with an elementary wisdom. They are far superior to me in life experience and insight and thereby also in general knowledge. What should I tell them? If neither my professional know-how nor my insight into life is actually relevant to them, why should they listen to me?"[33] We will return to this question of the qualifications one needs for the preaching office.

The fixation on the preacher having to "continually deliver the Word of God" as a reason for preaching has, in homiletic theory as well as in the practice of preaching, fostered the misconception that a sermon means to patiently listen to words of revelation concerning how one should cope with the unintelligible, faith-less reality of everyday life which lacks in faith. Delivering and listening to a sermon mainly comes out of the need to continually reaffirm one's faith in the worship service – the faith one already "has" and masters everyday life with.

---

**33** K.-P. Hertzsch, 1990, 18f.

### 2.1.2 Preaching as an Expression of the Presence of God

On the other hand (and at the same time) a sermon is an expression of the presence of God. In the language of the Old Testament: "The heavens are telling the glory of God, and the firmament proclaims his handiwork. Day to day pours forth speech, and night to night declares knowledge. There is no speech, nor are there words, their voice is not heard" (Ps 19:1–3). With this we come to the *credenda* of Homiletics which have already been cited several times: God is experienced, "heard", "seen" and understood wherever people live, love and suffer. God is always present somehow, perhaps even particularly when he is not spoken *about*. "God speaks" – this also belongs to the *credenda* of Homiletics – not only through the sermon (not even predominantly through a sermon) but becomes "visible" in many forms of communication through which people relate to one another. The Sunday sermon is *one* specific expression of the presence of God – one that is specifically cultivated in the worship service and is as such connected with all other signs which "proclaim God" each in their own way.

With this approach, the homiletic capacity of the theological attempt to fix the communication of the gospel exclusively to particular forms of the "Word of God" in the Old and New Testaments and moreover to postulate an "immediate" process of revelation through the sermon, is called into question. This rationale of the sermon, represented in different ways by dialectical theology, runs the risk of, first, attributing too little weight on and undervaluing the impact of the presence of God as well as, secondly, the inevitably conveyed, medial character of the "revelation" in the preaching event. Nothing is "communicated" or "revealed" without being entrusted to a medium. In each individual case, there is a need of some signs in order for something – words, pictures, gestures, rituals, sacraments – to be perceived as an expression of the presence of God.

The principle according to which the presence and work of God inspires "preaching" today, may have contributed significantly to the formation of the Old and New Testaments. Whether one begins with the experiences of the Fathers, with the Exodus or with the events of Sinai: All these tales begin and find their climax when human beings become aware of what they understand to be a sign of the presence and work of God, and all these stories end in the fact that people can interpret and experience their current life as a part of "salvation history". In a similar way, this is true for the New Testament and the "sermons" contained therein, articulated with reference to perceived signs of the presence of God which determined the appearance, speaking and actions of Jesus, his story and his fate.

We thus conclude that the sermon exists not only because the congregation cannot suppress the communication of their faith but also because the story of God's dealing with humanity extends into the present and inspires sermons as a testimony of faith. The presence of God awaits ever new verbal "expressions".

In this regard, one can describe the sermon as a never-ending commentary on the presence of God and his dealings with humanity. Looked at theologically – and often enough empirically – it is naturally not merely a "commentary" but is itself a sequence of the story of salvation. In the context of the presence of God, people experience in, with and through the sermon that their own present appears to them in a new light, that their future opens up again, that they begin to experience freedom and that the "sense of certainty"[34] with regard to their own life is strengthened etc.

## 2.2 On the Conception of the Human Being in Preaching

The inevitability of preaching with a particular anthropology[35] and thereby taking up a theological position becomes particularly evident in the homiletic focusing on "freedom", "love" and "sin".

### 2.2.1 "Freedom" in the Sermon

On the question of human *freedom* there has been a markedly bipolar discussion which determined pastoral theology from the end of the 19th into the 20th century and correspondingly had an effect on the practice of preaching: At one end of this curve of tension, freedom is understood above all as freedom from sin, death and the devil, which is why in sermons "doom" and "salvation" are spoken of primarily in the context of sin and forgiveness. At the other end of the discourse – in the course of the reformulation of psychological discoveries in Homiletics – human freedom is mainly considered as freedom from guilt, false self-images, oppressive authorities, fear, hurts etc., that is, in the context of experiences which are not directly associated with the freedom from being sinful and lost.

Even though the representatives of the corresponding perspectives frequently argued about the reach of their understanding of freedom, they went united in that in both cases it is a matter of *freedom from* something which the listeners do not have or should not be. And both ideas of freedom presuppose that human beings constantly find themselves in a state of crisis from which they must be "freed".

---

**34** Wilhelm Gräb sees as a significant effect of good sermons in an "interpretation of life which strengthens certainty" (2013, 69).
**35** On this problem cf. already above, III.1.1.

However, a sermon in which the freedom of living by faith is to become evident cannot limit itself to the surmounting of individual moments where a lack of freedom is felt. It must unfold what it means to be able to *lead* a life in freedom. Freedom for its part is an experience which is not only gained through words of encouragement but is also the result of a constant, life-long process of appropriation. If one desires to strengthen this aspect of freedom in the sermon, one must abstain from indulging in sweeping condemnations of the human striving for freedom and autonomy. After all, humans are, as part of God's creation, not merely sinners. In this context, being created in the image of God[36] thus means that freedom is part of their integrity and a constitutive feature of their being, which might become damaged but may – also with homiletic means – be restored.[37] Here a person's will plays an important part, because the well-reflected and deliberated use of one's free will (i.e. acquired in a process of appropriation characterized by distance and approximation) is experienced by the person as an elementary form of exercising one's freedom. Such a will, in turn, is an essential prerequisite for being able to experience oneself as subject of that action or attitude which the sermon advises.[38]

### 2.2.2 "Love" in the Sermon

Not only freedom, but also *love* belongs to the human characteristics arising from the *imago dei* through which people experience themselves *as human beings*. Love, however, almost exclusively finds expression as an announcement of deficiency (people in principle love too little) or as an appeal (people should finally love more). In thousands of sermons humans are portrayed as a cripple where love is concerned, who selfishly care just for themselves, are interested

---

36 On the discussion of the *imago dei* in relation to the experience of "freedom" and "love" cf. the contribution by W. Pannenberg, 1968.

37 Cf. some attempts at this in essays by W. Engemann, 2007a.

38 On the practical-theological discussion of freedom of will cf. W. Engemann, 2006a. The work of Martin Kumlehn on the "Predigtverständnis Johann Gottfried Herders im Kontext seiner philosophischen Anthropologie" (2009) ("Johann Gottfried Herder's Understanding of the Sermon in the Context of his Philosophical Anthropology") deserves special recognition in view of the few homiletic works that consider anthropology in their historical deliberations on sermons or Homiletics. As Kumlehn points out, Herder emphasizes the necessity of an individual, personal appropriation and individual modification or adaption of the understanding of oneself and the world as promoted by the Christian religion. A sermon should be structured in such a way that its listeners get a chance to react to what they have heard in the context of their own experiences of life and faith and to deepen these. Cf. M. Kumlehn, 2009, esp. 137–250.

in relationships only for the sake of particular advantages and are inherently incapable of forming commitments. Only through the advance of God's care and threatening social sanctions does the individual reveal a certain social conduct. It is astonishing what a triumphal march Charles Darwin's image of humanity – which was otherwise met with massive criticism by theology and the church in connection with his theory of evolution – was able to undertake in theological anthropology and in the sermon: The human individuals[39], who – in the struggle for survival – triumph over their weaker counterparts, fit all too well with the soteriological concept of *incurvatus in se ipsum*. The strongest and most unscrupulous prevail. The supposedly atrophied or not at all existent human willingness to form relationships and to cooperate becomes the basic motive of their sinfulness in the sermon, which is often accompanied by the accusation of narcissism.

This, however, disregards the fact that human beings certainly experience themselves as loving and that the reception and granting of love is one of their most important motivations.[40] Most of what people undertake in the course of their lives is oriented on social relationships in which care, attentiveness and esteem are received and granted. People are in principle not focused on egoism and rivalry but on cooperation, response and love. It is as if the person who gives and receives love is "on drugs" – and as if the best drug for a person is another person. People panic and become aggressive when relationships in which they experience affection, love and recognition are threatened, destroyed or break down. Successful relationships mean everything to people. Cooperation, solidarity and love make people happy. And yet, it is not a means to obtain salvation. Love does not keep sin at bay. However, it is of no help to the listener if the sermon continually stresses that God only ever loves "despite" the fact that they as human beings are not capable of love – and to be told that, in any case, it is better to love than to be loved.

In contrast to this, sermons should contribute to people finding their way back in the double track of giving and receiving love or remaining in it, including the acknowledgement of their ability to feel and give love and to reinforce this ability.

A classical problem of the sermon which results from an oversimplified anthropology is the defamation of loving oneself: "We think too much of our own good and are ourselves our own neighbor." In the individual case this may happen – perhaps more often than the individual would like to admit. But this should not lead to pleading in the sermon for a more rigorous dealing with oneself, because in principle loving oneself is a desirable virtue. It is not by chance that in the

---

**39** Cf. C. Darwin [1859] 1872, esp. 48–61.
**40** J. Bauer, 2006, esp. 34, 52.

Double Command of Love it is presupposed as a suitable measure for the love towards God and one's neighbor. It becomes a problem only – as with all virtues – if one does not interpret it properly and confuses it, for example, with the strength of one's purchasing power. From the descriptions of society in the last 20 years there emerges more a loss of the virtue of self-love which is why in this area – said with tongue in cheek! – sin is gaining ground: People are prepared to wear themselves out in the workplace to the point of threatening their identity. They are hard on themselves and, to the point of unconsciousness, they fulfil demands made on them from the outside. They are exhausted from continuously having to give more, and from the demand to redefine themselves from week to week.

With that said, it thus is becoming for a sermon derived from the gospels to also be a Christian guide to loving oneself.

### 2.2.3 "Sin" in the Sermon

One can learn much about the implicit anthropology of a sermon if one visualizes its *understanding of sin*. For the history of the sermon one can observe, over and above the observations made in III.1.5, a broad, thematically differentiated spectrum of perspectives with regard to human beings as sinners.[41] In so doing one can follow the epochs in the history of the church or Christianity and see how "sin", as it were, corresponds like a mirror image with the contemporary ideal pictures of a living by faith.

- In the time of *Orthodoxy* humankind stands out above all as sinners when they boycott the acts of salvation with their supposed free will. From a lack of humility, they are always in danger of gambling away their status as children of God to the devil who tempts people to follow their own evil inclinations.
- The sermon of *Pietism* frequently makes momentary snapshots from the day-to-day life of a depraved world when it depicts people as sinners: People are sinners to the extent that they succumb to the "temptations of the world". The battle against sin is correspondingly a "battle against the world". In this view of the world, the kingdom of God lies precisely in the other direction: Renunciation of the world, of desire – particularly in the area of sexual sensuality – play a large part in the battle against sin. Here already the points are switched for the specification of sin on individual socially ostracized deeds and thereby placed in the direction of a moralistic understanding of sin.
- In the Homiletics and preaching of the *Enlightenment* sin is regarded in a particular way as a result of a lack in or a bad education and upbringing: Insufficient religious and moral orientation leads to a person behaving "immorally". Consequently, the task of the sermon is to put a stop to the general moral decline and arouse the interest of the people again for what is true, beautiful and good.
- *Friedrich Schleiermacher* contradicted these ideas of sin which were descending into moralism and ethicism. He made restitution of the *theological* significance of sin when – arguing both

---

**41** Cf. also the examination by J. Block, 2010, 71–73.

theoretically and christologically – he interpreted it as a disruption of the "feeling of utter dependency on God" and therewith as a disruption of the experience of freedom. This disturbance is overcome in that God makes himself known to us, which has a redeeming effect: because of the self-presentation of God in our consciousness, we become aware of the paralysing blockage in our life and our relationship with God – which, nevertheless, never completely breaks off. This modern approach to the problem of sin offers various homiletic possibilities of interpretation: "sin" may manifest itself as lack in zest for life, which according to Schleiermacher is an expression of a disturbed awareness of oneself and God. The "actual sin" consists in tolerating a discordant attitude in oneself that is "a secret contradiction to the awareness of God" which cannot be separated from our self-awareness. To sin then practically means to betake oneself into bondage through a particular action or attitude and, thus, to not live according to the freedom suggested by our consciousness of God and ourselves.[42]

Consequently, in the history of preaching and Homiletics, we are not only met with a moralistic sharpening of "sin" but people are also seen in their complex, multi-layered existence which they must preserve in the face of multitudinous life situations, when they come up against barriers and feel as if they are embroiled in guilt. This, however, does not call their redemption through Christ into question; their existence as sinners does not result in a breaking of their relationship with God. One could, however, say that the fact that *humans experience themselves as sinners always means that their intended life in freedom is threatened.*

It is particularly due to the liberal Homiletics of the late nineteenth and early twentieth centuries that the understanding of sin was further removed from moralistic constrictions, and that sin was no longer equated with the dramatic loss of the divine relationship to God. Friedrich Niebergall (1866–1932), in an analysis of the "branded and presumed conditions"[43] in the sermons of his time, quoted impressive examples of how "sin" can be thematized in the analysis of the actual reality of human everyday life which is full of problems. In this way people were made aware of their present, including the roles which they, nolens volens, take over in day-to-day life.

"Apart from the constant features in every person's life quite a few lines are drawn to make the listeners aware of their present. The sense of the inexorable reality is impressed upon them with all that is part of it: neglected creatures in both sexes, lonely people, cold people, misunderstandings [...] and other crosses such as the work which wears them down – which is a special characteristic of the present. [...] In this way, the impression is always upheld that it is an important concern of life and not a matter of fine festive words that invoke rapture and admiration. The different sides of the human heart are used in changing images to serve as a foil for the light of the gospel of the Good News. Time and again, rather than suffering in general, there

---

42 Cf. F. D. E. Schleiermacher, 2016 [1835], 271, 305.
43 F. Niebergall, 1929, 170–176.

is talk of disappointments that come from the realm of our work, our family, our traffic. In each case this consideration for the outer and inner condition of the listener is a post on the winning side of the modern sermon which dare not be lost. If the sermon is to be regarded more highly again it must get out of the schematic bringing into play of conditions. This practice is certainly very comfortable; but if one simply talks of 'affliction' and 'sin' there is the danger that the words are taken up with feelings instead of things arising in the consciousness." We must "get away from all the biblical, ecclesiastical schema and jargon to show our listeners things as it were *en plein air*." It is a matter of opening the listeners' eyes for "the inhibitions of life", for the "compulsion to always ask what other people think of us", for "being willing and unwilling at the same time", for the "temptations because of one's own misfortune compared to the luck of another", for "the power of the press over pit thinking" and for "the feelings of inferiority which hide behind vanity". "If we suggest things like that, then people would take notice in quite another way than when we drone on about sin and affliction. For then our listeners have [...] the feeling that the preacher and his word are not flying around up there in the blue but are standing on the solid ground of reality. May those who wish to envision themselves away from this reality into the fair world of beautiful pictures and music then flee from such a prosaic [...] preacher to one who is more uplifting. Those who remain there are stuck in such conditions and search in them for our help."[44]

One of the biggest problems in the current homiletic (and liturgical) allusions to sin I see in the widespread practice of *holding up before people the limits of their existence as humans, i.e. their human existence itself*: "we were not open enough for one another, we have not shown enough kindness although you, God, have always provided us sufficiently with love" etc. – thus the homiletic (and liturgical) jargon. As if openness to everyone, permanent readiness with help and understanding, or constant friendliness and leniency were in principle reasonable solutions – or even the opposite of sin. No one wants to, is able to or should be this way! That we cannot adapt ourselves with the same good attitude to every person and occasionally draw back, that we are always programmed to understand and help but also deliberately refuse to do something, that we do not always appear as kind but can also be aggressive – these are not relapses into sin which must be forgiven. This is how we *must* be and should desire to be: like human beings. We cannot desire to be something other than human. To be like this is part of the person whom we have become. And we should not only tolerate this person but love him.

Otherwise the sermon stands less in the danger of preaching "cheap grace", but "takes the easy way out" with a concept of "cheap guilt": When one reproaches people with their humanity – namely, if one accuses them of falling into sin because their behavior deviates from the person whom they did not even want to be – one takes away their possibility of winning an *adequate* view of

---

44 F. Niebergall, loc. cit., 171, 174–177.

guilt which can lead to repentance. In the homiletic "traipsing around" fictitious deficits, the listeners never get the opportunity to become the subject themselves, to look over their own shoulder, to catch a glimpse of the possibilities of another existence, indeed to experience remorse, to do penance – and in all this to take a step into freedom. For, to recognize that one could have acted differently – which is why one experiences remorse – means always discovering room to move. No, it is too cheap to complain about the humanity of the listener and to make them feel guilty about the experience of the internal defence.

Therefore, it makes sense to bring up "sin" in the form of images, scenes and stories of failure to live in freedom and love. People yearn for a life, when freedom and love are not necessarily at odds with aggression, loving oneself, separation and the experience of pain.[45] To be sure, it is a life with unreasonable demands, but not with the demand that, to experience freedom and love, one should discard one's existence as a human being.

## 2.3 The Sermon as a Recommendation of Faith

Sermons always also imply the recommendation of a particular way of believing[46] but are sometimes – for that very reason – perceived as a warning against faith if with their recommendation of faith to the listeners they expect an attitude which has nothing to do with the "freedom of a Christian". A sermon as a recommendation of faith – that is naturally not a definition; a sermon should also stimulate faith as well as deepen and strengthen faith. In this chapter, we are concerned with the question of *which concept of faith theologically determines the homiletic work,* and which way of believing is accordingly suggested in the sermon. An examination which – analogous to the concept of sin[47] – investigates the question of what kind of faith is actually recommended to the listeners in the course of

---

45 W. Engemann, 2009a, esp. 278–286.

46 This thesis of the sermon as a "recommendation of faith" which first appeared in the second edition of my "Introduction to Homiletics" (2011), 424–432, was reinforced by Bernhard Kirchmeier in a doctoral dissertation. In his view "through the falling back on the concept of recommendation [...] emphasis is put on the appellative or intentional dimension which is the basis of all human attempts to communicate". What is more "with the use of the concept of faith as opposed to the concept of the gospel, the homiletic field of vision is extended in that one understands the gospel not only as a logical beginning or dogmatic heart of faith but rather also as an expression of a personal life of faith [...]. On the basis of the understanding of the sermon as a recommendation of faith, human faith can be understood as an anticipated purpose of preaching and can be analyzed" (B. Kirchmeier, 2017, 19).

47 Cf. above, III.2.2.3, p. 448–451.

the sermon event is still to come.[48] Nevertheless a test-reading of sermons from various epochs of the history of faith and the church already shows that here, too, the theological views and basic religious attitudes of the respective period are expressed.

### 2.3.1 Accents in the History of Faith

Since the sermon of Lutheran orthodoxy practiced the communication of faith as a kind of explanatory teaching of doctrine,[49] in *Pietism* faith appears more strongly as a *fulfillment of life*. "A true Christian is not justified simply by faith in Christ but also through his faith he becomes a dwelling-place and temple of Christ and the Holy Spirit."[50] "True faith" grows from the "rebirth", from the "conversion" which is the aim of the sermon. The individual is urged to live up to their "living faith" by leading a pious life.

The sermon cries out from a dead fictitious faith the true, zealous faith which is not satisfied with the "what is right" in some statements of faith but desires to be "uplifted". In his sermons P. J. Spener emphasizes that such faith "does not exist in a useless deliberation" but proves itself in that it changes people, in the sense that they bear fruit and have a real chance in the battle against sin. The believers draw their strength from the certainty that they are reconciled with God through Christ. Because Christians, through their faith, have a "means of salvation" at their disposal, they owe themselves, the other, and God a life in the light – a life which is fit to be seen.[51]

In the Homiletics and sermon of the *Enlightenment* the idea of a *personal acquisition* of faith which was already apparent in Pietism was continued. One disputed not only that the acceptance of dogmas which appeared unreasonable was what mattered for faith, but theology and specifically the sermon made a problem of such contents which demanded all too great a sacrifice from rational thinking.

---

**48** For the present, Bernhard Kirchmeier has submitted a relevant analysis (2017, 133–374).
**49** The homiletic exhortation of J. B. Carpzow (1565–1624) to abstain from theological jargon when explaining texts or dogmatic topoi and to bring one's language onto the linguistic level of the *rudissimi* (the simplest-minded) should prove as an indication of this practice. Cf. A Beutel, 2002, esp. 41f.
**50** J. Arndt, 1605, II, 4, 1. Already the sub-title of this work is significant and programmatic for the communication of faith in the pietistic sermon: "it is about healing, penitence, sincere remorse and sorrow for sin and true faith, also a devout life and way of living for the true Christian".
**51** Cf. P. J. Spener, [1686] 2006, 170.

Faith emerges as something which is reasonable, natural and sensible for a human being. It helps them to acquire a conscientious way of life, appropriate for their own life, serving their fellow humans and benefiting to society. Here faith appears as the Christian way of leading a life related to religion in harmony with other reasonable insights, whereby one's own experience is never avoided or circumvented. Moreover, faith and corresponding Christian maxims result in a good feeling of being alive.

*Liberal theology and Homiletics* go one step further in the question of the acquisition of faith: it no longer requires the individual to live with a faith that would not help them in the acquisition of freedom. The communication of faith is also expressed in a determined "worldliness" in preachers, whereby they do not condemn "the world" and everyday life but they are seen as given places for the experience and development of faith. It is very important for faith to recognize a *meaningful connection* in life. Faith is then something for people who have "a longing for some sense in their world which has become vast". "However, meaning for them is the connection of events in life and the world with something that has value and significance."[52]

In the dialectic-theological approaches to the nature of faith, faith is developed more in the direction of the so-called *fides qua creditur*[53]; the theology of experience, and above all anthropological arguments, tend to discuss faith on the basis of a *fides quae creditur*. In both cases, this has far-reaching consequences for the faith a sermon suggests:

To acknowledge by faith that one is related to God as subject is thereby connected with risking the "leap into the darkness of the unknown", "into empty air"[54]. Later Barth explained that faith amounts to "acknowledgement", "recognition" and "confession"[55] – whereby elements of the *fides quae creditor* at least come into play. For Barth faith is above all a cognitive category which actually has the character of an assent, as the verbs used to show.

In contrast, Gerhard Ebeling brought the radical relationship of faith to experience into play and considered only the faith which one can relate to experiences, which are accessible to everyone, as recommendable.[56] Consequently, faith is not an act of obedience, not a mere acknowledgement of a relationship which developed for the individual only through

---

52 F. Niebergall, 1929, 9.
53 *Fides qua creditur* (the faith through which one believes) – this expression dating from the time of Lutheran Orthodoxy directs one's attention to faith *as an act of faith*, to the development of trust and confidence, to faith as an expression of a relational event. As *fides quae creditur* (the faith which is believed) faith is seen more closely in relation to its content through which it reveals itself as *Christian* faith which differentiates itself from other expectations.
54 K. Barth, 1968, 98.
55 Cf. idem, 1953, KD IV, 1. 846–850.
56 Cf. G, Ebeling, 1975, 25, 232. Accordingly, faith "does not separate from experience but leads into it" (loc. cit., 186).

the Word of revelation, but the *experience* of owing thanks to God.[57] Nevertheless, Ebeling sees the person's relation to the concept of faith anchored in an action of the Word: "Faith corresponds to the Word of God. [...] Faith is always expressed in words and consequently has something to say and empowers to the use of the Word. [...] The declared belief in Christ and the sudden dominance of the Word 'faith' [in the New Testament] belong together and form one single fact."[58]

Wolfhart Pannenberg goes a step further in the question of possible (accessible to the person's own perceptive faculty) handicaps for the orientation of faith. To be sure he, too, sees in the act of trusting the root-character of faith, but this trust is not unfounded nor unconditional: "Thus a person does not come to faith blindly, but by means or an event that can be appropriated as something that can be considered reliable." In so saying, Pannenberg turns away from the temptation to communicate faith as an "unfounded risk".[59]

In the practice of preaching, the whole tension between an understanding of faith as *fides qua creditur* and *fides quae creditur* can be drawn up to the present day. The testimonials of faith stretch from the advice "simply to depend upon God", to decide against all scepticism and to have more trust, up to the attempt to wring the listeners' consenting "yes" with observations and arguments about the knowledge of faith. In the argumentation of both directions it is noticeable that "faith" is mainly talked about as an *object* or *subject*, far more rarely in the sense of an attitude or even "behavior". It thus follows that both perspectives are in danger of suggesting, with the recommendation of faith, decisions or contents which primarily represent a cognitive effort and with which it remains questionable how it can become *the person's own* and could belong to them – i.e. *which way of having faith* they are actually suggesting.

### 2.3.2 Challenges of the Homiletic Communication of Faith

Two problems arise from the observations just made: on the one hand, the communication of faith as an underivable and freely given assurance that is beyond empirical examination (*fides qua creditur*) results in that having faith is cut off from all human attempts to see oneself, God and the world as connected and to recognize in them grounds for belief. The "act of believing" paradoxically finds

---

57 Loc. cit., 318. Therefore, faith is not an "empty sack" which is crammed full in the sermon with "specific objects", i.e. certain prescribed topics of the Christian faith, and then dragged away by the listener (G. Ebeling, 1962, 19).

58 Loc. cit., 293, 308.

59 W. Pannenberg, 1968, 138. Particularly relevant for Homiletics is Pannenberg's idea that the essence of faith is not distorted by evidence but by the fact that it "appears as an unfounded risk" (cf. idem, 1982, 110).

*no* connection to what happens through people, what is possible for them or might emanate from them.[60] On the other hand, a one-sided fixation on particular contents of faith (*fides quae creditur*) fosters the misunderstanding that faith primarily means that one approves the basic principles of a particular confession. To escape from the problems arising from this it is imperative to extend the spectrum of argumentation and, above all, to look at the emotional dimension of faith, its relevance for the person's feelings of being alive (2.3.2.1) and the communication of faith as a confession (2.3.2.2).

### 2.3.2.1 On the Emotional Dimension of the Act of Faith

To understand the act-characteristics of faith, does not only imply to understand it as a "cognitive event"[61], but also to perceive its emotional implications. *People who believe, feel their faith in a certain way.* If it is not an ailing, compulsive or fearful faith, it will influence their feeling of being alive in a positive way and become a resource from which they can take steps into freedom and have experiences of an impassioned life. But this presupposes that this faith belongs to these people in the same way as their emotions which e.g. accompany their wishes, volition, decisions and actions – emotions which people experience day by day as subjects. Otherwise they do not fall away from faith but faith falls away from them.[62]

The forms of expression of faith which occur in the biblical stories not only manifest themselves very frequently in particular emotions of expectation, of hope, of courage or of gratitude etc. Often the sincerity or strength of faith is seen *as it is expressed in feelings which control the existence* and imparts something for the freedom of the individual and for the relationships in which a person lives in. Thereby two basic experiences or basic feelings are most important: the feeling of space (as a basic feeling of freedom) and the feeling of depth (as a basic feeling of love). The main point of faith appears to lie in being able to live a life in freedom and in love granted and received, a life which is then experienced as an ardent life. Correspondingly there exist strong convergences between concrete feelings in the context of the experience of freedom and particular facets of faith: *Faith reveals itself for example*

---

**60** This depends inter alia on the almost exclusively soteriological and christological development of the conception of faith, i.e. on its embedding in an event "extra nos" and on the worry that a person's (ability to have) faith is misunderstood as a good work and an achievement.
**61** K. Barth, 2009b, KD IV, 1, 247.
**62** Cf. W. Engemann, 2009b, esp. 292–297.

- in that it has an emotive-visionary component and thereby is able *to fulfill the expectations of a person in terms of content,*
- *in that* it is connected with a feeling of responsibility and motivates people to make their own judgments and then stick to it independently,
- in that it takes shape in the feeling of hope and courage, and that people, thanks to their faith, can "risk" relationships and throw themselves into them,
- in that faith can be seen not least in the feeling of gratitude and can be connected with correspondingly deeper and more passionate devotion.

| Basic Aspects of Human Behavior | Respective Feelings | Respective Facets of Faith |
|---|---|---|
| Wishing | feeling of expectation | anticipatory |
| | anticipation | visionary |
| | sense of value etc. | creative |
| Decision-making | feeling of freedom | motivated |
| | sense of responsibility | assertive |
| | feeling of ego strength etc. | reasoned |
| Volition | feeling of courage | adventurous |
| | feeling of hope | risk-aware |
| | feeling of curiosity etc. | committed |
| Action | feeling of consistency | devoted |
| | sense of triumph | dedicated |
| | sense of gratitude etc. | passionate |

**Fig. 33:** Correspondences between feeling and faith

The experience of faith in the context of love is similar: Since faith is indisputably an event of relationship, it cannot be lived without emotions, cannot be "conjured". It is sparked off and develops in, with and under the receiving and giving of care. From this there arises the precedence of love before faith in Paul: "So faith, hope, love abide, these three; but the greatest of these is love" (1 Cor 13:13).[63]

---

63 In this context, one can perhaps even gain something from the ambiguous conception of the "battles of faith" colored by the pathos of historical pietism, as long as this does not mean the mere struggle for certainty, but a struggle for relationships. To understand a sermon inter alia as "support in the battles of faith" then means to support people in their relationship struggles, including their relationship to God, and the experience of love connected to it, to stand by their side in their desire and ability to remain in this love, and to be able to understand a threatening or existing loss of love and care as a cause of the "battles of faith". Faith that has not grown out

The faith which a sermon communicates should be a good recommendation for coping with the present and future life. If it relates to the basic experiences of freedom and love and to the problems connected to it (experiences of lack of freedom and failing relationships) a sermon can show clearly what the sentence "Your faith has made you well"[64] means for the entirety of life. This way of communicating faith also contributes to a *good feeling of life* in the listeners. This is important and a chance for the sermon since the attitude towards life is important in how people generally perceive their life. The *feeling of life* is that feeling in which the individual is both confronted and connected with his environment: People's feeling for themselves and for their world and for others are two aspects of the same, extensive feeling of life. This – good or bad – basic human feeling is at the same time a kind of felt general conclusion; in fact, it represents an evaluation of their own life and is thereby an expression of a valuing attitude towards one's own life.

It is without question that the homiletic communication of faith can play a positive part in the individual's feeling of life as long as it keeps in sight the emotional side of faith and its relevance for experiences of freedom and love to the extent to which the development of faith is connected to emotions as they are named as examples in Fig. 33 above (p. 456). That this faith, precisely because of the strongly emotional reality of the experiences connected to it, is not in every case "sound" has been verified since[65] and, from a homiletic standpoint, is also a question of the theology which underlies the sermon on each occasion.

### 2.3.2.2 On the Communication of Faith as Confession

For a draft of a concept of faith in the sense of a *fides quae creditur* it is correct, that the communication of faith is related to contents. One cannot recommend the Christian faith without having "concepts" of God, humanity, the world, forgiveness, blame, "eternal life" etc. In short: One cannot preach faith without reflecting on "who Jesus Christ is for us today". It is completely justified that one expects from someone who enters the pulpit of a church that they can express what they mean when they talk about "resurrection", "eternal life" or the "kingdom of God" and expects this to cause

---

of the experience of affection and is not practiced in the struggle for (or in the shaping of) love, evaporates.

**64** Cf. esp. Matt 9:22, Mark 10:52, Luke 7:50.

**65** Cf. R. Grossarth-Maticek, 2016.

a strengthening of faith. The extent to which a preacher can do this is a question of the *acquisition* of faith, and in no way a question of mere knowledge.[66]

However, it is not self-evident what "emerges" as faith in the course of the theological development and spiritual maturation of a preacher – whether it really helps others with their confession or rather obscures their access to living by faith. The history of the theology and faith of Christianity shows that the "topics" of the Creed were interpreted quite differently. The Apostles' Creed, which has been repeated in worship services for centuries, has remained the same apart from a few variations; how individuals – and naturally individual preachers – interpreted it is subject to powerful changes as well as to contemporary and personal focuses.

In the communication of faith in the sermon, however, one cannot hide behind the theologically interesting variety of interpretations and connotations. Here lies the perhaps greatest challenge of the contemporary communication of faith; to test and find a language in which one can and is willing to articulate what one believes in order to develop the models, keystones, vanishing-points and cornerstones of one's own faith while preparing a sermon.

Preachers are in general well-trained to work with theological constructs and to communicate with abstract concepts who "God" is, the extent to which he could be God and yet "become man", what the "trinity" signifies, the extent to which a human needs the "justification" which cost Jesus of Nazareth his life etc. Most occupational theologians will answer such theological questions in their sleep, so to speak. But in a sermon – more or less unexpectedly slotted into the verbosity – they are scarcely any help. For the formulae of Christian theology *which have become necessary in their time* but are also *conditioned by their time* are not themselves a gospel but strategic models to get onto the track of the gospel in preparing a sermon. That is why the systematic theological considerations in the run-up to the sermon are imperative.

For many pastors, however, at least part of the explanatory pattern of the broad stream of dogmatic traditions is in fact no longer an aid for their work.[67] Certain theological concepts are ignored without any substitute, which may lead

---

66 Cf. also the chapter on the person of the preacher (I.2), especially the considerations of the creed specific to their person (I.2.2.1 and I.2.3.2.2) and the "assimilation" of dogmatics or the Christian confessions (I.2.3.2.2 and I.2.4.2.2).

67 Cf. K.-P. Jörns 2008, 53. The "pluralism within religion" (54) observed by Jörns, can be seen e.g. in the answer to the question of the divinity of Jesus: In West Germany in 1992 only 54%, in the East 71% of the pastors questioned, confessed that "Jesus Christ, as the Trinitarian faith has laid down dogmatically, is with God the Father and God the Holy Spirit God in a Trinity and should be worshipped as God" (54). Only for 36% of the pastors does the Bible count as holy (55). That humanity needs redemption and that God is necessary for this is widely disputed among pastors. But there are great differences in the question of *from what* humanity must be redeemed.

to a sermon being drafted without any theological system of coordinates at all. Occasionally, some dogmatic teachings are used out of a certain embarrassment or a sense of duty, although the preachers realize that they are offering little support on the terrain of the Late Modern Age. In both cases the congregation will have problems in understanding, when listening to the sermon, which faith is actually being recommended to them.

*Therefore, it is essential to acquire a language for the sermon whose contents are an adequate expression of faith in the language of that time.* Preachers, as theologians, should be companions who, as believers, can respond to the questions of our time in the language of our time. In doing so, it might help if one occasionally remembers that the contents of the faith which is to be communicated in the sermon are not fused for time and eternity with particular dogmatic phraseology, which is why faith by no means signifies intellectually reproducing theological figures of speech, concepts or combinations of words and then being able to endorse them.

In this context, Jesus' comment quoted above – "Your faith has helped you" – may serve as a leitmotif for the sermon: Those who preach are challenged to express what living by faith means for them and the extent to which faith is a way of living and how it relates to freedom, love and hope – in short: the extent to which faith is connected to a "good feeling of being alive" which includes an affirmative answer to existence. To preach in this way is fundamentally different from making the usefulness of faith plausible on the basis of a worthwhile biography (even one's own!). Those who preach expose the extent to which they themselves are dependent on having faith.

---

The most questioned theological explanation is the statement that our mortality is a result of the Fall. This is only approved by 13% of the pastors. Cf. also idem, 1999, 137, 254.

# 3 The Task of the Sermon

## 3.1 The Task of the Sermon in the Light of the New Testament

There are no documents of systematic reflection on "proclamation" and the task which accompanies it from the time of the New Testament. Nevertheless, the inclusion of this period in the topic to be handled here is important: On the one hand, inter alia the service in the synagogue was a godparent in the development of the Christian worship service. On the other hand, already in that early period the synagogal sermon was noticeably transformed in the context of Christian-religious practice. Both aspects are to be appreciated homiletically.

### 3.1.1 Communication of the Gospel in the Context of the Jewish Sermon

Two elements of the sermon that are still characteristic today, their "attachment to a given word and a congregation gathered together"[68] already held true for the sermon in the synagogue which was practiced in the second part of the worship service after one or more readings from Scripture (Acts 13:15). Although the development of the synagogue-sermon clearly began with a return to the prophetic practice, the practice of preaching in the synagogue allows us to discern that a certain prophetic trait has become established in the understanding of the sermon itself: it is not primarily the cultic rituals in which lively communication between God and humankind took place, but this cooperation is expressed primarily in the sermon, even if, to a large extent, it related to the "very limited area of the law and its regulations"[69]. Hence, the *task of the sermon* was seen as teaching the listeners this "law" both as a text as well as instructing them how to convert it in their everyday lives. One of the central questions up to the present time was: How do I, a believing Jew, act properly? Although the sermon in early Christianity set other accents, there are noticeable points of contact in conception and a common rooting between the Christian and synagogal sermon.

Hellenistic-Jewish sermons are today – after a time when they were often called "legalistic" – "valued for what they are: talk of God"[70]. They do not simply narrate and instruct but also argue and, in so doing, reveal a missionary interest. However, to relate to the situation of the listeners is rather alien in these sermons. On the one hand, this may have had political grounds and was

---

68 A. Niebergall, 1955,186.
69 Loc cit., 190.
70 F. Siegert, 1992, 293.

https://doi.org/10.1515/9783110440256-013

connected with the bad experiences regarding the Roman Empire; on the other hand, this seems to have corresponded to the understanding of the sacredness of Scripture, that its meaning was not seen as something to be presently *ascertained* but *amplified* at best. An eschatological reception of the concept of σωτηρία (salvation, redemption – initially a "fashionable word of the time") which emerged particularly in the Christian tradition, cannot be detected in the Hellenistic-Jewish sermons. The "spiritual salvation" was understood there more as stoic and (middle) platonic.[71]

The influence of the practice of preaching in the synagogue on the Christian proclamation is clear in the conceptional respect. The dependence on Jewish models on questions of the methodology of biblical exegesis is unmistakable. "The Christian interpretation of the Bible with the models it possessed [needed ...] to risk far less than those Jews who knew Greek, which had to first apply what they learned in literature lessons to the Bible. Looked at with regard to content, the Christian interpreters of Scripture had nothing much else to do than to insert Christ at the place where in Hellenistic-Jewish theology the [...] Logos had stood."[72]

In the beginning, compared with the Jewish sermon in the synagogue, the Christian proclamation was less thought of as an orientation for a Christian *praxis pietatis*. It had – for ears accustomed to the lectures or stylized philosophical conversation[73] – an unusual note. Among Christians, the talk was not held in elegant speech about the affairs of justice, the cult or everyday life, but those listening became suddenly themselves the target of the speech, "those concerned" in the event.

### 3.1.2 "Sermon" in the New Testament

Because the Christian sermon as a public speech only became the rule at a later date, there is no adequate specialist term in the New Testament for what we understand today as sermons. The early Christian apostles had scarcely to reckon with the audience of ancient orators. In places such as on the Areopagus or in the theatre one had to be publicly invited, and in the synagogue Christian speakers were at best tolerated. From the cultural and social conditions at that time, to which particularly the high status of a masterly public speech and a correspondingly inexorable public belonged, we can also infer "that men like Paul must have been pleased when someone placed a larger living-room at their disposal"[74].

---

71 Loc cit., 295, 310.

72 Loc cit., 316f. Further significant points of contact between sermon and Derasha have been brought out in a comprehensive examination by Alexander Deeg (2006).

73 Here we are thinking of the genre of the *diatribe*. This concept is derived from the verb διατρίβειν (to crush) and here should be understood in the sense of *detailed arguing*. In this form of lecture, inter alia ethical and philosophical – for laymen in any case difficult questions – were "broken up" and made understandable in an elaborate speech.

74 Cf. F. Siegert, 1992, 315f., following the research of S. K. Stowers, 1984, esp. 72–82.

Even if we cannot reconstruct a picture of the Christian sermon in New Testament times and cannot receive any *direct* answer to the question of the understanding of the task of preaching, we find significant verbs in the New Testament with which the communication of the gospel is characterized in various contexts. These concepts produce a varied but, in view of the intention of this event, clear picture (cf. Fig. 34) which is still central for the question of the task of the sermon.

| Examples from the New Testament | Translation in Context |
|---|---|
| **1. διδάσκειν – to teach** | |
| καὶ εὐθὺς τοῖς σάββασιν εἰσελθὼν εἰς τὴν συναγωγὴν <u>ἐδίδασκεν</u> (Mk 1:21) | And when the Sabbath came, he entered the synagogue and <u>taught</u>. [They were appalled at his teaching.] |
| καὶ ὡς εἰώθει πάλιν <u>ἐδίδασκεν</u> αὐτούς (Mk 10:1) | [And crowds again gathered around him;] and, as was his custom, he again <u>taught</u> them. |
| <u>διδάσκων</u> ἐν ταῖς συναγωγαῖς αὐτῶν καὶ κηρύσσων τὸ εὐαγγέλιον τῆς βασιλείας (Mt 4:23) | [Jesus went throughout Galilee,] <u>teaching</u> in their synagogues and proclaiming the good news of the kingdom of God. |
| **2. καταγγέλλειν – to (ceremoniously) proclaim, to announce something, to declare something** | |
| τὸν Χριστὸν <u>καταγγέλλουσιν</u> (Phil 1:17,18) | The others <u>proclaim</u> Christ out of selfish ambition, not louder. What does it matter? Just this, that Christ is proclaimed in every way. |
| διὰ τούτου ὑμῖν ἄφεσις ἁμαρτιῶν <u>καταγγέλλεται</u> (Acts 13:38) | Let it be known to you therefore, [my brothers,] that [through this man Jesus] forgiveness of sins is <u>proclaimed</u> to you. |
| φῶς μέλλει <u>καταγγέλλειν</u> τῷ τε λαῷ καὶ τοῖς ἔθνεσιν (Acts 26:23) | [Paul sums up his sermon: I am his witness saying nothing but what the prophets and Moses said would take place: that Christ must suffer, and that, by being the first to rise from the dead,] he would <u>proclaim</u> light both to our people and to the Gentiles. |
| **3. κηρύσσειν – to speak loudly of something in public, to continue to make something public** | |
| τὸν Χριστὸν <u>κηρύσσουσιν</u> (Phil 1:15) | Some <u>proclaim</u> Christ from envy and rivalry, but others from goodwill. |
| ἄγωμεν ἀλλαχοῦ εἰς τὰς ἐχομένας κωμοπόλεις, ἵνα καὶ ἐκεῖ <u>κηρύξω</u> εἰς τοῦτο γὰρ ἐξῆλθον (Mk 1:38) | [He said unto them:] Let us go on to the neighboring towns, so that I may <u>proclaim the message</u> there also; for that is what I came out to do. |

**Fig. 34:** The New Testament terminology for the communication of the gospel

| Examples from the New Testament | Translation in Context |
|---|---|
| κατὰ πόλιν καὶ κώμην <u>κηρύσσων</u> καὶ εὐαγγελιζόμενος τὴν βασιλείαν τοῦ θεοῦ (Lk 8,1) | [Jesus went on through cities and villages,] proclaiming and <u>bringing the good news</u> of the kingdom of God. |
| <u>κηρύσσων</u> ὅσα ἐποίησεν αὐτῷ ὁ Ἰησοῦς (Lk 8:39) | So he [the healed Gerasene] went away, <u>proclaiming</u> [throughout the city] how much Jesus had done for him. |
| ἀπέσταλκέν με, <u>κηρύξαι</u> αἰχμαλώτοις (Lk 4:18) | [In the synagogue, Jesus refers to Is. 61:1: The Spirit of the Lord is upon me.] He has sent me <u>to proclaim</u> [release] to the captives [and recovery of sight to the blind, to let the oppressed go free, to proclaim the year of the Lord's favor.] |
| **4. εὐαγγελίζεσθαι – to bring/proclaim the good news** | |
| κατὰ πόλιν καὶ κώμην κηρύσσων καὶ <u>εὐαγγελιζόμενος</u> τὴν βασιλείαν τοῦ θεοῦ (Lk 8:1) | He [Jesus] went on through cities and villages, proclaiming and <u>bringing the good news</u> of the kingdom of God. |
| πνεῦμα κυρίου [...] ἔχρισέν με <u>εὐαγγελίσασθαι</u> πτωχοῖς (Lk 4:18) | [Jesus proclaimed:] The Spirit of the Lord [...] has anointed me <u>to bring good news</u> to the poor. |
| <u>εὐαγγελιζόμεθα</u> τὴν πρὸς τοὺς πατέρας ἐπαγγελίαν γενομένην (Acts 13:32) | And we <u>bring you the good news</u> that what God promised to our ancestors. |
| τὸν Ἰησοῦν καὶ τὴν ἀνάστασιν <u>εὐηγγελίζετο</u> (Acts 17:18) | He [Paul] was <u>telling the good news</u> about Jesus and the resurrection. |
| τοῖς ἔθνεσιν <u>εὐαγγελίσασθαι</u> τὸ ἀνεξιχνίαστον πλοῦτος τοῦ Χριστοῦ (Eph 3:8) | [Paul:] [This grace was given to me] to <u>bring</u> to the Gentiles <u>the news</u> of the boundless riches of Christ. |
| **5. ἀπαγγέλλειν – to report, to testify, to tell, to announce, to proclaim** | |
| <u>ἀπαγγεῖλαι</u> τοῖς μαθηταῖς αὐτοῦ (Mt 28:8) | [So they (the women) left the tomb quickly, and ran] <u>to tell</u> the disciples of the resurrection. |
| μαρτυροῦμεν καὶ <u>ἀπαγγέλλομεν</u> ὑμῖν τὴν ζωὴν τὴν αἰώνιον [...] ὃ ἑωράκαμεν καὶ ἀκηκόαμεν, <u>ἀπαγγέλλομεν</u> (1 Jn 1:2f.) | We testify and <u>proclaim</u> to you the life that is eternal [...]; What we have seen and heard we <u>tell</u>. |
| **6. διαμαρτύρεσθαι – to persuade, to testify, to witness, to preach** | |
| [...]συνείχετο τῷ λόγῳ ὁ Παῦλος <u>διαμαρτυρόμενος</u> [...]εἶναι τὸν χριστὸν Ἰησοῦν (Acts 18:5) | Paul was occupied with proclaiming the word, <u>by testifying</u> [...] that the Messiah was Jesus. |
| <u>διαμαρτύρασθαι</u> τὸ εὐαγγέλιον τῆς χάριτος τοῦ θεοῦ (Acts 20:24) | If only I [...] accomplish the task [...] of <u>preaching the good news</u> of the grace of God. |

**Fig. 34:** (continued)

| Examples from the New Testament | Translation in Context |
|---|---|
| **7. ἐξαγγέλλειν – to proclaim far and wide, to make known all over the world** | |
| τὰς ἀρετὰς <u>ἐξαγγείλητε</u> τοῦ ἐκ σκότους ὑμᾶς καλέσαντος εἰς τὸ θαυμαστὸν αὐτοῦ φῶς (1 Pet. 2:9) | You shall <u>proclaim</u> the mighty acts of him who called you out of darkness into his marvelous light <u>in all the world</u>. |
| **8. ἀναγγέλλειν – to repeat something, to pass on a message, to circulate something** | |
| <u>ἀναγγέλλομεν</u> ὑμῖν, ὅτι ὁ θεὸς φῶς ἐστιν (1 Jn 1:5) | This is <u>the message we have heard from him and proclaim to you</u>, that God is light [and in him there is no darkness at all.] |
| **9. λαλεῖν – to speak, to recite, to proclaim, to say the word** | |
| <u>ἐλάλει</u> αὐτοῖς τὸν λόγον (Mk 2:2) | He was <u>speaking</u> the word to them. |
| <u>τὸν λόγον λαλεῖν</u> (Phil 1:14) | [And most of the brothers and sisters, having been made confident in the Lord [...] dare] <u>to speak the word</u> [with greater boldness and without fear.] |
| **10. ἡ ἀκοή – hearing, sense of hearing, tidings, rumour, sermon, news**<br>**ἀκούειν – to hear** | |
| ὡς ὡραῖοι οἱ πόδες τῶν εὐαγγελιζομένων [τὰ] ἀγαθά. Ἀλλ' οὐ πάντες ὑπήκουσαν τῷ εὐαγγελίῳ. Ἡσαΐας γὰρ λέγει· κύριε, τίς ἐπίστευσεν <u>τῇ ἀκοῇ</u> ἡμῶν, ἄρα ἡ πίστις ἐξ ἀκοῆς, ἡ δὲ <u>ἀκοὴ</u> διὰ ῥήματος Χριστοῦ (Rom 10:15b-17) | [Paul quotes Isaiah to comment on his preaching experience:] How beautiful are the feet of those who bring good news! But not all have obeyed the good news; for Isaiah says, Lord, who has believed <u>our message</u>? So faith comes from <u>what is heard</u>, and <u>what is heard</u> comes through the word of Christ. |
| ἵνα ὁ λόγος Ἡσαΐου τοῦ προφήτου πληρωθῇ ὃν εἶπεν· κύριε, τίς ἐπίστευσεν <u>τῇ ἀκοῇ</u> ἡμῶν;καὶ ὁ βραχίων κυρίου τίνι ἀπεκαλύφθη; (Jn 12:38) | [Commentary of the Gospel of John on the preaching experience of Jesus, citing Isa. 53.1:] This was to fulfill the word spoken by the prophet Isaiah: Lord, who has believed our message? |
| τοῦτο μόνον θέλω μαθεῖν ἀφ' ὑμῶν, ἐξ ἔργων νόμου τὸ πνεῦμα ἐλάβετε ἢ ἐξ <u>ἀκοῆς</u> πίστεως; (Gal 3:2) | The only thing I want to learn from you is this: Did you receive the Spirit by doing the works of the law or by believing <u>what you heard</u>? (Luther: from the <u>preaching</u> of the faith)? |
| Subsequently to the preaching ministry of Jesus (διδάσκων ἐν ταῖς συναγωγαῖς αὐτῶν καὶ κηρύσσων τὸ εὐαγγέλιον τῆς βασιλείας) it says: Καὶ ἀπῆλθεν <u>ἡ ἀκοὴ</u> αὐτοῦ εἰς ὅλην τὴν Συρίαν (Mt 4:23f.) | Subsequently to the preaching ministry of Jesus (teaching in their synagogues and proclaiming the good news of the kingdom and curing every disease and every sickness among the people) it says: So <u>the news of him</u> spread throughout all Syria. |
| Ἐν ἐκείνῳ τῷ καιρῷ ἤκουσεν Ἡρῴδης ὁ τετραάρχης <u>τὴν ἀκοὴν</u> Ἰησοῦ (Mt 14:1, cf. also Mk 1:28) | At that time Herod the ruler <u>heard reports</u> about Jesus. |

These insights yield significant clues for the character and task of the sermon:

1. *Preaching differs from ritual acts of religious communication.* The New Testament knows no sacred terminus technicus for the sermon as a communication of the gospel but describes this process on the basis of a wealth of concepts which aim at interaction, which all have especially one thing in common: they arise from everyday communication and refer to various aspects of a largely disorganized connection between speaking, listening and understanding. At the same time, they mark the important facets of the sermon.

The semantically widely diversified concept of the word ακοή[75] combines several requirements and characteristics of the sermon: it refers e.g. to the fact that the gospel originally came into circulation "as a rumor" of which Herod got wind (and was frightened). The concept also reminds us that the good news is passed on not only from the pulpit but also from person to person in everyday life and here as then it relies on an open ear, and it stresses that the most splendid speech does not reach its goal if it does not lead to a process of acquisition on the part of the listeners. The concept of ακοή shows how firmly these two perspectives belong together in that it in fact applies to both sides of the same medal and can indicate both "sermon" and also "what is heard".[76]

2. *The sermon has a dual reference to existence*: the communication of the gospel is an event of transmission in speaking, listening and hearing with a strong focus on existence – and in terms of both the one speaking and those who listen. In the process of preaching the scope and range of living by faith is visualized together, which presupposes an existential concern also in the preacher, as becomes clear from the healed Gerasene (Luke 8:39). By contrast, the German concept of "Verkündigung" (proclamation) embodies (from its significance and effect in dialectical theology) a bizarre problematic nature of the obedient passing on of messages and is, as such, definitely not a key concept for understanding a so complex process as that of preaching.

Homiletic approaches which were close to dialectical theology have, in the theological foundation of their understanding of the sermon, preferred to emphasize the expression κηρύσσειν. In pre-biblical use, this verb indicated the role of the herald, the κῆρυξ who – without having to bother about how his message was received – simply had to deliver or announce it in the name of his client. While the heralds in the time of Homer still appear as a kind of adjutant who are particularly close to their lord and are enlisted for more personal services (such as preparing

---

75 Cf. in the table (Fig. 34) the example in section 10.
76 Many aspects of the "Auredit" (cf. above, p. 11) can be found again in the "Homiletics" of the New Testament in phrases which call one to "listen with one's ear" i.e. to desire to understand, internalize and acquire what one has heard.

the bath) their function and social status changed considerably in the time after Homer. "Now only something completely superficial is demanded from the herald, namely this, that he has a good, pleasant-sounding voice"[77] so that he can read out the commands of his king clearly to anybody. If one reduces how Jesus or the apostles preached to this interpretation of the terms κῆρυξ or κηρύσσειν, one takes away the actual point of the New Testament understanding of the communication of the gospel. When a sermon is preached, it is not simply a matter of mere proclamation but that something happens "in, with and under" the sermon in favor of the listeners. It is all about a fundamental *hearing* experience (cf. above the concept of ἀκοή) which involves the *occurrence* of freedom, remorse, forgiveness, confidence etc. Consequently, the thesis that a preacher is "nothing more than a 'herald', the bearer of the news, the 'ambassador in the place of Christ'"[78] is more than dubious.

3. *Preaching has much to do with the proclamation of life*: In more than 50 instances, Jesus' "preaching" is described as *teaching*. Sometimes synonymous in connection with other verbs from the table above, sometimes simply alone – as, e.g., in the advance notice to the Sermon on the Mount according to Matt 5:1: "Then he began to speak, and taught them." What then follows is a kind of summation of his message. If one wants to win clues for the task of the sermon from this observation, one aspect in particular emerges: Jesus does not simply extend information about salvation which one can at best believe, but he mediates a way of life in a deeper sense: He teaches life. He gives people their lives; he gives them a new way of understanding themselves – which can initially release a very disturbing effect, even "dismay" (Mark 1:21f.). Therefore, a sermon does not simply name objects of faith in order to appeal that one should believe them, but it introduces far-reaching learning-processes which lead to a new understanding of living by faith.

4. A central point of reference of the communication of the gospel (for Jesus himself) is a "life lived in freedom" under the "grace of God"[79] or (for the apostles) in "Christ". *To preach* and to *testify to Christ* are thereby interchangeable concepts, a sermon without the stereotype "τον Χριστὸν" is unthinkable even when it is not expressly stated.[80] All the contents of a sermon – like the forgiveness of

---

77 H.-J. Thilo, 1986, 21.
78 G. Voigt, 1973, 54. Of course, the renowned Leipzig Practical Theologian Gottfried Voigt is to be credited with the fact that in his sermons he by no means "played the herald" but, using the whole of his being with great passion and dedication, in his own words, with vivid pictures and "existential interpretations" of the biblical texts, struggled for the listeners' understanding. His meditational sermons are an impressive witness to this (cf. G. Voigt, 1965–1970, 1978–1984).
79 Cf. the beginning of Jesus' activity as a preacher according to Luke 4:14–18.
80 In Phil 1:14–18 three different expressions are used for the same occurrence: (14) "And most of the brothers and sisters, having been made confident in the Lord by my imprisonment, dare *to speak the Word* (λαλεῖν τον λόγον) with greater boldness and without fear. (15) Some *proclaim*

sins (Acts 13:38), the reminder of the promise of faith (Acts 13:32), the question of the resurrection (Acts 17:18) etc. – are to lead towards a "life in freedom" or "under the grace", i.e. a gospel of a "life in Christ".

5. On the one hand, preaching is a *traditional concept* which is concerned with "transmission" and "reproduction"; but it stands no less for visions, for the imagining of a changed reality. Consequently, preaching includes, along with the speech act of "narrating" and "testifying" the presentation of new stories and one's own insights won through experience. A person who preaches is faced with the challenge of relating to a faith which, in the sense of what has already been said, (cf. 4) is "Christian" but must also let it be seen to what extent this faith is needed for today and in the future and in what way it may be of help.

6. A sermon is never just about content that can be summarized in objective statements or assertions. The meaning of the word εὐαγγέλιον can only be adequately understood in relation to the whole process of communication, i.e. a process with the character of an event in which something happens with, to and for humankind. Therefore, it is one of the characteristics of the "Good News" that it is communicated verbally and cannot be separated from the situation connected to the communication (and therefore also not completely absorbed in what is written).

7. Overall, the New Testament concepts have a certain programmatic character in that they represent the diversity of speech acts offered in the sermon. It is a matter of transmitting, teaching, narrating, witnessing, crying out, questioning, appealing, challenging, acknowledging, forgiving, repeating etc. Preaching does not mean simply passing on messages of salvation in the manner of a herald but means communicating the gospel by attracting and directing attention through storytelling, by working with arguments and (re)shaping worldviews, by "speaking plainly" out of personal concern and by generally addressing something that is helpful and useful and lasting for everyday life; something good is done to the hearers when the history of faith in the congregation is connected to and becomes part of the tradition of Christianity.

---

(κηρύσσειν) Christ from envy and rivalry, but others from goodwill. (16) These proclaim Christ out of love, knowing that I have been put here for the defense of the gospel (17) the others *proclaim* (καταγέλλειν) Christ out of selfish ambition, not sincerely but intending to increase my suffering in my imprisonment. (18) What does it matter? Just this, that Christ is proclaimed in every way, whether out of false motives or true; and in that I rejoice."

## 3.2 The Task of Preaching in the Light of Reformation Theology

Important insights of the theology of the Reformers first came to fruition in Martin Luther's understanding of the task of the sermon. In the teaching on the sermon it becomes clear in an exemplary way what it amounts to when the "Word of God" becomes the central perspective of theology. In the same way, the Word of God created the world in the beginning and, in the person of Jesus Christ, not only conveyed the message of salvation but had a healing, forgiving, reconciling and redeeming effect. Therefore, the sermon is to be understood as a continuation of the event of redemption in our time and for the individual listener. The sermon should continuously enable the individual to be opened to the possibilities of living by faith which have been made available though the saving work of Christ. In this sense, Jesus Christ and faith in him are the "generalis scopus"[81] of every sermon. The church could – so Luther speculated – possibly do without everything else, but not without the preached Word of God. "Everything but the word can be left aside. And nothing is better to push forward than the word."[82]

Here the argumentation structure of "law and gospel" plays a special part – though not in such a way that it could be used to construct a pattern according to which the gospel is expected in the last third of the sermon, only after the listeners have already been given all sorts of un-accomplishable performance goals in the first two-thirds, on the impossibility of which they would otherwise despair. Luther essentially developed the concept of law as functional. Through the law a person's sins are uncovered. To uncover sins, however, does not mean to preach *about the sin*, as generally in the practice of preaching the ever-popular descriptions of sin have no business in the address from the pulpit – and certainly not with the aim of worrying the listeners in order then to comfort them. *"To preach the law means simply: to allow the person to see their own reality"*[83] *and in so doing to appeal to their deepest being, their conscience.*

However, the expectation that the gospel touches a person's whole existence and the respect of the reality of the person's life into which the gospel should be proclaimed, demands that one sees his *whole* existence, whereby the dimension of sin must not be faded out. Otherwise the preachers remain in debt to the listeners. They remain in debt to those who could possibly become aware of suppressed, burdensome and self-incurred living conditions in which the gospel should prove its liberating power. In this sense, it is imperative that the law has

---

**81** M. Luther, WA 36, 180.
**82** Cf. M. Luther, WA 12, 37. 29f.
**83** M. Josuttis, 1995a, 27.

a place in the sermon for the revelation of the significance of the gospel in the actual life of the listener.

With recourse to Luther's homiletic differentiation between law and gospel it is, however, frequently overlooked that his concept of the sermon includes a third aspect: the liberation and strengthening of the conscience.

"Tria predicanda. Primo est deicienda, secundo erigenda, tertio ressolvenda seu evolvenda ex his, quae ei dubia sunt, primo per legem, secundo per euangelium, tertio per expositionem illorum, quae est sententia et quid continetur in toto verbo Dei, etiam in exemplis, simultudin-ibus, primum ex scriptura , alia duo ex rebus, quas ipsi vidimus aut experti sumus."[84] – "Three things must be preached: first, one should overcome the conscience, second, raise it again, third, free it or lead it from everything which is dubious for it. The first [occurs] through the law, the second through the gospel, the third by presenting all those aspects that are included as the basic idea and guiding principle in the Word of God as a whole, as well as by examples and para-bles. The first [is won] from Scripture, both the others [i.e. examples and parables] we draw from what we have ourselves experienced and learned."

By considering the concept of conscience, one is considering the human being in his unmistakable individuality, in the core of his existence but also as "a person before God". However, in order for the individual to realize the importance of faith for a "good conscience" and a life in freedom, the preacher should have an earnest look at his doubts. The work of the sermon is not done if individuals, in listening to the sermon, cannot also take a step into freedom after their con-science – corresponding to the third aspect of this homiletic sketch of the task of the sermon – is supplied with arguments upon which they can fall back on when dealing with themselves and their doubts. Here again, the essential signif-icance of the teaching dimension of the communication of the gospel (cf. above διδάσκειν) comes into play in the context of the task of the sermon.

The quotation above is not to be understood as a suggestion for a stereotypi-cal formation of a sermon in three steps as Luther's own sermons reveal. Rather, it basically concerns the three tasks of the sermon: a sermon should (1) contribute to the self-awareness of the problem of the difficulties of the individual (before God), it should (2) open up the possibilities available for the individual by having faith in God – in view of how things stand. To do so in promises, statements of acceptance or appeals, which lead one to believe that one might receive a life in faith as a gift and retract oneself as subject from the responsibility for one's own life is not, however, enough. Consequently, a sermon should (3) open up the pos-sibility that one can also intellectually acquire the basic Christian idea of living by faith to which belongs deepening the biblical presentations of a fulfilled life,

---

**84** M. Luther in one of his "Tischreden", WA TR 4, 479.

looking into the ways it depicts freedom, describing the significance of the giving and receiving of love, encouraging to an attitude of tolerance, teaching to love oneself etc.

In this, the experience of both the preacher and the listener is given special significance.[85] As for the preacher, it is experience not in the sense of professional experience in the art of speaking, but in the light of the experience received in his testimony, or in relation to the experiential side of his faith, which has grown through his own doubts. The experience of the individual, in turn, is at the vanishing point of the sermon, when, with what is essentially to be said from the perspective of the law and the gospel about a person's life, it is linked to present existential experience – and when the "experience with experience" related in the sermon finds a continuation in the individual ability to believe and live in "John and Jane".

Luther's basic homiletic ideas amount to a sermon which inspires *both* "repentance" *and* thankfulness for God's loving kindness – and, furthermore, is able to unfold what it means for the individual to engage in living by faith. In so doing the argumentation is both theologically and educationally in the sense of Rom 2:1.4.[86] Therefore, this dialectic is set in motion not by the law, but by the gospel. Luther's basic homiletic principle thus reads "Nihil nisi Christus praedicandus".[87] In the expectation that Christ himself is the effective and salutary content of the sermon, for Luther the preached word is the first and most important way "through which his [i.e. Christ's] promise is publicized and on which the faith of the listeners should be kindled or restored"[88]. In this context, Luther awards the sermon a *sacramental character.* This understanding implies an answer to the question of the task of the sermon which was revolutionary for his time: In giving the sermon a sacramental definition, Luther does not intend to give the Word of God some effectiveness of its own, but in characterizing the preached word as a sacrament, he sees a saving event in the *communicative process of preaching itself.* This process only reaches a

---

**85** Cf. on this the empirical focus in the brief portrayal of Martin Luther's Homiletics by Dietrich Rössler (2002).

**86** "Therefore you have no excuse, whoever you are [...] Or do you despise the riches of his kindness and forbearance and patience? Do you not realize that God's kindness is meant to lead you to repentance?"

**87** M. Luther, WA 16, 113.

**88** A. Niebergall, 1955, 266. Recently Sybille Rolf, in an excellent "Studie zum imputativen Aspekt in Martin Luthers Rechtfertigungslehre und zu seinen Konsequenzen für die Predigt des Evangeliums" ("Study on the imputation aspect in Martin Luther's doctrine of justification and its implications for the preaching of the gospel"), has made it clear what it means theologically to hold a justifying sermon (cf. S. Rolf, 2008, esp. 343–375).

preliminary goal when the individual has become aware of the *pro me* in that event of salvation and is stimulated, instructed and finally enabled through the sermon to grasp it.

The consequence of this is that "justification by faith" cannot be the main *topic* of the sermon. The individual has to *experience* justification in, with and through the sermon. "The *pro me* of the gospel message – it happened for me, for us – is not a subsidiary addition to the event of salvation; it is contained in the event itself and thus intrinsically included in it. The result of this is that the event of salvation is only completed where – precisely in the medium of the word, the address – it grasps the individual effectively. [...] The non-verbal or "over-verbal ('sacramental') way of presenting salvation, as the medieval situation characterized it, is superseded in Luther by a way of presentation which is in the strict sense verbal. If [then] Luther occasionally applies the concept of sacrament to the word, the 'automatism of salvation' is not [...] testified for but, inversely, the 'character of the word' of sacrament – which aims at a believing acceptance, grants a personal relationship – is expressed."[89]

After all, the task of the sermon according to Luther also has an *eschatological component:* Preaching is imperative, because the final chapter has not yet been written, because the "second coming" it still to come, because "Satan" must still be driven out. The "devil" is less afraid of holy water than of the sermon, because in it Christ is alive, in it he comes among the people and forces him to retreat. But that, according to Luther, is connected to temptations. In order to persist, the individual needs a sermon that knows about such temptations and, so to speak, "resists" them with reference to Christ, a sermon which takes the power of "temptation"[90] seriously so as not to proclaim Christ in a world in which the listeners do not live at all. Of course, this task is not fulfilled in such a way that "temptations" or everyday problems are simply made the topics of the sermon. (That would – as Luther would say – "delight the Devil".) The task of the sermon is fulfilled when life as it is, is spoken of in the light of the gospel, when individuals realizes through the sermon how they can live in the conditions of this world, as citizens of the kingdom of God.

"The real subject of a Christian address is not a biblical text [...] but rather nothing other than the day-to-day reality of the life of the listener himself – in the light of the promise. That is why the old homiletic scheme of *explicatio* and *applicatio* is so unsatisfactory. It gives the impression as if first, there is the text and how one understands it, and then, secondly, there is the question of how the understanding of the text can be related to the life of the listener. But this concept [...] bestows the sermon with the wrong task. To preach means: I talk with the listener about his life,

---

89 K.-H. Bieritz, 1984, 127f.
90 Lange refers to 'temptation' as the perception and experience of the opposition of the situation which is marked by "the language of the facts". Correspondingly, the sermon serves that "the promise of Christ is made relevant for a specific situation" E. Lange, 1976, 63f.

[...] his hopes and disappointments [...]. He, the listener, is my topic, surely: he the listener before God. [...] I speak with the listener about his life, not from the foundation of my experience of life, my religious education, my deep wisdom, my religious inspiration. I speak with him in the light of Christ's promise."[91]

Martin Luther's insistence on simplicity and comprehensibility was modified *rather by hermeneutics than by pedagogy*. The clarity of the address should serve to foster everyone's understanding of the gospel. Subsequently, one should not describe Luther's grounds for the task of the sermon primarily as "educational".

This conclusion cannot be expanded to "the understanding of the sermon of the reformers". John Calvin, for example, considered the sermon primarily as a process of learning. His sermons contain clear signals that indicate the extent to which he was interested in the didactic value of a sermon.[92] He sees the main task of the sermon in the teaching of obedience to God, an obedience which also becomes apparent in one's lifestyle. In this sense, the task of the sermon for Calvin is above all catechetical.[93] Thereby the task is associated with placing the personal and public life under the will of God and an education to use the Bible independently, whereby "claims and obligations which God lays upon his congregation strongly come to the fore".[94] For Calvin the task of the sermon is not fulfilled if it does not lead to salvation.

Philipp Melanchthon and Andreas Hyperius did not suggest a new definition of the Lutheran understanding of the sermon, but allowed *first signs of a Protestant doctrine of preaching* to be seen in that they concerned themselves systematically with the *"how"* of the sermon. Their attempt to connect ancient rhetoric, especially the division of the address into particular genres, with biblical details on the variety of effects of the Word of God (e.g. teaching and consolation) links the two reformers conceptually.[95] As far as Melanchthon and Hyperius comment on the task of preaching, pedagogical considerations are even more evident than in Calvin's case: Preachers turn to the congregation as a "gathering like a crowd of pupils"[96]. They must do everything to the best of their knowledge and belief in order – in accordance with the intention of the Word of God which arises from the text and its genre – to influence the will and emotion of those listening so that the way in which the congregation acts gradually changes. These impulses already show

---

91 E. Lange, loc. cit., 58, 62.
92 Cf. the places where this is found, quoted by E. Winkler (1990, 586–588).
93 A. Krauß sums up: Calvin's sermons are "actually catecheses" (1884, 228).
94 A. Niebergall, 1955, 283, 286f.
95 Thus, for example, Melanchthon, with reference to 1 Tim 4:13 and 1 Cor 14:3. Referring to 2 Tim 3:16 and Rom 15:4, Hyperius arrives at five genres of sermons, or, more specifically, added three further *genera* between the *doctrina* and *consolatio* after Melanchthon: refutation, homily (here: a sermon with a strong moral accent) and reprimand. A sixth *genre* is probably to be understood as a tribute to the not always clearly defined sermon situation (cf. E. Winkler, 1990, 589f.).
96 P. Melanchthon, 1559, StA II. 2, 480.

features of pedagogization, which later gave the sermon its sometimes debilitating character and had a lasting effect on the understanding of the task of preaching.

## 3.3 The Task of the Sermon in the Light of its Publicity

As certain as in the communication of the gospel – this belongs to the homiletic legacy of the Reformation – "each individual personally" is considered "and their personal answer" is expected, it is a matter of "this individual as a part of their [i.e. God's] beloved world"[97]. In the spectrum of the tasks of the sermon there is also its service for the world as a whole, for a public which reaches out beyond the context of the congregation. Naturally, the sermon is not the only form of the congregation's effectiveness in public, which is why the determination of the tasks of the sermon by no means coincides with the spectrum of tasks of the church in all her welfare as well as social and political relations. This, of course, also implies a limitation and concretization of the task of preaching compared to other forms of the communication of the gospel.

### 3.3.1 Historical Aspects

In the question of the effectiveness and function of the sermon in public, two poles come into view, between which the meaning of the sermon for the society can be roughly classified: From its beginnings up to the present, the sermon has on the one hand been a *factor of critique and renewal* of church and society; on the other, it fulfilled *stabilizing and ordering functions* in church and society. Hence, in the course of its history, the sermon has in part questioned the existing conditions, partly supported them. As a rule, this happened *indirectly* in both of the aforementioned perspectives, in that the Christian tradition answered, for example, the subversive question of obedience to every form of society by the "lordship of Christ", or by individuals becoming effective publicly as "witnesses". Even the component of sermons which stabilize society – apart from famous exceptions – has mainly been inductive: Since the emergence of early Christianity, the sermon has contributed to circulating the concept of a "virtuous life in the spirit of the

---

97 H. Gollwitzer, 1962, 103.

gospel"[98]; therewith it became extremely useful – especially in the theology of the Enlightenment – for the upholding of a well-ordered and peaceful co-existence.

Today, considered from a legal point of view, the tradition of the sermon participates in public life by virtue of the fact that – through contracts between church and state – the office of preaching is an integral part of the ordering of society. However, the basic interest of society at large in the existence of the institution that is the sermon, has, despite all discrepancy and discord surrounding it, probably always been of a pragmatic nature: In this way, for example, Charlemagne's engagement for the sermon was based on the expectation that this institution would contribute to safeguarding particular moral norms.[99] On the part of the general public, the task of the sermon grew to provide a contribution to the internalization of particular values which were relevant to society as a whole. In later epochs, too – especially at the time of the Reformation, in the Enlightenment and in Pietism – the Protestant sermon was "a part of a functioning social order. Through it was passed on inter alia what a good person must do. The proper sermon is consequently protected by the authorities"[100].

In a similar way, we can mention many examples of the sermon as catalyst for reforms. The reformatory movements between the 11th and 14th century received significant impulses from sermons which were ventured in public, e.g. by the Waldenses, the Wycliffe Movement or the Hussites. Even if they were classified as "heretical" in church history, they nevertheless drew their potential for argumentation from Scripture; their sermons constantly proved to be a danger to particular hierarchical principles. The sermons before and during the "Wende" ("The Turnaround") in Germany (1989/1990) also "wanted something" for society as a whole; they also expressed what could be concretely desired in society in view of how things were. Preachers saw their task – as before them Martin Luther King and others – as anticipating a new reality and encouraging people to approach this reality as something real.[101]

Nevertheless, the processes of secularization and individualization of the late 19th and 20th century have contributed to the fact that the Christian religion is no longer considered as a central guarantee of the norms and values of society. This

---

**98** Cf. T. Specht in: Augustine, 1913, X.

**99** Cf. K.-F. Daiber, 1991a, 44.

**100** Loc cit., 45. The replacement of the office of priest with the office of preacher in the Protestant churches, set in motion by the Reformation, however, proved to be a political change in society with far-reaching consequences. The sermon became a new, personal form of religious communication in which the individual, as the antipole to the collective orientation, was given a heavier weight. "Sermon as address and individual faith as answer [...] become symbols of a changing spiritual orientation" (loc cit., 47).

**101** Examples of sermons can be found in W. Engemann, 1993b.

has consequences for the public interest in (or the understanding of) the sermon which, as before, is in demand, still present in the media of television and radio and still observed by many people. Therefore, it is necessary to deal theologically with the question of the publicity of the sermon.

### 3.3.2 Theological Aspects

#### 3.3.2.1 Pre-Considerations on the Question of the Sermon in Public

At first sight the question how the sermon is related to the general public is quickly answered. The requirements of public preaching formulated in the Confessio Augustana are ostensibly unambiguous and related to the vocation of the clergy.

"No one should teach publicly [publice docere] in the churches or preach or administer a sacrament without a proper vocation" (CA XIV). According to the CA, those commissioned with a "proper vocation" are the *rite vocati*. Only these may teach "publice". Of course, it is not precisely laid down in which sense "publice" is to be understood. In his explanation of "publice docere" Ernst Sommerlath listed three possible senses which could claim to be simultaneously valid: (1) "Before a greater part of the *congregation*." Here it is a matter of the communication of the gospel which "extends beyond the narrow frame of a household community or a closed circle." (2) Directed to the whole world, not simply to individual visitors of a worship service or groups of congregational members for whom – scarcely noticed by the general public – is preached in any church. Finally, there is (3) a meaning of "publice" which extends beyond the obvious area of influence (cf. 1 and 2). This implies a *determination of the content and a standard:* Therefore, the public character of a sermon could also be seen in that it is commissioned by the church and should be an expression of her teaching.[102]

Nevertheless, the *publice docere* contains – against the background of the religious practice of the Late Middle Ages – a spectacular, new, quasi-democratic component from the church's practice of communication: While so far, all religious questions had been discussed in advance in a small group, frequently even in secret, laid down and authorized so that after publication only agreement needed to be asked for, public now became the actual scene of event. Anyone who

---

**102** Cf. on this E. Sommerlath, 1953, 64f. D. Pirson (1999) points out that today the church and her message - and thus the core of her identity - are presented neither publicly nor primarily through preaching in public, but also by other "media, which has not been commissioned to do so" (217). From this, of course, he does not conclude that there is no purpose in insisting that a "representative of the church" speaks as a *rite vocatus* in the church and congregation, but he demands of the church that it should care about what is conveyed as its identity beyond the publicity of the pulpit.

preached exposed himself in public to the judgment of the congregation and gave them the opportunity of judging what had been heard against the background of their own experience.[103]

Of course, this principle did not guarantee that the sermon was "public" in the sense of that it is also perceived by a wider public. The willingness to expose oneself as a preacher to a wider public is not a sufficient basis for formulating a claim on any public (beyond the congregation) to listen to the sermon. In order to estimate the true relevance of the gospel for the world, in Homiletics, Christological arguments were primarily used as well as pointing out the reach of "the person and work of Jesus". In this way, the public nature of the sermon is neither referred to nor asserted – particularly since this perspective highlights requirements of the sermon which are equally true for small numbers and a limited public reception. But what is the significance of drawing on Christological arguments this context?

If the person and work of Jesus are fundamentally relevant to the theological foundation and content of the sermon, each sermon participates in the character of the communication of the gospel in the sense of Jesus. After all, from all that has been reconstructed of Jesus' practice of teaching it entailed (1) confronting people *in public* with the possibilities of living by faith, (2) asserting God's acts of salvation against existing *conditions of power and injustice* and demonstrating faith as a form of dealing with people and issues. When Jesus preached he showed (3) that he was in complete *solidarity* with those who were in need of immediate help. Here, in the homiletic sense, the so-called "Offices of Christ" come into view.

At the root of these "offices", the descriptions of functions relating to the person and work of Jesus Christ, lies the attempt to, on the one hand, describe the lasting significance of Jesus Christ in history and in the present and, on the other, to be able to reconstruct and define them anew. Already in the Early Church there were attempts which in the New Testament fixed the mediator function of Jesus (cf. 1 Tim 2:5f.) on the basis of "offices" (Prophet, High Priest, Shepherd, King, Lord). Developed first by Calvin as a detailed Three-Office-Doctrine (Prophet [or teaching office], Priest and Shepherd) this became known particularly in the structure of Orthodoxy (*officium propheticum, officium sacerdotale, officium regium*). This model has become part of a long history of reception, both in the Roman Catholic and Protestant theology, including a variety of different emphases which we cannot go more closely into here.[104]

---

**103** Cf. M. Luther's title: "Das eyn Christliche versamlung odder gemeine recht vnd macht habe, alle lere ztu urteylen vnd lerer tzu beruffen, eyn vnd abtzusezen [...]" ("That a Christian assembly or congregation has the right and power to judge all teachings as well as to appoint and dismiss those teaching [...]"), WA 11, 408–416.
**104** Cf. W. Kasper, 1981, 252–268.

### 3.3.2.2 Christological Aspects of the Public Character of the Sermon

The three characteristic features of the teaching of Jesus – (1) to disseminate into the streets and open spaces and not to exclude anyone, (2) to remain by the truth, even when it is not pleasant to hear and (3) to provide solidarity for those who need guidance – suggest the differentiation between three aspects of publicity. In the context of Homiletics, it is possible to assign them to the functions of the three offices of Christ, which results in three separate concepts, namely a *categorial*, an *intentional* and an *actual* concept of the public.

#### a) The Affected Humanity. Towards a Categorial Concept of "Public"

Traditionally, when "Christ's office as King" is mentioned, it is a matter of a *categorial concept of publicity*: "Because Christ is the Lord over all flesh, because salvation lies only in his name, because the sermon is the preaching of his eternal rule, the sermon is a public act"[105] in the true sense. With this understanding of public action founded on the "proclamation of the rule of Christ" the "quality of publicity does not depend upon the *quantity* of the group addressed but [lies] in the *content* of the proclamation".[106] Important in this position is the attempt that one can develop a "virtual" concept of publicity which is independent of political consciousness on the part of the individual preacher, independent of the number of listeners at the time and also independent of the medial possibilities of circulating the sermon. "Virtual" in this context means that there is a constant movement towards this publicity which is related to the communication of the gospel (also beyond homiletic paths). The world is actually always in view when a sermon is held in any region. What is true of the enlightened citizen aware of the environment – thinking globally, acting regionally – is also true of the sermon. If the kingdom of God is not only proclaimed in the sermon but is also based on its coming, it is an act which basically concerns the *whole* of the general public whether they follow the sermon or not. As a theological premise this category fulfils, among others, an ensuring function: The content of the gospel is related to the will of God who is concerned with humankind and wants to build his "kingdom" with them.

One of the shortcomings of this premise is that it dismisses empirical evidence altogether and ignores the experiences of Christians who have little regard for the theologically proclaimed lordship of Christ or possibly ignore it. Therefore, homiletic reflection should not restrict itself to a categorical understanding

---

**105** A. de Quervain, 1939, 7. Cf. Matt 28:18.
**106** M. Josuttis, 1988, 41–50, here: 44; emphasis W. E.

of the public as a theological fiction. And yet, it also cannot avoid asking about the consequences this may have for the content and character of the sermon, if the premises of the lordship of Christ are to be more than the desperate attempt to burnish the self-image of an attention-depraved church.

Nonetheless, we must ask: if the general public is not interested in the fact that they "are subordinate" to God's kingship, to what extent is this publicity of the sermon important for them? That the worship service, the general meeting of the church in which the sermon is heard, has become simply a "remnant"[107] of the congregation cannot be overlooked. And since "from the universal validity of a message [...] its general accessibility by no means [follows]"[108] we must ask, how such a global concept of publicity can be taken into account homiletically. To do so, it is necessary to deepen the understanding of the general public on a second level.

### b) The Society Addressed: The General Public Intended

A sermon which does not also concern and have an effect upon the *res publica*, the interests of the general public, can hardly refer to the gospel. In this context, I use the concept of a *general public intended*. The gospel is always communicated in competition to other messages. Anyone who preaches, speaks with a definite purpose which has consequences for the society in which the sermon is held. Thus, those who preach should be aware of the extent to which what they believe they must say is related to the societal and socio-political discourse.[109]

Hans-Eckehard Bahr goes so far as to demand that the sermon should be guided by the effectiveness of other public forms of communication (mass media), to accept their premises (novelty, intelligibility, expertise, unambiguity, openness), to, at the most, keep up with them and, if possible, to succeed them. It is a matter of nothing less than a "determined position on a specific problem". This entails consequences which are not only formal and related to communication but are also related to their content: "The proclamation avoids the danger of becoming *pre*-public where it dares to be information in the qualitative sense, i.e. where it no longer makes an impression of being a socially free-floating speech-event but where, in the time of prophetic tradition, it leaves itself open to the political religious conflict about the internal and external constitution of society."[110]

---

107 Ch. Schröter, 1975, 74.
108 M. Josuttis, 1988, 47.
109 Cf. H.-E. Bahr, 1968, 108.
110 Loc. cit., 120, 114f.

A sermon that makes its voice heard by intervening can first of all appeal to the prophetic tradition: prophetic speech has the function "of proclaiming the direct will of God in a concrete historical situation. [...] Consequently, the promise and call for a change in one's ways are necessary hallmarks and, naturally, also the threat in the case of obstinacy. [...] This entails a necessary change, breaking off and new beginning; it means speaking and acting in responsibility from a historical point of view."[111]

All this is not only somehow linked to the prophetic ministry of Christ; however, from the way Jesus acted as a prophet a number of aspects may be yielded for the public sermon. Above all, one must keep in mind that the sermon is not simply delivered in a vacillating way and does not merely consist in rigid repetitions of theological truths. To proclaim Jesus Christ as "the truth" means to preach concretely, not extra-historically. Such a sermon should in no way appear pretentious but may be accompanied by doubts and have a limited range. Nevertheless, it may "blow up" situations revealing hidden possibilities, moving to repentance or provoking contradiction. Prophetic preaching aims to show that the truth which is Jesus Christ "proves himself to be truth, standing the test of historical situations"[112]. This includes countering falsehoods, naming blame and demanding justice.[113]

It is, of course, doubtful whether such an intended publicity must be primarily developed from the *concept of information* as H.-E. Bahr had in mind in 1968. Those who declare the essence of the sermon to be that it informs about injustices, denounces inhuman legislation, names constraints in society, presses for remedial action and proclaims the gospel in the actual socio-political context of our society *only in this way*, do indeed go into opposition, however, they must allow us to ask: "What should an ecclesiastical 'mirror' [Spiegel] provide, if the socially critical SPIEGEL[114] can already be bought at every kiosk?"[115] Apart from the overestimation of the achievement or effect of such an information-sermon compared to similar, already existing socio-critical efforts, such a strategy is in danger of suppressing information. If information is provided only relevant when it serves one's criticism of society, pieces of information which play a part beyond counterarguments are in danger of being disregarded.

Here we would also do well to remember that in the communication of the gospel it is not mainly a matter of publicizing deficits. Christian preaching has "positive"

---

**111** W. Dantine, 1972, 290.
**112** W. Kasper, 1977, 260.
**113** In this context cf. Sebastian Kuhlmann's examination of Martin Niemöller's prophetic preaching (S. Kuhlmann, 2008, esp. 336–340).
**114** Der SPIEGEL ("The Mirror") is a German weekly news magazine.
**115** Cf. Josuttis' critique of Bahr's ideas of a "proclamation as information" in: M. Josuttis, 1988, 54f.

grounds. It should serve living when it expresses options of living by faith, in freedom and responsibility. This, however, includes that a sermon, motivated by the gospel, also addresses issues of public nature, especially when it claims to be "prophetic" or "political" – and when the first addressees of the sermon are the members of the congregation.

### c) The Congregation Present: Factual Public

The *factual public of the sermon* is initially the congregation who hears the sermon when it is delivered. In the debates about the public effectiveness of the sermon it is sometimes regretted that the sermon has no "real publicity" and apparently "only" serves to edify a nucleus or remainder of a congregation. Here one overlooks that the congregation consists of human beings who – each for themselves – in different ways all participate in the "global public" by living and working in it. The significance of the individual members of the congregation is underestimated if one does not recognize the given connection of the congregation to the general public: Members of the congregation represent a cross-section of the most varied occupations, social strata and cultural milieus. From these they come to the sermon, and after the sermon they return to them. Even when a sermon is heard only by listeners who are more or less "ecclesiastically socialized" it still has a surplus of publicity to the extent that those present are themselves part of a wider public, of society as a whole.

Because of the fixation on the relatively modest percentage of those Christians who attend a service every or almost every Sunday, it is overlooked that, seen as a whole, the worship service has a significant "audience rating": "Around one million people in Germany visit a Protestant worship service every Sunday. Moreover, on average, a million Christians watch the Sunday worship service on television." On special occasions such as the Harvest festival, the number of churchgoers doubles. On Christmas Eve they even accept inconveniences and long periods of waiting to take part in the service – and that with a continuously increasing tendency. More than nine million people go to church on that day – not only members of the congregation. Especially in the former GDR member churches, where – in terms of figures – the service on Christmas Eve is visited by more than 60 per cent of the church members, many non-Christians also attend the Christ Vesper. One can reckon with around 70 million annual visitors to the worship service. Not included in this reckoning are the guests for baptisms and weddings which take place outside the congregational service as well as people who celebrate church services for special personal reasons.[116] These numbers are not intended to trivialize but to show how many people are regularly reached and influenced through worship services, unlike any other secular institution.

---

116 Kirchenamt der EKD, 2009, 14f. For more recent statistics cf. above under I.6.1, p. 269, footnote 703.

Preaching is also "public" in this sense: Those who have stayed away are included in the sermon in that they meet people who have heard a sermon, had a good look at it and, in so doing, have possibly changed a little in their thinking and attitudes. In this way others have an indirect part in the effect of the sermon. In this context, we should also remember the New Testament concept of ακοή[117]: Even important information can initially circulate as a rumor and thereby become effective in the general public.

Decisive processes of passing on information and forming opinions also take place without institutional resolutions. "Even in the age of technically-conveyed mass communication the decisive processes of changing human opinions and conduct take place almost exclusively in interpersonal contacts. [...] Appeals for change in the sermon, but particularly in the local press and radio, remain futile as long as the addressees are not provided with a living space molded by a community and an area where they can learn and practice the new attitude [...]. The gospel today still has to rely on its being handed on from person to person, from mouth to mouth."[118]

Attempts have been made to interest people in the cultural heritage of preaching, and to give this form of communication a more representative factual publicity by inviting representatives of public life (politicians, scientists, artists) to the pulpit, whereby also non-Christians were invited.[119] This led, at least for the duration of the project, to people hearing a sermon who had hardly any or no experiences with this medium. In many cases the relevance of the sermon for questions of public interest emerged in a completely new way.[120]

To the task of the sermon with regard to its factual publicity belongs the attitude of absolute solidarity with those present in the worship service. They should

---

**117** Cf. the corresponding table (Fig. 34) above on p. 463–465.
**118** M. Josuttis, 1988, 58, 62, 64f.
**119** The project, initiated by the *Evangelischen Akademie Thüringen* in the context of the events of the "Kulturstadtjahres Weimar 99" arranged that from the First of Advent 1998 till Last Sunday in the church year in 1999 each of the sermons delivered was not held by "theologically professional" preachers but by "responsible people in the town, region or state": "Politicians, craftsmen, artists, doctors, white-collar workers [...]. To this group also belong people from other denominations, other religions and some without any religious affiliation" (Dokumentation des Thüringer Kanzelstreits [Documentation of the Thuringian Pulpit Dispute], 1999, 12).
**120** Cf. F. Hiddemann/J. Reifarth, 2000. The attempt "to bring [the sermon] anew into general discussion" on the occasion of a city becoming a 'Capital of Culture' for the year – this was one of the explanations for setting-up the concept – had, in this respect at least, a considerable effect. The debate surrounding this series of sermons also showed the considerable extent to which the question as to *who* may preach is connected to the question of the *task of the sermon*. Cf. on this III.4.5 and W. Engemann, 1999, 25–45.

experience that *the service and sermon take place publicly for their benefit,* and that it is a matter of their lives. This attentiveness to those present is not only concerned with "registered members". Anyone can listen to a sermon; no one should be prevented from doing so. It is an expression of the "priestly" character of Jesus' "practice of preaching". Jesus turned *to all.* To emphasize this, he frequently and explicitly addressed and showed solidarity with those to whom no one else spoke without having personal reasons for doing so – such as "tax-collectors and sinners", without restricting himself to this group.[121] It is people of flesh and blood, it is those who are not selected, some who have been pushed to the side, as well as some representatives of the general public who listen to a sermon on a Sunday. To preach *for them* requires that the sermon is understandable for everyone and does not remain restricted to a particular congregational milieu. Moreover, the homiletic respect for the factual public demands those who preach to be aware of the contemporary form of their lives, i.e. to know in what ways the search for a successful life manifests in the present and which problems come with it.

The three levels of the publicity of the sermon mentioned are very closely connected. They result in a sermon which is not directed at those beyond the church walls and abstains from a virtual dressing-down of those responsible and irresponsible in the church and in society at large who are not present at the time of speaking. On the contrary, the sermon does far more justice to its claim of being public when it retains its character of a direct address to proclaim if it explores *possibilities of living by faith under the given circumstances with those present.* At the same time, this presents a form exerting influence on the intended general public. It takes place with the expectation of a change in the "given conditions". Preaching is anything but the attempt to freeze situations rhetorically. However, this expectation is homiletically untenable without working with a categorial concept of the general public, or in theological terms: it is to see individuals as part of humanity *coram deo*, to imagine their changeability and renewability and, when working on a sermon, to reckon with an open future which brings "salvation". One can imagine the interactions of the various levels of publicity as is shown in the diagram above (cf. Fig. 35):

---

121 In the christological justification of her homiletic principles L. Susan Bond refers to, above all, feminist aspects (cf. L. S. Bond, 2014).

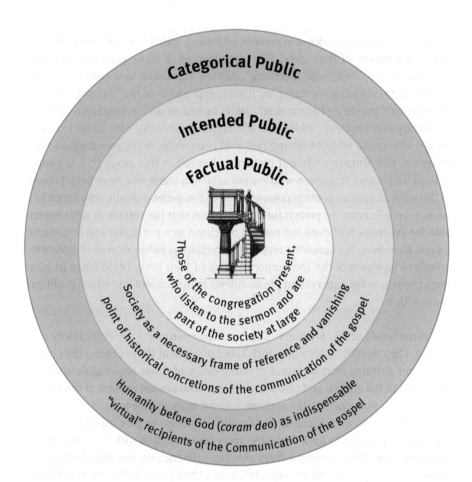

**Fig. 35:** Categories of the publicity of the sermon

# 4 Communication as a Theologically Essential Characteristic of Preaching

The fact that, after a detailed communication-theoretical discussion in Part I, we must now take up the question of preaching *as an event of communication* again, has theological grounds. Despite being implicitly connected to the situations, phases and components of the preaching process, these grounds require explicit consideration. A coherent theology of preaching must relate to the conditions of human speaking, listening and understanding in order to avoid the accusation of postulating the invalidation of the conditions of human communication as soon as "God" is involved.

The term "communication" already indicates that preaching does not only have to do with "revealed messages", with being able to comprehend and follow true and correct ideas. Along with a cognitive dimension, communication processes always also have an emotional dimension. They do not merely impact the *thoughts* and *judgments* of those involved, but also their *feelings and sense of life*. They manifest themselves as *experience*. Communication is consequently considerably more than "making *pieces of information available*"[122]: it is, in fact, always also a sign of participation that reflects the sort of relationship which connects the communicating parties. All of this has wide-ranging consequences for the theology of preaching.

## 4.1 Preaching as an Event of Communication and Relationship

It is one of the fundamental insights of communication studies that processes of communication and understanding take place on at least two levels – on the *level of content* and on the *relationship level*. When people speak to and with one another they refer, on the one hand, to the "objects and circumstances" surrounding their environment and lives: They talk about the weather, upcoming holidays, partnerships, books, and ideas, about good or bad experiences etc.

---

122 Cf. the brief definition by S. Maser (1971, 168). According to him, it is the aim of communication to generate actions and behavior. This definition, however, lacks the dimension of *communication as an event of participation* to a certain extent. But the fact that, in processes of communication, individuals are a part as well as participants of relationships, that communication has an active as well as passive side through which the communicating subject is affected, becomes involved and is changed, essentially belongs to this process. On the fashioning of communication as participation cf. W. Engemann, 2000b, 142–154.

https://doi.org/10.1515/9783110440256-014

These "things" make up the content of their communication. However, in, with and beneath what people say – on the *level of description* – they also express their attitude towards each other: They come closer to one another or distance themselves – to point out just two poles of a wide range of potential positions. Without having to express it in words we can let the other know: "Don't be!" – but also "It is good to have you here." The *relationship level* in communication does not simply indicate how what is said is *meant* in a particular case – nicely or contemptuously, ironically or encouragingly. It moreover contributes to the definition of the relationship.

There are a number of different terms or interpretation models which can be used to delineate the ambiguity of human communication, corresponding to the many different disciplines that have attempted to approach the phenomenology of human communication. Here the models of Eric Berne[123] and Paul Watzlawick[124] rank among the most informative and most widely received ones. Significant preliminary work in the field of the communication science has been carried out in this respect by people such as Fritz Künkel[125], Karl Voßler[126] and Karl Löwith[127], and there are, of course, also the psychological studies of Sigmund Freud, who was one of the first to attempt to analyze the ambiguity of human communication in the context of relationships.[128]

It would be erroneous, from a communication theoretical perspective, to detach the level of content from that of relationship. To the same degree it would be homiletically obsolete to abstract human understanding from the dimension of relationship in working out a theology of preaching: preaching, too, is not simply an act of merely "transmitting" the gospel in terms of providing bare facts, sometimes referred to as "facts of salvation", but of articulating a life lived by faith in freedom – as a life in the (already existing) relationship with God. Further, a sermon enunciates consequences for people's relationship to themselves and others, which is once again a relationship in which the individual experiences himself as a subject entitled to live a life in freedom. Thus preaching is at heart an act of dealing with an individual's existing relationships with God, with himself

---

123 E. Berne speaks of the "social" and "psychological" level of communication (1967, 32f.).
124 The popular differentiation between "content level" and "relationship level" goes back to P. Watzlawick (1967, 51–54).
125 F. Künkel, 1940, 162.
126 K. Voßler, 1960, 45.
127 K. Löwith, 1969, 125.
128 Cf. Freud's understanding of the Conscious and Unconscious (1984, 125–162) and his discussion on the *Psychopathology of Everyday Life*, in which he traces slips in communication – among them slips of the tongue – back to relationship conflicts (1922, esp. 94, 119).

and with others. In this sense a sermon is, in fact, a kind of "relationship maintenance process".

In what follows these considerations will be exemplarily applied to individual aspects of a convergent theology of preaching.

## 4.2 Preaching is Personal Communication. Christological and Pneumatological Aspects of Homiletics

What kind of facts are we actually looking at when we – quite naturally – speak of the "work of the Holy Spirit in the sermon" or of the "presence of Christ in the sermon"? Frequently such expectations, formulated as assertions, are linked to the premise of viewing the event of preaching as an exclusive way of God establishing contact with humanity (and vice versa of humanity contacting God). Accordingly, expectations and demands are high – at least in theory; in practice, however, preacher and listener often settle for some sort of Christian, biblically-theologically based "small talk". In contrast to this, a theology of preaching should have the function of sermon communication within the frame of the above-mentioned relationships to God, to oneself and to others in mind.

### 4.2.1 The Personal Character of the Sermon as Expression of the Incarnation of God

As a process of communication a sermon is realized between people, which lends it a *character of personal transmission.* Anyone who preaches has a "face"[129] through which all that is said attains an individual character. It is hardly possible for preachers to get an idea across without revealing something about themselves in the act – without signalizing, for example, how they feel about the things they say, or whether they enjoy preaching or if they are quite indifferent. They cannot take on the role of the impartial observer, nor are they supposed to try and withdraw themselves from "the message" to suggest it is not *them* who must convey it.

What we are told by someone within the course of a lively communication differs fundamentally from everything we hear through machines such as audioguides or MP3 players. As a rule, technical sound-carriers have an instrumental

---

129 In the history of the concept, as a correlate expression for *persona,* the concept of ("face", "countenance", in the context of the theatre also "mask") may be identified. In the Septuagint this term stands for the "face of God" (cf. E. Lohse, 1974, 769–781).

function, i.e. they are not part of the information. They can, at most, be out of order and thus disrupt the flow of information. When functioning properly, they serve the purpose of transmitting news which always remain the same – no matter how often they are repeated. By contrast, what we are told in a sermon does not come through to us as if prerecorded or canned, nor directly through a conserved text, but reaches us in a fundamentally different way: Because the preacher is an individual, what is said in the sermon has "a personal touch". The "Word" is presented to us with something additional which was previously not part of the "Word" and is, in fact, not the "Word" but something that comes from the person who speaks it. We cannot have one without the other. Even in the process of the communication of the gospel the "witness" cannot hide himself behind his testimony.[130]

What the gospel means or in what way it is important for the acquisition of faith is shown to advantage in a sermon under the specific conditions of personal communication. It is a short-sighted conception that the real dilemma of the communication of the gospel is to be seen in the person of the preacher.[131] Instead, one must recall the elements of the concept of person.

The term *persona*, as it has been used since the time of Tertullian[132], is associated with the acquisition of particular roles including their visualization by individual actors on stage. "The concept of person thus by its very origin includes the feature of an event unfolding in dialogue and relations (roles). The concept must, therefore, almost inevitably have suggested itself when it was a question of representing in concepts the mode in which God meets us in redemption history, especially in Jesus Christ [...]. The divine person is not essence and substance, but rather pure mutual regard, pure actuality in reciprocal giving and receiving."[133] If the gospel takes action and enters into a relationship with humankind in the person of Jesus, it bears in itself the very nature of personal self-communication. The practice of the gospel of Jesus – to be its subject in person – in turn corresponds to the personal nature of human communication. Consequently this implies more than the mere proclamation of the biblical salvation history in the here and now. In the communication of the gospel salvation history *currently* takes place, integrated in the story about and with humans. In the context of personal communication the "salvation in Christ" becomes reality. This experience, however, has an anthropological downside: human beings experience themselves in this event as persons in a specific manner: On the one hand as being loved in their inconvertible uniqueness, wanted as an "unsubstitutable self"[134], and on the other hand as being equipped with a dynamic openness for something different, new, yet unknown – and as being able to enter into a relationship with other people and with "God".

---

130 Cf. H. Barié, 1972.
131 Cf. I.2.2.3, p. 34–37.
132 Cf. C. Andresen, 1961, esp. 10–20.
133 W. Kasper, 1981, 241.
134 Loc. cit., 279.

People appear as themselves – in their individual uniqueness – only in relation to other people, one could also say: through communication. (Even Jesus became "Christ" *by* entering into relationships with other people in person.) In the context of theological anthropology the concept of the human person does not only imply the above mentioned communication structure in regard to other persons but also "participation in the essence of God" and thus the "impartation"[135] of freedom and love as the essential features of the gospel. The fact that the person of the preacher plays a constitutive, comprehension-enhancing and guiding role in the preaching process is hence not to be considered a handicap but as the modus operandi in communicating the gospel. Because God became human "the Word of God" also takes shape as gospel under the conditions of personal human communication.

### 4.2.2 The Personal Character of "Preaching in the Holy Spirit"

#### a) The Believed and the Composed Sermon – Credenda and Facienda of Homiletics

The homiletic debate on the work of the Holy Spirit in the sermon is located between two opposing principles, one of which postulates in numerous variations the "the inability to have command over the Word of God". Here the Holy Spirit appears either to participate in the preaching event as a kind of unfathomable whim of God – and, in doing so, to guide humanity in leading a life in freedom and the experience of the receiving and granting of love – or not. In this case, one can only plead and hope for the preparation of the sermon not to remain fruitless and that the Spirit takes care of this human talk to become something that fundamentally goes beyond what is humanly possible. The second principle reflects the insight that a "sermon in" or "from the Holy Spirit" is a statement on being "according to Christ" in the communication of the gospel. This means: it is basically possible to recognize – and that means also to theologically assess – whether a sermon does justice to its function of contributing to the expansion of the experience of freedom or the deepening of the experience of love – and to take care of this homiletically.

In this context, the *credenda* and *facienda* of Homiletics appear on the scene once again: What can we *for one thing* believe and accept, what can we depend upon, what can keep us calm in view of the requirement to preach in the same spirit as Jesus did when he brought the gospel to the people? For another thing:

---

135 Loc. cit., 280.

what are we meant to homiletically consider and to do in order not to merely acci-
dentally come across this track? Provided they are based on homiletically appropriate premises, both approaches have their own right.

It would, for example, be a homiletically disastrous attitude to wish to wait for a "sermon in the
Holy Spirit" as if for a pneumatological illumination or falling star and in the meantime to reject
those "mostly average sermons"[136] from a feeling of spiritual superiority. For the communication
of the gospel "in the Holy Spirit" there is no need to create any special conditions; the given
conditions of a personal communication which answer to people and their faith are already sufficient. These conditions, on the one hand, include the premises which *actually can be taken care
of* by the preacher particularly because they lie within the scope of the possibilities of communicating faith and *belong to the facienda of* Homiletics. On the other hand there are – among other
things, also pneumatological – requirements for a successful sermon *no one needs to take care
of* because – as credenda – they remain mere postulates in the work on the sermon which does,
however, not exclude but rather include their clarification, rationales and discussion and makes
them central threads in the theology of preaching.

The *facienda* of a sermon "in the Holy Spirit" includes, above all, everything
that relates, in terms of content, to what Luther referred to as "was Christum
treibet" [what promotes Christ]. This refers to the sermon's focus on experiences linked to the ideas of freedom and love. Access to and dealing with such
experiences is the fundamental concern of the communication of the gospel,
the homiletic key point of all christological-pneumatological reasoning in
Homiletics. According to the biblical records, these experiences are *the actual*
scope of work and an activity of the Holy Spirit. A sermon which risks taking
experiences of the lack of freedom seriously, a sermon which struggles for
freedom and which takes up the lost, refused, forgotten experience of affection,
love and appreciation, a sermon which is capable of addressing the ability to
believe as a revival and protection of humanity's relationship (to God) – such a
sermon is a sermon "in the Spirit of Christ".[137] For the phrase "in the Spirit"[138],
in the end, expresses that for one thing a sermon serves the purpose of the
appropriation and acquisition of freedom and, for another thing, that it is a
groundbreaker for the experience of the receiving and granting of love, acceptance and appreciation. We cannot only hear and judge whether a sermon is
preached in this Spirit or not; additionally we can also strive to achieve this on
a hermeneutical, verbal, exegetical etc. level.

---

**136** Cf. this observation in R. Bohren, 1993, XX.
**137** Cf. W. Engemann 2009b and above III.2.2.1–2 (p. 445–448) and III.2.3.2.1 (p. 455–457).
**138** "Where the Spirit of the Lord is, there is freedom" (2 Cor 3:17). "The Spirit of the Lord is upon
me, [...] to proclaim release to the captives, [...] to let the oppressed go free" (Luke 4:18). "The fruit
of the Spirit is love" (Gal 5:22); "because God's love has been poured into our hearts through the
Holy Spirit that has been given to us" (Rom 5:5).

The *credenda* regarding the pneumatological nature of the sermon, on the other hand, involve acknowledging that in the experiences of freedom and love each person – and every preacher – "has something of God" and "knows God" without having to be like God. Freedom and love are no categories alien or inaccessible to the nature of humankind but are, in fact, fundamental categories of their existential experience and determination. If preachers are ready to accept this as the basis of communicating faith and to "bear witness" without, in doing so, abstracting from their own experiences, certain effects are likely to occur, since in the history of faith and theology in Christianity they have been believed and described as effects of the Spirit of God. These reflections of divine freedom and love within the human are structural features of the pneumatological character of the sermon. The sermon "in the Spirit" is consequently an event for the sake of freedom and love, determined by the belief that the foundations for the experience accompanying this event are given to every person and that God does not at times obstruct them, at times allow them as the fancy takes him.

Approaching the question of the work of the Holy Spirit in the act of the sermon implies that Christology and pneumatology relate to the same event: The New Testament describes everything that happened through, or with, the person of Jesus as a *happening in the Holy Spirit*.[139] Consequently all that can be said about the Holy Spirit in turn also refers to the appearance, speaking and acting of Jesus as practice of the communication of the gospel.

In the New Testament the Christ event is described in all its phases – i.e. also with regard to God's Incarnation – as a pneumatological event. In this sense the Holy Spirit functions as "the medium" "in which God graciously acts in and through Jesus Christ"[140]. The Spirit is the possibility space to speak about Jesus' human nature *and* divine sonship without relativizing God's divinity or revoking humanity's human nature. "The spirit as the personal bond of the freedom of the love between Father and Son is the medium into which the Father freely and out of pure grace sends the Son, and in which he finds in Jesus the human partner in whom and through whom the Son obediently answers the Father's mission in a historical way." As an event in the Spirit, God's Incarnation neither leads to a leveling nor to a gradation of the difference between God and humanity but is an expression of the unique freedom in which God and the individual

---

**139** Mary conceives Jesus through the power of the Holy Spirit (Luke 1:35; Matt 1:18.20); it is the Spirit through whom Jesus is appointed to his messianic office at his baptism (Mark 1:10–11); Jesus works for people in the power of the Spirit (Matt 12:28; Luke 4:14); Jesus' death on the ross is understood as a sacrifice in the Spirit (Heb 9:14); Jesus is resurrected in the power of the Spirit (Rom 1:4;8:11) etc.

**140** W. Kasper, 1981, 251. For more detail see below.

person enter into a relationship. "The greater the proximity to God [is], the greater [is] the intrinsic reality [Ger.: Freisetzung] of the human being."[141]

Characterizing the Holy Spirit as place of encounter between the human being and God corresponds to relating him to the dynamic processes that are typical for any kind of encounter. In this context Welker speaks of the emergence of a "force field"[142], of a space in which something decisive, actually relevant for the human being, which changes and renews them, happens – something which at heart is related to experiences in the context of freedom and love. These experiences are, in fact, the result of "was Christum treibet" [what promotes Christ] and in this way prove to take place in the Holy Spirit.

### b) Homiletic Myths: "Desubjectification" and "Unavailability"

The question of the working of the Holy Spirit has often been posed hermeneutically and related to the "impossible possibility of understanding the Word of God". In varied formulations (e.g. "unavailability of the Word of God") it has time and again been stressed that neither the understanding of the divine Word nor certain anticipated effects are within the realms of homiletic and thus human possibility: "There is no guarantee that the individuality of the preacher becomes the vessel of the Spirit [...]. The spark will not spring over on every occasion and the study of the Bible become a *real* encounter with the Word"[143], for the Holy Spirit only appears in the sermon as giver and gift of the Word if he wishes so.[144]

Rudolf Bohren's Homiletics represents an attempt to develop the pneumatological character of the sermon from the idea of a "theonomous reciprocity"[145]. This model emphasizes the primacy of the authority of God not only in terms of the question of the sermon's justification but also in respect of the clarification of its tasks and practical realization. Here the Holy Spirit comes into play, for what characterizes the work of the Spirit [...] is that *he* puts us to work. [...] He activates

---

141 Loc. cit., 251f.

142 M. Welker, 1992, 224. According to Welker "the force field of this Spirit (works) in a way that human experiences and expectations, human contact and human agreement, human care and human withdrawal become possible *in the Spirit*" (loc. cit., 225).

143 J. Rothermundt, 1984, 133.

144 Cf. R. Bohren, 1993, 82–88, esp. 87.

145 He was inspired to this by a thought from A. A. v. Ruler: "Theonóme reciprociteit: het is de Geest, die het alles doet en geeft, die bijvoorbeeld onze wil vrijmaakt, zó dat we een vrije wil krijgen. Maar reciprociteit: hét kenmerkende van het werk van de Geest is, dat het ons aan het werk zet" (A. A. van Ruler, 1964, 214). In his introductory thesis (1993, 65) Bohren calls him *Anton* A. Ruler though his real name is actually *Arnold* Albert van Ruler.

us by being himself active. [...] The presence of the Spirit becomes the presence of mind of the speaker and listeners."[146] The homiletic premises of this approach imply the observation that "as preacher, I do not have the Word in myself [...]. The Spirit becomes the communication instructor of the disciple and the disciple the spokesman of the Spirit. It is not the disciple who speaks but the Spirit; but the Spirit needs the mouth of the disciple, and the disciple himself must speak [...]. *The [Holy] Spirit does not only provide the Word but also its articulation.*"[147]

Other authors, too, relate the working of the Spirit in the sermon to reducing all that is human and thwarting humanity's desire to do something in order to create scope for the speaking and acting of God himself. The arguments against such a *depersonalization* of the homiletic process and against the use of the Holy Spirit as an *argument for the unavailability* of the "proper understanding of the Word of God" are obvious:

*Argument 1:* Processes of communication are, in fact, inherently "unavailable". It is basically part of the essence of communication itself, as well as of the human conditions of understanding that intentions may be heard or not heard, that something well-intended may come across badly, that we may talk past each other or understand the exact opposite (or even nothing at all) of what someone wishes to say. Such phenomena are neither a characteristic nor a whim of the Holy Spirit. It is also part of the essence of communication that one may "understand" the other before they have even finished speaking, that the addressee may occasionally be able to tell more precisely than the speakers (preachers) themselves what the consequences of particular statements in a particular situation are. Wanting to reserve the working of the Holy Spirit for the loss of information between speaker and listener means having to engage the Holy Spirit as a stopgap for any kind of mutual exchange and understanding between human beings.

*Argument 2:* Invoking the Holy Spirit in order to be able to eliminate the preachers as subjects from the moderating event of the preaching process by reducing them to a mere "mouthpiece" and by urging them to recede behind their witness means to give up the sermon's Christological basis.[148]

*Argument 3:* Setting the role of the Holy Spirit as the unavailable, merely miraculous overcoming of the spiritless preacher, furthermore leads to a wealth of aporiae

---

**146** R. Bohren, 1993, 76. P. Clayborn (2010) champions a similar approach.
**147** Loc. cit., 82f. Emphasis W. Engemann.
**148** Cf. above, 4.2.1.

which include the statement that the working of the Holy Spirit in the sermon is, in fact, totally unpredictable, but still can be destroyed through the art of rhetoric.[149]

No matter how passionately Rudolf Bohren, by his own admission, preaches, in his Homiletics he frankly confesses "not to be able to say in the same breath" that he enjoys listening to sermons in the same way: "What I hear in sermons is *mostly unpleasing*. There are very few occasions in which somebody talks past me with such verbosity as in a sermon."[150] If this what is "mostly unpleasing" makes the bad sermon a rule, it poses the question why the Holy Spirit works so rarely. Why is the "unavailable miracle" of a sermon, in which the preacher is the mouthpiece of the Spirit, the exception? What hinders the Spirit if the preacher is not capable of adding anything significant anyway? According to Bohren, it is, for one thing, the eloquence of the preacher that is to blame: "As a rule, the greatest misery comes over me when listening to preachers who know how to talk." On the other hand he renders the preachers' lack of fear for their own salvation responsible.[151] That, of all things, the Spirit is hindered precisely through the homiletic virtue of rhetoric (rather than through incompetence or thoughtlessness regarding the use of language), that he steers clear of the sermon if – instead of the notorious fear for one's salvation – trust is involved, seems a little narrow-minded and leaves the assumed "unpredictability" rather unrecognizable. If one were to follow this perspective one would find that the Spirit is astonishingly choosy: He is not fond of rhetoric and finds it attractive when people fear for their salvation!

It leads to such aporiae if the Holy Spirit is misunderstood as an eccentric being who at times co-operates in the sermon, but yet at other times lets the preachers down with all their shortcomings and imperfections and leaves the listeners out in the cold, just as he pleases. It leads to further aporiae if one assumes that preachers are "mostly" – i.e. as a rule – such spiritually deficient beings that the Holy Spirit – not even for the sake of the congregation – seems unable to win through, that the human word is just *too* dead to be filled with the Spirit.

The pneumatological model favored here, which regards a sermon "in the Holy Spirit" as the *communication of the gospel within a qualified space of relationship and encounter between people,* implies certain consequences for the understanding of the roles of preacher and listener in the homiletic process: They do not act as transmitters or receivers of a message which is subject to approval, but are repeatedly – yet each time anew – made familiar with what it means to live by faith. They acquire through practice, as it were, a particular attitude towards themselves, towards others and towards God as well as a perception of the scopes of their lives.

---

149 Cf. also Merkel's criticism of a pneumatology which plays off the effect of the Spirit against practical-theological principles and, de facto, allows Homiletics itself to appear as a "godless enterprise" (F. Merkel, 1992, 65).

150 R. Bohren, 1993, 22f. Emphasis W. E.

151 Loc. cit., 23f.

This is also reflected in the structure of the homiletic process itself, which needs to be recalled once again in this context: the preacher has to deal with concepts and ideas of a particular given text. But the text needs the preacher in person in order to be able to become a "living", "spiritual" word. The text gives leeway to the preachers in finding their own words, which in turn open up in the communication with the congregation scopes for a life in freedom and love, for the broadening of horizons, for keeping the future open etc. The listeners for their part use these scopes in that, through the sermon, they allow themselves for their part to be affected by the sermon, and independently continue what they have heard in their own lives.[152]

Finally we cannot avoid a christological argumentation in pneumatological questions of the sermon: that God became human in Christ means that communication about our life by faith also takes place under the conditions of personal communication. Any argument that the "personal sermon" discussed above[153] is not "an event in the Spirit" because the preacher is *too much* of a person, an individual and subject would be amiss. On the contrary: the more reflective and self-aware a preacher appears before the congregation – instead of copying an idealized preacher or authoritarian mouthpiece – the better will the listeners be enabled to take up an attitude of their own and, in consequence, to step into freedom.

## 4.3 Preaching is Acting Communication. Creation-Theological Aspects

Theological approaches to preaching as well as to the biblical tales of creation coincide in their strong reference to the reality-creating power of language: in both cases reality is created and structured through language so that something takes place, through communication, which would not have happened otherwise. It seems thus reasonable to take a closer look at the theological significance of the analogies between the event of creation and the event of preaching.

### 4.3.1 On Preaching as a Speech Act

In the discussion of the significance of the Speech Act Theory in Homiletics[154] we proceeded from the assumption that people act *in that* they say something. The *content* (p – for "proposition") of a speech is, in fact, not communicable if it is not

---

152 Cf. the overview in I.1, p. 3–13.
153 Cf. the discussion in I.2.4, p. 80–85.
154 Cf. above, 1.5.3.1, p. 226–241.

linked to action, without having a particular *function* (f). A speech act is therefore characterized by outlining wherein the communicated function of a particular content (F[p]) in a particular situation consists, i.e. by explaining in what way what has been said intervenes in reality, forms relationships and creates new facts.

From this perspective creation and sermon can be compared to one another as analog acts: The cosmos in the story of creation is called into being from nothing just because God *speaks.* The creation is described as speech act par excellence, in which the Word and the effect of the Word are distinguishable but nevertheless belong together inseparably.

"By the word of the LORD the heavens were made, and all their host by the breath of his mouth. He gathered the waters of the sea as in a bottle; he put the deeps in storehouses. Let all the earth fear the Lord; let all the inhabitants of the world stand in awe of him. For he spoke and it came to be; he commanded, and it stood firm" (Ps 33:6–9). In that God speaks he forms and organizes the world. Things are as they are because God called them by name. "Then God said: 'Let there be light! And there was light" (Gen 1:3). The blessing spoken over people is to be understood as a constitutive act, as an enablement and empowerment of humanity to fulfill their destiny. Accordingly the first chapter of the Bible makes the "address of God" to humanity conclude with the succinct phrase: "And it was so" (cf. Gen 1:28–30).

The sermon for its part is not just understood as an "address as such" but as an effective "address to someone",[155] as a speech-event which is capable of changing particular circumstances. The sermon refers to reality in order to bring it to our minds, to protect it and to penetrate further into it – or to question and influence it. All these "references" are to be regarded as specific ways of influencing reality. *Because* people listen to a sermon and expose themselves to the communication of the gospel, they enter into a reality which, in spite of entirely belonging to the world they come from, stretches, extends, reshapes this world. Here once again the afore-mentioned relevance of the "virtual" dimension of the sermon becomes apparent.[156]

The reality structured through speech acts involves, first of all, the relationship between the communication partners established in the event of communication. Speech acts are interactive, i.e. anyone who speaks treats their communication partners in one way or another and, in doing so, creates a specific "reality of relationship". What an address achieves cannot be separated from the kind of relationship with the addressee the speaker enforces. Against this background it needs to be stressed that a sermon, due the very activity character

---

155 In his reception of the Speech Act Theory, B. Casper distinguishes between an "address as such" in the sense of a statement addressed to no one in particular and an "address to someone", which implies a functional orientation, namely a stimulus for action. Cf. B. Casper, 1975, 53.

156 Cf. the excursus on "The Virtual Perspective: The Sermon as a Construction of the World" (p. 205–207).

of language, *always* accomplishes *something.* In consequence, preachers do not only have to ask themselves whether they actually know what they are saying but also whether they have taken into consideration what they *do* when they preach. Beyond effectionalistic expectations on the sermon's impact one also has to think about what should (or should not) be achieved in the outcome of the sermon, i.e. which reality should be striven for, what should, in fact, be changed. Whenever the preacher approaches his task in the pulpit, he should be aware that he can *indeed intervene in stories*, perhaps influence the course of human fates; that, at least, his specific way of communication does not go by the listener without a trace.[157]

The interactive nature of human communication is relevant to the sermon in that the communication of the gospel effectively implicates dealing with relational structures which affect the individuals' relationship to God, to others and to themselves.

### 4.3.2 On Preaching as an Act of Raising Awareness for Life and as Keeping Open the Future

One of the core creation-theological premises of Homiletics is the assumption of an analogy between God's act of creation and the "call to existence" which arises through the sermon. This thesis is not linked to the rhetoric of dialectical theology according to which the individual is in a constant situation of response or obedience and soon is faced with problems in listening, soon with problems in obeying. A sermon rather participates in the character of creation in that it is concerned with *calling people into their own lives,* with allowing them to become present, with supporting them in appearing and "being there completely", with assisting them in treading into existence and leading their own lives as free and beloved creatures.

This approach corresponds to the New Testament talk of the "New Creation" and its reference to a life which is not to be postponed but instead takes place in the here and now. Bursting into one's own life is triggered, among other things, through the act and as a consequence of the communication of the gospel, the content of which is "Christ".[158] The sermon takes place in order to call people to

---

157 One might contradict this view, as a boring sermon does not seem to be particularly "moving". On the other hand discontent, frustration and annoyance actually represent very strong forms of being affected. They are experienced as an emotional "significance" of the sermon and felt to be quite hurtful.
**158** Cf. 2 Cor 5:17; Gal 6:15.

a life in love and freedom – that is the content and intention of the gospel.[159] A sermon which calls to life has, above all, consequences for the amount of freedom in which people lead their lives and for the remaining in love – the basis of all viable relationships which sustain, protect and enrich life.

Another, by no means less significant, analogy between the life-opening impacts of the event of creation and the act character of the sermon refers to the undetermined state of humanity's future – in an entirely positive sense: entering into existence, the arrival into life offers a vision. Life as it is, the things as they are wait, as it were, for the appearance of humanity, for their decisions, for their actions, for what they, as of then, take care of independently and self-reliantly. The situation in which people come to hear a sermon often appears to them as a situation with a "closed" future, as hopeless, as a sort of frozen present, as a life in which there seems to be no longer space for development. (Even "Paradises" may be perceived as worlds which indeed seem to offer everything without, however, one being able to experience an echo of one's own ideas and decisions in these worlds.[160]) A sermon can contribute to keeping the future open or pushing open doors, to moving a stone, pushing back a bolt so that people once again find access to the experience of being an active subject in their own lives, of wanting and being able to do something – even when and particularly after experiencing failure or their own unpredictability.

Being able to "see" the future and to find hope requires imagination, ideas for alternatives, visions which tentatively show in what direction things might turn. A sermon requires courage to state and approach desirable conditions, to visualize promising prospects, to think of the world in a different way. The initially seemingly presumptuous theological demand that the sermon should "orient itself by the event of creation" points to its anticipatory power. It means the ability to verbally imagine what a person's history of faith or God's history with humanity amounts to, what we can expect if in the course of listening to, understanding and further developing the sermon something of what the sermon is about actually materializes. "Humankind lives in God's horizon of possibility, no matter how disguised this horizon [...] may be. It is the task of the sermon to imagine humankind in God's horizon of possibility."[161]

---

**159** "I live and you should also live" (John 14:19). "God's love was revealed among us in this way: God sent his only Son into the world so that one might live through him" (1 John 4:9).
**160** In this context cf. John Milton's "criticism of Paradise" in "Paradise Lost" (1978) and W. Engemann 2007d.
**161** A. Grözinger, 1995, 98.

## 4.4 Preaching is Committing Communication. Eschatological Aspects

To homiletically speak of a sermon's "eschatological earnestness" can actually mean two things: For one – and this corresponds to the theological line of this Introduction – it can denote the *sermon's radical existential orientation*: Whenever a sermon is delivered, people are addressed in respect to their life lived by faith, i.e. in particular regarding perspectives and problems which arise from the challenge of leading a life in freedom and love. For another thing, the "eschatological earnestness" of the sermon can be seen in the task of calling from the pulpit for a *decision for or against God*, for or against faith, for or against life etc. – and in this way of "putting people [every Sunday] into a situation" in which they have to decide whether they desire to belong to God or not.

### 4.4.1 On the Radical Existential Orientation of Preaching

The sermon poses the question of leading one's own life as a question of leading a *life by faith*. This question is, in fact, the actual reason for the aforementioned homiletic focus on the *existential categories of freedom and love:* People should be able to live their own lives ardently, thankfully and responsibly. This implies that they should be able to "explain" their lives before themselves, before others and before God, that they know their own wishes and desires and how to deal with them and that they are able to make sound decisions and act accordingly.

In this sense, the talk of the "sermon's earnestness" means the homiletic equivalent of the "earnestness of life": A sermon should offer something against life's uneasiness, help us in finding a way of our own in the light of the vast number of life choices we are constantly faced with. Consequently one might say that it is an effect of the eschatological dimension of the sermon if – through listening to a sermon – people regain touch with their own life experiences, if they experience themselves as free subjects and become aware of scopes of action which they were previously not aware of. This includes, among other things, the experience of repentance as this may lead to the insight that we are free rather than determined in our actions – and consequently not forced to renew "false" decisions. This means a sermon which takes people seriously in the way they lead their lives, relates to them, and helps them, for example, to evaluate their own wishes, to sound out possible alternatives for action, to reconsider reasons for or against particular attitudes and actions and to take decisions which do not contradict their own convictions. In this way their life becomes "earnest" in that they truly begin to live (again).

Eschatological preaching additionally means to provide for the listeners' participation in the sermon's structural level, allowing them to co-operate. From its very beginning the communication of the gospel has been pervaded by an irrevocable "It's your turn now!", by a *successio hermeneutica*, a sort of hermeneutic existentialism.[162] The quintessence of this process ("message") can only be comprehended if demands are made on the person, and if they agree to the demands on behalf of what is to be understood.

This procedure can be traced in every stage of the formation of Christian tradition and is – as Rudolf Bultmann argues – not the result of a liberalistic annulment of theological categories into anthropocentric heresies.[163] It might be helpful in the profiling of the eschatological aspect of the sermon to draw Bultmann's demythologization program more consistently into Homiletics: Just as biblical texts remain "unfulfilled" when only dealt with from the pistic perspective as to whether we believe them or not, it would not be right to view the sermon's main goal as either gaining the listeners' general approval or their rejection. A sermon has certainly not yet reached the individual listener if it simply makes him the proud approver of incomprehensibilities and improbabilities. This would certainly not open up any opportunities for the listeners to appear in the communication of the gospel and to be won over for composing their own life. Hence the eschatological character of a sermon does not so much consist in the fact that it deals "with the last things" or challenges the congregation's conception of the world but rather in its hermeneutical achievement of inviting the listeners to understand their life here and now and assisting them in participating in the way outlined above.

The one who has understood the sermon best is not the one who can repeat it by heart but the one who *appeared in the sermon himself* and in the course of the communication of the gospel has arrived in the present and center of his own life.

### 4.4.2 On the Homiletic Problem of the "Call to Reason"

Homiletic eschatology may also be expressed in a "call to reason". Representatives of this approach, often with reference to arguments of dialectical theology, invoke a fundamentally appellative character "of the Word of God" mostly

---

162 Cf. W. Engemann, 2003c, 145–156.
163 "A true address is only a word which reveals people to themselves, teaches them to understand themselves not through a theoretical instruction about them but in a way that the event of the address opens for them a situation of existential self-understanding which, in fact, must be embraced. An address does not present us with a number of options to arbitrarily choose from, but places ourselves in the center of the decision as to whom we wish to become through the address and our answers to it" (R. Bultmann, 1964, 283).

in allusion to biblical quotations. According to them, the listeners become "prisoners of God", are driven "into a corner"[164], and a decision on life or death is demanded from them.[165] In the sermon listeners are "cornered" in as far as they can in fact only choose between either accepting it or rejecting God (!).

This understanding of the "call to decision", too, has a long tradition in the practice of preaching in which the possible consequences of the communication of the gospel are in fact reduced to the approval or rejection or a yes/no decision respectively.[166] The eschatological nature of the sermon lies in its incessant calling of the listeners to repentance and the reason of faith – because they constantly become separated from God and incur guilt. Such an argumentation does not only operate with a particularly crude understanding of "believing"[167] but additionally puts the listeners under stress by constantly doubting their relationship to God.

Such an eschatological accentuation of the sermon contests the meaning of communicating the gospel in all kinds of different ways, which was rediscovered in the course of the Reformation. This consists in the fact that, in view of how things are, people are "comforted" by assuring them of their relationship with God, which does not, however, imply a threat but promises a life lived out of the experience of love. Humanity's relationship to God is not the result of homiletically induced decision-offensives taking place among Christians on Sunday mornings but is the prerequisite for people being enabled to live by faith, each in their own personal way.

---

**164** Cf. K. Barth, 1925, 121, 134.

**165** Cf. R. Bultmann, 1964, 283. Cf. also W. Trillhaas: "The decision the sermon sometimes invites us to take can in fact only contain the affirmative answer that the decision on humankind is settled. A decision against this fact is the rebellion of unbelief" (1954, 51f.).

**166** "One cannot avoid the decision [...] Every Sunday the bells call out. And every time man must decide [...] Every evening he must decide whether the day will end with Jesus [...] And on Good Friday everyone must decide whether, as far as he is concerned, Jesus Christ has died in vain or he wants to stay under his Cross along with the Christian congregation [...] Everything depends upon this decision: [...] whether we shall be with God in all eternity or not. But anyone who has decided for him should be aware that this decision must be made anew every day" (O. Dibelius, 1952, 36f.).

**167** On this problem cf. III.1.2, p. 432f. and III.2.3, p. 451–459.

## 4.5 Preaching is Mandated Communication. Ecclesiological Aspects

In a certain way the church herself may be considered as an effect of preaching, "for where Christ is not preached, there is no Holy Spirit to create, call, and gather the Christian church!"[168] As an event in the Spirit the sermon takes on the function of founding and constructing a church, it is a form of God's service to the church: "To this end, in his boundless kindness and mercy, God provides for the public proclamation of his [...] holy and only saving Gospel of his eternal Son, our only Saviour and Redeemer, Jesus Christ. Thereby he gathers an eternal church for himself out of the human race."[169] As a public form of the communication of the gospel, a church-shaping function is ascribed to the sermon, and through this it has a determining influence on the nature of the church: the sermon clarifies what the church is all about and what it means to belong to her. The church becomes visible in her preaching. The sermon is a prominent expression of the essence of the church.[170]

### 4.5.1 The "Ministry of the Word". A Mandate for the Congregation as well as the Individual

Due to the fundamental importance of the communication of the gospel for the existence and the life of the church[171] the question arises as to who is entitled to preach in public and, in doing so, to represent something of the church's self-understanding.

To answer this question one needs to recall that "the Word comes in vogue" (M. Luther), even if it is not vitalized by a professional preacher. As a rule, the practice of the communication of the gospel is not subject to permission but is encountered wherever there are Christians. What may be referred to as

---

168 M. Luther in the explanation on the Third Article of the Apostles' Creed in the Large Catechism, 1959, 416.
169 Formula of Concord, Art. II: Free Will, 1959, 830f., par. 50.
170 Homiletic works interested in the connection between sermon and church are indeed very rare. As a rule, they also deal less with contemporary challenges but are predominantly devoted to historical questions as e.g. on the ecclesiological dimension of homiletic outlines of the 19th century. Cf. in this context the profound analysis by Ruth Conrad, 2012.
171 Particularly from an ecclesiological point of view it becomes apparent how ludicrous this fixation on the public act of preaching regarding the "proclamation", the "passing on the Word of God" etc. actually is. In the early days of the church and the emerging congregations the focus clearly was on individual perceptions, on hearsay, rumors and personal testimonies.

"Christian" is usually discerned through people who call themselves Christians or are regarded as Christians, without them having to be obliged to "proclaim" (the gospel). Here "messages" are circulated which – just like an "open letter of Christ" – are known, read and interpreted by all people (2 Cor 3:2f.) and which influence the public image of the church. Over and above this general level of perception the *Smalcald Articles* teach us that the gospel does not become known only through the publicly "spoken word" "by which the forgiveness of sin (the peculiar function of the gospel) is preached to the whole world". With reference to Matt 18:20 they explain that the gospel also finds quite concrete expression in the "mutual conversation and consolation of brethren" (*per mutuum colloquium et consolationem fratrum*)[172].

As a matter of fact, these circumstances of Christian congregational prac- tice are linked to the *general priesthood of all believers*. This rightly lauded topos of Reformation's communal theology does not regulate who may preach *in public* on Sundays but, at least, contradicts the priest's "role as a mediator" with regard to the salvation of the individual; it strengthens the relevance of the individual faith and settles some important *premises* regarding the appointment to ministry:

–   The fact that all Christians are priests results from baptism or from the associated "ordi- nation" to a personal testimony; one could also say, from their factual competence to give testimony which all Christians acquire in the course of their lives through their individual faith. Anyone who believes is capable of saying in their own words who – as D. Bonhoeffer puts it – "Jesus Christ [is] for us today".

–   Luther's talk of the general priesthood of all believers has an apologetic point: When it comes to one's own salvation there is no need for a mediating priest, for someone else to appease God, as in this matter everyone is their own priest: As believers we are in a direct and immediate relationship with God and do not need any further intercession. The dignity of a general priesthood bestowed on every Christian is linked to the annulment of any kind of "economy of salvation" which made the individual dependent on clerics in the question of salvation. The appointment of priests and pastors does not exist because – without it – Christians would otherwise not have the chance of achieving salvation.

–   Each and every individual can advocate for others in a priestly way, can with the same "effectiveness" as ordained priests pray for others and act in a priestly manner. The individ- ual Christian is, as a member of the Body of Christ and through his basic capability of com- municating the gospel "the point of intersection of the congregatio [...] and ministerium". In every Christian "ministry and congregation" are one.[173]

---

172 The Smalcald Articles, Art. Gospel, 1959, 310, par. 45.
173 C. H. Ratschow, 1993, 612.

The consequence of the idea of the general priesthood is certainly not that *everybody* should preach. But from a homiletic point of view it implies that the whole congregation is a potential subject of the communication of the gospel and that it, as a whole, is tasked with doing so. This task is assumed by the congregation in various forms – among others through deacons, through church elders, musicians, teachers etc. They are all "messengers in the place of Christ" (cf. 2 Cor 5:20).

From this general basis, in the course of the church's emergence the preaching office developed for various reasons. With this office the congregation appointed someone *to be their counterpart*, since "despite all Christians being priests, not all are pastors"[174]. In this manner the congregation takes into account not only the vis-à-vis-structure of the communication of the gospel but also ensures a standard of professionalism in preaching, which is why a book like this one has to be written and read. What that means in detail will be outlined in what follows under the headline of the "intrinsic logic" of the preaching office as well as in the light of the question what preaching competence might actually mean.

### 4.5.2 On the Intrinsic Logic of the Preaching Office

#### a) Personal Commitment in the Preaching Office

The congregational practice in the New Testament already reveals that different offices were assumed by different people, which was due to the need of different forms of the communication of the gospel, various functions of the congregation and the individual distribution of talents. "We have gifts that differ according to the grace given to us: prophecy in proportion to faith; ministry, in ministering; the teacher in teaching" (Rom 12:6–7). This implies a unique and personal condition of the individual offices, connected to the basic idea that the individual members – in view of their different gifts – should assume their given function instead of allowing themselves to be substituted by others, i.e. that they cannot hand over the responsibility for their tasks. This statement refers to a certain in-exchangeability of the individual who is at the congregation's disposal with *his* ministries so that the congregation as a whole accomplishes their mission in the world.

#### b) Structuring the Communication of the Gospel

The task of preaching is dependent on people who publicly practice what, in fact, all Christians in a certain way practice through their personal testimony. "What

---

174 M. Luther in his interpretation of Psalm 82, in: WA 31/1, 211.

the Church does is *publice*, i.e. cosmopolitan, intended for the world, not curled in upon the congregation itself. Public teaching and proclamation demands that the congregation 'appoints' 'suitable' Christians for this office. This means that the congregation bears the 'public' service of these men and women to the world and for the world."[175] The channeling of particular functions and processes always also implies the possibility of their reexamination, in this case the reexamination of the contentual continuity between the individual sermon and biblical tradition in view of the danger of false interpretations and heresy.[176] This means that insisting on the preaching office is also based on the conception that the spreading of the gospel does not simply happen through gradual percolation of the Good News but implies a deliberate *discussion* which again implies adroitness and skillfulness in the sense of professionalism. The fact that "heresy" is canonically relevant until today and that preachers are explicitly demanded to deal with potential misunderstandings and misinterpretations clearly shows that the purity of their preaching is *in no way* attested merely *qua office* to the individual preachers. By entrusting someone with the preaching office we expect him to take up the challenge of dealing with the matter of the gospel in a theologically correct and homiletically skillful manner.[177]

### c) The "Vis-à-Vis" Situation of the Sermon

Even though by taking part in the priesthood of all believers every Christian is called to witness to his faith, it is certainly not possible for the whole congregation to step into the pulpit – not even "virtually" or "symbolically". That would be the case if, for example, in the run-up to the service a group of congregational members democratically voted on what should be said in the pulpit on Sunday only to subsequently delegate the proclamation of this message to a random member of the congregation. The concrete event of the communication of the gospel, however, is not a jointly decided communiqué but, in fact, an expression of faith of an individual who stands facing other people or another individual. It is, however, indeed a different thing to impart one's understanding of a life by faith to one single conversational partner than to do so in the form of a homiletically elaborate public speech. It is thus important to assign the preaching office to

---

175 C. H. Ratschow, 1993, 613.
176 While justifying the preaching office with being a "defense against heresy" hardly plays a role in the practice of the church today, this argument had considerable weight in the Early Church and the Middle Ages: The sermon was consequently bound to an office (and therewith to certain possibilities of control) in order to institutionalize the necessary differentiation of the gospel, among other things, from the teaching of the Arians, Pelagians and Donatists.
177 On the criteria of this expectation cf. III.4.5.3.

people who are familiar with the conditions of a theologically responsible public religious address. This is why the Reformers set such great value – among other things through accredited ordination – upon "proven quality": "No one should be allowed to administer the Word and the sacraments in the church unless he is duly called"[178].

In this way, however, the rootedness of the office in the congregation as a whole is not abandoned but, in fact, "reinforced"[179], as it is reflected precisely in the fact that the congregation appoints and accepts particular people to preach. The holders of the preaching office should above all exercise their functions towards the *congregation* in that they–"an stad vnd befehl der andern"[180] – exemplarily show in the form of their own testimony what it means to live by faith in the here and now. The congregation has to make sure that there is someone amongst them who is competent to do so. But this competence does not involve any "policy-making power" (which unquestionably resides with the congregation as a whole); therefore it is neither indisputable nor basically universally valid or generally binding.

In order to explain the vis-à-vis position of the sermon, Ernst Lange refers to the *threefold externality* of the gospel: *First*, no one is able to achieve a testimony of his own faith without being caught up in the perspectives of the gospel by another, by a "brother". *Second:* Anyone who approaches another person as a witness to faith has certainly not invented the gospel which has minted his own faith, "he has it from Scripture [...], consequently it is also external to him; he, too, must be told in order to be able to pass it on". *Third:* Holy Scripture is not *per se* the Word of God, "it *becomes* so *in usu:* in being preached I encounter it as the Word of God". Here, too, E. Lange resorts to the "secret of externality". Although all three aspects are homiletically relevant, it is the second, "the connection of Scripture to the ministry of the Word", that leads "with a certain necessity to the institutionalization of that vis-à-vis" of preacher and congregation.[181]

The installation of the preaching office within and through the congregation is the attempt to regulate the complex task of communicating the gospel in public in a way that is understandable to the individual believer as well as to the public, appropriate to the self-understanding of the church and in accordance with the personal commitment to the Christian culture of testimony.

### d) The Sermon's Relation to Tradition

The analysis of biblical texts during the preparation of the sermon implies that the homiletic work is highly concerned with interpretation, with the

---

178 Apology of the Augsburg Confession, Art XIV (Ecclesiastical order), 1959, 214.
179 Cf. M. Luther, On the Misuse of the Mass, WA 8, 495, 28f.
180 Loc. cit., 412, 32.
181 Cf. E. Lange, 1976, 110.

exegesis of texts as central parts of the Christian tradition. Provided that the Bible is to be considered as a "Book of the Church"[182] i.e. not as a book of God, the one who preaches in church as well as in the interest of the church and, in doing so, draws on Holy Scripture and thus participates in the renovation (reformation) and extension (mission) of this church must also participate in her tradition of interpretation. What this means is explained in detail in chapter I.3 above.

Of course there is no such thing as one single correct interpretation for each text. A text may even infer perspectives and open up insights the author could not have foreseen but which nevertheless correspond to its original intention. Incidentally, a sermon should not exhaust texts but be in accordance with Scripture and – also in the light of the old written traditions of faith – illuminate our life by faith in the here and now. Consequently the sermon's "scripturality" presupposes the *knowledge of the Christian history of interpretation within the frame of the Confessions of the Church* in which the congregation expresses its religious consent.

As certain as the need and ability for interpretation of a text is not eradicated by an individual sermon (and as certain as another sermon at another time in another place can have another accentuation) there is, among the premises mentioned, a "true", and a "false", an "appropriate" and an "inappropriate" – as formulated by the Reformers: a true and false doctrine.[183] So the congregation for its part is not released from its task "to judge every doctrine"[184]. They are needed in this function precisely when a preacher takes his office seriously and, relating to the biblical text (i.e. on the basis of his understanding of this historical text), comes to a new, current contemporary text which is directly capable of connection. Through the communication of the gospel in the form of a sermon the members of the congregation for their part are challenged to mediate independently and autonomously in their own

---

**182** Cf. the programmatic work of W. Marxsen, 1967.

**183** Cf. e.g. M. Luther's comments on the first petition of the Lord's Prayer in the Large Catechism: "Since we see that the world is full of sects and false teachers, all of whom wear the holy name as a cloak and warrant for their devilish doctrine, we ought constantly to cry against all who preach and believe falsely and against those who attack and persecute our Gospel and pure doctrine [...]. For there is nothing he [God] would rather hear than to have his glory and praise exalted above everything else and his Word taught in its purity and cherished and treasured" (Luther, 1959, 426).

**184** Cf. M. Luther: "That a Christian assembly or congregation have the right and power to judge all doctrine and to call, install and depose, reason and cause from Scripture", 1523, WA 11, 408–416.

everyday lives between tradition and situation and thereby 'to carry the tradition further'.[185]

### e) Functional Legitimation of the Preaching Office

Neither does the preaching office bestow the preacher a special spiritual quality nor a particular dignity. As we have seen its legitimation is a functional one. In this vis-à-vis structure, however, there is something special which distinguishes it from other offices. The gifts practiced in the Corinthian congregation, for example, and the functions allocated to individuals are not present in today's congregations to the same degree (cf. 1 Cor 12:8–10) which does not mean, however, that the congregations are less worthy of being called a church. A church which refrained from the public communication of the gospel, on the other hand, should be fundamentally questioned. If this communication were abandoned – metaphorically speaking – the cardiovascular system of the church would collapse. In this sense it seems to be justified to describe the preaching office as "the ultimate or basic office of the church"[186] with which it stands or falls: "For of all acts of worship that is the greatest, most holy, most necessary, and highest, which God has required as the highest in the First and the Second Commandment, namely, to preach the Word of God. For the ministry is the highest office in the church. Now, if this worship is omitted, how can there be knowledge of God, the doctrine of Christ, or the Gospel?" ("Denn der allergrößte, heiligste, nötigste, höchste Gottesdienst, welchen Gott im ersten und andern Gebot als das Größte hat gefordert, ist Gottes Wort predigen; denn das Predigtamt ist das höchste Amt in der Kirche. Wo nun der Gottesdienst ausgelassen wird, wie kann da Erkenntnis Gottes, die Lehre Christi oder das Evangelium sein?")[187]

---

**185** Cf. W. Engemann, 2003e, 138.
**186** C. H. Ratschow, 1993, 617.
**187** Apology of the Augsburg Confession, Art. XV (Human traditions in the church), Die Bekenntnisschriften der Ev.-Luth. Kirche, vol. I, par. 44, 305. In his Tractatus de potestate papae (Treatise on the Power and Primacy of the Pope) Melanchthon emphasizes in par. 25–27: "The person adds nothing to the word and office commanded by Christ. No matter who preaches and teaches the word" ("Und tut die Person gar nichts zu solchem Wort und Amt, von Christo befohlen, es predige und lehre es, wer da wolle"). In this article Melanchthon explains that, the "rock" upon which the Lord wants to build his church (cf. Matt 16:18) does in fact, not refer to Peter but to "preaching and ministry". For "it is certain that the church is not built on the authority of a man, but on the ministry of the confession" ("muss man je bekennen, dass die Kirch nicht auf einigs Menschen Gewalt gebaut sei, sondern sie ist gebaut auf das Amt, welches das Bekenntnis [weiterträgt]") (Die Bekenntnisschriften der Ev.-Luth. Kirche, 1978, vol. II, 497). Because the different German and English versions of the Apology of the Augsburg Confession/

Because the church substantially depends on the communication of the gospel, which finds particular expression in the sermon, she thoroughly examines the quality and aptitude of the holder of the preaching office, not only before but also after the ordination. Such "examinations" are only rarely carried out by means of explicit "assessment measures" which, e.g., may be part of visitations, but emerge ideally from the *self-regulating communication between congregation and preacher.* This is the reason why preachers depend on their congregations, not in spite, but because of the office passed on to them. With the same determination with which congregations acknowledge their preachers' competence and aptitude they must, for the preachers' own sake, stay in dialog with them, give them feedback, address potential problems and from time to time report what has emerged from a particular sermon – i.e. how it fared outside the church walls. Preachers must rely on their congregations, i.e. allow themselves to be supported by them. Their office should be an expression of deep solidarity with the basis and not of a difference or distance between them. Preachers cannot perform their office without the congregation confiding in them and thereby leading them to the places where their preaching is needed.

### 4.5.3 On the Question of Aptitude for the Preaching Office. Demands made by the Church and the Congregation

When considering the preconditions of the ministry of the Word, it is not enough to point to the above-mentioned 'intrinsic logic' of this institution. Whoever takes on this task must possess certain competences, as listed and substantiated in the following.

#### a) Shared Identity

The aptitude for the preaching office is above all based on the willingness of the preachers to place themselves, together with their congregation, in a shared tradition, and thus to be part of a "shared identity". Such willingness implies joining the congregation in continually seeking this identity anew, and to make it a palpable fact. This is why the calling of a preacher presupposes a fundamental "consent"[188] to the beliefs of the church which count as constitutive from a theological perspective. In the final analysis, these documents of faith reflect the experience and deeply held beliefs of the congregation condensed

---

the Tractatus Papae all display various stages of editing, the passage used here will remain in its original German version.
**188** C. H. Ratschow, 1993, 615.

into key pronouncements, which it also expects to be constituents of the preacher's identity. It does not follow from this expectation, though, that – by appealing to the overall consensus prevalent in the confessional documents of the church – there should be no more arguments as to specific details. *After all, the relevant texts received their profile and pithiness in a process of concrete, historic argument and in debates guided by specific interests.* These documents are the outcome, the interim conclusion derived from the *interrelationship between tradition and concrete situation* which still impacts the congregation today. The identity-forming function of these creeds derives mainly from the fact that topical questions of a faith-based life are dealt with *in the light of answers previously established and of "enduring questions"*, i.e. guided by a constant and earnest dialog with tradition.

In other words: On the one hand, the members of the congregation have the right to know where their preacher stands. The starting point of a shared identity *and* its mutually agreed continual pursuit legitimize the congregation's desire "to query the teaching". On the other hand, the preacher is beholden to the congregation to utilize his competence – gained in consequence of his training and education – to interpret the old creeds and to keep them alive in the congregation. In this, a stimulating dialog between his personal identity and the suprapersonal identity of the church (the community of believers) should be a crucial concern to ensure that the sermon does not degenerate into a thoughtless regurgitation of dogmatic maxims (traditionalism) or only reflects an uncontrolled, self-centered display by the preacher (individualism).

There is also another side to the precondition of a shared identity: the preacher should face the members of his congregation as *one of them,* in the sense that he has to cope with the same challenges of life and faith as all the others, including concomitant problems, anxieties and doubts. The parish pastor must be able to get across that he himself is on a journey traditionally referred to as "discipleship". Which does not, however, mean that the preacher must constantly and explicitly point that out; rather, this fact should transpire from the communicative and participative behavior of the preacher himself. To the extent that, as a consequence of the preaching office, "this old flesh" should be "killed" every day ("der alte Adam täglich getötet werde") and "begin a new and eternal life"[189] the preacher also faces the challenge, daily new, of "plunging into Baptism and daily coming forth again"[190].

---

**189** Apology of the Augsburg Confession, Art. XXIV (On the Mass), in: Die Bekenntnisschriften der Ev.-Luth. Kirche, 1978, Vol. I, par. 34, 360.
**190** Luther summarizes his statements on baptism as follows: "This is what it means to plunge into Baptism and daily come forth again" (Large Catechism, Part 4: On Baptism, 1959, 445).

What is noteworthy is that "creeping back to Baptism" is principally described as a process, not necessarily as an iterative event. What, however, is referred to as a "daily" occurrence is the struggle against a relapse into the old life characterized by a lack of freedom: *emerging* from baptism, the constantly renewed reappearance in life is necessarily a daily reoccurring event in which the efficacy of baptism itself is not in the balance. So, this "coming forth through baptism" – in a homiletic context – is about re-emerging and going forth into public life, which both the preacher and the congregation are tasked with achieving. It is the "appearance" in one's own existence, a daily exercise, that is the focus of the shared interest of preacher and listener; it can also be called "sanctification".

In other words: Anyone who takes up the challenge of communicating the gospel to the congregation in a sermon, should be aware of the situations that preacher and listeners are familiar with, situations they share and also perceive as being a link between them. "A precondition of successful communication is the *participation* of the speaker in the situation of the listeners, the interest, the intrinsic involvement of the church in the situation which is the motivation for the sermon [...]. Participation is the precondition underpinning a responsible ministry of the Word."[191]

### b) Owed Competence

It seems obvious that mere *readiness* to adopt the approach outlined above and the *willingness* to participate in the life of the congregation are not sufficient qualifications for a preacher. To be able to meet the complex requirements of the preaching office, *specific competences* are needed: A sermon results from, among other things, a theologically and hermeneutically reflected reading of biblical texts, from critically reflected – i.e. not superficial – perception and interpretation of current life and reality, from a sound linguistic awareness and concomitant rhetorical skills, as well as from detached introspection, to list a few essential aspects.[192]

These are taxing preconditions, and also cogent reasons why the congregation, or the church, has put assessment procedures in place to establish to what extent would-be pastors meet these preconditions. This is mainly done by the theological assessment offices installed by the church in the respective countries. Their verdict decides who can apply to be a candidate for ordination. Any ordination is preceded by a kind of "assessment test" which must *fully satisfy*

---

191 E. Lange, 1976, 113, 115.
192 The ability to apply the categories and criteria named and discussed in Part I precisely reflects the expected "spectrum of competence" and is therefore not explained here again. Cf. I.2.4, I.3.4, I.4.4, I.5.4, I.6.4, I.7.4.

the respective church that a specific candidate meets the preconditions for the preaching office with respect to communicating the gospel.

The pronouncement that the incumbent of the preaching office must be *rite vocatus*[193] does not refer to the niceties of the ordination process as such. Rather, it focuses on the fundamental personal and professional aptitude for communicating the gospel.[194] *Rite vocatus* – this phrase sets out that there are cogent reasons for officially tasking a specific person with administering the duties of a pastor and preacher.[195]

Naturally, the church's identification with a candidate *rite vocatus* to preach in public does not encompass everything these people are likely to say or do later on. True, the ordination is the liturgical manifestation in which the church assumes responsibility for a pastor's competence to communicate the gospel. However, this assumption of responsibility is not based on the ordination itself, it derives from a personnel-related decision. "This decision is based on the expectation that – in light of his assessed aptitude, and relying on the assistance of the Holy Spirit – the ordinand will be able to interpret the Christian message."[196] So, the church's responsibility (not guarantee!) that a pastor's preaching activities amount to communicating the gospel does not rest on a sacramental ritual but on a decision taken outside a church service and based on verifiable reasons.

Practical Homiletics requires subject knowledge which cannot necessarily be expected of the whole congregation: Whoever delivers a sermon will have to take into account considerations which may be beyond the grasp of the congregation as a whole but are indispensable if the sermon is to achieve its aim. The preacher needs the qualification to *act as a theologian* when delivering a sermon, i.e. to underpin the sermon with sound theology.[197] What he has to say cannot only be the result of theological insights gained *otherwise* or simply borrowed. Since communicating the gospel itself is the source and objective of all theology, a preacher must also be able to do it justice in his theological work.[198]

---

**193** "It is taught among us that nobody should publicly teach or preach or administer the sacraments in the church without a regular call (*nisi rite vocatus*)" (The Augsburg Confession, 1959, par. XIV, 36).

**194** Cf. also C. H. Ratschow, 1993, 614.

**195** "Rite vocatus" is an umbrella term for various forms of appointment and should therefore not be equated with the term "ordination" (cf. S. Hell, 2006).

**196** D. Pirson, 1999, 214.

**197** The cover design with the pulpit of the *Zionskirche* in Berlin (using a construction drawing by the architect August Orth [1828–1901]) hints at the interest of this book to view the art of preaching as "téchne" in the sense of Aristotle, i.e. as an "artistry". Due to the effect of the preachers preaching from this pulpit (including, among others, Dietrich Bonhoeffer) in resisting National Socialism and the importance of Zionskirche in the struggle for freedom and justice under the dictatorship of the SED regime in the GDR, the drawing also stands for the demand on the sermon to be contemporary – that is, relevant.

**198** In this context cf. the ardent plea of Ch. Grethlein for the role of theology as an occupational science: Ch. Grethlein, 2009, esp. 104–130.

Just to make sure there is no misunderstanding in this respect: What was said in the previous paragraph does not mean that, in principle, not *all* members of the congregation can participate in the communication of the gospel. A qualified pastor, however – when working on a sermon – can surely be expected to be able to do so in a more captivating way, more in line with tradition, with a better trained eye for the complex homiletic situation, in short *in a more professional manner*. This does not exclude the "manifold participative possibilities, also encompassing the honorary pastoral professional key roles as lectors", but explicitly includes them. The manifold possibilities of communicating the gospel imply "a specific dynamic which enables participation in spiritual communication also independent of the pastors"[199].

It is against this backdrop that Isolde Karle has, in numerous publications, posed the question of the pastor as a professional, which triggered a plethora of important follow-up discussions. Karle takes as her starting point a comprehensive analysis of the term professional[200], or starts from classic professions characterized by dealing with "central questions and problems of human life in society, such as illness, guilt and salvation of the soul"[201]. This puts the focus on professions such as medical doctors, lawyers, teachers and theologians. What these professions have in common is the prevalence of communicative situations requiring an "*interactive*, personal encounter with physically present humans". This gives a "dominant position to these profession (within systems shaped by a variety of occupation, such as health, law, education and religion) and makes them representative of a system as a whole"[202].

This key position of these professions, bestowed and at the same time exacted by society as well as the church, corresponds to the differentiated roles in modern society. "A clear differentiation between roles greatly lowers the barrier to participation in the system of religion. For, as distinct from just any member of the church, a Protestant Christian can with some justification expect their pastor to be the first port of call when it comes to spiritual matters, the baptism or confirmation of their child, and that he will conduct prior talks as well as the ceremony itself with the requisite decorum, in an appropriate manner, and with diligence and responsibility."[203]

To be able to meet such expectations, pastors should possess a variety of basic competences, which are focused on by the churches in different regions in accordance with varying assessment models (exams, assessment procedures). In this, the focus is (1) on "subject-related" competences in matters

---

**199** I. Karle, 2000, 510f.
**200** Cf. I. Karle, 2001, 31–58.
**201** I. Karle, 2000, 508.
**202** Loc. cit., 509f.
**203** Ibid.

of theology, which include familiarity with the practical-theological basics of communicating the gospel; (2) on communication-related competences, above all the ability to interact. Finally, (3) professional-ethical challenges have to be taken into consideration. The following provides a closer look at these competences:

- *Theological competence*: The above-mentioned complex balance between tradition and a concrete situation, the critical examination of the implications of one's own faith prior to delivering the sermon etc. – all these things are not self-evident. "From a theological-professional point of view, the task is to bridge a gap with reference to gospel-based teaching and in this manner to depict and expound difficult central issues of the Christian faith, such as the cross, the resurrection of Jesus, or baptism and Holy Communion, comprehensibly and in accordance with the teachings of the church."[204]

- *Communicative competence*: A number of homiletic concepts relating to the criteria of communicative competence have been developed, among others, in person- (I.2.3.4) and language-related (I.5.3) contexts. The considerations on the "shared identity" also belong in this context. Among the preconditions of professional communication, Isolde Karle points out that "continuity with regard to the one pastoral professional" also plays a role, as well as a "local environment", a "neighborhood" which is not detrimental to the requirements of interactive communication between congregation and pastor.[205]

- *Professional-ethical competence*: Karle emphasizes the professional-ethical repertoire of behavioral features available to the pastor. The fundamental need for them results from the issue of trust, which is a pervasive element of this profession:[206] "Like doctors, judges and teachers, pastors are constantly concerned with critical situations of human life, and hence with core existential questions of human identity. All official ecclesiastical acts and ceremonies represent such typical professional problem situations in which sensitive, prudent and professional assistance by the pastor is of the essence. Thus, in the event of bereavement, a pastor will generally encounter people who, in the face of death and dying, are deeply upset emotionally

---

**204** I. Karle, loc. cit., 520. In his examination David A. Jacobsen (2015) quite rightly points out that the sermon is not only to be considered as the final result of the theological work, but also the site, starting-point and mode of theological reflection. In reference to the task of the sermon, the different themes and facets of theology come into play in a contemporary accentuation.
**205** Cf. I. Karle's criticism of the Impulse paper, "Church of Freedom" (I. Karle, 2009).
**206** For more detail cf. I. Karle, 2001, 72–82.

and existentially uprooted. In such a situation of distress, the members of the congregation must be able to rely on the unconditional *protection of trust*."[207] Even if, as is the case here, Isolde Karle justifies the need for professional competence in the context of situations encountered in the course of ecclesiastical acts, her elucidations are equally relevant to the homiletic context and the preaching office.

If it is not possible, e.g. through the above-mentioned concept of a shared identity or through sensitive relationship-building between preacher and congregation, to achieve a certain level of trust, there is little scope for any sermon. As it is, the perception of the role of the preacher is linked to unreasonable demands deriving from the Scandalon-Character of the gospel (cf. 1 Cor 1:23), from the prophetic-critical function of the sermon and, last but not least, from the idiosyncrasies of the preacher's personality. If, "in spite of it all", the congregation is to be induced to participate willingly in a gospel-based discourse on freedom and love, such trust-building signals as "professional sensitivity, willingness to accept responsibility [...] and being there for the congregation"[208] are indispensable.

---

207 I. Karle, 2000, 515.
208 Loc. cit., 517.

## Epilog

In order to make progress in the homiletic métier and become "adept" at it, it is not necessary to deal with all the perspectives of reflection developed in this book when preparing each and every sermon. However, the measure of *academic distance* achieved through such perspectives, questions and highlighted problems is a precondition for being aware of the challenges inherent in one's daily work on sermons, and also of coming up with clearer ideas of a "solution" or a rational theological approach to them. The more familiar one is with respective homiletic topics, the more likely one is – and the less inhibited – to discover or explore one's own individual paths in matters of Homiletics.

This switch-over from an academic, critical distance towards the homiletic trade to a joyful approach to preaching depends in no small amount on the extent to which pastors view their work on the sermon as a particular *chance for themselves*: It is a great privilege – in the course of one's job, as it were – for oneself "to be the theme" once a week. Which does not mean – as we have shown – being obliged to preach "about one's own life"; but it is indispensable for any good sermon (only then can it be relevant to *somebody*) *to be perceived as relevant to the preacher himself and as filling a personally experienced need.* When working on a sermon, everything that is part of life – one's view of life, the evaluation of past experience as a trigger for reflecting on consequences, the perception of certain customary situations, awareness of one's own expectations and ideas of the future, resolving the elementary question of what one really stands for in certain situations of life etc. – all this needs to be on the desk if the sermon is to reflect life.

Considering life in a sermon as a life "before God" or within the scope of the gospel, is all the more inspiring since it is the life *we are leading*, and not one that is constantly missed, postponed and moaned over, or one that needs to be talked up. Viewed from this angle, sermons are journeys of discovery into real life, a specific manner of exploring the gift of life and a guide to the art of living it.

## Part IV: **Guidelines for Sermon Preparation Process**

# A Model for Preparing a Sermon

## How to Use this Model

Good sermons are not just the result of a carefully followed guide. As a rule, they are the result of a long process of experience and reasoning, in which one gradually tackles the homiletic challenges, discussed in Parts I to III of this book. The theoretical and practical analyzing of the various homiletic questions – which can already be seen in the course of a single homiletic seminar for advanced students – undoubtedly helps to avoid serious mistakes in the field of preaching.

Therefore, the following references presuppose the study of the preceding chapters of this book. "Guidelines" are sometimes used with the misconception that one could do without the detailed examination of the basic questions of a field of research, knowledge and practice, i.e. in this case, that one could compose a sermon on the basis of a *"follow me"* in the sense of an IKEA assembly instruction. That is a pipe-dream! Such a guideline can offer no more than a standard program for composing a sermon which is entirely *based on recollection*. It is recommended, as has already been indicated above, to pay particular attention to a single homiletic focus for a while (i.e. in several sermons in succession) in order to adequately explore the possibilities and problems of dealing with texts, with one's own subjectivity, with today's reality of life etc.

Generally speaking, neither all aspects have to be worked through equally intensively, nor must their order always be the same. Sometimes one point merges seamlessly with the other, or prefigures on a case-by-case basis, something that comes to the fore later in this program. Sometimes one point leads smoothly into the next or occasionally anticipates something which is to be considered at a later point in this program. Above all, however, each further step can be accompanied by modifications, corrections and improvements to views and decisions already made. Consequently, the steps for the work should not be thought of as rigidly linear but are subject to a certain circularity. The same applies to the very detailed questions listed in each work step. These cannot and should not be worked through each time, but above all indicate in which direction to think. The questions signal what is at stake in the individual steps and should inspire to formulate one's own questions.

Depending on the text and the problem, and depending on the homiletic experience and competence, the steps explained below will be fruitful in varying degrees according to the individual. Some will gain relevance and plausibility

https://doi.org/10.1515/9783110440256-part IV

of their sermon through careful exegesis others through creative play with the textual motifs and another through a deliberate, attentive engagement with questions of our time. Especially in view of professional or individual preferences, however, the *other steps and elements* of preparing a sermon may add a correcting and horizon-expanding function; constantly omitting them would have a detrimental effect on the homiletic work.

# 1 The Preparatory Stage

## 1.1 The Homiletic Diary

The *homiletic diary* represents everyday reality in the preparatory phase of the sermon. Those who work on a sermon need "material". They should relate to authentic perceptions which reflect something of what takes place among people, what moves them, what causes them suffering, upon what they orient themselves, what priorities they choose, the fears and expectations they have etc. Small sequences of everyday life can shed light on human existence. It is not absolutely necessary to start a special booklet for this. The pocket calendar which one always carries, a piece of paper and a pencil in the pocket, the dictation function in the mobile phone are sufficient to achieve in this way an informative "scribbling-pad [...] for things seen, heard (and) read" in which "one may include short pieces of reflection"[1]. One should not rely too much on one's memory in this respect because the perceptions of unpleasant realities are very quickly suppressed; other observations on the other hand are hard to remember because of their randomness or banality.

The *homiletic diary* frequently helps in the unreflected dilemma of reversing the relationship between the relation of reality and text, or situation and tradition: Instead of allowing *actual realities of life* (as a rule a concrete *sequence* or a *segment* from the general context of experienced reality) to challenge the biblical text and the history of its interpretation, a reversal of this principle can frequently be observed: Events and occurrences are constructed to illustrate biblical texts. In the course of this we find reports in sermons of pseudo-real, abstract and also strongly stylized "cases" of insufficient love of one's neighbor, lack of faith etc. to make Paul or some other author of the Bible understandable. The truly contemporary sermon is based on a contrary procedure: The biblical text is brought up because both preacher and listener *need* it in view of how life is, in order to see and be able to understand *experienced reality in the light of the gospel,* to recapitulate it or, if need be, to rethink and change it.

---

1 G. Otto, 1982, 20. The idea of a homiletic diary is about a lively, conscious contemporaneity in order to connect the sermon to the "strong current [of the] present" (cf. I. Bachmann, 1984, 61).

The homiletic diary should not be drawn up selectively so that it is kept with an eye on the putative "answers" of the sermon text. Otherwise significant perceptions could be lost simply because, at first sight, they cannot be connected to the respective text. Precisely the independence of the homiletic diary from the thematic perspective of a text or Sunday is important for the view of the tension, which arises between "promise" and "reality". Questions like the following might guide what is noted:

- What has angered and shocked or moved, touched and pleased me in the past week?
- What disputes on which issues have I encountered?
- With what or whom have I – inwardly or explicitly – spontaneously declared solidarity?
- When I saw someone weeping, laughing or in a rage: What was the reason or cause?
- Have I seen pictures, which made me pause? What did I see in them?
- Which scenes fascinated me, which repelled me – and what were the reasons?

## 1.2 Reading the Text

The attentive reading of the sermon text in English presents a step of its own in the preparation of the sermon. The text should first – otherwise one might perhaps not even get around to it – simply be read. For preachers who are familiar with Greek and Hebrew it is barely possible to read a piece of the original text without viewing it with "exegetical" eyes. As important as the exegetical perspective is at a later point, immediately at the beginning of the preparatory stage it can move one's attention away from the *non*-historical-critical implications of the text and thereby obstruct an immediate productive understanding. Without the concentrated, careful attention of simply reading a text, one possibly throws away a surprising increase of insight, which may later reappear when rereading the text, first of all read in English, in its original form but "with new eyes".

It is helpful for the development of an idea for the sermon to hold back the premature or, in the course of time, the routine question of how one could "say this today". At this point questions, which serve the approach to the narrated world of the text have priority:

- What is actually told? What is the text about? What topics does it bring up?
- On which questions or problems does the text focus thematically?
- Which position does it represent on this matter?
- What interest or intention may the author have had?
- Who can relate to such a tale? To whom does it apply? Who "benefits" from hearing it?
- What does the text to contribute argumentatively to the matter it has brought up? What does it teach?
- In the face of which situation does the text say what it says?
- What is the text intended to achieve?

– Against what is it directed?
– What premises does the text have in its pros and cons?
– To what genre does the text belong (epistle, prayer, hymn etc.)?
– What does that mean for its original function?
– What headline would I give the text in order to get to the heart of what it is telling?

Of course it won't always deter the homiletic work-process to immediately write down what appears to be a "good idea" at the time, when it comes to mind. The "appearance" of such ideas in this first reading and understanding is frequently simply the recognition of favorite ideas, topics or theses, which one has in mind anyway. The associations and intentions which arise with this are present when one looks at the text again even without being recorded. The ensuing reading of the sermon text, not under pressure – particularly not under the pressure of wishing to apply it – is a good prerequisite for something to get under way which is not primarily influenced by commentaries, aids to preaching or one's own "theo-logic" but at least to a certain extent is due to the effect of the text itself.

## 1.3  The Perception of Aspects of Relation and Content

Processes of communication between people take place on a level of content and relation. This is also true in a certain way for the reading and understanding of texts: While we satisfy ourselves on "what is in the text" there are also emotions at work which make a task either sympathetic or unsociable, which can result in satisfaction or annoyance, in pleasure or frustration. Consequently, in the course of the reception of texts, not only are contents detected but moods are evoked, memories which accompany them are brought to mind, sometimes one becomes conscious of fears and other reactions. After all, the texts with which we preach were often written under circumstances when emotions were high.

The questions listed in 1.2 in this chapter related exclusively to the content level. The approach to the text is now to be supplemented by questions of the relationship level, which are similar to those dealt with in the context of the pastoral-psychological analysis of the preaching process (III.2.2.1).

– What mood (thankfulness, resignation, grief, indignation etc.) predominates in the text and clearly resonates in the author's contact with the reader?
– With what emotional state does the author of the text count upon on the part of the reader? What mood is apparently assumed?
– What feelings does the text arouse in me?
– Why is it that I react to this text with quite specific emotions? What previous experience do I have with this text?
– Does this text contradict or correspond to fundamental convictions of my thinking and faith?
– Does this text trigger any emotions in me at all or can I only deal with it on the level of intellect for the moment?

When the feelings which particular statements and concepts in a text arouse are not detected, they have an unconscious effect on the reception and interpretation of the text. Ventures on the emotional level are – exactly like the questions on the reading relating to content – completely *text-related* observations; they are part of an approach to the text based entirely on observation and have no need (initially) of further instruments. From the impact of the text in the day-to-day field of experience (homiletic diary) statements gradually arise and unexpected material comes forth: Threads of daily or even extraordinary experiences intertwine with the threads of other experiences which in part are rich in tradition – even such experiences which at that time have led to the respective text in front of us.

These perceptual approaches to the text can be deepened through various exercises. This includes, for example, the attempt to see the text in a specific atmospheric context, i.e. together with the situational context. For this purpose, the participants in a homiletic seminar receive their sermon text in a sealed envelope. "With the sealed envelope, the groups betake themselves into specific 'atmospheres' made known to them in advance. One group, for example, is given the task of travelling the suspension railway in Wuppertal from one terminus to the other. Another group is to "walk" the pedestrian zone of the Wuppertal inner city for two hours."[2] It would be just as stimulating 'to spend time' in a railway-station, an industrial estate, a department store etc., and then, after entering into the particular atmosphere of that place, to read the text and, with that in mind, "to establish the respective atmosphere". After an intensive exchange about their perceptions the members of the group must agree on a 'group result': What is the quintessence of the joint perceptions?"[3] The unique effect of this 'experimental arrangement' is that the participants are in a way witnessing the extent to which what they have perceived affects the text and, conversely, how the text begins to relate to particular atmospheres or situations and thus indicates how it is relevant.

Without the creative act of reflection and focused perception, without allowing hunches, interpretations and insights to come and go in the preparatory phase of the sermon, there is a danger that one will either say what one already always thought anyway, or that one restricts oneself to equating the theme of the sermon with the results of the exegesis. This would result in an impoverishment of the possibilities of interpreting the text and naturally also the perspectives of the sermon.

---

**2** A. Grözinger, 1996, 188f.
**3** Loc. cit., 189.

## 2 The Analytical Phase

The first reading of the text is aimed at bringing the thematic and emotional accents into view which the text, without employing exegetical-hermeneutic specialist knowledge, divulges through that which it itself "tells" and reveals. In the second step, it is a matter of ascertaining the historical world depicted in the text. To be able to classify it historically and understand it "in a relatively correct way" one must establish its context at the time of writing from which it was brought into circulation. In so doing the following aspects must be taken into consideration.

### 2.1 The Question of the Historical Situation which Needed the Text and Provided it with a "Sitz im Leben"

Anyone who preaches on a text does not do so simply because the order of pericopes drawn up years ago established that it is the "turn" of this text on this particular Sunday in the church year. We relate to texts because they are concrete forms of experiences of a life lived by faith and documents of the communication of the gospel. In order to understand these experiences and documents it is indispensable – which is generally the prerequisite for the understanding of experiences and documents – that one should throw light on the historical circumstances which led to this text, i.e. *to understand the situation which needed this text*. Thus, in this step, we do not immediately jump from the text to our situation, but first try to go back to the situation dealt with in the text. Here, for example, the following questions must be discussed:

- In which historical context does this text belong?
- Which historical experience determines this text?
- In the face of what kind of problems was this text written or used?
- For which problem does this text provide a solution?
- What or who should change in the view of this text?
- Against which attitudes or expectations is this text directed?
- Which attitudes or expectations does it acknowledge?
- In which sphere of life did this text have its place at that time?

### 2.2 The Question of the Texture of the Present, in the Field of which the Sermon will Achieve its "Sitz im Leben"

Our lives today are also determined by concerns and events in which we gather experiences, in which we learn to live and believe. Sometimes these occurrences are *compressed into texts* in letters, diaries, newspapers and novels. Because of their sign character, other forms (beyond spoken and written words), not simply verbal utterances, mean something, too. In a culture, everything which can be perceived, "read" and interpreted, everything which can be taken as a "sign" (that is, everything which is considered to be "significant" in any respect) makes its mark in the world of the text which is intended to be understood. It tells us something of how people saw themselves at that time, about their worldview, their feelings and perception of life and much more. The understanding of a text necessarily involves the acquisition of some basic knowledge of milieus, issues of time, politics, socio-political facts, intercultural and interreligious issues, and so on.

However, the study of texts and messages that circulate in our socio-cultural environment does not aim at providing the sermon with the necessary input so that one can speak on politics and the social situation in one's own country or serving the clichés of ailing, postmodern humanity. The deciphering of such present-day texts is nevertheless a decisive requirement for understanding the reality of people alive today and for obtaining a contemporary, authentic frame of reference for the sermon to be developed. The following questions (which naturally do not need to be dealt with anew before every sermon but rather aim for a certain familiarity with authentic present-day occurrences in the sense of a general knowledge of the world today) may help in this:

- How do people find orientation in their lives?
- Which values are generally considered desirable?
- What is understood – possibly varying in differing milieus – as a rewarding, fulfilled, wasted or lost life?
- What is considered as a hindrance to a fulfilled life?
- What are people afraid to lose and what are they hoping to gain?
- To which particular difficulties and risks are the people of today exposed?
- In what context are experiences of lack of freedom or the feeling of being lost, excluded, oppressed etc. made?
- In which contexts of life is the tension between individuality and conformity particularly evident?
- What role does the idea of "self-fulfillment" play, and what in general is understood by this?

## 2.3 The Comparison of the Historical Situation of the Text to the Current Situation of the Sermon

Just as the first listeners or readers of a text later recorded in the Bible were encouraged, uplifted, or warned with a fresh, living text written just for them, so the congregation needs to know how useful, helpful or even beneficial it was for them to have come to service today and to have heard a sermon. This experience presupposes that the sermon is suited to their situation and emerged from the analysis of their life as it is. The approach to this reality of everyday life does not occur (in the case of a sermon from a biblical text) without a comparison of the situation today with the situation then. Here it is a matter of questions like the following:

- Are there similarities or analogies between the situation which, at that time, led to the actual biblical text and the situation in which the sermon today is expected to be received?
- Are there "anthropological constants" which extend from the situation then to the situation today? In which experiences were they then and are they now evident?
- How did the text at that time influence people's thinking and action? At what kind of (re-) thinking and action must a sermon aim which will achieve what is relevant today?
- In what sense are the relationships between individuals or their relationship to God, which emerge in the text, relevant to the relationships between people and their relationship to God today?

Each of the steps mentioned so far under point 2 is based on an *interrelation* between situation and tradition both with regard to the formation of the text as well as to the emergence of the sermon: Text *and* sermon are documents of the experience of the Christian religion. Both are the result of the fact that, *on the one hand,* the situation continually brings a new challenge to tradition and puts a strain on it in a certain sense as well as claims it in a deeper sense of the word; *on the other hand,* tradition as a handing down of faith can always contribute to the clarification, interpretation, correction, questioning and stabilizing of situations.

## 2.4  The Question of the Motifs of the Sermon Text

In this step, we examine with which motifs (concepts, ideas, illustrations) the situation then was described, reflected upon and influenced. This analysis uncovers the text's repertoire of interpretation, reveals its semantic structure, discloses its implied tensions and differences, i.e. the semantic parameters mentioned above (cf. II.1.4) which determine a text: rich – poor, close – distant, large – small, strong – weak, profit – loss, worthwhile – futile, first – last etc.[4] To ascertain the individual elements of the structure of argumentation in the text is part of the

---

4 Naturally these motifs need not appear in pairs in the text. But they describe what they describe on the basis of an actual polarity or oppositionality. The oppositions to be established do not always correspond to the common lexical adversatives: "Poor" must in no way always describe the opposite of "rich" but can, for example, stand in opposition to "spiritually arrogant" and "put on show" (cf. Matt 5:3), i.e. mean "authentic" or "genuine".

analysis. Here the forms of historic-critical exegesis may be used, which can possibly lead to revisions or a reduction of the perspectives already pursued in steps 1.3 and 2.2. The questions, which are dealt with in this step are, for example:

- Which basic ideas, illustrations and illusions determine the text?
- Which semantic oppositions determine the construction and message of this text?
- What is the significance of these motifs, illustrations and ideas in other biblical contexts?
- What is their *specific* significance in the text in front of us?
- Upon which arguments does the text build its message?
- Which scale of values does the text imply?
- Which values rank as at the top and which as at the bottom?
- Which concepts or allusions are used to talk about humanity, faith and God?

"Unfortunately, there is a series of sermon texts which, according to the current understanding, baulk so strongly at a meaningful interpretation that you should then take the liberty of enriching the text from the entire biblical records or concentrate on one single motif in the text as your theme. No 'cutting theology', which simply beats a narrow clearing in the thicket of the forest! In any case, each individual text should be understood as representative of the whole gospel."[5]

## 2.5 The Question of the Points of Contact between the Motifs in the Text and Societal Discourse

Once again it is a matter of a juxtaposition: After having analyzed the sermon text linguistically, semantically and considered its significance, now the question arises as to how the text relates to the semantics and linguistics, i.e. the general ways of communicating in society today. In doing so, we encounter "rifts" and "bridges" between the imagination and language of an ancient text and those of our day. Since the social discourse on questions of existence, of social life today, the challenges of our time etc. reflects the respective social situation in linguistic form, it is important in the run-up to the sermon to consider the following questions:

- Which ensemble of expectations currently determines the daily lives of people in our country?
- On the basis of which categories, with which scales is the value of life generally characterized and measured?
- What is generally considered as "beneath the dignity" of the person? What does one really "need" in order to be considered a "human being"?

---

**5** From the "Leitfaden zum homiletischen Verfahren der Predigtstudien" ("Guide to the Homiletic Process of Sermon Studies") published by Kreuzverlag, developed by Roman Roessler (Bremen 2001, 5).

- What are people easily won over for and eagerly become committed to?
- What is frowned upon? What counts as unreasonable? What is taboo?
- Who is acknowledged and respected?
- Who can be certain of the greatest contempt?
- What counts as politically correct and what as incorrect?

Furthermore, we must ask at which point the current discourse of our society is (apparently) directly affected by the discussion of the text, where it is reinforced by it, collides with it or offers resistance. A text which is 2000 years old and the "Zeitgeist" naturally reveal and discuss questions about life in different ways and each with their own legitimacy. Both discourses require a systematic theological mediation which aims to relate varying theological (e.g. soteriological, eschatological or creation-theological) patterns of argumentation of traditional and contemporary theology to one another. In this phase, it is therefore not a question of allowing "the text" or "the faith" to prevail over the present time.

- Which dogmatic patterns of argumentation might be used to further one's theological and situational understanding of the text?
- To what extent can the text – in the context of a hermeneutic experiment – be considered a form of theological sharpening of current existential questions?
- Which experiences may complicate a sermon with this text under current conditions?
- Which statements in the text appear "as if written for today"?
- Is there a danger of misunderstandings in the sense of an obvious faulty reception?
- Which problems, themes or experiences do I assume, when using this text in a sermon that is (hopefully) relevant to contemporary listeners?

At this point at the latest one should consult various *homiletic literature for sermon preparation* and see, what others have to say about the text and the situation, the hermeneutical problems and the theological accentuation for a sermon with this text. In particular, three types of homiletic literature should be considered.

1. *Sermons*: One should frequently refer to sermons on the same text by other authors. Alongside collections of sermons by individual authors[6] and publishers[7] as e.g. in the *Homiletischen*

---

6 Cf. M. Beintker/G. Klein/H. Stoevesandt, 2002; W. Engemann, 1993b, 2001a, 2007a; H.-G. Heimbrock, 2003; G. M. Martin, 2003; H. R. Reuter, 2012. As examples for contemporary preaching, certain historical collections of sermons with certain emphases are highly recommended. For example, the politically explosive sermons of Martin Niemöller, edited by M. Heymel, 2001, and the sermons of Dietrich Bonhoeffer, edited by Isabel Best, 2012.

7 Cf. for example the sermons and sermon studies, published by Concordia Publishing House (South Jefferson St. Louis, MO) in the Quarterly Journal "Concordia pulpit resources" (https://books.cph.org/cpr). See also Ch. Dinkel, 2008–2013. This six-volume edition offers sermons of prominent theologians on all sermon texts for the liturgical year. Sermons on the texts

*Monatshefte* (Homiletic Monthly) circulated by Vandenhoeck & Rupprecht with the basic pattern: Interpretation of the text, consideration of the translation, literature, suggestions for the hymns, readings, sermon and prayer.

2. *Regularly appearing sermon meditations or sermon studies:* Here we refer to two "classics" proved in practice:

(1) The *Predigtstudien* (sermon studies) of the Kreuz-Verlag are published in two half-volumes per year. They differ from the other homiletic literature for sermon preparation in that *two* authors are entrusted with the preparation of the sermon and come to an understanding between themselves on it: Author A attends to the pattern *beginning – examination of the text – homiletic-end-result* with the central question: "How do I hear and understand the sermon text?" Author B initially has a critical look at what the author of the first part has done (*Dialog with A*) and then in two further steps (*the homiletic situation – the sermon and the worship service*) discusses the question: "How do I speak to those listening to the sermon?"

(2) The *Göttinger Predigtmeditationen* (Göttingen sermon meditations) correspond in a structural respect to the way "from the text to the sermon". Based on the findings of the exegesis and having considered theological aspects and hermeneutic questions, the authors then offer thoughts and suggestions for the content and task of the sermon. The sermon meditations frequently offer compact, theologically informative texts that can be a significant aid in the intensification of one's own preparation of the sermon.

3. Finally there are also several already *completed series on preparing a sermon.* One homiletic aid which might be somewhat "dusty" in its language but is exegetically rich in points, exciting in the systematic-theological deciphering and hermeneutically stimulating is the series *Homiletische Auslegungen der Predigttexte* (Homiletic Interpretation of the Sermon Texts) by Gottfried Voigt. The author has thoroughly edited all six series of pericopes twice (before and after the Revision of 1977)[8] and in so doing submitted a reliable sermon aid.

If one consults commentaries and homiletic literature for sermon preparation already at the very beginning in the process of writing a sermon, without first trying to establish one's own ideas for the task of the respective sermon, one risks becoming heavily influenced by other's ideas and suggestions. One will use the contributions of others with a greater profit if one has earlier adopted a position for oneself and made one's own concept of the difficulties and possibilities which are mentioned or overseen in the texts of other authors.

---

of the current pericope order can also be found in the "Lesepredigten" (sermons for reading, cf. footnote 402, p. 162) published by Evangelische Verlagsanstalt (Leipzig) and the "Pastoralblätter" (pastoral journal) published by Kreuz-Verlag (Hamburg).

**8** Cf. G. Voigt, 1965–1970, 1978–1984, reprinted 2003.

# 3 The Stage of the Draft

## 3.1 Reflections on the Theme of the Sermon

On the basis of the previous results we can formulate a working hypothesis which is equivalent to constructing a focus for the further homiletic reflection. This can take place in the form of a motto which is rich in associations, a provisional sermon title or a striking central idea which suddenly allows an existential question or a particular problem related to the situation to appear and at the same time touches on a central idea of the text. This all has to do with working out a "sermon corpus". This formulation should not represent any abstract declaration of intent (for instance looking at the text Rom 3:21–28: "I should like to encourage the congregation in their justification"), but should 1. express the core of the contents of the sermon, 2. be formulated from the stand-point of the potential listeners and 3. have an eye on the expected effect of the sermon.

- What do I want to express with my sermon?
- What behavior do I wish to encourage or which attitude corresponds to what I want to say?
- Why am I preaching? What can perhaps change through my sermon, what should be reinforced or strengthened?
- Who, apart from myself, deals with this topic which I should like to bring up (e.g. which institution, which field, which professions) and to what conclusions do they come?
- What have I as a theologian to say on this?
- In what respect do I consider my sermon to be helpful for life?
- Who can use what I wish to say – and how so?

Without having a main idea for the sermon that wishes to bring home a certain "point" the address from the pulpit is in danger of becoming an exegetical essay. Manfred Josuttis considers the main sermon-idea to be the "center of crystallization for the whole of the sermon", the "basic idea [...] which should characterize the individual statements"[9]. This is why it is important to be so long adamant on this point until one has – at least for oneself! – the impression that one has found a plausible, relevant "springboard" or goal. The imagination essential for this step can be aided by reading, through using quotations[10], through conversation with a preparatory group etc.[11]

---

9 M. Josuttis, 1970, 630f.
10 "As speaker, I rely on taking 'loans', on one occasion more, on another less. This is permitted if the one lending is halfway solid and if I use the loan sensibly, i.e. thoughtfully and reflected upon. The one who should be scolded is the one who has nothing to say but does not admit to this but talks away cheerfully – a nuisance for the listeners" (G. Otto, 1994, 123). Cf. also the paperback *Zitate für die Predigt* ("Quotations for the Sermon") (H. Hamdorf-Ruddies et al., 1993).
11 Cf. M. Josuttis, 1970, 638–642.

## 3.2 The Structuring of a Semantic Field

The main idea, however, needs real material, which might have found expression in the homiletic diary. How does what is written there conform to the motto that I am attempting to explain? A good possibility of making progress here consists in playfully "translating" the discourse presented in the text into the contemporary social discourse.

This can have the result that one uses the text in an unusual way by transferring it into another situation and changes the people sketched in the text into figures from everyday life. Other possibilities of using the text playfully are to replace individual words with synonyms or antonyms. One can "intervene at one place and continue in a new direction; convert the text into illustrations, bring it on stage; construct an anti-text; record the text on tape and listen to it; present the text as the content of a letter, tell it to someone's face; devise actions without speaking; work the text into the course of the argumentation of a disputation; sing the text; compose an address to a jury; refute the text; [...]; draw a caricature; put the text into the mouths of various types of people [of the present]; allow atheists to argue and pious people to quote"[12].

This creates new connections between the texture of the experience gained in the texts and the texture of current experience. Meanwhile, the sermon text becomes more and more concrete, "inevitable" and limited in its many possibilities of expression – at least with regard to the impending sermon.

## 3.3 The Draft of the Manuscript

A sermon needs a well-founded construction plan which can arise in various ways:[13] Its "bricks" can be obtained initially in a fairly rough state and laid aside for later use and then – metaphorically – appropriately "cut" and "made to fit". A construction plan can change or be discarded during the process and lead to a new beginning. At the end of such a process, however, one should be able to explain the plan of one's own sermon and provide information as to why it is so and how the sermon – if it is to fulfill what is expected of it – should "work": Why *this* beginning, why *this* story, why *this* confrontation, why *this* conclusion? On the basis of which homiletic principles can one – gauged on

---

12 A. Horn, 2009, 149f. Cf. also the thoughts on a playful approach to the task of the sermon in S. Wolf-Withöft 2002, esp. 109–124.

13 Cf. the book on homiletic practice by M. Nicol and A. Deeg (2005) and the thoughts of V. A. Lehnert (2006) on the "pruning" of manuscripts (79–88), on drafting index cards and on "performance" (89–143) connected to examples inter alia for a dialogical speech, the beginnings of sermons and narratological sermons.

professional and human standards – assume that the sermon is received in the way one intended? Here there are initially two tasks to master: One must find a *stringent structure* (i.e. above all: a fitting sequence of thoughts) and a *suitable beginning.*

When *structuring* the sermon, it is important to ensure that the argumentation is consistent and coherent. Here, for example, (a) either the model of a common "vanishing-point" of different trains of thought can form the basis or (b) the model of the development of a picture or a "core of crystallization" in various ways. One can also (c) argue dialectically on the basis of thesis, antithesis and synthesis or (d) reinforce the main thought of the sermon in such a way, that general experiences and insights are transformed into something concrete and individual.[14] The individual parts of the sermon should be arranged in such a way that they provide the listeners with sufficient clues and aids to see "the bigger picture". This, however, can only succeed if the one preaching has first developed a "bigger picture" in the course of the sermon preparation. This is also where the guidelines discussed above (see I.4.3) in relation to the principles of the psychology of learning as well as narratological, dialogical, semiotic and virtual ways of structuring the sermon are discussed. For beginners the perspective of the psychology of learning – with the "fivefold" elements of motivation, delimitation of problems, trial and error, offering of a solution, reinforcement of the solution – is perhaps particularly suitable, since the implementation of the individual steps of this model seems easier to apply than the other models for structuring.

In the *introduction,* one must pay heed that it leads stringently *in medias res* and that the listeners are shown the factual grounds for the sermon, e.g. a conflict, an ambivalent experience, a reasonable way of looking at a problem, in short – a need for discussion and communication is revealed through which the sermon obtains a comprehensible relevance. This can take place through the description of a scene, through a brief anecdote or a metaphor in which the focus of the sermon is highlighted. Only in rare cases one will continue an idea for the introduction which one had at the very beginning of the homiletic work, since one can only go *in medias res* if one already has a clear idea on the subject, the content and the point of the sermon. This, for its part, usually comes at a relatively late stage of the homiletic reflection.[15]

---

14  Cf. the compilation in A. Härtner/H. Eschmann, 2001, 107–113.
15  On this cf. suggestions made by M. Bernstorf/T. Thomsen, 2012, 26, 42, 66, 73f., 82, 94, 117, 130.

Since the draft of the manuscript requires very complex considerations, which, depending on the chosen concept for the sermon, entail very different decisions, only a selection of relevant questions can be offered here.

- Which central ideas, that have become apparent in the preliminary work as relevant to the sermon, must be differentiated from which secondary thoughts and facets of the theme?
- From which basic experience or which basic problem does my sermon start?
- Which standpoint is suitable as a beginning and guide to the "center of crystallization" of the sermon?
- On which material do I fall back (homiletic diary, further texts, novels, books of non-fiction, pictures etc.) to become proficient in the subject?
- How should the individual thoughts of the sermon be arranged in order to form a coherent overall structure? In short: what structure does my sermon have?
- What title and what sub-titles does the sermon have?[16]
- Which formal or stylistic signals motivate to listen?
- Which exegetical, theological or "specialist" pieces of information are really indispensable for understanding my sermon?

The "model for preparing a sermon" presented in this chapter is not ultimately about a technical optimization of crafting a sermon, but about embedding the homiletic work in the ongoing personal and theological process of development which those preaching find themselves in. Accordingly, Annette Müller presents her empiric analysis of crafting a sermon (which leads into homiletic teaching methods) in the expectation of encouraging the "process of growth in the person preaching towards more insight and a greater freedom of action". Those who preach should be able to write "theologically reliable, individually consistent, linguistically appealing sermons [that those listening can] connect to". This has to do with "self-regulation as a grasping of options", with the perception of "room for maneuver in the sermon preparation", which leads to preaching willingly, even considering the occasionally "unreasonable demands of the profession of pastor".[17] Anyone wishing to learn more about empirical research on the preferred strategies and routines for the weekly preparation of the Sunday sermon of pastors and desires to adopt them will find excellent suggestions in this study by A. C. Müller.[18]

---

**16** Such working-titles and subdivisions naturally need not be communicated to the congregation like a lecture; but they challenge the preacher to lay a clear trail which the listeners can follow.
**17** A. C. Müller, 2014, 378.
**18** On the basis of twelve examples, a range of specific ways towards crafting a sermon are presented. These are analyzed and assessed with regard to categories and criteria of both Homiletics and writing research. As such, the advantages and disadvantages of certain strategies for preparing a sermon are made clear.

## Guidelines for the Preparation of a Sermon Draft within the Homiletic Seminar and for Theological Examinations[19]

For a homiletic paper, which is to be presented in the context of a seminar or a theological examination and should include a sermon and the respective preliminary work, the following structure is recommended:

1. *Introductory remarks* (optional): The work may begin with introductory remarks if, for example, a special method of working on the text diverges from the usual structure of such a draft or a unique focus on a specific homiletic perspective of reflection characterizes the work in a specific way (at most one page). It is not necessary to give a commentary on the steps which are expected anyway.

2. *Exegetical-hermeneutic commentary*: The focus of the exegetical-hermeneutic commentary is on the clarification of the overall message of the text, thus serving to formulate a main idea. It must be clarified to what extent this text serves to document experiences of faith.

   To establish this, one must ask questions such as: For which problem should this text be the "solution" or at least an orientation? Which arguments come into play? How was the text received? How is the text different from similar statements in other texts? This step closes with a brief résumé of the central statements or "core experience" of the text (total length approx. three pages). In the course of the exegesis one should compose one's own *translation* which – if the text is very long – may also be added as an appendix.

   The presentation of a translation does *not* mean that one must also *use* it in the sermon. The choice of the form of the text then used in the sermon must of course – especially when there are abridgements or divergences from the exegetically acquired text – be commented on with hermeneutical, didactic or similar arguments *in the homiletic commentary. In the end, the sermon text must appear and be quoted as a whole in the version and in the place in which it will appear in the sermon.* The rare cases in which the text itself is not explicitly mentioned or not discussed as a unified quotation in the sermon, require an explanation within the homiletic commentary.

3. In a systematic-theological commentary, dogmatic or ethical categories and patterns of argumentation of also contemporary systematic theology (of the twentieth and twenty-first century), should be used to elaborate, which

---

**19** In order to use this guideline accordingly, it is highly recommended to have read part I-III of this book.

theological questions the sermon touches upon and how they are relevant to the vital questions of humankind – while also taking the exegetical insights and the main idea for the sermon into account. This step serves, on the one hand, *to further the theological insights of the text* as a documentation of experiences of faith as well as, on the other hand, a *theological discussion of the relevance of the sermon* for a life lived by faith today. In this context, anthropological aspects always play a part; they help to discern in which respect, on what grounds, with which goal and what right people can be approached about their existence and their faith. (Total length approx. three pages)

4. The analysis of the situation can be compared to a beam of light, which illuminates a detail of the complex reality of life today. It describes and comments on the difficulties and possibilities of living by faith, on the basis of a definable problem or with reference to a specific question. Mind you: This is not about the application of the text[20] to a situation constructed for it, but about the *search for an authentic situation*, a given situation or circumstance that needs to be understood, endured, respected, shaped, subverted or combated etc. Consequently, the analysis of the situation gives an answer to the simple question as to *why this sermon should be delivered*. Which experience, which dilemma do I assume when I work on a sermon with this text and the background of its experience? With what objections must I reckon? (Total length approx. two pages)

5. The homiletic commentary brings the *concrete task of the sermon* to its focal point. This includes explaining the task or aim of the sermon *from the listener's point of view*. Hence not: "I wish to...", "I would like to...", but: "The listeners should understand, be enabled to..." etc. Hence it is not simply a matter of mere declarations of intent but of well-founded expectations with regard to the "condition" (including their thought, faith and action) of the listeners as a result or effect of the sermon.

In this step, *the design* of the sermon should be justified homiletically: with arguments for its structure, its language, for the use of pictures[21] and symbols, with explanations for the particular form of the sermon (story, fictitious letter, sermon using a picture). In short, in relation to homiletic arguments and

---

**20** This means: Because the text has to offer "X" as a solution, "Y" must be seen as a problem so that the text proves that it is useful.

**21** In his study on working with real, i.e. visually receivable instead of merely verbal images, R. A. Jensen (2005) points to the special opportunities of homiletic communication based on pictures. Cf. in particular his considerations on "Religious Imagination" (loc. cit., 86–90).

insights[22] one must explain what was done in a technical respect so that the sermon will be heard and understood in a way corresponding to its intention.

In this context, one must also discuss the place or context in which the sermon text should be brought up in the sermon (total length approx. four pages).

6. A liturgical commentary fits the sermon *according to chosen liturgical elements in an exemplary way in the overall context of the worship service* and thereby marks the "golden thread" of the service.

Here one should relate *to the proper or the leitmotif of the particular Sunday*[23] and therewith to the church year. In two or three examples, it should be demonstrated how that which is treated in the sermon is touched upon in other parts of the service or possibly also is contrasted by these. This can be done by e.g. a short commentary on quoted or autographic Kyrie-prayers, a rendering of Psalms, through suggestions for hymns, references to the spatial arrangement, visual elements, stimuli for the celebration of Communion (special "words of offering"), words of blessing or through a "prayer after the sermon".

7. Sermon (total length approx. five pages)

8. Besides the cover page and the table of contents, a bibliography must also be included in every homiletic seminar or examination paper. All the homiletic literature for sermon preparation one has quoted or used as a guideline (Sermon Studies, Sermon Meditations, Collections of Sermons etc.) is to be listed under the name of the authors of the cited contributions and not as anonymous reference books.

---

22 Here it is a matter above all of relating to the homiletic repertoire discussed in I.1–I.7.
23 Cf. the short portraits of the Propria for Sundays and Holidays in K.-H. Bieritz, 2000, 681–720.

Part V: **Appendix**

# Bibliography

*On the use of the bibliography:* In order to make it easier for readers to quickly find the publications they are looking for, an additional principle of classification has been introduced in the alphabetical list of references. Since many authors have several publications listed – the respective year of publication is indicated in the footnotes directly after the name – the corresponding works were additionally listed according the year of their publication. If there are several publications by the same author with the same year of publication, minuscules were added as a means of further subdivision (e.g.: R. J. Allen, 1998a, 23). Where necessary in order to avoid ambiguity, the first year of publication was added just after the publication title in square brackets.

## A

1899    **Achelis**, Ernst Christian: Homiletik, in: Idem: Praktische Theologie, Mohr, Freiburg, 3rd ed., 1899, 119–167

1990    **A Four Year Lectionary**, ed. by Joint Liturgical Group (Ed. G. Tellini), Canterbury 1990

1985    **Albrecht**, Horst: Predigen. Anregungen zur geistlichen Praxis, Kohlhammer, Berlin/Stuttgart/Köln/Mainz 1985

2002    **Albrecht**, Christian/**Weeber**, Martin (Eds.): Klassiker der protestantischen Predigtlehre. Einführungen in homiletische Theorieentwürfe von Luther bis Lange, Mohr Siebeck, Tübingen 2002

1998a   **Allen**, Ronald J.: Interpreting the Gospel. An Introduction to Preaching, Chalice Press, St. Louis/Mo. 1998

1998b   Idem (Ed.): Patterns of Preaching. A Sermon Sampler, Chalice Press, St. Louis/Mo. 1998

2002    Idem: Preaching is Believing. The Sermon as Theological Reflection, Westminster John Knox Press, Louisville/Ky. 2002

2005    **Allen**, O. Wesley: The Homiletic of All Believers. A Conversational Approach, Westminster John Knox Press, Louisville/Ky. 2005

1966    **Althaus**, Paul: Die christliche Wahrheit. Lehrbuch der Dogmatik, G. Mohn, Gütersloh, 7th ed., 1966

1963    **Altmann**, Eckhard: Die Predigt als Kontaktgeschehen, Evangelische Verlagsanstalt, Berlin 1963

1975    **Amberg**, Ernst-Heinz: Der Ort der Predigt im Verkündigungsauftrag der Gemeinde, in: Helmut Zeddies (Ed.): Immer noch Predigt?, loc. cit., 1975a, 9–17

1985    **Anderegg**, Johannes: Sprache und Verwandlung, Vandenhoeck & Ruprecht, Göttingen 1985

1961    **Andresen**, Carl: Zur Entstehung und Geschichte des trinitarischen Personbegriffs, in: ZNW, Vol. 52, 1961, 1–39

2002    **Andrews**, Dale: Practical Theology for Black Churches, Westminster John Knox Press, Louisville/Ky. 2002

2009    **Apel**, Kim: Predigten in der Literatur. Homiletische Erkundungen bei Karl Philipp Moritz (= PThGG, Vol. 7), Mohr Siebeck, Tübingen 2009

1959    **Apology of the Augsburg Confession** [1537], in: The Book of Concord. The Confession of the Evangelical Lutheran Church, ed. by Theodore Tappert, Fort Press, Philadelphia, 6th ed., 1959, 97–245

https://doi.org/10.1515/9783110440256-015

1972    **Arens**, Heribert: Predigt als Lernprozess, Kösel, München 1972
1975    **Arens**, Heribert/**Richardt**, Franz/**Schulte**, Josef: Predigt als Lernprozess, in: Peter Düsterfeld/Hans Bernhard Kaufmann (Eds.): Didaktik der Predigt, loc. cit., 1975, 41–81
1935    **Aristotle**: The "Art" of Rhetoric, ed. by John H. Freese, William Heinemann & G. P. Putnam's Sons, London/New York 1935
1610    **Arndt**, Johann: Vier Bücher vom wahren Christentum, das ist von heilsamer Buße, herzlicher Reue und Leid über die Sünde und wahrem Glauben, auch heiligem Leben und Wandel der rechten wahren Christen, Duncker, Vol. I, Braunschweigk 1606; Vol. II–IV, Braunschweigk 1609; Vol. I–IV, Francke, Magdeburg, 2nd ed., 1610
2013    **Arnold**, Jochen/**Fuchs**, Frank/**Stäblein**, Christian (Eds.): Dem Leben auf der Spur. Mit Literaturgottesdiensten durch das Kirchenjahr (= GGG, Vol. 23), Lutherisches Verlagshaus, Hannover 2013
1937    **Asmussen**, Hans: Das Kirchenjahr (= Gottesdienstlehre, Vol. 2), Chr. Kaiser, München, 2nd ed., 1937
1959    **Augsburg Confession** [1530], in: The Book of Concord. The Confession of the Evangelical Lutheran Church, ed. by Theodore Tappert, Fort Press, Philadelphia, 6th ed., 1959, 23–96
1913    **Augustine**: Vorträge über das Evangelium des heiligen Johannes (= BKV, Vol. 1), transl. and introduced by Thomas Specht, Kempten, 2nd ed., 1913
1962a   Idem: Confessiones, in: CChrSL, Vol. XXXII, 1962, 1–273
1962b   Idem: De doctrina Christiana, in: CChrSL, Vol. XXXIII, 1962, 1–167
1962    **Austin**, John L.: How to do Things with Words. The William James Lectures delivered at Harvard University in 1955, Harvard University Press, Cambridge/Mass. 1962


**B**

1984    **Bachmann**, Ingeborg: Werke, Vol. 4, ed. by Christiane Koschel et al., Piper, München/ Zürich, 3rd ed., 1984
1968    **Bahr**, Hans-Eckehard: Verkündigung als Information. Zur öffentlichen Kommunikation in der demokratischen Gesellschaft, Furche-Verlag, Hamburg 1968
1997    **Bal**, Mieke: Narratology. Introduction to the Theory of Narrative, University of Toronto Press, Toronto, 2nd ed., 1997
2000    **Ballod**, Georg/**Ballod**, Matthias: Predigthilfen aus dem Rechner? Computergestützte Predigtanalysen, Berg Verlag, Marnheim 2000
1972    **Barié**, Helmut: Kann der Zeuge hinter sein Zeugnis zurücktreten? in: EvTh, Vol. 3., 1972, 19–38
1925    **Barth**, Karl: Menschenwort und Gotteswort in der christlichen Predigt, in: ZZ, Vol. 3, 1925, 119–140
1968    Idem: The Epistle to the Romans [1919], Oxford University Press, London/Oxford/New York 1968
1991    Idem: Homiletics [1987], Westminster John Knox Press, Louisville/Ky. 1991
2009a   Idem: Dogmatics, Vol. I.1, The Doctrine of the Word of God [1932], ed. by Geoffrey W. Bromiley and Thomas F. Torrance, T&T Clark, London 2009
2009b   Idem: Church Dogmatics [1953], Vol. IV.1, The Doctrine of Reconciliation, ed. by Geoffrey W. Bromiley and Thomas F. Torrance, T&T Clark, London 2009
1974    **Barthes**, Roland: S/Z, Blackwell/Hill and Wang, New York 1974

1994    Idem: La mort de l'auteur, in: Œuvres complètes, ed. by Éric Marty, Seuil, Paris 1994, 419–495

1987    **Barwise**, Jon/**Perry**, John: Situations and Attitudes, MIT Press, Cambridge/Mass. 1983

1965    **Bastian**, Hans-Dieter: Verfremdung und Verkündigung. Gibt es eine theologische Informationstheorie? Chr. Kaiser, München 1965

2006    **Bauer**, Joachim: Prinzip Menschlichkeit. Warum wir von Natur aus kooperieren, Hoffmann und Campe, Hamburg 2006

1999    **Bayer**, Oswald: Schöpfung, systematisch-theologisch, in: TRE, Vol. 30, 1999, 326–348

2006    **Beck**, Ulrich: Risikogesellschaft. Auf dem Weg in eine andere Moderne, Suhrkamp, Frankfurt/M., 18th ed., 2006

1998    **Behler**, Ernst: Ironie, in: Historisches Wörterbuch der Rhetorik, Vol. IV, Niemeyer, Tübingen 1998, 599–624

2002    **Beintker**, Michael/**Klein**, Günter/**Stoevesandt**, Hinrich: Geschenktes Leben: Die Rechtfertigungsbotschaft in Predigten, Evangelische Verlagsanstalt, Leipzig 2002

1978    **Die Bekenntnisschriften** der evangelisch-lutherischen Kirche, 2 Volumes, Evangelische Verlagsanstalt, Berlin, 2nd ed., 1978

1999    **Benjamin**, Walter: Doctrine of the Similar [1933]. Selected Writings, Vol. 2, Part 2, ed. by Michael W. Jennings, Harvard University Press, Cambridge/Mass./London 1999

1956    **Berelson**, Bernard: Content Analysis, in: Gardner Lindzey (Ed.): Handbook of Social Psychology, Vol. I, Cambridge/Mass., 2nd ed., 1956

1951    **Berggrav**, Eivind Josef: Man and State [1946], Muhlenberg Press, Philadelphia 1951

1966    **Berne**, Eric: Principles of Group Treatment, Oxford Univ. Press, New York 1966

1972    Idem: What Do You Say After You Say Hello? The Psychology of Human Destiny, Grove Press, New York 1972

1967    Idem: Games People Play – The Psychology of Human Relationships. The basic Handbook of Transactional Analysis, Ballantine, New York 1967

1972    **Bernstein**, Basil: Studien zur sprachlichen Sozialisation, Pädagogischer Verlag Schwann, Düsseldorf 1972

2012    **Bernstorf**, Matthias/**Thomsen**, Thorge: Selbst Verständlich Predigen? So geht's! Vandenhoeck & Ruprecht, Göttingen 2012

2012    **Best**, Isabel (Ed.): The Collected Sermons of Dietrich Bonhoeffer, Fortress Press, Minneapolis/Minn. 2012

2016    **Beute**, Marinus: Wie ben ik als ik preek? Bronnen en herbronning van het homiletisch zelfbeeld, Boekencentrum Academic, Zoetermeer 2016

2002    **Beutel**, Albrecht: Aphoristische Homiletik. Johann Benedikt Carpzovs ‚Hodogeticum' (1652), ein Klassiker der orthodoxen Predigtlehre, in: Christian Albrecht/Martin Weeber (Eds.): Klassiker der protestantischen Predigtlehre, loc. cit., 2002, 26–47

1989    **Beutel**, Albrecht et al. (Eds.): Homiletisches Lesebuch. Texte zur heutigen Predigtlehre, Katzmann-Verlag KG, Tübingen 1989

2010    **Bieler**, Andrea/**Gutmann**, Hans-Martin: Embodying Grace. Justification in the Real World, Fortress Press, Minneapolis/Minn. 2010

1970    **Biemer**, Günter (Ed.): Die Fremdsprache der Predigt, Patmos-Verlag, Düsseldorf 1970

1983    **Bieritz**, Karl-Heinrich: Die Predigt im Gottesdienst, last published in: Idem: Zeichen setzen, loc. cit., 1995, 137–158

1984    Idem: Verbum facit fidem. Homiletische Anmerkungen zu einer Lutherpredigt, last published in: Idem: Zeichen setzen, loc. cit., 1995, 123–136

1985    Idem: Kritik der Kritik. Beispiele, Strukturen und Funktionen von Predigtkritik, in: ZGDP, Vol. 3, 1985, 25–33

1990    Idem: Predigt und rhetorische Kommunikation, in: Karl-Heinrich Bieritz/Christian Bunners et al. (Eds.): Handbuch der Predigt, loc. cit., 1990, 63–98

1995    Idem: Zeichen setzen. Beiträge zu Gottesdienst und Predigt (= PTHe, Vol. 22), Kohlhammer, Stuttgart 1995

1998    Idem: Offenheit und Eigensinn. Plädoyer für eine eigensinnige Predigt, in: Erich Garhammer/Heinz-Günther Schöttler (Eds.), loc. cit., 1998, 28–50

2000    Idem: Der Gottesdienst im Kirchenjahr. Einführung in das *proprium de tempore*, in: Evangelisches Gottesdienstbuch, loc. cit., 2000, 681–720

2004    Idem: Liturgik, de Gruyter, Berlin 2004

2009    Idem: Ritus und Rede. Die Predigt im liturgischen Spiel, in: Wilfried Engemann/Frank Lütze (Eds.): Grundfragen der Predigt, loc. cit., 2nd ed., 2009, 303–319

1990    **Bieritz**, Karl-Heinrich/**Bunners**, Christian et al. (Eds.): Handbuch der Predigt, Evangelische Verlagsanstalt, Berlin 1990

2004    **Blank**, Udo: Wer hilft hier wem? Predigt zu Lk 6, 36–42, in: Jürgen Gohde (Ed.): Diakonisch predigen, loc. cit., Stuttgart 2004, 46–49

1980    **Blasig**, Winfried: Welche Predigt hilft?, in: Werkstatt Predigt, Vol. 8, 1980, 41–50

2010    Idem: Indikativisch, narrativ und befreiend? Homiletische Anmerkungen zur Predigt von der Sünde, in: Mareile Lasogga/Udo Hahn (Eds.): Gegenwärtige Herausforderungen und Möglichkeiten christlicher Rede von der Sünde, Amt der VELKD, Hannover 2010, 67–88

1989    **Bloom**, Harold: Ruin the Sacred Truths. Poetry and Belief from the Bible to the Present, Harvard University Press, London/Cambridge/Mass. 1989

1968    **Bohren**, Rudolf: Unsere Kasualpraxis – eine missionarische Gelegenheit? (= TEH, Vol. 147), Chr. Kaiser, München, 3rd ed., 1968

1971    Idem: Die Gestalt der Predigt, in: Gert Hummel (Ed.), Aufgabe der Predigt, loc. cit., 1971, 207–231

1980    Idem: Predigtlehre [1971], Chr. Kaiser, München, 4th ed., 1980

1981    Idem: Die Differenz zwischen Meinen und Sagen. Anmerkungen zu Ernst Lange, Predigen als Beruf, in: PTh, Vol. 70, 1998, 416–430

1993    Idem: Predigtlehre [1971], Chr. Kaiser, München, 6th ed., 1993

1989    **Bohren**, Rudolf/**Jörns**, Klaus-Peter (Eds.): Die Predigtanalyse als Weg zur Predigt, Francke, Tübingen 1989

1999    **Bond**, L. Susan: Trouble with Jesus. Women, Christology and Preaching, Chalice Press, St. Louis/Mo. 1999

1937    **Bonhoeffer**, Dietrich: Nachfolge, Chr. Kaiser, München 1937

2010    Idem: Letters and Papers from Prison (= Dietrich Bonhoeffer Works, Vol. 8), ed. by John W. de Gruchy, Fortress Press, Minneapolis/Minn. 2010

2005    Idem: Ethics (= Dietrich Bonhoeffer Works, Vol. 6), ed. by Clifford J. Green, Fortress Press, Minneapolis/Minn. 2005

1965    Idem: Gesammelte Schriften, ed. by Eduard Bethge, Vol. IV, Chr. Kaiser, München 1965

1998    Idem: Predigten – Auslegungen – Meditationen (1925–1945), ed. by Otto Dudzus, Chr. Kaiser, Gütersloh 1998

2000   **Brinkmann**, Frank Thomas: Praktische Homiletik. Ein Leitfaden zur Predigtvorbereitung, Kohlhammer, Stuttgart 2000

2014   **Brothers**, Michael A.: Distance in Preaching. Room to Speak, Space to Listen, Eerdmans, Grand Rapids/Mich. 2014

2005   **Brown**, Sally A. (Ed.): Lament. Reclaiming Practices in Pulpit, Pew and Public Square, Westminster John Knox Press, Louisville/Ky. 2005

1932   **Brunner**, Emil: Die Frage nach dem „Anknüpfungspunkt" als Problem der Theologie, in: ZZ, Vol. 10, 1932, 505–532

1949   **Brunner**, Peter: Die Schriftlesung im Gottesdienst an Sonn- und Feiertagen, in: Joachim Beckmann/Peter Brunner et al.: Der Gottesdienst an Sonn- und Feiertagen. Untersuchungen zur Kirchenagende I/1, Bertelsmann, Gütersloh 1949

1965   **Buber**, Martin: Das dialogische Prinzip, Lampert Schneider, Heidelberg, 2nd ed., 1965

1994   **Bühler**, Axel (Ed.): Unzeitgemäße Hermeneutik. Verstehen und Interpretation im Denken der Aufklärung, Klostermann, Frankfurt/M. 1999

2011   **Bühler**, Karl: Theory of Language. The Representational Function of Language [1934], John Benjamins Publishing, Amsterdam/Philadelphia 2011

1995   **Bukowski**, Peter: Predigt wahrnehmen. Homiletische Perspektiven, Neukirchener Verlag, Neukirchen-Vluyn, 3rd ed., 1995

1955   **Bultmann**, Rudolf: Essays, Philosophical and Theological, SCM Press, London 1955

1964   Idem: Glaube und Verstehen, Vol. I, Mohr, Tübingen, 5th ed., 1964

1969   Idem: Faith and Understanding, Vol. I, ed. by Robert Funk, Harper & Row, New York/ Evanston 1969

1972   Idem: Glaube und Verstehen, Vol. II, Mohr, Tübingen, 7th ed., 1972

1985   Idem: New testament and mythology [1941], in: Idem: New testament and mythology and other basic writings, selected, ed. and transl. by Schubert M. Ogden, SCM Press, London 1985, 1–44

1990   **Bunners**, Christian: Die Hörer, in: Karl-Heinrich Bieritz/Christian Bunners et al. (Eds.): Handbuch der Predigt, loc. cit., 1990, 137–182

1990   **Burbach**, Christiane: Argumentation in der „politischen Predigt". Untersuchungen zur Kommunikationskultur in theologischem Interesse (= ErTh, Vol. 17), Peter Lang, Frankfurt/M. et al. 1990

1987   **Buttrick**, David: Homiletic. Moves und Structures, Fortress Press, Philadelphia 1987

2002   Idem: Speaking Jesus. Homiletic Theology and the Sermon on the Mount, Westminster John Knox Press, Louisville/Ky. 2002

2007   Idem: Speaking Conflict. Stories of a Controversial Jesus, Westminster John Knox Press, Louisville/Ky. 2007

## C

1929   **Calvin**, Jean: Christianae religionis Institutio [1536], in: Joannis Calvini Opera Selecta, ed. by Peter Barth, Wilhelm Niesel and Dora Scheuner, Vol. I, München 1929

1960   Idem: Auslegung der Heiligen Schrift [1546], Neue Reihe (AHS.NR), ed. by Otto Weber, Vol. 16, Verlag der Buchhandlungen des Erziehungsvereins, Neukirchen 1960

2002   **Campbell**, Charles L.: The Word Before the Powers. An Ethic of Preaching, Westminster John Knox Press, Louisville/Ky. 2002

2012   **Campbell**, Charles L./**Cilliers**, Johann H.: Preaching Fools. The Gospel as a Rhetoric of Fully, Baylor University Press, Waco/Tex. 2012

2006    Campbell, Charles L./Saunders, Stanley P.: The Word on the Street. Performing the Scriptures in the Urban Context [2000], Reprint Wipf and Stock, Eugene/Oreg. 2006

2002    Cannon, Katie Geneva: Teaching Preaching. Isaac Rufus Clark and Black Sacred Rhetoric, Continuum, New York 2002

1975    Casper, Bernhard: Sprache und Theologie, Herder, Freiburg/Basel/Wien 1975

2012    Charbonnier, Lars/Merzyn, Konrad/Meyer, Peter (Eds.): Homiletik. Aktuelle Konzepte und ihre Umsetzung. Vandenhoeck & Ruprecht, Göttingen 2012

1998    Childers, Jana: Performing the Word. Preaching as Theatre, Abingdon Press, Nashville/ Tenn. 1998

2008    Childers, Jana/Schmit, Clayton J. (Eds.): Performance in Preaching. Bringing the Sermon to Life, Baker Academic, Grand Rapids/Mich. 2008

1976    Cicero: De oratore. Lateinisch-deutsche Ausgabe. Übersetzt, kommentiert und mit einer Einleitung, ed. by Harald Merklin, Reclam, Stuttgart, 2nd ed., 1976

2010    Clayborn, Patrick: Preaching as an Act of Spirit. The Homiletical Theory of Howard Thurman, Homiletic, Vol. 35, 2010, 3–16

2012    Conrad, Ruth: Kirchenbild und Predigtziel. Eine problemgeschichtliche Studie zu ekklesiologischen Dimensionen der Homiletik (= PThGG, Vol. 11), Mohr Siebeck, Tübingen 2012

1984    Cornehl, Peter: Nachwort zu Ernst Lange, Chancen des Alltags, loc. cit., 1984, 346–349

2001    Cornelius-Bundschuh, Jochen: Die Kirche des Wortes. Zum evangelischen Predigt- und Gemeindeverständnis (= APTLH, Vol. 39), Vandenhoeck & Ruprecht, Göttingen 2001.

1995    Crüsemann, Frank/Romberg, Walter: Sondervotum zur „Stellungnahme der Theologischen Ausschüsse von EKU und VELKD zum ‚KLAK-Votum‘", in: Streit um das Gottesdienstbuch, loc. cit., 1995, 30f.


D

1990    Daewel, Hartwig: Der Weg zur Predigt, in: Karl-Heinrich Bieritz/Christian Bunners et al. (Eds.): Handbuch der Predigt, loc. cit., 1990, 497–541

2001    Dahlgrün, Corinna: Nicht in die Leere falle die Vielfalt des irdischen Seins. Von der Notwendigkeit eschatologischer Predigt, Peter Lang, Frankfurt/M. et al. 2001

2005    Dahm, Karl-Wilhelm: Frust und Lust im heutigen Pfarrberuf, in: DtPfrBl, Vol. 105, 2005, 232–237.

1991a   Daiber, Karl-Fritz: Predigt als religiöse Rede. Homiletische Überlegungen im Anschluss an eine empirische Untersuchung (= Predigen und Hören, Vol. 3), Chr. Kaiser, München 1991

1991b   Idem: Verschränkung der Orte: Politische Predigt, in: Idem (Ed.): Predigt als religiöse Rede, loc. cit., München 1992, 172–185

1983    Daiber, Karl-Fritz/Dannowski, Hans Werner et al.: Predigen und Hören. Ergebnisse einer Gottesdienstbefragung, Vol. 2, Chr. Kaiser, München 1983

1979    Dalferth, Ingolf Ulrich: Religiöse Sprechakte als Kriterien der Religiosität? Kritik einer Konfusion, in: LingBibl,Vol. 44, 1979, 101–118

1973    Dannowski, Hans Werner: Möglichkeiten und Grenzen der Contentanalyse. Dargestellt anhand einer Untersuchung der Ordinationspredigt M. Kruses, in: Werkstatt Predigt, Vol. 1, 1973, 28–36

1975    Idem: Sprachbefähigung in der Ausbildung, in: Peter Düsterfeld/Hans Bernhard Kaufmann (Eds.): Didaktik der Predigt, loc. cit., 1975, 163–175

1981    Idem: Ansätze zu einer Typologie von Erzählpredigten, in: Horst Nitschke (Ed.): Erzählende Predigten, Vol. 2, loc. cit., 1981, 152–157

1985    Idem: Kompendium der Predigtlehre, G. Mohn, Gütersloh 1985

1972    **Dantine,** Wilhelm: Die prophetische Dimension des Amtes der Versöhnung, in: Andreas Baudis et al. (Eds.): Richte unsere Füße auf den Weg des Friedens. H. Gollwitzer zum 70. Geburtstag, Chr. Kaiser, München 1972, 285–298

1872    **Darwin,** Charles: The Origin of Species. By Means of Natural Selection, or the Preservation of Favoured Races in the Struggle for Life, John Murray, London, 6th ed., 1872

1989    **Debus,** Gerhard et al.: Thesen zur Predigtanalyse, in: Rudolf Bohren/Klaus-Peter Jörns (Eds.): Die Predigtanalyse als Weg zur Predigt, loc. cit., 1989, 55–61

2006    **Deeg,** Alexander: Predigt und Derascha. Homiletische Textlektüre im Dialog mit dem Judentum, Vandenhoeck & Ruprecht, Göttingen 2006

2014    **Deeg,** Alexander/**Garhammer,** Erich/**Kranemann,** Benedikt (Eds.): Gottesdienst und Predigt – evangelisch und katholisch (= EKGP, Vol. 1), Neukirchener Verlagsgesellschaft, Neukirchen-Vluyn 2014

1979    **Denecke,** Axel: Persönlich predigen. Anleitungen und Modelle für die Praxis, G. Mohn, Gütersloh 1979

2004    **Deselaers,** Paul: Psalmen predigen. Ermutigung aus der neuen Psalmenforschung, in: Frank-Lothar Hossfeld/Ludger Schwienhorst-Schönberger (Eds.): Das Manna fällt auch noch heute. Beiträge zur Geschichte des Alten Testaments (= HBS, Vol. 44), Verlag Herder, Freiburg/Basel/Wien 2004, 158–173

1952    **Dibelius,** Otto: Predigten, Verlag Die Kirche, Berlin 1952

1939    **Diem,** Hermann: Warum Textpredigt? Predigten und Kritiken als Beitrag zur Lehre von der Predigt, Chr. Kaiser, München 1939

1971    Idem: Der Theologe zwischen Text und Predigt [1960], in: Gert Hummel (Ed.): Aufgabe der Predigt, loc. cit., 1971, 278–294

2008–   **Dinkel,** Christoph (Ed.): Im Namen Gottes. Kanzelreden (6 Bde.), Radius-Verlag, Stuttgart
2013    2008–2013 (Vol. 1, Erste Predigtreihe, 2008; Vol. 2, Zweite Predigtreihe, 2009; Vol. 3, Dritte Predigtreihe, 2010; Vol. 4, Vierte Predigtreihe, 2011; Vol. 5, Fünfte Predigtreihe, 2012; Vol. 6, Sechste Predigtreihe, 2013)

1921    **Dobschütz,** Ernst von: Vom vierfachen Schriftsinn. Die Geschichte einer Theorie, in: Harnack-Ehrung. Beiträge zur Kirchengeschichte, ed. by Adolf von Harnack, Hinrichs'sche Buchhandlung, Leipzig 1921, 1–13

1940    **Doerne,** Martin: Luther und die Predigt, in: Luther. Mitteilungen der Luthergesellschaft, Vol. 22, 1940, 36–42

1999    **Dokumentation des Thüringer Kanzelstreits.** Reden über Gott und die Welt – 52 Sonntagspredigten, ed. by Landesstelle für Jugendarbeit der Ev.-luth. Landeskirche in Thüringen, Eisenach 1999

1975    **Düsterfeld,** Peter/**Kaufmann,** Hans Bernhard (Eds.): Didaktik der Predigt. Materialien zur homiletischen Ausbildung und Fortbildung, Comenius-Institut, Münster 1975

1992    **Düwel,** Bernd: Bilder für den Prediger. Ein Beitrag zur Spiritualität des Predigtdienstes, EOS, St. Ottilien 1992

2004 **Dutzmann**, Martin/**Potthoff**, Karlheinz: Der vorgeschlagene Predigttext. Kritische Anmerkungen zweier Prediger, in: Perikopenordnung in der Diskussion, loc. cit., Hannover 2004, 53–56

# E

1962 **Ebeling**, Gerhard: The Nature of Faith, Muhlenberg Press, Philadelphia 1962

1975 Idem: Wort und Glaube, Vol. III: Beiträge zur Fundamentaltheologie, Soteriologie und Ekklesiologie, J. C. B. Mohr, Tübingen 1975

1979 Idem: Dogmatik des christlichen Glaubens, Vol. I, J. C. B. Mohr, Tübingen 1979

1989 Idem: Fundamentaltheologische Erwägungen zur Predigt, in: Albrecht Beutel et al. (Eds.): Homiletisches Lesebuch, loc. cit., 1989, 68–83

1972 **Eco**, Umberto: Einführung in die Semiotik, Fink Verlag, München 1972

1977 Idem: Das offene Kunstwerk, Suhrkamp, Frankfurt/M. 1977

1985 Idem: Trattato di semiotica generale, Bompiani, Milano, 10th ed., 1985

1987 Idem: Streit der Interpretationen, Universitätsverlag Konstanz, Konstanz 1987

2006 **Edgerton**, W. Dow: Speak to Me That I May Speak. A Spirituality of Preaching, Pilgrim Press, Cleveland/Oh. 2006

1995 **Egli**, Andreas: Erzählen in der Predigt. Untersuchungen zu Form und Leistungsfähigkeit erzählender Sprache in der Predigt, Theologischer Verlag Zürich, Zürich 1995

2005 **Ehrensperger**, Alfred: Die westlichen, gallikanischen Liturgien, in: Veröffentlichungen der Liturgiekommission evangelisch-reformierten Kirchen der deutschsprachigen Schweiz, Zürich 2005, Lieferung AZ III B 08, 1–27, 1

1996 **Engels**, Johannes: Genera causarum, in: Historisches Wörterbuch der Rhetorik (Vol. 3), ed. by Gert Ueding, Max Niemeyer Verlag, Tübingen 1996, 701–721

1984 **Engemann**, Wilfried: Die Verkündigung als transaktionales Ereignis zwischen Prediger und Hörer. Eine Studie zur Anwendbarkeit der Transaktionsanalyse auf homiletische Fragehinsichten – Relevanzen und Probleme, Diss. A, Univ. Rostock, 1984

1989 Idem: Kritik der Homiletik aus semiotischer Sicht. Ein Beitrag zur Grundlegung der Predigtlehre, Habilitationsschrift, Univ. Greifswald 1989

1990 Idem: Wider den redundanten Exzess. Semiotisches Plädoyer für eine ergänzungsbedürftige Predigt, in: ThLZ, Vol. 115, 1990, 785–800

1992a Idem: Persönlichkeitsstruktur und Predigt. Homiletik aus transaktionsanalytischer Sicht, Evangelische Verlagsanstalt, Leipzig, 2nd ed., 1992

1992b Idem: Semiotik und Theologie – Szenen einer Ehe, in: Wilfried Engemann/Rainer Volp (Eds.): Gib mir ein Zeichen. Zur Bedeutung der Semiotik für theologische Praxis- und Denkmodelle, de Gruyter, Berlin/New York 1992, 3–28

1992c Idem: Semiotischer Essay über die eine und andere Predigt, in: PSt(S), Vol. I, 1992, Kreuz Verlag, Stuttgart 1992, 9–24

1992d Idem: Wie beerbt man die Dialektische Theologie? Kleine homiletische Studie, in: Wilfried Engemann/Rainer Volp (Eds.): Gib mir ein Zeichen. Zur Bedeutung der Semiotik für theologische Praxis- und Denkmodelle, de Gruyter, Berlin/New York 1992, 162–173

1993a Idem: Semiotische Homiletik. Prämissen – Analysen – Konsequenzen (= THLI, Vol. 5), A. Francke Verlag, Tübingen/Basel 1993

1993b Idem: Wider die Verdummung des Salzes. Predigten aus dem Bauch der „Dicken Marie", Evangelische Verlagsanstalt, Leipzig 1993

1996    Idem: Der „moderne Mensch" – Abschied von einem Klischee. Fragen zur Problematik der kulturanthropologischen Prämissen Praktischer Theologie und kirchlichen Handelns heute, in: WzM, Vol. 48, 1996, 447–458. Reprint of an edited version in: Wilfried Engemann, 2003b, 346–358

1998a   Idem: Der Spielraum der Predigt und der Ernst der Verkündigung, in: Erich Garhammer/ Heinz-Günther Schöttler (Eds.): Predigt als offenes Kunstwerk, loc. cit., 1998, 180–200. Reprint of an edited version in: Wilfried Engemann, 2003b, 141–166

1998b   Idem: „Und dies habt zum Zeichen." Spezifische Gesichtspunkte der Semiotik Umberto Ecos in praktisch-theologischer Engführung, in: Bernhard Dressler/Michael Meyer-Blanck (Eds.): Religion zeigen. Religionspädagogik und Semiotik, LIT-Verlag, Münster 1998, 300–324. Reprint of an edited version in: Wilfried Engemann, 2003b, 167–188

1999    Idem: Wie kommt ein Prediger auf die Kanzel? Elemente zu einer Theologie der Predigt im Kontext des Weimarer Predigtstreits – 21 Thesen (= Wechselwirkungen. Traktate zur Praktischen Theologie und ihren Grundlagen, Vol. 33), Spenner, Waltrop 1999

2000a   Idem: Texte über Texte. Die Beziehungen zwischen Theologie, Literaturwissenschaft und Rezeptionsästhetik, in: PrTh, Vol. 35, 2000, 227–245. Reprint of an edited version in: Wilfried Engemann, 2003b, 232–245

2000b   Idem: Zum Problem der Maschinisierung der Kommunikation. Herausforderungen für den Erwerb und die Pflege von Religiosität in der Gegenwart, in: WzM, Vol. 52, 2000, 141–155.

2000c   Idem: Semiotik, praktisch-theologisch, in: TRE, Vol. 31, 2000, 134–142

2001a   Idem: Ernten, wo man nicht gesät hat. Rechtfertigungspredigt heute (mit einem Geleitwort von Karl-Heinrich Bieritz), Luther-Verlag, Bielefeld 2001

2001b   Idem: Predigen und Zeichen setzen: Eine homiletische Skizze mit Beispielen, in: Uta Pohl-Patalong/Frank Muchlinsky (Eds.): Predigen im Plural. Homiletische Perspektiven, EB-Verlag, Hamburg 2001, 7–24

2001c   Idem: Predigt als Schöpfungsakt: Zur Auswirkung der Predigt auf das Leben eines Menschen, in: Idem (Ed.:) Theologie der Predigt, loc. cit., Leipzig 2001d, 71–92

2001d   Idem (Ed.): Theologie der Predigt. Grundlagen – Modelle – Konsequenzen, Anniversary publication in honour of Karl-Heinrich Bieritz (= APrTh, Vol. 21) Evangelische Verlags-anstalt, Leipzig 2001

2002    Idem: Lebenskunst als Beratungsziel. Zur Bedeutung der Praktischen Philosophie für die Seelsorge der Gegenwart, in: Michael Böhme et al. (Eds.): Entwickeltes Leben. Neue Herausforderungen für die Seelsorge, Anniversary publication in honour of Jürgen Ziemer, Evangelische Verlagsanstalt, Leipzig 2002, 95–125

2003a   Idem: Die Person als Subjekt pastoralen Handelns. Positionen und Perspektiven, in: Wilfried Engemann: Personen, Zeichen und das Evangelium, loc. cit., 2003c, 273–292

2003b   Idem: Personen und Beziehungen. Predigt und Transaktionsanalyse, in: Wilfried Engemann: Personen, Zeichen und das Evangelium, loc. cit., 2003c, 293–319

2003c   Idem: Personen, Zeichen und das Evangelium. Argumentationsmuster der Praktischen Theologie (= APrTh, Vol. 23), Evangelische Verlagsanstalt, Leipzig 2003

2003d   Idem: Rezeptionsästhetik und Theologie. Konvergente Perspektiven, in: Wolfgang Adam et al. (Eds.): Wissenschaft und Systemveränderung. Rezeptionsforschung in Ost und West, Universitätsverlag Carl Winter, Heidelberg 2003, 295–317

2003e   Idem: „Unser Text sagt. . .“ Hermeneutischer Versuch zur Interpretation und Überwindung des „Texttods“ der Predigt [1996], in: Wilfried Engemann: Personen, Zeichen und das Evangelium, loc. cit., 2003c, 108–140

2004   Idem: Die Lebenskunst und das Evangelium. Über eine zentrale Aufgabe kirchlichen Handelns und deren Herausforderung für die Praktische Theologie, in: ThLZ, Vol. 129, 2004, 875–896

2006a   Idem: Aneignung der Freiheit. Lebenskunst und Willensarbeit in der Seelsorge, in: WzM, Vol. 58, 2006, 28–48

2006b   Idem: Erschöpft von der Freiheit – Zur Freiheit berufen. Predigt als Lebens-Kunde unter den Bedingungen der Postmoderne, in: Hanns Kerner (Ed.): Predigt in einer polyphonen Kultur, loc. cit., 2006, 65–91

2007a   Idem: Aneignung der Freiheit. Essays zur christlichen Lebenskunst, Kreuz-Verlag, Stuttgart 2007

2007b   Idem: Kommunikation des Evangeliums als interdisziplinäres Projekt. Praktische Theologie im Dialog mit außertheologischen Wissenschaften, in: Christian Grethlein/ Helmut Schwier (Eds.): Praktische Theologie. Eine Theorie- und Problemgeschichte (= APrTh, Vol. 33), Evangelische Verlagsanstalt, Leipzig 2007, 137–232

2007c   Idem: Praktische Theologie. Eine Einführung in Selbstverständnis, Struktur und Methodik der Praktischen Theologie, in: Wolfgang Marhold/Bernd Schröder (Eds.): Evangelische Theologie studieren. Eine Einführung, 2nd ed., LIT-Verlag, Münster 2007, 137–170

2007d   Idem: Paradies verloren – Leben gewonnen. Über unseren Weg in die Welt, in: Wilfried Engemann: Aneignung der Freiheit, loc. cit., 2007, 147–158

2007e   Idem: Wohlan denn, Herz, nimm Abschied und gesunde. Buchbericht zu Klaus-Peter Jörns: Notwendige Abschiede. Auf dem Weg zu einem glaubwürdigen Christentum, Gütersloh, 2nd ed., 2004, in: WzM, Vol. 59, 2007, 405–410

2008a   Idem: Ein Fall für die Predigt: Gefährdete Freiheit. Überlegungen zur homiletischen Grundsituation der Sonntagspredigt, in: Kristian Fechtner/Lutz Friedrichs (Eds.): Normalfall Sonntagsgottesdienst? Gottesdienst und Sonntagskultur im Umbruch, Kohlhammer, Stuttgart 2008, 130–140

2008b   Idem: Virtuelle Realität und die Welt des Glaubens – oder: Der Wirklichkeitsbezug religiöser und theologischer Praxis. Ein Geleitwort, in: Ilona Nord: Realitäten des Glaubens. Zur virtuellen Dimension christlicher Religiosität, Verlag De Gruyter, Berlin 2008, XI–XXXI

2009a   Idem: Das „Lebensgefühl“ im Blickpunkt der Seelsorge. Zum seelsorglichen Umgang mit Emotionen, in: WzM, Vol. 61, 2009, 271–286

2009b   Idem: Die emotionale Dimension des Glaubens als Herausforderung für die Seelsorge, in: WzM, Vol. 61, 2009, 287–299

2009c   Idem: Die Problematisierung der Predigtaufgabe als Basis homiletischer Reflexion. Eine Methode der Predigtvorbereitung, in: Wilfried Engemann/Frank Lütze (Eds.): Grundfragen der Predigt, loc. cit., 2nd ed. 2009, 411–427

2010a   Idem: Homiletische Literatur zu Beginn des 21. Jahrhunderts. Schwerpunkte, Problemanzeigen und Perspektiven (Teil I), in: ThR, Vol. 75, 2010, 163–200

2010b   Idem: Homiletische Literatur zu Beginn des 21. Jahrhunderts. Schwerpunkte, Problemanzeigen und Perspektiven (Teil II), in: ThR, Vol. 75, 2010, 304–341

2013    Idem: Lebensgefühl und Glaubenskultur. Menschsein als Vorgabe und Zweck der religiösen Praxis des Christentums, in: WzM, Vol. 65, 2013, 218–237

2016a    Idem (Ed.): Handbuch der Seelsorge. Grundlagen und Profile, Leipzig, 3rd., newly revised and extended ed., 2016

2016b    Idem: Homiletische Literatur zwischen 2010 und 2015. Schwerpunkte, Problemanzeigen und Perspektiven (Teil I), in: ThR, Vol. 81, 2016, 1–34

2016c    Idem: Homiletische Literatur zwischen 2010 und 2015. Schwerpunkte, Problemanzeigen und Perspektiven (Teil II), in: ThR, Vol. 81, 2016, 117–178

2009    **Engemann**, Wilfried/**Lütze**, Frank (Eds.): Grundfragen der Predigt. Ein Studienbuch, Evangelische Verlagsanstalt, Leipzig, 2nd ed., 2009

2002    **Ergänzungsband zum Evangelischen Gottesdienstbuch** für die Evangelische Kirche der Union und für die Vereinigte Evangelisch-Lutherische Kirche Deutschlands, ed. by Kirchenleitung der VELKD und im Auftrag des Rates der Kirchenkanzlei der EKU, Verlagsgemeinschaft „Evangelisches Gottesdienstbuch", Berlin et al. 2002

1966    **Erikson**, Erik H.: Ontogeny of Ritualization in Man, in: Philosophical Transactions of the Royal Society of London. Series B, Biological Sciences, Vol. 251, No. 772: A Discussion on Ritualization of Behaviour in Animals and Man, 1966, 337–349

1995    **Eßer**, Hans Helmut: Die Lehre vom „testimonium Spiritus – Sancti internum" bei Calvin, in: Verbindliches Zeugnis II. Schriftauslegung – Lehramt – Rezeption, ed. by Wolfhart Pannenberg and Theodor Schneider (= DiKi, Vol. 9/II), Herder, Freiburg i. Br. 1995, 246–258

2000    **Evangelisches Gottesdienstbuch**. Agende für die Evangelische Kirche der Union und für die Vereinigte Evangelisch-Lutherische Kirche Deutschlands, ed. by Kirchenleitung der VELKD, Verlagsgemeinschaft „Evangelisches Gottesdienstbuch", Berlin et al. 2000


**F**

2007    **Fechtner**, Kristian: Im Rhythmus des Kirchenjahres. Vom Sinn der Feste und Zeiten, Gütersloher Verlagshaus, Gütersloh 2007

1931    **Fendt**, Leonhard: Die alten Perikopen, Mohr, Tübingen 1931

1941    Idem: Die neuen Perikopen, Mohr, Tübingen 1941

1970    Idem: Homiletik, revised by Bernhard Klaus, de Gruyter, Berlin, 2nd ed., 1970

1957    **Fischer**, Martin (Ed.): Einer trage des anderen Last. Vom geordneten Dienen in der Gemeinde. Ein diakonischer Predigtband, Lettner-Verlag, Berlin 1957

1951    **Forck**, Bernhard Heinrich: Predigt zu Mt 9,35–38, in: Wilhelm Herbst (Ed.): Das Zeugnis der Kirche in der Gegenwart, Buchverlagsgesellschaft für christliche Literatur, Nürnberg 1951, 298–302

1997    **Fremde Heimat Kirche**. Die dritte EKD-Erhebung über Kirchenmitgliedschaft, ed. by Klaus Engelhardt, Hermann von Loewenich and Peter Steinacker, G. Mohn, Gütersloh 1997

2010    **Franz**, Ansgar: Unterschiedliche Lesarten. Perikopenordnung in der Ökumene, in: Auf dem Weg zur Perikopenrevision. Dokumentation einer wissenschaftlichen Fachtagung, ed. by Kirchenamt der EKD, Amt der UEK and Amt der VELKD, Hannover 2010, 153–177

2013    Idem: Das theologische Verständnis der Auswahl von Verkündigungstexten für die Liturgie, in: Birgit Jeggle-Merz/Benedikt Kranemann (Eds.): Liturgie und Konfession. Grundfragen der Liturgiewissenschaft im interkonfessionellen Gespräch, Freiburg/Basel/Wien 2013, 17–28

1922    **Freud**, Sigmund: Zur Psychopathologie des Alltagslebens. Über Vergessen, Versprechen, Vergreifen, Aberglaube und Irrtum, Internationaler Psychoanalytischer Verlag GmbH, Leipzig et al., 8th ed., 1922

1964    Idem: New Introductory Lectures On Psycho-Analysis and Other Works (= The Standard Edition of the Complete Psychological Works of Sigmund Freud, Vol. XXII [1932–1936]), ed. by James Strachey, The Hogarth Press and the Institute of Psychoanalysis, London 1964

1984    Idem: Psychoanalyse. Ausgewählte Schriften [1915], Reclam, Leipzig 1984

2000    **Freund**, Annegret: Aggression als Lebensenergie? Kain und Abel im homiletischen Feld. Eine Predigt und einige Auredite, in: Klaus Petzold/Klaus Raschzok (Eds.): Vertraut den neuen Wegen. Praktische Theologie zwischen Ost und West, Anniversary publication in honour of Klaus-Peter Hertzsch, Evangelische Verlagsanstalt, Leipzig 2000, 219–245

2008    **Friedrichs**, Lutz: Kasualpraxis in der Spätmoderne. Studien zu einer Praktischen Theologie an den Übergängen (= APrTh, Vol. 37), Evangelische Verlagsanstalt, Leipzig 2008

2001    **Früh**, Werner: Inhaltsanalyse. Theorie und Praxis, Universitätsverlag Konstanz, Konstanz, 5th ed., 2001

1978    **Fuchs**, Ottmar: Sprechen in Gegensätzen. Meinung und Gegenmeinung in kirchlicher Rede, Kösel, München 1978

**G**

2000    **Gärtner**, Stefan: Gottesrede in (post)moderner Gesellschaft. Grundlagen einer praktisch-theologischen Sprachlehre, Schöning, Paderborn et al. 2000

1998    **Garhammer**, Erich/**Schöttler**, Heinz-Günther (Eds.): Predigt als offenes Kunstwerk. Homiletik und Rezeptionsästhetik, Don Bosco Verlag, München 1998

2006    **Garhammer**, Erich et al. (Eds.): Kontrapunkte. Katholische und protestantische Predigtkultur (= ÖSP, Vol. 5), Don Bosco, München 2006

1978    **Geest**, Hans van der: Du hast mich angesprochen, Theologischer Verlag Zürich, Zürich 1978

1991    Idem: Das Wort geschieht. Wege zur seelsorgerlichen Predigt. Mit 25 Predigtskizzen, Theologischer Verlag Zürich, Zürich 1991

2013    **Gidion**, Anne/**Arnold**, Jochen/**Martinsen**, Raute (Eds.): Leicht gesagt! Biblische Lesungen und Gebete zum Kirchenjahr in Leichter Sprache (= GGG, Vol. 22), Lutherisches Verlagshaus, Hannover 2013

1988    **Göttert**, Karl-Heinz: Kommunikationsideale. Untersuchungen zur europäischen Konversationstheorie, Verlag Ludicium, München 1988

1998    Idem: Konversation, in: Historisches Wörterbuch der Rhetorik, Vol. 4, ed. by Gert Ueding, Max Niemeyer, Tübingen 1998, 1322–1333

1979    **Götzinger**, Karl: Predigtanalyse, in: Rolf Zerfaß/Franz Kamphaus (Eds.), Die Kompetenz des Predigers, loc. cit., 1979, 165–170

2004    **Gohde**, Jürgen (Ed.): Diakonisch predigen. Predigten aus dem Erfahrungsfeld der Diakonie, Kohlhammer, Stuttgart 2004

1962    **Gollwitzer**, Helmut: Erwägungen zur politischen Predigt, in: Idem: Forderungen der Freiheit. Aufsätze und Reden zur politischen Ethik, Chr. Kaiser, München 1962, 97–112

1987    **Gräb,** Wilhelm: Rechtfertigung von Lebensgeschichten. Erwägungen zu einer theologischen Theorie der Amtshandlungen, in: PTh, Vol. 76, 1987, 21–38.

1990a   Idem: Arbeit an Lebensdeutungen. Religionspädagogische Überlegungen zur gegenwärtigen Lage, in: EvErz, Vol. 42, 1990, 266–277

1990b   Idem: Der hermeneutische Imperativ. Lebensgeschichte als religiöse Selbstauslegung, in: Walter Sparn (Ed.): Wer schreibt meine Lebensgeschichte? G. Mohn, Gütersloh 1990, 79–89

1991    Idem: Wofür das Christentum heute steht. Überlegungen zum Stellenwert systematisch-theologischer Reflexion in der Predigtvorbereitung, in: PSt(S), Vol. II, 1/1991, 7–16

1993    Idem: Kirche als Ort religiöser Deutungskultur. Erwägungen zum Zusammenhang von Kirche, Religion und individueller Lebensgeschichte, in: Ulrich Barth/Wilhelm Gräb (Eds.): Gott im Selbstbewusstsein der Moderne. Zum neuzeitlichen Begriff der Religion, G. Mohn, Gütersloh 1993, 222–239

1997a   Idem: „Ich rede mit dem Hörer über sein Leben." Ernst Langes Anstöße zu einer neuen Homiletik, in: PTh, Vol. 86, 1997, 498–515

1997b   Idem: Lebensgeschichtliche Sinnarbeit. Die Kasualpraxis als Indikator für die Öffentlichkeit der kirchlichen Religionskultur, in: Volker Drehsen et al. (Eds.): Der ‚ganze Mensch'. Perspektiven lebensgeschichtlicher Identität, Anniversary publication in honour of Dietrich Rössler, de Gruyter, Berlin/New York 1997, 219–240

2013    Idem: Predigtlehre. Über religiöse Rede, Vandenhoeck & Ruprecht, Göttingen 2013

1812    **Gräffe,** Johann Friedrich Christoph: Über den Werth academischer homiletischer Vorübungen nebst Beschreibung meines homiletischen Seminariums, Dieterich, Göttingen 1812

2007    **Grethlein,** Christian: Grundinformation Kasualien. Kommunikation des Evangeliums an Übergängen des Lebens, Vandenhoeck & Ruprecht, Göttingen 2007

2009    Idem: Pfarrer – ein theologischer Beruf! Edition Chrismon, Frankfurt/M. 2009

2013    Idem: Was gilt in der Kirche? Perikopenrevision als Beitrag zur Kirchenreform (= ThLZ.F, Vol. 27), Evangelische Verlagsanstalt, Leipzig 2013

2014    Idem: Mut zu größerer Flexibilität. Die aktuelle Perikopenrevision und viele offene Fragen, in: DtPfrBl, Vol. 114, 2014, 77–81

2002    **Grevel,** Jan Peter: Die Predigt und ihr Text. Grundzüge einer hermeneutischen Homiletik, Neukirchener, Neukirchen-Vluyn 2002

1979a   **Grice,** Herbert Paul: Intendieren, Meinen, Bedeuten, in: Georg Meggle (Ed.): Handlung, Kommunikation, Bedeutung, Suhrkamp, Frankfurt/M. 1979, 2–15

1979b   Idem: Sprecher-Bedeutung und Intention, in: Georg Meggle (Ed.): Handlung, Kommunikation, Bedeutung, Suhrkamp, Frankfurt/M. 1979, 16–52

1991    **Grözinger,** Albrecht: Die Sprache des Menschen. Ein Handbuch. Grundwissen für Theologinnen und Theologen, Chr. Kaiser, München 1991

1995    Idem: Praktische Theologie als Kunst der Wahrnehmung, Chr. Kaiser, Gütersloh 1995

1996    Idem: Spielend bei der Sache. Hochschuldidaktische Konsequenzen einer phänomenologischen Religionspädagogik, in: Bernd Beuscher et al.: Prozesse postmoderner Wahrnehmung: Kunst – Religion – Pädagogik, Passagen-Verlag, Wien 1996, 183–190

2004    Idem: Toleranz und Leidenschaft. Über das Predigen in einer pluralistischen Gesellschaft, Gütersloher Verlagshaus, Gütersloh 2004

2008    Idem: Homiletik (= Lehrbuch Praktische Theologie, Vol. 2), Gütersloher Verlagshaus, Gütersloh 2008

2016    **Grossarth-Maticek,** Ronald: Wahrnehmung der eigenen Gottesbeziehung und Gesundheit. Ergebnisse aus den Heidelberger prospektiven Interventionsstudien, in: Wilfried Engemann (Ed.): Menschsein und Religion. Anthropologische Probleme und Perspektiven der religiösen Praxis des Christentums (= WFTR, Vol. 11), Vandenhoeck & Ruprecht, Göttingen 2016, 65–86

## H

1971    **Habermas,** Jürgen: Vorbereitende Bemerkungen zu einer Theorie der kommunikativen Kompetenz, in: Jürgen Habermas/Niklas Luhmann, Theorie der Gesellschaft oder Sozialtechnologie. Was leistet die Systemforschung? Suhrkamp, Frankfurt/M. 1971, 101–141

1972    Idem: Theorie der kommunikativen Kompetenz, in: Horst Holzer/Karl Steinbacher (Eds.), Sprache und Gesellschaft, Hoffmann und Campe, Hamburg 1972, 208–236

1976    Idem: Universalpragmatik, in: Karl-Otto Apel (Ed.): Sprachpragmatik und Philosophie, Suhrkamp, Frankfurt/M. 1976, 235–246

1981    Idem: Theorie des kommunikativen Handelns, Vol. I, Suhrkamp, Frankfurt/M. 1981

2015    **Haendler,** Otto: Grundriss der Praktischen Theologie, Berlin 1957, in: Otto Haendler: Praktische Theologie. Grundriss, Aufsätze und Vorträge, ed. and introduced by Wilfried Engemann (= OHPTh 1), Evangelische Verlagsanstalt, Leipzig 2015, 113–480

2017a   Idem: Die Idee der Kirche in der Predigt, Theol. Habil. Universität Greifswald 1930, Archiv der Humboldt-Universität zu Berlin, NL Haendler F 21, maschinenschriftlich, in: Otto Haendler: Homiletik. Monographien, Aufsätze und Predigtmeditationen, ed. and introduced by Wilfried Engemann (= OHPTh 2), Evangelische Verlagsanstalt, Leipzig 2017, 43–204

2017b   Idem: Die Predigt. Tiefenpsychologische Grundlagen und Grundfragen [1941], Berlin, 3rd ed., 1960, in: Otto Haendler: Homiletik. Monographien, Aufsätze und Predigt-meditationen, ed. and introduced by Wilfried Engemann (= OHPTh 2), Evangelische Verlagsanstalt, Leipzig 2017, 269–632

2001    **Härtner,** Achim/**Eschmann,** Holger: Predigen lernen. Ein Lehrbuch für die Praxis, Christliches Verlagshaus, Stuttgart 2001

1993    **Hamdorf-Ruddies,** Hildegard et al. (Eds.): Zitate für die Predigt. Mit einer Einführung von Manfred Josuttis, Vandenhoeck & Ruprecht, Göttingen 1993

1996    **Handbook for the Revised Common Lectionary,** ed. by Peter C. Bower, Westminster John Knox Press, Louisville/Ky. 1996

1837    **Harms,** Claus: Der Prediger: Wie ihn die Pastoraltheologie Seyn und Thun lehret, hinsichtlich der Predigt, der Kinderlehre und der Vorbereitung der Confirmanden, Universitätsbuchhandlung, Kiel, 2nd ed., 1837

1978    **Harnack,** Theodosius: Praktische Theologie [1878], Vol. 2, Deichert, Erlangen 1978

1973    **Harris,** Thomas A.: I'm ok, you're okay [1969], Avon Books, New York 1973

2010    **Hauschildt,** Eberhard/**Kohler,** Eike/**Schulz,** Claudia: Milieus praktisch. Analyse- und Planungshilfen für Kirche und Gemeinde, Vandenhoeck & Ruprecht, Göttingen 2010

1990    **Haustein,** Manfred: Sprachgestalten der Verkündigung, in: Karl-Heinrich Bieritz/ Christian Bunners et al. (Eds.): Handbuch der Predigt, loc. cit., 1990, 459–496

1974    **Hedman**, Fride: Optimal Responding. A pastoral Dialogue with Transactional Analysis (= Publications of the Institute of Practical Theology at Åbo Akademi, Vol. 9), Åbo 1974

1986    **Hegel**, Georg Friedrich Wilhelm: Werke in 20 Bänden, ed. by Eva Moldenhauer and Karl Markus Michel, Suhrkamp, Frankfurt/M. 1986

1986    **Hegewald**, Wolfgang: Zur Bedeutung des Poetischen für Prediger und Predigt, in: Joachim Dyck/Walter Jens/Gert Ueding (Eds.): Rhetorik, Vol. 5: Rhetorik und Theologie, Verlag Niemeyer, Tübingen 1986, 39–60

1998    Idem: Vom achten Gebot. Nachrichten aus einer Werkstatt der Wörtlichkeit, in: Neue deutsche Literatur, Vol. 46, 1998, 36–44

1996    **Heidegger**, Martin: Being and Time. A Translation of Sein and Zeit, State University of New York Press, Albany 1996

2003    **Heimbrock**, Hans-Günther: Spuren Gottes wahrnehmen. Phänomenologische Impulse für Predigt und Gottesdienst, Stuttgart 2003 (= Christentum heute, Vol. 5), Kohlhammer, Stuttgart 2003

2010    **Hein**, Martin/**Bockelmann**, Thomas (Eds.): Inspiriert! Theater im Gottesdienst – 12 ausgewählte Predigten, Evangelischer Medienverband, Kassel 2010

1979/    **Heine**, Heinrich: Historisch-kritische Gesamtausgabe der Werke, ed. by Manfred
1986    Windfuhr, Hoffmann und Campe, Hamburg, Vol. 8.1, 1979; Vol. 7.1, 1986

2006    **Hell**, Silvia: „Ordnungsgemäß berufen". Eine Empfehlung der Bischofskonferenz der VELKD zur Berufung zu Wortverkündigung und Sakramentsverwaltung nach evangelischem Verständnis – Kritische Anmerkungen zur Amtstheologie, in: Virtueller „Leseraum" der Universität Innsbruck vom 18. 12. 2006, http://www.uibk.ac.at/theol/leseraum/texte/674.html

1990    **Henkys**, Jürgen: Ansätze des Predigtverständnisses, in: Karl-Heinrich Bieritz/Christian Bunners et al. (Eds.): Handbuch der Predigt, loc. cit., 1990, 27–62

1989    **Hermelink**, Jan: Bibliographie zur Predigtanalyse seit 1945, in: Rudolf Bohren/ Klaus-Peter Jörns (Eds.): Die Predigtanalyse als Weg zur Predigt, loc. cit., 1989, 179–186

1992    Idem: Die homiletische Situation. Zur jüngeren Geschichte eines Predigtproblems, Vandenhoeck & Ruprecht, Göttingen 1992

1995    Idem: Predigt in der Werkstatt. Zur Bedeutung der Predigtanalyse in der theologischen Ausbildung, in: BThZ, Vol. 12, 1995, 40–57

1995    **Hermelink**, Jan/**Müske**, Eberhard: Predigt als Arbeit an mentalen Bildern. Zur Rezeption der Textsemiotik in der Predigtanalyse, in: PrTh, Vol. 30, 1995, 219–239; Reprinted in: Wilfried Engemann/Frank Lütze (Eds.): Grundfragen der Predigt, loc. cit., 2nd ed., 2009, 365–387

2010    **Herrmann**, Florian: Leseordnungen in der Gemeinschaft der Evangelischen Kirchen in Europa, in: Auf dem Weg zur Perikopenrevision. Dokumentation einer wissenschaftlichen Fachtagung, ed. by Kirchenamt der EKD/Amt der UEK/Amt der VELKD, Hannover 2010, 185–197. An English version of this text can be found on http://www.leuenberg.net/sites/default/files/media/PDF/liturgie/lectionaries_en.pdf

1990    **Hertzsch**, Klaus-Peter: Predigtlehre: Erwartungen und Möglichkeiten, in: Karl-Heinrich Bieritz/Christian Bunners et al. (Eds.): Handbuch der Predigt, loc. cit., 1990, 11–26

1995    Idem: Die Predigt im Gottesdienst, in: Handbuch der Liturgik. Liturgiewissenschaft in Theologie und Praxis der Kirche, ed. by Karl-Heinrich Bieritz and Hans-Christoph Schmidt-Lauber, Evangelische Verlagsanstalt/Vandenhoeck & Ruprecht, Leipzig/Göttingen 1995

1997    Idem: Christliche Predigt über Texte aus dem Alten Testament, in: BThZ, Vol. 14, 1997, 3–13

1994    **Hess-Lüttich,** Ernest W. B.: Dialog, in: Historisches Wörterbuch der Rhetorik, Vol. 2, ed. by Gert Ueding, Max Niemeyer Verlag, Tübingen 1994, 606–621

1975    **Heue,** Rolf/**Lindner,** Reinhold: Predigen lernen, Schriftenmissions-Verlag, Gladbeck 1975

1995    **Heyen,** Heye: Lebensbejahung und Lebensverneinung auf der Kanzel, tuduv-Studien, München 1995

2007    Idem: Warum die Predigt das 21. Jahrhundert überleben wird, in: Gottfried Bitter/Heye Heyen (Eds.): Wort und Hörer. Beispiele homiletischer Perspektiven, Lit-Verlag, Münster 2007, 137–149

2011    **Heymel,** Michael (Ed.): Martin Niemöller: Dahlemer Predigten. Kritische Ausgabe, Gütersloher Verlagshaus 2011

2013    Idem: Die Lesepredigt als eigene Gattung, in: ThBeitr, Vol. 44, 2013, 23–38

1992    **Hiddemann,** Frank: Geheimnis und Rätsel. Studie zum Gebrauch zweier Begriffe in Theologie und Ästhetik, in: Wilfried Engemann/Rainer Volp (Eds.): Gib mir ein Zeichen. Zur Bedeutung der Semiotik für theologische Praxis und Denkmodelle (= APrTh, Vol. 1), de Gruyter, Berlin 1992, 73–94

2000    **Hiddemann,** Frank/**Reifarth,** Jürgen: Öffentlich predigen. Prominente Predigten aus dem Thüringer Kanzelstreit, Gütersloher Verlagshaus, Gütersloh 2000

1978    **Hindelang,** Götz: Auffordern. Die Untertypen des Aufforderns und ihre sprachlichen Realisierungsformen, Verlag Alfred Kümmerle, Göppingen 1978

1936    **Hirsch,** Emanuel: Das Alte Testament und die Predigt des Evangeliums, Mohr, Tübingen, 1936

1964    Idem: Predigerfibel, de Gruyter, Berlin 1964

1978    Idem: Christliche Rechenschaft, ed. by Hayo Gerdes, Vol. 2, Die Spur (GmbH), Berlin et al. 1978

1988    **Hirschler,** Horst: Biblisch predigen. Lutherisches Verlagshaus, Hannover, 2nd ed., 1988

1996    **Hober,** David: Die Radiopredigt. Ein Beitrag zur Rundfunkhomiletik (= PTHe, Vol. 25), Kohlhammer, Stuttgart 1996

1932    **Holl,** Karl: Luthers Bedeutung für den Fortschritt der Auslegungskunst, in: Idem: Luther. Gesammelte Aufsätze zur Kirchengeschichte, Vol. I, Mohr, Tübingen, 6th ed., 1932, 544–582

1979    **Hollenweger,** Walter J.: Interkulturelle Theologie. Vol. 1: Erfahrungen der Leibhaftigkeit, Chr. Kaiser, München 1979

1973    **Homiletische Arbeitsgruppe:** Die Predigt bei Taufe, Trauung und Begräbnis. Inhalt, Wirkung und Funktion. Eine Contentanalyse, erarbeitet von der Homiletischen Arbeitsgruppe Stuttgart, Frankfurt/M. et al. 1973

2009    **Horn,** Andreas: Der Text und sein Prediger. Hoffentlich entlastende Bemerkungen zu einer Phase der Predigtvorbereitung [1983], in: Wilfried Engemann/Frank Lütze (Eds.): Grundfragen der Predigt, loc. cit., 2nd ed., 2009, 141–150

1982    **Hornig,** Gottfried: Analyse und Problematik der religiösen Performative, in: NZSTh, Vol. 24, 1982, 53–70

1971    **Hummel,** Gert (Ed.): Aufgabe der Predigt, Wissenschaftliche Buchgesellschaft, Darmstadt 1971

# I

| 1976 | **Iser,** Wolfgang: Der implizite Leser. Kommunikationsformen des Romans von Bunyan bis Beckett, W. Fink, München, 2nd ed., 1976 |
| 1994 | Idem: Der Akt des Lesens. Theorie ästhetischer Wirkung [1976], W. Fink, München, 4th ed., 1994 |
| 1934 | **Iwand,** Hans Joachim: Die Predigt des Gesetzes, in: EvTh, Vol. 1, 1934/35, 55–78 |
| 1979 | Idem: Briefe, Vorträge, Predigtmeditationen. Eine Auswahl, ed. by Peter-Paul Sänger, Evangelische Verlagsanstalt, Berlin 1979 |
| 1984 | Idem: Predigtmeditationen [1963], Vandenhoeck & Ruprecht, Göttingen, 4th ed., 1984 |

# J

| 2015 | **Jacobsen,** David S.: Homiletical Theology. Preaching as Doing Theology, Wipf and Stock, Eugene/Oreg. 2015 |
| 1974 | **James,** Muriel/**Savary,** Louis M.: The Power at the Bottom of the Well: Transactional Analysis and Religious Experience, Harper& Row, New York 1974 |
| 2005 | **Jensen,** Richard A.: Envisioning the Word. The Use of Visual Images in Preaching, Fortress Press, Minneapolis/Minn. 2005 |
| 1978 | **Jentsch,** Werner: Prediger und Predigt. Zur seelsorgerlich-missionarischen Verkündigung heute, G. Mohn, Gütersloh 1978 |
| 1910 | **Jerome:** S. Eusebii Hieronymi Epistulae, Pars I, Epistulae I–LXX, CSEL LIV, Wien 1910 |
| 1964 | Idem: S. Hieronymi Presbyteri, Opera, Pars I, Opera Exegetica 4, Commentariorum in Hiezechielem libri XIV, CChrSL, Vol. LXXV, Typographi Brepols Editores Pontificii, Turnhout 1964 |
| 1986 | **Jetter,** Werner: Symbol und Ritual. Anthropologische Elemente im Gottesdienst, Vandenhoeck & Ruprecht, Göttingen, 2nd ed., 1986 |
| 1999 | **Jörns,** Klaus-Peter: Die neuen Gesichter Gottes. Was die Menschen heute wirklich glauben, Verlag C. H. Beck, München, 2nd ed., 1999 |
| 2008 | Idem: Notwendige Abschiede. Auf dem Weg zu einem glaubwürdigen Christentum [2004], Gütersloher Verlagshaus, Gütersloh, 4th ed., 2008 |
| 1998 | **Jörns,** Klaus-Peter/**Großeholz,** Carsten (Eds.): Was die Menschen wirklich glauben. Die soziale Gestalt des Glaubens – Analysen einer Umfrage, Chr. Kaiser/Gütersloher Verlagshaus, Gütersloh 1998 |
| 1969 | **Josuttis,** Manfred: Zum Problem der politischen Predigt, in: EvTh, Vol. 29, 1969, 509–522 |
| 1970 | Idem: Über den Predigteinfall, in: EvTh, Vol. 30, 1970, 627–642 |
| 1972 | Idem: Was können die GPM leisten? in: GPM, Vol. 61, 1972/73, 131–139 |
| 1973 | Idem: Gesetz und Gesetzlichkeit im Politischen Nachtgebet, in: EvTh, Vol. 33, 1973, 559–578 |
| 1974 | Idem: Der Vollzug der Beerdigung. Ritual oder Kerygma? in: Idem: Praxis des Evangeliums zwischen Politik und Religion, loc. cit., 1988, 188–206 |
| 1983 | Idem: Die Bibel als Basis der Predigt, in: Hans-Georg Geyer et al. (Eds.): Wenn nicht jetzt, wann dann? Anniversary publication in honour of Hans-Joachim Kraus, Neukirchener Verlag, Neukirchen-Vluyn 1983, 385–393 |
| 1985a | Idem: Rhetorik und Theologie in der Predigtarbeit. Homiletische Studien, Chr. Kaiser, München 1985 |

1985b    Idem: Verkündigung als kreatorisches Geschehen [1972], in: Idem: Rhetorik und Theologie, loc. cit., 1985, 29–46

1986    Idem: Politische Kultur auf der Kanzel? Radius, Vol. 31, 1986, 38–40

1988    Idem: Praxis des Evangeliums zwischen Politik und Religion [1974], Chr. Kaiser, München, 4th ed., 1988

1991    Idem: Der Weg in das Leben. Eine Einführung in den Gottesdienst auf verhaltenswissenschaftlicher Grundlage, Chr. Kaiser, München 1999

1995a    Idem: Die Predigt des Gesetzes nach Luther [1962], in: Idem: Gesetz und Evangelium in der Predigtarbeit. Homiletische Studien, Vol. 2, Chr. Kaiser, Gütersloh 1995, 22–41

1995b    Idem: Gesetzlichkeit in der Predigt der Gegenwart [1966], in: Idem: Gesetz und Evangelium in der Predigtarbeit. Homiletische Studien, Vol. 2, Chr. Kaiser, Gütersloh 1995, 94–181

1996    Idem: Die Einführung in das Leben. Pastoraltheologie zwischen Phänomenologie und Spiritualität, Chr. Kaiser, Gütersloh 1996

1997    Idem: „Unsere Volkskirche" und die Gemeinde der Heiligen. Erinnerungen an die Zukunft der Kirche, Chr. Kaiser, Gütersloh 1997

2009    Idem: Der Prediger in der Predigt. Sündiger Mensch oder mündiger Zeuge? [1974] in: Wilfried Engemann/Frank Lütze (Eds.): Grundfragen der Predigt, loc. cit., 2nd ed., 2009, 81–103

1968    Jüngel, Eberhard: Das Verhältnis der theologischen Disziplinen untereinander, in: Die Praktische Theologie zwischen Wissenschaft und Praxis (= SPTh, Vol. 5), Chr. Kaiser, München 1968

1972    Jung, Carl Gustav: The Relations between the Ego an the Unconscious [1928], in: Collected Works, Vol. 7, ed. by. Herbert E. Read: Two Essays on Analytical Psychology, Princeton/N.J. 1972, 123–244

## K

1972    Kaempfert, Manfred: Religiosität als linguistische Kategorie? Über einige allgemeine Eigenschaften religiöser Texte, in: LingBibl, Vol. 17/18, 1972, 31–53

1998    Kalivoda, Gregor: Jargon, in: Historisches Wörterbuch der Rhetorik, Vol. 4, ed. by Gert Ueding and Max Niemeyer, Tübingen 1998, 712–717

2000    Karle, Isolde: Pastorale Kompetenz, in: PTh, Vol. 89, 2000, 508–523

2001    Idem: Der Pfarrberuf als Profession. Eine Berufstheorie im Kontext der modernen Gesellschaft, Chr. Kaiser/Gütersloher Verlagshaus, Gütersloh 2001

2002    Idem: Den Glauben wahrscheinlich machen. Schleiermachers Homiletik kommunikationstheoretisch betrachtet, in: ZThK, Vol. 99, 2002, 332–350

2009    Idem: Wozu Pfarrerinnen und Pfarrer, wenn doch alle Priester sind? Zur Professionalität des Pfarrberufs, in: DtPfrBl, Vol. 109, 2009, 3–9

1981    Kasper, Walter: Jesus the Christ, Burns & Oates/Paulist Press, London/New York 1981

2003    Kay, James F.: Reorientation. Homiletics as Theologically Authorized Rhetoric, in: The Princeton Seminary Bulletin, Vol. 24, 2003, 16–35

2007    Idem: Preaching and Theology, Chalice Press, St. Louis/Mo. 2007

1985    Keel, Othmar: Politisches in der Predigt, in: Orientierung, Vol. 49, No. 23/24, 1985, 251–256

2006    **Kerner**, Hanns (Ed.): Predigt in einer polyphonen Kultur, Evangelische Verlagsanstalt, Leipzig 2006

1843    **Kierkegaard**, Søren A.: Furcht und Zittern/Wiederholung [1843] (= Sören Kierkegaard. Gesammelte Werke, Vol. 3), Verlag Diederich, Jena, 2nd ed., 1909

1990    **Kiesow**, Ernst-Rüdiger: Der Prediger, in: Karl-Heinrich Bieritz/Christian Bunners et al. (Eds.): Handbuch der Predigt, loc. cit., 1990, 99–135

2009    **Kirchenamt der EKD** (Ed.): Evangelische Kirche in Deutschland. Zahlen und Fakten zum kirchlichen Leben, Hannover 2009

2016    Idem (Ed.): Evangelische Kirche in Deutschland. Zahlen und Fakten zum kirchlichen Leben, Hannover 2016

2017    **Kirchmeier**, Bernhard: Glaubensempfehlungen. Eine anthropologische Sichtung zeitgenössischer Predigtkultur (= APrTh, Vol. 67), Evangelische Verlagsanstalt, Leipzig 2017

1935    **Klausner**, Theodor: Das römische Capitulare Evangeliorum, Vol. I: Typen, Aschendorff, Münster/Westf. 1935

1973    **Kleemann**, Jürg: Verkündigung als Sprachproblem, in: NH, No. 65, 1973, 98–112

1997    **Klein**, Günter: Rudolf Bultmann – ein unerledigtes Vermächtnis, in: ZThK, Vol. 94, 1997, 177–201

2003    **Klie**, Thomas: Zeichen und Spiel. Semiotisch und spieltheoretische Rekonstruktion der Pastoraltheologie (= PThK, Vol. 11), Gütersloher Verlagshaus, Gütersloh 2003

1934    **Knolle**, Theodor/**Stählin**, Wilhelm: Das Kirchenjahr. Eine Denkschrift über die Kirchliche Ordnung des Jahres. Im Auftrag der Niedersächsischen Liturgischen Konferenz und des Berneuchener Kreises, Stauda-Verlag, Kassel 1934

1982    **Koch**, Ernst: Der Prediger als Problem der Predigt in der Homiletik des 19. und 20. Jahrhunderts, in: Hans Seidel/ Karl-Heinrich Bieritz (Eds.): Das lebendige Wort. Beiträge zur kirchlichen Verkündigung, Anniversary publication in honour of Gottfried Voigt, Evangelische Verlagsanstalt, Berlin 1982, 218–240

1907    **Köstlin**, Heinrich A.: Die Lehre von der Seelsorge [1895], Reuter & Reichhard, Berlin, 2nd ed., 1907

2009    **Konferenz Landeskirchlicher Arbeitskreise Christen und Juden** (Ed.): Die ganze Bibel zu Wort kommen lassen. Ein neues Perikopenmodell, in: Begegnungen. Zeitschrift für Kirche und Judentum, Vol. 92 (Sonderheft), Hannover 2009

1970    **Kopperschmidt**, Josef: Kommunikationsprobleme der Predigt, in: Günter Biemer (Ed.): Die Fremdsprache der Predigt, Patmos-Verlag, Düsseldorf 1970, 30–57

1976    Idem: Allgemeine Rhetorik. Einführung in die Theorie der persuasiven Kommunikation, Kohlhammer, Stuttgart, 2nd ed., 1976

1977    Idem: Von der Kritik der Rhetorik zur kritischen Rhetorik, in: Heinrich F. Plett (Ed.): Rhetorik. Kritische Positionen zum Stand der Forschung, Fink, München 1977, 213–229

1989    Idem: Methodik der Argumentationsanalyse, Frommann-Holzboog, Stuttgart/Bad Cannstadt 1989

1990    Idem: Rhetorik, 2 Volumes, Wissenschaftliche Buchgesellschaft, Darmstadt 1990

1883    **Krauß**, Alfred: Lehrbuch der Homiletik, Verlag Friedrich Andreas Perthes, Gotha 1883

1981    **Krüger**, Horst: Widerstände von Predigern gegen Predigttexte. Sprechaktanalyse an ausgewählten Beispielen, in: Werkstatt Predigt, Vol. 41, 1981, 36–67

1940    **Künkel**, Fritz: Einführung in die Charakterkunde, Verlag S. Hirzel, Leipzig, 10th ed., 1940

1983 **Kugler**, Georg: Die Wahrheit und die Richtigkeiten. Über eindeutiges Reden, in: ZGDP, Vol. 1, 1983, 9–20

2008 **Kuhlmann**, Sebastian: Martin Niemöller. Zur prophetischen Dimension der Predigt (= APrTh, Vol. 39), Evangelische Verlagsanstalt, Leipzig 2008

2009 **Kumlehn**, Martin: Gott zur Sprache bringen. Studien zum Predigtverständnis Johann Gottfried Herders im Kontext seiner philosophischen Anthropologie (= PThGG, Vol. 4), Mohr Siebeck, Tübingen 2009

1955 **Kunze**, Gerhard: Die Lesungen, in: Leiturgia. Handbuch des evangelischen Gottesdienstes, Vol. II, ed. by Karl Ferdinand Müller and Walter Blankenburg, J. Stauda-Verlag, Kassel 1955, 87–180

2008 **Kuttler**, Iris: Pfarrer in der Krise? Zusammenhänge zwischen Arbeitsanforderungen im Pfarrberuf und dem Burnout-Syndrom, Konstanzer Online-Publikations-System (KOPS), Konstanz 2008, http://www.ub.uni-konstanz.de/kops/volltexte/2008/4964/

## L

2002 **Lämmlin**, Georg: Die Lust am Wort und der Widerstand der Schrift. Homiletische Re-Lektüre des Psalters, LIT-Verlag, Münster/Hamburg/London 2002

1968 **Lange**, Ernst: Die verbesserliche Welt. Möglichkeiten christlicher Rede – erprobt an der Geschichte vom Propheten Jona, Kreuz Verlag, Stuttgart/Berlin 1968

1976 Idem: Predigen als Beruf. Aufsätze, ed. by Rüdiger Schloz, Kreuz Verlag, Stuttgart/Berlin 1976

1984 Idem: Chancen des Alltags, Kreuz Verlag, Stuttgart 1984

2009 Idem: Funktion und Struktur des homiletischen Aktes (shortened version of: Zur Theorie und Praxis der Predigtarbeit [1968]), in: Wilfried Engemann/Frank Lütze: Grundfragen der Predigt, loc. cit., 2nd ed., 2009, 157–169

1999 **LaRue**, Cleophus J.: The Heart of Black Preaching, Westminster John Knox Press, Louisville/Ky. 1999

2010 Idem: I Believe I'll Testify. Reflections on African American Preaching, Westminster John Knox Press, Louisville/Ky. 2010

1967 **Lausberg**, Heinrich: Elemente der literarischen Rhetorik. Eine Einführung für Studierende der klassischen, romanischen, englischen und deutschen Philologie, Hueber, München, 3rd ed., 1967

1990 Idem: Handbuch der literarischen Rhetorik. Eine Grundlegung der Literaturwissenschaft, Franz Steiner Verlag, Stuttgart, 3rd ed., 1990

2006 **Lehnert**, Volker A.: Kein Blatt vorm Mund. Frei predigen lernen in sieben Schritten. Kleine praktische Homiletik, Neukirchener Verlagshaus, Neukirchen-Vluyn 2006

1993 **Leipold**, Heinrich: Anknüpfung I. Systematisch-theologisch, in: TRE, Vol. 2, 1993, 743–747

2010 **Lektionar für evangelisch-lutherische Kirchen und Gemeinden**. Mit Perikopenbuch [1985], ed. by Liturgische Konferenz on behalf of Vereinigte Evangelisch-Lutherische Kirche Deutschlands (VELKD), Lutherisches Verlagshaus, Hannover, 5th ed., 2010

1957 **Lilje**, Hanns: Was und wie sollen wir heute predigen? In: Lutherisches Kirchenamt Hannover (Ed.): Die Predigt, loc. cit., Berlin/München 1957, 9–23

1976    **Link,** Hannelore: Rezeptionsforschung. Eine Einführung in Methoden und Probleme, Kohlhammer, Berlin et al. 1976

1996    **Linke,** Angelika et al. (Eds.): Studienbuch Linguistik, M. Niemeyer Verlag, Tübingen, 3rd ed., 1996

1999    **Lips,** Hermann von: Das Medium ist die (frohe) Botschaft. Beobachtungen zur Verwendung von εὐαγγέλιον und εὐαγγελίζεσθαι im Neuen Testament, in: Christoph Kähler/Martina Böhm/Christfried Böttrich (Eds.): Gedenkt an das Wort, Anniversary publication in honour of Werner Vogler, Evangelische Verlagsanstalt, Leipzig 1999, 93–106

1995    **„Lobe mit Abrahams Samen."** Stellungnahme der KLAK und des Zentralvereins der EA, in: Streit um das Gottesdienstbuch (Erneuerte Agende), loc. cit., 1995, 2–14

1953    **Löhe,** Wilhelm: Agende für christliche Gemeinden des lutherischen Bekenntnisses [1844, 2nd ed. 1853], in: Idem: Gesammelte Werke, Vol. VII/1, Freimund-Verlag, Neuendettelsau 1953

1969    **Löwith,** Karl: Das Individuum in der Rolle des Mitmenschen, Wissenschaftliche Buchgesellschaft, Darmstadt, 2nd ed., 1969

1974    **Lohse,** Eduard: Grundriss der neutestamentlichen Theologie (= ThW, Vol. 4), Kohlhammer, Stuttgart 1974

2013    **Lorensen,** Marlene Ringgaard: Dialogical Preaching. Bakhtin, Otherness and Homiletics (= APTLH 74), Vandenhoeck & Ruprecht, Göttingen 2013

2003    **Lose,** David J.: Confessing Jesus Christ. Preaching in a Postmodern World, Eerdmans, Grand Rapids/Mich. 2003

2006    **Lütze,** Frank M.: Absicht und Wirkung der Predigt. Eine Untersuchung zur homiletischen Pragmatik (= APrTh, Vol. 29), Evangelische Verlagsanstalt, Leipzig 2006

1989    **Luther,** Henning: Predigt als Handlung. Überlegungen zur Pragmatik des Predigens, in: Albrecht Beutel et al. (Eds.): Homiletisches Lesebuch, loc. cit., 1989, 222–239

1883    **Luther,** Martin: Werke. Kritische Gesamtausgabe. „Weimarer Ausgabe" (WA), Weimar 1883 ff.

1959    Idem: Large Catechism [1529], in: The book of concord – the confession of the Evangelical Lutheran church, ed. by Theodore Tappert, Fort Press, Philadelphia, 6th ed., 1959

1982    Idem: Acht Sermone D. M. Luthers von ihm gepredigt zu Wittenberg in der Fasten [1522], in: Martin Luther, Studienausgabe Vol. II, ed. by Hans-Ulrich Delius, Evangelische Verlagsanstalt, Berlin 1982, 520–558

1957    **Lutherisches Kirchenamt Hannover** (Ed.): Die Predigt. Das Gespräch über die Predigt auf der Lutherischen Generalsynode 1957 in Hamburg, Gemeinschaftsverlag Ev. Presseverband Bayern und Lutherisches Verlagshaus, Berlin/München 1957

1995    **Lutz,** Samuel: Huldrych Zwingli, in: Christian Möller (Ed.): Geschichte der Seelsorge in Einzelporträts, Vol. 2: Von Martin Luther bis Matthias Claudius, Vandenhoeck & Ruprecht, Göttingen 1995, 65–84

## M

1994    **Madonna,** Luigi C.: Die unzeitgemäße Hermeneutik Ch. Wolffs, in: Axel Bühler (Ed.): Unzeitgemäße Hermeneutik, loc. cit., 1994, 26–42

1989    **Man,** Paul de: Blindness and Insight. Essays in the Rhetoric of Contemporary Criticism, Introduction by Wlad Godzich, Routledge, London, 2nd ed., 1989

1983    **Martianus** Capella: De nuptiis Philologiae et Mercurii, ed. by James A. Willis, Teubner, Leipzig 1983

1984    **Martin**, Gerhard Marcel: Predigt als „offenes Kunstwerk"? Zum Dialog zwischen Homiletik und Rezeptionsästhetik, in: EvTh, Vol. 44, 1984, 46–58

2003    Idem: Predigt und Liturgie ästhetisch. Wahrnehmung – Kunst – Lebenskunst (= Christentum heute, Vol. 6), Kohlhammer, Stuttgart 2003

1957    **Marxsen**, Willi: Exegese und Verkündigung, Chr. Kaiser, München 1957

1967    Idem: Das Neue Testament als Buch der Kirche, Evangelische Verlagsanstalt, Berlin, 2nd ed., 1967

1971    **Maser**, Siegfried: Grundlagen der allgemeinen Kommunikationstheorie. Eine Einführung in ihre Grundbegriffe und Methoden, Berliner Union GmbH/Kohlhammer, Stuttgart 1971

1883    **Matthesius**, Johann: Martin Luthers Leben. In siebzehn Predigten dargestellt, ed. by Evangelischer Bücherverein, Berlin, 3rd ed., 1883

2001    **McClure**, John S.: Other-wise Preaching. A Postmodern Ethic for Homiletics, Chalice Press, St. Louis/Mo. 2001

2004    **McClure**, John S./**Allen**, Ronald J. et al.: Listening to Listeners. Homiletical Case Studies, Chalice Press, St. Louis/Mo. 2004

2003    **Meinhard**, Isolde: Ideologie und Imagination im Predigtprozess. Zur homiletischen Rezeption der kritischen Narratologie (= APrTh, Vol. 24), Evangelische Verlagsanstalt, Leipzig 2003

1963    **Melanchthon**, Philipp: Elementorum rhetorices libri duo [1531/1542], in: Corpus Reformatorum, Vol XIII [1846], ND 1963

1959    Idem: The Treatise on the Power and Primacy of the Pope [Tractatus de potestate papae], in: The Book of Concord – The Confession of the Evangelical Lutheran Church, ed. by Theodore Tappert, Fort Press, Philadelphia, 6th ed., 1959, 319–335

1992    **Merkel**, Friedemann: Predigt in ‚freier' Rede, in: Sagen – Hören – Loben. Studien zu Gottesdienst und Predigt, Vandenhoeck & Ruprecht, Göttingen 1992, 47–68

1995    **Merten**, Klaus: Inhaltsanalyse. Einführung in Theorie, Methode, Praxis, Westdeutscher Verlag, Opladen, 2nd ed., 1995

1975    **Mertens**, Alfred: Kritische Kommentierung zum Thema „Predigt als Lernprozess", in: Peter Düsterfeld/Hans Bernhard Kaufmann (Eds.): Didaktik der Predigt, loc. cit., 1975, 82–98

1992    **Merz**, Georg: Der Pfarrer und die Predigt, introduced and ed. by Friedrich Wilhelm Kantzenbach, Chr. Kaiser, München 1992

2009    **Metz**, Johann Baptist: Kleine Apologie des Erzählens [1973] in: Wilfried Engemann/ Frank Lütze (Eds.): Grundfragen der Predigt, loc. cit., 2nd ed., 2009, 217–229

2014    **Meyer**, Peter: Predigt als Sprachgeschehen gelebt-religiöser Praxis. Empirisch-theologische Beiträge zur Sprach- und Religionsanalyse auf der Basis komparativer Feldforschung in Deutschland und in den USA (= PThGG, Vol. 15), Mohr Siebeck, Tübingen 2014

1995    **Meyer-Blanck**, Michael: Vom Symbol zum Zeichen. Symboldidaktik und Semiotik (= Vorlagen, Neue Folge, Vol. 25), Lutherisches Verlagshaus, Hannover 1995

1997    Idem: Inszenierung des Evangeliums. Ein kurzer Gang durch den Sonntagsgottesdienst nach der Erneuerten Agende, Vandenhoeck & Ruprecht, Göttingen 1997

1999 Idem: Tiefenpsychologie und Strukturtheologie: Otto Haendler, in: Geschichte der Praktischen Theologie. Dargestellt anhand ihrer Klassiker, ed. by Christian Grethlein and Michael Meyer-Blanck (= APrTh, Vol. 12), Evangelische Verlagsanstalt, Leipzig 1999

2006 Idem: Predigt und Lesungen im evangelischen Gottesdienst, in: Erich Garhammer et al. (Eds.): Kontrapunkte, loc. cit., München 2006, 150–163

2007 Idem: Die Dramaturgie von Wort und Sakrament. Homiletisch-liturgische Grenzgänge im ökumenischen Horizont, in: PTh, Vol. 96, 2007, 160–171

2008 Idem: Das Rhetorische und das Pädagogische in der Jugendpredigt, in: Michael Meyer-Blanck et al. (Eds.): Jugend und Predigt, loc. cit., München 2008, 219–227

2009a Idem: Entschieden predigen, in: LS, Vol. 60, 2009, 8–12.

2009b Idem: Liturgie und Liturgik. Der Evangelische Gottesdienst aus Quellentexten erklärt, Chr. Kaiser, Gütersloh, 2nd ed., 2009

2010 Idem: Heilsame Nähe. Sünde und Vergebung im Gottesdienst, in: Johannes Block/ Holger Eschmann (Eds.): Peccatum magnificare. Zur Wiederentdeckung des evangelischen Sündenverständnisses für die Handlungsfelder der Praktischen Theologie, Vandenhoeck & Ruprecht, Göttingen 2010, 95–103

1999 **Meyer-Blanck**, Michael/**Weyel**, Birgit: Arbeitsbuch Praktische Theologie. Ein Begleitbuch zu Studium und Examen in 25 Einheiten, Chr. Kaiser, Gütersloh 1999

2008 **Meyer-Blanck**, Michael/**Roth**, Ursula/**Seip**, Jörg (Eds.): Jugend und Predigt. Zwei fremde Welten? (= ÖSP Vol. 6), Verlag Don Bosco, München 2008

1959 **Mezger**, Manfred: Die Sprache der Predigt, in: SThU, Vol. 29, 1959, 106–121

1963 Idem: Die Amtshandlungen der Kirche als Verkündigung, Ordnung und Seelsorge. Vol. I: Die Begründung der Amtshandlungen, Chr. Kaiser, München 1963

1971 Idem: Die Anleitung zur Predigt. Rudolf Bultmann zum 75. Geburtstag [1959], in: Gert Hummel (Ed.): Aufgabe der Predigt, loc. cit., 1971, 382–406

1989 Idem: Die Verbindlichkeit des Textes in der Predigt [1964], in: Albrecht Beutel et al. (Eds.): Homiletisches Lesebuch, loc. cit., 1989, 88–110

2009 Idem: Die eine Wirklichkeit. Vorspiel zur Freude an der Predigt [1970], in: Wilfried Engemann/Frank Lütze (Eds.): Grundfragen der Predigt, loc. cit., 2nd ed., 2009, 19–28

2009 **Micklich**, Thomas: Kommunikation des Glaubens. Gottesbeziehung als Kategorie praktisch-theologischer Theoriebildung (= APTLH, Vol. 58), Vandenhoeck & Ruprecht, Göttingen 2009

1983 **Möller**, Christian: Seelsorglich predigen. Die parakletische Dimension von Predigt, Seelsorge und Gemeinde, Vandenhoeck & Ruprecht, Göttingen 1983

1992 **Muck,** Herbert: Umwertungen im Raumgefüge „Kirche". Eine semiotische Darstellung der wechselvollen Raumbeziehungen, in: Wilfried Engemann/Rainer Volp (Eds.): Gib mir ein Zeichen. Zur Bedeutung der Semiotik für theologische Praxis- und Denkmodelle (= APrTh 1), de Gruyter, Berlin/New York 1992, 232–245

1954 **Müller**, Alfred Dedo: Grundriss der Praktischen Theologie, Evangelische Verlagsanstalt, Berlin 1954

2014 **Müller**, Annette C.: Predigt schreiben. Prozess und Strategien der homiletischen Komposition (= APrTh, Vol. 55), Evangelische Verlagsanstalt, Leipzig 2014

1983 **Müller**, Hans Martin: Gottesdienst nach reformatorischem Verständnis, in: ZGDP, Vol. 1, 1983, 2–8

1996    Idem: Homiletik. Eine evangelische Predigtlehre, de Gruyter, Berlin/New York 1996

2002    Idem: Emmanuel Hirschs Bedeutung für die Predigt, in: Christian Albrecht/Martin Weeber: Klassiker der protestantischen Predigtlehre, loc. cit., 2002, 202–224

2015    **Müller**, Konrad: Wort und Wirkung. Zur Grundlegung der Predigt, Evangelische Verlagsanstalt, Leipzig 2015

1971    **Müller**, Max: Erfahrung und Geschichte. Grundzüge einer Philosophie der Freiheit als transzendentale Erfahrung, Alber, Freiburg/München 1971

1993    **Müller**, Theophil: Evangelischer Gottesdienst. Liturgische Vielfalt im religiösen und gesellschaftlichen Umfeld, Kohlhammer, Stuttgart/Berlin/Köln 1993

1993    **Müller-Lauter**, Wolfgang: Existenzphilosophie/Existentialismus, in: TRE, Vol. 10, 1993, 714–732

1957    **Müller-Schwefe**, Hans-Rudolf: Wie spricht die Kirche des Wortes heute? in: Lutherisches Kirchenamt Hannover (Ed.): Die Predigt, loc. cit., Berlin/München 1957, 38–58

1958    Idem: Zur Zeit oder zur Unzeit. Eine Anthologie moderner Predigten, Kreuz Verlag, Stuttgart 1958

1993    Idem: Anknüpfung II. Praktisch-theologisch, in: TRE, Vol. 2, 1993, 747–752


**N**

1968    **Neidhart**, Walter: Die Rolle des Pfarrers beim Begräbnis, in: Rudolf Bohren/Max Geiger (Eds.): Wort und Gemeinde. Probleme und Aufgaben der Praktischen Theologie, Anniversary publication in honour of Eduard Thurneysen, EVZ-Verlag, Zürich 1968, 226–235

1989    Idem: Erzählbuch zur Bibel 2. Geschichten und Texte für unsere Zeit weiter-erzählt, Benziger, Köln 1989

2014    **Neuordnung der gottesdienstlichen Lesungen und Predigttexte**. Entwurf zur Erprobung, ed. by Kirchenämter von EKD, UEK und VELKD, C.H. Beck, Nördlingen 2014

2005    **Nicol**, Martin: Einander ins Bild setzen. Dramaturgische Homiletik, Vandenhoeck & Ruprecht, Göttingen, 2nd ed., 2005

2009    Idem: PredigtKunst. Ästhetische Überlegungen zur homiletischen Praxis, in: Wilfried Engemann/Frank Lütze (Eds.): Grundfragen der Predigt, loc. cit., 2nd ed., 2009, 235–242

2005    **Nicol**, Martin/**Deeg**, Alexander: Im Wechselschritt zur Kanzel. Praxisbuch Dramaturgische Homiletik, Vandenhoeck & Ruprecht, Göttingen 2005

1960    **Niebergall**, Alfred: Der Prediger als Zeuge, G. Mohn, Gütersloh 1960

1909    **Niebergall**, Friedrich: Wie predigen wir dem modernen Menschen? Teil 1: Eine Untersuchung über Motive und Quietive, Mohr, Tübingen, 3rd ed., 1909

1917    Idem: Die Kasualrede. Praktisch-theologische Handbibliothek (Vol. I), Vandenhoeck & Ruprecht, Göttingen, 3rd ed., 1917

1929    Idem: Die moderne Predigt. Kulturgeschichtliche und theologische Grundlage, Geschichte und Ertrag, J. C. B. Mohr (P. Siebeck), Tübingen 1929

2004    **Nielsen**, Bent Flemming: Genopførelser. Ritual, kommunikation og kirke, Forlaget Anis, København 2004

1982    **Nietzsche**, Friedrich: Die fröhliche Wissenschaft, in: Nietzsche, Werke, Kritische Gesamtausgabe, ed. by Giorgio Colli and Mazzino Montinari, 5. Abt., Vol. II, W. de Gruyter, Berlin/New York 1982

2008    **Nisslmüller**, Thomas: Homo audiens. Der Hör-Akt des Glaubens und die akustische Rezeption im Predigtgeschehen, Vandenhoeck & Ruprecht unipress, Göttingen 2008

1976    **Nitschke**, Horst (Ed.): Erzählende Predigten, Vol. 1, G. Mohn, Gütersloh 1976

1981    Idem (Ed.): Erzählende Predigten, Vol. 2, G. Mohn, Gütersloh 1981

1848    **Nitzsch**, Carl Immanuel: Praktische Theologie, Vol. II, Marcus, Bonn 1848

2008    **Nord**, Ilona: Realitäten des Glaubens. Zur virtuellen Dimension christlicher Religiosität, de Gruyter, Berlin 2008

1991    **Nüchtern**, Michael: Kirche bei Gelegenheit. Kasualien – Akademiearbeit – Erwachsenenbildung, Kohlhammer, Stuttgart/Berlin/Köln 1991

**O**

1979    **Öffner**, Ernst: Pastoralsoziologische Grundlegung: Der Pfarrer und sein Kommunikationsproblem, in: Bernhard Klaus et al. (Eds.): Kommunikation in der Kirche, G. Mohn, Gütersloh 1979, 57–110

1975    **Ohnesorg**, Peter: Aspekte zum Thema Glaube und Sprache, in: Werkstatt Predigt, 1975, 37–42

1981    **Ordo Lectionum Missae**. Missale romanum ex decreto sacrosancti oecumenici concilii vaticani II instauratum auctoritate Pauli PP. VI promulgatum [1969], Roma, 2nd ed., 1981

1976    **Origen**: De principiis libri IV, hg., übers., mit krit. und erl. Anmerkungen versehen v. Herwig Görgemanns und Heinrich Karpp (= TzF, Vol. 24), Wissenschaftliche Buchgesellschaft, Darmstadt 1976

1989    Idem: Homélies sur Ézéchiel, Latour-Maubourg, Paris 1989

1995    Idem: De principiis, in: Ante-Nicene Fathers, Vol. 4, ed. by Alexander Roberts and James Donaldson, Hendrickson, Peabody/Mass. 1995, 349–382

1970    **Otto**, Gert: Vernunft. Aspekte zeitgemäßen Glaubens, Kreuz-Verlag, Stuttgart 1970

1982    Idem: Wie entsteht eine Predigt? Ein Kapitel praktischer Rhetorik, Chr. Kaiser, München 1982

1994    Idem: Die Kunst, verantwortlich zu reden. Rhetorik – Ästhetik – Ethik, Chr. Kaiser, Gütersloh 1994

1999    Idem: Rhetorische Predigtlehre. Ein Grundriss, Grünewald/Evangelische Verlagsanstalt, Mainz/Leipzig 1999

2009    Idem: Predigt als Sprache. Eine Zusammenfassung in sechs kommentierten Thesen, in: Wilfried Engemann/Frank Lütze (Eds.): Grundfragen der Predigt, loc. cit., 2nd ed., 2009, 259–279

2015    **Oxen**, Kathrin: „Nur noch kurz die Welt retten." Die politische Predigt von heute als Herausforderung für die homiletische Aus- und Fortbildung, in: Helmut Schwier (Ed.): Ethische und politische Predigt, loc. cit., 2015, 157–183

**P**

1857    **Palmer**, Christian: Evangelische Homiletik [1842], Steinkopf, Stuttgart, 4th ed., 1857

1968a   **Pannenberg**, Wolfhart: Der Mensch – Ebenbild Gottes? In: Beiträge zu einer modernen Anthropologie, ed. by Süddeutscher Rundfunk im Rahmen der Senderreihe „Das Heidelberger Studio", 43. Sendefolge, R. Piper & Co., München 1968

1968b   Idem: Revelation as History, Macmillan, London 1968

1982    Idem: Jesus, God and Man, Westminster Press, Philadelphia, 2nd ed., 1982

2004    **Perikopenordnung in der Diskussion**, ed. by der Gemeinsamen Arbeitsstelle für gottes-dienstliche Fragen der EKD, Vol. 18, Hannover 2004

1997    **Peters**, Albrecht: Abendmahl III/4, in: TRE, Vol. 1, 1993, 131–145

1975    **Piper**, Hans-Christoph: Einflüsse psychischer Strukturen auf Predigt und Seelsorge, in: EvTh, Vol. 35, 1975, 60–71

1976a   Idem: Die Predigtanalyse, in: Seelsorgeausbildung. Theorien. Methoden. Modelle, ed. by Werner Becher, Vandenhoeck & Ruprecht, Göttingen 1976, 91–105

1976b   Idem: Predigtanalysen. Kommunikation und Kommunikationsstörungen in der Predigt, Vandenhoeck & Ruprecht/Herder, Göttingen/Wien 1976

1999    **Pirson**, Dietrich: „Publice docere" im kirchlichen Handeln der Gegenwart, in: Festschrift für Martin Heckel, ed. by Karl-Hermann Kastner et al., Mohr Siebeck, Tübingen 1999, 208–217

1998    **Pitzele**, Peter: Scripture Windows. Toward a Practice of Bibliodrama, Torah Aura Productions, Los Angeles 1998

1999    Idem: Bibliodrama. Ein Ruf in die Zukunft, Lernort Gemeinde, Vol. 17, 1999, 50–54

2014    **Plate**, Christian: Predigen in Person. Theorie und Praxis der Predigt im Gesamtwerk Otto Haendlers (= APrTh, Vol. 53), Evangelische Verlagsanstalt, Leipzig 2014

1952    **Plato**: IV: Laches, Protagoras, Meno, Euthydemus, with an English Translation, ed. by Walter R. M. Lamb, Harvard University Press/William Heinemann, Cambridge/Mass./London 1952, 259–371

1982    Idem: Sämtliche Werke, Bde. 1–3, ed. by Erich Loewenthal, Verlag Lampert Schneider, Heidelberg 1982

2006    **Pörksen**, Uwe: Was taugt die Rede in unserer medialen Welt und was ihre Bauform als Grundriss einer Predigt?, in: Hanns Kerner (Ed.). Predigt in einer polyphonen Kultur, loc. cit., Leipzig 2006, 93–108.

2001    **Pohl-Patalong**, Uta: Predigt als Bibliolog. Homiletische Anstöße zu einer neuen Predigtform, in: Uta Pohl-Patalong/Frank Muchlinsky: Predigen im Plural, loc. cit., 2001, 258–268

2003    Idem: Bibliolog. Predigen mit der ganzen Gemeinde, in: DtPfrBl, Vol. 103, 2003, 33–35

2009    Idem: Bibliolog. Vol. 1: Impulse für Gottesdienst, Gemeinde und Schule. Grundformen, Kohlhammer, Stuttgart 2009

2009    **Pohl-Patalong**, Uta/**Aigner**, Maria E.: Bibliolog. Vol. 2: Impulse für Gottesdienst, Gemeinde und Schule. Aufbauformen, Kohlhammer, Stuttgart 2009

2001    **Pohl-Patalong**, Uta/**Muchlinsky**, Frank: Predigen im Plural. Homiletische Aspekte, EB-Verlag, Hamburg 2001

1984    **Preuß**, Horst Dietrich: Das Alte Testament in christlicher Predigt, Kohlhammer, Stuttgart et al. 1984

1989    Idem: Das Alte Testament in der Verkündigung der Kirche, in: Albrecht Beutel et al. (Eds.): Homiletisches Lesebuch, loc. cit., 1989, 125–140

## Q

1696    **Quenstedt**: Theologia didactico-polemica I [1685], Fritsch, Lipsia, 3rd ed., 1696

1939    **Quervain**, Alfred de: Der Öffentlichkeitsanspruch des Evangeliums (= ThSt, Vol. 4), Verlag des Evangelischen Buchhandels, Zollikon/Zürich 1939

2006    **Quicke**, Michael J.: 360-Degree Leadership. Preaching to Transform Congregations, Baker Books, Grand Rapids/Mich. 2006

1995    **Quintilian**: Institutionis oratoriae libri XII. Ausbildung des Redners, 12 Bücher, Lat.-Germ., transl. and ed. by Helmut Rahn, 2 Bde., Wissenschaftliche Buchgesellschaft, Darmstadt, 3rd ed., 1995

## R

1958    **Rad**, Gerhard von: Theologie des Alten Testaments, Vol. 1, Chr. Kaiser, München, 2nd ed., 1958

1967    **Rahner**, Karl: Schriften zur Theologie, Vol. VIII, Verlag Benziger, Zürich 1967

2000    **Ramsey**, G. Lee: Care-full Preaching. From Sermon to Caring Community, Chalice Press, St. Louis/Mo. 2000

1847    **Ranke**, Ernst: Das altkirchliche Perikopensystem aus den ältesten Urkunden der Römischen Liturgie – dargelegt und erläutert, Reimer, Berlin 1847

2000    **Raschzok**, Klaus: Der Thüringer Kanzelstreit. Praktisch-theologische Anmerkungen, in: Klaus Petzold/Klaus Raschzok (Eds.): Vertraut den neuen Wegen. Praktische Theologie zwischen Ost und West, Anniversary publication in honour of Klaus-Peter Hertzsch, Evangelische Verlagsanstalt, Leipzig 2000, 121–152

2014    Ders: Predigt als Leseakt. Essays zur homiletischen Theoriebildung, Evangelische Verlagsanstalt, Leipzig 2014

1993    **Ratschow**, Carl Heinz: Amt – Ämter – Amtsverständnis VIII, in: TRE, Vol. 2, 1993, 593–622

1999    **Ratzmann**, Wolfgang: Was ändert sich an unserem Gottesdienst durch die Einführung des Evangelischen Gottesdienstbuches? In: Amtsblatt der Ev.-Luth. Landeskirche Sachsens, No. 18, 1999, B 57–60

2006    Idem: Die Predigt als Element des protestantischen Gottesdienstes. Das Verhältnis von Predigt und Abendmahl, in: Erich Garhammer et al. (Eds.): Kontrapunkte, loc. cit., München 2006, 178–190.

2010    Idem: Empirische Studie zur Perikopenordnung. Kommentar aus praktisch-theologischer Sicht, in: Empirische Studie zur Perikopenordnung (Abschlussbericht), epd-Dokumentation Nr. 44 vom 2. November 2010, 29–58

2005    **Reusser**, Kurt: Problemorientiertes Lernen. Tiefenstruktur, Gestaltungsformen, Wirkung, in: Beiträge zur Lehrerinnen- und Lehrerbildung, Vol. 23, 2005, 159–182

2012    **Reuter**, Hans Richard: Beim Wort genommen. Predigten, Radius-Verlag, Stuttgart 2012

2000    **Reuter**, Ingo: Predigt verstehen. Grundlagen einer homiletischen Hermeneutik (= APrTh, Vol. 17), Evangelische Verlagsanstalt, Leipzig 2000

1992    **Revised Common Lectionary**. Includes Complete List of Lections for Years A, B and C, ed. by Consultation on Common Texts, Nashville/Tenn. 1992

1994    **Rhetorica ad Herennium** [ca. 90–80 v. Chr.]. Ausgabe Lateinisch-Deutsch, ed. and transl. by. Theodor Nüßlein, Verlag Artemis und Winkler, Düsseldorf 1994

1989    **Richter-Böhne**, Andreas: Unbekannte Schuld. Politische Predigt unter alliierter Besatzung, Calwer Verlag, Stuttgart 1989

1996    **Riemann**, Fritz: Grundformen der Angst. Eine tiefenpsychologische Studie [1961], Verlag Reinhard, München, 33rd ed., 1996

2009    Idem: Die Persönlichkeit des Predigers aus tiefenpsychologischer Sicht [1974], in: Wilfried Engemann/Frank Lütze (Eds.): Grundfragen der Predigt, loc. cit., 2nd ed., 2009, 61–77

1976    **Ritschl**, Dietrich/**Jones**, Hugh O.: „Story" als Rohmaterial der Theologie, Chr. Kaiser, München 1976

2000    **Ritter**, Werner H.: Kindliche Religion und Phantasie – dargestellt an einem exemplarischen Kapitel der Religionspädagogik, in: Idem (Ed.): Religion und Phantasie. Von der Imaginationskraft des Glaubens, Vandenhoeck & Ruprecht, Göttingen 2000, 151–180

2002    **Rössler**, Dietrich: Beispiel und Erfahrung. Zu Luthers Homiletik, in: Christian Albrecht/Martin Weeber (Eds.): Klassiker der protestantischen Predigtlehre, loc. cit., Tübingen 2002, 9–25.

2001    **Roessler**, Roman: Theologie im Spiegel heutiger Predigtpraxis. Brief an einen Mitstreiter der homiletischen Zunft, in: Wilfried Engemann (Ed.) Theologie der Predigt, loc. cit., Leipzig 2001d, 61–67

2004    Idem: Was lange währt . . . Anstöße zu einer Revision der Perikopenordnung aus homiletischer Sicht, in: Perikopenordnung in der Diskussion, loc. cit., 2004, 57–63

2008    **Rolf**, Sybille: Zum Herzen sprechen. Eine Studie zum imputativen Aspekt in Martin Luthers Rechtfertigungslehre und zu seinen Konsequenzen für die Predigt des Evangeliums, Evangelische Verlagsanstalt, Leipzig 2008

1993    **Roloff**, Jürgen: Amt–*Ämter*–Amtsverständnis IV, in: TRE, Vol. 2, 1993, 509–533

1997    **Rose**, Lucy: Sharing the Word. Preaching in the Roundtable Church, Westminster John Knox Press, Louisville/Ky. 1997

1984    **Rothermund**, Jörg: Der Heilige Geist und die Rhetorik. Theologische Grundlinien einer empirischen Homiletik, G. Mohn, Gütersloh 1984

2011    **Ruffing**, Janet K.: To Tell the Sacred Tale. Spiritual Direction and Narrative, Paulist Press, Mawah/N.J. 2011

1964    **Ruler**, Arnold Albert van: Structuurverschillen tussen het christologische en het pneumatologische Gezichtspunt, in: De spiritu sancto, Bijdragen tot de leer van de Heilige Geest bij gelegenheid van het 2e eeuwfeest van het Stipendium Bernardinum, ed. by J. de Graaf, Kemink & Zoon, Utrecht 1964, 205–227

**S**

1948    **Sartre**, Jean-Paul: L'imaginaire. Psychologie phénoménologique de l'imagination, Gallimard, Paris 1948

2008    **Schaap-Jonker**, Hanneke: Before the face of God. An Interdisciplinary Study of the Meaning of the Sermon and the Hearer's God Image, Personality and Affective State, Lit Verlag, Berlin/Münster et al. 2008

1978    **Schade**, Herwarth von: Perikopen. Gestalt und Wandel des gottesdienstlichen Bibelgebrauchs (= RGD, Vol. 11), Lutherisches Verlagshaus, Hamburg 1978

1973    **Schäfer**, Manfred: Bericht zu Anlage, Durchführung und Ergebnissen der Contentanalyse, in: Homiletische Arbeitsgruppe, loc. cit., 1973, 18–52

1985    **Scharfenberg**, Joachim: Einführung in die Pastoralpsychologie, Vandenhoeck & Ruprecht, Göttingen 1985

1992    Idem: „Gib mir ein Symbol." Identitätsfindung durch religiöse Symbole, in: Wilfried Engemann/Rainer Volp (Eds.): Gib mir ein Zeichen. Zur Bedeutung der Semiotik für theologische Praxis- und Denkmodelle, de Gruyter, Berlin/New York 1992, 247–254

1980    **Scharfenberg**, Joachim/**Kämpfer**, Horst: Mit Symbolen leben. Soziologische, psychologische und religiöse Konfliktbearbeitung, Walter-Verlag, Olten/Freiburg 1980

1975    **Scheler**, Helmut: Kritischer Kommentar zum Thema „Sprechakttheorie in der Homiletik", in: Peter Düsterfeld/Hans Bernhard Kaufmann (Eds.): Didaktik der Predigt, loc. cit., 1975, 206–225

1912    **Schian**, Martin: Orthodoxie und Pietismus im Kampf um die Predigt. Ein Beitrag zur Geschichte des endenden 17. und des beginnenden 18. Jahrhunderts, Verlag A. Töpelmann, Gießen 1912

1957    **Schieder**, Julius: Unsere Predigt. Grundsätzliches, Kritisches, Praktisches, Chr. Kaiser, München 1957

1995    **Schieder**, Rolf: Der „Wirklichkeitsbezug" der Predigt. Vom Nutzen einer diskurstheoretischen Predigtanalyse, in: EvTh, Vol. 55, 1995, 322–337

1964    **Schillebeeckx**, Edward: Kirche und Menschheit, Conc(D), Vol. 1, 1964, 29–40

1993    **Schlegel**, Leonhard: Handwörterbuch der Transaktionsanalyse. Sämtliche Begriffe der TA praxisnah erklärt, Herder, Freiburg et al. 1993

1843    **Schleiermacher**, Friedrich D. E.: Predigten. Neue Ausgabe, Vol. I, Reimer, Berlin 1843

1850    Idem: Praktische Theologie. Die Praktische Theologie nach den Grundsätzen der Evangelischen Kirche im Zusammenhang dargestellt, ed. by Jacob Frerichs, in: Sämtliche Werke, I, 13, Berlin 1850 (reprint: de Gruyter, Berlin/New York 1983)

1960    Idem: Der christliche Glaube nach den Grundsätzen der evangelischen Kirche im Zusammenhang dargestellt [1821], de Gruyter, Berlin, 7th ed., 1960

1988    Idem: Christian Caring. Selection from Practical Theology, ed. by James O. Duke and Howard W. Stone, Fortress Press, Philadelphia 1988

2016    Idem: The Christian Faith, ed. by Hugh R. Mackintosh and James S. Stewart, Bloomsbury T&T Clark, London et al. 2016

1991    **Schmalstieg**, Olaf: Bibel-Träume. Friedenskuss, Zeichen im Sand, Himmel auf Erden. Predigten zur Symbolsprache der Bibel, Edition Servet, Grand-Lancy 1991

1973    **Schmid**, Wolf: Der Textaufbau in den Erzählungen Dostoevskijs, in: Beihefte zu Poetica, W. Fink Verlag, München 1973, 5–53

1973    **Schmidtchen**, Gerhard: Gottesdienst in einer rationalen Welt. Religionssoziologische Untersuchungen im Bereich der VELKD. Mit einer Einführung und einem theologischen Nachwort v. Manfred Seitz, Univ. Erlangen-Nürnberg/Calwer Verlag, Stuttgart 1973

1992    **Schmidt-Lauber**, Hans-Christoph/**Seitz**, Manfred (Eds.): Der Gottesdienst. Grundlagen und Predigthilfen zu den liturgischen Stücken, Calwer Verlag, Stuttgart 1992

1979    **Schmölders**, Claudia: Die Kunst des Gesprächs, Deutscher Taschenbuchverlag, München 1979

1982    **Schnath**, Gerhard: Fantasie für Gott. Gottesdienste in neuer Gestalt, Kreuz-Verlag, Stuttgart, 2nd ed., 1982

1968    **Schnell**, Uwe: Die homiletische Theorie Philipp Melanchthons, Lutherisches Verlagshaus, Berlin/Hamburg 1968

1990    **Schönherr**, Albrecht: Predigt und Fragen der Zeit, in: Karl-Heinrich Bieritz/Christian Bunners et al. (Eds.): Handbuch der Predigt, loc. cit., 1990, 379–408

1936    **Schreiner**, Helmut: Die Verkündigung des Wortes Gottes, Verlag Friedrich Bahn, Schwerin 1936

1975    **Schröter**, Christoph: Die Bedeutung der Gemeindesituation für die Predigtgestalt, in: Helmut Zeddies (Ed.): Immer noch Predigt?, loc. cit., 1975, 66–78

1982a   **Schüepp**, Guido (Ed.): Handbuch zur Predigt, Benziger, Köln 1982

1982b   Idem: Struktur und Faktoren der Predigtkommunikation, in: Idem, Handbuch zur Predigt, loc. cit., 1982, 36–76

1972   **Schütz**, Werner: Geschichte der christlichen Predigt, de Gruyter, Berlin 1972

1981   Idem: Probleme der Predigt, (= Dienst am Wort, Vol. 41), E. Klotz Verlag, Göttingen 1981

1990   **Schulz**, Hansjürgen: Predigt im Vollzug, in: Karl-Heinrich Bieritz/Christian Bunners et al.: Handbuch der Predigt, loc. cit., 1990, 543–569

1993   **Schulze**, Gerhard: Die Erlebnisgesellschaft. Kultursoziologie der Gegenwart [1992], Campus, Frankfurt/M., 4th ed., 1993

1986   **Schwarz**, Alois: Praxis der Predigterarbeitung. Neue Homiletik, Verlag Styria, Graz et al. 1986

2008   **Schwarz**, Norbert: „...denn wenn ich schwach bin, bin ich stark." Rezeptivität und Produktivität des Glaubenssubjekts in der Homiletik Hans Joachim Iwands, Vandenhoeck & Ruprecht, Göttingen 2008

1848   **Schweizer**, Alexander: Homiletik der evangelisch-protestantischen Kirche, Weidmannsche Buchhandlung, Leipzig 1848

2009   **Schwier**, Helmut: Homiletik: Predigen (nicht nur) für alte Menschen, in: Thomas Klie et al. (Eds.): Praktische Theologie des Alterns, de Gruyter, Berlin 2009, 431–447

2015   Idem (Ed.): Ethische und politische Predigt. Beiträge zu einer homiletischen Herausforderung, Evangelische Verlagsanstalt, Leipzig 2015

2008   **Schwier**, Helmut/**Gall**, Sieghard: Predigt hören. Befunde und Ergebnisse der Heidelberger Umfrage zur Predigtrezeption (= Heidelberger Studien zur Predigtforschung, Vol. 1), LIT-Verlag, Berlin/Münster 2008

2013   Idem: Predigthören im konfessionellen Vergleich (= Heidelberger Studien zur Predigtforschung, Vol. 2), LIT-Verlag, Berlin 2013

1969   **Searle**, John R.: Speech Acts. An essay in the philosophy of language, University Press, Cambridge 1969.

1972   Idem: Was ist ein Sprechakt, in: Horst Holzer/Karl Steinbacher (Eds.): Sprache und Gesellschaft, Hoffmann und Campe, Hamburg 1972

1975   Idem: A Taxonomy of Illocutionary Acts (= Minnesota Studies in the Philosophy of Science, Vol. VII), Minneapolis/Minn. 1975

1979   Idem: Expression and Meaning. Studies in the Theory of Speech Acts, Cambridge University Press, Cambridge/London et al. 1979

1980   **Seidel**, Hans: Auf den Spuren der Beter. Einführung in die Psalmen, Evangelische Verlagsanstalt, Berlin 1980

1577   **Selnecker**, Nicolaus: Acta Formulae Concordiae, in: Scriptores rerum Germanicarum, Arab. Zählung 6, 1–12, Moenum, Frankfurt 1577

1581a   Idem: Kurze Erinnerung. Von dem christlichen Buch der Concordien, Berwaldt, Leipzig 1581

1581b   **Selnecker**, Nicolaus/**Crato**, Adam: Weihnacht Predigten. Von der Person Jesu Christi. Von der persönlichen Vereinbarung göttlicher und Menschlicher Natur in Christo [...], Berwaldt, Leipzig 1581

2016   **Sendler-Koschel**, Birgit: In Kommunikation mit Wort und Raum. Bibelorientierte Kirchenpädagogik in einer pluralen Kirche und Gesellschaft (= ARP, Vol. 58), Vandenhoeck & Ruprecht, Göttingen 2016

1959   **Sick**, Hansjörg: Melanchthon als Ausleger des Neuen Testaments, Mohr, Tübingen 1959

1992  **Siegert**, Folker: Drei hellenistisch-jüdische Predigten II. [...] Kommentar nebst Beobachtungen zur hellenistischen Vorgeschichte der Bibelhermeneutik, in: WUNT, Vol. 61/II, Mohr, Tübingen 1992

2005  **Sloterdijk**, Peter: Im Weltinnenraum des Kapitals. Für eine philosophische Theorie der Globalisierung, Suhrkamp, Frankfurt 2005

1959  **Smalcald Articles** [1537], in: The Book of Concord – The Confession of the Evangelical Lutheran Church, ed. by Theodore Tappert, Fort Press, Philadelphia, 6th ed., 1959, 287–318

1959  The **Solid Declaration of the Formula of Concord** [1577], in: The Book of Concord – The Confession of the Evangelical Lutheran Church, ed. by Theodore Tappert, Fortress Press, Philadelphia, 6th ed., 1959, 463–636

1953  **Sommerlath**, Ernst: Amt und allgemeines Priestertum, in: Friedrich Hübner (Ed.): „Allgemeines Priestertum" im Neuen Testament (= SThKAB, Vol. 5), Lutherisches Verlagshaus, Berlin 1953, 40–89

1791  **Spalding**, Johann J.: Über die Nutzbarkeit des Predigtamtes und deren Beförderung [1722], Bossische Buchhandlung, Berlin, 3rd ed., 1791

1589  **Spangenberg**, Cyriacus: Theander Lutherus [21 Predigten], Mansfeld 1589

2002  **Spener**, Philipp Jakob: Die erste Wiederholungspredigt, gehalten in Frankfurt am Main, den Pfingstmontag, 24. Mai 1686, in: Die Werke Philipp Jakob Speners, Vol. II: Der christliche Glaube, ed. by Kurt Aland et al., Brunnen-Verlag, Gießen 2002, 157–168

1958  **Stählin**, Wilhelm: Tägliches Geleit. Auslegung der täglichen Lesungen aus der Heiligen Schrift nach dem Kirchenjahr, Stauda-Verlag, Kassel 1958

2016  **Statistisches Bundesamt** (Ed.): Statistisches Jahrbuch. Deutschland und Internationales, Wiesbaden 2016

2006  **Stebler**, Christoph: Die drei Dimensionen der Bestattungspredigt. Theologie, Biographie und Trauergemeinde, Theologischer Verlag Zürich, Zürich 2006

1981  **Steinwede**, Dietrich: Biblisches Erzählen nach Beispielen aus Grundschule und Kindergarten für Aus- und Fortbildung, Vandenhoeck & Ruprecht, Göttingen 1981

1995  **Stellungnahme der Theologischen Ausschüsse** von EKU und VELKD zum „KLAK-Votum", in: Streit um das Gottesdienstbuch (Erneuerte Agende), loc. cit., 1995, 15–28

2015  **Stetter**, Manuel: Wie sagen, was gut ist? Überlegungen zu drei Verfahrensweisen ethischer Predigt, in: Helmut Schwier (Ed.): Ethische und politische Predigt, loc. cit., 2015, 184–195

1979  **Stollberg**, Dietrich: Predigt praktisch. Homiletik – kurz gefasst. Mit 10 Predigtentwürfen, Vandenhoeck & Ruprecht, Göttingen 1979

1984  **Stowers**, Stanley Kent: Social Status, Public Speaking and Private Teaching, in: NovTest, Vol. 26, 1984, 59–82

1995  **Streit um das Gottesdienstbuch** (Erneuerte Agende): Theologie nach Auschwitz oder Theologie „als wäre nichts geschehen"? Ed. by Ev. Arbeitskreis Kirche und Israel in Hessen und Nassau, Heppenheim 1995

**T**

1975  **Tacke**, Helmut: Glaubenshilfe als Lebenshilfe. Probleme und Chancen heutiger Seelsorge, Neukirchener Verlag, Neukirchen-Vluyn 1975

1994  **Theißen**, Gerd: Zeichensprache des Glaubens. Chancen der Predigt heute, Chr. Kaiser, Gütersloh 1994

2005    **Thiele**, Michael: Portale der Predigt. Kommunikation, Rhetorik, Kunst, Bayerischer Verlag für Sprechwissenschaft, Regensburg 2005

1947    **Thielicke**, Helmut: Predigt am Karfreitag 1947, in: Andreas Richter-Böhne (Ed.), Unbekannte Schuld. Politische Predigt unter alliierter Besatzung, Calwer, Calw 1989, supplement I–X

1974    **Thilo**, Hans-Joachim: Psyche und Wort. Aspekte ihrer Beziehungen in Seelsorge, Unterricht und Predigt, Vandenhoeck & Ruprecht, Göttingen 1974

1986    Idem: Beratende Seelsorge. Tiefenpsychologische Methodik – dargestellt am Kasualgespräch [1971], Vandenhoeck & Ruprecht, Göttingen, 3rd ed., 1986

1955    **Thimme**, Hans (Ed.): Verkündigung der Kirche heute. Vorträge und Entschließungen auf der Landessynode und auf einzelnen Kreissynoden der Evangelischen Kirche von Westfalen im Jahre 1954 (2 Volumes), Luther Verlag, Witten 1955

1971    **Thurneysen**, Eduard: Die Aufgabe der Predigt [1921], in: Gert Hummel (Ed.): Aufgabe der Predigt, loc. cit., 1971, 105–118

1962    **Tillich**, Paul: Religionsphilosophie, Kohlhammer, Stuttgart 1962

1967    Idem: Systematic Theology. Three volumes in one, The University of Chicago Press, Chicago 1967

1997    **Tisdale**, Leonora Tubbs: Preaching as Local Theology and Folk Art, Fortress, Minneapolis/Minn. 1997

2008    Idem: Exegeting the congregation, in: Thomas G. Long/Leonora Tubbs Tisdale: Teaching Preaching as a Christian Practice. A New Approach to Homiletical Pedagogy, Westminster John Knox Press, Louisville/Ky. 2008, 75–89

2010    Dies.: Prophetic Preaching. A Pastoral Approach, Westminster John Knox Press, Louisville/Ky. 2010

1978    **Track**, Joachim: Analogie, in: TRE, 1978, Vol. 2, 625–650

1938    **Trillhaas**, Wolfgang: Ein Jahrgang Predigten, Vandenhoeck & Ruprecht, Göttingen 1938

1954    Idem: Evangelische Predigtlehre, Evangelische Verlagsanstalt, Berlin, 4th ed., 1954

**U**

1994    **Ueding**, Gerd/**Steinbrink**, Bernd: Grundriss der Rhetorik. Geschichte, Technik, Methode, Metzler, Stuttgart/Weimar 1994

1961    **Urner**, Hans: Gottes Wort und unsere Predigt, Evangelische Verlagsanstalt, Berlin 1961

2005    **Usarski**, Christa: Jesus und die Kanaanäerin (Matthäus 15,21–28). Eine predigtgeschichtliche Recherche (= PTHe, Vol. 69), Kohlhammer, Stuttgart 2005

**V**

1857    **Vinet**, Alexandre: Homiletik oder Theorie der Predigt [fr. 1830], Bahnmeier, Basel 1857

1944    Idem: Ausgewählte Werke, Vol. 3: Vinet als Professor der Theologie im Zeitalter des vordringenden Radikalismus: 1837–1845, ed. by Ernst Staehelin, Zwingli-Verlag, Zürich 1944

1934    **Vischer**, Wilhelm, Das Christuszeugnis des Alten Testaments, Chr. Kaiser, München, Vol. I, 1934; Vol. II, 1942

1979    **Völzing**, Paul-Ludwig: Begründen, Erklären, Argumentieren. Modelle und Materialien zu einer Theorie der Metakommunikation, Quelle und Meyer, Heidelberg 1979

1971    **Vogel**, Heinrich: Die Verantwortung unserer Predigt, in: Gert Hummel (Ed.): Aufgabe der Predigt, loc. cit., 1971, 151–164 – First published in: MPTh, Vol. 26, 1930, 246–255

1965–   **Voigt**, Gottfried: Homiletische Auslegung der Predigttexte, Evangelische Verlags-
1970    anstalt, Berlin 1965–1970

1973    Idem: Mitten unter ihnen. Zum Verständnis des Gottesdienstes, Evangelische Verlags-anstalt, Berlin 1973

1978–   Idem: Homiletische Auslegung der Predigttexte. Neue Folge, Evangelische Verlags-
1984    anstalt, Berlin 1978–1984; Vandenhoeck & Ruprecht, Göttingen, 2nd ed., 1984; reprint: Spenner 2003

1993    **Voigt**, Kerstin: Otto Haendler – Leben und Werk. Eine Untersuchung der Strukturen seines Seelsorgeverständnisses, Peter Lang, Frankfurt/M. 1993

1992    **Volp**, Rainer: Liturgik. Die Kunst, Gott zu feiern, Vol. 1: Einführung und Geschichte, G. Mohn, Gütersloh 1992

1994    Idem: Liturgik. Die Kunst, Gott zu feiern, Vol. 2: Theorien und Gestaltung, G. Mohn, Gütersloh 1994

1960    **Voßler**, Karl: Geist und Kultur in der Sprache, Verlag Dobbek, München, 2nd ed., 1960

## W

1983    **Wacker**, Bernd: Zehn Jahre „Narrative Theologie" – Versuch einer Bilanz, in: Willy Sanders/Klaus Wegenast (Eds.): Erzählen für Kinder, Erzählen von Gott, Kohlhammer, Stuttgart 1983, 13–32

1977    **Wagner**, Heinz: Polylogpredigt, in: Der Sonntag, ed. by Evangelisch-Lutherische Landeskirche Sachsens vom 11. 9. 1977

1978    Idem: Die Diakonie, in: Handbuch der Praktischen Theologie. Vol. III, ed. by Heinrich Ammer/Jürgen Henkys et al., Evangelische Verlagsanstalt, Berlin 1978, 263–317

1997    **Walter**, Nikolaus: Urchristliche Autoren als Leser der „Schriften" Israels, in: BThZ, Vol. 14, 1997, 59–77

1973    **Warning**, Rainer: Imagination, in: Historisches Wörterbuch der Philosophie, Vol. IV, 1976, 217–220

1967    **Watzlawick**, Paul et al.: Pragmatics of Human Communication. A Study of Interactional Patterns, Pathologies and Paradoxes, W. W. Norton & Co, New York 1967

1993    **Weimar**, Klaus: Enzyklopädie der Literaturwissenschaft [1980], A. Francke Verlag, Tübingen/Basel, 2nd ed., 1993

1964    **Weinrich**, Harald: Tempus. Besprochene und erzählte Welt. Kohlhammer, Stuttgart 1964

2009    Idem: Narrative Theologie [1973], in: Wilfried Engemann/Frank Lütze (Eds.): Grundfragen der Predigt, loc. cit., 2nd ed., 2009, 243–251

1992    **Welker**, Michael: Gottes Geist. Theologie des Heiligen Geistes, Neukirchen-Vluyn 1992

1988    **Wilson**, Paul S.: Imagination of the Heart. New Understandings in Preaching, Abingdon, Nashville/Tenn. 1988

2001    Idem: God Sense. Reading the Bible for Preaching, Abingdon, Nashville/Tenn. 2001

1955    **Wingren**, Gustav: Die Predigt, Evangelische Verlagsanstalt, Berlin 1955

1990    **Winkler**, Eberhard: Aus der Geschichte der Predigt und Homiletik, in: Karl-Heinrich Bieritz/Christian Bunners et al. (Eds.): Handbuch der Predigt, loc. cit., 1990, 571–614

1997    **Winkler**, Klaus: Seelsorge, de Gruyter, Berlin/New York 1997

1901    **Winter,** Friedrich Julius: Der Erfolg der Predigt, NKZ, Vol. 12, 1901, 974–997

1969    **Wintzer,** Friedrich: Die Homiletik seit Schleiermacher bis in die Anfänge der „dialektischen Theologie" in Grundzügen (= APTh, Vol. 6), Vandenhoeck & Ruprecht, Göttingen 1969

2006    **Wöhrle,** Stefanie: Predigtanalyse. Methodische Ansätze – homiletische Prämissen – didaktische Konsequenzen, LIT-Verlag, Münster 2006

1971    **Wölber,** Hans-Otto: Die Predigt als Kommunikation [1957], in: Gert Hummel (Ed.): Aufgabe der Predigt, loc. cit., 1971, 359–381

2002    **Wolf-Withöft,** Susanne: Predigen lernen. Homiletische Konturen einer praktisch-theologischen Spieltheorie (= PTHe, Vol. 58), Kohlhammer, Stuttgart 2002

2004    Dies.: Homiletik und Gender. Beobachtungen zu einer phänomenalen Lücke, in: PTh, Vol. 39, 2004, 164–167

1986    **Wonneberger,** Reinhard/**Hecht,** Hans Peter: Verheißung und Versprechen. Eine theologische und sprachanalytische Klärung, Vandenhoeck & Ruprecht, Göttingen 1986

## Z

1957    **Zahrnt,** Heinz: Trachtet zuerst nach der Predigt, in: Das Sonntagsblatt. Christliche Wochenzeitung für Politik, Wirtschaft und Kultur, ed. by Hanns Lilje, Verlag Sonntagsblatt, Hamburg, 19. 5. 1957, Nr. 20, 24

2000    Ders: Glauben unter leerem Himmel. Ein Lesebuch, Piper-Verlag, München/Zürich 2002

1975a   **Zeddies,** Helmut (Ed.): Immer noch Predigt? Theologische Beiträge zur Predigt im Gottesdienst, erarbeitet im Auftrag der Kommission für Theologie des Bundes der EKiDDR, Evangelische Verlagsanstalt GmbH, Berlin 1975

1975b   Idem: Zum Öffentlichkeitscharakter der Predigt, in: Helmut Zeddies (Ed): Immer noch Predigt?, loc. cit., 1975a, 94–111

1979    **Zerfaß,** Rolf/**Kamphaus,** Franz (Eds.): Die Kompetenz des Predigers im Spannungsfeld zwischen Rolle und Person, Comenius-Institut, Münster 1979

1990    **Ziemer,** Jürgen: Der Text, in: Karl-Heinrich Bieritz/Christian Bunners et al. (Eds.): Handbuch der Predigt, loc. cit., 1990, 207–245

2015    Idem: Seelsorgelehre. Eine Einführung für Studium und Praxis, Vandenhoeck & Ruprecht, Göttingen, 4th, newly revised and extended ed., 2015

1892    **Zunz,** Leopold: Die gottesdienstlichen Vorträge der Juden, historisch entwickelt. Ein Beitrag zur Altertumskunde und biblischen Kritik [...], Frankfurt/M. 1892, reprographischer Nachdruck der 2., verm. Auflage (m. einem Register v. N. Brüll), Olms, Hildesheim 1966

# Index of Names

https://doi.org/10.1515/9783110440256-016